THE USSR IN 1989:
A RECORD OF EVENTS

Published in cooperation
with Radio Free Europe/Radio Liberty

The USSR in 1989:
A Record of Events

Compiled by

Vera Tolz

Edited by MELANIE NEWTON

Foreword by Vladimir G. Treml

Westview Press
BOULDER, SAN FRANCISCO, & OXFORD

Robert Farrell is general editor of the annual chronology of events.

Copyright © 1990 by Westview Press, Inc.

Published in 1990 in the United States of America by Westview Press, Inc., 5500 Central Avenue, Boulder, Colorado 80301, and in the United Kingdom by Westview Press, 36 Lonsdale Road, Summertown, Oxford OX2 7EW

Library of Congress Cataloging-in-Publication Data
Tolz, Vera.
    The USSR in 1989 / compiled by Vera Tolz : edited by Melanie Newton.
        p. cm.
    ISBN 0-8133-8016-2
    1. Soviet Union—Politics and government—1985- —Chronology.
2. Soviet Union—History—1953- —Chronology. I. Newton, Melanie.
II. Title.
DK286.T65   1990
947.085′4′0202—dc20   90-32326
                                                                                         CIP

Printed and bound in the United States of America

The paper used in this publication meets the requirements
of the American National Standard for Permanence of Paper
for Printed Library Materials Z39.48-1984.

10   9   8   7   6   5   4   3   2   1

DK
286
T65
1990

Contents

Foreword, by Vladimir G. Treml   vii

Preface   ix

Acknowledgments   xi

———————————

The Month of January   1

The Month of February   61

The Month of March   123

The Month of April   186

The Month of May   231

The Month of June   283

The Month of July   341

The Month of August   409

The Month of September   470

The Month of October   525

The Month of November   589

The Month of December   653

Key to Articles Published in *Report on the USSR* in 1989   705

Name Index   707

Subject Index   723

Foreword

A chronological record of events in a given country is always useful for those writing or learning about that country, not to mention for those shaping policy towards it or doing business with it. With respect to the USSR in 1989, it might be said that such a record becomes indispensable, because both the year's events and the nature and extent of the information made available about them by the Soviet media were extraordinary. There were labor strikes, interethnic conflicts and violence, calls for sovereignty by various constituent republics, demonstrations and counter-demonstrations, widespread shortages of consumer goods, and trials of former leading officials. *Glasnost'* continued to gain ground, but many attempts to exercise censorship occurred. The role played by the new parliament, the Congress of People's Deputies, and by the revamped USSR Supreme Soviet assumed increasing importance, while political factions emerged within the Communist Party and signs of a multiparty system became evident outside it. A large number of *samizdat* works were officially published, and extensive coverage was given to newly released statistics on social problems such as crime. Analyses of the poor performance of the economy were abundant, as were discussions of reform. Add to this reports of the dramatic changes that were taking place in Eastern Europe and accounts of the USSR's relations with other parts of the world, and the yield was a torrent of information, one that virtually inundated Western observers of the Soviet scene in 1989.

By bringing much of this information together in a single volume and giving it some form and order, *The USSR in 1989: A Record of Events* will help considerably in understanding the historic transformations taking place in the Soviet Union and in evaluating what often seem to be the contradictory and tortuous developments in the country's efforts to modernize. Based on the regular feature "The USSR This Week" in Radio Liberty's weekly publication *Report on the USSR*, the volume contains citations of original sources and references to related materials. A historian in her own right, Vera Tolz (University of Leningrad and University of Birmingham), who prepares "The USSR This Week" and is the compiler of the volume, is well known for her insightful analyses and thoughtful articles on a variety of Soviet topics. She brings these same qualities and this same versatility to *The USSR in 1989: A Record of Events*. Repeatedly, the volume demonstrates her exceptional skill and foresight both in identifying those people and events that have subsequently proved to be of importance and in choosing those Soviet sources that have offered more considered views than others. If any issues or happenings have inadvertently been missed, they are few and far between. The coverage is balanced and thorough, creating a vivid kaleidoscope of the cultural, economic, political, and social changes in the USSR in 1989. News-oriented, the entries are brief but nonetheless more than mere summaries, frequently giving analytical and background notes that place events in a larger contemporary and historical perspective. The volume has been edited by

Melanie Newton (University of Bristol), who is a long-time member of the publications staff at RFE/RL. As the first in an annual series of such reference works, *The USSR in 1989: A Record of Events* is certainly to be welcomed as a lasting and useful contribution to knowledge of the Soviet Union.

VLADIMIR G. TREML
Duke University

Preface

A chronology of developments in and relating to the Soviet Union, *The USSR in 1989: A Record of Events* aims at providing those interested in Soviet affairs with a substantial yet handy reference work. The volume is organized on a day-by-day basis and divided into chapters for each month. Headlines are used for each entry to facilitate locating information. Entries for a given day have been arranged roughly in descending order of importance. Where a story runs over several days or even weeks—as is often the case with state visits, parliamentary sessions, and ethnic disputes—its sequential parts have been grouped together in a single entry on the day it began.

For its information, *The USSR in 1989: A Record of Events* draws on the wide range of Soviet and non-Soviet media reports at the disposal of RFE/RL and makes extensive reference both to primary sources and, where appropriate, to other pertinent materials. One consequence of the campaign for *glasnost'* has been that various Soviet media organs often present differing and at times conflicting pictures of the same event. In such instances, information offered by the official media has, if possible, been checked against *samizdat* and other independent sources. In addition, the coverage of developments provided by the most outspoken liberal Soviet periodicals, such as *Moscow News* and *Ogonek*, has generally been regarded as more reliable than that provided by those media organs still adhering to pre-*glasnost'* practices.

The sheer quantity of information issuing from the USSR in 1989 inevitably meant that some degree of selection had to be exercised in compiling the volume. Besides seeking to cover all the major developments in or involving the Soviet Union that attracted broad attention both inside and outside the country during the year, the compiler has sought to focus on some of the less newsworthy but nonetheless interesting happenings that proceeded from or had a bearing on the current Soviet reform process. The decision about which of the latter to include, while guided by overall considerations of relative importance and scope and distribution of coverage, has naturally been to some extent a matter of predilection.

Frequently, an event or topic that is dealt with in the volume has been described or analyzed more fully in an article that appears in Radio Liberty's weekly publication *Report on the USSR*. For reasons of space, these articles have been referred to simply by their "RL" numbers. To illustrate, the entry headlined "*Pravda* Carries Letter Criticizing *Ogonek*" on page 54 carries a reference to RL 51/89. To assist the reader who may wish to locate RL 51/89, there is a Key at the back of the volume showing in which issue of *Report on the USSR* the article was published. Some of the entries in the volume cite *RFE/RL Special* as a source. This is a designation for reports filed by RFE/RL's own correspondents. A comprehensive index is an essential part of any reference work of this kind if users of it are to find information quickly and easily. *The USSR in 1989: A Record of Events* contains two indexes—one of persons only and one of subjects and proper names other than those of persons. Because some persons are mentioned literally hundreds of times in the volume, the index entries of their names are further subdivided into subject categories.

MELANIE NEWTON AND VERA TOLZ

Acknowledgments

Though only the names of the two principals—the compiler, Vera Tolz, and the editor, Melanie Newton—appear on the cover of this volume, many other people were involved both directly and indirectly in its preparation. A particularly valuable contribution was made by members of the research staffs of Radio Liberty and Radio Free Europe, whose specialized knowledge and writings helped to make authoritative coverage of such a vast range of topics possible. Their commentaries for the daily media survey *RFE/RL Daily Report* were drawn on extensively. Of enormous help too were the summaries of news agency reports put together by RFE/RL's News and Current Affairs Division, the reports filed by RFE/RL's own correspondents, and the numerous telephone interviews with people in the Soviet Union conducted by members of RFE/RL's broadcasting services. As director of the Radio Liberty Research Department, Keith Bush inaugurated the weekly chronology of events known as "The USSR This Week" some years ago.

Without the encouragement of E. Eugene Pell, president of RFE/RL, Inc., *The USSR in 1989: A Record of Events* could not have been produced. At the heart of the volume is his interest in making part of the immense flow of information now emanating from the Soviet Union and being evaluated by RFE/RL in connection with its broadcasts available to the Western public in a convenient, lasting, and usable form. S. Enders Wimbush, director of Radio Liberty, gave his unstinting support to the project from beginning to end.

The preparation of the volume was under the general charge of Robert Farrell, assistant director of RFE/RL publications, who conceived the idea for it. Karen Whitehouse, production editor in the RFE/RL Publications Department, typeset and copyfit the entire text on a Macintosh® using Microsoft Word® and PageMaker®. She also carried out corrections and made technical and other adjustments in the text right up to the last minute. The kind help of Rebecca Ritke, acquisitions editor at Westview Press, is gratefully acknowledged. She and Libby Barstow, also of Westview Press, patiently and conscientiously shepherded the volume through the complicated process of reproduction. Finally, a public expression of gratitude is owed to the indexer, whose labors contributed significantly to the volume's usefulness as a reference work.

MN
VT

The Month of January

Gorbachev Sends New Year's Message to the American People

Soviet leader Mikhail Gorbachev expressed gratitude to the American people for coming to the aid of the victims of the Armenian earthquake. In a New Year's message he said that, seeing the response by the United States and other countries to the tragedy, one cannot help thinking that all people, however different, are really one family. US President Ronald Reagan expressed his "deepest sympathy" for the earthquake victims in his reciprocal New Year's message to the Soviet people. Gorbachev said 1988 had brought many improvements in relations. He said, "fears and suspicion are gradually giving way to trust and feelings of mutual liking" (*TASS*, in English, January 1). On January 2, *Pravda* carried the text of Gorbachev's address to the American people, followed by Reagan's address to the USSR.

Yulii Daniel Dies

It was reported that Yulii Daniel, a Soviet satirist and poet who spent five years in prisons and labor camps for illegally publishing his works abroad, had died in Moscow on December 30. His former wife, Larisa Bogoraz, said Daniel had died after suffering a stroke. He was sixty-three and had been in ill health for some time. Daniel's trial in 1966, together with another writer, Andrei Sinyavsky, gave birth to the dissident movement in the Soviet Union. In July, 1988, *Ogonek* published some of Daniel's poems—the first such publication in more than twenty years. Daniel was buried on January 2 in Moscow's Vagankovskoe cemetery (*AP, RL Samizdat*, December 31; *Reuters*, January 2). On January 3, Sinyavsky made history when he became the first outstanding dissident writer allowed to return to the USSR. Sinyavsky traveled to Moscow for a five-day visit in connection with Daniel's death (*The Daily Telegraph*, January 4).

Ban Imposed on Exports of Some Consumer Goods and Foodstuffs

The Soviet Union announced that it would impose a ban on individual exports of some consumer goods, clothing items, and foodstuffs. The ban is to come into effect on February 1 and last until the end of 1990. Customs duties

1

are also being imposed on some other privately exported goods, ranging from 20 to 100 percent of their retail prices. The measures affect goods being exported by people who live overseas and have been in the USSR as tourists or on business. Radio Moscow (1500) said the ban covers television sets, refrigerators and freezers, washing and sewing machines, children's clothing and footwear, coffee, and caviar. The items affected by the imposition of customs duties include some household electrical appliances, some radios and cameras, and some car accessories and car parts. The resolution of the USSR Council of Ministers bringing the ban into effect also stipulates that the overall value of consumer goods exported from the Soviet Union by a single individual must not exceed 100 rubles. Commenting on the measures in *Trud* on January 3, economist Tat'yana Koryagina said they were a logical step to protect the domestic market, but she said that they would not solve the Soviet Union's problem of short supplies. At a news conference on January 5, Vitalii Boyarov, first deputy head of Soviet customs, rejected suggestions that the new measures could result in a trade war between the USSR and its Comecon trading partners. He conceded, however, that the ban, which follows similar curbs by the GDR, Poland, and Czechoslovakia, would slow longstanding plans to make Comecon an integrated trading bloc (*Reuters*, January 5).

Intellectuals Call for Replacement of Anti-Reform Officials

Moscow News (No. 19) carried an open letter from six Soviet intellectuals to Gorbachev declaring their support for his policies and calling for the replacement of officials opposed to reform. The letter was signed by the scientist Roald Sagdeev, the writer Daniil Granin, the filmmaker Elem Klimov, the actor Mikhail Ulyanov, the editor of *Znamya*, Grigorii Baklanov, and the playwright Aleksandr Gel'man. The letter said reforms are being hampered by conservative Party officials and members who make up what the letter-writers call "a dictatorship of mediocrity." It called for such people to be replaced. It also called for greater cooperation with people regarded as dissidents, saying that this would strengthen rather than weaken the authority of *perestroika*.

Medvedev on Solzhenitsyn

In an interview with *Moskovsky komsomolets*, Soviet historian Roy Medvedev said he wished the USSR would allow publication of essays he had written criticizing the works of exiled Soviet writer Aleksandr Solzhenitsyn. He also called for the publication of Solzhenitsyn's works so that they could be subjected to criticism. Medvedev said negotiations were under way to publish more of his own works in the USSR, including his book on Stalin, *Let History Judge*. On December 3, 1988, Medvedev sharply attacked Solzhenitsyn's works for alleged "slander of Lenin." In an interview with the Riga newspaper *Sovetskaya molodezh'*, Medvedev suggested that Solzhenitsyn's *Gulag Archipelago* should either not be published at all in the USSR, or, if published, then with commentaries. In criticizing Solzhenitsyn, Medvedev attributed to him some statements that Solzhenitsyn never made in his works.

Armenian Activist Says Threatening Letter Is Fake

Armenian activist Rafael Papoyan said a letter threatening violence if leaders of the Karabakh Committee are not freed from jail is a fake. The letter appeared unsigned in the Armenian Party daily *Kommunist* on December 28. Papoyan said the letter—purportedly written by Armenian militants—was an attempt by Soviet officials to discredit the banned Karabakh Committee, which has led the campaign for the transfer of Nagorno-Karabakh from Azerbaijan to Armenia. *Kommunist* claimed the letter had been received by law-enforcement officials and the KGB. Sergei Grigoryants, a dissident editor who is half Armenian and has been monitoring ethnic unrest in the Transcaucasus, agreed that the letter was a fake. He told a Moscow news conference on January 2 that it was written in well-constructed Russian and had probably been drafted by a Russian or an Armenian living outside Armenia (*AP, Reuters,* January 1 and 2).

Ogonek Describes Corruption in 1970s

Ogonek (No. 1) carried the first part of a four-part article by correspondent Dmitrii Likhanov on the corrupt activities of Uzbek officials and Brezhnev's son-in-law Yurii Churbanov in the 1970s. Churbanov and the Uzbek officials described in the article were sentenced in Moscow on December 30, 1988, to various terms of imprisonment for their actions. See also *Ogonek*, Nos. 2, 3, and 4.

Monday, January 2

Official Says Party Lags Behind in Perestroika

Pravda carried an article by Leon Onikov, an official identified as an inspector in the CPSU Central Committee's Propaganda Department, saying that the CPSU was lagging far behind the rest of Soviet society in implementing *perestroika*. Onikov said many undemocratic

3

principles of Party organization introduced by Stalin remained in place. He said small groups of officials were still responsible for issuing resolutions, monitoring their implementation, and reporting on their effects. Plans for *glasnost'* in the Party to be implemented by November, 1986, had remained unfulfilled, he said, and Gorbachev had subsequently urged Party bodies to draw up legal guarantees for *glasnost'*. Onikov urged officials to begin work now to draw up new statutes for the Party prior to its twenty-eighth congress. On January 3, *Pravda* published further criticism of the CPSU, saying some Party members were showing indulgence towards "interethnic emotions and anti-Socialist and extremist attacks." It also criticized the Soviet press for not reporting on manipulations by ministries and departments aimed at "sabotaging" a decision to reduce administrative personnel.

Arms Plants Switched to Manufacturing Farm Equipment

TASS said about 250 arms-manufacturing plants had been drawn into an effort to design and build thousands of new machines to improve the Soviet food-processing industry. The move, announced in an interview with Deputy Prime Minister Igor Belousov, serves Gorbachev's goal of diverting some resources from the military to improve conditions for Soviet consumers. Huge quantities of food are currently lost in transportation and storage.

Ethnic Relations Center Set Up in Kazakhstan

TASS said an interethnic relations center had been established in Kazakhstan to look at ways of improving ethnic relations in the USSR. It said the center in the Kazakh capital Alma-Ata brings together scientists, Party workers, economists, cultural workers, and public figures. Kazakh Central Committee Secretary Uzbekali Dzhanibekov told TASS such a center was particularly important in Kazakhstan because the republic's 16 million people represent more than 100 ethnic groups. (Nationalist riots in Alma-Ata in December, 1986, left at least two people dead, including a policeman, and scores more were injured.) Details about the center, which is attached to the Kazakh Academy of Sciences, were first given in *Kazakhstanskaya pravda* on December 25, 1988.

Tuesday, January 3 ⸻

Jail Sentences Passed on Looters in Quake Zone

Sovetskaya Rossiya said the Armenian Supreme Court had passed jail terms on a number of people caught looting in areas hit by last month's earthquake. The newspaper said

4

a Erevan driver had been sentenced to eight years in prison for stealing food worth over 1,600 rubles from a Leninakan warehouse the day after the quake. Another man received a five-year sentence for posing as a doctor and stealing valuables from dead and wounded pulled from under the rubble in Spitak and Kirovakan.

Moscow Rabbi to Participate in World Jewish Congress

The chief rabbi of Moscow has asked to participate in meetings of the World Jewish Congress. Rabbi Adolf Shaevich, spiritual leader of Moscow's choral synagogue, made his request in a letter to WJC President Edgar Bronfman. Shaevich said that he was not a member of the Soviet Union's Anti-Zionist Committee and that the committee had been disbanded. Shaevich said he regretted that such a group had existed. He said he had never taken part in actions against Jews or the state of Israel. A WJC spokesman said Shaevich would be granted observer status at WJC international meetings. WJC Executive Director Elan Steinberg said the group was delighted with the development (*Reuters, UPI,* January 3).

***Pravda* Criticizes Georgian Protests**

Pravda criticized recent demonstrations and hunger strikes in Georgia. Western reports last November said that 200,000 people had demonstrated in Tbilisi and that several hundred had held a week-long hunger strike. The protesters opposed planned Soviet constitutional changes that they said violated the rights of the Union republics. *Pravda* accused the organizers of the protests of "adventurism, inhumanity, and barbarism." It said protest leaders had incited disorder and urged people to hand in their CPSU and Komsomol membership cards. It said they had also urged strikes and demanded that Georgia secede from the Soviet Union.

***Izvestia* Publishes Two Pages of Western Advertising**

Izvestia carried two pages of advertising, mostly for Western companies. Western reporters in Moscow said this was the first Western advertising to appear in a Soviet newspaper. One full-page advertisement was for a French firm that had recently signed a contract to build a large aluminum factory in Armenia. The second page was taken up with advertisements from Soviet, West German, and Belgian firms and a West German bank. *Izvestia* announced its acceptance of the advertising in a front-page story. It said the purpose was to give Western businessmen a chance to start "a direct dialogue" with Soviet companies.

USSR Ready to Help Track Down Pan Am Bombers

Soviet Foreign Ministry spokesman Vadim Perfil'ev told journalists in Moscow that the Soviet Union was ready to help find the people who bombed a Pan Am jet last month, causing the loss of 270 lives. He said those responsible should be found and punished so that such a tragedy is never repeated. He added that the Soviet Union was prepared to join international efforts "to rid human civilization of terrorism" (*AP*, *UPI*, January 3).

US Ambassador Meets KGB Chief in Moscow

US Ambassador to Moscow Jack Matlock held talks with the chief of the KGB, Vladimir Kryuchkov, a US embassy spokesman said. The spokesman said the meeting, which was held at Matlock's request, marked the first time that a US ambassador to the Soviet Union had met a KGB chief. The spokesman said Matlock and Kryuchkov had discussed matters of mutual interest, but he declined to give details. TASS also reported the meeting but did not divulge any details (*Reuters*, *AP*, January 4).

Soviet Citizen Complains His Letters to VOA and BBC Were Lost

Izvestia carried a letter from D. Shesterkin, a reader from Krivoi Rog, criticizing the Soviet postal service. Shesterkin said several letters that he had sent to the VOA and the BBC had failed to arrive. Shesterkin said he suspected that the letters had deliberately not been sent by the Soviet post, because its officials disliked the addressees.

Wednesday, January 4

Britain and US Declare Agreement in Principle to Moscow Conference

Britain and the United States told the Soviet Union they would agree to attend a human-rights conference in Moscow in 1991 if the Soviet Union continues to improve its human-rights record. Diplomats in Vienna said that Britain and the United States could refuse to go to Moscow any time before 1991 if the USSR did not honor the human-rights commitments made by Gorbachev. (The most likely deadline for a final decision will be around mid-1990.) The diplomats said the decision to go to Moscow had followed a series of recent Soviet actions, including the release of political and religious prisoners, an easing of emigration restrictions, and the end to jamming of Western radio broadcasts. Jewish groups in the United States and Britain criticized the decision, saying it was not yet time to reward the Soviet Union with a human-rights conference in Moscow. Soviet human-rights activist Andrei Sakharov said that holding the conference must depend on the situation in Armenia. He said he was very worried about what was happening there. He mentioned in particular the arrests of members of the Karabakh Committee (*RFE/RL Special*, January 4 and 5).

Radio Tashkent (0230) said a six-month-old child had been killed and nineteen other people injured when Afghans staged a riot in the city on January 1. The report said the rioters were "hooligan elements from among Afghan citizens staying in Tashkent" and were intoxicated by alcohol and narcotics. It said Afghans had thrown stones at pedestrians and passing vehicles near a market. On January 5, Radio Moscow (0700) said two more people had died as a result of the riot.

Afghan Riot in Tashkent Reported

Gorbachev met Ayatollah Abdullah Javadi Amoli, a personal envoy from Iranian leader Ayatollah Khomeini, in the Kremlin (*Pravda*, January 5). Amoli was heading a delegation to Moscow that included Iranian Deputy Foreign Minister Mohammed Javad Larijani. Amoli delivered a personal message to Gorbachev from Khomeini. Iran's official news agency said the message was the first Khomeini had sent to a foreign leader since the Islamic revolution in Iran in 1979. Details of the message were provided by Khomeini's son, Seyyed Ahmad, who said Khomeini told Gorbachev the failure of communism had become evident and asked him "to think about and do research on Islam in a serious way." He told Iranian television his father's message praised Gorbachev for courage in his restructuring efforts and in facing up to world realities. The letter marked a clear turnabout for Khomeini. In the past, the Iranian religious leader has lumped the Soviet Union together with the United States and Britain as one of the world's three "great satans."

Gorbachev Meets Khomeini's Personal Envoy in Kremlin

The authorities in Armenia and Azerbaijan issued a joint appeal to people in both republics to resist attempts to stir up ethnic passions. Radio Baku said the appeal, published on the front page of several republican newspapers, was aimed at tens of thousands of Armenians and Azerbaijanis who fled their homes last year to avoid ethnic unrest and violence triggered by the territorial dispute over Nagorno-Karabakh. The appeal is signed by the Armenian and Azerbaijani Communist Party Central Committees, Supreme Soviet Presidiums, and Councils of Ministers. In an interview with TASS, Soviet investigator Vasilii Novikov said special teams had been set up in the

Joint Armenian-Azerbaijani Appeal to Refugees

two republics to examine criminal aspects of ethnic unrest in the region. Novikov said that 101 criminal cases had been filed by January 1 and that eighteen people had already been tried and sentenced.

Soviet Historian Says NKVD Hired Trotsky's Murderer

In an article in *Literaturnaya gazeta*, Soviet historian Nikolai Vasetsky said that Stalin had ordered the assassination of Leon Trotsky and that the NKVD had carried it out. Vasetsky said the NKVD had trained a Spanish Communist, Ramon Mercader, to kill Trotsky. Trotsky was killed in Mexico City in 1940 while in exile. Until recently, the Soviet Union has said he was killed by disillusioned followers. On November 10, 1988, *Kazakhstanskaya pravda* said Stalin was responsible for Trotsky's murder.

Markov Retires as Chairman of USSR Writers' Union

The chairman and former first secretary of the USSR Writers' Union, Georgii Markov, is retiring. TASS said Markov's resignation request would be submitted at a plenum of the Writers' Union to be held this month. Markov, who is seventy-seven, served as first secretary of the Writer's Union from 1971 to 1986, when he was replaced by Vladimir Karpov. Markov was then given the largely ceremonial post of union chairman.

***Ogonek* Sharply Increases Circulation**

Radio Moscow (0900) reported that 3.2 million copies of the first issue of *Ogonek* for this year had been printed. This represents an increase of almost 1.5 million copies over last year's weekly printing of 1.7 million. Some 2.8 million of the 3.2 million copies will be subscription copies. Last month, *Ogonek's* chief editor, Vitalii Korotich, said he wanted to sever the magazine's ties with the publishing house operated by *Pravda*. This, he said, would allow *Ogonek* to increase its circulation, make its own decisions about how to spend income, and sell copies abroad to earn hard currency.

Soviet Consular Officers Told to Help Emigrés

Soviet Deputy Foreign Minister Boris Chaplin said Soviet diplomats had been told that Soviet citizens who live abroad are not "unpatriotic" and deserve much better treatment. He told a Moscow news conference that consular officers had been instructed to protect the rights of emigrants, prevent discrimination against them, and provide social and legal assistance (*TASS*, in English, January 4). The official Soviet attitude towards émigrés has changed drastically over the last year. Soviet officials,

8

including Foreign Minister Eduard Shevardnadze, have called for more cooperation with émigrés. The Soviet press has also started to present émigrés in a positive light, departing from its previous practice of portraying them as traitors (see, for instance, an article by Leonid Pochivalov in *Literaturnaya gazeta*, December 28, 1988).

South Korean-Soviet Fishing Agreement Signed

A South Korean firm has signed a contract with Moscow to acquire fish from Soviet territorial waters and develop a joint-venture seafood-processing plant on Soviet soil, a company spokesman said. Lee Soo-Il, managing director of Korea Tuna Company, said the contract initially allows his company to acquire 100,000 tons of fish per annum from Soviet fishing boats inside the Soviet 200-mile exclusive fishing zone. In return, Korea Tuna will provide money, technology, and equipment. The arrangement is the first of its kind between a South Korean firm and the Soviet Union. Seoul has no diplomatic relations with Moscow (*UPI, Reuters,* January 4).

Thursday, January 5

Sakharov Nominated to Congress of People's Deputies

Soviet human-rights activist Andrei Sakharov was nominated for a seat in the new Congress of People's Deputies. Sakharov was nominated by the Ivan Pavlov Institute of Physiology in Leningrad. Two hundred and sixteen votes were cast in favor of his nomination and twenty-nine against. Sakharov was nominated for one of seventy-five seats in the congress reserved for nominees of the country's scientific workers (*TASS,* January 5).

Soviet Official Indicates Jamming Was Hazardous

USSR Deputy Minister of Communications Gennadii Kudryavtsev said in an interview published by TASS that Soviet jamming of Western radio broadcasts was dangerous because of the high levels of electromagnetic radiation it produced. This was apparently the first time that a Soviet official made such an admission about jamming, which went on for decades before gradually being phased out over the past several years. "The jamming stations were usually placed in the center of towns, and the electromagnetic radiation in adjacent areas exceeded the safety norms," Kudryavtsev said. He did not say what the levels were or explain the effects of prolonged exposure to high levels. He said that, now that jamming has ceased, outdated jamming stations will be dismantled and modern ones used for local radio broadcasting.

Soviet Reaction to Downing of Libyan Planes

Soviet Foreign Ministry spokesman Gennadii Gerasimov said Moscow had received with "indignation" the news of the United States' downing of two Libyan fighter planes. He told a news conference in Moscow that such actions are a show of "adventurism" and "state terrorism" that could have serious consequences. He said the action ran counter to efforts in the world community to find political solutions to conflicts (*TASS*, in English, January 5).

Ignalina Controversy Debated in Moscow

Radio Vilnius (0200) said a government commission of leading Soviet specialists had discussed the future of the controversial Ignalina nuclear power plant in Lithuania and were divided over whether to build a third reactor at Ignalina. The report said Konstantin Frolov, a vice president of the USSR Academy of Sciences, signed a document prepared by Lithuanian scientists calling for a halt to work on the third reactor. About one-third of the scientists on the commission, however, failed to sign the document and are strongly opposed to its conclusions. Environmentalists have raised doubts about the safety of the Ignalina plant and believe that expanding it would involve ecological hazards. The Ignalina reactors are more powerful versions of the one that exploded at Chernobyl' in 1986.

New Limits Imposed on Cooperatives

The Soviet government has imposed new limits on a range of cooperatives. The rules, issued on December 31, 1988, by the USSR Council of Ministers without any preliminary public discussion, are the first specific limits imposed since the introduction of a law in June, 1988, expanding the rights of cooperatives. In addition, the CPSU Politburo today announced new measures aimed at putting pressure on cooperatives to lower their prices. TASS said the government would give preferences in state loans, tax rates, and supplies of raw materials to businesses that sell their goods and services at state-controlled prices. Georgii Golubov, a Justice Ministry official, told a news conference that the restrictions had been imposed in response to "hundreds and thousands" of complaints from consumers about the poor quality and high prices at cooperatives. The new rules ban some kinds of private business entirely, including the organization of general-education schools; producing or showing "cinema and video productions"; publishing "works of science, literature, and art"; the manufacture of religious items; wine-making; pawn shops; and "amusement houses." Other business activities are allowed only if a cooperative works under contract to a state factory or official organization.

The rules also prohibit a range of private medical services, including all types of surgery, treatment of pregnant women, and work-related checkups (*The New York Times*, January 6).

_____ *Friday, January 6*

In a speech to a congress of the West German Communist Party in Frankfurt, CPSU Politburo member Aleksandr Yakovlev said the new ideas generated by *perestroika* must not be judged by how well they conform with Communist dogma. Yakovlev said only those who study Marxism without bearing direct responsibility for human beings can rest upon the illusion that dogma is more important than life. Yakovlev said *perestroika* should instead be judged by what it produces for human progress, workers, countries, and socialism (*DPA*, *TASS*, January 6). For the text of Yakovlev's speech, see *Izvestia*, January 7.

Yakovlev Attends West German CP Congress

Izvestia said that documents had been removed from the Foreign Ministry's restricted list concerning the case of Marshal Mikhail Tukhachevsky, a deputy war minister under Stalin. Tukhachevsky was executed in 1937, after being charged with conspiracy in connection with reports of contacts between the German army and leaders of the Red Army. *Izvestia* said the documents now released include communications from Soviet diplomats in Czechoslovakia and France showing that the Nazis passed along information to Czechoslovak President Eduard Benes about "so-called contacts" between the German army and leaders of the Red Army. The revelations were contained in an article entitled "The USSR Ministry of Foreign Affairs Opens Its Archives." While the Soviet press from time to time publishes reports about making previously secret archive materials available to the public, Soviet specialists in the humanities continue to complain about problems they still face in gaining access to archives. One of the main articles condemning the restrictions imposed on the use of archives in the USSR was published by historian Boris Ilizarov in *Ogonek* (No. 2).

Tukhachevsky Documents Taken Off Security List

Pravda published the text of a CPSU Central Committee resolution "On Additional Measures for the Restoration of Justice to Victims of Repressions That Took Place in the 1930s, 1940s, and Early 1950s." The resolution stipulated

Central Committee's Decree on Rehabilitation of Stalin's Victims

11

that people sentenced (often to death) without trial by the so-called three-man groups (*troiki*) and "special assemblies" (*osobye soveshchaniya*) should be automatically rehabilitated. The number of people sentenced in this way is estimated to be in the millions. The resolution added, however, that people convicted of being Nazis, members of nationalist groups, murderers, executioners, and traitors should not be rehabilitated. On January 16, the Presidium of the USSR Supreme Soviet adopted a decree on the matter. On January 31, *Pravda* carried an interview with the chief military prosecutor, Boris Popov, commenting on the resolution and the decree. Popov said about 25,000 individuals whose cases came under the jurisdiction of the military prosecutor would be rehabilitated under the decree. Popov said that the number of applications for rehabilitations from people sentenced during World War II had tripled recently but that many applications had been turned down. He said that every fifth request for rehabilitation is rejected.

Three Armenian Prosecutors Dismissed after Ethnic Unrest

Pravda said three district prosecutors in Armenia had been dismissed for failing to deal with ethnic unrest. *Pravda* said four other prosecutors had been strongly reprimanded and a fifth told he should quit at the end of his term. More than sixty people died in Armenia and Azerbaijan last year in disturbances linked to the Nagorno-Karabakh issue.

***Pravda* Says USSR Hoped to Control World Weather**

An interview conducted in 1963 with Sergei Korolev, the founder and chief designer of the Soviet space program, was published for the first time. In the interview, in *Pravda*, Korolev revealed that, when it launched its aggressive space program in the 1950s, the USSR hoped satellites would allow it to manipulate global weather patterns, controlling droughts and even hailstorms. *Pravda* said that under the current policy of *glasnost'* the interview, which had been confined to sealed newspaper archives, could now be published. In the interview, Korolev, who died in 1966, defended the potential benefits and spinoffs for the civilian economy of the space program.

***Sobesednik* on 1947 Famine in Bessarabia**

The youth journal *Sobesednik* (No. 3) carried a letter from Igor Sokolov of Krasnoyarsk Krai, who wrote that in 1947 a famine had been organized in Bessarabia (in Moldavia) similar to the famine in Ukraine in 1933. Sokolov said that he had lived in Bessarabia from the 1940s to the 1960s and that he recalled how all the grain and other food products were confiscated from peasants in Bessarabia [to suppress their resistance against forced collectivization].

Literaturnaya Rossiya carried an essay by Vladimir Tsybin on Russian philosopher Nikolai Berdyaev. Berdyaev, together with other Russian idealist philosophers, had been banned in the USSR until last year.

Literaturnaya Rossiya on Berdyaev

Saturday, January 7

Pravda carried an interview with Vyacheslav Pankin, head of the USSR Ministry of Internal Affairs' Criminal Investigation Department, on the ethnic unrest in Armenia and Azerbaijan. Pankin stated that forty-three people had been killed and that there had been 3,000 pogroms and cases of arson in the two republics since the resurgence of unrest in November. This brings the death toll to more than eighty since ethnic strife began last February. AP quoted a spokesman for the Azerbaijani Foreign Ministry as saying 160,000 Azerbaijanis had fled Armenia to escape unrest and the effects of the earthquake. In Armenia, the 90,000 refugees from Azerbaijan have been joined by 500,000 who lost their homes in the earthquake.

New Figures on Death Toll in Ethnic Unrest

Novosti press agency reported that "Interfront," a counter organization to the Popular Front of Latvia, held its founding meeting in Riga today. Novosti said the new organization, the overwhelming majority of whose members are Russians living in Latvia, agrees with the Popular Front on many issues, including the need for Latvian citizenship and giving priority to Latvian culture. It disagrees, however, with making Latvian the only state language and opposes creating a separate Latvian Olympic Committee. Novosti said the new group also wants the USSR Public Prosecutor to continue appointing Latvia's Public Prosecutor and is opposed to putting the entire republic on a full cost-accounting basis. The Popular Front holds the opposite opinion on both these issues. The same day, Latvian Communist Party First Secretary Janis Vagris complained about "an intolerable split" within the Latvian Party, saying it was caused by members working for both the Popular Front and "Interfront" (*TASS, AFP*, January 7). On January 20, *Sovetskaya Latviya* carried a letter from the chairman of the Popular Front of Latvia,

Controversy over International Front in Latvia

13

Dainis Ivans, to the Council of "Interfront." In the letter Ivans rejected the possibility of cooperation between "Interfront" and the Popular Front. He rejected claims that on many issues the two fronts have similar positions and said the goals of the two organizations are completely opposed. On January 26, *Sovetskaya Latviya* carried an article reporting on a discussion of "Interfront" by the Latvian Party Central Committee. While praising the front, the Latvian Party leadership pointed out that some sectors of the population of Latvia had a negative attitude towards the front.

Armenian Activists Arrested

The authorities in Erevan arrested a group of Armenian activists, including four more members of the Karabakh Committee, according to various Western news agency reports quoting activist Rafael Papoyan and relatives of the detainees. Papoyan was quoted as saying the latest arrests raise doubts about whether the five members of the Karabakh Committee who were sentenced in December to thirty days in jail will be released (*AP, AFP*, January 9). On January 9, the Armenian minister of internal affairs, Usik Arutyunyan, told a press conference in Erevan that charges would be brought against several members of the Karabakh Committee under a law covering "participation in group disorders." Arutyunyan said the charges would be brought by both the Armenian and USSR Public Prosecutors (*Reuters*, January 10).

Foreign Travel Reported to Be Easier

The latest issue of *Argumenty i fakty* contained a statement by the head of the Soviet visa office OVIR, Rudolf Kuznetsov, that most Soviet citizens now need only an invitation from an acquaintance abroad in order to obtain a tourist visa to travel outside the USSR. Kuznetsov added that emigration visas are easier to obtain as well. He said last year more than 90,000 Soviet citizens had been allowed to emigrate, most of them Jews, Armenians, and Soviet Germans. A spokesman for the US embassy in Moscow said that the number of Soviet citizens who received US visitor visas rose to 20,354 in 1988 from 5,987 in 1987.

Ogonek Publishes Defense of Lev Kopelev

Ogonek (No. 2) carried a letter signed by fifty-two prominent Soviet intellectuals, among them Andrei Sakharov, Bulat Okudzhava, Yurii Karyakin, Fazil Iskander, Anatolii Pristavkin, and David Samoilov, condemning an attack against the émigré writer Lev Kopelev that appeared in *Sovetskaya Rossiya* on December 21, 1988. The signers of the letter termed the anti-Kopelev article a deliberate provocation against *perestroika*, similar to the letter by Nina Andreeva published in the same newspaper on March 13, 1988. Kopelev is one of the émigré community's most enthusiastic supporters of current Soviet policy. On January 1, *Moscow News* (No. 1) also condemned the attack on him by *Sovetskaya Rossiya*.

In an interview with the Italian newspaper *la Repubblica*, Boris El'tsin said that he expects a reconciliation with Gorbachev soon. He blamed the rift between himself and Gorbachev on Egor Ligachev. El'tsin added that Ligachev should be removed, and he again complained about the pace of *perestroika*, saying that restructuring efforts should have been concentrated in areas that affect people's lives, such as food, consumer goods, and services.

El'tsin Predicts Reconciliation with Gorbachev

TASS said that heavy snow and hurricane-force winds had disrupted the western part of Georgia and that some people were being evacuated. It said there had been "human losses" in the area but gave no figures. According to TASS, electricity had been cut off in some towns and villages, and roads through mountain passes were blocked, and a government commission had ordered the evacuation of the population from "the disaster area." On January 8, it was reported that at least six people had died in the storms (*Reuters*, January 8).

Heavy Snow and Winds in Georgia

Sunday, January 8

Soviet Foreign Minister Eduard Shevardnadze announced at the international conference on chemical weapons in Paris that the USSR intends to destroy its stocks of chemical weapons this year at an installation specially constructed for this purpose. He said the Soviet position on chemical weapons had "changed radically" in the past two years, explaining that the USSR used to make such weapons and conceal the fact, while now it wants to eliminate them and is ready to accept "the most stringent international verification," including on-site inspections without any right of refusal. He declared that the Soviet Union had not deployed chemical weapons beyond its territory and had never transferred them to another state (*UPI, TASS*, in English, January 8). The United States welcomed the Soviet announcement.

USSR to Destroy Its Chemical-Weapons Stocks

Gorbachev Calls for Defense Cuts to Trim Budget

The Soviet press published details of the speech Soviet President and CPSU General Secretary Gorbachev gave to a meeting of scientists and cultural figures on January 6. In the speech Gorbachev stressed that the problem of the state budget deficit, whose existence had been concealed until last year, is so acute that defense spending may have to be cut. Gorbachev said a preliminary study showed that defense expenditures could be cut without reducing the level of security. He said the war in Afghanistan, the Chernobyl' nuclear disaster, the Armenian earthquake, the fall in oil prices, and the sharp fall in revenues from alcohol sales had all contributed to the budget problem. From these and other recent statements the shortfall during the period 1985–88 may be estimated at about 131 billion rubles. Much of Gorbachev's speech focused on problems of *perestroika*. He criticized those who blame *perestroika* for the country's economic, social, and ethnic problems. He said *perestroika* had merely exposed these problems and offered opportunities for finding ways of solving them. He also said the Communist Party was being attacked by "those who wish to wreck *perestroika*" and added that some people were trying to sow doubt about socialism, questioning whether "the framework of socialism is too narrow for *perestroika*." He said ideas about political pluralism, and private property are also cropping up (*Pravda*, January 8).

Shevardnadze Has Meeting with Arens

Soviet Foreign Minister Eduard Shevardnadze met with Israeli Foreign Minister Moshe Arens in Paris. TASS said Shevardnadze told Arens that the realistic stance of the Palestinian leadership meant there was a historic chance for a breakthrough in a Middle East settlement. Shevardnadze said the world was waiting for an adequate Israeli response. After the meeting, Arens said the Soviet Union was allowing the Israeli consular mission in Moscow to expand its activities. He said Shevardnadze told him the USSR now considers the Israeli mission "an address for political activities" (*Reuters*, *AP*, January 8).

Yakovlev Appears on West German Television

CPSU Politburo member Aleksandr Yakovlev said in an interview on West German television that it was a mistake for the USSR to have followed blindly the armaments spiral. He said the USSR now favored a policy of balanced and moderate levels of armaments. Yakovlev also said it was possible that one day the Berlin Wall would go, but he said the wall was not built by the USSR and is part of relations between East and West Germany (*DPA*, *ARD*,

January 8). On January 9, Yakovlev met West German Chancellor Helmut Kohl in Bonn to discuss arms control and Gorbachev's visit to Bonn. West German government spokesman Friedhelm Ost said Yakovlev and Kohl emphasized the interest they have in Gorbachev's visit leading to an improvement in mutual relations (*DPA*, *Reuters*, *AFP*, January 9).

Armenian Nuclear Power Plant to Be Closed by March 18

Armenian Party First Secretary Suren Arutyunyan told a Party conference in Erevan that the nuclear power plant near the city will be closed down completely by March 18. He was quoted as saying the Central Committee shared the concern and anxiety of the population about the safety of the plant following last month's earthquake in Armenia (*Moscow Television, Reuters, AFP*, January 8). On January 11, *Izvestia* published a report saying that factories in Armenia would face an electricity shortage when the plant is closed. *Izvestia* said a resolution of the USSR Council of Ministers called for a speeding up of construction of another nuclear power station, at Rostov-on-Don, to meet the shortfall. The same day, *Pravda* published a letter from ten scientists calling for a halt to construction of a nuclear power plant in the Crimea. The letter said that the site of the plant is subject to severe seismic and volcanic activity and that the plant is not built to withstand an earthquake of the size liable to occur in the Crimea. It said no nuclear plant should be built in a densely populated area like the Crimea, where 2 million people live.

Number of Suicides in USSR Revealed

Meditsinskaya gazeta revealed that there were 54,000 suicides in the USSR in 1987, a figure that suggests an all-Union suicide rate of around 19 per 100,000 of the population. The article said that the suicide rate in the USSR ranges from between 2 and 8 per 100,000 in the Caucasus and the Central Asian republics to between 23 and 29 in the RSFSR and the Baltic republics. It quoted a specialist as saying this difference can be attributed to "the greater respect for religious traditions" in the southern republics. This is not the first time the suicide rate has been published in the Soviet press. Last spring, *Argumenty i fakty* (No. 22, 1988) said the suicide rate stood at "around 20" per 100,000 of the population; see RL 290/88.

Moscow News and Nedelya Interview Sinyavsky

Moscow News (No. 2) carried an interview with émigré Russian writer Andrei Sinyavsky and his wife Mariya Rozanova. (The trial in 1966 of Sinyavsky and writer Yulii

Daniel gave birth to the Soviet dissident movement.) In the interview Sinyavsky spoke about his imprisonment, emigration, and literary work. Another interview with Sinyavsky appeared in *Nedelya* (No. 1). Sinyavsky gave both interviews in Paris. On January 13, *Knizhnoe obozrenie* (No. 2) published an interview with Sinyavsky and his wife that they gave while in Moscow in connection with the death of Daniel.

Monday, January 9

Tax Break to Encourage Inventors

The chairman of the State Committee on Inventions and Discoveries, Ivan Nayashkov, told a news conference that new incentives for inventors will include a three-year tax-free period. Additional changes will bring Soviet patent and copyright law into line with that of other countries. The changes are included in a new draft law published in late December (*Reuters, AP*, January 9).

Afghan Guerrillas Break Off Talks with Vorontsov

In an angry statement issued in Islamabad, Sibghatullah Mojaddedi, the spokesman of the Pakistan-based Afghan guerrilla alliance, said the *mujahidin* had decided to break off talks with Soviet negotiators because "they use threats, look for war rather than peace, and disrespect the Afghans' right to self-determination" (*AP, Reuters*, January 9). Mojaddedi accused Moscow of trying to impose an alien government on the Afghan people and insisted that no further talks would be possible until all Soviet troops were out of Afghanistan and the People's Democratic Party of President Najibullah had been overthrown. The talks began on January 5. At a news conference on January 8, USSR First Deputy Foreign Minister and Ambassador to Kabul Yulii Vorontsov put the blame for the failure of the talks entirely on the *mujahidin*, accusing them of "medieval thinking." On January 10, Vorontsov told a news conference there was "a serious danger" the USSR might have to delay or suspend the withdrawal of its troops from Afghanistan because the resistance had rejected a broad-based future government. His remarks came as Western diplomats reported that the final phase of the troop withdrawal was being prepared and could get under way fully on January 15 (*Reuters, AP*, January 10). On January 15, the commander of Soviet Forces in Afghanistan, Lieutenant General Boris Gromov, said all his troops would be out of the country by February 15 (*Reuters, TASS*, January 15).

TASS reported that the Central State Archive has opened half a million secret files on such subjects as the Russian Orthodox Church and the White Guard. Records on organizations liquidated during the 1920s and 1930s are now being declassified. According to TASS, specialists may now have access to court documents, and provision has been made for researchers to look at documents of the USSR Public Prosecutor's Office, the USSR Ministry of Health, the State Committee on Publishing, and the All-Union Council of Trade Unions.

Central Archive Opens Files

Former CPSU Politburo member Boris El'tsin again warned of the dangers of the concentration of power in the hands of one leader. He said in an interview with West German television (ZDF) that many people hope Gorbachev can resist that temptation. El'tsin also said *perestroika* was not making progress, because people are not getting what they have been promised. He said that there is still a shortage of consumer goods and that services are bad. He insisted that there is no organized resistance to *perestroika* among senior Soviet leaders but that "a concealed and delaying resistance cannot be denied."

El'tsin Speaks Out Again on Gorbachev and *Perestroika*

Soviet Foreign Minister Eduard Shevardnadze said information the United States gave him on a Libyan chemical factory does not prove the plant can make chemical weapons. Shevardnadze made the statement to reporters before leaving the chemical weapons conference in Paris. On January 8, US Secretary of State George Shultz briefed Shevardnadze on American findings that the plant is intended for making poison gas (*AP, UPI, DPA,* January 9).

Shevardnadze Says No Proof of Chemical-Weapons Production in Libya

Pravda carried an article by its Paris correspondent Vladimir Bolshakov on Soviet émigrés. Bolshakov praises those émigrés who are in favor of *perestroika* and attacks those who are not. Aleksandr Glezer and Julia Wishnevskaya are among those praised, while Aleksandr Zinov'ev and Vladimir Maksimov come under attack.

***Pravda* on Emigrés**

Tuesday, January 10

A plenum of the CPSU Central Committee met to discuss the nomination of Party members for the elections of the new Congress of People's Deputies. The Soviet media

Central Committee Plenum

19

reported that the plenum nominated 100 candidates from a list of 312; however, the names of the candidates were not immediately made public. In a speech to the plenum, Gorbachev said the campaign for the newly styled national elections faces difficulties, including "group egoism, ambition, and political careerism." He said a high level of organization and responsibility was important to ensuring the success of the campaign. Gorbachev expressed satisfaction that most of the congress candidates nominated so far are active supporters of *perestroika* (*TASS, Radio Moscow*, 1200, *Reuters, AP*, January 10).

Izvestia Criticizes Moscow Mail Service

Izvestia said it had received letters and telephone calls from Muscovites complaining that, because of the disorganized work of Moscow's post offices, many periodicals were failing to reach subscribers.

Shevardnadze Says Each People Has Right to Choose

Soviet Foreign Minister Eduard Shevardnadze said new Soviet thinking gives each people the right to choose the political system that best suits it. He also said that, when international relations are dominated by ideology, the ideals shared by all humanity are relegated to a secondary position. His remarks came in an interview published in the French newspaper *Le Figaro*. Shevardnadze reported a timetable was being prepared for the withdrawal of some Soviet troops from Czechoslovakia, Hungary, and East Germany. He said planned military cuts were accepted by "an overwhelming majority of our people" and by the leaders and personnel of the armed forces.

Demonstrations in Lithuania

About 50,000 people demonstrated for two hours in Vilnius to condemn the secret protocol to the Nazi-Soviet border and friendship treaty that provided for the transfer of Lithuania to the Soviet sphere of interest. The authorities had given permission for the rally, and there was no police interference. There were about twenty speakers from various unofficial groups. The speakers called for Lithuanian independence and the withdrawal of what they termed "the Soviet occupation army." Participants in the rally approved by acclamation a resolution addressed to the United Nations Decolonization Committee "protesting against the continuing colonization of the three Baltic States" and asked that this question be raised at the next session of the United Nations General Assembly (*Reuters, AP*, January 11).

Radio Moscow (0800) reported that an association for the defense of consumers' rights had been set up in Lithuania. The report said that the organization would work mainly for the setting of realistic prices for consumer goods and for better quality. It said the association would give advice to consumers and defend their rights if necessary.

Lithuanian Association for Defense of Consumers' Rights

The Soviet Union has formed a joint venture with an art dealer in the United States to sell Soviet art. Eduard Nakhamkin, a Russian who emigrated to the United States from Latvia, will buy Soviet artworks and resell them to US dealers. Soviet officials say they hope the project will increase the flow of hard currency to the Ministry of Culture and the Union of Soviet Artists (*AP*, January 10).

Agreement Signed for Soviet Artists to Sell at US Galleries

An Israeli basketball team, Maccabi Tel Aviv, flew to the Soviet Union to play its first game there since the USSR severed diplomatic relations with Israel at the time of the 1967 Middle East war. Maccabi will compete against CSKA Moscow in a European Champions Cup game on January 12. For more than twenty years, the two countries' teams have played on neutral courts in Western Europe (*Reuters*, January 10).

Israeli Basketball Team Goes to Moscow

_____*Wednesday, January 11*

The Soviet Union will soon require foreigners who want to stay in the country for more than three months to prove they are free of the AIDS virus. Soviet spokesman Gennadii Gerasimov told reporters in Moscow that those who do not have proof could be made to take an AIDS test. He said that people who try to avoid the test may be expelled and that the new measures are to go into effect on February 1. He also said Soviet AIDS tests had revealed that 334 foreigners were carrying the virus and that five of them had actually developed the disease. One hundred twelve Soviet citizens were found to be carriers, and three have developed the disease, one of whom has died (*Reuters, AP*, January 11).

New Soviet AIDS Policy Announced

Two Soviet activists were reported to have been confined to psychiatric hospitals last month. Activist Aleksandr Podrabinek told reporters in Moscow that Anatolii

Activists Reported Confined to Psychiatric Hospitals

Ilchenko was confined on December 23 in the Ukrainian city of Nikolaev. He said Ilchenko was accused of anti-Soviet propaganda. Podrabinek also said Vyacheslav Cherkashin was confined in Novosibirsk. Reports reaching the West said Cherkashin was confined on December 17. Cherkashin is a member of the unofficial Russian nationalist group "Pamyat'." Another activist, Aleksandr Novikov, told reporters he had been hospitalized as a schizophrenic after distributing leaflets on democratic rights. He said he had been confined in a hospital in Chernyakhovsk and had met seven political prisoners there. Novikov was released in October (*AP, AFP, RL Samizdat*, January 11). On January 12, the chairman of the Soviet Scientific Society of Psychiatrists and Neuropathologists, Georgii Morozov, was quoted by TASS as saying there are no political prisoners in Soviet mental hospitals. Morozov also said that, although the competence of individual doctors might be questioned, he ruled out "the possibility of deliberate wrong diagnosis." Morozov said a list of forty-eight patients of Soviet mental hospitals whose diagnosis had been questioned by the United States was being thoroughly studied. He said a delegation of American psychiatrists due to visit the Soviet Union next month will be allowed to review the condition of patients and their treatment.

Soviet Students Arrive in United States

Forty Soviet secondary school students arrived in the United States for a four-week stay that will include a meeting with US President Ronald Reagan. The students, all from Moscow schools, are the first contingent of Soviet pupils participating in a new exchange program called the US-USSR High School Academic Partnership Program. Students selected to participate will spend about a month studying at an American school and living with an American family. American students will begin going to Soviet schools next month (*RFE/RL Special*, January 12).

Marx's "Secret Diplomatic History" Published

Voprosy istorii (No. 1) carried a Russian translation of Karl Marx's *Secret Diplomatic History of the Eighteenth Century*. It is the first time the work has appeared in Russian translation in the Soviet Union. The collection of Marx's and Engels' works in Russian does not include the *Secret Diplomatic History*, because some of its statements are regarded as anti-Russian. In its introduction to the *Secret Diplomatic History, Voprosy istorii* also asserts that "some of [Marx's] statements about Russia are biased." Several Soviet historians and philosophers complained last year about the lack of a Russian translation of Marx's controversial works; see for instance, *Voprosy istorii* (No. 3, 1988) and *Ogonek* (No. 19, 1988).

Literaturnaya gazeta published an article by the lawyer Arkadii Vaksberg, who disputed the myth, still persistent in the Soviet Union, that officials under Stalin were very modest in their material demands, in contrast with the corrupt and pampered officials of the Brezhnev era. On the basis of archive materials, Vaksberg described how Stalin's prosecutor Andrei Vyshinsky used all kinds of tricks to build himself an enormous country house near Moscow at state expense. Vaksberg compared Vyshinsky's behavior with that of one of the most corrupt officials of the Brezhnev era, Nikolai Shchelokov.

Vaksberg on Corrupt Officials under Stalin

———————————————————————————*Thursday, January 12*

The 1989 population census officially began in the Soviet Union today. TASS said more than a million census-takers will spread out across the Soviet Union during the week-long process. The census has been under way in more remote areas since August, 1988. TASS said the 1989 census would, for the first time since 1926, contain questions about housing conditions. TASS also said officials had been instructed to record Soviet citizens' ethnic allegiance exactly as they express it in order to gain a more exact ethnic portrait of the people of the Soviet Union. For instance, it said, census takers would no longer be allowed to record the Guzuls as Ukrainians. The Guzuls are a group of highlanders who live in southwest Ukraine. The chairman of the State Committee for Statistics, Mikhail Korolev, said that the data would be kept confidential and that the information would be used to draw up plans for social and economic development. He said no questions would be asked about religion or wages.

1989 Census Begins

Moscow police broke up a demonstration by Crimean Tatars in front of the Kremlin, detaining about a dozen people who had unfurled red protest banners. The demonstrators, who were demanding the right to return to their homeland on the Black Sea peninsula, stood on the steps of the Lenin Library for about eight minutes before they were hauled away by police. In summer, 1988, a special Soviet government commission ruled that

Police Detain Crimean Tatars Demonstrating in Moscow

restrictions on the resettlement of Tatars be lifted, but the local authorities in the Crimea say they can only allow people to return if there are jobs and apartments available (*Reuters*, January 12).

Arrest of Former Moldavian Official

Trud reported that the former Party second secretary in Moldavia, Viktor Smirnov, had been arrested in connection with what it called "the Uzbek affair." *Trud* did not say on what charges Smirnov had been arrested, but it reported his arrest in a story about abuses in Uzbekistan and the convictions of Yurii Churbanov and Uzbek police officials on bribery charges. Smirnov retired as Party second secretary in Moldavia in November, 1988, apparently for health reasons. He had held the job since August, 1984, and is a candidate member of the CPSU Central Committee. A report on Smirnov's arrest also appeared in *Moscow News* (No. 4).

CPSU Publishes Election Platform

The CPSU published its platform for nationwide elections in March to the new Congress of People's Deputies. It promises improved living conditions and increased benefits for the elderly, large families, and families with low incomes. The document, adopted on January 10 by the CPSU Central Committee, says priority will be given to improving food supplies, boosting the output of industrial goods, and to trying to provide every family with its own apartment by the year 2000. It does not say how this will be achieved. The platform also envisages laws to strengthen individual rights, improve interethnic relations, broaden the rights of republics, and strengthen their sovereignty (*TASS*, in English, January 12).

"Special Form of Administration" Imposed in Nagorno-Karabakh

The Presidium of the USSR Supreme Soviet decided that the Nagorno-Karabakh Autonomous Oblast of Azerbaijan will retain its autonomous status but under "a special form of administration" (*osobaya forma upravleniya*). TASS said the Presidium decided the measure would be temporary. The announcement came after the Presidium had considered proposals from Party and state bodies in Azerbaijan and Armenia and from the Council of Nationalities. TASS said the Presidium's aim was to prevent continued aggravation of interethnic relations and stabilize the situation in the region. TASS did not explain what form the special administration would take. It said a decree of the Presidium would be published in the press. The text of the decree appeared in the Soviet press on January 15. The decree said the move, which suspends the powers of the oblast's soviet, was aimed at preventing persistent strains in interethnic relations from getting worse. It said that, starting on January 20, a special committee would assume full legislative and executive powers until a new oblast soviet is elected, but it did not indicate how long that would take. The committee is to be chaired by Arkadii Vol'sky, the special Kremlin envoy sent to the troubled region last year. The decree said the committee would have the authority to suspend the powers of all local governing bodies and to organize new elections of those bodies. It also empowered the committee to ban or suspend the activities of public organizations and unofficial groups that are deemed to violate the USSR's Constitution or laws (*Pravda*, January 15). On January 16, Vol'sky told Soviet television that the main task of the new committee was to calm people and "avert an interethnic war." He also criticized the local authorities for neglecting economic and social problems in the area. He said he had traveled a good deal in the Soviet Union but could not name a more neglected region than Nagorno-Karabakh. (A lengthy commentary by Vol'sky on the situation in Nagorno-Karabakh also appeared in *Pravda*, January 15).

Boris El'tsin gave a pessimistic assessment of the progress of reform in the Soviet Union. He told Radio Liberty in a telephone interview that he believed *glasnost'* was deteriorating and *perestroika* was slowing down. He said the media had initially stirred people from apathy but that there were now signs of tightening up in the media. As a result, he said, many people in the Soviet Union had begun losing interest in the central press. El'tsin mentioned an interview he had given to Soviet journalists last November. He said that he had answered 320 questions but that the interview had not been published in full anywhere. He said it was his policy not to leave any question unanswered, even tough and impolite ones (*RFE/RL Special*, January 12).

El'tsin Pessimistic about Perestroika

CIA Director William Webster said in an interview published in the US newspaper *USA Today* that there are signs the Soviet Union wants to help reduce the threat of terrorism. Webster said that he has not shared the view held by some that the USSR was responsible for much terrorism, especially a decade ago. He said that, to whatever extent Moscow may have been involved in the past

USSR Wants to Cooperate with Western Intelligence on Terrorism

in training, supplying, and shielding terrorists, this has now changed. He said he thinks Soviet intelligence would pass along to the United States any information it might have about last month's bombing of a US airliner over Britain (*AP, AFP*, January 12). On January 15, Radio Moscow's Hebrew Service broadcast a statement attributed to Deputy Chairman of the KGB Vitalii Ponomarev offering to cooperate with the CIA, British intelligence, the Israeli Mossad, and other such groups in fighting terrorism. The broadcast was monitored by Radio Israel. On January 30, Ponomarev was quoted by the Novosti press agency as reiterating the KGB's willingness to cooperate with Western intelligence services under "special circumstances."

Friday, January 13 ──────────────────────────────────

Estonian Ban on Exports Reported

A report on Radio Budapest said Estonia had banned the export of some goods to foreign countries and to other Soviet republics. The radio did not quote a source for its information. The report said it was unclear how the ban would be controlled and how Soviet tourists would be stopped from shopping in Estonia, since there are no customs borders between the republics. The report said it was now forbidden to take items in short supply, such as food, clothes, and articles of general use, out of Estonia (*Radio Budapest*, January 13, 1200 and 1400).

Gorbachev Addresses Food Problem at Moscow Conference

Gorbachev said that new approaches, including respectful treatment of the land, are needed to improve food supplies in the USSR and that many mistakes had been made in land improvement and farming systems. "We have simply been violating nature," Gorbachev said at a one-day conference in Moscow on upgrading management of the country's agroindustrial complex. Those attending included republican and regional Party leaders, farming specialists, and Agroindustrial Committee officials. Gorbachev said a Party plenum on agrarian policy set for March would deal with ways to improve food supplies and the lives of rural workers. He said no agrarian policy could be effective if it ignored the interests of rural workers (*Central Television*, 1900; see also *Pravda*, January 14).

Shevardnadze Goes to Kabul

Soviet Foreign Minister Eduard Shevardnadze joined Soviet Ambassador Yulii Vorontsov in Kabul. Shevardnadze's trip was unannounced. TASS described it as a working visit. At a news conference the same day, Soviet Deputy Defense Minister Vitalii Shabanov told reporters the second phase of the Soviet withdrawal from Afghanistan would begin soon. He said the Soviet Union considers it "a duty" to meet the February 15 deadline. On January 14, Shevardnadze met with Afghan President Najibullah. TASS said the Soviet side confirmed its total support for the Afghan leadership's political course and also its intention to continue to play an intermediary role in launching a general dialogue in Afghanistan. Moscow also said it would continue to supply Afghanistan with all-round assistance (*AP, Reuters*, January 13 and 14).

Saturday, January 14

Former Soviet Chief of Staff Sergei Akhromeev said he supports the unilateral military reductions announced by Gorbachev. Akhromeev said in an interview in *Sovetskaya Rossiya* that the reductions are correct politically and militarily. He said they would not affect Soviet military preparedness. Akhromeev's resignation for health reasons on December 7, 1988, coincided with Gorbachev's announcement of Soviet military cuts to the United Nations. Soviet officials said at the time that the two events were not connected.

Former Soviet Chief of Staff Supports Cuts

Kazakhstanskaya pravda published an article on the forced collectivization in Kazakhstan. The article described the brutal methods by which collectivization was conducted and the famine that resulted.

Collectivization in Kazakhstan Described

The Soviet Union's trade balance worsened in 1988, with exports slumping by 2 percent and imports increasing by 6.5 percent, according to official figures released today. Tadeusz Teodorovich of the USSR Ministry of Foreign Economic Relations said total trade turnover stood at 132 billion rubles in 1988, up from 129 billion the previous year. He told TASS the structure of Soviet exports remained unsatisfactory, with 70 percent derived from fuel and energy deliveries and engineering products accounting for 16 percent. The worsening of the trade position appears to have been caused primarily by falling prices for oil and raw materials (*Reuters*, January 14).

Soviet Figures Show Worsening Trade Balance

Council of Ministers Criticizes Enterprises with Low Plan Targets

At a meeting in Moscow the USSR Council of Ministers criticized enterprises that set the lowest possible targets in order subsequently to overfulfill them and obtain plan profits. The meeting heard that for some enterprises the lower the plan the more profitable it was and that the result was a fall in production. Prime Minister Nikolai Ryzhkov said this was "a dangerous tendency," particularly when formulating targets for the next five-year plan. He called for a close study of the problem (*TASS, AP,* January 15).

Sunday, January 15

El'tsin Nominated to Run for Congress Deputy in Moscow

It was reported that a Moscow district had nominated Boris El'tsin as a candidate for the new Congress of People's Deputies. *The New York Times* said El'tsin had received a majority of votes among the six people competing for the nomination. The report said El'tsin's nomination must still be approved by local election authorities. New Soviet laws prohibit USSR ministers from serving in the new congress. El'tsin is a first deputy minister but holds the rank of minister. If elected to the congress, El'tsin will have to give up his ministerial post. The aide was further quoted as saying Boris El'tsin had been nominated in other districts around the Soviet Union but had decided to run in Moscow.

Human-Rights Conference Opens in Moscow

A private East-West conference on human rights began in Moscow. TASS said the conference was being attended by prominent public figures, lawyers, and parliamentarians from Europe and North America. The conference was jointly chaired by Fedor Burlatsky, chairman of the Soviet Human-Rights Commission, and Rosalyn Carter, wife of former US President Jimmy Carter. Mrs. Carter said she thought the conference was unique because it began with each participant criticizing his own nation's human-rights situation. As three priorities for the Soviet Union, Burlatsky named religious freedom, first in practice and then in law; legal protection of human rights; and legalization of unofficial citizens' groups. Burlatsky said he hoped the USSR would pass a law guaranteeing religious freedom this year, but he added that the first draft was "a major problem." He said it was being written by bureaucrats with no contribution from religious believers (*AP,* January 16).

Mikhail Gorbachev said Soviet compromises had helped achieve agreement in Vienna on a package of disarmament and human-rights issues. TASS quoted Gorbachev as saying that months of hard bargaining at the Vienna conference had shown that peace is not a gift from above. The agreement, adopted formally on January 15 by the thirty-five states participating in the conference, calls for new talks on conventional forces in Europe and for broad guarantees in the area of human rights. The Soviet chief delegate in Vienna, Yurii Kashlev, said the document elevated the original Helsinki accords to "a qualitatively new level." He said its human-rights provisions were "a major breakthrough" (*Reuters, AP, RFE/RL Special,* January 16).

Soviet Union Hails Helsinki Final Document

Pravda said that current processes in Soviet society have influenced the style of Radio Free Europe and Radio Liberty. In a dispatch from RFE/RL headquarters in Washington, *Pravda* said RFE/RL had replaced the word anticommunism with the term democratic ideals. It said that, instead of urging a takeover of power in the USSR, the radios were now broadcasting appeals to improve the Socialist system. *Pravda* said that, although Radio Liberty editors pretend to be the forerunners of *perestroika* and *glasnost'*, in fact they are not interested in progress in the Soviet Union but are intent on kindling hostility and contradictions within Soviet society.

***Pravda* on Changes in RFE/RL Broadcasts**

Prime Minister Nikolai Ryzhkov, who heads a special Politburo commission overseeing earthquake relief efforts, returned to Armenia to resume supervising rebuilding of the area devastated by last month's earthquake. Accompanied by three other members of the commission, he toured Leninakan and Spitak. TASS said public transport and supplies of water, power, and gas have now been restored in Leninakan. It said construction work had begun on several new dwellings. On January 18, TASS announced plans to rebuild Leninakan, Kirovakan, and Spitak. TASS said that Spitak, which was closest to the earthquake's epicenter, would be rebuilt six kilometers southwest of its present location and that the former city would be turned into gardening lots, while the territory between the old and new Spitak would become a memorial park. TASS said most of the new housing in Kirovakan would be built west of the city. It said experts

Ryzhkov Returns to Armenia

were still undecided about where to rebuild Leninakan, Armenia's second largest city, because of high seismic activity in most of northwest Armenia. TASS also said all new houses would be built no higher than four stories and would withstand tremors of nine points on a twelve-point scale. The December 7 quake had a strength of at least ten points. On January 18, Ryzhkov told Soviet television that the estimated cost of reconstruction was rising towards 8 billion rubles to be spent over the next two years. He said that was almost half the expected annual increase in the country's national income.

Over 2,500 Officials in Azerbaijan Penalized for Unrest

TASS said more than 2,500 Communist Party members and government officials had been disciplined in connection with the ethnic unrest in Azerbaijan. Many were sacked from their jobs and expelled from the Party and the Komsomol. The people concerned had either been actively involved in riots and demonstrations, had assisted in them, or had failed to take measures to stop them, the report said. It did not give any names. On January 23, *Pravda* revealed that Azerbaijani Minister of Internal Affairs A. Mamedov had been given a strong reprimand and his deputy dismissed. The newspaper said two other ministers had also been punished but gave no details.

Writer Boris Vasil'ev Discusses Russian History

Izvestia (January 16, 17, and 18) carried a three-part article by liberal writer Boris Vasil'ev, who depicts the whole of Russian history as a gradual process of moral degeneration. He pays special attention to the Stalinist period, looking for the roots of Stalin's repressions in the early years of Bolshevik power. He regards the disbanding of the Constituent Assembly by the Bolsheviks as the turning point after which the democratic development of Russia became impossible.

Tuesday, January 17

Personnel Changes in Armenia

A plenum of the Armenian Central Committee replaced republican Party Second Secretary Yurii Kochetov with Oleg Lobov (*Radio Moscow*, January 17). (For more information on Lobov, see RL 60/89.) The main purpose of the plenum was to reduce the number of Central Committee departments and establish Central Committee commissions, as is being done in other republics. Today's issue of *Pravda* said that forty-nine leading Party, government,

30

and law-enforcement officials were dismissed in December and that the republican minister of internal affairs was reprimanded because of continuing ethnic unrest. TASS gave the number of dismissed officials as forty-eight and added that thirteen officials had been expelled from the Party for destabilizing the situation, inactivity, unlawful actions, and failing to prevent ethnic strife.

Zhdanov's Name to Be Removed from Towns and Institutions

The CPSU Central Committee has proposed removing the name of Stalin's chief ideologist, Andrei Zhdanov, from places and institutions named after him in the USSR. A committee resolution said Zhdanov organized mass repressions of innocent people in the 1930s and 1940s and was guilty of crimes. In its "Vremya" news program on January 17, Soviet television said a Ukrainian town on the Azov Sea named after Zhdanov would have its original name, Mariupol, restored. The move is in response to numerous letters to the Soviet Cultural Fund requesting the return of the old name. On January 17, Soviet television also revealed that Zhdanov's name would be removed from the Universities of Leningrad and Irkutsk and from factories, kolkhozes, and army units. Numerous materials have appeared during the past year in the Soviet press calling for Leningrad University to be renamed; see, for instance, Yurii Karyakin in *Ogonek* (No. 19,1988).

Belorussian Encyclopedia to Publish Unusual Volumes

The publishers of the *Belorussian Soviet Encyclopedia* are about to release a collection of biographies of soldiers who perished in Afghanistan. The commemorative volume, devoted to the Belorussian republic's war dead, is based on material drawn from 500 questionnaires, newspaper accounts, and the recollections of friends, teachers, and commanding officers. The profits will go to a hospital treating soldiers wounded in Afghanistan. The encyclopedia is also preparing a similar volume on Stalin's victims, particularly those Party, government, cultural, and academic figures whose encyclopedia entries now end with the words "died in 1937" (*Radio Moscow-2*, January 17, 0910).

Gerasimov Reiterates Soviet Stand on Wallenberg's Death

At a press conference in Moscow, Soviet Foreign Ministry spokesman Gennadii Gerasimov repeated the official Soviet view that Swedish diplomat Raoul Wallenberg died in a Soviet prison in 1947. Many reports have said Wallenberg was seen in Soviet prison camps long after that date. Wallenberg saved tens of thousands of Hungar-

31

ian Jews from the Nazi death camps during World War II by giving them Swedish papers. He was arrested by Soviet troops in Budapest forty-four years ago. Gerasimov confirmed a Swedish press report that Swedish and Soviet officials discussed the Wallenberg case a month ago (*TASS*, January 17).

Soviet Citizens Hopeful about Bush Administration

TASS said a poll taken by the Institute for Sociological Studies last November found that 64 percent of respondents believe relations between the United States and the USSR will improve during the Bush administration. The same percentage of respondents said they had friendly feelings towards the United States.

TASS Journalists to Stand Trial in Estonia

On January 17, Radio Stockholm reported that members of the Estonian Popular Front had appealed to a court to punish two TASS journalists in Tallinn who "distorted the truth in their reporting from Estonia." (The trial of the two journalists had been scheduled for December, 1988, but the two defendants failed to appear in court.) Among reports to which the Popular Front objected was one alleging that its leadership had been going around factories in Tallinn destroying machines. Another TASS report, carried by *Pravda*, accused the leadership of the front of trying to influence the deputies of the Estonian Supreme Soviet on the eve of the emergency session on November 16, 1988, at which the Estonian Parliament voted for the republic's sovereignty from Moscow.

*Wednesday, January 18*_____

Estonia Approves New Language Law

The Estonian Supreme Soviet approved a controversial language law that requires most civil servants, doctors, shop employees, and factory directors to speak both Estonian and Russian and specifies how Estonian is to be used in everyday dealings. Members of Estonia's large Russian minority had opposed the law since many cannot speak Estonian. Most Estonians, however, can speak Russian. Under the law, Russians in public service in Estonia must be able within the next four years to converse and conduct their affairs in Estonian. The voting, according to Estonian television, was 204 in favor and 50 against. There were six abstentions. Estonian Party ideology chief Mikk Titma has said Russian is a good language for affairs between Soviet republics but not for communication within republics (*TASS*, January 18). On January 19, Titma called the new law "a vigorous step towards Estonian sovereignty." He told Radio Tallinn that Estonians feel "considerably more secure" now that the law has been passed. He said they sense they can be masters of their own land (*Radio Tallinn*, *AP*, January 19). See *Izvestia*, January 21. The text of the law was published in *Sovetskaya Estoniya* on January 22.

Physicist and human-rights activist Academician Andrei Sakharov failed to win nomination by the USSR Academy of Sciences for one of the thirty seats allocated to it in the new Congress of People's Deputies. Sakharov was turned down, along with several other leading scientific and cultural figures at a twelve-hour-long meeting of the academy's Presidium. Sakharov's name had been proposed on January 5 by the Ivan Pavlov Institute of Physiology in Leningrad. Roald Sagdeev, director of the Soviet Space Research Institute, who also failed to win nomination, said: "If I had to summarize those not elected, I would say it is the group of the most outspoken proponents of *perestroika*. I am proud to be in such company" (*Reuters*, *UPI*, January 19). On January 20, Sakharov criticized the academy's selection of candidates as "undemocratic." Sakharov criticized the academy's Presidium for rejecting a proposal that the academy's candidates be chosen by the full academy membership. The Presidium instead selected its own list of candidates. The same day, amid a public outcry at his rejection by the academy, Sakharov was nominated as a candidate for the Oktyabr'skaya District of Moscow by the Lebedev Physics Institute (*Reuters*, January 20). On the nomination of candidates at the Academy of Sciences see also *Sotsialisticheskaya industriya*, January 24. See also an attempt to defend the rejection of Sakharov and other reformists by the Presidium of the academy in *Pravda*, February 1.

Academy of Sciences Rejects Sakharov as Parliamentary Candidate

Pravda carried a letter accusing *Ogonek* and other Soviet media of printing distorted articles "under the cover of vital slogans." *Ogonek* is an outspoken advocate of *perestroika* and *glasnost'*. The *Pravda* letter is signed by "prominent Soviet cultural personalities," including film actor Sergei Bondarchuk and Siberian writer Valentin Rasputin. Both have associated themselves with Russian nationalist causes and have criticized *Ogonek* in the past. The *Pravda* letter says history is being distorted,

Pravda* Carries Letter Criticizing *Ogonek

the social achievements of the people are being rewritten, and cultural values are being vulgarized in some articles in the Soviet press. The letter said these tendencies appear in many articles in *Ogonek*. On January 28, *Pravda* hit back at the conservative cultural figures for their letter against *Ogonek*. In its editorial on January 28, *Pravda* said it had been bombarded with critical messages from readers following publication of the letter. It said a group of ten leading [liberal] writers, including Vasyl Bykov and Evgenii Evtushenko, had complained about the letter's content and bitter tone. The editorial also called on the Soviet people to be tolerant and said "tolerance and the ability to listen to an opponent and understand his arguments are an integral part of the culture of discussion, of Socialist pluralism of opinion." For further details and an analysis of the attack, see RL 51/89.

Gorbachev Details Military Budget and Troop Cuts

Gorbachev said the Soviet military budget would be trimmed by 14.2 percent. He said this would include a 19.5 percent reduction in the manufacture of arms and military technology and a 12 percent cut in the armed forces. He did not say over what period the cuts would be carried out, nor did he give a figure for the current Soviet military budget. The official Soviet figure is 20.2 billion rubles, but Western estimates put it at about six times higher. Gorbachev was speaking at a Kremlin meeting with former US Secretary of State Henry Kissinger, former French President Valery Giscard D'Estaing, and former Japanese Prime Minister Yasuhiro Nakasone. The three men were in Moscow as part of a delegation representing the Trilateral Commission, a private Western organization set up to discuss international affairs (*Reuters*, *AP*; *TASS*, in English, January 18). See, *Pravda*, January 19.

Shevardnadze Rebuffs Calls to Dismantle Berlin Wall

Soviet Foreign Minister Eduard Shevardnadze said the Berlin Wall is not a subject for the Helsinki review conference in Vienna. US Secretary of State George Shultz and British Foreign Secretary Geoffrey Howe both called at the Vienna conference this week for the wall to be taken down. Shevardnadze told reporters on arrival in Vienna today that each state had a right to build its frontiers as it wished. He said: "we must proceed from that and respect the sovereignty of states" (*Reuters*, January 18). Howe later told Shevardnadze at a meeting that Britain's attendance at a human-rights conference in Moscow in 1991 depended on the Soviet human-rights record. US Secretary of State-Designate James Baker also said the United States would attend the meeting if there were further improvements in Soviet human rights (*RFE/RL Special*, January 18).

Radio Moscow (1700) cautioned Soviet reformers about the possible consequences of their reforms and cited increasing poverty in Hungary as an example of what can happen. The radio said recent big price increases in Hungary had created more poverty and tension. It cited figures broadcast on Hungarian television a week ago that said the number of poor people in Hungary had risen from 1.9 million in 1987 to over 2.5 million today.

Radio Moscow Cites Hungary in Caution to Soviet Reformers

The town of Beruni in northern Uzbekistan has nominated an ecological activist to represent it in the new Congress of People's Deputies. TASS said the vote was unanimous for thirty-six-year-old Roza Baltaeva. The agency said Baltaeva is well known in Beruni for her work to protect the environment. It said she was instrumental in having a polluting asphalt plant moved out of the town and in reducing leaks from other plants. Beruni is located on the shores of the Aral Sea. TASS quoted Baltaeva as saying that, if she is elected, she will try to make sure that government programs to save the shrinking body of water are actually put into effect.

Uzbek Town Nominates Ecological Activist

Twelve leading Armenian activists arrested last month have been transferred from Armenia to a prison in Moscow, Reuters quoted an Armenian source as saying. The source, speaking by telephone from Erevan, said all but one of those transferred were leading members of the outlawed Karabakh Committee. The arrests have dismantled the leadership of the committee, which has been coordinating the campaign for the transfer of Nagorno-Karabakh to Armenia from Azerbaijan.

Arrested Armenian Activists Transferred to Moscow

Thursday, January 19

Radio Moscow (0900) said seventy-two people had been poisoned over the past week by emissions from the Orenburg natural-gas-processing plant on the Ural River. The report said the gas plant had not taken the safety steps required by local authorities eight days ago. It said those

Seventy-two People Poisoned by Gas Plant

affected had been hospitalized. The broadcast said the local health authorities had demanded the plant cut its output by 30 percent. The plant management, citing a gas shortage and the need to fulfill the plan, failed to do so.

Rising Crime Rate

USSR Minister of Internal Affairs Vadim Bakatin said that crime in the USSR rose almost 17 percent last year but that this figure does not reflect the seriousness of the situation. He was quoted by *Pravda* as saying the true crime rate is considerably higher than official statistics suggest. He said that street crime had risen by 40 percent and that attacks on policemen were becoming more frequent. Bakatin complained police had not responded to the challenge of increased crime. He also said there was a disregard for the truth in the police force that has led to a moral decline.

China Welcomes Soviet Troop Withdrawal from Border Areas

China welcomed Gorbachev's announcement that Moscow would withdraw 200,000 troops from East Asia over the next two years. Soviet troop concentrations along the border with China and in Monoglia have long been seen by China as a major obstacle to normal relations. China's Foreign Ministry spokesman Li Zhaoxing told reporters China welcomed the withdrawal of Soviet troops and hoped the process would continue. Soviet Foreign Minister Shevardnadze is due in Beijing on February 2 to prepare for the first Sino-Soviet summit since 1959; it is expected to take place in the first half of 1989 (*Reuters*, January 19).

Friday, January 20 —————————————————————————

Zhukov's Memoirs Shatter Stalin's War Image

Pravda shattered the image of Stalin as a war hero by publishing previously secret sections of the World War II memoirs of Marshal Georgii Zhukov that blame Stalin for "the annihilation of thousands of Soviet citizens." (Zhukov was deputy commander in chief of the Soviet Armed Forces during the war. He is considered a hero for his role in the defense of Moscow and Stalingrad.) *Pravda* quoted Zhukov's daughter, Mariya, as saying the marshal's memoirs have often been cited by Stalinists as proof that Stalin was a magnificent leader rather than the criminal portrayed in recent Soviet publications. She said a key section of her father's writings was still hidden in his safe for publication at some future date. The full page of new excerpts published in *Pravda* includes Zhukov's report that Stalin played no role in directing the war effort but often had front-line commanders issue orders devised by the general staff as if they were his own. *Pravda* said that Zhukov wrote an entire chapter on Stalin's repressions of the army but that virtually all of it was deleted from the originally published version of his memoirs.

Moscow Party First Secretary Lev Zaikov criticized the work of the Moscow Party organization under his predecessor, Boris El'tsin. Zaikov said the previous leadership had been unable to meet the social and economic development targets set for Moscow in 1986. Zaikov was speaking at a meeting of the Moscow City Party Committee. The meeting was attended by Gorbachev. In his speech, Zaikov also said the current leaderships in a number of Moscow districts were losing control. He described this as "a dangerous tendency" (*TASS*, January 20).

Zaikov Attacks Moscow Leadership under El'tsin

Gorbachev sent a congratulatory telegram to George Bush on the day of his inauguration as US president. Radio Moscow-1 (2100) quoted Gorbachev as saying Bush had become president at a time of improving US-Soviet relations. Gorbachev said further US-Soviet efforts would help to bring solutions to the most painful problems of our time. Meanwhile, Soviet journalists in Washington complained that they had experienced delay in receiving accreditation to cover the inauguration (*TASS*, January 20).

Gorbachev Congratulates Bush

Pravda carried a distorted account of the events in Czechoslovakia by publishing almost verbatim the tendentious comments of CTK, the Czechoslovak press agency, and of the TASS correspondent in Prague. The Soviet Party daily claimed that the demonstrations in Prague's Wenceslas Square, which have been going on for a whole week in commemoration of the self-immolation twenty years ago of the Czech student Jan Palach, were seeking to undermine "the incipient process of democratization" allegedly taking place in the country under the leadership of the Czechoslovak Communist Party.

***Pravda* Distorts Events in Czechoslovakia**

Saturday, January 21

Andrei Sakharov was quoted as saying that progress in the sphere of human rights in the Soviet Union had taken a step backwards. In an interview released today by the

Sakharov Reports Setback in Human-Rights Situation

37

US weekly *US News and World Report*, Sakharov was quoted as saying that, while Gorbachev had acted courageously in the international arena, there were "some very serious shortcomings in his domestic policies." Sakharov mentioned the arrest of members of the Karabakh Committee in Armenia, saying this was "absolutely unnecessary." Sakharov added: "Since there are now prisoners of conscience in the USSR again, plans for a human-rights conference in Moscow in 1991 should be suspended" (*Reuters*, January 21).

Gorbachev Addresses Moscow City Party Conference

Gorbachev rejected calls to import more consumer goods to make up for shortages, saying such a strategy would mean that the USSR would not be forced to learn to manufacture its own products. "If we take a credit of a billion dollars and buy goods for one or two years, they will be on the market. But what will happen in the third year?" he asked rhetorically in a speech to a meeting of the Moscow City Party Committee. Gorbachev said the USSR had in the past used oil revenues to finance imports of consumer goods. But, Gorbachev said, "we can't continue selling raw materials for Western consumer goods." Gorbachev said that, in addition to the drop in oil prices, the state's finances had also been adversely affected by "Chernobyl', Armenia, and Afghanistan—our old sins." Referring to his antialcohol drive launched in 1985, Gorbachev said that, although the campaign had lost the state 40,000 million rubles, "we don't regret it" (*Radio Moscow-2*, 2140, January 21). For the text of the speech, see *Pravda*, January 24.

Ballerina Makarova to Dance in Leningrad

Ballerina Natal'ya Makarova said she was planning to return to the USSR for the first time since she defected in 1970 and dance again with her old company, the Kirov Ballet in Leningrad. In her interview with AP, Makarova said that she had been invited to Leningrad by the Kirov Theater and that the first of her two appearances during a two-week visit would be on January 26. In the interview, Makarova praised Gorbachev for his liberal cultural policies.

Authorities Round Up Ukrainian Activists to Prevent Meeting

KGB and police officials detained dozens of members of the unofficial Democratic Union who had come from various parts of the USSR to participate in a meeting in Kiev, an activist said. In a telephone interview with AP, Yurii Mityunov said about sixty people had been expected at the meeting. He said at least fourteen of those arrested were released by the evening. Those who were not residents of Kiev were forced to leave the city, he said. The detentions succeeded in preventing the meeting. (Members of the Democratic Union, which advocates a multiparty system in the USSR and rejects socialism, are regularly subjected to harassment, including detentions, by the authorities.)

Report on Grain Harvest Shortfall Says Food Situation Tense

A report released by the State Committee for Statistics said last year's harvest had totaled 197 million tons, 2 million tons higher than the preliminary estimate given last week. The official target for 1988 had been 235 million tons. The report said that grain imported to the USSR last year, which consisted mostly of fodder, had amounted to 36 million tons and that growth in agricultural production was slower last year than in 1987. It said that the output of meat, eggs, and milk had increased but that potato, vegetable, and fruit output had declined in many parts of the country. The report said the food situation in the USSR continued to be tense (*TASS*, in English, January 21).

TASS Says USSR Helping to Ease Food Shortage in Afghanistan

TASS said six Soviet transport planes loaded with flour had arrived at Kabul airport to try to help ease a severe food shortage in the Afghan capital. The agency and Radio Moscow said Kabul was experiencing great hardship because resistance forces were trying to organize an economic blockade. Resistance attacks have been reported recently along the Salang highway, which links Kabul with the USSR. Radio Moscow also reported fierce fighting between government troops and resistance forces in two provinces. The radio said the Afghan army had been forced to leave a number of security posts in the eastern border province of Nangarhar. On January 22, Soviet television's veteran reporter Mikhail Leshinsky said Kabul had fallen under siege by the resistance. On January 23, Major General Lev Serebrov, who is political officer at the Soviet military high command in Kabul, said the Afghan government was at least partly to blame for the current severe lack of food in the Afghan capital. Serebrov told Western reporters in Kabul that the local authorities did not speak out in time when they realized extra food would be needed (*AP*, January 23).

Falin and Peres Discuss Middle East Bilateral Ties

In Bonn, the head of the CPSU Central Committee's International Department Valentin Falin met with Israeli Finance Minister (former Foreign Minister) Shimon Peres.

39

An Israeli spokesman said they discussed the Middle East, bilateral relations, and Soviet Jews. He said that Falin had presented some Soviet ideas on the possibility of expanding bilateral relations and that Peres had brought up the idea of direct flights between the two countries. No details were given. Falin and Peres were in Bonn after attending a luncheon on January 20 honoring former West German chancellor Willy Brandt (*RFE/RL Special*, January 21).

Trud and *Izvestia* on Nagorno-Karabakh

In an interview with the newspaper *Trud*, Major General A. Kolomitsev, identified as commandant of the Nagorno-Karabakh "special area," said the situation in Nagorno-Karabakh had "largely stabilized." Kolomitsev said there had been no strikes or rallies in the region recently, nor was there any disorder. He added, however, that security forces in Nagorno-Karabakh were continuing to find people illegally in possession of weapons and explosives and that occasional calls for strikes were heard. Kolomitsev said more than fifty people had been arrested in the region's capital Stepanakert during ethnic clashes. The same issue of the newspaper analyzed the nomination in Nagorno-Karabakh of candidates for elections to the new USSR Congress of People's Deputies. The newspaper complained that some of the nominees were people who had destabilized the situation in the region. Meanwhile, *Izvestia* reported that hundreds of millions of rubles would be spent on developing the Nagorno-Karabakh Oblast. The newspaper said the money would mostly be spent on housing, roads, new schools, and recreation facilities and on reequipping neglected and technically obsolete enterprises. The newspaper also said that the Party boss of Nagorno-Karabakh, Genrikh Pogosyan, who strongly defended demands for the oblast to be transferred from Azerbaijan to Armenia, was retiring due to health problems.

Sunday, January 22

Soviet Commander on Pullout from Afghanistan

Major General Lev Serebrov told Western correspondents in Kabul that his country's forces were leaving Afghanistan with "a sense of not having accomplished their mission to the end." Serebrov claimed that Soviet forces entered Afghanistan nine years ago entrusted with "an honorable task." He said Soviet forces still aimed to be out of Afghanistan by the February 15 deadline set in the Geneva accords (*AP*, January 22).

Moscow News (No. 4) carried an interview with émigré Soviet writer Georgii Vladimov, who now lives in West Germany. Only last year, *Literaturnaya gazeta* and other Soviet newspapers sharply attacked Vladimov. Vladimov's anti-Stalinist novel *Vernyi Ruslan* (Faithful Ruslan) was published in the February issue of the journal *Znamya*.

Moscow News Interviews Georgii Vladimov

Moscow News carried an interview with lawyer Aleksandr Yakovlev, who was identified by the weekly as one of the authors of the new Principles of Criminal Legislation. Yakovlev commented on a provision of the new Principles that calls for the Criminal Codes of the fifteen union republics to be brought into line with international convenants signed by the USSR. As an example, Yakovlev cited the infamous Soviet law punishing "parasitism"—i.e, failure to work in the public sector—which in the past was used to sentence to imprisonment or internal exile nonconformist writers, such as Josef Brodsky and Andrei Amal'rik, or Jewish scholars who had lost their jobs because they had applied for emigration. According to Yakovlev, the "parasitism" law will not be included in the new RSFSR Criminal Code.

Moscow News on New Criminal Legislation

Andrei Sakharov was nominated as a Moscow candidate for the new USSR Congress of People's Deputies. Western correspondents said that Sakharov was nominated unanimously by about 1,000 people at a meeting at the Dom Kino. Reuters quoted Sakharov as saying he was moved and excited by the trust placed in him at the nomination meeting and would do everything in his power to justify this trust. Sakharov's nomination must still be approved by an electoral commission. If approved, Sakharov will compete in March elections against Vitalii Vorotnikov—Politburo member and chairman of the Presidium of RSFSR Supreme Soviet—and Boris El'tsin. Sakharov was also nominated as a congress deputy on Janaury 20 by workers at Moscow's Lebedev Physics Institute. Today's nomination, however, would supersede the previous one.

Sakharov Gets Nomination from Moscow

Ogonek (No. 5) carried an article by Anatolii Golovkov, who said many of those jailed for antistate activity in the post-Stalin period should be rehabilitated. Golovkov argued that measures being taken to restore the reputation of the victims of Stalin's purges should also be extended to the victims of his successors. "We would be

Ogonek Urges Rehabilitation for Former Dissidents

even more grateful if they [the authorities] would concern themselves with those who suffered under Khrushchev and Brezhnev," Golovkov declared, referring to dissidents of the 1960s and 1970s. "They suffered only because they did not want to believe barefaced lies, hypocrisy, and empty promises," he said, adding that they expressed some of the very ideas that have emerged as official policy under Gorbachev.

Soviet Nuclear Test Conducted

The USSR conducted an underground nuclear test explosion near the city of Semipalatinsk in Kazakhstan. TASS said the test was aimed at upgrading military technology and produced a yield of between 20 and 150 kilotons (*TASS*, in English, January 22).

Monday, January 23 ────────────────────────────────────

Earthquake in Tajikistan

Western correspondents in Moscow quoted official sources as saying two villages in Tajikistan had been buried in landslides set off by a big earthquake there (*Reuters, AP*, January 23). Reuters quoted a spokesman at the Tajik representation in Moscow as saying the total population of the two villages was just over 1,400. TASS said that 104 people had been hospitalized in the Tajik capital Dushanbe and that special medical teams had been sent from Moscow to treat the injured. It gave a figure of 1,000 killed in the disaster (see also *Pravda*, January 24).

On January 24, however, Foreign Ministry spokesman Gennadii Gerasimov said estimates of the number of victims of the Tajikistan earthquake had been revised downwards by one-third. TASS quoted Gerasimov as saying residents of the village of Kukulibalo had been presumed to be among the victims of the quake, but it was later learned that some of the villagers had managed to leave their homes and flee into the mountains before the landslide descended on their village.

On January 25, Tajikistan's prime minister, Izatullo Khaeev, said 274 people were known to have died in the earthquake. He said the final death toll might be higher, but not by more than five or seven (*DPA, AFP, Reuters*, January 25). January 25 was also declared a day of mourning for the victims of the earthquake (*TASS*, January 25).

On January 27, a representative of the UN disaster relief office arrived in Tajikistan to assess the scale of the destruction and help determine the type and scope of international assistance needed. President of the Tajik Academy of Sciences Sagit Negmatullaev said that seismologists knew in advance an earthquake was going to hit the republic but that a lack of good communications and other technical facilities meant they were unable to warn citizens about where it would strike (*TASS*, in English, *APN*, January 27).

Politburo Member Criticizes Abortions, Lack of Contraceptives

The only woman on the CPSU Politburo, Aleksandra Biryukova, said there were too many abortions being performed in the Soviet Union. She blamed a lack of contraceptives. Candidate Politburo member Biryukova told a news conference in Moscow "it is not normal when the number of abortions is about equal to the number of births." Biryukova was responding to an article published in *Moscow News* (No. 4) about the fact that 90 percent of first pregnancies in the USSR end in abortion. She said she had asked Minister of Health Evgenii Chazov to investigate (*AP*, January 23).

Hungarian Named to Head Soviet Nuclear Research Institute

A Hungarian has been chosen as the first non-Soviet scientist to direct the Soviet Nuclear Research Institute, located at Dubna, north of Moscow. Hungary's MTI news agency said Dezso Kiss, a Budapest nuclear physicist, was chosen last week and will take over the post in March. MTI said the Dubna institute has a staff of 7,500. It said half of them are Soviet citizens and the rest come from Comecon countries and North Korea.

Victimized Author of Letters to Brezhnev Now Praised

A man who was victimized for writing a letter of complaint to Leonid Brezhnev has been defended in an article appearing in *Pravda*. The newspaper said that its story was intended to serve as a rehabilitation of Teimuraz Avaliani, former director of a shoe factory in Kiselevsk in the RSFSR. The newspaper said Avaliani complained to Brezhnev in 1980 that the Party Politburo and the government were not fulfilling their obligations and that delays in assessing the methods of the leadership could be costly to the Soviet people. *Pravda* said Avaliani had been victimized for the letter. The newspaper said a deputy of the RSFSR Supreme Soviet, Valentina Panina, wrote to the CPSU CC asking for full rehabilitation for Avaliani. She called him a courageous and honest Communist. *Pravda* said the Party Control Committee had agreed to her request and that this was why *Pravda* was printing Avaliani's story.

Two Men Go on Trial for Erevan Airport Blockade

Two men accused of organizing disturbances at Erevan's Zvartnots Airport last July went on trial before the Armenian Supreme Court. TASS said Albrik Genoyan and Artur Pogosyan were charged with leading demonstrators who blockaded the airport and hindered landings for several days. TASS said some fifty flights were suspended because of the demonstration, and doors were broken and windows smashed at the air terminal.

Tuesday, January 24 ————————————————————————————

Uzbek President Resigns Following Charges of Abuse of Office

Uzbekistan's President Pulat Khabibullaev resigned after being accused of misusing his official position. *Izvestia* said the Bureau of the Uzbek Party Central Committee had approved his request to be transferred to a scientific job.

Izvestia Advocates Return of Soviet Citizenship to Rostropovich

Izvestia urged the Soviet authorities to return Soviet citizenship to cellist Mstislav Rostropovich, more than a decade after his passport was taken away. The newspaper published an interview with Rostropovich detailing his ill-treatment by the Soviet authorities in the 1970s.

Lyubimov Returns to Taganka to Direct *Alive*

Theater director Yurii Lyubimov returned to Moscow to direct a play at the Taganka Theater. Lyubimov was stripped of his Soviet citizenship while working in the West in the early 1980s. TASS said Lyubimov would stay in the Soviet Union for about three months and would direct the play *Alive* by Boris Mozhaev. It said Lyubimov tried to put on the play twenty years ago but was turned down by Soviet cultural officials. TASS said Lyubimov would also direct a second play during his visit, possibly *The Devils* by Dostoevsky.

Korotich Nominated to Congress of People's Deputies

Vitalii Korotich, the chief editor of *Ogonek*, has been nominated for a seat in the new Congress of People's Deputies. Korotich was nominated to represent Moscow's Dzerzhinsky Raion. He received nearly 800 of about 1,000 votes cast. It was the third time Korotich's supporters had tried to nominate him. He was passed over as a candidate for the USSR Writers' Union. An attempt to nominate him in the Dzerzhinsky Raion fifteen days ago ended with scuffles and an exchange of shouts between conservative opponents of Korotich and those backing him (*AP, AFP*, January 24).

44

A Soviet film producer has won a court battle against a Leningrad factory that accused him of libel. TASS said the management of the Kirishi biochemical plant near Leningrad felt it had been libeled by a film called *Against the Current* produced by Dmitrii Delov. The agency said the Kirishi plant was notorious for discharging hazardous wastes into the atmosphere and was the target of mass demonstrations last year. This prompted Delov's film which, TASS said, made officials of the Ministry of the Medical and Biological Industry feel "wounded and unhappy." The ministry supervises the Kirishi plant. TASS quoted Delov as saying he had been subjected to both pressure and threats from officials and finally sued for libel. TASS quoted Leningrad city court judge Boris Prokhorov as saying Delov's film was "by no means offensive to the plant." The judge said the film's main message was that technological progress must not be allowed to conflict with the environment.

Factory Loses Lawsuit against Producer of Environmental Film

TASS said competition would be held in Belorussia to design a memorial to the victims of Stalinist repressions from 1937–1941. (Stalin's purges in Belorussia have recently attracted special attention in the USSR and in the West in connection with the discovery last year of a mass grave of people shot by the NKVD during these years in the Kuropaty Woods near the Belorussian capital of Minsk.)

Monument to Stalin's Victims in Belorussia

The deputy chairman of the Soviet Chamber of Commerce and Industry, Vladimir Golanov, has invited forty South Korean businessmen to visit Moscow and Siberia in March. Officials at the Federation of Korean industries said the aim of the trip would be to discuss Siberian development projects. Golanov left Seoul after a three-day visit that included talks about plans for Moscow and Seoul to exchange trade offices in March. A spokesman for South Korea's biggest conglomerate—the Hyundai group—said Moscow and Seoul have also agreed in principle to set up joint ventures this year. He said the agreement calls for the formation of joint ventures in construction, manufacturing, and fisheries with Hyundai (*Reuters, UPI*, January 24).

Moscow Agrees to Set Up Joint Ventures with Seoul

On January 24, *Izvestia* published a response to a reader who had complained about the unavailability to the Soviet public of the text of the 1948 UN Universal Declaration of Human Rights. The reader said only 20,000 copies

***Literaturnaya gazeta* Republishes Human-Rights Declaration**

45

of the Declaration had been published in the Soviet Union in a collection of official documents on international law. In its reply, *Izvestia* said that, since April, 1988, the Declaration had been reprinted in a number of Soviet journals with a total circulation of 356,000. On January 25, the text of the Declaration was published in the weekly *Literaturnaya gazeta*, thus adding another 6,277,000 copies to the existing 376,000.

Wednesday, January 25

Izvestia Reports Fire-Bombing of Moscow Co-op Café

Izvestia reported the fire-bombing of a cooperative café in Moscow. TASS quoted the paper as saying a café manager and several patrons were knifed by unidentified assailants who forced their way inside the café and then threw bottles of petrol to start a fire on the night of January 18. *Izvestia* quoted the chairman of the café cooperative, Anatolii Rutkovsky, as saying the café "was caught between two warring gangs." There have been official reports of extortion attempts against cooperative enterprises in Moscow, including cafés.

Abalkin on Budget Deficit

Reuters quoted Academician Leonid Abalkin as saying the true Soviet budget deficit totals 100 billion rubles. This amounts to 20 percent of the Soviet state budget and 11 percent of Soviet Gross Domestic Product (as compared with the US budget deficit, which makes up 3–4 percent of US GNP). Abalkin, who was recently nominated for election to the new Soviet parliament, offered a number of solutions to this problem: first, cut investments in long-term development projects that do not show quick results; second, bring about a rapid extension of cooperative housing; and third, end subsidies to loss-making enterprises and farms. Agreeing with the economist Nikolai Shmelev, Abalkin also said he thought that, in the present situation, continuing with a price reform would be disastrous and could lead to social unrest.

Call for Unification of Tatar and Bashkir Republics Criticized

Pravda carried an article by the Tatar writer Rafael Mustafin, in which he revealed that a meeting of informal groups in Naberezhnye Chelny in Tataria had called for the unification of the Tatar and Bashkir Autonomous Republics into one Union republic. Mustafin confirmed reports in the Tatar press that a number of informal groups interested mainly in nationality issues had emerged in the

46

Tatar capital of Kazan. Mustafin was evidently quite critical of the call for the unification of the Tatar and Bashkir republics, asking its authors if they had consulted the Bashkirs about the idea. It should be recalled that a Tatar-Bashkir Autonomous State called Idel-Ural existed from November, 1917, to April, 1918, and that the Bolsheviks called in March, 1918, for a Soviet Socialist Tatar-Bashkir republic; but in 1919 and 1920 separate Bashkir and Tatar ASSRs were set up.

Plan to Create Free Economic Zones

Deputy Chairman of the State Foreign Economic Commission Ivan Ivanov told reporters that a plan to create free economic zones on Soviet territory would be ready by the summer. TASS quoted Ivanov as saying some fifteen Soviet regions had shown interest in the scheme, including the Far Eastern Primorsky Krai, Sochi, Odessa, Murmansk, and Vyborg. Estonia, whose capital Tallinn is a prime candidate, was not mentioned.

Sakharov Gives Interview to *Süddeutsche Zeitung*

In an interview with the West German newspaper *Süddeutsche Zeitung*, Academician Andrei Sakharov said he saw no alternative to *perestroika*. He added, however, that he feared Gorbachev could be overthrown or could fall under the control of others. Sakharov said support should be given not so much to Gorbachev himself as to the reform process in general. In the interview, Sakharov also criticized the new Soviet electoral system, saying that it was not democratic enough. On January 25, TASS reported that the Presidium of the RSFSR Supreme Soviet had complained at its meeting about the way candidates had been nominated for the March 26 elections to the Congress of People's Deputies. TASS said the presidium found that authorities in the central Russian district of Orel and in some other regions had failed to implement the democratic principles of the electoral law.

Soviet Observers Attend OPEC Meeting for First Time

It was reported that the Soviet Union had sent observers to London's meeting of OPEC members and independent oil-producing countries for the first time. The Soviet Union is the world's largest oil producer and a substantial exporter (*AP*, January 25).

Kuropaty Investigation to Be Resumed

Nina Mazia, deputy chairwoman of the Belorussian Council of Ministers, told *Izvestia* that the government's investigation into the Kuropaty Woods massacre had been resumed. (Last year, it was reported that mass graves of people shot by the NKVD in the period 1937–1941 had been found in the Kuropaty Woods near Minsk.) Belorussian intellectuals have expressed their dissatisfaction with the incompleteness of the official investigation, and it seems that the resumption of work is a response to this criticism. The Latvian journal *Daugava* (No. 1, 1989) charged that the conclusion of the investigation on November 14, 1988, was a scandalous attempt "to bring down the curtain on a national tragedy."

Thursday, January 26

Demonstration Reported in Kishinev

Radio Kishinev said there had been a large, unauthorized demonstration in the Moldavian capital on January 22. It said "provocative slogans" were shouted against leading officials. It quoted the Moldavian Party Buro as saying that city officials had acted too late and that police had been unable to stop the demonstrators. The radio said the demonstration had been organized by members of the Alexei Mateevici Club. The Mateevici literary and musical club was set up last summer. It has become one of the main independent movements in Moldavia.

Turkmen Central Committee Holds First Contested Election

A Turkmen who campaigned for improved water supplies has been elected a secretary of the republic's Communist Party. Radio Moscow said Baba Sakhatmuradov told the Turkmen Party plenum that if elected he would try to ensure a safe supply of drinking water for rural residents. The radio said Sakhatmuradov won by seven votes in the first contested election for such a high post in Turkmenistan. His opponent was Nurmukhamed Ashirov, first secretary of the Tedzhen Oblast Party Committee. Sakhatmuradov told the radio that the ecological situation in Turkmenistan had deteriorated in the past few years. He said that water sources had been polluted and that this was the cause of a high death rate among children and a high incidence of infectious disease (*Radio Moscow-1*, 1900, January 26).

Jewish Anti-Fascist Committee Publicly Rehabilitated

The Soviet Politburo Commission studying crimes of the Stalin era publicized the rehabilitation of the leaders of the Jewish Anti-Fascist Committee. Radio Moscow-2 (1400) said the Jewish Committee had been active in rallying public opinion against fascism during World

War II but that the committee had been disbanded in 1948 and many of its members were arrested on "groundless accusations." It said these accusations had led to sentences of death in 1952 and long prison terms for its leaders. The radio said that, although the USSR Supreme Court revoked the sentences three years later, this act and the Party rehabilitation of the committee's leaders had been kept secret. The radio said the Politburo commission had decided the rehabilitations should be publicized.

Expert Says USSR Cannot Publish Military Budget Yet

Soviet arms expert Oleg Grinevsky said the Soviet Union is not yet able to publish details of its military budget because it does not know what the figures are. Grinevsky, who is Soviet ambassador at large for security and arms control, was speaking in London to the Royal Institute of International Affairs. He revealed publication of the Soviet Union's military budget had been delayed because officials had not finished establishing "the real prices" of the goods and services the military uses. Publication of the figures would, he said, have to await the reform of prices in the USSR. Grinevsky said other information on the number of Soviet troops and armaments would be published by the end of this month (*RFE/RL Special*, January 26).

Vol'sky Tells Azerbaijan Party Chief What Is Needed

The Soviet government's special envoy in Transcaucasia, Arkadii Vol'sky, met with Azerbaijani Party leader Abdul-Rakhman Vezirov in Baku. TASS said Vol'sky explained to Vezirov what needs to be done in Nagorno-Karabakh in order to normalize the situation and speed up efforts to improve living conditions there. TASS said Vol'sky explained how the region would be converted to economic self-management and how Azerbaijani agencies could help. Interethnic relations in Transcaucasia were also discussed at a meeting of Party first secretaries of Armenia, Azerbaijan, and Georgia in Tbilisi on January 24. At the meeting it was decided to prepare a long-term program for the improvement of interethnic relations in the area. Particular attention was focused on the problem of persuading refugees who fled their homes in Armenia and Azerbaijan last year to return home (*Radio Moscow-1*, 1300, January 24). On January 27, TASS reported that the chief prosecutors of Armenia and Azerbaijan had met in Erevan and decided to intensify cooperation in coping with the refugee problem.

Lithuania Issues Decrees on Language and National Holiday

Details have been published of Lithuania's decision to declare Lithuanian the official language of the republic. TASS reported that a decree issued on January 25 by the Presidium of Lithuania's Supreme Soviet said Lithuanian would be used to conduct business in state and public bodies and to adopt laws and other acts. The decree said people who did not speak Lithuanian "should be provided with service in another language." It said there would be preschool institutions and schools to teach the Lithuanian language to non-Lithuanians living in the republic. TASS said another Lithuanian decree issued on January 25 had declared February 16 a national holiday. The date marks Lithuania's declaration of independence in 1918.

***Glasnost*' Editor Wins Publishers Award**

Western agencies reported that the editor of the independent Soviet magazine *Glasnost'*, Sergei Grigoryants, has been awarded the Golden Pen of Freedom Prize of the International Federation of Newspaper Publishers. Despite the political liberalization that has taken place in the Soviet Union under Gorbachev, Grigoryants continues to be persecuted by the Soviet authorities for his independent publishing activities (*AP, Reuters*, January 26).

Friday, January 27 ——————————————————————

Sakharov's Election Platform Published

Komsomol'skaya pravda published the main points of Academician Andrei Sakharov's election platform. They include such provisions as the promotion of ecological movements; freedom to choose one's country of residence; the opening of the archives of the NKVD and the MGB to the public; the introduction of trial by jury (*sud prisyazhnykh*); the abolition of capital punishment; a rapprochement between the Capitalist and Socialist systems; locating nuclear power stations underground; and the elimination of restrictions on personal income. In answer to a reader's question, "Whose candidate is A. Sakharov?", *Komsomol'skaya pravda* related how Sakharov had failed to be nominated by the USSR Academy of Sciences and how he had won nomination from Moscow Election District No. 1.

Children in Kalmyk Republic Infected with AIDS

Trud said that twenty-seven children in the Kalmyk Autonomous Republic had been infected with the AIDS virus because of the "criminal negligence" of hospital staff.

Trud quoted Valentin Pokrovsky, who is head of the AIDS laboratory at the central epidemiology institute in Moscow, as saying an investigation was under way and court proceedings would follow. The daily said the children, most of them under the age of two, had been infected because medical staff at a hospital in the Kalmyk capital of Elista had used unsterilized syringes. The original carrier of the virus has not yet been identified, however. On January 28, *Komsomolskaya pravda* also reported the incident. It quoted Pokrovsky as saying 3,000 children would be tested for the AIDS virus. He predicted that the number of those infected could grow.

At a press conference held on the eve of the founding meeting of the anti-Stalinist organization "Memorial," a number of leading Soviet writers and intellectuals pledged to expose all aspects of Stalin-era repression and seek to ensure it would never be repeated. They told reporters that they aimed to put Stalinism on trial and cleanse the nation of its legacy. The group includes leading anti-Stalinist writers Anatolii Rybakov and Ales Adamovich, poet Evgenii Evtushenko, and historian Yurii Afanas'ev (*Reuters*, January 27).

Writers Pledge to Put Stalin Repressions under Spotlight

Pravda carried a lengthy report by Chairman of the Soviet Peace Committee Genrikh Borovik and a member of the presidium of the committee, Vladimir Gubarev, on their meeting with Pope John Paul II in the Vatican. The influence of *perestroika* on the situation of believers in the USSR was one of the themes of their meeting. The report in *Pravda* also included details of the pope's biography.

***Pravda* Reports Meeting between Soviet Journalists and Pope**

Saturday, January 28

Arkadii Vol'sky, the Soviet government's special representative in Nagorno-Karabakh, urged tighter economic, social, and cultural ties between Nagorno-Karabakh and Armenia. In Erevan, Vol'sky, who heads a special committee that is temporarily administering Nagorno-Karabakh, discussed the situation in the oblast with Armenian Party First Secretary Suren Arutyunyan. Vol'sky also explained measures the committee was taking to set up independent economic associations, to expand the leasing system, and to sharply increase housing construction. He said that the recent decision by the Soviet authorities to give the region

Vol'sky Urges Tighter Ties with Armenia

a special status puts greater responsibility on the Armenian and Azerbaijani Party bodies and that they must work for a normalization of ethnic relations, an improvement in the political atmosphere in the oblast, and the creation of conditions that would permit refugees to return to their homes (*TASS*, January 28).

Soviet, US, and Cuban Officials Discuss Cuban Crisis

Soviet, US, and Cuban officials involved in the 1962 Cuban missile crisis, which brought the world close to nuclear war, ended a two-day conference in Moscow. One of the participants was Theodore Sorensen, who was a special counselor to the US president at that time, John Kennedy. He said after the conference that he was not sure all the participants had learned the lessons of the crisis. He said some speakers still blamed everyone but themselves for letting the crisis get out of hand. Mikhail Gorbachev and George Bush sent messages to the conference. Both said world security would improve if the Cuban missile crisis were better understood (*TASS*, *Reuters*, January 28).

Azerbaijan Has New Prime Minister

Radio Baku said that Ayaz Mutalibov had been appointed on January 27 to replace Gasan Seidov as chairman of the Council of Ministers of Azerbaijan. The radio said Seidov had asked to be relieved of his duties for health reasons. Mutalibov had been a deputy prime minister. Official reports did not link Seidov's departure to the ethnic unrest in Transcaucasia.

Founding Conference of "Memorial" Society

The all-Union constituent assembly of "Memorial," the society established to honor victims of Soviet political repressions, was held in Moscow over the weekend. The meeting was reported by TASS and various Western agencies. Five hundred delegates from some 100 Soviet cities are said to have attended the congress. The assembly approved a charter and confirmed Andrei Sakharov as chairman. On January 29, Sakharov told a news conference that only a fortnight before the congress opened it was unclear whether the authorities would allow the assembly to take place; he said that "Memorial" activists had met several times with members of the CPSU Central Committee and that "there was a certain tension at these meetings." But another "Memorial" activist, the Belorussian writer Ales Adamovich, told the assembly that Gorbachev's own attitude towards the objectives of "Memorial" was "most favorable" (*Reuters*, January 29). The assembly decided that the society would act on behalf of the victims of all periods of political persecution in the USSR, whether before or after the days of Stalin, including the members of the outlawed Armenian Karabakh Committee, who were arrested last year. One resolution asked that the nations deported under Stalin, in particular the Crimean Tatars, be allowed to return to their homelands; however, "Memorial" rejected, at Sakharov's insistence, a demand that officials of Stalin's Ministry of Internal Affairs who were guilty of taking part in repressions against innocent people be put on trial. The assembly was also addressed by Vitalii Korotich, the editor of *Ogonek*; Grigorii Baklanov, the editor of *Znamya*; the poets Andrei Voznesensky and Evgenii Evtushenko; the actor Mikhail Ulyanov; and the historian Yurii Afanas'ev. At the news conference, Afanas'ev, the chairman of the Moscow branch of "Memorial," attacked *Pravda* for misinforming the Soviet public about events in Armenia; Afanas'ev's outburst is reported to have been loudly applauded by other delegates. The charter of "Memorial" was published in *Ogonek*, No. 4, 1989. The television program "Vzglyad" gave coverage of the congress on February 3. Afanas'ev, head of the organizing committee for the congress, told the "Vzglyad" interviewer that the work of "Memorial" had been obstructed by the USSR Ministry of Culture. He said the ministry had even managed to freeze the bank account that was opened by the society's council to finance a monument and research center in honor of victims of Stalin's terror. The council had not received any information about the state of its account since January 12, the moderators of "Vzglyad" said.

Canadian Secretary of State for External Affairs Charles Clark said the Soviet authorities had again denied an exit visa to Aleksandr Rabinovich, a Soviet refusednik who has been trying to emigrate to Canada for more than ten years. It is the fifteenth time his visa application has been rejected. Clark said he was disappointed by the decision, which came a week after he had interceded for Rabinovich with Soviet Foreign Minister Eduard Shevardnadze at the Helsinki review conference in Vienna (*RFE/RL Special*, January 28).

Soviet Refusednik Again Denied Exit Visa

Two correspondents from *Trud* who talked to Soviet Germans in Kazakhstan reported that many of them regard the restoration of Soviet German autonomy, abolished in 1941, as necessary to preserve their national culture

***Trud* on Ethnic Germans in Kazakhstan**

and to restore justice. The correspondents made the point that, as a result of the scant attention paid to Soviet Germans in the media, many Soviet citizens were virtually unaware of their existence. The article is one of several on the Soviet Germans that have been published in the central press in the past few months. The tone is noticeably more sympathetic than that in reporting on the Crimean Tatars. On February 3, *Izvestia* carried a letter from an ethnic German, Andrei Shelenberg, who said he was about to emigrate to West Germany and explained that he had decided to do so because ethnic Germans are still discriminated against in the USSR. Shelenberg added that he was also discriminated against as a religious believer.

Sunday, January 29 ───────────────────────────────

First Issue of New Central Committee Journal Published

The Soviet media said the CPSU Central Committee had published the first issue of a new journal *Izvestiya TsK KPSS* (CPSU Central Committee News). TASS said the journal will publish official documents from both the past and present, citizens' letters, and biographies of current Party and government leaders. The first issue of the journal features a message from Gorbachev, in which he says the journal must help Soviet people form opinions about *perestroika* on the basis of accurate information and genuine documents. Gorbachev said the Central Committee wanted the journal to strengthen and enliven ties between the Party leadership and the people. He said these ties had been "seriously violated" in the past, when the system was run by command and injunction and decisions were based on exclusion and secrecy (*TASS*, January 29).

Former NKVD Officer Criticizes Stalinist Power System

A former officer of the NKVD called for the total destruction of the system of power established by Stalin and his accomplices. The officer, retired Police Colonel Aleksandr Litvintsev, said this should be done despite opposition from admirers of Stalinism. Litvintsev's remarks were published in *Sotsialisticheskaya industriya*. Litvintsev spoke about "the mechanism of mass repressions in the 1930s" and about how this mechanism was established and operated. He said the repressions had sparked fear among people and had twisted the minds of several generations. The newspaper asked why other members of the security forces at that time were still keeping quiet.

54

Marshal Sergei Akhromeev, former chief of General Staff and now a defense adviser to Gorbachev, said in an interview with *Moscow News* that the USSR and its Warsaw Pact allies would not continue to make unilateral moves towards disarmament if NATO does not respond with measures of its own. Concerning his resignation from the post of chief of General Staff, Akhromeev said he had resigned because at the age of sixty-six it had become difficult for him to work the fourteen or fifteen hours a day that his job demanded.

Moscow News Carries Interview with Akhromeev

_____ *Monday, January 30*

According to Major General of Technical Troops Viktor Kutsenko, who served as a military adviser in Afghanistan for three years, there are about 2.5 million "explosive objects" scattered around the country. In an interview carried by Novosti on January 30, Kutsenko insisted that Soviet forces had stopped laying mines in Afghanistan after June 15, 1988, when they started their withdrawal. He also claimed that the particularly dangerous plastic mines, which have maimed so many Afghan children, were of Pakistani and French manufacture and were exclusively used by the resistance.

Soviet Military Official on Mines in Afghanistan

Pravda carried a statement by Warsaw Pact defense ministers on the military balance between NATO and the Warsaw Pact in Europe. This is the first time Moscow has published detailed tables for each category of troops and weapons. The statement said each side's ground and air forces are roughly equal, while NATO has roughly twice as many naval vessels and personnel and "enjoys a considerable margin of superiority" in naval warplanes and aircraft carriers but not in submarines. NATO leaders have been maintaining for some time that the Warsaw Pact has overall superiority in conventional and tactical nuclear forces in Europe, especially in armor, tactical missile launchers, and artillery.

Warsaw Pact Data on Military Balance in Europe

Despite empty shelves, long lines, and grumbling consumers, economic figures show Gorbachev's drive for efficiency is improving the performance of the Soviet economy, according to Mikhail Korolev, chairman of the State Committee for Statistics. Writing in *Pravda*, Korolev cited a growing Gross National Product and increased

Top Soviet Statistician Says Economy Improving

production of many food items as proof that the reforms are having a positive impact on the Soviet economy. But he said the effectiveness of *perestroika* was difficult to spot in the shops because the Soviet consumer's demand for goods and services had grown even faster than production. Korolev said the Soviet Gross National Product grew by 5 percent last year and by 13.3 percent compared with 1985. The national income increased in 1988 by 4.4 percent over the 1987 figure, Korolev said.

USSR Shifting to Hydroelectric Power after Chernobyl'

An energy expert said in an interview with *Pravda* that the increasing danger of nuclear power and pollution from thermal stations had prompted the Soviet authorities to embark on a mass shift to hydroelectric power. Boris Kartelev, director of the Soviet Institute for Hydraulic Engineering, said hydroelectric stations were safest for the environment and the best way to create an efficient national grid, as long as they were built correctly.

Sakharov Denounces Repressions in Czechoslovakia

Academician Andrei Sakharov condemned repressions in Czechoslovakia and the Soviet media's reporting on recent demonstrations there. Sakharov's criticism came in an appeal also signed by his wife, Elena Bonner, and by Soviet activists Lev Timofeev and Larisa Bogoraz. The appeal said the violent action by Czechoslovak police to break up demonstrations in Prague earlier this month violated the human-rights guarantees recently agreed to in Vienna by the thirty-five signatory states of the Helsinki accords. It also criticized the Soviet media for failing to condemn the Czechoslovak repressions and for distorted reporting on the Prague demonstrations (*Reuters, AFP*, January 30). The Soviet media, including *Pravda*, simply repeated reports on the event issued by the official Czechoslovak news media.

Medvedev Arrives in Bucharest

Politburo member and chief Soviet ideologist Vadim Medvedev arrived in Bucharest on a working visit. (*TASS*, January 30). On January 31, Medvedev met with Romanian leader Nicolae Ceausescu. See *Pravda*, January 31.

Deficit Affecting RSFSR Economy

The Council of Ministers of the RSFSR said the republic's growing budget deficit was hampering the development of the national economy. Participants in today's session in Moscow said radical reforms had led to positive trends in the economic development of the republic, but at the same time they complained that the positive trends were not yet becoming permanent. They said the republic's financial situation was difficult. They also complained that there was too much money in circulation and not enough consumer goods and services. RSFSR Prime Minister Aleksandr Vlasov outlined measures to improve the republic's financial situation. They include changes in the republic's investment policy, cuts in construction projects, and the dismantling of loss-making enterprises. The republic's agroindustrial complex was told to do everything to step up the supply of foodstuffs and cut losses (*TASS*, January 30).

Sakharov Asks Jackson's Help for Jailed Armenians

Academician Andrei Sakharov is reported to have asked visiting American civil rights campaigner Jesse Jackson for help in gaining the release of jailed members of the Karabakh Committee. Jackson is in the USSR to raise funds for Armenian earthquake victims. He met with Sakharov on January 30 and was given a list of the jailed members of the Karabakh Committee. Sakharov was quoted as telling Jackson that the arrest of the committee members "flies in the face" of everything Gorbachev has done regarding reforms and the release of political prisoners (*Reuters*, January 30). Meanwhile, *Literaturnaya gazeta* (No. 4) carried the text of a speech delivered at the latest plenum of the USSR Writers' Union by the Armenian poetess, Silva Kaputikyan, in which she also urged that the members of the Karabakh Committee be released. On February 1, Jackson went to Erevan, where he met with Armenian Patriarch Vazgen and with Armenian Party First Secretary Suren Arutyunyan (*Reuters*, February 1).

Tuesday, January 31

USSR to Reduce Conscription

Colonel General Bronislav Omelichev, deputy chief of the General Staff of the USSR Armed Forces, told a press conference in Moscow that the military draft will be cut by about a quarter over the next few years in line with the cuts in troop strength promised by Gorbachev in December (*UPI*, January 31).

Bonner Objects to Publication of Interview

Elena Bonner, the wife of Andrei Sakharov, told a Radio Liberty correspondent that she had been misquoted by the French journalist Jean-Pierre Barou in an interview that appeared in *Süddeutsche Zeitung*, *Le Figaro*, and

57

other Western newspapers last week. She also said that the talks with Barou were supposed to have been an informal conversation, not a formal interview. She was particularly annoyed at what she said was Barou's misquotation of her remarks about the probability of Gorbachev's being overthrown. Bonner told RL that she had actually drawn attention to the fact that under the new election system Gorbachev or any other head of state could be overthrown because the congress and not the people elects the head of state. (The journalist quoted Bonner as saying that she would not bet on Gorbachev, because he might be overthrown.) In fact, Bonner said, she had come out in support of Gorbachev, saying he was the only leader the USSR had and the people would elect him if given the chance. On February 2, *Izvestia* published an editorial attacking Sakharov and Bonner over the interview published by Barou.

Korotich on Gorbachev's Salary

Vitalii Korotich told today's *Washington Post* (and, according to Reuters, *Molodezh' Moldavii*) that Gorbachev's salary is over 1,500 rubles a month. Korotich did not attempt to estimate the value of the acompanying fringe benefits available to the Soviet leader. He did, however, disclose that other Politburo members earn 1,200–1,500 rubles a month, while top military men may earn as much as 2,000 rubles.

Disagreement between Soviet Officials and German "Greens"

Soviet officials and members of the West German Green Party disagreed on nuclear energy policies at a recently concluded seminar in West Germany. The "Greens," however, said contacts would be resumed in Moscow later this year. The "Greens" told a Bonn news conference the two sides differed on many nuclear energy issues, including the links between civilian and military use and the consequences of the Chernobyl' disaster. Meanwhile, an international ecology conference opened today in Moscow. The secretary of the Foreign Relations Commission of the Supreme Soviet, Vadim Zagladin, told delegates there was no place for confrontation in environmental cooperation. The conference, which took up the question of environmental protection in Northern Europe, brought together parliamentary officials from Eastern and Western Europe, the USSR, and Canada. In Washington, Soviet officials were also attending a three-day international ecology conference that started at the US State Department on January 30 (*RFE/RL Special*, *TASS*, January 31).

The commander of Soviet forces in Hungary has given more details of the withdrawal of over 10,000 Soviet troops from Hungary. Colonel General Matvei Burlakov told Radio Budapest that an armored division and an armored training division would be withdrawn during May and June and that an airborne assault batallion and a regiment of fighter planes would be pulled out later this year. He said a chemical warfare battalion would be withdrawn next year. In addition to the troops, the general said, the families of 1,800 soldiers would also return to the USSR. Radio Budapest said the Soviet soldiers would leave twenty-two garrisons, which would then become Hungarian property.

Soviet General Gives Details of Withdrawal from Hungary

A conference at the Party headquarters in Moscow heard calls for greater economic independence for the country's Union republics. TASS quoted speakers as saying a number of economic functions must be transferred from the central authorities to the republics. It did not identify the speakers. TASS said there was much talk of increasing the rights of the republics and allowing them more self-government and self-financing. The agency said the meeting also considered ways to accelerate the social and economic development of the republics, increase their contributions to the country's economy, and improve relations between the republics. TASS said the meeting was called to prepare for a Party Central Committee plenum on ways to improve ethnic relations in the Soviet Union.

Party Group Debates Economic Independence for Republics

Making trips over the border will be easier for residents along both sides of the Hungarian-USSR border starting in March. Radio Budapest said that residents of Szabolcs-Szatmar in northeastern Hungary would be allowed to visit Transcarpathian border areas within the USSR with a permit from district police. It said a letter of invitation would no longer be required. The radio said the bilateral agreement would also allow Soviet citizens of Transcarpathia to travel several times a year to Hungary. A large number of ethnic Hungarians live in the Transcarpathian area, which was once part of Hungary but now belongs to the Ukraine.

USSR-Hungary Border Travel Eased

Uchitel'skaya gazeta said history exams for Soviet students, canceled last year because textbooks had been outdated by media exposures about the country's past, would be held again this year, but using a new system.

On Soviet History Exams

Under the new system, teachers will be able to devise their own exams, and students will be permitted to disagree with their teachers and textbooks without receiving lower grades, the newspaper said.

MVD to Publish Crime Statistics

The USSR Ministry of Internal Affairs said it was making available previously classified crime statistics. The deputy head of that ministry's press bureau, Police Colonel Yurii Arshenevsky, said in *Trud* that journalists would be able to obtain the data by applying directly to the ministry's press bureau. TASS reported Arshenevsky as saying the ministry plans to publish a statistical bulletin that will eventually be available to all interested subscribers. Arshenevsky said 93 of the 111 murders committed in the USSR this month had been solved. He said most of them had been committed in the home as a result of drunkenness and jealousy.

Gromov on Situation in Afghanistan

The Soviet military commander in Afghanistan described how his forces had battled to keep open the main road between Kabul and the Soviet border for withdrawing convoys. Lieutenant General Boris Gromov told a Kabul news conference that civilian and resistance losses had been heavy in fighting for the Salang Highway. He mentioned four Soviet dead. He rejected US accusations that the Soviet operations amounted to a scorched earth policy. He blamed the fighting on the resistance, saying their attacks had to be countered. He said that offers to negotiate with local resistance leader Ahmad Shah Masood had been rejected and that, following the fighting, the resistance was now too weak to block Soviet convoys withdrawing on the highway (*AP*, January 31). On February 1, Foreign Ministry spokesman Gennadii Gerasimov said Soviet bombing was necessary to keep open the route for a Soviet military withdrawal from Afghanistan and the supply line to Kabul. Gerasimov was speaking at a press conference in Istanbul (*RFE/RL Special*, February 1).

The Month of February

Soviet Foreign Minister Eduard Shevardnadze arrived in China for three days of talks to prepare for the first Sino-Soviet summit in thirty years. His talks included meetings with Foreign Minister Qian Qichen and Chinese leader Deng Xiaoping. Topics of discussion included Cambodia, defusing tensions along the Sino-Soviet border, and Soviet leader Mikhail Gorbachev's visit to China, which was formally scheduled for May (_Pravda_, February 4 and 5). Speaking to reporters on February 4, Shevardnadze said his talks in China had produced agreement on Cambodia and Afghanistan as well as ways to address Sino-Soviet concerns about military tensions along common borders (_TASS_, Western agencies, February 4). The same day, Shevardnadze left Beijing for Islamabad for talks with Pakistani leaders (_AP_, _Reuters_, February 4). On February 5, Shevardnadze met with Pakistani Foreign Minister Sahabzada Yaqub Khan. Later the same day, he talked with Prime Minister Benazir Bhutto. Shevardnadze discussed with the Pakistani leaders a political settlement in Afghanistan following the Soviet military withdrawal from the country (_Reuters_, _AFP_, February 5). On February 6, Shevardnadze left Pakistan without meeting leaders of the Afghan resistance (_Reuters_, February 6). Speaking to reporters before leaving Islamabad, Shevardnadze said his talks with Pakistani officials had failed to produce an agreement for ending the war in Afghanistan (_AP_, February 6; _Pravda_, February 7). Meanwhile, Afghan resistance leaders criticized Shevardnadze's visit to Pakistan. One of them, Gulbaddin Hekmatyar, said Soviet insistence on the survival of the current Afghan government would mean continuation of the war (_AP_, February 6).

Shevardnadze in China and Pakistan

Cuba said Admiral Vladimir Chernavin, commander in chief of the Soviet Navy, had arrived in Havana at the head of a Soviet military delegation. AP quoted the Cuban official news agency as saying Chernavin would tour Cuban armed forces installations during his visit.

Soviet Navy Chief in Cuba

61

Commission Set Up for Ties with Emigré Soviet Scientists

Soviet scientists and engineers have set up an international commission to maintain contacts with colleagues who have emigrated from the USSR. Commission member Yurii Gulyaev said "we will look for contacts and interact with people whom only yesterday many of us tried not to recall." Gulyaev is director of the Radio Engineering and Electronics Institute of the USSR Academy of Sciences. His comments appeared in *Sotsialisticheskaya industriya*. He said the commission planned to set up joint laboratories, enterprises, and research institutes abroad with the help of Soviet émigrés.

Minister Blamed for Poisoning of Orenburg Population

USSR Minister of the Gas Industry Viktor Chernomyrdin and two of his deputies have been blamed for leaks of poisonous emissions from a natural-gas-processing plant in Orenburg in the RSFSR in mid-January. Radio Moscow-1 (0800) quoted a special commission studying the incident as saying that Chernomyrdin and his deputies had been directly involved in the construction of the plant and knew it had no filtering system. The commission said that seventy-six people had suffered gas poisoning and that twenty-seven of them had been hospitalized.

KGB Chief in Uzbekistan Is Dead

Izvestia reported that the KGB chief in Uzbekistan, Lieutenant General Vladimir Golovin, had died suddenly on January 26 at the age of sixty-six. Golovin was appointed head of the KGB in Uzbekistan in August, 1983.

Economist Says *Perestroika* an International Phenomenon

Soviet economist Oleg Bogomolov said *perestroika* was becoming an international phenomenon among Communist countries. In an interview with Novosti, Bogomolov said that economic reforms had started in China ten years ago and were followed by reforms in Poland and Hungary. Soviet *perestroika* then prompted Bulgaria, Czechoslovakia, Mongolia, and Vietnam to recognize their own needs for change. East Germany, he said, still had not joined the reform "mainstream," and Romania, Cuba, and North Korea were still trying to cope with difficulties "by command and whip-cracking." He said that, although the need for reform varied in each country, pressure for change was mounting (*APN*, in English, February 1).

Memorial Plaque Unveiled for Stalin Victim

Officials in Moscow unveiled a memorial plaque for Lev Karakhan, a Soviet diplomat who was executed under Stalin. TASS said the plaque had been placed in the building that used to house the People's Commissariat for Foreign Affairs. First Deputy Foreign Minister Aleksandr Bessmertnykh said at the ceremony that Karakhan had played a great role in developing Soviet diplomacy. Karakhan was Soviet ambassador to Poland, China, and Turkey. He was shot in 1937 and rehabilitated under Khrushchev.

Leningrad Worker Stages Hunger Strike after Failing to Be Nominated

TASS said Gennadii Bogomolov, a Leningrad worker who went on a hunger strike after failing to be nominated as a candidate for the Congress of People's Deputies, had ended his fast when a different group put his name forward. Bogomolov started the fast on January 30 after his factory boss and the unit's Party group had refused to discuss his nomination, even though the majority of his co-workers wanted him to be their candidate. "He considered this to be discrimination on the part of the company management and Party organization for his pro-worker, self-management stand," TASS said. The agency added that Bogomolov had eventually been nominated by the Leningrad Engineering and Physics Institute.

Thursday, February 2

Demonstrators Demand Resignation of Academy's Presidium

Some 2,000 supporters of Andrei Sakharov demonstrated to demand the resignation of the Presidium of the USSR Academy of Sciences. According to TASS and various Western news agencies, the primary objective of the demonstration was to express anger over the Academy's failure to nominate Sakharov and other reformers to the Academy's list of candidates for the Congress of People's Deputies. Television coverage showed Sakharov at the demonstration, but he did not address the crowd. Academy President Gurii Marchuk was reported to have said that the Presidium would consider the protesters' demands next week. _Moscow News_ (No. 5) carried an article by correspondent Len Karpinsky, condemning the Presidium for not nominating Sakharov and other reformists from its ranks.

Voroshilov's and Suslov's Names to Be Removed

On February 2, _TASS_ and _Izvestia_ reported that the names of some former leading officials were to be removed from places of honor in Moscow. TASS reported that the name of one of Stalin's closest associates, Marshal Kliment Voroshilov, would be removed from the museum in the

63

capital that carries it. TASS said the museum's directors had decided to turn the building into a museum of local history and put most of the Voroshilov exhibits in storage. In the course of the *glasnost'* campaign, the Soviet press has discussed extensively Voroshilov's negative role in history, including his role in the purge of the military in 1937. *Izvestia* said the CPSU Central Committee and the USSR Council of Ministers had ordered the plaque on the Moscow University building honoring former chief ideologist Mikhail Suslov to be removed. The move follows numerous complaints in the press about the plaque on the part of students and professors at the university. There is still a street in Moscow named after Suslov, and the youth journal *Sobesednik* (No. 5) carried a complaint about this. In addition, *Ogonek* (No. 4) published a very critical article about Suslov's activities as Party ideologist.

Kulikov Replaced

It was reported that Soviet Army Marshal Viktor Kulikov had been replaced as commander in chief of the armies of the Warsaw Pact. The sixty-seven-year-old Kulikov had held the post for more than twelve years. His replacement is Army General Petr Lushev, a first deputy defense minister (*Radio Moscow-1*, February 2).

TASS Analyst Predicts Problems at Military Factories

A TASS military specialist predicted that there would be problems converting Soviet military factories to civilian production. Vladimir Chernyshev said workers would have to take wage cuts and lose bonuses and other prerogatives. He went on to say that managers would also have to change the way they do business. Chernyshev explained that converting from military to civilian production would cause planning problems because there was not enough information about the Soviet Union's military industries.

Two Waterways Projects Halted

Two Soviet waterways projects, one in Ukraine and the other on the lower Volga, have been halted. Soviet media said the Ukrainian Council of Ministers had ordered a halt to work on a giant dam and reservoir at the firth of the Bug and Dnieper rivers east of Odessa. TASS said the project had been deemed undesirable after public bodies had drawn attention to the ecological hazards involved. Radio Moscow said construction had also been stopped on a canal that was supposed to link the lower Volga River with the Chogray River on the border of the Kalmyk republic.

The Estonian Popular Front won official recognition, giving it the right to compete in local elections against the Communist Party. An Estonian journalist told Reuters the Presidium of the Estonian Supreme Soviet had registered the charter of the Popular Front. The Popular Front has grown into a powerful force in Estonia since its emergence in 1988.

Estonian Popular Front Wins Official Recognition

In its "Vremya" news program, Soviet television revealed that the government of Belorussia had covered up the full extent of the radiation danger caused by the 1986 Chernobyl' disaster and had only now ordered the evacuation of twenty contaminated villages. The report said residents of the unidentified settlements, most of them farming communities, had been left alone to live and grow crops in soil highly contaminated by radioactive fallout from Chernobyl'. The size of the population of the endangered villages was not disclosed.

Contaminated Villages in Belorussia to Be Evacuated Only Now

_____ *Friday, February 3*

"Vzglyad," the Soviet Union's most popular television show, was largely devoted this week to problems of foreign policy and military matters. In a series of street interviews, the moderators of "Vzglyad" asked people whether the USSR had committed any mistakes in foreign policy. The respondents identified as mistakes: the invasion of Afghanistan, the invasion of Czechoslovakia in 1968, the Cuban crisis, and the Soviet Union's involvement in secret diplomacy. Furthermore, all the respondents, including two or three junior army officers, also spoke in favor of replacing the present system of military conscription with a volunteer army. (Among these officers was a captain nominated for a seat on the Congress of People's Deputies.) Also interviewed was a member of the Afghan Communist Party who said that, following the departure of Soviet troops from Afghanistan, his party would be unable to remain in power and would be replaced by Islamic fundamentalists; the Afghan people, he told "Vzglyad," "will not support us," because of the Communist government's mistreatment of religion.

"Vzglyad" on Foreign Policy and Military Matters

Komsomol'skaya pravda reported that the director of a hospital in the Kalmyk capital of Elista, where twenty-seven children were infected with AIDS, had been dis-

AIDS in Elista Hospital

missed. The children, all aged about two, picked up the virus after nurses at the hospital in Elista had injected them with unsterilized syringes, according to press reports last week. Five of the children were reported to have passed the disease on to their mothers, and doctors were said to have started testing 12,000 local people for the virus. On February 4, *Sel'skaya zhizn'* said that, in addition to the children, four women had been infected with the AIDS virus in the Elista hospital. On February 16, *Sovetskaya Rossiya* quoted the RSFSR Minister of Health, Elenora Negovitsina, as saying the source of infection was apparently a man who caught AIDS while serving in the military in Africa. She said his wife had become infected and then their child, who was treated at the Elista hospital.

Novosti Publishes Book on Stalin's Victims

TASS said Novosti press agency had published a book on Soviet state and Party figures and scientists who were repressed in the Stalin period. Those discussed include close associates of Lenin, such as Nikolai Bukharin, Grigorii Zinov'ev, and Lev Kamenev. TASS said part of the proceeds of the book will go to build a memorial to Stalin's victims. It said the two-volume book is entitled *Returned Names* and contains articles by writers, journalists, and historians.

Estonian Komsomol Newspaper on Casualty Figures in Afghanistan

The Estonian Komsomol newspaper *Noorte Haale* carried an article saying that 50,000 Soviet military personnel had died in Afghanistan—a figure much higher than previous official Soviet reports. Last May, the Soviet authorities gave a figure of 13,310 for the number of Soviet soldiers who had died in Afghanistan.

Authorities Order Crackdown on State Enterprises

The Soviet authorities have ordered a crackdown on state enterprises for exploiting shortages of consumer goods to increase profits. The order from the USSR Council of Ministers requires factories to produce some inexpensive consumer goods and bars them from increasing prices without improving quality. The order follows complaints in the Soviet media that expensive goods are being produced instead of cheap but indispensable articles. (State-owned factories now have to show a profit. To do so, many have cut their output of inexpensive goods—which bring in little money—and have increased the production of expensive items.) According to Radio Moscow and TASS, the order reproaches ministries and departments for allowing exploitative price increases.

TASS said some 200 Moslems from Uzbekistan, Kazakhstan, and Tajikistan had staged a three-hour demonstration on February 3 after prayers in Tashkent's Tilla-Sheikh Mosque. According to the news agency, there were no clashes with police, who took measures to safeguard public order. It said the protesters had sought government intervention in the affairs of the Moslem Religious Board of Central Asia and Kazakhstan. On February 6, it emerged that the demonstration had been organized by a group of religious activists called "Islam and Democracy," who demanded the removal of the head of the Religious Board, Shamsutdin Babakhanov, because of his alleged drinking, womanizing, and excessive subservience to secular authorities (_The New York Times_, February 6). A day later Babakhanov was reported to have resigned and to have been replaced temporarily by M. Mamayusupov.

Moslems Stage Rally in Tashkent

The Azerbaijani Russian-Language Party and government daily _Bakinsky rabochii_ published what is to be the first in a weekly series of Azerbaijani language lessons "for those studying the language of our republic." The first lesson consists of approximately fifty basic phrases but no explanation of grammatical rules. A recent press article disclosed that some residents of Azerbaijan who did not speak Azerbaijani had begun attending private courses in the language.

Azerbaijani Lessons for Russian Residents

Pravda carried an interview with V. Sorokin, the newly elected president of the Union of Cooperators, which held its first congress recently. In the interview, Sorokin complained about the December 29 decree of the USSR Council of Ministers, which banned several types of cooperatives. Sorokin said the new Union of Cooperators consisted of 21,000 cooperatives, in which 411,000 people were employed. Sorokin said one of the first goals of the union was to set up a juridical consultation center for Soviet cooperators.

Pravda Interviews President of Union of Cooperators

The latest issue of _Argumenty i fakty_ carried an article by historian Roy Medvedev, who said that the full extent of Stalin's repressions would probably never be known. Medvedev, however, gave his own estimates, which he said were not exact. Medvedev said approxi-

Roy Medvedev on Number of Stalin's Victims

mately 40 million people were repressed by the Soviet dictator. He estimated that about 20 million of these had died in labor camps, or through executions, forced collectivization, and famine. Medvedev's article in *Argumenty i fakty* is a longer version of an article he published in *Moscow News* in November, 1988. Meanwhile, on February 3, the Soviet media reported that a mass grave had been uncovered by construction workers in Gornoaltaisk in Siberia. The reports said the remains of about fifty people examined there so far showed that they had been shot through the head. The grave is near the site of a Stalin-era prison camp (*TASS*, February 4).

Knizbnoe obozrenie on Voinovich

Knizbnoe obozrenie (No. 4) devoted two full pages to material by and about émigré writer Vladimir Voinovich. The items published include Voinovich's letter to the leadership of the Moscow writers' organization, written on the eve of his expulsion from the USSR Writers' Union in February, 1974, and the letter Voinovich wrote to Brezhnev after being deprived of his Soviet citizenship in July, 1981, on the grounds that he had damaged the prestige of the USSR. In the letter to Brezhnev, Voinovich pointed out that he could not have damaged the prestige of the Soviet state, because the Soviet state had no prestige to damage, thanks to the activities of its leaders. In an article about Voinovich accompanying the letters, critic Benedikt Sarnov identified as Voinovich's enemy in the Moscow writers' organization "the former KGB general, Viktor Il'in."

Military Cuts Vital for Improvement in Soviet Life

The Soviet Union cannot hope to achieve improvements in its standard of living without large military cuts, a senior Soviet commentator said in *Izvestia*. Stanislav Kondrashev, analyzing last week's publication of the Warsaw Pact's troops and arms levels in Europe, praised the disclosure as a step towards realizing Moscow's repeated promises to publish details of its defense budget. Kondrashev complained that the Soviet Union's relative contribution to the Warsaw Pact far outweighed that of the United States to NATO, with Moscow providing a far greater proportion of aircraft, ships, and other hardware.

Soviet People's Attitudes towards United States

Izvestia carried a short article reporting the results of an opinion poll conducted among the Soviet population by the Institute of Sociology together with the USSR Foreign Ministry on the attitudes of Soviet citizens towards the

68

United States. The poll was conducted in connection with the presidential elections in the United States. According to the poll, 7 percent of those questioned had a highly positive attitude towards the United States, 64 percent a positive attitude, 12 percent said they were cautious, and only 0.2 percent had clearly negative feelings.

Ogonek on Travel Regulations

Ogonek (No. 5) carried a lengthy interview on changes in Soviet travel regulations with an employee of the human-rights section of the Institute of State and Law, Doctor Vladimir Kartashkin. A correspondent of the journal had initially tried to obtain information on the isssue from the Soviet Visa and Registration Office (OVIR) and the Ministry of Justice, but was unsuccessful. In the interview, Kartashkin expressed his opinion on travel regulations. He suggested they should be similar to those existing in Western democratic countries. He also said the Soviet practice of depriving people emigrating to Israel of Soviet citizenship violated not only international but Soviet law.

Soviet Press on Situation in Poland

Ogonek (No. 5) published the text of a conversation between the journal's editor Vitalii Korotich and Polish film director Andrzej Wajda, who discussed the situation in Poland. While saying that there was no need at present to create new political parties in Poland, Wajda spoke of the need for pluralism of opinion, including on political issues. Wajda also proposed that a digest of the most interesting articles in the Soviet press be published in Poland so that Poles could become better acquainted with current Soviet debates on *perestroika*. DPA of February 10, reported that the latest issue of the journal *Novoe vremya* (New Times) carried interviews with "Solidarity" leaders Lech Walesa and Adam Michnik.

Sunday, February 5

Sakharov in Italy

On February 5, Academician Andrei Sakharov and his wife Elena Bonner arrived in Rome on a visit to Italy (*AP, Reuters*, February 5). On February 6, Sakharov was received by the president of the Italian Senate, Giovanni Spadolini. He then went on to the Vatican for a private audience with Pope John Paul II. Sakharov also met Cardinal Myroslav Lubachivsky, head of the Ukrainian Catholic Church. Lubachivsky was quoted as saying that Sakharov had told him he would do what he could to press for the legalization of the Ukrainian Catholic Church in the Soviet Union (*Reuters, AP*, February 6). On February 7, Sakharov met with Italian Socialist Party leader Bettino Craxi. During the meeting, Sakharov said the West should press the USSR for the release of the jailed members of the Armenian Karabakh Committee (Western agencies, February 7). On February 8, Sakharov attended a ceremony at Bologna University, where he was presented with an honorary doctorate. Speaking after the ceremony, Sakharov said the world's scientific community must defend not only its own members but "anyone who is a victim of repression" and "all those who are called prisoners of conscience." He said in the last two years great changes had taken place in the Soviet Union in the field of human rights. He also said he had great respect for Gorbachev and his reform policies. Sakharov said he hoped for the success of *perestroika* but called the process extremely complex and contradictory. He again drew attention to the plight of the members of the Karabakh Committee (*RFE/RL Special, Reuters*, February 8). Soviet television reported the ceremony in Bologna but did not carry the text of Sakharov's speech. The same day, Sakharov and Bonner left for Siena. Speaking at Siena University on February 9, Sakharov urged more religious freedom in the USSR and the legalization of the Ukrainian Catholic Church (*Reuters, AP*, February 9). On February 10, Sakharov visited Florence, where he received honorary citizenship of the city (*Reuters*, February 10).

Moscow News Interviews Sakharov

Moscow News (No. 6) carried an interview with Academician Sakharov concerning his nomination as a candidate for the Congress of People's Deputies. In the interview, Sakharov gave details of his election platform.

Volga River, Caspian Sea on Verge of Ecological Disaster

Sovetskaya Rossiya carried a report on "the critical ecological situation" of the Volga River. The newspaper gave a full-page report on the founding conference of a public committee called "Save the Volga." It said the conference adopted a motion saying the Volga and the Caspian Sea into which it flows are on the verge of "ecological disaster." The motion said unskilled and ecologically harmful "economic activity" was mainly to blame.

Soviet "Prisoners of Conscience" Freed

USSR Deputy Minister of Internal Affairs Leonid Sizov told *Komsomol'skaya pravda* that the Soviet Union had freed all detainees known in the West as "prisoners of conscience." According to Sizov, these include all those held for religious activities. A year ago, forty-five people were still being held on charges related to religious activity, Sizov said. Sizov also argued that Western reports saying there were 300 prisoners of conscience in the USSR were unfounded. A similar statement was made by Soviet Prosecutor V. I. Andreev in an interview with *Ogonek*(No. 4).

Disagreement over New Price Regulations

A State Price Committee official and the newspaper *Komsomol'skaya pravda* expressed differing opinions over new regulations intended to prevent unjustified price increases. The newspaper said the new measures erected a barrier over which economic reform might stumble. But in an interview with *Sovetskaya Rossiya*, the deputy chairman of the USSR State Price Committee, Ivan Gorbachev, said the new regulations would prevent "speculation and grabbing" and protect living standards. *Komsomol'skaya pravda* said prices were not going up because of bad intentions but because they had not been set at full market values. It also blamed the domination of monopolies. The price committee official said unjustified price increases should be stopped "at any cost." (A resolution by the USSR Council of Ministers published on February 3 ordered a crackdown on state enterprises that exploited shortages in consumer goods to increase their profits.)

Mass Celebrated in Vilnius Cathedral

A mass was held in Vilnius Cathedral to celebrate its being handed back to the Church. A Reuters correspondent said the cathedral was packed as Vilnius Apostolic Administrator Bishop Julijonas Steponavicius led the reconsecration ceremony. Several thousand people listened to the mass outside the cathedral on loudspeakers. The cathedral was seized by the Soviet authorities in 1949, and since then it has served as a secular building.

Manipulation of Election Campaign

The Soviet media reported that "deliberate manipulation" of the election law was widespread as local electoral commissions sought to carry out the task of interpreting the articles pertaining to the registration of candidates for election to the Congress of People's Deputies (*Radio Moscow*, February 6; *TASS*, February 5). The inquiries of the commissions into the qualifications of the nominees were reported to be taking on a personal and "intimate" nature. According to the chief of the juridical group of the Central Electoral Commission, such inquiries were inappropriate (*Izvestia*, February 5).

Monday, February 6 ————————————————————————————

Izvestia Reprints Sakharov's Rebuttal

Izvestia carried a letter from Andrei Sakharov rebutting the newspaper's criticism of comments attributed to him by a French journalist. An interview that Sakharov and Elena Bonner had supposedly given to journalist Jean-Pierre Barou, in which the couple expressed doubts that Gorbachev would last long in office, appeared in *Le Figaro*, the *Süddeutsche Zeitung*, and other West European newspapers in January. Sakharov, in his letter to *Izvestia*, denied that he had given a formal interview to Barou and said Barou's account of Sakharov's conversation with him contained a number of inaccuracies. In pointing out these inaccuracies, some of which drew unfavorable comment by *Izvestia* last week, Sakharov succeeded in communicating some of the main points of his conversation with Barou to the Soviet reader, including his call for direct rather than indirect elections in the Soviet Union.

Aganbegyan Says *Perestroika* Is Moving Too Slowly

Leading Soviet economist Academician Abel Aganbegyan said *perestroika* had run into unexpectedly strong opposition and was moving far too slowly. Writing in *Pravda*, Aganbegyan said that *perestroika* had brought changes in society and in foreign policy but that the living standards of Soviet citizens were rising too slowly. He said the changes must be made "two or three times more quickly."

Tuesday, February 7 ————————————————————————————

USSR Asks Turkey to Mediate for Release of POWs

The Soviet Union was reported to have asked Turkey to help mediate for the release of Soviet prisoners of war held by the Afghan resistance. Turkey's Anatolia news agency said the Soviet ambassador to Turkey, Albert Chernyshev, had told reporters Moscow had made the request and had asked Pakistan for help as well (*Reuters, AP*, February 7).

Soviet Deputy Premier Meets Thatcher

British Prime Minister Margaret Thatcher had talks in London with Soviet Deputy Prime Minister Vladimir Kamentsev. TASS said they discussed economic restructuring in the USSR and Soviet readiness to develop trade and economic relations with the West. Before meeting Thatcher, Kamentsev talked with British Trade and Industry Secretary Lord Young on the expansion of Anglo-Soviet trade. The

Soviet official is on a four-day visit to Britain (*TASS*, February 7). On February 9, Kamentsev went to the Confederation of British Industry in London for talks on how British firms could cooperate with the Soviet Union (*RFE/RL Special*, February 9).

Politburo Criticizes Armenia over Nuclear Plant

The Politburo commission created to deal with the aftermath of the earthquake in Armenia criticized the authorities in the Caucasian republic for failing to prepare fast enough for the impending shutdown of a controversial nuclear power station near Erevan. The station, long a source of discontent because of its siting in a seismic zone, was ordered closed by mid-March. The commission said work on boosting power-generating capacity to compensate for the closure had been going too slowly. The commission was quoted by TASS as saying the Armenian authorities were not telling people enough about the power shortages they would face (*Izvestia*, February 8).

Demonstration in Lithuania to Protest Europarliament Visit

Thousands of people were reported to have demonstrated in the Lithuanian capital of Vilnius on February 6 to protest against a visit there by five members of the European Parliament. The parliamentarians were on a tour of the Baltic States. The protesters expressed fears that the visit might lead to indirect recognition of Lithuania's incorporation into the USSR (*RFE Lithuanian Service*, February 7). It was reported that the members of the European Parliament were given a statement from the Lithuanian Popular Front "Sajudis" that unequivocally (and emphatically) reiterated the nation's commitment to the reattainment of independence (*Lithuanian Service*, February 8). On February 8, the EEC delegation went to Latvia. On February 9, they met with members of the Latvian Popular Front and the Latvian National Independence Movement (*Latvian Service*, February 9).

Soviet Crime Rate Up

USSR Public Prosecutor Aleksandr Sukharev told a meeting of the coordinating council of all-Union and republican law-enforcement agencies that these agencies were not coping with the rising crime rate in the Soviet Union. The meeting was reported by the "Vremya" television news program; this was the first time such a session was open to journalists. Sukharev was quoted as saying that improved crime prevention was needed in order to keep the penal system humane while at the same time protecting the public. According to data provided at the meeting, in 1988 the overall crime rate rose 10 percent; there was also a higher rate of unsolved crimes than in 1987. The murder rate rose 14 percent, and the number of murders of police officials doubled.

Soviet Death Toll in Afghanistan

At a press conference in Moscow, a USSR Foreign Ministry spokesman gave the official toll for Soviet troops killed in Afghanistan as "up to 15,000" (*AP*, February 7). This is to be compared with the previous toll of 13,310 covering the period December, 1979, through May 1, 1988.

Revised Casualty Figures for Nagorno-Karabakh

The total number of dead and wounded in unrest arising from the campaign to transfer Nagorno-Karabakh from Azerbaijan to Armenia over the past year has again been revised upwards. In early January, the official number of deaths stood at eighty-two, of whom forty-three had died during the latest round of violence in November and December. At a press conference on February 7, a senior official of the USSR Ministry of Internal Affairs, Major General Nikolai Vashko, disclosed that a total of ninety-one persons, including four soldiers from the Soviet Army and MVD troops, had died and that 1,500 civilians, 117 troops, and 32 policemen had been injured since the beginning of the unrest last February (*TASS*, February 7).

USSR to Build Power Station in Iraq

Soviet and Iraqi ministers launched work on a 700 million dollar power station south of Baghdad. Reuters and AP quoted the Iraqi media as saying the ceremony was performed by Iraq's Industry and Military Industrialization Minister Hussein Kamel Hassan and Soviet Minister of the Petroleum Industry Vasilii Dinkov. The agencies said the station, to be Iraq's biggest, would be built by the Soviet firm Tekhexport and in operation by the mid-1990s.

Wednesday, February 8 —————————————————

Most Important Event of 1989

According to an article by Aleksandr Bovin in *Izvestia*, Gorbachev's China visit and a complete normalization of Sino-Soviet relations will be the most important events of 1989, not only for the Soviet Union but for the world in general. He predicted that the normalization of Sino-Soviet relations would have a favorable impact on the situation in Asia and in the Asia-Pacific region in general.

The director of the Institute of the Economics of the World Socialist System, Oleg Bogomolov, said Stalinist socialism and key parts of Marxist theory were wrong, and he added that the USSR would soon act on that conclusion by selling private homes and land. Speaking at a press conference at the Soviet Foreign Ministry, Bogomolov said: "We still adhere to Marxist theory, but much of this theory should be adjusted because many of the conclusions of Marx have failed to stand the test of time." Bogomolov said the Soviet Union had found that banning private property left farmers with no concern for the land and long-term development. He predicted that the pending legalization of family farms would go further than previously stated and allow farmers to choose their own crops and sell them at market prices. Bogomolov also admitted that "the Stalinist system . . . was imposed on other countries." He said Socialist countries should now choose their own way of repairing the damage (*AP*, February 8). Bogomolov said it was theoretically possible for a country like Hungary to become a Western-style "bourgeois democracy" and still remain a member of the Warsaw Pact.

Oleg Bogomolov on Marxism

According to Aeroflot chief pilot M. Tereshenko, eighty-five people died in crashes on the state airline Aeroflot last year. Tereshenko said the figure was higher than the number killed the previous year but lower than comparable figures worldwide (*AP*, February 8).

Eighty-Five Soviet Citizens Died in Aeroflot Crashes in 1988

The Soviet Union's new chief of staff, Colonel General Mikhail Moiseev, said the days were over when the Soviet military was immune to budget cuts. Speaking to TASS, Moiseev said the military must now learn to save. He also said the Soviet military must be reorganized into "a more pronounced defensive posture." But, he said, it must not slip behind in battle-readiness and find itself unable "to prevent attempts at international bullying." TASS quoted Moiseev as saying the military budget would be cut by 14.2 percent "in the next few years." This was the budget cut announced by Gorbachev last month.

Chief of Staff Says Military Must Learn to Save

Soviet-born cellist and conductor Mstislav Rostropovich, who was stripped of his Soviet citizenship in 1978, has been readmitted to the Soviet Composers' Union. The readmission was announced in Moscow by the union's officials (*TASS*, February 8).

Rostropovich Readmitted to Soviet Composers' Union

Shevardnadze Meets West European Envoys

TASS reported that on February 7 Foreign Minister Eduard Shevardnadze had met with the ambassadors of the twelve countries of the European Community accredited in Moscow. Gorbachev sent the ambassadors good wishes and stressed the significance of the first formal dialogue between the Soviet Union and the EEC countries. Shevardnadze emphasized in his address the need to establish official relations between the USSR and the EEC as well as between Comecon and the EEC (*Pravda*, February 8).

Poland Demands Publication of Katyn Findings

Radio Warsaw and the Polish press announced that Ryszard Wojna, a Communist deputy of the Sejm (parliament), had demanded that findings about the Katyn massacre and other crimes against Poles during the Stalin era be published. Despite the fact that a commission of Polish historians handed over their conclusions about the Katyn massacre to their Soviet colleagues a year ago, the Soviet side has not yet come out with a satisfactory finding. Wojna further said that all Poles were entitled to know what was in these documents and that Soviet historians should realize that such painful matters could not be kept confidential forever.

Official Registration Denied to Latvian Popular Front

Radio Moscow carried an interview with Latvia's chief prosecutor, Janis Dzenitis, in which he said that the legal registration of the Popular Front of Latvia had been canceled because some provisions of its charter were in conflict with current law and with the USSR and Latvian Constitutions. He did not give any example of this but noted that the Popular Front might seek to re-register after the new USSR Supreme Soviet passed new laws governing public organizations.

***Neva* Criticizes Party**

The January issue of the Leningrad literary journal *Neva* carried an article critical of the Communist Party's place in Soviet life. Commentator Sergei Andreev wrote in the article that, given the Party's leading role, it was logical to conclude that it was the Party that had brought the Soviet Union to economic crisis and moral decline. Commenting on his article, Andreev told *The Washington Post* (February 8) he was personally not against Gorbachev. He said that he knew the article was dangerous but that he regarded it as a kind of "dialogue" with the Party. Andreev wrote in the article that, unless the Party were to become answerable to the vast majority of the Soviet population who are not Party members, Soviet democracy would be defective. He further said the Party organization and "the new class" of manager-bureaucrats were one and the same. These people, he said, stand to lose position and power through current changes and are sabotaging the reform process.

Literaturnaya gazeta carried a lengthy article giving a sophisticated evaluation of the activities of Ukrainian anarchist Nestor Makhno, a prominent figure in the Civil War. Makhno, who three times made pacts with the Bolsheviks but in the end broke completely with Soviet power, has traditionally been condemned in the USSR as a mouthpiece of "petty bourgeois sentiments of peasants." *Literaturnaya gazeta*, however, tried to show that the break between Makhno and the Bolsheviks had quite complicated roots. The article suggested that the Bolsheviks shared part of the blame for the break. The policy of the Bolsheviks towards peasants during the Civil War was based on the Marxist assumption that peasants were "the last bourgeois class." Condemning such an approach towards peasants as a serious mistake, *Literaturnaya gazeta* suggested that it had contributed to the souring of relations between the Bolsheviks and peasant movements, including Makhno's. The article also drew a parallel between the transformation of the Makhno movement into a dictatorship and the evolution of Bolshevism into Stalinism. In both cases, the article said, the leaders of the respective movements saw themselves as the sole representatives and executors of the people's will and, as such, not subject to the limits imposed by laws or rules. See RL 115/89.

Newspaper Reevaluates Nestor Makhno

Thursday, February 9

Komsomol'skaya pravda reported on the abuse of a prisoner by Afghan secret police and on a Soviet soldier who deserted to the resistance. A correspondent for the newspaper, Vladimir Snegirev, said he had seen three Afghan interrogators take the headwrap of a captured resistance fighter and wrap it tightly around his neck until he was gasping for air. The report did not say what happened to the prisoner. The correspondent also related the story of a Soviet soldier in Afghanistan who had deserted and served with the resistance for a year. The report said the soldier had deserted after being accused of selling Soviet army supplies. He was later recaptured.

Soviet Report on Abuse by Afghan Soldiers

77

Economist Says State Budget Deficit Dangerous

Soviet economist Leonid Abalkin said that the USSR's state budget deficit had reached a dangerous level and that the growth of personal income was moving out of control. Abalkin, who is director of the Economics Institute of the USSR Academy of Sciences, was quoted by TASS as saying a special program was needed to consolidate the financial system in the next two to three years. He also said attitudes towards production must be reformed so as to make *perestroika* irreversible. In his view, this required the development of cooperatives and individual labor and the introduction of new forms of state property, such as the leasing and self-supporting systems.

Komsomol'skaya pravda* Praises *Samizdat

Komsomol'skaya pravda carried an article praising *samizdat* of the pre-*glasnost'* era. It condemned the practice of sentencing people distributing *samizdat* to terms of imprisonment. The article said *samizdat* still exists in the USSR. As an example, it mentioned the unofficial journals of informal groups, which have started to proliferate in the past few years.

Moscow Historians Denounce Soviet Anti-Zionism as Hitlerian

Two Moscow historians, Sergei Rogov and Vladimir Nosenko, denounced Soviet anti-Zionist campaigning over the past two decades, comparing it with Nazi anti-Semitism and saying it had helped create a climate that had led thousands of Jews to emigrate. The historians' attack in *Sovetskaya kul'tura* appeared on the eve of the opening in Moscow of a new center to promote Jewish culture in the USSR. Rogov and Nosenko said leading anti-Zionist Vladimir Begun, who for years set the tone for official propaganda on the issue, "seeks to sow mistrust towards Soviet Jews." The historians compared Begun's views on Zionists with Adolf Hitler's condemnation of the Jews. *Moscow News* (No. 6) carried an article by poet Evgenii Evtushenko, who complained about the anti-Semitic slogans used at public meetings of "Pamyat'" and other similar informal groups. See RL 98/89.

Yazov Proposes Special Talks on Naval Force Reductions

Soviet Defense Minister Dmitrii Yazov said NATO and the Warsaw Pact should start immediate, separate talks on cutting naval forces. Writing in *Pravda*, Yazov said NATO had far more sailors, major surface ships, and ships carrying cruise missiles than does the Warsaw Pact. Yazov said the naval talks should include confidence-building measures for naval forces and for "independent activities of air forces." He did not elaborate on these measures. Yazov added that European security requires immediate action to do away with existing imbalances in forces and to substantially reduce the most dangerous offensive weapons. He said military forces on both sides should be restructured to give them a purely defensive character.

One-fifth of Belorussia is contaminated by radioactive fallout from the Chernobyl' nuclear power plant explosion to the point that the authorities are constantly monitoring the health of more than 300,000 residents, TASS reported. The agency asked why over two years had passed since the world's worst nuclear accident before residents were told about the extent of the threat to their health. Last week, Soviet television reported the evacuation of residents of several Belorussian villages contaminated after the 1986 accident. The television report also asked why the evacuation had only taken place more than two years after the disaster; see also *Pravda*, February 11.

Soviet Media on Chernobyl' Contamination in Belorussia

_____ *Friday, February 10*

Pravda carried an editorial devoted to informal groups. The newspaper said there were more than 60,000 such organizations in the country. (In 1988, *Argumenty i fakty* gave a figure of 30,000 informal groups.) The *Pravda* editorial praised the groups involved in the preservation of historical and cultural monuments and called on Soviet Party and state bodies to pay more attention to independent activities. The editorial made clear that the Soviet leadership is worried about the growing number of informal groups concerned with nationalities issues. The newspaper said "in some places, under the cover of democracy and *glasnost'*, of national self-assertion, overt criticism of our system is voiced." In an apparent reference to the popular fronts in the Baltic republics and groups like the Democratic Union, *Pravda* complained about "attempts to create political structures in opposition to the Party organs." The newspaper complained that local authorities had shown themselves incapable of dealing with such informal activities. It reiterated the allegation, used lately by the Soviet leadership, that "extremists" were trying to use nationalistic feelings for their own dubious purposes. As an example of an informal group whose existence should not be allowed, the editorial cited

Soviet Press and Officials on Informal Activities

79

the Karabakh Committee in Armenia. A number of other attacks on "anti-Soviet" trends within the informal groups movement followed the *Pravda* editorial. Speaking in Moldavia on February 10, Politburo member Viktor Chebrikov complained that "there exist anti-Socialist elements that attempt to create political structures opposing the CPSU." He warned that such attempts would not be tolerated. On February 12, *Sotsialisticheskaya industriya* carried an article that attacked, in very strong terms, the independent activists Lev Timofeev, Sergei Grigoryants, and Valerii Senderov, accusing them of taking money from Western intelligence agencies.

Newspaper Publishes 1929 Speech of Bukharin

Sovetskaya Rossiya carried the text of a statement made by Nikolai Bukharin, Aleksei Rykov, and Mikhail Tomsky at a plenum of the Bolshevik Party held on November 12, 1929. (This statement denied Stalin's accusations against the so-called "right-wing opposition." A statement of "the right-wing opposition" was nonetheless rejected by the plenum.) On February 3, *Pravda* denounced the suppression of "the right-wing opposition" at the end of the 1920s, calling it a turning point in Soviet history that paved the way for the establishment of Stalin's totalitarian system.

Newspaper Says Moscow's Air and Water Seriously Polluted

Sotsialisticheskaya industriya complained that Moscow's air and water were seriously polluted. It blamed surrounding farms for letting fertilizer into the water supply and the failure of a plan to move factories out of city.

Chazov Says There Are 2,000 Afghan War Invalids

USSR Minister of Health Evgenii Chazov said about 2,000 Soviet soldiers had been left disabled from the war in Afghanistan and would need rehabilitation. Speaking at a press conference in Helsinki, where Chazov is on an official visit, he said the injured men would be treated in six special centers throughout the country. One center near Moscow that, according to Chazov, was originally built for Party officials, is already in operation, and two others, in the RSFSR and Ukraine, will be opened soon (*Reuters*, February 10).

KGB Holds Open House

Nedelya (No. 5) reported on a "normal" working day at KGB headquarters. The report was accompanied by seventeen photographs ranging from a view of the KGB Communications Center to a class of cadets receiving instruction at a KGB training academy. The report also contained the biographies of seven people described as "typical" middle-ranking KGB officials. These include the secretary of the Communist Party organization in the central KGB apparatus, Colonel Nikolai Nazarov; a staffer of the KGB press bureau, Colonel Vladimir Prelin; and a professor at the KGB higher education school, Aleksandr Ignat'ev. All the biographies were accompanied by photographs. In describing the KGB's daily activities, *Nedelya* selected those likely to appeal most to popular opinion: attempts to prevent the transfer of illegal drugs from Asia to the West via Soviet territory; the KGB's involvement in the recent hijacking by three Soviet criminals of an aircraft to Israel; the fight against the illegal export of valuable Russian artifacts to the West; and, last but not least, the KGB's participation in the investigation of Stalin's crimes and the rehabilitation of his victims.

Pravda on CPSU Spendings

In response to a reader's letter, *Pravda* carried an article commenting on CPSU spending. The article said measures are under way to cut CPSU spending and turn some of the Party buildings (especially in Uzbekistan) into hospitals or sanatoriums for the general public. See also *Izvestiya TsK KPSS* (No. 1).

Zaikov Announces Measures to Solve Health Service Problems

Lev Zaikov, Politburo member and first secretary of the Moscow City Party Committee, has announced measures aimed at solving problems in Moscow's health service. TASS quoted Zaikov as saying that more funds had been allotted for the wages of medical personnel and for hospital repairs. Zaikov also said that Soviet disarmament policy would free capacity in many defense industry enterprises and that this capacity would be used for, among other things, meeting demand in health care. TASS said Zaikov had made his comments at a meeting of Moscow medical authorities earlier this week.

Khrushchev Hailed as Great Reformer at Moscow Meeting

Nikita Khrushchev was hailed as a great reformer at a packed meeting at the Moscow Aviation Institute. The meeting was part of a series of unofficial lectures on Soviet history that started last year. Speaking at the meeting, historian Roy Medvedev said, "We owe Khrushchev a tremendous debt. He laid the ground for what is happening in our country today." Khrushchev's son Sergei, who also addressed the meeting, said his father "was a man of his time who made mistakes because he did not manage to break away from the system that formed him." Sergei

Khrushchev also told the gathering that memoirs published in the West and attributed to his father were genuine. Soviet officials until recently have denounced the memoirs as a fabrication (*Reuters*, February 11).

Historian Links Lenin to Arrests

The term "enemy of the people," which is associated with Stalin's mass purges, was first applied by Vladimir Lenin, Army General and philosopher Dmitrii Volkogonov told *Moskovskaya pravda*. Volkogonov, who is writing the first official Soviet biography of Stalin, cited an example of a draft decree introduced soon after the revolution by Lenin "calling for the arrest of prominent members of the Party Central Committee as enemies of the people and for them to be tried by a revolutionary tribunal." Volkogonov said the decree was adopted by the Council of People's Commissars with only Stalin voting against it. "This little-known episode testifies to the fact that Stalin went through a grotesque change in his development," Volkogonov stated. "He was not always a vampire," he added.

Soviet Banker Says Government Should Be Charged Interest

Deputy Chairman of the USSR State Bank Vyacheslav Zakharov told reporters in Moscow that the government should pay interest on money it borrows to finance its budget deficit. Zakharov said that his bank was required to lend the government some money interest-free this year, but would not part with "one kopeck more" to finance the budget unless the government pays interest. Asked how the government would finance its budget deficit without a loan, Zakharov said that was the problem of the Ministry of Finance. Zakharov suggested that a method for financing deficits could be included in a new law on banking that is now being written (*Reuters, AP*, February 10).

Saturday, February 11 ───────────────────────────────

Soviet Writers Form Pressure Group to Support Reforms

A group of prominent liberal Soviet writers, including Vladimir Dudintsev, Anatolii Pristavkin, and Bulat Okudzhava, announced the formation of a special committee to support Gorbachev's reform process. A letter to the latest issue of *Ogonek* from twenty-six writers said the new committee, called "Writers in Support of *Perestroika*," is aimed at strengthening the influence of the literary community "on all spheres of life." On February 13, TASS announced the creation of another informal group, called the Russian (*Rossiisky*) Popular Front for the Support of *Perestroika*. According to TASS, the pro-claimed goals of the front are the promotion of democracy and opposition to "any sort of nationalism."

TASS reported from Baghdad that Soviet and Iraqi delega-tions had signed a protocol on economic cooperation that will be of major importance to Iraq. The USSR will coop-erate in the construction of major oil, gas, and energy in-stallations, as well as irrigation projects (*Pravda*, February 12).

New Treaty of Cooperation between Iraq and USSR

Soviet Deputy Foreign Minister Igor Rogachev was re-ceived by the foreign minister of Mongolia, Gombosuren Tserenpilyn, in Ulan Bator. According to TASS, Rogachev is visiting Mongolia to discuss the implications of Soviet troop reductions. Regional conflicts in Asia (Afghanistan, Cambodia, and the Korean Peninsula) were also dis-cussed. See *Izvestia*, February 12.

Rogachev in Ulan-Bator

Soviet television said that construction of the controver-sial Volga-Chogray canal was continuing, despite recom-mendations by a body of government experts that work be halted. The report said concerned citizens held rallies in several Soviet cities today to protest against the project. The report complained that the Ministry of Land Reclama-tion and Water Resources and the State Agroindustrial Committee had ignored experts' advice.

Volga Canal Project Goes Ahead, Protest Meetings Held

The Presidium of the USSR Supreme Soviet has submitted for public debate draft legislation on quality control and protection for Soviet consumers. TASS said the legislation would open the eyes of manufacturers and tradespeople to the fact that they had in the past often exercised "a monopolistic *diktat*." TASS said a consumer protection society and customers' legal advice agencies had been set up in the USSR. It said the policy of *glasnost'* had helped citizens to know their rights and demand recognition of them. For the text of the draft, see *Pravda*, February 12.

Draft Law on Consumer Protection Submitted for Public Debate

A spokesman at the US embassy in Thailand said two So-viet citizens had defected to the United States in Bangkok. The spokesman said the two people, whom he did not identify, had been granted asylum and had flown to the

Soviet Embassy Official in Bangkok Defects to US

United States. According to the newspaper *Bangkok Post*, the defectors are the medical officer at the Soviet embassy in Bangkok, Vladimir Zhila, and his wife Olga (*AFP*, *Reuters*, February 11).

Sunday, February 12

Invasion of Afghanistan Condemned as Catastrophic Stupidity

The Baltimore Sun quoted a Soviet official as sharply condemning the Soviet invasion of Afghanistan in 1979. The newspaper said Leonid Mironov, who was *Pravda's* first correspondent in Afghanistan, described the invasion as "a catastrophic stupidity" at a meeting of the Soviet Peace Committee. He said: "It seems our marshals believed that, in this little area [Afghanistan], we could show the Americans, the imperialists, that we knew how to fight. . . . It did not turn out that way . . . the decision to invade in 1979 was wrong from the beginning."

New "Open Dialogue" Column in *Pravda*

Pravda started a new column entitled "Open Dialogue" for its readers. It is to carry letters and "polemical notes" from Soviet and foreign readers. The first column was devoted to Afghanistan.

Baltic Republics Ban Export of Goods to Rest of USSR

Moscow News (No. 7) reported on a ban by Estonia and Latvia on the export of "goods in great demand" to the rest of the USSR. The weekly said that such goods included color televisions, refrigerators, and vacuum cleaners.

Chief of Staff Says Volunteer Army Would Cost Too Much

The Soviet Armed Forces chief of staff said it would cost too much for the Soviet Union to switch to a volunteer, professional army. Colonel General Mikhail Moiseev told Soviet television the change would require at least a fivefold increase in the defense budget. He said he opposed such a change now and in the immediate future.

Jewish Cultural Center Opens in Moscow

A Jewish cultural center bearing the name of Solomon Mikhoels opened in Moscow. The center's namesake was a prominent actor who was also the universally recognized leader of the Soviet Jewish community. He died in 1948 in a traffic accident that is thought to have been arranged by the Soviet security services. On February 13, TASS, in English, reported that Soviet Foreign Minister Eduard Shevardnadze had met with the president of the

World Jewish Congress, Edgar Bronfman, who was in
Moscow in connection with the opening of the Jewish
center. Shevardnadze and Bronfman discussed a number
of topics, including Jewish culture, religion, emigration,
and the plight of Jewish refusedniks.

**Language Demonstration
Dispersed in Kishinev**

Another mass demonstration was reported to have taken
place in Kishinev. According to AFP (February 14), about
10,000 people gathered in the Moldavian capital today to
demand official status for the Moldavian language and the
introduction of the Latin script. Several dozen demonstrators were arrested. The Knight-Ridder news service reported that "several thousand" people had been dispersed
by police. This is the second demonstration in Kishinev in
three weeks. On January 22, the A. Mateevici Club organized a rally that was subsequently condemned in the
Party press (*Sovetskaya Moldaviya*, January 27). The disturbances point to continued dissatisfaction in the republic, despite the steps that have recently been taken to meet
the language demands of the Moldavian intelligentsia.

**Official Says Nagorno-
Karabakh Should Be
Governed from Moscow**

In an interview with Radio Moscow, a Party official from
Nagorno-Karabakh, Robert Kacharyan, said there must be
"urgent and rapid changes" in the life of the oblast or
"everything could return to what it was before." (Kacharyan is the Party secretary at the Stepanakert silk mill, the
region's largest industrial enterprise.) He said the majority
of Nagorno-Karabakh residents wanted the administrators
sent from Moscow to take action. He said the sooner
people felt they were really being governed by Moscow,
the calmer things would become and the more work
would be done (*Radio Moscow-2*, 1830, February 12).

**Soviet Television Criticizes
Ayatollah Khomeini**

The Soviet television program "Mezhdunarodnaya panorama" criticized Ayatollah Khomeini and the executions of
political prisoners in Iran. One commentator said that
Khomeini had reneged on promises he made when the
Shah was ousted ten years ago and that he operates
according to the idea that "Islam is a tree that can only
grow if it is watered by young blood."

**Latvian Journalists' Union
Criticizes Central Press**

Moscow News (No. 7) carried a report on an extraordinary
(*vneocherednoi*) congress of the Latvian Journalists'
Union, which discussed, among other things, the coverage of events in Latvia by the central press. Echoing the

evaluation of the central press by Estonians, the Latvian journalists expressed dissatisfaction with what central newspapers write about *perestroika* in Latvia and condemned central press coverage as one-sided. *Moscow News* said the congress had adopted a special resolution to this effect and another calling for the publication in Russian of a digest of the most interesting articles from the Latvian-language press. In addition, the congress called for the publication of a Latvian version of *Moscow News*.

"Moscow Tribune" Holds Inaugural Meeting

According to *Moscow News* (No. 7), an informal group of Moscow intellectuals called "Moscow Tribune" held its inaugural meeting on February 4. The group, which was formed by Andrei Sakharov, Yurii Afanas'ev, Ales Adamovich, and other reform-minded intellectuals, will discuss topical issues of sociopolitical life in the USSR. *Moscow News* reported that "Moscow Tribune" would work in cooperation with employees of institutes of the USSR Academy of Sciences, where unofficial seminars have been held to discuss topical aspects of *perestroika*.

New Leningrad Newspaper

Moskovskaya pravda reported that the Leningrad branch of the Union of Soviet Journalists had started publishing a new newspaper, entitled *24 chasa* (24 Hours). The new publication is a collection under one cover of the most interesting articles published in Soviet newspapers and journals.

Monday, February 13 ———————————————————————

New Regulations for Soviet Journalists

Izvestia carried an interview with the chief of the press bureau of the USSR Ministry of Internal Affairs (MVD), Colonel Boris Mikhailov, who commented on the "Regulations on the Procedure for Representatives of the Mass Media to be Admitted to, and to Remain in, Localities Where Measures to Ensure Public Order Are in Operation." Issued last month, the regulations stipulate that journalists will be given access to rallies, meetings, and the scene of emergencies (for instance, accidents) only with special passes issued to them by the MVD. If journalists attempt to cover any of the above-mentioned events without a special pass, they will be regarded as being in breach of the law. Mikhailov attempted to justify the measure by saying that it had been introduced for the journalists' own safety. The *Izvestia* correspondent, however, expressed the fear that as a result of the regulations "every commonplace situation will be turned into an emergency, that a journalist will not be able to get to where he should be without a pass, and that the police will simply refuse to talk to people without special passes." *Izvestia's* fears were confirmed by Belorussian Minister of Internal Affairs V. Piskarev, who said that journalists would need passes to cover any event.

The founding conference of the Taras Shevchenko language society ended in Kiev with a call for the restoration of official status to the Ukrainian Language. Radio Kiev said the meeting was attended by Ukrainians from other parts of the USSR, Czechoslovakia, Poland, and the West. The radio quoted Ukrainian Deputy Prime Minister Mariya Orlik as saying the Presidium of the Ukrainian Supreme Soviet supports the idea of making Ukrainian an official language. The radio said the conference closed on February 12 after adopting a charter and electing poet Dmytro Pavlychko as chairman of the society (*Radio Kiev*, February 12 and 13).

Ukrainians Call for Restoration of Ukrainian as State Language

Izvestia criticized the authorities in the industrial town of Nizhnii Tagil for barring an independent environmental organization from spreading information and staging demonstrations, pointing out the smog in this town in Sverdlovsk Oblast was so bad that people could hardly breathe. *Izvestia* said the informal group, called "Ochishchenie" (Cleanup), had been trying to tell people that industrial planners and not the industries themselves were responsible for the smog. The newspaper said the group had been barred from staging a demonstration in October and a march in November and from putting up posters and giving lectures in plants. It said an attempt had been made to take the leaders of the organization to court.

***Izvestia* Criticizes Ban on Environmental Group**

Reuters reported that tens of thousands of Russian and Polish speakers had demonstrated in Lithuania against a decree making Lithuanian the language of business and government in the republic. The agency quoted local journalists as saying the protest in Vilnius was staged on the weekend by a movement of mainly non-Lithuanians called "Edinstvo" (Unity). On February 10, Radio Vilnius, in English, reported that the governing soviet in the small Rukainiai district of the Vilnius Raion, which is inhabited mostly by Poles, had declared itself a "Polish National

Backlash in Lithuania against New Language Law

Administrative District" not subject to laws requiring use of the Lithuanian language. Radio Vilnius said the action was illegal under Lithuanian law.) On February 14, Lithuania's Party First Secretary Algirdas Brazauskas said on Soviet television that giving official status to the Lithuanian language did not infringe on the rights of other nationalities in the republic.

Tuesday, February 14

MVD Releases Crime Statistics

For the first time since 1933, the USSR Ministry of Internal Affairs released crime statistics for the Soviet Union (*TASS*, February 14). Major General Anatolii Smirnov, the chief of the MVD's Main Information Center, described the figures to journalists as "not consoling." The overall number of reported crimes in the USSR rose to 1,867,223 in 1988—an increase of almost 4 percent over 1987. Premeditated murders were up (16,710 in 1988 versus 14,651 in 1987), as were rapes (17,658 versus 16,765), violent robberies, break-ins, holdups, and cases of assault and battery. In 1987, the MVD started releasing information on the number of convictions for various crimes; this is the first time, however, that the actual number of reported crimes has been made public.

First Issue of "Memorial" Newspaper

The first issue of *Vedomosti Memoriala*, an eight-page newspaper published by the "Memorial" society to honor the victims of political repression in the USSR, has been obtained by Radio Liberty's *Samizdat* Department. The issue was prepared on the eve of the society's founding congress and is dated January 28. The newspaper is printed by the "Kniga" Publishing House on the presses of *Gudok*, the railway workers' publication. Its print run is only 5,000 copies, making *Vedomosti Memoriala* a bibliographic rarity from the start. Among the contributors to the first issue are prominent reformist intellectuals, including Anatolii Rybakov, Yakov Etinger, Grigorii Baklanov, Lev Razgon, Evgenii Evtushenko, Yurii Afanas'ev, and Marieta Chudakova, as well as former *samizdat* "best-selling" authors such as Andrei Sakharov, Grigorii Pomerants, Larisa Bogoraz, and Mikhail Gefter. Aleksandr Daniel, son of Bogoraz and the late writer Yulii Daniel, and the former political prisoners Arsenii Roginsky and Vyacheslav Igrunov were among those who put together the first issue. There is no indication in the newspaper of how often it will appear.

Gorbachev appealed to Soviet workers to hold out through "this most difficult period" and to be patient with the difficulties and problems created as his reforms go into effect. He begged people to believe that the purpose of the reforms is "to heal our society" and improve the way of life of ordinary people. At the same time he dismissed the idea of a multiparty system as "nonsense." He said what was needed were democratic institutions that enabled people to exercise genuine control. Gorbachev was addressing a special meeting at the Moscow headquarters of the Party Central Committee. The meeting was attended by leading workers from all over the Soviet Union. Gorbachev's opening and closing speeches were shown on Soviet television on February 14. On February 15, Soviet television broadcast excerpts from the speeches of some twenty-five workers' representatives. See *Izvestia* and *Pravda*, February 16.

Gorbachev Appeals for Support of Working Class

The Council of Ministers of the Latvian SSR has decided to block immigration from the rest of the Soviet Union into the republic. The Council of Ministers reached the decision after intense debates on February 13. Sources told RFE/RL that Justice Minister Viktors Skudra and Council Chairman Vilnis Bresis strongly supported the measure. Latvian sources also said the immigration decision would probably be followed by a proposal to introduce distinct Latvian citizenship. (Last year, during his visit to Latvia and Lithuania, Politburo member Aleksandr Yakovlev opposed the idea of introducing republican citizenship.) The ministers also agreed that Latvia should move its clocks one hour behind Moscow time, starting in the spring (*Reuters*, February 14).

Latvian Leaders Decide to Block Immigration

The new commander of the Warsaw Pact Armed Forces General Petr Lushev said in an interview with TASS that international tensions were relaxing but that there was no guarantee this would continue. Lushev said this was why the Warsaw Pact Armed Forces would remain combat ready while they were being restructured. TASS described the interview as the first by Lushev since he took over command of the Warsaw Pact forces from Marshal Viktor Kulikov earlier this month.

Lushev Interviewed by TASS

Radio Vilnius said Lithuania's minister of culture, Jonas Bielinis, and the head of the republican radio and television system, Juozas Kuolelis, had retired early. The report

Two Officials Retire in Lithuania

said Bielinis had retired after twelve years on the job. No reason was given, and no successor was mentioned. Kuolelis was said to have retired last week "after having compromised himself." The report said Kuolelis had been replaced as radio and television chief by Domas Sniukas, the Lithuanian correspondent of *Pravda*. Sniukas was elected last month as chairman of the Lithuanian Journalists' Union (*Radio Vilnius*, 0400, February 15).

Eight Economists Defend Zaslavskaya and Aganbegyan

Sovetskaya kul'tura carried a letter from eight Soviet economists, including Oleg Bogomolov, Nikolai Petrakov, and Vitalii Shatalin defending Academicians Tat'yana Zaslavskaya and Abel Aganbegyan against attacks leveled against them by conservative writers at the plenum of the RSFSR Writers' Union at the end of last year. The letter said that the main critic of Zaslavskaya and Aganbegyan, A. Salutsky, had sharply distorted the views of the academicians in an effort to prove they were responsible for the degeneration of Soviet villages in the 1970s.

Wednesday, February 15

Withdrawal from Afghanistan

TASS reported this morning that the last Soviet soldier to walk over from Afghanistan into the Soviet Union across the "Friendship Bridge" was, as planned, Lieutenant General Boris Gromov, the Soviet military commander in Afghanistan. Soviet Foreign Ministry spokesman Gennadii Gerasimov suggested in an article in *Sovetskaya kul'tura* that Afghanistan could easily turn into another Lebanon. He blamed the perilous situation in Afghanistan on its long history of isolation and hostility towards outsiders. "Even the presence of a common enemy . . . could not unite the warring factions," Gerasimov wrote. The same day, the Soviet media for the first time reported an atrocity committed by Soviet troops during the war. *Literaturnaya gazeta* printed a story of the apparent execution of a carload of Afghan civilians, including two children, by Soviet troops simply because they refused to stop at a border checkpoint. *Pravda* also carried a commentary on Afghanistan, assuring its readers that the USSR has not pursued, and is not pursuing, any expansionist ambitions in Afghanistan. Meanwhile, UN Secretary General Perez de Cuellar confirmed that the USSR had completed the withdrawal of its troops from Afghanistan. The Soviet authorities issued two statements following completion of the withdrawal. A government statement, carried by

TASS, called for an immediate cease-fire between the warring Afghan factions and for an end to all foreign arms shipments to Afghanistan. The second statement was a message of thanks from the CPSU and the Soviet government to Soviet soldiers returning home "after fulfilling their patriotic and international duty" in Afghanistan (*Pravda*, February 16).

Demonstrations in Lithuania

Thousands of Lithuanians gathered in Kaunas to open a celebration marking the anniversary of the proclamation of Lithuanian independence in 1918. For the first time the celebrations were official. Many of the participants gathered in front of a city theater to listen to a reading of the declaration of independence at a meeting of the Lithuanian Popular Front (*AFP*, February 15). US Secretary of State James Baker sent greetings to the people of Lithuania on the independence anniversary (*RFE/RL Special*, February 15). On February 16, the celebrations continued in Vilnius and Kaunas. Many of the festivities were broadcast by Lithuanian television, including a call by a leader of the Lithuanian Restructuring Movement for "autonomy in Lithuania" (*Reuters*, February 16). The same day, an assembly of the Restructuring Movement approved a resolution calling for economic independence and state sovereignty for Lithuania (*Reuters*, February 17).

Working Group on Expanding Rights of Soviet Republics

There was a meeting in Moscow of a working group set up to draft proposals on expanding the rights of individual republics in the economic, social, cultural, and legal spheres. The group was formed by the Presidium of the USSR Supreme Soviet. TASS said many speakers stressed the need for stronger guarantees of the rights of republics in using their natural resources. They also discussed the need to set up legal mechanisms to settle possible conflicts on matters such as environmental protection, health care, and education. TASS said the working group instructed its editorial commission to continue work on proposals for the redistribution of power between the central authorities and the republics. See, *Izvestia* and *Pravda*, February 16. On February 17, *Pravda* reported on a Politburo meeting the day before that had approved measures designed to give more economic autonomy to the USSR's constituent republics. The newspaper said that, among other things, a republic's government would have the power to set tax rates for private cooperatives and to decide how to handle environmental problems on its territory.

Economist Says Paying More Would End Grain Shortage

Ukrainian economist Ivan Lukinov said the Soviet Union could end its grain shortages by paying farmers more for their products. Lukinov wrote in the latest issue of the CPSU Central Committee journal *Kommunist* that the USSR paid 150 dollars on the international market for one ton of grain. At the same time, he said, the government paid state and cooperative farms only 100-140 rubles per ton. Lukinov said production costs had increased so much that Soviet farms no longer make a profit on grain. Lukinov is the director of the Kiev Economics Institute of the Ukrainian Academy of Sciences.

Changes in Military Leadership

Radio Moscow announced personnel changes in the higher military establishment. The former commander of Soviet troops in Afghanistan, Lieutenant General Boris Gromov, has been appointed commander of the Kiev Military District; Army General Valentin Varennikov, first deputy chief of general staff of the USSR Armed Forces, who has been responsible for the Soviet troop withdrawal from Afghanistan, becomes the new commander in chief of the USSR Ground Forces and USSR deputy minister of defense (replacing Army General Evgenii Ivanovsky). Following the promotion of Army General Konstantin Kochetov to the post of USSR first deputy minister of defense, Lieutenant General Nikolai Kalinin has been nominated commander of the Moscow Military District. Kalinin had been commander of Soviet Airborne Troops since 1987. Another important change was made in the command of Chemical Troops. Colonel General Vladimir Pikalov, who had been commander of the Chemical Troops since 1969, has now been replaced by Major General Stanislav Petrov, former head of the Chemical Troops of the Group of Soviet Forces in Germany. In addition to these changes, it was announced that the newly appointed chief of general staff, Mikhail Moiseev, the new chief of staff of the Warsaw Pact Joint Forces, Vladimir Lobov, and the commander of the Belorussian Military District, Vladimir Shuralev, had all been promoted to the rank of Army General.

Thursday, February 16

Vorontsov Meets with Gandhi

Reuters reported from New Delhi that Soviet First Deputy Foreign Minister Yulii Vorontsov, who is also Moscow's ambassador to Kabul, had arrived in India for unannounced talks on Afghanistan with Prime Minister Rajiv

Gandhi. An Indian spokesman said Vorontsov also met with Foreign Minister Narasimha Rao. The spokesman said India wanted to see an independent and nonaligned Afghanistan following the Soviet military withdrawal (*UPI, AFP*, February 16).

USSR Signs First Foreign Investment Protection Accords

TASS said the Soviet Union had signed agreements with two Western countries—Finland and Belgium—on protecting capital investments by foreign business partners. TASS said the agreements were the first of their kind and would be ratified this summer. It said a similar agreement was being negotiated with Britain.

Popular Front Proposed in Ukraine

A Popular Front—similar to those in the Baltic States—has been proposed in Ukraine. Radio Kiev said the draft program for the Popular Front had been published in the literary journal *Literaturna Ukraina*. Formation of a Popular Front, which has been urged by Ukrainian writers, has run into official opposition. Radio Kiev also reported that an official commission charged with rehabilitating and honoring victims of Stalin's repressions in Ukraine had held its first meeting. The radio said the commission was headed by retired Ukrainian Prime Minister Oleksandr Lyashko and composed of representatives of the Ukrainian Supreme Soviet, the government, and the public.

Soviet and Chinese Scientists Sign Cooperation Pact

A pact calling for direct cooperation in research work between Soviet and Chinese scientists was signed in Beijing. China's Xinhua news agency said it would cover about seventy projects in fields such as study of the oceans and the atmosphere, water resources, and environmental protection.

Documentary on Party Conference Delayed

TASS reported that the USSR State Committee on Cinematography had delayed the premiere of a documentary on last summer's Nineteenth Party Conference. The film, entitled *Pluralism*, was made by Moscow director Aleksandr Pavlov. A secretary of the USSR Cinema Workers' Union told a group of Soviet and foreign journalists attending the premiere that the documentary, which TASS said gives an objective picture of the sharp debates at the conference, was apparently not to the liking of officials on the committee. See also a report on the film in *Moscow News* (No. 9).

Draft Law on Freedom of Conscience Prepared

Novosti press agency reported that on February 14 representatives of various religious confessions gathered at the Council of Religious Affairs to become acquainted with the text of the draft law on freedom of conscience before it is published for nationwide discussion. Meanwhile, *Sovetskoe gosudarstvo i pravo* (No. 2) carried the text of "recommendations" for the draft law on freedom of conscience written by a lawyer at the Institute of State and Law, Yurii Rozenbaum. Rozenbaum was one of the few Soviet lawyers who, in the early 1980s, started to advocate the idea of giving "the right of a person in law" to religious communities. (Lenin's decree of 1918 "On the Separation of Church and State" and Stalin's legislation "On Religious Associations" of 1929 emphasized that religious communities did not enjoy "the right of a person in law." See RL 332/86.)

Official Historian Says Hitler-Stalin Pact Was Mistake

Colonel General Dmitrii Volkogonov, who is working on the first Soviet official biography of Stalin, said the nonaggression pact that the USSR signed with Nazi Germany in 1939 was "a great political mistake." Volkogonov, who heads the Institute of Military History at the USSR Ministry of Defense, was interviewed by Radio Moscow. He said his institute was studying documents that had been inaccessible for a long time and that cast more light on the 1939 pact. He did not elaborate (*Radio Moscow-1*, 1000, February 17). *Moscow News* (No. 7) carried an interview with Volkogonov and another Soviet writer on Stalinism, Roy Medvedev. In *Moscow News*, Volkogonov explained why he had decided to write a biography of Stalin.

Former Moldavian Party Chief Defends His Actions

Former Moldavian Party First Secretary Ivan Bodiul (Bodyul) said his administration had not ignored the interests of Moldavians in favor of dictates from Moscow. In fact, Bodiul said, he had opposed orders from Moscow. Novosti press agency, which reported his comments, said "a different opinion prevails" in Moldavia, where Bodiul is considered "an apologist of stagnation." It also said Bodiul was "very close to Brezhnev." Novosti said Bodiul defended his administration in an interview with a reporter from the Moldavian-language magazine *Nistru*. It said Bodiul on that occasion denied an accusation by intellectuals that he had created obstacles to the devel-

94

opment of the Moldavian language and literature and to the cultural development of other nationalities in Moldavia.

USSR Warns Pakistan against Intervention in Afghanistan

Soviet Deputy Foreign Minister Yulii Vorontsov accused Pakistan of deploying artillery in Afghanistan and warned that Moscow could not remain indifferent if Pakistan intervened militarily to back the Afghan resistance. He accused Pakistan of deploying artillery to aid resistance forces surrounding the eastern Afghan city of Jalalabad, a charge that Pakistan denies. Vorontsov was speaking at a press conference in New Delhi (*Reuters*, February 17).

Lawyers Say Directives Fail to Protect Psychiatric Patients

Novosti press agency quoted two Soviet lawyers as saying directives issued to protect Soviet psychiatric patients are too vague and do not do the job. The lawyers, Boris Protchenko and Aleksandr Rudyakov, were quoted by *Kommunist* (No. 3) as saying that, despite the new rules, psychiatrists still have too much authority over psychiatric patients. It said the lawyers criticized one rule that allows physicians to order involuntary psychiatric examination of citizens who violate "the rules of conduct in a Socialist society." Novosti said the lawyers wrote that the record of the use of psychiatry as a weapon against dissidents shows how such provisions are abused by dishonest politicians. Novosti said the lawyers also criticized the Presidium of the Supreme Soviet and the Ministry of Health for issuing the directives in 1988 without consulting ordinary psychiatrists or lawyers.

TASS Urges Cooperation from Hungary in Evaluating Events of 1956

A TASS commentary said Hungary should cooperate with the USSR in evaluating the 1956 uprising in Hungary. Commentator Aleksandr Kondrashev said it was necessary to look objectively at all the reasons behind the Soviet leadership's decision to resort to such an "extreme move" as to use armed forces to stop "a counter-revolution" in Hungary in 1956. Kondrashev's comments came amid continuing debate in Hungary about the true nature of the events of 1956. The Hungarian Central Committee earlier this week described the events as a genuine popular uprising that later took on the characteristics of a counterrevolution. Kondrashev said it was impossible to ignore such obvious factors as Western inspiration of antigovernment actions and the participation in them of "reactionary emigrant circles." He also said the evaluation of events given by other Socialist countries, including Yugoslavia and China, should be studied.

Founding Congress of Independent Group in Tatar Republic

TASS said a new informal group called the Tatar Public Center was holding its founding congress in Kazan, the capital of the Tatar Autonomous Republic. TASS said the new association will form the core of an informal movement started by artists and other intellectuals in Tataria. The group's platform, published earlier, says Union republics and Autonomous republics in the USSR do not have equal conditions for economic and social development. The platform says the Tatar Public Center will work to remove these differences.

USSR Appoints Ambassador to EEC

The Soviet Union has appointed an ambassador to the European Community. He is Vladimir Shemyatenkov, an economics specialist. The announcement came as the EEC and the USSR ended two days of exploratory talks in Brussels over a possible trade agreement. The EEC Commission statement said that the talks had been positive and should now be quickly followed by concrete proposals. The commission said it should soon be possible to ask member governments for a mandate to begin formal negotiations with the Soviet Union on a trade and cooperation agreement. Comecon formally recognized the EEC last year. Since then, Hungary and Czechoslovakia have signed trade agreements with the EEC (*AP, Reuters*, February 17).

USSR Conducts Nuclear Test

The USSR exploded a nuclear device underground at the Semipalatinsk test range in Kazakhstan. TASS reported that the blast was designed to test the results of research into the physics of nuclear explosions.

***Pravda* Reports Narcotics Seizures in Azerbaijan, Kazakhstan**

Pravda reported major narcotics seizures in Azerbaijan and Kazakhstan. The newspaper said more than 118 kilograms of marijuana had been discovered in one cache in the Chuisk Valley, which runs through Kazakhstan and Kirgizia. The newspaper said this was the largest amount of narcotics ever to have been found in that area. The newspaper also reported that narcotics had been seized in Azerbaijan. The newspaper called for the establishment of special antinarcotics units within the Ministry of Internal Affairs.

96

Boris El'tsin said nationwide referendums, not just nation-wide discussions, should be held on important issues. He also said political struggle should be made a part of normal life rather than something in which people risk being labeled "an enemy of the people" if they get involved. Western reports said El'tsin was speaking after a meeting at which he was nominated by Moscow's Kuntsevo election district as a candidate for the Congress of People's Deputies (*la Repubblica*, February 17).

El'tsin Calls for Nationwide Referendums

Argumenty i fakty (No. 6) carried an article by V. Lordki-panidze, whose father worked for the NKVD, on the assassination of Sergei Kirov in 1934. In his article, Lordki-panidze said that, before the Leningrad resident Leonid Nikolaev assassinated Kirov, it was well known in the NKVD that Kirov's life was in danger. He said it was most likely that Stalin participated in the organization of the assassination of Kirov, although there are no documents to prove this.

***Argumenty i fakty* on Assassination of Kirov**

—————————————————————— *Saturday, February 18*

In the second installment of his book *On Stalin and Stalinism*, published in the February issue of *Znamya*, historian Roy Medvedev reveals that, since the summer of 1987, the USSR State Prosecuter's Office has been preparing materials to rehabilite the victims of the show trials of 1930–31—i.e., those of "the Industrial Party" and "the Union Buro of Mensheviks."

Forthcoming Rehabilitations

Czechoslovak Prime Minister Ladislav Adamec completed an official three-day visit to the USSR (*TASS*, February 18). Before leaving Moscow, Adamec told Radio Prague that Gorbachev understands well Czechoslovakia's restructuring problems. He said that during their meeting on February 17 Gorbachev had shown "very detailed interest in the restructuring situation" in Czechoslovakia.

Adamec Leaves Moscow

—————————————————————— *Sunday, February 19*

Soviet Foreign Minister Eduard Shevardnadze and Syrian President Hafez Assad discussed the Middle East conflict at a meeting in Damascus. (Shevardnadze is in Syria on

Shevardnadze's Visit to Syria

97

the first stage of a five-country tour in the Middle East.) The same day he met Syrian Vice President Abdel-Halim Khaddam (*UPI*, February 18). Speaking at a dinner in his honor in Damascus on February 18, Shevardnadze said the USSR would press the UN Security Council to convene an international conference to try to resolve the conflict in the Middle East. He said a peace conference should involve all the parties in the conflict, including the PLO (*UPI*, *Reuters*, February 19; *Izvestia*, February 20).

Trotsky's Grandson Submits Appeal for Trotsky's Rehabilitation

In *Moscow News* (No. 8) Mikhail Belyat, the weekly's correspondent in Mexico, described the local museum of Leon Trotsky. Belyat's article also contained an interview with Esteban Volkov, Trotsky's grandson. It was disclosed in the interview that Volkov, together with his four daughters, had formally appealed to the USSR Supreme Court for Trotsky's rehabilitation.

***Pravda* Reports Pipeline Accident in Siberia**

Pravda reported that workers deliberately detonated gases from a leaking pipeline in Siberia in order to protect nearby villages and a railway station. It said that the pipeline began leaking last week creating a huge cloud of explosive gases about 1.5 kilometers from the station and villages and that workers on board a rescue-repair helicopter fired a flare pistol at the cloud. This caused a big explosion and fire but also eliminated the danger.

***Krasnaya zvezda* on Ethnic Unrest in Transcaucasia**

Krasnaya zvezda said Armenians were continuing to leave their homes in Azerbaijan as ethnic tensions persist in the two republics. The newspaper said over 166,000 refugees had arrived in Armenia from Azerbaijan as of February 16. This represents an increase of 7,000 over the official figure for mid-November, 1988. It said this showed the situation in the area was still strained, despite apparent calm. The newspaper said some Armenians wanted to stage demonstrations in Erevan to commemorate the first anniversary of the ethnic violence in Sumgait. The newspaper noted, however, that curfew regulations in force in Erevan prohibit marches and demonstrations.

Report Says Sakharov Has Withdrawn All Candidacies

Moscow News (No. 8) carried a statement by Andrei Sakharov in which the academician said he had withdrawn from the elections to the Congress of People's Deputies. Sakharov is at present in Canada, where he and his wife Elena Bonner were awarded honorary doctorates by the University of Ottawa on February 14. According to *Moscow News*, Sakharov has decided that if he cannot be a candidate of the USSR Academy of Sciences he does not want to run for office. Sakharov's nomination was rejected by the academy on January 18. He has since been nominated in a number of other constituencies. *Moscow News* said Sakharov had rejected all these nominations and appealed to those who nominated him to vote for "the genuine and constant supporters of restructuring." The newspaper also carried a letter from twenty employees of institutes of the USSR Academy of Sciences, calling on another academician, Roald Sagdeev, to continue his election campaign. *Moscow News* (No. 7) quoted Sagdeev as saying he was likely to withdraw from the elections. Sagdeev was also rejected as a candidate by the USSR Academy of Sciences.

Moscow News (No. 8) said that the cancer rate had doubled in the region affected by the Chernobyl' disaster and that an abnormally high number of animals with congenital defects had been born in the last three years on a kolkhoz near Zhitomir. A veterinarian interviewed by *Moscow News* pointed out that fodder for the kolkhoz's cattle had been grown on contaminated fields.

Moscow News on Aftermath of Chernobyl'

The editor of *Pravda* hit back at the editor of *Ogonek* in a new round in the battle between conservative and liberal intellectuals. Writing in *Komsomol'skaya pravda*, Viktor Afanas'ev charged that *Ogonek*'s editor, Vitalii Korotich, had not always been such an avid supporter of reform as he is now under Gorbachev. Afanas'ev also rejected a charge by Korotich, published this month in the weekly *Sobesednik*, that as editor of *Pravda* he (Afanas'ev) was a theoretician of Party policy under Brezhnev. Afanas'ev argued that he had not crafted Kremlin policies but had been engaged in explaining Party and state documents. In trying to show that Korotich does not have a better past than he, Afanas'ev recalled that, in an article in *Literaturnaya gazeta* in 1979, Korotich highly praised Brezhnev's memoirs. Last month, *Pravda* published a letter from conservative writers denouncing Korotich. When ten liberal intellectuals, including Evgenii Evtushenko, wrote a letter to *Pravda* supporting Korotich, Afanas'ev declined to print it. It was published in *Ogonek* earlier this month. This is the first time that Afanas'ev has put his name to an attack on Korotich.

Pravda's Editor Hits Back after Liberals' Attack

50,000 Rally in Minsk

About 50,000 people were reported to have attended a rally at a Minsk stadium organized by a number of unofficial Belorussian groups. In a telephone interview with Radio Liberty, a Belorussian journalist said it was the first time local authorities had allowed such a meeting. He said the main goals of the organizers were the consolidation of democratic forces in Belorussia; focusing public attention on ecological, political, and social problems; and discussing the new system for election of people's deputies. On February 21, TASS reported on the rally. It quoted the chairman of the Belorussian Popular Front, Vasilii Yakovenko, as saying rallies and broad and open discussions were the only way to achieve "Socialist pluralism of opinion" in Belorussia.

Congress of Latvian Independence Movement Adopts Program

Reports reaching the West said the Latvian National Independence Movement held its first congress in Riga this weekend. At the congress, delegates adopted a program of reform proposals intended as steps towards independence. Among the proposals are a halt to non-Latvian immigration, the adoption of Latvian as the republic's official language, and local control of the republic's affairs. The congress also voted to elect a sixty-eight-member managing council. The reports said more than 400 delegates attended the meeting. Among them were several Latvians from abroad and two representatives of the board of the Popular Front of Latvia. Reports said the principles of Baltic solidarity were underscored by the congress, and representatives of the Estonian independence movement and the Lithuanian Freedom League delivered addresses (*RFE Research and Latvian Service*, February 21).

Monday, February 20 ————————————————————————————————

Gorbachev Visits Ukraine

On February 20, Gorbachev, accompanied by his wife Raisa, left Moscow for Kiev. His visit to Ukraine had not been previously announced. The first item on Gorbachev's agenda, as reported by TASS, was to lay flowers at a Kiev monument to Lenin. TASS said Gorbachev then became involved in a frank discussion with onlookers. He discussed the progress of *perestroika* and the need to support it with real deeds. Gorbachev told his audience there would be no progress in restructuring unless the people showed more initiative (*Radio Moscow-2*, 1500, February 20). He also discussed with them the Chernobyl' nuclear accident. He said a nuclear power station being built in the Crimea would not go into operation if experts advise against it. He also answered numerous complaints about food shortages and other everyday problems. Gorbachev promised there would be no action taken on prices for two or three years. The discussion was shown on Soviet television. See, *Pravda*, February 21.

On February 21, Gorbachev went to the Western Ukrainian city of Lvov, where he met with local cultural figures. On February 23, *Pravda* carried the remarks made by Gorbachev in Lvov. He was quoted as accusing some elements in Soviet society of using *perestroika* for their own ends. The same day, it was reported that a number of activists of the Ukrainian Helsinki Group had been detained in Lvov. A spokesman for the group said it was believed the detentions were connected with Gorbachev's visit to the city (*RL Ukrainian Service*, February 21). After Gorbachev left the city, the detained activists were released (*RL Ukrainian Service*, February 22).

On February 22, Gorbachev visited Donetsk, accompanied by Ukrainian Party First Secretary Vladimir Shcherbitsky and other republican leaders. TASS said that, after laying flowers at a monument to Lenin, Gorbachev had his first meeting with Donetsk residents. He also visited a local machine-building factory and talked to workers. Gorbachev then met with Donetsk miners and heard about the problems of the Donets Basin coal mines. TASS quoted Gorbachev as telling the workers that the working class was the principal moving force of *perestroika*. Gorbachev also told them that "any political leader on the middle level who puts sticks in the wheels of *perestroika* will have to be moved out of the way." Gorbachev also spoke about the danger of ethnic disturbances such as those in Transcaucasia over the Nagorno-Karabakh Autonomous Oblast: "You can only imagine what would happen if disruptions [like those] were to begin in such a republic as Ukraine" with its population of 51 million. Gorbachev claimed that special attention and respect had always been given in the Politburo to the development of the Ukrainian culture and language and that, if the language had not developed to its fullest in Ukraine, Moscow was not to blame (*Central Television*, February 22). Gorbachev said he planned talks with Ukrainian leaders on progress made in the republic in the last three years.

On February 22, AP reported that hundreds of people had staged a demonstration in Kiev. Some of the demonstrators carried banners demanding the ouster of the Ukrainian Party leader, Shcherbitsky. On February 23,

Gorbachev visited Chernobyl', where he met with workers and managers of the nuclear plant. TASS reported that safety measures were discussed. It was Gorbachev's first visit to the site of the world's worst nuclear accident. After Chernobyl', Gorbachev visited Slavutich, a town that was built to house workers who were evacuated because of the accident (see *Pravda*, February 24). TASS said Gorbachev returned to Kiev later the same day and addressed a meeting of workers, farmers, Party activists, municipal authorities, military men, and intellectuals. In his address Gorbachev said the Soviet Union was starting to see the results of *perestroika*. He said housing construction and spending on health care and education were increasing. He said that the attitude of the West towards the Soviet Union had improved, and he cited international aid for the victims of the Armenian earthquake as "an amazing indicator" of a new international situation. Gorbachev admitted, however, that many people continue to complain about the shortage of consumer goods and even suspect that at a certain level of society "sabotage" of *perestroika* is going on (*TASS*, February 23). On February 24, Gorbachev met in Kiev with Ukrainian writers pressing for improvements in the cultural, economic, and environmental spheres. Gorbachev was reported to have voiced his support for the writers' calls. Gorbachev also met with republican Party officials and criticized them for the low level of ideological work in the republic and for adapting to *perestroika* too slowly (*TASS*, February 24; *Pravda*, February 25).

Shevardnadze in Jordan

Eduard Shevardnadze arrived in Amman for talks with Jordan's King Hussein (*AP*, *Reuters*, February 20). After the talks, Shevardnadze said there were signs that a peace conference on the conflict in the Middle East would convene next year, but he added that much depended on Israel's position on the Palestinian issue. See, *Izvestia*, February 20.

Radio Moscow Comments on Katyn Report in Polish Weekly

Radio Moscow-2 (0730) carried a commentary on the publication by the Polish official weekly *Odrodzenie* (February 18, 1989) of a report issued in 1943 by the Polish Red Cross on the Katyn massacre. The report said that, "judging from the papers found on the corpses [of the Polish officers killed in Katyn] the murder took place in March or April, 1940," more than a year before the Germans invaded the Soviet Union. In its commentary, Radio Moscow said that, if the date given by the Polish report

was correct, then "there could have been only one per-
petrator of the action, the People's Commissariat of
Internal Affairs" (predecessor of the KGB). The radio's
commentary marks a major breakthrough in Soviet media
treatment of the Katyn massacre. It is the first time that the
Soviet side has admitted the possibility that the murder
was committed not by the Germans but by the Soviet
secret police. Meanwhile, on February 21, Polish government spokesman Jerzy Urban said the inscription would
be changed on the Katyn monument (near Smolensk)
commemorating the wartime massacre of the Polish
officers. (The inscription at present says the officers were
murdered in the Katyn forest in the USSR by the invading
German army.) Urban did not say what the inscription
would be changed to. On February 24, TASS summarized
a speech delivered the same day in the Sejm by Polish
Foreign Minister Tadeusz Olechowski. The summary,
however, excluded the minister's demand for clarity over
the Katyn massacre. See RL 112/89.

Eduard Shevardnadze opened talks in Cairo with Egyptian President Hosni Mubarak. Egypt's foreign minister,
Esmat Abdel-Maguid, said the two men agreed on the
need for an international peace conference on the Middle
East involving all parties in the region, including the PLO.
Shevardnadze invited Mubarak to visit the USSR (*AP*,
Reuters, February 20; *Pravda*, February 21). He also met
with Abdel-Maguid. An Egyptian Foreign Ministry spokesman said the two discussed Israeli opposition to an international peace conference (*Reuters*, *UPI*, February 21).
Speaking at a dinner in Cairo on February 21, Shevardnadze said an Arab-Israeli settlement was no mirage and
was vital to the USSR because the region was close to its
borders (*AP*, *Reuters*, February 21).

On February 22, Shevardnadze met separately with
Israeli Foreign Minister Moshe Arens and PLO chairman
Yasser Arafat (*Pravda*, February 23). After the meetings,
Shevardnadze said he thought Israel will one day realize
it is imperative for it to accept the idea of an international Middle East peace conference with PLO participation. Shevardnadze said such a conference would also
mean guarantees for Israel's security, which he said
Israel badly needs. He added, however, that there
could be no solution without Israeli good will. Shevardnadze said that his talks with Arens were useful and
frank but that difficulties remained. Back in Israel, Arens
said he had left Shevardnadze in no doubt that Israel
regarded the PLO as an obstacle to peace and not as a

**Shevardnadze Visits Cairo,
Meets Arens and Arafat**

partner in negotiations. In his turn, Arafat said he was prepared to open talks with the Israelis in Moscow if necessary (*Reuters, UPI*, February 22).

On February 23, Shevardnadze said in Cairo that the USSR and Israel could restore full diplomatic ties if Israel accepted an international peace conference with the participation of the PLO. He also called on UN Secretary General Perez de Cuellar to appoint an envoy to the Middle East to lay the foundation for such a conference. Shevardnadze criticized the United States' efforts to limit Soviet influence in the Middle East. (US President George Bush earlier this week welcomed Shevardnadze's current visit but said Moscow's role in the Middle East should be limited.) The same day, Shevardnadze left Cairo for Iraq (*Reuters, UPI, AP*, February 23).

On February 24, Israeli Prime Minister Yitzak Shamir rejected Shevardnadze's proposals for talks on the Middle East. He said Israel would never accept the Soviet conditions for a resumption of diplomatic relations (*Reuters, AP*, February 24). In Iraq, Shevardnadze met with Iraqi Foreign Minister Tariq Aziz and Iraqi President Saddam Hussein (*UPI*, February 24; *Pravda*, February 25).

Armenian Earthquake Caused 10 Billion Rubles in Damage

The Armenian Committee for Statistics said last December's earthquake in Armenia had caused 10 billion rubles worth of damage. TASS reported the committee as saying the quake affected 40 percent of Armenian territory. On February 21, TASS said that a new quake had struck northern Armenia during the night; there were no casualties.

Pravda Quotes Oleg Tumanov as Attacking Radio Liberty

Despite its report earlier this year citing improvements in the work of Radio Liberty, *Pravda* today repeated its standard attack on the US radio station. *Pravda* carried an interview with former acting chief editor of RL's Russian Service, Oleg Tumanov, who defected to Moscow in 1987. In his interview, Tumanov called the radio "a subversive propaganda tool" engaged in espionage activities.

New Approach to Soviet Invasion of Czechoslovakia

A commentary in *Sovetskaya Rossiya* (February 18), reprinted in the Czechoslovak Party daily *Rude Pravo* (February 20), admitted that the Soviet-led invasion of Czechoslovakia in 1968 provoked anti-Soviet feelings and "deep disillusionment" in Czechoslovakia. The commentary said Czechoslovakia's ruling Communists, put into power by Moscow after 1968, had underestimated the opposition to them. This seems to be the first time that a Soviet commentary has openly admitted that the 1968 invasion was not seen by all Czechoslovaks as a necessary move.

In an interview on Hungarian television, Boris El'tsin discussed his relations with Gorbachev and Egor Ligachev. El'tsin said that his initial good relations with Gorbachev had soured and that Ligachev was partly to blame. El'tsin said his differences with Ligachev were over the pace of *perestroika*, the antialcohol campaign, and whether there should be special stores for officials.

El'tsin Discusses His Relations with Gorbachev and Ligachev

Tuesday, February 21

A commission has been set up in Kazakhstan to fight swindling and abuses in the distribution and sale of goods in high demand. It is chaired by Kazakhstan's Party first secretary, Gennadii Kolbin. *Izvestia* said that last year in Kazakhstan goods worth 5 million rubles had been stolen and criminal proceedings instituted against 1,000 people.

Commission to Fight Market Crime in Kazakhstan

Quoting dissident sources in Leningrad and Kiev, UPI reported today that university students from across the Soviet Union had met on February 6–8 in Leningrad to adopt a resolution calling for military education to be made noncompulsory. The students, who are said to have represented ninety institutes of higher education in forty-five cities, also made plans to boycott classes at university military departments (*voennye kafedry*) from February 27 to March 5. They also intend to hold "a constitutional meeting" on March 11 to form a nationwide student union of the USSR, UPI said. Protests and boycotts of military preparation classes—which are currently mandatory in the second, third, and fourth years of university, regardless of previous military service—have been reported before, in any number of cities from Riga to Irkutsk, Leningrad to Tashkent. In October, students from Kiev State University's Physics Department organized a picket in front of the *kafedra*'s classrooms and managed to obtain significant concessions from the university authorities (for example, those who have already served in the military will no longer be required to go through drill exercises or study the Statutes of the Armed Forces). There have been indications that the

Mounting Campaign against Military Obligations

105

Ministry of Defense and the State Committee for Public Education are already working on a draft for the reform of military preparation departments. For more information, see RL 36/89.

Soviet Anti-Zionist Committee Still Exists

Argumenty i fakty (No. 6) carried an interview with General David Dragunsky, the chairman of the Anti-Zionist Committee of the Soviet Public. Dragunsky revealed that, despite numerous Western reports to the contrary, the committee has not been disbanded, and he implied that it would not be disbanded in the near future. The Anti-Zionist Committee was set up under Yurii Andropov and has gained a bad reputation worldwide for its attacks against the Jewish religion and the Jewish state. Among its charges was the highly publicized claim that "Zionists" were responsible for the Nazi genocide against "Soviet people" during World War II. With one possible exception, all of the committee's leadership, including Dragunsky and his deputy Samuil Zivs, are Jewish. It was Zivs who was widely quoted in the Western media as the source for assurances that the Anti-Zionist committee had ceased to exist. In his interview with *Argumenty i fakty*, however, Dragunsky tried to portray the Anti-Zionist Committee as a non-Zionist, Jewish organization that helps to promote Jewish culture and even defends Soviet Jews against manifestations of anti-Semitism. He claimed that it was not a state-sponsored, anti-Israeli body.

Soviet Newspapers on AIDS Situation

Pravda and *Trud* published alarming reports on the AIDS situation in the USSR. The Party daily quoted specialists as saying that by the year 2000 there will be 15 million HIV carriers and 200,000 AIDS victims in the Soviet Union. The trade-union paper was more encouraging, quoting Deputy Minister of Health Aleksandr Kondrusev as saying that, "according to preliminary calculations," there will be 55,000 HIV carriers and 1,300 cases of the disease in the USSR by the end of the century. Both newspapers were reporting on a conference of the Emergency Commission on AIDS held in Moscow on February 20. The conference was chaired by Minister of Health Evgenii Chazov, who drew attention to deficiencies in Soviet efforts to combat the disease. One of the most serious problems is the lack of disposable hypodermic syringes. Lax hygienic procedures in Soviet clinics and hospitals have also contributed to the spread of the disease. The Soviet media have carried numerous reports on what happened in the city of

Elista (Kalmyk ASSR), where at least twenty-seven children and five mothers in a children's hospital were infected via improperly sterilized syringes.

The Lithuanian Party leadership issued a warning to nationalists to avoid confrontation. TASS said a plenum of the Party's Central Committee in Vilnius had warned that confrontation along national lines could lead to a split in Lithuanian society. TASS said this should not be permitted. The plenum was quoted as urging resolute measures to bring about cohesion of Lithuania's Party organizations and demanded that attempts to excite chauvinism and national hostility be nipped in the bud. The Lithuanian Party daily *Tiesa* quoted the republic's Party leader Algirdas Brazauskas as saying at the plenum that the situation in Lithuania is nearing a stage at which special rule might have to be imposed on the republic as was the case in Nagorno-Karabakh. TASS said there was criticism of "Sajudis," the Lithuanian restructuring movement (see *Pravda*, February 22). The plenum was quoted as saying that "extreme standpoints" recently had started to dominate the movement's activities and that some of its members were turning to "anti-Socialist demands" for the withdrawal of Lithuania from the USSR. On February 23, Reuters reported that the Lithuanian authorities had halted a twice-weekly television show broadcast by "Sajudis" until after the elections to the Congress of People's Deputies. (On February 22, a spokesman for "Sajudis" said the group was not worried about criticism from the republic's Central Committee. The spokesman, Virgilijus Cepaitis, told Reuters that the Party was "frightened" by a recent "Sajudis" call for Lithuanians to be allowed to decide their own form of government.) Another representative of "Sajudis," Kazimiras Antanavicius, said in the *Globe & Mail* (Toronto) of February 22 that the perception in Moscow and the West that the reform movement wanted to cut Lithuania's ties with the Soviet Union was incorrect. He said that in fact "Sajudis" would like the Soviet republics to operate like the European Community states. TASS of February 21 also said the Lithuanian Party secretary in charge of ideology, Lionginas Sepetys, had retired and been replaced by Valerijonas Baltrunas, a physician and the former first secretary of the Lithuanian Komsomol. Sepetys had held the post for thirteen years. The same day, the Lithuanian Council of Ministers ordered the use of the Lithuanian language by government and other public bodies and by the courts (*AP*, *TASS*, in English, February 21).

Lithuanian Party Warns Nationalists

Soviet Historian Urges Review of Events in Hungary in 1956

Moscow News (No. 9) carried an article by historian Andranik Migranyan calling for a joint Soviet-Hungarian review of the events of 1956, when Soviet tanks rolled into Budapest to crush an uprising and remove the country's prime minister. The rebellion had been officially regarded in both countries as an attempt at counterrevolution until last month, when a leading reformer in the Hungarian leadership, Imre Pozsgay, called it an uprising against an oligarchy humiliating the nation. The Hungarian Party Central Committee later ruled that the remark by Pozsgay was premature and avoided stating clearly whether the events of 1956 were a counterrevolution or popular uprising. Writing in *Moscow News*, Migranyan said: "It seems to me that the Hungarian Party Central Committee plenum found the most sensible course for the time being to deal with the problem." He said the decision taken by the plenum "invites us to undertake a joint review of the events of 1956."

Article Cites Problems with Medical Care in Moscow

An article in *Znamya* (No.3) said that, despite having more physicians and hospital beds than New York, Moscow has a higher mortality rate and lower life expectancy. The article said that for decades officials were more interested in producing "showcase statistics" than in learning whether increasing the number of hospital beds and physicians really improved the country's health-care system.

Problems with Soviet Exports Reported

The journal *Pravitel'stvennyi vestnik* reported problems with exports last year and urged the introduction of new economic methods to improve the situation. The journal said the USSR continued to produce outdated airplanes, cars, and agricultural machines that were inferior to Western goods. It said that the target output of important raw materials for export was not reached last year and that the production of various export goods for this year was already behind planned targets. It also said trade ties with Socialist countries were unsatisfactory.

Soviet Official Says No Plans to Publish Rushdie Book

Chairman of the USSR State Committee for Publishing Houses, Printing Plants, and the Book Trade Mikhail Nenashev said the USSR had no immediate plans to publish *The Satanic Verses* by British author Salman Rushdie. (Rushdie's book has been regarded as blasphemous by many Moslems, and Iran's Ayatollah Khomeini has ordered Rushdie's assassination.) Speaking to reporters in New Dehli, Nenashev claimed that Soviet policy generally prohibits the publication of work that is offensive to either the religious or national sentiments of any country (*UPI, AFP*, February 22).

Estonian Writers Protest Havel Sentence

Estonian novelist Arno Valton said the entire leadership of the Estonian Writers' Union has signed a protest letter demanding the immediate release of Czechoslovak playwright Vaclav Havel. In an interview with RFE, Valton said members of the leadership were among more than thirty leading writers in the union who signed the protest letter. The letter was sent to the Czechoslovak government as well as PEN International. In another interview, Estonian writer Sirje Ruutssoo told RFE that the Estonian literary organization "Wellesto" had also sent a protest telegram to the Prague authorities demanding the release of Havel and other activists on trial in Prague.

Air-Traffic Controllers on Strike

Literaturnaya gazeta reported that, exasperated by what they consider inadequate salaries, bureaucratic inertia, and outdated equipment, Moscow's air-traffic controllers have resorted to a novel form of strike. According to the newspaper, instead of refusing to work, 350 controllers at Moscow's central flight-control installation have spent the last two months refusing to collect their pay. By such an unusual action they are trying to attract the attention of the authorities to their demands for a fairer distribution of wages, better job descriptions, and other improvements. The action is the latest in a series of labor confrontations in the Soviet Union in recent months.

Smirnov Expelled from Moldavian Central Committee

The Central Committee of the Moldavian Communist Party expelled its former second secretary, Viktor Smirnov. TASS said the action had been taken because Smirnov "had compromised himself." Smirnov retired as Party second secretary in Moldavia last November, and *Trud* and *Moscow News* reported his arrest in Moscow last month. TASS said Smirnov faces charges of taking bribes and being involved in "a well-known corruption case in Uzbekistan." In a separate report on Smirnov's expulsion, TASS, in English, quoted Moldavian Party First Secretary Semen Grossu as saying Smirnov had caused serious damage to the prestige of the Party in Moldavia.

Thursday, February 23

Orthodox Church Reopens in Moscow

An Orthodox church that had been closed to believers for fifty years has been reopened in Moscow. TASS said a liturgy was conducted in the seventeenth-century church of the Archangel Michael in an area of apartment houses in southwestern Moscow. The agency added that there was much restoration work still to be done on the church.

Cooperative Taxation Left Up to the Republics

The Soviet leadership has decided to leave taxation on the income of cooperatives up to the individual republics. TASS said this decision was decreed by the Presidium of the USSR Supreme Soviet in an order published in *Izvestia*. It said the order becomes effective on July 1. TASS said cooperatives will be taxed on all profits that they do not contribute to charity. It said the republics will determine the tax rate. The decision was first made at the Politburo meeting on February 16 (*Pravda*, February 17).

Yazov in *Pravda*

Pravda carried an article by USSR Minister of Defense Dmitrii Yazov marking Soviet Army and Navy day. In the article, Yazov said Soviet plans to reduce its armed forces have raised a number of problems, such as how to provide housing and work for the discharged soldiers. The Soviet Union has said it will reduce its armed forces by 500,000 men over the next two years.

Korotich Rejected as Candidate

It was announced that Vitalii Korotich, the chief editor of *Ogonek*, had been rejected as a candidate for the elections to the Congress of People's Deputies in a Moscow district. Supporters of Korotich at a meeting of an election commission to choose candidates said Korotich felt the meeting was manipulated by the commission chairman (*Reuters*, February 23).

Discrimination against Kalmyks Reported

It was reported that residents of an area where more than two dozen children were infected with the deadly AIDS virus have been pelted with stones. Writing in *Izvestia*, Kalmyk poet David Kugultinov urged legislation banning discrimination against people suffering from the virus. In late January, the Soviet media reported that twenty-seven children had been infected with the virus in the Kalmyk capital of Elista through the use of dirty syringes. Several mothers were found to have been infected by nursing their babies. Now, Kugultinov said, residents of nearby areas have begun throwing stones at cars with Kalmyk license plates, "as if the cars are spreading AIDS." "The attitude towards students leaving the Kalmyk republic to study in neighboring republics has sharply changed; voices are calling out demanding that they be housed in separate dormitories," he said.

Cuts in KGB Suggested

Moscow News (No. 9) carried an article urging restructuring in the KGB. In the article, historian Mikhail Lyubimov argued that the KGB staff should be cut back. Mentioning the reductions in the Soviet armed forces, Lyubimov said "the work of the [Soviet] counterintelligence departments should correspondingly be reduced and reoriented." Lyubimov also suggested the creation of "a permanent joint organ with controlling functions [over the secret services], with the participation of representatives of the US Congress and the USSR Supreme Soviet."

Friday, February 24

USSR to Review Cases of Persons Stripped of Citizenship

The Soviet Union is to review cases of citizens stripped of their citizenship in connection with their emigration from the USSR. "We must review the cases of those who have been denied a homeland due to the biased red tape of stagnation," Yurii Reshetov, head of the Soviet Foreign Ministry's Humanitarian Cooperation and Human-Rights Section, told a news conference. "It cannot be ruled out that some legislative acts of the past may have to be changed," he added (*Reuters*, February 24). Earlier this year, *Ogonek* (No. 5) carried an interview with a Soviet lawyer, who said that, in stripping people of Soviet citizenship when they emigrated from the USSR, the Soviet Union had violated not only international law but its own legislation as well.

Lyubimov Interviewed by APN

Exiled Soviet theater director Yurii Lyubimov was quoted by Novosti press agency as saying *perestroika* must show economic results soon or people will become disillusioned and apathetic. Novosti also quoted Lyubimov as saying "*perestroika* has not yet asserted itself irreversibly." Lyubimov was stripped of his Soviet citizenship during a visit to London in 1983. He is now temporarily back in Moscow to stage several plays at the Taganka Theater. Novosti quoted Lyubimov as saying that he wanted to return to the USSR permanently but that the main obstacle was the decree that stripped him of his citizenship.

Moscow News Editor Says Glasnost' Does Not Always Work

Chief editor of *Moscow News* Egor Yakovlev said *glasnost'* does not always work "and quite a few things are still being hushed up" in the USSR. In an interview with Novosti press agency, Yakovlev said the country must take the next step and move from *glasnost'* to democratization of the mass media and create "a new kind of news media—bold, critical, and reflecting different points of view." Yakovlev said this was necessary because the current "docile mass media" in the USSR hinders the exercise of democratic controls. In the interview, Yakovlev also said media freedom was one of the planks in his platform in running for the Congress of People's Deputies.

Estonians Celebrate Independence Day

Estonia's blue, black, and white national flag was raised on Toompea, the old fortress in the capital of Tallinn, during an official ceremony marking the seventy-first anniversary of Estonia's independence. Estonian President Arnold Ruutel said national symbols should not be regarded as hostile to socialism. Ruutel said Estonia would continue to observe the anniversary of the founding of the Estonian Soviet Socialist Republic (*TASS*, February 24).

Saturday, February 25

Office Responsible for Rehabilitations Complains of Understaffing

Sovetskaya kul'tura carried an interview with an official from the Main Military Procurator's Office, Vladimir Provotorov, on the current work of the office on the rehabilitation of Stalin's victims. The office is responsible for the rehabilitation of military men and of civilians who were tried on charges of treason by a military tribunal. In the interview, Provotorov said that, between 1954 and 1964, 500,000 people were rehabilitated by the Military Procurator's Office, while in 1988 only 805 people were rehabilitated. Provotorov explained the low figure for 1988 by the fact that the section of the Military Procurator's Office dealing with rehabilitations is currently understaffed. There are at present forty people working on rehabilitations, whereas during the ten years after Stalin's death there were 500. Provotorov complained that, if the number of staff were not increased, at least 150 years would be needed to finish the job.

Newspaper Complains about New Regulations for Journalists

Sovetskaya kul'tura reported on the effects of the new "Regulations on the Procedure for Representatives of the Mass Media to Be Admitted to, and to Remain in, Localities Where Measures to Ensure Public Order Are in Operation," which stipulate that journalists must obtain special passes from the Ministry of Internal Affairs in order to cover rallies, meetings, and scenes of accidents and emergencies. The newspaper disclosed that a group of journalists, including a correspondent of *Pravda*, was refused access by the police to an electoral meeting of the Sverdlovsky and Dzerzhinsky Districts of Moscow on the grounds of not having special passes. The newspaper noted that, while the police are very efficient when it comes to preventing journalists from covering a certain event, they are extremely slow in issuing special passes. (See also an interview in *Krasnaya zvezda* on February 26 with an official from the USSR Journalists' Union who attempted to defend the regulations.) More than a month later, *Moscow News* (No. 14) and *Ogonek* (No. 13) carried attacks on the new regulations, written by leading Soviet journalists and writers.

Erevan Military Commander on Situation in Armenia

Lieutenant General Yurii Kuznetsov told *Krasnaya zvezda* that emergency measures in Armenia could not be lifted yet because ethnic protests were still flaring up. In an interview with the newspaper, Kuznetsov complained about the continuing activities of the banned Karabakh Committee. Kuznetsov said members of the committee "will not calm down." (All the leaders of the committee have been arrested.) Kuznetsov said there had been an illegal demonstration in Erevan last week that drew more than 1,000 people. He also gave a new death toll of eighty-three for the past year of unrest. Official figures earlier this month put the toll at ninety-one. The discrepancy was not explained. On March 3, *Krasnaya zvezda* again complained about the demonstration. It said the demonstrators had demanded the release of the leaders of the Karabakh Committee and urged a boycott of the upcoming elections to the new parliament.

Thousands Demonstrate in Tbilisi

Reports from Tbilisi said thousands of people took part in rallies protesting against the incorporation of Georgia into the Soviet Union. The rallies were held on the eve of the sixty-eighth anniversary of the event (*AFP*, February 25). According to Georgian dissident Zviad Gamsakhurdia, who spoke to RFE/RL by telephone, the demonstrations took place at four locations in Tbilisi. Demonstrators carried Georgian national flags and placards referring to the loss of Georgian independence and calling for the release of Georgian political prisoners. There were tanks, armored personnel carriers, and troops on the streets, and some streets were cordoned off. Troops beat up some of the demonstrators. The number of persons detained was estimated at between 150 and 500. They were later released.

Mozhaev on Situation in Agriculture

Pravda carried a lengthy interview with Soviet writer Boris Mozhaev, who said that the situation in agriculture has not improved in the period of *perestroika*. Mozhaev spoke about how much better the situation in Russian agriculture was in 1913 and in the period of the NEP than it is now.

Shevardnadze Leaves Baghdad, Goes to Teheran

Speaking in Baghdad before leaving Iraq, Soviet Foreign Minister Eduard Shevardnadze called for all foreign navies to be withdrawn from the Persian Gulf. He said Moscow was willing to withdraw its warships and hoped the United States would as well (*Reuters*, *AP*, February 25). The same day, Shevardnadze traveled to Teheran. See *Pravda*, February 26.

Politburo Member Urges Higher Output of Basic Foodstuffs

Politburo member Viktor Nikonov called for a higher output of bread, meat, sugar, and other foodstuffs to better supply the needs of the Soviet population. Nikonov is also the Central Committee secretary in charge of agriculture. He was speaking in the capital of Turkmenistan, Ashkhabad, where he is a candidate for next month's elections to the Congress of People's Deputies. He said the economic situation in the country was changing "slowly," and he called solving the food problem a "very urgent" issue. Nikonov said importing foodstuffs that should be produced in the Soviet Union could not be justified either economically or politically (*TASS*, February 25). For the text of Nikonov's speech, see *Izvestia*, February 26.

Rebuilding in Leninakan Criticized

The Politburo commission set up to deal with the aftermath of the Armenian earthquake criticized the pace of rebuilding housing and social and cultural facilities in the Armenian city of Leninakan. (The city was seriously damaged by the quake.) State construction organizations of the republic were accused of "sluggishness." The commission complained that the population had not yet seen the reconstruction plans for their cities and villages and that no public discussions had been held. The commission also accused the republic's news media of "passivity" and said criticism of them by the people was justified. Heading the session of the commission was Deputy Prime Minister Lev Voronin (*Izvestia*, February 26).

Soviet television reported the death of Ukrainian Party Central Committee member and USSR Supreme Soviet deputy Grigorii Tkachuk. The report said Tkachuk had died on February 23 at the age of seventy. An obituary issued by Party and state leaders praised him as a talented organizer in the kolkhoz movement and as a successful worker in the agricultural sphere. He was twice decorated as a Hero of Socialist Labor. His obituary was published in *Pravda* on February 26.

Ukrainian Party Central Committee Member Tkachuk Dies

TASS said one of two nuclear reactors at the nuclear power station near Erevan had been permanently shut down after twelve years in operation. It had been designed to last thirty years. (The second reactor at the plant is scheduled to be closed later this year. The decision to shut down the Armenian nuclear power plant was taken after the earthquake in the republic last December.)

Nuclear Reactor Closed in Armenia

TASS and *Izvestia* said participants in a meeting in Dushanbe on February 24 had called for a revival of ancient Tajik culture and for official status for the Tajik language. TASS said participants in the meeting in Dushanbe's central square had met with Tajik President Gaibnazar Pallaev and members of a commission preparing a proposal for giving the Tajik language official status. TASS said the meeting was told that a draft law on the Tajik language had been worked out and that it would be published in the press and submitted for public discussion.

Dushanbe Meeting on Revival of Tajik Culture and Language

TASS summarized a speech delivered on Moldavian television on February 24 by the Moldavian Party leader, Semen Grossu, who said preparation was under way of a series of draft laws on the status of the Moldavian language. Grossu said that a scheme was being worked out for making Moldavian the republic's state language and that problems connected with the conversion of written Moldavian to the Latin alphabet were being studied.

Party Chief Endorses Steps on Moldavian Language

Thousands of demonstrators have rallied in recent weeks in the Moldavian capital, Kishinev, to demand official status for the Moldavian language and the introduction of the Latin alphabet. In the television broadcast, Grossu condemned the demonstrations, saying that they were unsanctioned and that their organizers had "ignored the legal demands of the authorities to observe order." According to TASS, he said the protests were an example of "extremism, demagoguery, and irresponsibility." On February 27, reports from Kishinev said there had been another unofficial demonstration in the city over language issues. At least 2,000 people were reported to have taken part (*Reuters*, February 27). For information on recent developments in Moldavia, see RL 92/89, 93/89, and 94/89; on the language problem in Moldavia, see also *Sovetskaya Moldaviya*, February 15.

Soviet Ambassador Praises Central American Peace Move

The Soviet ambassador to Nicaragua praised the new Central American peace accords and said they proved regional conflicts did not have to be solved by military means. In what observers said was a rare news conference in Managua, Ambassador Valerii Nikolaenko said the Soviet Union viewed the results of last week's Central American summit in El Salvador with great satisfaction (*Reuters*, February 25). Last week's meeting of five Central American presidents agreed to work towards disbanding the US-backed anti-Sandinista *contra* movement in return for liberal reforms in Nicaragua.

Sunday, February 26

Shevardnadze in Teheran

Eduard Shevardnadze met in Teheran with Iran's spiritual leader Ayatollah Khomeini. TASS reported that Shevardnadze gave Khomeini a personal message from Gorbachev. The future of Soviet-Iranian relations was discussed (*Izvestia*, February 27). The Iranian news agency IRNA quoted Khomeini as telling Shevardnadze that Iran and the USSR should improve their relations in order to confront "devilish acts of the West." On February 27, Shevardnadze met Iranian President Ali Khamenei. IRNA quoted Shevardnadze as saying improved relations were possible despite ideological differences. It quoted Shevardnadze as telling Khamenei that Iran enjoys high international prestige and that the USSR had concluded that "it must acknowledge the beliefs of others and respect them." Radio Teheran said that, during the meeting with

Shevardnadze, Khamenei called on the Soviet Union to promote peace in the Gulf by putting pressure on Iraq to pull its remaining troops out of Iranian territory (*Reuters*, February 27). The same day, Shevardnadze and his Iranian counterpart Ali Akbar Velayati signed protocols expanding Soviet-Iranian political and cultural contacts. Shevardnadze then left Teheran for Moscow (*Reuters, AP*, February 27). On March 2, *Pravda* published an interview with Shevardnadze on his Middle East tour. See reports in *Pravda*, February 27 and *Izvestia*, February 28.

Thousands of people were reported to have taken part in an unofficial gathering in the Ukrainian city of Lvov in memory of the Ukrainian poet Taras Shevchenko. A spokesman for the Ukrainian Helsinki group, Anatolii Dotsenko, told RFE/RL that priests from the banned Ukrainian Catholic Church and the Russian Orthodox Church participated. He also said there had been a demonstration in Kiev to protest against the sentencing of two people arrested at an election rally on February 24. At the rally participants carried slogans demanding the ouster of Ukranian Party leader Vladimir Shcherbitsky.

Thousands Attend Shevchenko Memorial Service

Monday, February 27

Politburo member Aleksandr Yakovlev said only *perestroika* could conquer "the problems that have been piling up for decades" in the Soviet Union. TASS quoted Yakovlev as saying the problems include "increasing corruption, social injustice, local feudal structures, ecological crimes, and inadequate attention to national histories, languages, and ethnic cultures." TASS said Yakovlev was speaking at an election rally in Tbilisi, and it quoted him as saying the Party hoped the voters would elect pro-*perestroika* candidates to the Congress of People's Deputies. See, *Izvestia*, February 28.

Yakovlev Says Only *Perestroika* Can Overcome Ethnic Problems

A USSR Supreme Court judge said some crimes committed in Soviet penal camps were the fault of the camp administrators. TASS said judge Robert Tikhomirov, who heads the USSR Supreme Court's criminal division, told a Supreme Court plenum that 4,000 crimes had been committed in penal camps last year. Tikhomirov was quoted as saying the camp administrators sometimes

Judge Criticizes Administrators of Penal Camps

117

provoke the crimes by working convicts too long, failing to pay them for all their work, and ordering harsh punishments for minor violations of camp rules. Since last year, the Soviet press has been discussing the harsh conditions in Soviet penal camps, and calls have been made to make the Soviet penal system more humane. TASS said it had been announced at the plenum that fifty-seven penal camps had been closed down last year and that another thirty were scheduled to be closed this year.

Writers and Activists Protest Rushdie Death Sentence

A group of about fifteen independent activists demon-strated outside the Iranian embassy in Moscow to protest against Ayatollah Khomeini's death sentence on British author Salman Rushdie. The demonstration was organ-ized by the unofficial Democratic Union and the unofficial journal *Glasnost'*. In a statement handed out to passers-by, the demonstrators criticized the Soviet authorities for not condemning Iran's reaction to Rushdie's book *The Satanic Verses* (*AP, AFP*, February 27). On February 28, *Komsomol'skaya pravda* reported that another demon-stration condeming Khomeini's action had been held on February 26 by a group of young Soviet writers from the Moscow "Poeziya" Club. On February 28, Soviet Foreign Ministry spokesman Gennadii Gerasimov said the Soviet leadership was "concerned" about the death sentence on Rushdie and would try to resolve the issue at a meeting of foreign ministers in Vienna next week (*Reuters*, Febru-ary 28). On March 2, TASS said Khomeini may have had no choice under Moslem law but to denounce Rushdie. The commentary also said the world press had distorted and oversimplified Iran's position on Rushdie's book.

More Jewish Cultural Centers Created in USSR

TASS and Reuters reported that Jewish cultural centers were being established in Leningrad and Tashkent. In the past year, Jewish centers have been established in the Baltic republics, Minsk, Kishinev, Kiev, Lvov, and Moscow.

Yazov on Soviet Troop Withdrawal from Eastern Europe

USSR Minister of Defense Dmitrii Yazov said in *Izvestia* that the first Soviet military unit to be withdrawn from Eastern Europe this year would be a tank division from Veszprem in Hungary. He said the withdrawal would take place between May and August. Two further tank divi-sions will be pulled out this summer from Jüterbog and Vogelsang in East Germany. According to Yazov, these withdrawals will include twenty-four missile launchers and about 2,700 tanks. These divisions, he told *Izvestia*, will not only be withdrawn but also disbanded. Yazov said two more tank divisions would be withdrawn from East Germany and one from Czechoslovakia in the summer of 1990. He said the purpose of the withdrawals is to reduce military expenditures and support the Party's policy of "demilitarization of international relations."

Izvestia carried a report by its Vilnius correspondent attacking Elta, the Lithuanian equivalent of TASS. *Izvestia* complained that Elta had carried with sympathy and support all the pronouncements made at the celebrations of Lithuania's independence day by the unofficial "Sajudis" movement, even those pronouncements that were nationalistic in character or praised bourgeois Lithuania.

Izvestia Attacks Lithuanian News Agency

Tuesday, February 28

Andrei Sakharov said he stands by a statement he made at a press conference in Canada earlier this month that some Soviet soldiers in Afghanistan were shot by their own forces. Sakharov was quoted as saying some Soviet soldiers had been fired on by Soviet helicopters to prevent them being taken captive by the resistance. Lieutenant General Boris Gromov, who commanded the Soviet forces in Afghanistan, said in an interview with *Krasnaya zvezda* that "such monstrous events" never occurred. In response to Gromov's comments, Sakharov said he still believed his statement was accurate (*UPI*, February 28). On March 2, *Komsomol'skaya pravda* reported on a telephone interview with Sakharov in which he again confirmed his stand. The interview also contained remarks by Elena Bonner, calling for direct talks between the Soviet Union and Afghan resistance on POWs, with UN and Red Cross participation. Along with Sakharov's comments, the newspaper published a statement by former Soviet Armed Forces Chief of Staff Marshal Sergei Akhromeev, who rejected Sakharov's account.

Sakharov Says He Stands by Statement on Afghan Fighting

Hundreds of thousands of Armenians marched in Erevan to honor those killed in last February's Sumgait riots. AP and AFP quoted an Armenpress news agency spokesman as saying 600,000 to 800,000 people took part in the march. Demonstrations have been banned in Erevan for months, but the spokesman said the military authorities allowed today's march.

Armenians Commemorate Sumgait Victims

119

Arkadii Vol'sky on Situation in Nagorno-Karabakh

Moscow's special administrator in the Nagorno-Karabakh Autonomous Oblast said that the situation in the region had been normalized but that relations between local Armenians and Azerbaijanis remained tense. Vol'sky told *Krasnaya zvezda* that refugees had returned home to several areas of Nagorno-Karabakh, but he said mutual suspicion, mistrust, reproaches, and accusations persisted. Meanwhile, Radio Baku quoted the city's military commander as saying that the situation in Baku continues to normalize and that a curfew imposed after renewed violence last November is to be shortened by two hours (to 2400–0500 hours) starting March 2.

Burlatsky Says Gorbachev Is Safe

Fedor Burlatsky, who is believed to be an unofficial adviser to Gorbachev, appeared on Austrian television. Asked about the possibility of a coup d'état in the Kremlin, Burlatsky replied that Gorbachev is not in danger of being overthrown, because he has not alienated officials the way Khrushchev did twenty-five years ago and because nobody in the Politburo can present a serious alternative—either to Gorbachev as a leader or to his political reform program. According to Burlatsky, Gorbachev's position is also guaranteed by the fact that the country's main political forces—the army, the Party, and the KGB—are completely split over the path of reform and are not in a position to organize concerted action against Gorbachev. He said, however, that failure of the present leadership to improve the Soviet standard of living would cause social tensions in the country.

Tajikistan's "Greens" Reach Compromise with Authorities

TASS reported that environmentalists in Tajikistan had reached a compromise with the republic's Ministry of Power over construction of the Rogun dam. The republican "Green" movement has opposed the dam because of the high level of seismic activity in the region of the Vakhsh River. The compromise solution calls for a review of the project after the first of a planned six generating units goes into operation at the end of this year. At this stage the dam will be only fifty meters high, not 325 meters as planned.

New Lithuanian Constitution Conflicts with USSR Constitution

The official draft of Lithuania's new constitution was made public, and TASS said it contains provisions that conflict with the USSR Constitution. The agency disclosed that the Presidium of the Lithuanian Supreme Soviet has decided to seek changes in the USSR Constitution. TASS said the draft calls Lithuania "a sovereign Soviet Socialist state." It said the draft backs economic independence for the republic and interprets "statehood and sovereignty" more broadly than the current constitution of the USSR. The official draft of Lithuania's new constitution is, however, less radical than one issued by the independent "Sajudis" movement. According to RFE's Lithuanian Service, the latter draft includes proposals that laws passed by the USSR Supreme Soviet should only be valid in Lithuania if they have been approved by the Lithuanian parliament.

Italian Communist Party General Secretary Achille Occhetto met in Moscow with Gorbachev. Occhetto said later that they had discussed former Czechoslovak Party First Secretary Alexander Dubcek and his visit to Italy last November. Ochetto said he had talked to Gorbachev about the importance of democratization and "the historic importance" of Dubcek's 1968 reform program. Ochetto did not tell reporters what Gorbachev said (*Reuters*, February 28). See also *Pravda*, March 1.

Gorbachev Meets Occhetto

Four people accused of taking a busload of children hostage last December and demanding a plane to fly them to Israel went on trial in Moscow. TASS said a fifth man also went on trial for allegedly helping to plan the action. It said the five are being tried in open court by a panel for criminal cases of the RSFSR Supreme Court. Israel extradited the hijackers to the Soviet Union after the plane landed in Tel Aviv.

Hijackers Go on Trial in Moscow

In a ten-minute interview broadcast on Austrian television, sociologist Tat'yana Zaslavskaya, a leading reformer, described some of the problems of setting up the Soviet Union's first public opinion research institute. Zaslavskaya said that there is a shortage of paper and that the institute's computers have to be kept at a nearby airport, "where they are safe from being stolen." The most serious problem, however, is resistance on the part of local officials, who do not see the need for the institute and "inhibit our work wherever they can." Asked about the popular mood in the USSR, Zaslavskaya said the public's faith in *perestroika* seemed to be waning, and she cited a recent Gallup telephone poll, which showed that "now no more than 12 percent of Muscovites believe in an economic upswing; one year ago, it was 22 percent."

Zaslavskaya Interviewed on Austrian TV

She claimed that "a large part of the nationality conflicts" in the USSR had been organized by "conservative political lobbies," and she said 1989 would be "the crucial year for *perestroika.*" "At the end of this year, I see only two alternatives—either the radically democratic road, or the old, well-trodden, conservative road . . . paved with the usual old compromises," she said.

Soviet Psychiatrists Treating Fewer Patients since Anti-Abuse Law

A panel of leading Soviet doctors said psychiatrists are treating fewer patients following the introduction of new regulations designed to guard against abuses. Panel members told a Moscow news conference that case loads were down by about 30 percent. The panel, which includes chief Moscow psychiatrist Vladimir Tikhonenko, said the USSR has some 5.5 million mental patients. Tikhonenko said doctors want enforced treatment cut to a minimum. Soviet regulations covering psychiatric treatment were changed last year (*Reuters*, February 28).

Party Chief Urges Crackdown on Moscow's "Free-Speech" Street

Moscow city Party chief Lev Zaikov has demanded an end to "disorder" on the Arbat, a popular pedestrian area where artists vie with pavement poets on what has been dubbed "free-speech street." Moscow newspapers reported that Zaikov made his remarks at a meeting of the capital's Party organization on the weekend. Zaikov was quoted as saying that "an impermissible situation" had arisen on the street with "open anti-Sovietism" flourishing under the flag of democracy. He said, "we must wage a much more resolute struggle against extremists and nationalist-minded people and groups."

The Month of March

Politburo Resolution on "Informatization" of USSR

The first issue of the new Party monthly *Izvestiya TsK KPSS* contains a Politburo resolution on the conversion of the Soviet Union to "an information society." The resolution, dated July 15, 1988, claims that the USSR is between seven and twelve years behind the United States in computer technology and software development, and it also acknowledges Soviet backwardness in data communication, open data banks, the printing industry, and library science. Arguing that, if radical steps are not taken, the Soviet Union may never catch up with the advanced industrial countries, the resolution instructs the USSR Gosplan, the USSR Academy of Sciences, the State Committee for Computer Technology and Information Science, and other relevant organizations to devise models for transforming the USSR into "an information society." The draft proposals are to be published for public discussion during the first half of 1989 and later submitted to the USSR Supreme Soviet.

Soviet Election Official on Upcoming Balloting

The deputy head of the Soviet Central Electoral Commission, Dmitrii Golovko, said that, on average, two candidates would run for every seat in the elections to the Congress of People's Deputies on March 26 but that one in four of the constituencies would have only one candidate. He noted that 80 percent of the officially approved candidates were Party members, which he said was more than in previous elections. He revealed that his department had received thousands of letters with suggestions for improving the electoral system (*TASS*, March 1).

Medvedev Says *Glasnost'* Will Continue

TASS reported that Vadim Medvedev, the CPSU Politburo member responsible for ideological affairs, had told an election meeting in Minsk on February 28 that, despite "persistent pressure" for ideological censorship of public opinion, arising from the diversity of views expressed in the Soviet media and in public, the CPSU would continue its policy of *glasnost'* (*TASS*, in English, March 1). On March 2, *Pravda* carried the text of the speech by

123

Medvedev, in which he accused opponents of *perestroika* in the USSR of hiding behind dogma. Medvedev called for a reappraisal of the relationship between the economy and traditional Socialist thought. In an apparent reference to the Popular Front movements, Medvedev said the Party should learn to live in a society undergoing political change, where social movements and organizations have a role to play.

Gorbachev Donates Money to Earthquake Fund

Komsomolets Tajikistana said Gorbachev had donated 82,000 dollars from the US sale of his book *Perestroika* to the Tajikistan earthquake fund. (The quake took place in January.)

Historian Describes Activities of Azerbaijani "Homeland" Society

In an interview with the RL Azerbaijani Service, Azerbaijani historian Abulfaz Aliev of the republican Academy of Sciences described the activities of the unofficial "Yurd" (Homeland) Society, which enjoys great support among Azerbaijani intellectuals. According to Aliev, students and teachers at Baku University are particularly enthusiastic about the society, which also has an officially registered branch in Nakhichevan. Among the issues of concern to the members of "Yurd" are republican control of natural resources; the preservation of the Azerbaijani language, culture, and historic monuments; relations with Iranian Azerbaijan; democratization in the republic; and the struggle against conservative bureaucrats. Abulfaz Aliev also reported that the scholar Enver Aliev, who was reported by human-rights circles in Moscow to have been arrested on February 17 for his membership in "Yurd," had in fact been arrested because of his participation in demonstrations in Baku last year.

Bus Service to China

TASS reported that a daily bus service had started between Kazakhstan and Xinjiang. An agreement on setting up the service was signed in the Kazakh capital of Alma-Ata in December, 1988.

Lenin's Legend Challenged Again

Novyi mir, which broke with the taboo on criticizing Lenin's policies with the publication of an article by Vasilii Selyunin in May, 1988, carried another article indicating that Lenin began restricting democracy and limiting dissent not long after the October Revolution. The article by Igor Klyamkin, entitled "Why It Is Difficult to Speak the Truth," states that "even in Lenin's time, pluralism did not

124

coexist in harmony with the Party organization." The article also discusses the limits of Gorbachev's *glasnost'* campaign (*Novyi mir*, No. 2, 1989).

Yugoslavia and USSR Again Discuss Soviet Debts

The 1,700 million dollars worth of goods the Soviet Union owes Yugoslavia was discussed by Soviet and Yugoslav officials in Belgrade. Tanjug said the debt was brought up at talks between USSR Minister of Foreign Economic Relations Konstantin Katushev and Yugoslav Prime Minister Designate Ante Markovic and National Vice President Stane Dolanc. Tanjug reported that the same issue was also raised on February 28 during the talks between Katushev and Yugoslav Trade Minister Nenad Krekic. Yugoslav officials have complained that the trade imbalance that led to the Soviet debt has also contributed to Yugoslavia's high inflation rate. Tanjug said Katushev and Krekic signed a protocol on bilateral trade for 1989.

Slyun'kov Criticizes State of Uzbek Economy

Politburo member Nikolai Slyun'kov said Uzbekistan was moving too slowly to overhaul and reequip its factories. Slyun'kov also criticized the slow growth in skills of Uzbek workers and weak economic and work discipline. TASS said Slyun'kov was speaking at an election meeting in the Uzbek capital, Tashkent. See *Izvestia*, March 2.

Historian Argues Stalin to Blame for Cold War

Literaturnaya gazeta published an article by a specialist on the United States, Nikolai Popov, who argued that Stalin was largely to blame for the Cold War and for continuing Western suspicion of Moscow's policies. (Popov attracted public attention by being one of the first to say on the pages of the Soviet press [in *Sovetskaya kul'tura*, April 26, 1988] that the concentration of excessive power in the hands of the Bolshevik Party under Lenin contributed to the creation of Stalin's "perfect totalitarian state.") In the article in *Literaturnaya gazeta*, Popov also argued that it was "naïve or hypocritical" to condemn Western leaders at the time of the Anglo-French agreement with Hitler in Munich in 1938 for refusing to ally with Moscow. The reason lay not only in the West's lack of foresight, he said, but "also in the fact that Western public opinion put us on the same level as Fascist Germany and saw itself as having to choose between two evils." In a way, Popov's outspoken article is in line with "the new thinking." Last year, Eduard Shevardnadze said Stalin's domestic repressions had undermined international trust in Soviet foreign policy and thereby contributed to the Cold War. There are, however, some top Party officials who do not endorse this line. Valentin Falin is one of the main figures defending the traditional Soviet assessment of the Cold War and the pre-World War II period. In addition, in a speech in Tbilisi on February 27, Politburo member Aleksandr Yakovlev, the most liberal leader as regards Soviet domestic policies but a holder of sharp anti-American views, argued that the West had started the Cold War and was reluctant to abandon its anti-Communist stance.

Official Says KGB Informants Not in Conflict with Glasnost'

Izvestia published a response to a question posed by a reader of the provincial newspaper *Mariiskaya pravda* who asked how the use of KGB informants in virtually every work collective fitted in with the policy of *glasnost'*. The response carried by *Izvestia* was formulated by A. P. Burakov, a KGB official, who defended this practice. Burakov said: "The organs of the KGB have always regarded and still regard the organization of work with citizens' written and verbal communications as a way of using [citizens'] participation to ensure state security."

Draft Program of Proposed Ukrainian Popular Front Criticized

There has been more official criticism in Ukraine of plans by cultural figures to create a Ukrainian Popular Front similar to the ones in the Baltic States. *Radio Kiev* reported on a meeting of the Presidium of the Ukrainian Academy of Sciences at which the Ukrainian Central Committee secretary for ideology, Yurii Elchenko, attacked the proposed front's draft program as a political manifesto. The draft program has been strongly criticized recently by other Ukrainian Party ideologues and in letters in the Ukrainian press.

Thursday, March 2

"Sajudis" Candidate Withdraws, Clears Way for Lithuanian Party Chief

A member of Lithuania's restructuring movement, "Sajudis," has withdrawn his candidacy for the Congress of People's Deputies, clearing the way for the republic's Party chief to win the seat, "Sajudis" sources said. Since it was founded last year, "Sajudis" has posed an unprecedented challenge to the Party's influence in Lithuania, but it has recently come under increasing attack from the authorities. Reuters quoted a representative of "Sajudis" as saying the movement had decided that Arvydas Juozaitis, a young "Sajudis" activist and a candidate for election from

Vilnius, should step down in favor of Lithuanian Party chief Algirdas Brazauskas, a reformer who has expressed some sympathy for the movement.

Politburo member Egor Ligachev was quoted as criticizing the leasing system. At an election rally in the Omsk Oblast in Western Siberia, Ligachev was reported to have suggested that the leasing system contradicted traditional Socialist values (*The Baltimore Sun*, March 3, based on Central Television, "Vremya," of March 2). *The Christian Science Monitor* reported on February 23 that, at a meeting with conservative writers in Moscow, Ligachev had also dismissed leasing as a solution to the Soviet Union's agricultural problems. Soviet leader Mikhail Gorbachev, however, has strongly endorsed the lease system—most recently during his trip to Ukraine.

Ligachev on the Lease System

The Ukrainian authorities have consigned 430 formerly closed churches in Ukraine to the Russian Orthodox Church and allowed them to be reopened for worship. Representatives of the Ukrainian Catholic Church, which is banned in the USSR, said the move occurred last month. They said an estimated three-quarters of these churches had belonged to the Ukranian Catholic Church before it was forcibly abolished in 1946 (*RFE/RL Special*, March 2).

Churches in Ukraine Permitted to Reopen as Orthodox Churches

About twenty Soviet Jewish refusedniks staged a demonstration near the Kremlin to protest against the government's refusal to grant them exit visas. Security officials asked the group to disperse but made no attempt to use force. At a similar protest last year, police dragged demonstrators away to waiting buses (*AP, Reuters*, March 2).

Refusedniks Stage Protest near Kremlin

Hungarian Prime Minister Miklos Nemeth arrived in Moscow on a one-day visit. *Radio Budapest* said Nemeth planned to discuss bilateral ties and Comecon affairs. On March 3, Nemeth met with Gorbachev. Gorbachev was quoted by the Hungarian MTI news agency as saying he hoped "local conditions were mature" for the emerging political pluralism in Hungary. MTI quoted Gorbachev as saying the Soviet leadership accepts Hungary's decision to pursue pluralism and does so "with respect and great confidence" (*TASS*, March 3; *Izvestia*, March 4).

Nemeth Visit to Moscow

127

Friday, March 3 —————————————————————————————————————

Politburo on Farming

A draft report on agricultural policy outlining recommendations for changes in the way Soviet farms are owned and operated was published at the end of a two-day meeting of the CPSU Politburo. The Politburo recommended major changes to solve the Soviet Union's food supply problem. It advocated land-leasing and other alternatives to sovkhozes and kolkhozes. The Politburo's report will be submitted to a Central Committee plenum on March 15–16 (*TASS*, March 3; *Pravda*, March 4).

Andropov's Name Removed from Soviet City

The name of former Soviet President Yurii Andropov has been ordered removed from the city of Rybinsk, on the Volga River. TASS said the decision had been taken by the CPSU Central Committee and the Supreme Soviet at the request of residents of Rybinsk. It said Rybinsk was named after Andropov two weeks after his death in February, 1984. The names of other former Soviet leaders have been removed from cities and other places in recent years. (In contrast with the names of Brezhnev, Chernenko, and officials of the Stalinist era, Andropov's name has, however, always been mentioned with respect in the Soviet press.)

Muslim Leader Describes Improvements for Believers

A top Muslim leader in the USSR, Mufti Mahmud Gekkiyiev, said that *perestroika* has brought improvements for Muslims but that there is more to be done. In an article issued by Novosti, Gekkiyiev said there is still a shortage of religious books, but he cited plans for the publication of 50 million copies of the Koran this year. He said limitations on the import of religious literature from abroad had been lifted, and he pointed out that some mosques have been built but that more are needed. Gekkiyiev is the chairman of the Muslim Board for the Northern Caucasus. He said the board had received permission to build its first religious school in Daghestan.

USSR to Cut Oil Sales for Hard Currency

A Soviet trade official said the USSR will reduce its oil sales to hard-currency buyers during the first six months of 1989. *TASS* quoted Vladimir Arutyunyan as saying there will be a reduction of about 5 percent over last year's hard-currency sales. Arutyunyan is the general director of Soyuznefteksport, the Soviet trading organization responsible for oil sales.

The United States and the Soviet Union have agreed to expand their embassy staffs to cope with the extra workload created by improved relations. US State Department spokesman Charles Redman said that twenty additional positions had been added to each side's embassy and consulate last month and that fifteen more positions are scheduled to be added in August (*RFE/RL Special*, March 3).

USSR and United States to Increase Embassy Staffs

A Latvian candidate for the new Soviet parliament has denounced Moscow's troops as occupiers and the local Communist Party as collaborators and says he will work for Latvian independence. In a startling display of openness even for the progressive Baltic republic, Einars Repshe's opinions were published on the front page of the Latvian Komsomol newspaper *Sovetskaya molodezh'*. Repshe is twenty-seven. According to *Sovetskaya molodezh'*, he is a physicist and a member of the unofficial Movement for the National Independence of Latvia and editor of its newspaper.

Latvian Calls Soviet Army Occupiers

Saturday, March 4

Pravda published another article confirming previous Soviet media reports that *perestroika* has resulted in some people leaving the Communist Party. *Pravda* reviewed the cases of two such people, one of whom left the Party after it started to denounce his idols—Stalin, Molotov, and Voroshilov. The other, by contrast, agreed with criticism of the Soviet past but said he did not want to be a member of a Party that had committed so many crimes. *Pravda* was critical of both men but more so of the second one. The newspaper revealed that the term *otkazniki*, or refuseniks, has recently started to be used to describe people leaving the CPSU. Previously, this term was used to denote people who had been refused permission to emigrate, or refusedniks. See also a reader's complaint about people leaving the CPSU in *Izvestia*, March 1.

***Pravda* on People Leaving the CPSU**

On March 4, an estimated 500 people from throughout Ukraine attended the inaugural conference in Kiev of the Ukrainian "Memorial" Society. According to a report obtained by telephone from the Moscow representative of the Ukrainian Helsinki Union, the society's aims are to collect documentation about the victims of

Thousands Back Inauguration of Ukrainian "Memorial"

political terror in Ukraine, to help survivors and their families, to build a memorial complex to the victims, and generally to foster the development of Ukrainian culture and of democratization in the republic. The meeting adopted statutes and was addressed by, among others, Borys Oliinyk, a poet and a member of the Central Committee of the Ukrainian Communist Party. The new society sees itself as a separate organization from the original "Memorial" association founded in Moscow. On March 5, some 5,000 people were reported to have taken part in the Ukrainian "Memorial" Society's first public rally, which was held outside a Kiev stadium. From a report issued by *AP* on March 5, it appears that the meeting turned into a political demonstration and that many of the participants made it clear they consider Stalinism not only a problem of the past but also of the present in Ukraine. As one of them put it, "Stalinism Lives!" On March 6, Reuters quoted a spokesman for the Ukrainian Helsinki Union as saying the authorities in Kiev had pledged to look into claims that many thousands of victims of Stalinist repressions may be buried in a mass grave in the Bykovnya forest near Kiev. Meanwhile, *Komsomol'skaya pravda* (March 3) reported on a meeting held by the Karaganda Oblast branch of the "Memorial" Society and a group of MVD officials who had worked in the Karaganda camp complex in the period from the 1930s–1950s. (The first article on the camp complex appeared in *Kazakhstanskaya pravda* on July 24, 1988).

Solzhenitsyn's "Zhit' ne po lzhi" Published Again

The periodical *Vek XX i mir* (No. 2) published Aleksandr Solzhenitsyn's article "Zhit' ne po lzhi!"(Live Not By Lies!) It is the second time the article has been published in the Soviet Union. It appeared the first time on October 18, 1988, in *Rabochee slovo*, the newspaper for railway workers in Kiev (see RL 551/88). The publication of the article in *Vek XX i mir* is accompanied by a note by the critic Igor Vinogradov, who remarks it is a pity that Solzhenitsyn's calls could not have been heard by the Soviet public in the 1970s. *Vek XX i mir* (No. 1) carried a letter by writer Boris Mozhaev calling for the publication of Solzhenitsyn's works in the USSR.

Pravda Says Nuclear Town Not on Soviet Maps

Pravda said prisoners built the Soviet Union's first industrial nuclear reactor in a secret town that is still not on maps. *Pravda* said one of its correspondents was the first journalist to visit the town, which it reports now houses a plant for reprocessing spent nuclear fuels, but it did not name the town or give its location. It said construction work on the reactor and the town was directed by physicist Igor Kurchatov, who guided the development of the first Soviet nuclear weapons, and by Lavrentii Beria, the head of the NKVD. Zhores Medvedev, a Soviet biologist now living in England, described the USSR's secret towns in his book *Soviet Science*, published in 1978.

Near-Accident Aboard Soviet Nuclear Icebreaker

An incorrect order nearly caused a major accident aboard a Soviet nuclear-powered icebreaker, but safety mechanisms and crew action averted a disaster, Rostislav Nikolsky told the newspaper *Vodnyi transport*. Nikolsky, who is head of the State Committee on Safety in the Nuclear Industry, said in an interview with the newspaper that an order to open a drain valve to a working reactor aboard the icebreaker "Rossiya" had triggered a four-minute emergency while the vessel was undergoing maintenance last November. "If there had been further crew errors, the reactor would have been left with no cooling system and the fuel could have melted," Nikolsky said. The same day, TASS reported that the crew of a nuclear-powered lighter anchored off Vladivostok had gone ashore to allay fears among the population that the vessel represented an ecological threat. Earlier this month, dockers in Vladivostok and Magadan had said they would refuse to handle the vessel, intended for year-round use in Arctic waters. TASS quoted the ship's captain, Vasilii Smirnov, as saying the lighter's reactor had an advanced, three-layered protection system that ruled out contamination. On March 7, *Sovetskaya Rossiya* said the nuclear-powered lighter had been refused permission to dock at Vladivostok.

More Evacuations Urged around Chernobyl'

Izvestia said the health authorities had recommended the evacuation of the inhabitants of five more Ukrainian villages located near the Chernobyl' nuclear plant. The newspaper added, however, that tests of people who were exposed to the largest amounts of radiation following the accident in 1986 had shown no increase in radiation-related disease. It said the evacuation of the five villages in Kiev Oblast had been recommended in keeping with new guidelines on the maximum amount of radiation people should receive.

Large Soviet Supply Convoy Arrives in Kabul

TASS correspondent Yurii Tyssovsky reported the arrival in Kabul of the first column of 235 heavy trucks from the Soviet Union, carrying food, fuel, and other supplies.

Another 1,200 trucks were expected to arrive during the day via the Salang Highway. Tyssovsky said the only obstacle the convoy encountered was snow avalanches, but he reported no serious problems with the *mujahidin*. According to Reuters, the Najibullah government is said to have struck a deal with the rebels to let the convoy pass safely.

Sunday, March 5 ─────────────────────────────────────

Moscow Crowd Calls for Ligachev's Resignation

At a rally held in Gorky Park on March 5 to honor the memory of the victims of Stalin's terror on the thirty-fifth anniversary of the dictator's death, literary critic Yurii Karyakin told some 2,500 people that "the demand for Ligachev's resignation has become a demand of all the people." Amid cries of "El'tsin is the son of the people! Shame on Ligachev!" bystanders applauded at each mention of El'tsin's name. The poet Evgenii Evtushenko, the editor of *Glasnost'*, Sergei Grigoryants, and Valeriya Novodvorskaya, a member of the Democratic Union, were among those present. Other topics that drew applause included challenges to the one-party system, criticism of Soviet aid to Romania and North Korea, demands for the restoration of Soviet citizenship to Aleksandr Solzhenitsyn, and calls for the publication of *The Gulag Archipelago*. The Russian nationalist organization "Pamyat'" also held a rally on March 5 and placed a wreath on Stalin's grave in Red Square. "Pamyat'" leader Igor Sychov was reported to have worn black jackboots and to have been protected by bodyguards wearing T-shirts emblazoned with slogans such as "Down with the occupation of Jewish Nazis" and "We want the decolonization of Russia" (*Baltimore Sun* and *The Washington Post*, March 6, 1989).

Latvian Institute Withdraws Support for Soviet Deputy

A former leader of the Latvian Communist Party, August Voss, who is a senior official in the Soviet parliament, has been stripped of his parliamentary nomination. *Moscow News* (No.10) said that staff and students at Riga Polytechnic, which proposed Voss for the Supreme Soviet in 1984, had exercised their formal right to withdraw the nomination. As the parliament will be dissolved shortly and will not sit again before elections on March 26, the move was clearly aimed at discrediting Voss, who is seen as a former agent of central control over Latvia.

Moscow News (No. 10) carried an interview with customs officials, who said that foreign newspapers containing cartoons of Kremlin leaders are barred from the Soviet Union. One of the customs officials also revealed that, if issues of Western periodicals on sale in the USSR contain articles "aimed at undermining the Soviet state system" or articles with "anti-Soviet content," they are withdrawn from sale. The deputy chief of the customs Legal Department, Aleksandr Khromtsov, told *Moscow News* that publications of "well-known anti-Soviet and anti-Communist organizations" may not be imported into the USSR. He cited as an example the London-based journal *Index on Censorship*.

Customs Officials Reveal Restrictions on Sale of Western Publications

Moscow News (No. 10) revealed soaring grain import figures and said the country's inability to feed itself was shameful. It was the first time a chart giving a clear picture of the Soviet Union's huge grain imports has appeared in the central Soviet press, although the figures are published annually in *Vneshnyaya torgovlya*, an official journal on foreign trade.

Newspaper Cries "Shame" over Grain Imports

Boris El'tsin has decided to run for election for Moscow's national-territorial seat, which represents roughly 7 million people. His opponent is Evgenii Brakov, director of the ZIL automobile factory. El'tsin's long absence from the national media was broken on March 2, when he appeared on the television program, "Good Evening, Moscow." Responding to a viewer's call, El'tsin said that, while Soviet society and the CPSU were not yet ready for a multiparty system, a debate on the subject should be started and "maybe after that, in a year or a year and a half, it could be discussed on a nationwide scale and concrete conclusions drawn." According to the *The Independent* (March 2, 1989), El'tsin's campaign staff has accused the Moscow authorities of blocking their efforts to obtain halls for some twenty-six election meetings they have planned. El'tsin has also pronounced himself ready to run against Gorbachev for the post of chairman of the new Supreme Soviet (*The Observer*, March 7, 1989).

El'tsin to Run for Election to New Parliament in Moscow

Soviet Foreign Minister Eduard Shevardnadze arrived in Vienna to attend talks on conventional arms reductions in Europe. The Soviet chief delegate in Vienna, Yurii Kashlev, commented extensively on the talks in *Pravda* (March 4), as did Soviet Foreign Ministry spokesman

Talks on Conventional Arms Cuts Open in Vienna

Gennadii Gerasimov in the "International Panorama" program on Moscow television on March 5. On March 7, British Foreign Secretary Sir Geoffrey Howe and Shevardnadze put forward their proposals. The NATO proposals are more far-reaching and detailed than those of the Warsaw Pact and would require the Warsaw Pact to make bigger cuts. Howe argued at a press conference that this was common sense, since the USSR and its allies still enjoy a vast numerical superiority in conventional forces. Shevardnadze did not propose specific limits for any category of arms; he merely suggested 10 to 15 percent cuts below the lowest levels of either side, to be carried out during the first phase of two to three years. He said there should also be cuts in combat aircraft, helicopters, and multiple rocket launchers—which NATO has steadfastly opposed—in order to achieve "a strictly defensive character" at the end of the third phase—that is, in four to six years. Shevardnadze further proposed separate negotiations for eliminating short-range nuclear missiles still stationed by both alliances in Europe (Western agencies, *TASS*, March 6).

Medical Cooperatives on Way Out?

The New York Times reported that the restrictions on cooperatives adopted at the end of last year have forced many medical cooperatives out of business. According to the newspaper, "more than 30 percent of the estimated 4,500 registered private medical practices" in the Soviet Union have closed; and in Moscow, "about 65 of 200 such enterprises" have shut down since January. Although medical cooperatives have been accused of charging too much and catering to the better-off members of Soviet society, polls have shown that the bulk of their patients are workers with modest incomes who are dissatisfied with the low level of care in state-run polyclinics.

New Regulations on Cooperatives Attacked

Ogonek (No. 8) carried an article by Mariya Salykova that sharply attacked the decree issued by the USSR Council of Ministers on December 29, 1988, seriously limiting the activities of cooperatives. The article convincingly argued that medical cooperatives (which were particularly severely regulated) provide services that cannot be found elsewhere in the Soviet Union without a six-month wait. The article documented the preferable conditions (private or semiprivate rooms and toilet facilities) common to cooperative clinics and the availability of certain kinds of treatment that are rare or nonexistent under the state medical system. The article also described some of the difficulties of cooperatives in the filmmaking industry. *Moscow News* (No. 9) likewise carried criticism of the decree on cooperatives. The newspaper carried a letter signed by a group of leading Soviet scholars, who complained about a provision of the decree banning the production of icons by cooperatives. On February 20, *Izvestia* published a letter from a group of jurists, strongly criticizing the decree on cooperatives.

Expert Says Armenian Quake Might Have Been Forecast

Sovetskaya Rossiya quoted Professor Gennadii Sobolev as saying the Soviet authorities had ignored important data that might have been used to forecast last year's major earthquake in Armenia. Radio Moscow, which summarized the article, quoted Sobolev as saying the USSR should build a nationwide earthquake warning system. He said such a system would cost only a fraction of the estimated damage done by the Armenian quake.

Readers Meet with *Moscow News* Editorial Board

Moscow News (No. 10) carried a report on a meeting in Moscow between the newspaper's editorial board and staff writers and its readers. Some remarkable statements were made during the meeting. One reader suggested that, after doing so much harm to the country, the CPSU "should either step aside or move over at the helm of power." In response, journalist Len Karpinsky suggested that the Party should be given a chance to correct its mistakes. Problems in the current election campaign, the situation of Boris El'tsin, and how journalists should make the best use of the opportunities offered by *glasnost* were among other topics raised by the newspaper's readers.

_____ *Monday, March 6*

New Head of State for Uzbekistan Finally Appointed

At an extraordinary session of Uzbekistan's Supreme Soviet, Mirzaolim Ibragimov, the republic's permanent representative in Moscow, was named to succeed Pulat Khabibullaev as chairman of the Presidium of the Uzbek Supreme Soviet. Having served for less than a year in this post, Khabibullaev was retired at the end of January after an investigation that confirmed allegations that he had abused his official position by performing favors for relatives of the disgraced former republican leaders Sharaf Rashidov, Inamzhon Usmankhodzhaev and Narmakhonmadi Khudaiberdyev (*TASS*, March 6).

Soviet Coal Miners End Five-Day-Old Strike

More than 100 coal miners ended a five-day-old strike after the authorities agreed to resolve problems in their pay system, AP quoted dissident sources as saying. Sergei Grigoryants said 115 miners in the city of Vorkuta had staged the strike. *Izvestia* reported on the strike on March 10. The newspaper said that the minister of the coal industry, Mikhail Shchadov, had gone down into the pit to talk to the miners but that they had rejected his proposals and had held out until their demands were met. It said mine managers deemed responsible for the strike had been punished.

***Pravda* Supports Giving National Language Official Status**

Pravda carried an article that supported giving official status to national republican languages. The author of the article, Moscow University Professor Maya Vsevolodova, said such a move was both logical and justified. Her article said the only way to solve the country's language problems was to introduce complete bilingualism. On March 9, *Novosti* carried a commentary saying that Russification was an "irrational" policy enforced in the Baltic republics and other parts of the USSR. The agency blamed the policy on central ministries and departments but not on the CPSU. It also insisted that Moscow should not be blamed for the construction of ecologically unsafe enterprises in the Baltic republics.

International Movement Meeting in Estonia

DPA said there were calls for transferring northeastern Estonia to the Russian Federation at a meeting on March 5 of Estonia's mostly Russian "Interdvizhenie" (International Movement). A resolution adopted at the meeting said that, if the ethnic situation in Estonia worsens, the northeastern part of the republic should be detached and made an autonomous district of the Leningrad Oblast. On March 7, Estonian Party First Secretary Vaino Valjas criticized "Interdvizhenie" on Estonian radio and television. He called it an extremist group with whom no cooperation was possible.

Every Country's Fate Is in Its Own Hands

Asked about "the Brezhnev Doctrine," Soviet Foreign Ministry spokesman Gennadii Gerasimov said the fate of every East European country "is in its own hands." Speaking on Hungarian television, Gerasimov said the Soviet Union now holds the opinion that every country must make its own decisions. He said "we can give advice, we can discuss issues, but the right to decide is not ours." "The Brezhnev Doctrine" allows Warsaw Pact countries to interfere in the internal affairs of any country in the bloc if processes there seem to threaten socialism in other countries. The same day, US Secretary of State James Baker urged the USSR to renounce the doctrine.

Soviet Oil Minister Vasilii Dinkov announced that the Soviet Union would cut oil production and exports during the first half of 1989 (*TASS*, March 6). The policy will be reviewed at mid-year and may be continued if conditions so dictate. This shift in Soviet policy is seen by some observers as an attempt to bolster OPEC's efforts to raise world oil prices. The USSR views a price of about 20 dollars a barrel as high enough to justify production. World oil prices are currently in the 16–19 dollars a barrel range. The Soviet move follows similar steps by a number of non-OPEC oil producers, including Mexico and Egypt. Other analysts in the West argue that the measures are less a political move in support of OPEC than one driven by economic realities, such as mature oil wells and the increasing costs of petroleum production, which combine to restrict production possibilities rather severely, especially in the USSR.

USSR to Cut Oil Output

An article in the *Los Angeles Times* reported that several candidates to the Congress of People's Deputies are running on "a women's platform," promising that they will try to secure better working conditions for women as well as the right for women to stay at home if they wish. The article also stated that a third of the members of the last Supreme Soviet were women but that women comprise only one-fifth of the candidates running in the country's territorial constituencies for the forthcoming elections. According to a TASS report of March 7, the chairman of the Central Electoral Commission stated that women comprise only 17 percent of the 2,901 candidates registered for 1,500 seats; however, seventy-five seats belonging to the Soviet Women's Committee as well as an undisclosed number of the other seats given to public organizations (750 seats in all) will go to women.

Some Candidates to Congress Running on Women's Platform

Tuesday, March 7

US Secretary of State James Baker and Soviet Foreign Minister Eduard Shevardnadze met in Vienna to discuss international issues (see *Pravda*, March 8). The meeting,

Meeting between Shevardnadze and Baker

which Baker said had taken place in "a very positive atmosphere," covered bilateral relations, human rights, and regional issues such as the Middle East, Central America, Afghanistan, and Angola. Referring to Shevardnadze's tour of the Middle East last week, Baker said that the United States had reservations about convening a big international conference before necessary preliminary work, such as bringing together the Palestinians and the Israelis, had been done.

Baker commented on the term "new thinking," which is used to describe current Soviet diplomacy, saying that the United States was eager to see action and not just rhetoric, particularly regarding Iran and Central America.

Asked about *perestroika*, Baker said the United States believed that *perestroika* was good for the Soviet Union and for the rest of the world and hoped that it would succeed, but its success, Baker added, depended on what the Soviet Union did and not on the West.

Concerning human rights in the USSR, Baker told the press that progress had been good until last December but that there had been little visible progress since (*Komsomol'skaya pravda*, March 8, carried a front-page interview with Shevardnadze.)

Gerasimov's Comments on Afghanistan

Izvestia criticized "the ultraconservative forces in Pakistan's administration" for launching an anti-Soviet campaign accusing Moscow of having systematically destroyed the infrastructure of Afghanistan. The same day Gerasimov condemned the interim government and its search for international recognition. He said that President Najibullah's government was the only legitimate one.

Medvedev Meets with Mass Media

CPSU Central Committee Secretary for Ideology Vadim Medvedev summoned representatives of the Soviet mass media for a meeting at the CPSU Central Committee. He criticized journalists for paying too much attention to electoral platforms that do not correspond with the official views of the Party, saying that the press should not "merely reproduce declarative though obviously impracticable promises of some candidates " but should comment on them and criticize them. Medvedev urged the Soviet press not just "to register events of the election campaign" but to proceed more aggressively in promoting the political platform of the Communist Party (*TASS*, March 7; *Pravda*, March 8).

More than fifty Armenian refugees were reported to have gathered at a government office in Moscow to demand a meeting with Prime Minister Nikolai Ryzhkov. Reuters said the Armenians were unhappy about plans to force them to return to Azerbaijan, which they left during ethnic riots there. The Armenians were quoted as saying they were afraid to go back and want to resettle in Moscow or elsewhere.

Armenians Reported Unhappy about Going Back to Azerbaijan

Nikolai Ryzhkov held a press conference in Moscow at which he said "the theoretical foundations" of *perestroika* had been worked out two years before Gorbachev came to power in 1985. Speaking to women journalists gathered in the Kremlin Palace on the eve of International Women's Day, Ryzhkov also revealed that he was frustrated at the slow pace of reforms. During the briefing, he made no promises of quick dividends from *perestroika*, saying 40 percent of the country's factory equipment needed to be replaced (*AP*, March 7). In a separate report on the press conference, Reuters quoted Ryzhkov as saying the USSR hoped to have half its military-oriented industry switched over to civilian production by 1991. The press conference was shown on Soviet television on March 8.

Ryzhkov Holds Press Conference

Vladimir Tikhonov, a full member of VASKhNIL (the Academy of Agricultural Sciences) and a critic of Stalin's collectivization, has blamed "utterly senseless" pricing for low grain yields and persistent food shortages. In an interview with *Komsomol'skaya pravda*, Tikhonov said the USSR, although the world's third largest grain producer, had to import large quantities of grain because much of its wheat production was fit only for fodder. Soviet farmers, offered identical prices whatever the quality of their grain, had no incentive to produce wheat suitable for making bread, Tikhonov said.

VASKhNIL Academician Denounces Grain Imports

Eduard Shevardnadze said it was unfortunate Iran had broken off diplomatic relations with Britain over the Rushdie affair. Iran announced the decision today (*UPI*, *AP*, March 7). *Moscow News* (No. 11) carried an article by fourteen Soviet intellectuals, calling on Ayatollah Khomeini to revoke his death threat against Rushdie. The article was signed by, among others, Academician Roald Sagdeev, songwriter Bulat Okudzhava, and poet Evgenii Evtushenko.

Shevardnadze on Rushdie

**Urban on NKVD
Responsibility for
Katyn Massacre**

Polish government spokesman Jerzy Urban said at a press conference in Warsaw that the Soviet NKVD was responsible for the massacre of more than 4,000 Polish officers in the Katyn forest near Smolensk during World War II (*The New York Times*, March 7). TASS reported on the press conference but avoided mentioning Urban's statement on NKVD responsibility for the massacre. On March 9, in an interview with *Trybuna Ludu*, the Polish cochairman of the joint historical commission investigating the Katyn massacre, Jarema Maciszewski, also said evidence showed that Stalin's NKVD shot the Polish officers.

Wednesday, March 8————————————————————————

**Protest of Women
Refuseniks**

Jewish women refuseniks began a fast to attract attention to the plight of those who have been denied permission to emigrate from the USSR. The women said they were worried that the international popularity of *perestroika* would divert attention from the fact that some people are still being refused emigration visas. About forty-five women are participating in a three-day fast in nine Soviet cities. Participants are also writing to Raisa Gorbachev and Barbara Bush, seeking their support (*AP*, March 8).

**USSR Accepts Jurisdiction of
World Court**

USSR Deputy Foreign Minister Anatolii Adamishin said the USSR will now accept the jurisdiction of the World Court in the Hague to resolve certain human-rights cases. Adamishin told the UN Commission on Human Rights in Geneva that Moscow had dropped its previous reservations about unresolved rights cases appearing before the court. Adamishin told the commission there was no longer anyone imprisoned in the USSR for his or her political or religious convictions (*Reuters, AP*, March 8).

***Izvestia* Says Soviet AIDS
Cases Rising Fast**

Izvestia said the number of AIDS cases in the Soviet Union was rising at an alarmingly fast rate, with the number of infected or ill people forecast to increase almost ten times next year. It quoted Minister of Health Evgenii Chazov as saying AIDS now poses as much of a danger to the USSR as nuclear weapons. On March 9, Novosti said the number of Soviet AIDS carriers had reached 146 by the beginning of 1989. *Sem'ya* (No. 9) published a chart showing venereal disease rates in the Soviet Union for the years 1985 through 1987.

In an interview with TASS, a member of the Central Auditing Commission, Georgii Barabashev, denied charges of vote-rigging in elections to the new Congress of People's Deputies. "The growing number of Communists among candidates is not the result of any quotas set from above," he said; "it is evidence of their authority among the broad masses of the people."

Soviet Electoral Official Denies Vote-Rigging

———*Thursday, March 9*

Reuters and AP said there had been protests in the Ukrainian city of Rovno to demand the return of a former Orthodox church to believers. Reuters quoted an unnamed local official as saying about 250 people had been gathering in front of the former church each day and that four women were staging a hunger strike on its steps. Dissident sources, however, said the number of people gathering outside the church was much higher. They put it at 3,000. Reuters said the church was turned into a museum of atheism in the early 1960s. It said the protests were prompted by the refusal of the local soviet last month to agree to hand back the church to believers.

Protesters in Ukraine Demand Return of Church

Residents of Nagorno-Karabakh have begun a fresh wave of strikes to back demands for secession from Azerbaijan, a local official said. The strikes, which began on March 6 in Stepanakert, were the first reported protest of its kind since the oblast was placed under the direct control of Moscow in January (*Reuters*, March 9).

New Strike in Nagorno-Karabakh to Back Secession Demands

The chief Soviet delegate to new arms talks in Vienna said the USSR was interested in early agreement at the negotiations. Oleg Grinevsky spoke to reporters at the opening of talks on confidence- and security-building measures. The talks will run parallel with another set of talks in Vienna on reducing conventional forces in Europe, which opens this afternoon. Grinevsky warned, however, that the West should not assume that new policies in the USSR would make it open to unreasonable NATO demands. He said the USSR could not be expected to make force reductions without NATO doing the same (*Reuters*, *AP*, March 9). Meanwhile, in Moscow Soviet Deputy Foreign Minister Viktor Karpov said NATO's modernization of its tactical nuclear forces would have a negative effect on the progress of con-

Grinevsky on Vienna Arms Talks

ventional arms talks. He said he favored parallel talks on tactical nuclear weapons (*Reuters, AP, TASS*, in English, March 10).

Gorbachev's Aide on Electoral Campaign

Soviet political scientist Georgii Shakhnazarov, an aide to Gorbachev, said district election meetings had rejected some Party leaders as candidates for the Congress of People's Deputies. Shakhnazarov said those officials should lose their Party posts to people who are trusted and supported by both Party members and non-Party people. Shakhnazarov made his comments in an interview with Novosti. Meanwhile, in *Moscow News* (No. 10) economic journalist Andrei Nuikin complained that officials on electoral commissions had used tricks to get Party candidates elected even if they do not get the required votes.

Ligachev Says Czechoslovak Agricultural Experience Will Help USSR

Politburo member Egor Ligachev, who is on a four-day visit to Czechoslovakia, said he had been sent there to gather ideas for improving Soviet agriculture. He told Radio Prague that Soviet citizens hoped the CPSU could come up with a program that would make "a considerable improvement" in food supplies in the very near future. Official figures show that Czechoslovakia met its harvest goals last year but that the supply of food to Czechoslovak consumers fell owing to problems with processing and distribution (*Radio Prague*, March 9). On March 10, Ligachev met with Czechoslovak Party chief Milos Jakes and discussed restructuring in the economy (*AP*, March 10). On March 11, before returning home from Prague, Ligachev praised the performance of Czechoslovak agriculture as an example of what the USSR was trying to achieve. He made the comments on Czechoslovak television. Ligachev was also interviewed on the Soviet television program "Vremya." In this interview he said he had seen in Czechoslovakia "once again that the foundation of solving food questions is the development, by every means, of sovkhozes and kolkhozes, together with the extensive development of relations of financial autonomy."

Friday, March 10

Zaikov Rejects Talk of Multiparty System

Politburo member and Moscow city Party First Secretary Lev Zaikov said the USSR did not need debates about a multiparty system. Zaikov complained at a meeting of Moscow's Party and public organizations that it had become "fashionable" to talk about a multiparty system, but he said democracy in countries with multiparty systems "still serves a definite class" (*TASS*, in English, March 10; *Pravda*, March 11). By contrast, former Moscow Party First Secretary Boris El'tsin has said the Soviet Union could be ready to consider a multiparty system as early as next year.

Children's Disease in Estonia

Twenty-four children in Sillamae in northeast Estonia are suffering from a disease that causes loss of hair. TASS said seventeen children had been taken to a children's hospital in Moscow. TASS said people were asking if the children were suffering from the same disease that broke out in Chernovtsy in Ukraine last year. More than 130 children there were affected by a disease that caused loss of hair and nervous disorders and was believed to have been caused by thallium poisoning. TASS said that the children in Sillamae, who all go to the same kindergarten, were being examined by a special commission but that it was too early to make a diagnosis.

USSR Denies Links to Greek Government Scandal

In Athens, the Soviet embassy denied claims that it had bribed the Greek government to get a contract worth 550 million dollars to build an alumina plant in Greece. The accusation was made by the wife of a fugitive Greek banker who allegedly accepted millions of dollars in payoff from the Soviet Union on behalf of Greek Premier Andreas Papandreou's Socialist government (*RFE/RL Special*, March 10).

New President Chosen in Kazakhstan

Makhtari Sagdiev was reported to have been appointed the new president of Kazakhstan. Sagdiev, who is sixty, was formerly first secretary of Kazakhstan's Kokchetav Oblast. TASS said Sagdiev was chosen at a meeting of the Presidium of the Kazakh Supreme Soviet in Alma-Ata. He replaces Zakash Kamalidenov, who left the post last December. TASS said Kamalidenov had requested that he be released from the post on health grounds. He was fifty-two.

Iran to Trade Natural Gas for Soviet Machinery

The USSR has agreed to provide Iran with machinery in exchange for natural gas. TASS quoted Deputy Minister of the Gas Industry Sergei Kashirov as saying the deal was proposed by Iran during his visit to Teheran. Kashirov was quoted as saying the agreement also calls for the

USSR to service Iranian gas pipelines. Iran sold large amounts of natural gas to the USSR during the years when Iran was ruled by the Shah, but the USSR canceled the purchases shortly after the current Islamic regime came to power in Teheran ten years ago and raised the price of the gas.

Consumer Societies on the Increase in USSR

Novosti said consumer societies were springing up all over the USSR to fight against low-quality products and to campaign against shortages. The agency carried an interview with Anatolii Konnabikh, who heads a group that helps to set up the societies and that is attached to the Central Council of Trade Unions. Konnabikh said that consumer societies had already held inaugural conferences in thirteen regions of the country and that conferences would be held in another sixty regions this month. If enough societies were formed, he said, there could be a national association of consumers. Konnabikh praised a draft law on the quality of goods and consumers' rights published in *Izvestia* in February, but he said the law's enactment would not solve all the problems.

Orthodox Church Candidate Wants to Help Afghan Veterans

Metropolitan Pitirim of Volokolamsk and Yur'ev, who is a candidate in the forthcoming elections to the new parliament, told a meeting of voters that he will try "to write acts of mercy into law" if elected. He also said he was very concerned about Afghan war veterans. As quoted by Novosti, Pitirim said he and a friend of his who was wounded in Afghanistan had begun a program to find land in the Volokolamsk district near Moscow that veterans could lease. He also said there were many abandoned houses in rural parishes. These, he said, could be fixed up and given to the relatives of soldiers killed in Afghanistan. Pitirim also said he wanted to establish a rehabilitation center for veterans.

Pravda Says Nationalities Plenum Must Consider Ethnic Germans

Pravda said the forthcoming Central Committee plenum on interethnic relations should discuss the plight of ethnic Germans in the Soviet Union. The newspaper said that ethnic Germans were among the first victims of Stalinism and that the failure to publicly rehabilitate them had damaged their cultural and national development. The newspaper did not take a stand on the issue of German autonomy, but it printed letters from readers calling for the restoration of some form of statehood for Soviet Germans.

The chairman of the Popular Front of Latvia, Dainis Ivans, said that his group was concerned about the activities of conservative Communists in Latvia. He told a news conference in Stockholm on March 9 that there was a rift in the Latvian Communist Party between conservatives and supporters of *glasnost'*. He said the popular front was concerned because conservatives were trying to increase control of the media and because the authorities had failed to criticize an anti-*glasnost'* demonstration in Riga last month. Ivans is visiting Sweden with a delegation from the Popular Front (*AP*, March 10).

Latvian Popular Front Worried about Conservatives

The US National Aeronautics and Space Administration said the United States and the Soviet Union had agreed to a satellite hookup to exchange medical data to help people injured in December's earthquake in Armenia. NASA said that, under the plan, US medical facilities would be linked with Soviet hospitals and rehabilitation centers via satellite. NASA will provide a compatible satellite ground terminal to be installed in Armenia. The link will begin operation this spring (*UPI*, March 10).

Satellite Hookup to Help Armenian Quake Victims

TASS criticized the United States for ordering the expulsion on March 9 of a Soviet diplomat accused of spying. The expulsion order concerned a military attaché at the Soviet embassy in Washington, Yurii Pakhtusov. US officials say Pakhtusov was arrested by FBI agents when he was caught receiving classified documents on US computer systems (*AP*, March 10). TASS ridiculed the US charges against Pakhtusov. At a regular press conference in Moscow, Foreign Ministry spokesman Gennadii Gerasimov did not announce any retaliatory Soviet action but termed Pakhtusov's expulsion "a gross provocation" (*AP*, March 10).

Soviet Reaction to Expulsion of Soviet Spy from US

A Soviet military expert, Andrei Kokoshin, provided the US Congress with some details of the USSR's planned unilateral military reductions. Kokoshin is a deputy director of the Institute of the USA and Canada in Moscow and is only the second Soviet citizen with official standing to appear before the Congress. He told the US House of Representatives Armed Services Committee that the unilateral reductions were an integral part of a process that would make Soviet military doctrine more defensive (*Reuters*, *AP*, March 10).

Soviet Expert Gives Details on Soviet Military Reductions

Izvestia Carries Article by Ulam

Izvestia carried a lengthy article by leading US sovietologist Adam Ulam on US-Soviet relations and American perceptions of the Soviet Union. In the introduction to the article, *Izvestia* praised Ulam's scholarship and complained that for a long time his books were simply dismissed in the Soviet Union as anti-Soviet.

Saturday, March 11 ─────────────────────────────

El'tsin Identifies Four Who Decided on Afghan Invasion

Boris El'tsin said the decision to send Soviet troops to Afghanistan was made by just four people: the then Party chief Leonid Brezhnev; Defense Minister Dmitrii Ustinov; Foreign Minister Andrei Gromyko; and Politburo ideologist Mikhail Suslov. El'tsin's revelations came in a speech before 800 people at the Kuntsevo Theater, where he was campaigning for election to the new Congress of People's Deputies (*AP*, March 11).

US Psychiatrists Complete Inspection

A group of psychiatrists from the United States completed an unprecedented two-week inspection of Soviet psychiatric facilities, including some still under control of the USSR Ministry of Internal Affairs. The US psychiatrists refused to discuss their findings on whether the facilities were still being used to hold political prisoners and said their report would be published after their return to the United States. One of the group's members, Ellen Mercer, said that, as long as Soviet psychiatric officials refused to fully acknowledge past psychiatric abuse, the system was still open to abuse. The leader of the group, Professor Loren Roth, said that the Soviet authorities had caused some difficulties but that the US psychiatrists were eventually satisfied with the inspections and interviews with patients (*Reuters, DPA*, March 11).

Independent Psychiatric Association Formed

A group of Soviet psychiatrists have formed a new independent psychiatric association to campaign for higher standards in Soviet psychiatry. The group ended a two-day founding meeting in Moscow on March 11. Reuters quoted the group's leader, psychiatrist Viktor Lanovoi, as saying members of the group were opposed to Soviet readmission to the World Psychiatric Association until it releases all political prisoners from psychiatric facilities and punishes those guilty of signing orders committing dissidents to mental asylums.

146

Izvestiya TsK KPSS (No. 2) printed a transcript of the controversial speech Boris El'tsin gave to the October, 1987, Central Committee plenum. A report on the transcript shows that, among other complaints, El'tsin said he feared a new personality cult was growing around Gorbachev. He also accused Egor Ligachev of slowing the pace of reform. Foreign Minister Eduard Shevardnadze is quoted as defending Ligachev, and Gorbachev is quoted as calling El'tsin "politically illiterate."

Transcript of El'tsin's Controversial Speech Published

Sunday, March 12

Unofficial demonstrations were staged by the Democratic Union in Moscow and Leningrad. As is always the case with actions staged by the Democratic Union, the demonstrations were broken up by the police. A spokesman for the Democratic Union said about forty people were detained in Moscow and sixty-five in Leningrad. While the Leningrad demonstration was described by Reuters as a campaign meeting to discuss the upcoming elections to the new parliament, the Moscow demonstration was aimed at pressing for an official reappraisal of the revolution of February, 1917. In the course of the current reevaluation of history in the USSR, the February Revolution, which toppled Tsar Nikolas II and briefly set up a Social Democratic government, has gradually started to receive a more positive assessment. Reuters reported that the demonstrators in Moscow raised the prerevolutionary red, white, and blue Russian flag (see also *AP*, March 12). On March 13, AP and Reuters reported that the editor of the journal *Glasnost'*, Sergei Grigoryants, had been jailed for ten days and fined 150 rubles for participating in the Moscow demonstration. On March 14, the head of the International Federation of Newspaper Publishers, Giovanni Giogannini, appealed to Gorbachev for Grigoryants' release. He said the harassment of a journalist trying to do his job was intolerable and made a mockery of *glasnost'* (*AP*, March 14).

Unofficial Demonstrations in Moscow and Leningrad

Moscow News (No. 11) reported that two Armenians had been convicted on charges of organizing disturbances at the airport in Erevan during last year's unrest over Nagorno-Karabakh. The report said Albrik Gevoyan and Artur Pogosyan had both been sentenced to eighteen months in prison by the Armenian Supreme Court. The report said they were accused of organizing actions that

Two Armenians Jailed for Airport Disturbances

resulted in the shutdown of Zvarnots Airport last July. The sentences were affirmed by the Armenian Supreme Court on March 23. TASS said the airport shutdown resulted in the loss of 633,000 rubles in state income and inconvenienced 18,000 passengers.

Moscow News on Soviet Edition of Cohen's *Bukharin*

Moscow News (No. 11) published a report about the publication in the USSR of the Russian translation of Stephen Cohen's book *Nikolai Bukharin: A Political Biography.* The newspaper said that "the profits raised from the publication will be forwarded to the Memorial Fund dedicated to those who perished in the Stalinist repressions."

Moscow News Criticizes Georgian Informal Activists

Moscow News (No. 11) attacked members of informal groups in Georgia who on February 25 organized meetings in Tbilisi, calling for the independence of Georgia. (February 25 is the anniversary of the establishment of Soviet power in Georgia in 1921.) The demonstrators also observed "a day of mourning" in memory of those who died during the revolution. *Moscow News* called the demonstrators' slogans "anti-Soviet."

People's Front Demonstration in Riga

Western agencies said tens of thousands of Latvians took part in a demonstration in Riga in support of the Popular Front of Latvia. The reports said the demonstration was peaceful and unopposed by the police. An AP report quoted activist Boris Sokolov as saying the demonstration was to counter criticism from "Interfront," a largely Russian organization. "Interfront" has protested against moves by the People's Front of Latvia to restore Latvian as the dominant language in the republic. According to Sokolov, the participants in the demonstration agreed to send a message to Gorbachev and the Latvian parliament favoring democratization (*AFP*, March 12).

El'tsin Appears in Televised Election Debate

Boris El'tsin appeared in a television debate with his opponent in the election campaign for the Congress of People's Deputies, Evgenii Brakov, the director of the ZIL automobile plant. The two men are contesting a seat representing Moscow in the March 26 elections. During the debates, El'tsin complained that some of Gorbachev's polices were "half-baked." He was replying to a question about why he was still calling for reductions in defense spending and the space program when cuts had already been announced (*Reuters*, March 12).

Soviet Jewish engineer Yulii Kosharovsky arrived in Israel from the USSR after waiting eighteen years for an exit visa. Prime Minister Yitzhak Shamir was among those at the airport to welcome Kosharovsky (*Reuters*, March 12).

Soviet Jewish Engineer Arrives in Israel

A number of policemen were reported to have been injured on March 12 during an unofficial demonstration in the Moldavian capital of Kishinev. Radio Kishinev reported on March 13 that the injuries occurred when demonstrators broke through a police cordon. The radio said thousands of people took part in the demonstration. It gave no reason for the protest, but it noted that one of the placards demanded official status for the Moldavian language. The protest is the latest in a series of unauthorized demonstrations in Kishinev this year.

Another Demonstration in Kishinev

—————————————————————— Monday, March 13

Abe Stolar, an American who has lived in the USSR since his youth, arrived in Vienna after finally being allowed to leave. Stolar was born in Chicago and brought to the USSR by his parents in the 1930s. He began his campaign to leave the USSR with his family thirteen years ago (*AP*, March 13).

Soviet American Finally Allowed to Leave USSR

A leader of Estonia's Popular Front, Edgar Savisaar, was quoted by UPI as saying Estonia will need foreign allies if it is to succeed in its aims. He was speaking in Stockholm. Savisaar said one of the front's aims was a market economy that would accept pluralistic ideas of property ownership. As quoted, Savisaar criticized the present centralized Soviet command structure. He said the front wants sovereignty for Estonia. He also expressed hope that Estonia will be represented by new, more progressive people in the Congress of People's Deputies.

Estonian Popular Front Leader Outlines Aims

A Soviet official has denied what he said were Western press reports that radioactive waste might be buried in Latvia. The denial came in an interview given to TASS by Boris Semenov, first deputy chairman of the State Committee for the Utilization of Nuclear Energy. Semenov said the reports that nuclear waste might be buried in Latvia under a planned contract with West Germany had also appeared in *Atmoda*, an independent weekly published by the Popular Front of Latvia. Semenov said no such

Official Says Radioactive Waste Not Being Buried in Latvia

contract existed. Semenov told TASS the USSR had processed and enriched uranium for Western firms since 1973. He said the radioactive substance was transported through Latvia via the port of Riga but that this posed no danger. A number of letters and articles alleging higher than normal radiation levels in Latvia have appeared in the Latvian press over the past year.

Vote Taken in Favor of Changing Name of Lithuanian Town

A report from the small Lithuanian town of Kapsukas said residents had voted to change the name of the town back to Mariyampol. The town's name was changed to Kapsukas in 1955. The information was obtained by RFE/RL from Teodora Kazdailiene, a representative of the Lithuanian branch of the International Society for Human Rights. According to Kazdailiene, in a referendum held on March 12, about 47,000 people voted for the change and between 6,000 and 9,000 people voted against it.

Soviet Union Floats Third Bond Issue

The Soviet Bank for Foreign Economic Relations (*Vneshekonombank*) announced it will float a DM 750 million, seven-year bond issue on March 29. The yield on the bonds will be 7 percent, with a 0.25 percent premium above purchase price. The bonds will be issued in denominations of DM 1,000 or 10,000. This is the third such Soviet bond issue and follows a DM 500 million, seven-year issue at 6.75 percent last July and a 100 million Swiss Franc issue in January, 1988 (*Reuters*, March 13).

Tuesday, March 14 _____

International AIDS Conference Opens in Moscow

An international conference on the disease AIDS opened in Moscow. More than 150 participants from Eastern and Western Europe are taking part in the conference, organized jointly by the World Health Organization and the Soviet government. Organizers say the main objective of the four-day conference is to determine how to organize surveillance of drug users as part of efforts to control the spread of the disease (*DPA, Radio Moscow*, March 14). On March 17, Deputy Minister of Health Aleksandr Kondrusev said there had been an increase in the number of AIDS cases in the USSR and that part of the reason was a serious lack of disposable syringes for injections. He told reporters that the USSR produced 30 million disposable syringes last year but needs many more. Kondrusev and President of the USSR Academy of Medical Sciences

Valentin Pokrovsky said three Soviet citizens and three foreigners had so far died of AIDS in the USSR, while another 554 people, mostly foreigners, are known carriers. The figures are the highest yet given. Pokrovsky said the reuse of dirty syringes at a hospital in Elista in the Kalmyk Autonomous Republic had infected forty-nine people with AIDS, forty-one of them children. Last month, only thirty-six victims were reported. Both he and Kondrusev complained that most people in the USSR were utterly indifferent to the dangers of AIDS.

Draft Plans Published for Giving Republics More Autonomy

Soviet newspapers published a draft of plans to give the republics more autonomy. TASS said the draft proposes that republics and regions be given more control over the production of consumer goods and of most public services. It said these include housing, health, environmental protection, culture, local transport, and tourism. Moscow, however, would retain control of defense, national transportation, energy, machine-building, and the chemical and pharmaceutical industries. TASS said the guidelines for switching the republics to a system of self-government and self-financing should be ready before the start of the next five-year plan period in 1991.

Publication of New Testament Interrupted

A reader wrote to *Izvestia* to complain that publication of the New Testament, which began in *V mire knig* at the end of last year, was discontinued in the January issue of the journal. The reader said a telephone inquiry met with the response that "publication was interrupted for reasons outside the journal's control."

RFE/RL Says Reports of Renewed Jamming Incorrect

RFE/RL said reports that the Soviet Union had resumed jamming Radio Liberty's Russian-language broadcasts were incorrect. RFE/RL engineers in Munich said they had not detected any jamming activity since intentional interference with transmissions into the Soviet Union stopped on November 29, 1988. A press release issued by RFE/RL was prompted by a Western news agency report quoting a dissident in Moscow as saying a Radio Liberty broadcast had been jammed on March 13.

Russians Stage Demonstration in Estonia

Tens of thousands of ethnic Russians staged a demonstration in Tallinn. Reports said the demonstrators denounced a law making Estonian the republic's official language and attacked the reinstatement of the old Estonian national flag. They also threatened strikes if the Estonian Party and government do not grant their demands within two weeks. Estimates of the size of the crowd ranged from 20,000 to 100,000. The police were reported to have put the figure at 50,000. No incidents were reported. The protest was organized by "Interdvizhenie," a group formed to protect the rights of ethnic Russians and other non-Estonians in Estonia (*Western agencies*, March 14).

Lithuania's "Sajudis" Says It Is Denied Election Materials

Members of Lithuania's "Sajudis" said the authorities are reneging on a promise to print election materials for "Sajudis"-backed candidates in upcoming elections to the USSR's Congress of People's Deputies. "Sajudis" backs candidates who favor more autonomy for the republic. "Sajudis" member Andrius Kubilius said a government printing plant that had promised to print the materials now says it cannot do this in time for the campaign. Angonita Rupsyte, also a "Sajudis" member, said that the Communist Party has had huge print runs of leaflets and posters (*RFE Lithuanian Service, Reuters*, March 14).

Ukraine Says Chernobyl' Cleanup Cost Billions of Rubles

A Ukrainian delegate told a United Nations meeting in Vienna that the accident at the Chernobyl' nuclear power plant has forced the Soviet Union to divert "billions of rubles" from urgent social projects. Addressing the Commission for Social Development, Yurii Kostenko also referred to other "major industrial accidents" in Ukraine but provided no details. Kostenko told the commission that the early 1980s had seen "a marked slow-down" in Ukraine's economic growth and that there was a tilt towards "a technocratic bias," which he said meant that industry was favored over social services. He said the resulting situation had had a negative impact on people (*RFE/RL Special*, March 16).

Soviet Union Says It Will Cut Northern Forces

Soviet Foreign Ministry spokesman Gennadii Gerasimov said the USSR will cut military personnel in the Leningrad district and in its Northern Fleet by 20,000. He said the reductions are part of an already announced plan to reduce the Soviet armed forces by half a million over the next two years. Gerasimov told reporters in Moscow that there are no large tank divisions left in the north European part of the Soviet Union. He said some 700 tanks were removed in 1986 and 1987. He also said two ballistic missile submarines had been withdrawn from the Soviet Baltic Fleet (*Reuters, AP, TASS*, in English, March 14).

Activists in the Ukrainian city of Lvov said a demonstration was held there on March 12 to protest against alleged attempts by the authorities to rig the outcome of upcoming elections to the Congress of People's Deputies. Members of the Ukrainian Helsinki Union said the protesters accused Ukrainian Party First Secretary Vladimir Shcherbitsky of fixing procedures to ensure candidates loyal to him would be elected (*RL Ukrainian Service*, March 14).

Reports of Demonstration in Lvov

Wednesday, March 15

A two-day plenary session of the CPSU Central Committee focusing on agricultural reforms began in Moscow. In a speech to the plenum, Mikhail Gorbachev told delegates that agriculture was the key problem facing the USSR. He said the USSR was incapable of feeding itself and was slipping further and further behind other developed countries in food output. He said food shortages were creating social tension and generating not only criticism but real discontent. He called for "a green revolution" to improve living standards. Gorbachev said further delay was inadmissible. He said reforms should include cutting back agricultural bureaucracy; widening the use of land leasing, individual enterprise, and family farming; and increasing reliance on market mechanisms and monetary incentives. He proposed replacing the Agroindustrial Committee, Gosagroprom, with a state commission on food supplies and procurements (*TASS*, in English, *AP, Reuters, UPI*, March 15). On March 16, the Central Committee approved a new farm program. Politburo member Egor Ligachev promised that it would improve the country's food supply. Ligachev said the program includes the leasing of state land to private farmers and allows their families to inherit the leases. He said the farm program also includes major improvements in rural life such as better schools and medical care. The points listed by Ligachev matched those proposed by Gorbachev. Ligachev told foreign journalists he has no disagreements with Gorbachev on basic issues, including the farm program. He said people who call him "a reactionary" in opposition to Gorbachev either do not understand the issues or hope for a split in the Soviet leadership (*Reuters, UPI, AFP, AP*, March 16). In his closing speech to the plenum, Gorbachev said the leadership must do better with farm reforms than with other programs or "we shall all be bankrupt before the people." Gorbachev said that

Central Committee Plenum on Agriculture

there were serious shortcomings in programs to improve health care and engineering and that the leadership cannot afford to deal with agriculture the same way. The speech was broadcast on Soviet television on March 17 (*Reuters, TASS, Central Television*, 1900, March 17). See also *Pravda*, March 16 and 17. For Gorbachev's speech, see *Pravda*, March 18.

Anatolii Strelyanyi on Soviet Agriculture

The French daily *Le Figaro* published an interview with the outspoken Soviet journalist and agricultural specialist Anatolii Strelyanyi. Strelyanyi said that reforming Soviet agriculture is primarily a political and ideological question, since it affects "the philosophical and religious base of [Soviet] power." Asked whether returning the land to the peasants is not impossible at present, Strelyanyi replied: "It's not impossible, it's indispensable. From the simplest *muzhik* to the regional [Party] secretary everybody knows why it [agriculture] works better in the West: because they have capitalism there." Strelyanyi was not optimistic about the future. He predicted that a food-rationing system would be created in the next few months and that the USSR would return to the conditions of the late 1920s, when there was "an explosion of hatred against 'speculators' and 'kulaks'."

Pravda Reveals Existence of Secret Radio Jamming Department

Pravda revealed the existence of a now disbanded secret radio jamming department in the USSR Ministry of Communications that it said had spent nearly fifty years refining the art of disrupting foreign broadcasts to the USSR. The article noted that the former jamming transmitters are now used to broadcast regional radio programs and that there have been proposals to develop information channels to keep people abreast of medical services, road conditions, and entertainment in their areas.

Ligachev Candidacy Produces Largest Number of Critical Letters

The chairman of the CPSU Electoral Commission, Valentin Koptyug, said the candidacy of Politburo member Egor Ligachev for a seat in the Congress of People's Deputies had generated twenty-five critical letters. That was the highest total of critical letters received by Party leaders listed in a TASS report. TASS said three letters had been received complaining about the candidacy of Gorbachev on the grounds that he had been a member of the leadership prior to *perestroika*. All 100 Party candidates, including Gorbachev and Ligachev, were elected to Party seats in the Congress at the Central Committee plenum today.

Several hundred Soviet citizens chanting "Shame, shame!" demonstrated outside the US embassy in Moscow to protest against being refused admission to the United States as political refugees. The group, including many Armenians, said they had been informed they did not qualify for a refugee program under which Washington pays the airfare and other expenses for immigrants fleeing political persecution at home. They said they had been told they could go to the United States under the "Parole" program, which means they must have an affidavit from an American promising to pay their way and guarantee their support in the United States. One of the protesters said they had given up jobs, apartments, and residence permits in order to get Soviet exit visas and now had nowhere to go (*Reuters*, March 15).

Citizens Protest over Denial of US Refugee Status

An initiative group seeking to form a Popular Front in Azerbaijan is reported to have applied for official registration. A member of the group, E'tibar Mamedov, told RFE/RL by telephone that the group had sent a letter requesting registration to the Azerbaijan Supreme Soviet two days ago. Mamedov said the group would hold a congress later this month to set up a popular front in Azerbaijan. He said the group was made up of about twenty-five people, mainly scholars and journalists (*Azerbaijani Service*, March 15).

Popular Front Initiative Group Formed in Azerbaijan

The Soviet Union said it was expelling a US diplomat in retaliation for last week's expulsion of a Soviet military attaché from the United States for allegedly trying to buy computer secrets. Soviet Foreign Ministry spokesman Gennadii Gerasimov said the expulsion of the US assistant military attaché was "in reply to the provocation against Soviet diplomacy." He said the US diplomat had taken pictures of military facilities and tried to penetrate a closed area (*UPI, TASS*, in Russian, March 15). The tit-for-tat expulsions continued on March 23, with the expulsion of a member of the Soviet Trade Organization in New York (*RFE/RL Special*, March 23).

USSR Retaliates for Expulsion of Diplomat from US

The new Grand Mufti of Kazakhstan and Central Asia, Mukhammadsadyk Mamayusupov, commented on the dispute over Salman Rushdie's novel *The Satanic Verses*. He said the British writer's book should be judged in a forum where the author has a right to defend himself. In an interview with AP, Mamayusupov said the Muslims of

New Mufti Comments on Rushdie Affair

the Soviet Union "are also displeased that Rushdie has published a novel in which Islam is insulted." But he added: "I don't know who Rushdie is, I don't know in what circumstances he was writing. Therefore, I can't judge him." Meanwhile, commentator Aleksandr Bovin, writing in *Moscow News* (No. 12), denounced the Soviet leadership's refusal to condemn Ayatollah Khomeini's death threat against Rushdie, saying Moscow had placed politics above moral considerations.

Thursday, March 16 ————————————————————————————

Commission to Examine Allegations against El'tsin

Politburo member Vadim Medvedev said a Party commission will investigate allegations that former Moscow Party First Secretary Boris El'tsin has deviated from the Party line. Medvedev told a Moscow press conference that, during the plenum that ended today, El'tsin rejected criticism of his stand on several issues. Medvedev said El'tsin had denied advocating a multiparty system in the Soviet Union and said he had merely urged public discussion of the idea. El'tsin is still a member of the Central Committee although he lost his other Party posts in the fall of 1987. He is now seeking a seat representing Moscow in the Congress of People's Deputies (*TASS, Radio Moscow-2*, 2030, *Reuters, AFP*, March 16).

Landslides and Avalanches Hit Caucasus

Soviet television said several areas of the Georgian republic had again been hit by landslides, avalanches, and mudslides. It said the situation was particularly bad in the Adzhar-Imeret mountain regions, where many homes had been destroyed. The report said there had been casualties but gave no details. Radio Moscow said landslides and avalanches had also hit the neighboring Chechen-Ingush Autonomous Republic, damaging homes, roads, and power supplies, but causing no casualties (*Central Television, Radio Moscow-1*, 1300, March 16).

Vorontsov Says Pakistani Forces Helping to Take Jalalabad

The Soviet ambassador to Afghanistan Yulii Vorontsov said Pakistani military forces are helping the Afghan resistance in its attempt to seize the eastern Afghan city of Jalalabad. Vorontsov told a Kabul news conference that "it looks as if it is the beginning of the Pakistani-Afghan war." He said this was a grave situation, and he asked the international community to pay attention to it. Pakistan has previously denied it has troops in Afghanistan. The same day Western correspondents in Kabul said the Soviet Union had resumed its airlift to the Afghan capital. Journalists said at least twenty Soviet transport planes carrying arms had landed on March 15. Vorontsov acknowledged during the press conference that Moscow was supplying weapons to the Afghan government (*Reuters, AP, AFP*, March 16).

Soviet Writer Says He Is Fearful for Future of Independent Press

Soviet writer Lev Timofeev told the US Commission on Security and Cooperation in Europe that he was fearful for the future of the independent press in the Soviet Union. Timofeev, editor of the unofficial journal *Referendum*, spoke by telephone from Moscow with members of the commission holding a hearing in Washington. Timofeev said he was concerned that a draft Soviet press law would leave the independent press without recognition or even outlawed. He said "not a single independent publication has been registered or officially recognized." He said the government was maintaining a monopoly on the printed word (*RFE/RL Special*, March 17).

Soviet Minister Depicted in Satirical Photo Montage

For the first time in the Soviet Union a Soviet minister has been made the subject of a satirical photo montage. The satirical magazine *Krokodil* carried a picture of the minister for water resources, Nikolai Vasil'ev, sitting at his desk faced by a huge mechanical digger against a background of a landscape laid bare by construction workers. The picture was accompanied by a caption saying "Not only have we drained millions of hectares of land, we have irrigated them as well." Until now, caricatures of government officials have been forbidden in the Soviet Union and the import of foreign newspapers containing cartoons of Soviet ministers not permitted (*AFP*, March 16).

Friday, March 17

Ordzhonikidze Hijackers Get Long Prison Terms

Four men from the northern Caucasus received long prison terms for hijacking a busload of schoolchildren last December 1 and using them as hostages in order to obtain money and a flight to Israel. The leader of the gang received fifteen years in prison. The other three received fourteen years each. An accomplice who did not take part in the actual hijacking received a three-year sentence. The men were taken into custody upon arrival in Israel and handed back to the Soviet authorities (*Reuters, AFP, TASS*, March 17).

Controls Established for Soviet Foreign Trade

TASS said all Soviet enterprises that intend to engage in foreign trade must be registered with the government. It said this includes cooperatives and joint ventures as well as individual Soviet factories. The agency said the Ministry for Foreign Economic Relations has been authorized to regulate exports and imports of specific goods and services as well as trading with specific countries or groups of countries. It said licensing of quotas will be enforced "whenever required by the balance of payments and other economic and political conditions." TASS said the purpose of the new rules is "to streamline foreign economic activity."

Lithuanian Government Permits Registration of "Sajudis"

TASS reported that the Council of Ministers of Lithuania had decided to permit the registration of "Sajudis," the unofficial Lithuanian Restructuring Movement. TASS said the "Sajudis" charter supports *perestroika* as initiated by the Soviet Party leadership "on the basis of democracy and humanism." "Sajudis" is the second popular front movement in the Baltic States to be officially registered after the Estonian Popular Front. The Popular Front of Latvia was registered, but the move was later revoked.

Second Reactor at Armenian Nuclear Power Plant Shut Down

A Soviet nuclear power official said the shutting down of the Armenian nuclear power plant had been completed. One of the plant's two reactors was shut down permanently last month, and TASS quoted Erik Pozdyshev of the Ministry of Atomic Power as saying the second reactor had been shut down on schedule today. The decision to shut down the plant came in response to popular appeals after the earthquake in Armenia in December.

Komsomol and Cultural Fund Elect Deputies

The Komsomol elected seventy-five deputies to the new Congress of People's Deputies. TASS said the seventy-five were elected by secret ballot from ninety-eight candidates at a plenum of the Komsomol Central Committee. TASS said the Soviet Cultural Fund also elected its five deputies today. They are: fund chairman Dmitrii Likhachev, Orthodox Metropolitan Pitirim, poetess Gulrukhsor Safieva, artist Mikhail Savitsky, and Soviet Cultural Fund member Ivan Samoilov.

TASS said Soviet scientists have tested a new, low-toxic defoliant for use by Soviet cotton farmers. It said that, whereas until recently farmers were using as much as 24 kilograms of toxic defoliant per hectare of cotton to make the leaves drop off before harvesting, 500 grams of the new substance will be enough. TASS said this considerably reduces the risk of poisoning and environmental damage. The USSR banned the use of a dangerous defoliant, Butifos, in 1987, but reports last year said it was still being used because nontoxic defoliants were in short supply.

TASS Says Low Toxic Defoliant Created for Cotton Fields

Saturday, March 18

Boris El'tsin told a crowd of at least 10,000 people at a Moscow election rally that he will fight to make the Communist Party subject to control by the people. Reuters quoted El'tsin as saying he had come to realize how far removed the Party apparatus is from the people. It was also reported that El'tsin's supporters had decided to send a letter to Mikhail Gorbachev, saying allegations that El'tsin had deviated from the Party line were fabricated. A commentator for the Novosti press agency, Mikhail Poltoranin, who was chief editor of *Moskovskaya pravda* at the time when El'tsin was Moscow Party boss and has remained close to him ever since, suggested on the television program "Vzglyad" on March 17 that there was a campaign to undermine El'tsin's candidacy. The directors of Gosteleradio subsequently issued an apology to "those viewers who might have been offended by the unworthy comments made on 'Vzglyad'." On March 19, several thousand people demonstrated in central Moscow in support of El'tsin and his campaign for election to the new parliament. The police did not attempt to stop the crowd (*Reuters*, March 19). The demonstrations in support of El'tsin continued in Moscow from March 20 to 22. The demonstrators shouted slogans against Egor Ligachev and also criticized bureaucracy and the privileges enjoyed by Party members. Addressing the demonstrators, El'tsin complained that Party officials were trying to block his election, and he criticized *Moskovskaya pravda* for being biased against him. (*Moskovskaya pravda* criticized El'tsin on March 19.) On March 21, *Moskovskaya pravda* published El'tsin's election platform but omitted two key points: his views on the idea of a multiparty system and his call for the CPSU to be subject to public control. *Moscow News* (No. 12) carried an article by correspondent

El'tsin Continues to Campaign for Election

Vitalii Tret'yakov who said that some anonymous leaflets had been distributed that sought to disgrace El'tsin and prevent his election to the new parliament.

Priests Elected to Parliament for First Time

Two representatives of the Russian Orthodox Church have been elected to the Congress of People's Deputies. Metropolitan Pitirim will represent the Soviet Cultural Fund (as will its chairman, Academician Dmitrii Likhachev). In addition, Metropolitan Aleksei of Leningrad and Novgorod has been elected to represent the Soviet Charity Fund, whose members unanimously elected five deputies from fifteen candidates. This is the first time that members of the clergy have won seats in the Soviet parliament (*TASS*, March 17 and 18).

Sunday, March 19 ————————————————————————————————————

CPSU Deputies' Mandate Published

According to the election law, deputies to the Congress of People's Deputies are to be given mandates by their constituents. These mandates are legally binding, and deputies who do not fulfill them will be subject to recall. The CPSU deputies have been given an ambitious mandate that includes "enhancing the authority of the CPSU, preventing the adoption of laws that could entail breaches of the principle of social justice, and strengthening the unity of the USSR." They have also been charged with adopting laws that will eradicate corruption and increase the responsibility of parents for their children's upbringing and with introducing measures to aid women and to improve medical services, consumer services, and education. Deputies should "take a careful approach to working out price formation policy, with priority being given to consumers' interests." They are to formulate a law on defense and be guided by the concept of reasonable sufficiency when determining defense expenditures (*TASS*, March 19).

Pravda Publishes Tally of Votes for CPSU Deputies

Pravda published the results of the Central Committee election held on March 15. Although all 100 of the candidates received more than the minimum number of votes necessary for election, they were not all elected unanimously. Of the plenum's participants, 641 were eligible to vote; thirty-five (mostly ministerial and defense personnel) were not. Twelve votes were cast against Mikhail Gorbachev, and seventy-eight—the highest number of negative votes received by any candidate—were cast against Egor Ligachev. Aleksandr Yakovlev received fifty-nine "no" votes, while the chief editor of *Pravda*, Viktor Afanas'ev, received thirty-eight.

In an interview in the latest issue of *Ogonek*, Army General Valentin Varennikov, who was in recent years a senior representative for the USSR Ministry of Defense in Kabul, criticized former Defense Minister Dmitrii Ustinov for deciding in favor of the intervention in Afghanistan in 1979 against the advice of top military officials. Varennikov says that the former chief of general staff, Marshal Nikolai Ogarkov, and his deputy, Marshal Sergei Akhromeev, opposed Ustinov because they were pessimistic about Soviet prospects in Afghanistan. Only last week, former Moscow Party boss Boris El'tsin claimed that the decision to intervene in Afghanistan was made by Ustinov, Brezhnev, Suslov, and Gromyko without consulting their colleagues in the Politburo. KGB defectors are believed to have claimed that the then KGB boss Andropov and Prime Minister Kosygin vigorously opposed the decision to send troops to Afghanistan on the grounds that there was little enthusiasm for a Marxist revolution among the Afghan population.

Article Says General Staff Opposed Afghan Intervention

In an interview with *Komsomol'skaya pravda*, historian Roy Medvedev said that, apart from several attacks on Lenin and one assassination attempt on Brezhnev, there have been no attempts on the lives of Soviet leaders. Specifically, Medvedev denied that the wife of the disgraced minister of internal affairs, Nikolai Shchelokov, had tried to shoot Andropov. His statement also implicitly rejected rumors of assassination attempts on Gorbachev and his wife, which have surfaced quite frequently over the past few years.

Assassination Rumors Denied

Radio Erevan said the Armenian Council of Ministers had declared a holiday on April 24 to commemorate the 1915 massacre of tens of thousands of Armenians in Turkey. The move followed legislation passed in the republic in November formally condemning "the 1915 genocide of the Armenians in Ottoman Turkey." Calls for official commemoration of the day followed an outbreak of ethnic unrest between Armenians and Azerbaijanis over the Nagorno-Karabakh issue last year (*Reuters*, March 19).

Armenia to Commemorate 1915 Armenian Massacre

Congress of Consumer Cooperatives Opens

The Twelfth National Congress of Consumer Cooperatives opened in Moscow. Radio Moscow reported that Gorbachev attended this morning's session of the three-day congress, along with Ryzhkov, Ligachev, and other Kremlin leaders. Nikonov was absent. See, *Pravda* and *Izvestia*, March 21 and 22.

Soviet Journal on Rehabilitation of Mensheviks

Sovetskaya bibliografiya (No. 1) confirmed that another case fabricated by Stalin is to be reviewed. The journal said that people sentenced in March, 1931, for alleged membership in the so-called "Union Bureau of the Mensheviks" are to be rehabilitated. The journal published a political biography of Vladimir Groman, the leading figure sentenced at the Menshevik trial, together with a list of his publications.

***Pravda* Publishes Map of Chernobyl' Radioactivity**

Pravda published a map showing areas still contaminated as a result of the Chernobyl' nuclear disaster of 1986. In addition to the Chernobyl' area itself, the map showed contamination in other parts of Ukraine, in Belorussia, and in the Bryansk area of the RSFSR; it also showed radiation on the Kola peninsula in the far north, in the southern Caucasus, and along the southern coast of the Gulf of Finland.

Preparatory Meeting for Central Committee Plenum on Ethnic Relations

A meeting was held in the Central Committee as part of preparations for a Central Committee plenum on interethnic relations (*TASS*, March 21, *Pravda*, March 22). The meeting was attended by officials of the Presidium of the USSR Supreme Soviet, as well as officials of Union-republican supreme soviets and the soviets of various autonomous territories, legal experts, and Party officials from a number of republics and autonomous territories. The discussions covered a wide range of topics including delimiting the powers of the USSR and Union republics, strengthening the legal status of Autonomous republics, regulating the development and use of languages, legislation on citizenship, the national rights of people who live outside their national territory or who do not have one, and the new functions of the Council of Nationalities of the USSR Supreme Soviet. The TASS report gave no details of any of the proposals made. It did, however, make plain Moscow's strong reservations about plans (notably in the Baltic republics) to introduce some form of restrictive republican citizenship, stating that "the unity of rights and obligations of all citizens of the USSR regardless of their place of residence on the territory of the USSR should be strictly observed and guaranteed." It also confirmed that Gorbachev's call last year for a strengthening of the law against kindling ethnic hostility had not been forgotten.

Gorbachev and Yakovlev in Rome

Mikhail Gorbachev said it had been a long time since Soviet society had lived through such a political and intellectual upsurge as the one brought about by *perestroika*. Gorbachev spoke in a videotaped message to the Italian Communist Party Congress in Rome. The Soviet leader said this was not just a spontaneous explosion of a feeling of freedom after so many years of stagnation and restrictions. He said it was also the recognition of responsiblity for renewal of the country, for a new quality of socialism. Gorbachev said *perestroika* marked the rebirth of the original values of the October Revolution (*Reuters*, March 20 and *Pravda*, March 21, carried the text of Gorbachev's message). The congress of the Italian Communist Party was attended by Politburo member Aleksandr Yakovlev. On March 20, Yakovlev spoke in Rome before members of the Italian Parliament and representatives of the press. In his speech he called for the abolition of "the iron curtain" that has divided Europe for the past forty years (*TASS*, March 20; *Pravda*, March 21). Yakovlev praised the concept of "a common European home" and said that world politics should be guided by common European political and cultural traditions and values.

Zhdanov's Name Removed from Town, Raion in Azerbaijan

The name of Stalin's associate Andrei Zhdanov has been removed from a town and a raion in Azerbaijan. Radio Baku said the Presidium of the Supreme Soviet of Azerbaijan had ordered the changes "taking into consideration the wishes of the population." It said both the town of Zhdanov and the raion had been renamed Deilagan (*Radio Baku*, 0304, March 19).

Rally Calls for Official Use of Uzbek Language

Reports from Tashkent said there had been a demonstration in the city on March 19 in support of the use of Uzbek as a state language (*Reuters*, *AP*, March 20). At least 1,000 people, most of them young, took part. Uzbekistan's new president Mirzaolim Ibragimov told them that possibilities for the official use of Uzbek were being investigated.

Candidate Says He Wants to Break Culture Ministry Monopoly

The chairman of the Union of Soviet Composers said the union wanted to "break the monopoly" on music held by the Ministry of Culture. Tikhon Khrennikov told TASS the ministry had been "absolutely impotent" in providing musical "enlightenment" for the Soviet people. Khrennikov is one of the union's ten deputies elected to the new Congress. TASS quoted him as saying he considered it his public duty to "free professional musicians and music lovers from the dictates of bureaucrats." In fact, Khrennikov is himself regarded by many members of the union as a bureaucrat who made his career under Stalin. In the course of the *glasnost'* campaign calls have been made for the removal of Khrennikov from the post of chairman of the union.

Preferential Treatment for Official Cars Abolished

Radio Moscow reported that the traffic police have abolished rules covering preferential treatment for official vehicles in Moscow. It has been standard practice for many years to put special sound and light signals on vehicles used by senior ministerial officials and the staff of other government bodies and Party offices. Radio Moscow reported that from now on such privileges would be granted only to ambulances, firefighting vehicles, and other emergency services.

USSR and Japan Fail to Reach Agreement on Peace Treaty

Reports said two days of Soviet-Japanese consultations had failed to bring the two countries closer to a peace treaty formally ending World War II hostilities. The Soviet and Japanese deputy foreign ministers, Igor Rogachev and Takakazu Kuriyama, headed the talks. Japan insists that there can be no peace treaty until Moscow hands back the Kurile islands that the Soviet Union has occupied since the end of World War II. TASS said that during the Tokyo consultations both sides had restated their wish to improve bilateral ties, but the agency made no direct reference to the territorial dispute (*Reuters*, March 20).

Elections in Komsomol

On March 20, Soviet television showed the election of the Komsomol's seventy-five nominees for the Congress of People's Deputies, which took place on March 17. One interesting feature was that candidates were allowed for the first time to address the Komsomol Central Committee in their own languages; one young Uzbek woman was shown doing so.

Andrei Sakharov and other Soviet academics, including Politburo member Vadim Medvedev, were shown on Soviet television on March 20 as they cast their votes for the Academy of Sciences' nominees for the Congress of People's Deputies. Sakharov addressed the academy meeting on March 20 and 21, criticizing its Presidium for the undemocratic procedure that was used in January for selecting candidates for election to the congress. (On that occasion, Sakharov, Zaslavskaya, Sagdeev, and other reform-minded academicians were rejected by the academy's Presidium as election candidates.) On March 21, only eight of the academy's twenty-three nominees received the required number of votes. They are lawyer Sergei Alekseev; physicists Zhores Alferov, Andrei Gapanov-Grekhov, Yuri Osipyan, and Karl Rebane; chemist Oleg Nefedov, radio-physicist Nikolai Karlov; and mathematician Vladimir Platonov (*TASS*, March 21). On March 22, Andrei Sakharov, Roald Sagdeev, Abel Aganbegyan, Nikolai Shmelev, and other *perestroika* advocates were proposed by the academy for seats in the Congress of People's Deputies (*AFP*, March 22). These proposals were not formal nominations; such nominations cannot be made for two weeks. In accordance with an earlier decision of the Central Electoral Commission, vacant seats must be filled no sooner than two weeks and no later than two months after the first election.

Academy of Sciences Elects Parliamentary Delegates

Argumenty i fakty (No. 9) published an interview with an historian, Major Aleksandr Kolesnikov, on the fate of General Andrei Vlasov, who in 1942 defected to the Germans and later headed the Nazi-sponsored Russian Liberation Army. Following the traditional Soviet line on Vlasov, Kolesnikov condemned the general as a traitor, but he added an unorthodox explanation for Vlasov's action that seems to suggest a change in the standard interpretation of the Vlasov case. Kolesnikov said the main thing that pushed Vlasov to defect was the poor performance of the Second Shock Army, which was under Vlasov's command. According to Kolesnikov, Vlasov was afraid Stalin would have him executed for the failures of his army. Condemning Stalin's policy of executing military commanders for unsuccessful operations, Kolesnikov argued that Vlasov was also, in a way, a victim of Stalinism; however, Kolesnikov rejected suggestions that, even before his defection, Vlasov was an active opponent

Argumenty i fakty on General Vlasov

of Stalinism. Kolesnikov said the available documentary evidence shows that Vlasov supported Stalin's policies until they began to affect him personally. Moreover, he had been a member of a garrison military tribunal that sentenced many innocent people to death.

Elections at Various Organizations

The election of deputies from the Unions of Soviet Writers, Filmmakers, and Journalists, from the Academy of Agricultural Sciences (VASKhNIL), and from the Soviet Red Cross, among others, also took place today. Some of the more prominent deputies to the Congress include the head of the Central Committee's International Department, Valentin Falin, cosmonaut Valentina Tereshkova; the recently appointed director of TASS, Leonid Kravchenko; El'tsin-associate Mikhail Poltoranin; and the chief of Lithuania's State Commission for Television and Radio, Domas Sniukas. The Writers' Union chose Viktor Astaf'ev, Valentin Rasputin, Oles Honchar, Vasyl Bykov, and writers from Moldavia, Lithuania, Uzbekistan, and Georgia. Sergei Zalygin, editor of *Novyi mir*, and Yurii Voronov, editor of *Literaturnaya gazeta*, were also elected (*TASS*, March 21).

Ammonia Explosion in Lithuania

Izvestia carried a report on an ammonia explosion in Lithuania on March 20. It said the explosion at a plant in Ionava had killed four people and injured fifty. The newspaper said about 30,000 people were evacuated. The newspaper said the plant where the explosion occurred had often been mentioned as an environmental hazard. On March 22, the death toll in the explosion in the ammonia plant was put at seven (*Radio Moscow*, March 22).

RL Interviews Soviet Editor Who Published Solzhenitsyn

Radio Liberty interviewed the chief editor of the Soviet journal *Vek XX i mir*, who in February published Aleksandr Solzhenitsyn's essay *Zhit' ne po lzhi* (Live Not By Lies). (Solzhenitsyn's wife Natalya recently made a statement saying that *Vek XX i mir* had a limited circulation and therefore not enough people would be able to read Solzhenitsyn's essay.) In the interview with Radio Liberty, the journal's chief editor Anatolii Belyaev said his journal had not submitted the Solzhenitsyn essay to Glavlit, the main Soviet censorship body, before publication. Belyaev called Solzhenitsyn "the greatest Russian writer of today." He said there was no sense in banning the publication of his works in the USSR.

Russian Orthodox believers were reported to have demonstrated recently in the city of Ivanovo for the return of a church to their community. Dissident sources in Moscow told RFE/RL by telephone on March 22 that some 300 people took part in the demonstration on March 19.

Orthodox Believers Demonstrate for Return of Church

Izvestia complained about the secrecy surrounding the costs of Soviet space missions. It said the figures should be published. The newspaper quoted election candidates as calling for a reduction in the cost of space programs. *Izvestia* said that this had upset many space specialists but that public appeals to bring secret subjects into the open could only be welcomed.

***Izvestia* Criticizes Secrecy around Space Mission Costs**

The Soviet Union welcomed the European Community's decision clearing the way for a return of ambassadors from EC member-states to Iran. A Soviet Foreign Ministry spokesman said Moscow viewed the decision as a positive step towards easing the tensions that arose over Salman Rushdie's book *The Satanic Verses*. The spokesman said the decision is in line with Soviet efforts made at meetings in Teheran and Vienna to help resolve the dispute (*TASS*, March 22).

USSR Welcomes EC Decision in Rushdie Affair

Antinuclear activists in Kazakhstan have set up a group seeking to end nuclear weapons testing and production there. TASS said poet and Supreme Soviet deputy Olzhas Suleimenov had been elected chairman of the group, which calls itself "Nevada," after the state where US nuclear tests are conducted. The organization wants the closure of nuclear test sites in the area around Semipalatinsk in northeast Kazakhstan. TASS said the group also wants to phase out plants that produce nuclear materials for the military and to conduct public inspections of dump sites for radioactive waste.

Group Wants End to Nuclear Tests in Kazakhstan

Pravda sharply criticized the political situation in Estonia. The newspaper said some groups had exploited the development of democratization and *glasnost'* and were saying whatever they liked. The article said the Estonian Communist Party had taken a passive stance in this

***Pravda* Criticizes Political Situation in Estonia**

167

situation. The newspaper criticized the Estonian Popular Front by name, saying its leaders were "constantly getting carried away."

Arbatov Fails in Bid for Parliamentary Seat

Georgii Arbatov, for almost two decades Moscow's top specialist on the United States and director of the Institute of the USA and Canada, failed in his bid to win a seat in the new Soviet parliament. TASS said Arbatov's defeat in a secret vote to choose five delegates from the Soviet Peace Committee might have been due to an open letter criticizing him for dictatorial methods. The letter, which, according to TASS, was signed by a group of Moscow scientists, criticized Arbatov's "power and pressure methods" in running the USA and Canada Institute.

Shevardnadze on Foreign Policy

Eduard Shevardnadze urged major changes in the way the USSR makes foreign policy decisions. *Izvestia* quoted Shevardnadze as saying that foreign policy must be explained to the people. He predicted that in the future open hearings in the Supreme Soviet, referendums, and public opinion polls would be considered before fundamental foreign policy decisions were made. He said that if experts had been consulted over the Soviet intervention in Afghanistan, they would have told the leadership that a military solution in that country was impossible.

Latvian Journal Publishes Bunin's *Okayannye dni*

The Latvian literary weekly *Daugava* began to serialize in its March issue Ivan Bunin's book *Okayannye dni* (The Accursed Days). The book is one of the most bitter attacks on the Bolsheviks and their postrevolutionary policies.

Thursday, March 23 ————————————————————————————

Shevardnadze Denies Involvement in Afghan Intervention

In an interview with *Izvestia*, Foreign Minister Eduard Shevardnadze categorically denied playing any role in the decision to send Soviet troops to Afghanistan in December, 1979. The minister stated that the decision had been taken "behind closed doors" by "a few, very high-ranking officials" and that candidate members of the Politburo, such as he was, were presented with a *fait accompli*. The same day, TASS quoted Shevardnadze as saying Moscow would react "most decisively" if Soviet embassy personnel in Kabul are threatened by the Afghan resistance. He did not tell TASS what actions Moscow might take. He said the

USSR would continue to supply arms to government forces. *Pravda* said the Afghan resistance had cut nearly all the main roads leading out of Kabul. The report said the government of Afghanistan can communicate with most of the country's provincial capitals only by air.

Vice President of the USSR Academy of Medical Sciences Leonid Il'in said some people exposed to radiation in the Chernobyl' nuclear plant explosion could develop thyroid cancer. Il'in said some people may suffer enlarged thyroids by 1994 that in some instances could become malignant by 1996 (*TASS*, March 23).

Official Says Some Chernobyl' Victims Risk Thyroid Cancer

A report from Frunze said an earthquake on March 22 in Kirgizia caused "extensive damage." The report, broadcast by Radio Baku, gave no details of the damage. It confirmed a previous TASS report on the strength and location of the earthquake, whose epicenter was in the Pamir mountains about 160 kilometers southwest of Naryn. TASS said that the shock of the quake was cushioned by the mountains and that there were no reports of damage in Naryn or nearby villages.

Reports on Damage from Kirgizia Earthquake

Egor Ligachev, denounced by thousands of demonstrators on the streets of Moscow during the week leading up to the elections to the Congress of People's Deputies, was quoted by APN as saying there was no opposition in the ruling Politburo. The APN reporter, Vladimir Ostrovsky, said Ligachev told him that debates within the Politburo were often "free and animated" with decisions taken by consensus but that none of the Politburo could be said to constitute "an opposition."

Ligachev Interviewed by Novosti

A report in *Pravda* said that organized crime in the Soviet Union was flourishing and that some cooperative workers had been forced to buy guns for self-defense. The report said that mafia members used fast cars, computers, and electronic listening devices in their criminal activities and that, even if they were caught, gang leaders bribed local law-enforcement officials and members of the judiciary. It also said that many cooperatives were trying to lure policemen away from public service into the security business by offering them salaries as much as three times the average as well as other inducements. The newspaper said the murder rate rose 14 percent last year and armed

***Pravda* on Mafia**

169

robberies by more than 40 percent. It attributed almost 20,000 crimes in the period 1987–1988 to the work of 2,607 organized groups. On March 24, *Pravda* quoted USSR Deputy Prosecutor General Aleksandr Katusev as saying the Soviet Union needed new laws to combat economic crime. Katusev said criminals find loopholes in the law that allow them to invest stolen money.

Talks on Conventional Forces Adjourn in Vienna

The Soviet Union has given the Vienna conference on reducing conventional forces in Europe a list of NATO and Warsaw Pact combat aircraft that it said should be included in the negotiations. The list was presented at the final meeting before the arms talks adjourned. The Soviet Union says that combat aircraft should be included in the first phase of reducing conventional forces, but NATO believes that the first phase should be limited to tanks, artillery, and armored troop-carriers (*RFE/RL Special*, March 23).

Unofficial Organization of Soviet Writers

Vadim Sokolov, secretary of a new Soviet pro-*perestroika* writers' organization called "April," said the group had called for the rehabilitation of Aleksandr Solzhenitsyn. Sokolov told RFE/RL that the call came in a resolution adopted at the group's first meeting three weeks ago, which also urged the rehabilitation of other writers subjected to repression and persecution in the past. Sokolov said the new group was an alternative to the conservative USSR Writers' Union, which he said had become like a government ministry. The group's members include such reform-minded writers as Anatolii Pristavkin, Anatolii Strelyanyi, and Yurii Chernichenko. On March 15 and 22, *Literaturnaya gazeta* reported briefly on the group's first meeting and goals.

Former Central Committee Member Medunov Expelled from Party

Sergei Medunov, once a senior official in the CPSU, was reported to have been expelled from the Party for allowing corruption to flourish in Krasnodar Krai, where he was first secretary during the Brezhnev era. In 1982, Medunov was dismissed from the post after nine years in office and named USSR deputy minister of the fruit and vegetable industry. Shortly after his retirement, he was expelled from the Central Committee for "shortcomings in his work." TASS said Medunov headed the Party organization in a region where corruption and embezzlement flourished and where people who tried to expose the illegalities were persecuted.

Hungarian Party chief Karoly Grosz arrived in the Soviet Union on March 23 to brief Soviet leaders on the course of economic and political reforms in Hungary (*TASS*, March 23). Speaking on Soviet television the same day, the Hungarian Party leader said reforms in the USSR and Hungary have much in common. On March 24, Grosz met Gorbachev. TASS said the two men exchanged expertise and information on "pressing issues of Socialist construction" in their countries. They also discussed bilateral cooperation and foreign policy. Speaking to reporters before leaving Moscow, Grosz said he and Gorbachev agreed on every issue they discussed during several hours of talks. The Hungarian Party boss said Gorbachev had expressed no objection to his country's plans to create a multiparty system (*Reuters*, March 24).

Grosz in USSR

The youth journal *Sobesednik* (No. 11) carried an article saying that notwithstanding the reform process under way in the USSR, many Soviet citizens still want to emigrate. The article spoke about "the fourth wave" of emigration from the Soviet Union. It said that many current would-be émigrés are young people who think that they have too few opportunities to make careers in their homeland.

***Sobesednik* on Fourth Wave of Emigration**

Pravda reported that millions of Soviet citizens live on the breadline with totally inadequate wages or pensions. "We write very rarely about poor people—pensioners, labor veterans, and invalids living on low incomes, about young families living from hand to mouth—yet there are very many of them in our country," the newspaper said. Fifteen million people in the USSR live on a pension of less than 60 rubles a month, it added. *Pravda* quoted a letter from a war veteran on a fifty-seven-ruble monthly pension who complained she had felt little effect from Gorbachev's reform program.

***Pravda* on "Poor People" in USSR**

Lithuanian Party First Secretary Algirdas Brazauskas said his party has submitted its own program to the CPSU Central Committee based on proposals made by many Lithuanian Communists for a program "proceeeding from the currently prevailing situation" in Lithuania. He also said the Lithuanian Party will continue to follow "the

Lithuanian Party Submits Its Own Program

general Party line," but "at the same time pursuing our own local goals." According to TASS, Brazauskas made his statement in the latest issue of *Argumenty i fakty.* TASS quoted Brazauskas as saying the Lithuanian proposals have also been addressed to the coming Central Committee plenum on nationalities issues.

Vagris Says He'll Work for Latvia's Economic Independence

Latvia's Party First Secretary Janis Vagris said he will work to make the republic self-financing if elected to the Congress of People's Deputies. Vagris told Soviet television that Latvia, like the other Soviet republics, needs more economic independence to solve problems such as housing and inflation. Vagris, who was interviewed at a Riga construction site, said his main concern was to solve the housing problem.

Ukrainian Mass Grave Found to Hold Victims of 1930s Repression

TASS said a Ukrainian official had confirmed that bodies discovered in a mass grave near Kiev last year were victims of repressions in the 1930s. Ukrainian State Prosecutor Viktor Kulik heads an investigation commission set up by the Ukrainian Council of Ministers to examine the circumstances leading to the deaths of people whose remains have been found near the village of Bykovnya in the Darnitsk forest. He said the commission had been able to establish the names of some of the victims and that further examination of local archives had confirmed that the dead had been charged in the 1930s with counter-revolutionary and nationalist activities. Kulik said he believed there were more graves in the area that have yet to be discovered.

Saturday, March 25 ———————————————————————

Rallies Held on Eve of Elections

On the eve of the elections to the Congress of People's Deputies, many rallies were held in various cities of the USSR. On March 24, *Izvestia* attacked "nationalists" in Estonia, accusing them of trying to disrupt the election campaign. The newspaper claimed a leaflet had been found in Tallinn urging people to boycott the election. In Riga, one of the candidates for election, Juris Dobelis, a member of the Latvian National Independence Movement, said he was standing for election on the platform of independence for Latvia from the USSR (*Reuters,* March 25). In Moscow, thousands of people rallied once more in support of Boris El'tsin (*UPI,* March 25).

TASS said that some 300,000 persons in Riga participated in an observance commemorating Latvian victims of repression under Stalin's rule. The agency said that a meeting and procession of mourning commemorated more than 40,000 Latvians who were deported forty years ago during the campaign to collectivize Latvian agriculture. March 25 is the fortieth anniversary of the start of the second wave of mass deportations of Latvians to remote parts of the USSR; the first wave started in 1941. Estonians gathered on the same day to commemorate the deportation of their countrymen in similar circumstances (*TASS*, March 25).

Stalin's Victims Commemorated in Latvia and Estonia

USSR Minister of Internal Affairs Vadim Bakatin said that the problem of rising crime in the USSR was "cause for alarm and food for thought." TASS said Bakatin's comments came in an interview in the latest issue of the weekly *Nedelya*. He was quoted as expressing particular concern over the increase in crime committed by young people. Bakatin said that juvenile delinquency grew in 1988 by 11 percent and that 55 percent of all criminals convicted last year were under the age of thirty.

Interior Minister Says Growing Crime "Reason for Alarm"

Police have started clamping down on poets who display and sell their politically charged verses on the Arbat. Earlier this year, Lev Zaikov, the Moscow city Party boss, charged that on the Arbat, "under the flag of democracy, banalities have blossomed and sometimes overt anti-Soviet propaganda."

Poets on Moscow's Arbat Reported Hushed by Police

Some 20,000 people demonstrated in Tbilisi against a campaign in the Autonomous Republic of Abkhazia aimed at reducing Georgian control. AFP quoted Georgian sources as providing the information. (On March 18, it was reported that several thousand Abkhaz held a meeting in a small town in their republic to demand that Moscow give them the status of a Union republic.)

Georgians Demonstrate against Minority Demands

Sunday, March 26

March 26 was the day of elections for 1,500 of the seats in the new Congress of People's Deputies. Two or more candidates competed in about three quarters of the constituencies; in the rest, there was only one candidate.

Elections to Congress of People's Deputies

Mikhail Gorbachev was shown on Soviet television voting for deputies to the new parliament. Speaking to reporters after the voting, Gorbachev said that his policies of pressing for more democracy and *glasnost'* were "the key to tapping the potential of our Socialist system." Asked about the prospects for a multiparty system, Gorbachev said that this would not be the solution to the Soviet Union's problems. Gorbachev was also quoted by AP as saying that he was not satisfied with the results of *perestroika.* He said he would like it to be more energetic (*Reuters, UPI,* March 26). Reuters reported that human-rights activists in the Ukrainian city of Lvov boycotted the elections. Followers of the banned Ukrainian Catholic Church also said they would stay away from the polls, while members of an independent cultural association called "The Lion Society" said they were voting against everyone on the ballot (*Reuters,* March 26).

El'tsin on Housing Problem

The Sunday Telegraph published an interview with Boris El'tsin. Among other things, he voiced doubts about the CPSU's promise to provide every Soviet family with an apartment or house of its own by the year 2000: "Here we've been following old habits—making a declaration and asking afterwards if it can be done. We have declared that by the year 2000 every Soviet family will have an apartment. Then we did our sums, and it turned out that it is almost impossible. If we don't fulfill the promise we will have betrayed the people again." (The Third Party Program, adopted at the Twenty-second Congress of the CPSU in 1961, promised that every Soviet family would have its own apartment by 1980. That promise was not kept.) Today, some 14 million Soviet families and individuals are on the waiting list for better housing (*Pravda,* January 22).

Eltsin's Victory, Soviet Leaders' Popularity Scale

As early as March 26, Reuters reported the first results of the elections, which showed Boris El'tsin's sweeping victory in the campaign to become deputy for Moscow to the new Soviet parliament. On March 27, it became known that El'tsin had won 89 percent of the vote in Moscow. This overwhelming victory—won in open contest—counts for more than the election of the top Soviet leaders who won by a margin of over 90 percent at an internal Party vote during the recent plenum of the Central Committee. In the uncontested Central Committee elections of Party deputies to the Congress of People's Deputies, Mikhail Gorbachev, Nikolai Ryzhkov, and

Viktor Chebrikov all received 98 percent—the biggest votes for Politburo members. These percentages were exceeded, however, by those obtained by a candidate member of the Politburo, Anatolii Luk'yanov, and a Central Committee secretary, Baklanov, both of whom received 99 percent of the vote. The results of the Party elections were published in *Pravda* on March 19. Of the other Members of the Politburo, Nikolai Slyun'kov and Vadim Medvedev ranked second in popularity inside the Party, taking 97 percent of the votes. Lev Zaikov and Viktor Nikonov won 96 percent, while Aleksandr Yakovlev seems to have enjoyed less support from the Central Committee, receiving only 91 percent. In a stunning display of dissatisfaction with his conservative views, the Central Committee gave Egor Ligachev only 88 percent of its votes at the plenum—less than his opponent El'tsin received in the "open" election.

Protest March in Erevan

Protesters marched for about an hour in the Armenian capital of Erevan before being dispersed by the police. The number taking part in the demonstration was put between 2,000 and 3,000. Armenian sources told AFP and AP that at least one person was detained. Mehat Gabrillyan, an Armenian activist, was quoted by AP as saying some of the marchers carried posters referring to the elections to the Congress of People's Deputies. The protest called for an independent Armenia and for the release of members of the Karabakh Committee detained last year.

Soviet Diplomat in Iraq during Saudi King's Visit

Vladimir Polyakov, who heads the Near East and North Africa Department at the Soviet Foreign Ministry, visited Iraq over the weekend where he was said to have held talks with the Iraqi Foreign Minister, Tariq Aziz. King Fahd of Saudi Arabia was in Baghdad for talks with Iraqi leaders at the same time as Polyakov. The Soviet Union and Saudi Arabia do not have diplomatic relations but have had high-level contacts over the past year. Western and Iraqi reporters said Polyakov delivered a message from Eduard Shevardnadze to the Iraqi Foreign Minister. There has been no official comment concerning Polyakov's visit (*UPI, AP*, March 26).

Easter Celebrations in USSR

TASS reported that Easter was celebrated by the Roman Catholic and Protestant Churches in the Baltic republics and in the Lvov area of Western Ukraine. TASS said Roman Catholic Cardinal Julians Vaivods attended a mass in Riga. In Lithuania, masses were held in Vilnius and in Klaipeda. Easter was also observed in twenty-six Lutheran parishes in Lithuania, and the Evangelical-Lutheran Church of Estonia celebrated Easter with special services. TASS said that Catholics attended masses in Lvov and other parts of Western Ukraine.

Moscow News Interviews Conquest

Moscow News (No. 13) published a lengthy interview with Robert Conquest conducted by an American journalist from the journal *Nation*. Conquest focused primarily on his books *The Great Terror*, which is to be serialized in the Soviet journal *Neva*, and *Harvest of Sorrow*. Conquest said that the current revelations about Stalinism in the Soviet press have confirmed the main conclusions he reached in his books. *Voprosy istorii* (No. 3) carried a letter from Conquest defending his estimates of the number of victims of the famine in Ukraine in 1932–33. Last year, *Voprosy istorii* published a letter by a leading Soviet specialist on peasant history, V. Danilov, who criticized Conquest, saying he had overestimated the number of deaths from the famine. The editorial introduction to the interview in *Moscow News* claims that *The Great Terror* reached the Soviet Union through *samizdat* channels soon after it was published in the West in 1968. The introduction mentioned that, on reading the book, the Soviet intelligentsia immediately came to regard it as "one of the most important Western research works on Soviet history."

Monday, March 27 ───────────────────────────────────

More Information on Drug Addicts in USSR

Novosti reported that the number of people with "a drug habit" in the Soviet Union now stands at 120,000. This includes 46,000 registered drug addicts and 4,744 "sniffers of toxic substances." Eighty percent of Soviet drug users are young people under twenty-five, and the main centers of teen-age drug abuse are in Turkmenia, Uzbekistan, Kazakhstan, Ukraine, and some parts of the RSFSR. According to official figures, almost 90 percent of Soviet addicts use homemade preparations of poppy or hemp; "heroin, LSD, and marijuana practically do not exist in the USSR." Novosti said studies have shown that "the most important objective reasons for drug addiction among teen-agers are poor academic progress, overambitiousness in career goals, and constant conflicts and alcoholism in the family."

The literary monthly *Raduga* (No. 2) contains an article by Mikhail Shilov, who declares that the one-party system in the Soviet Union was "the chief precondition" for the creation of Stalin's personality cult. The author points out to readers that Lenin established the system but did not envisage the consequences. Shilov adds that the one-party system continues to create problems in the Soviet Union even in the period of *perestroika*, noting that the ruling Politburo makes mistakes like any normal group of working people but that there is no one to criticize the Politburo's performance. Shilov rejects as absurd the claim often made by Soviet officials that a one-party system has a strong historical tradition in the Soviet Union. Shilov says that party pluralism should be allowed in the USSR because a one-party system is incompatible with democracy.

Strong Attack on One-Party System Published

Nedelya (No. 11) carried an interview with Aleksandr Tsipko, the philosopher who became famous for a four-part article in *Nauka i zhizn'* (Nos. 11 and 12, 1988; and Nos. 1 and 2, 1989) in which he attributed the Soviet Union's great failures and tragedies to flaws inherent in Marxism, on the basis of which the Bolsheviks tried to build a new society in Russia. In the *Nedelya* interview, Tsipko reiterated his criticism of some of the postulates of Marxism, such as Marx's ideas on "nonmarket socialism." The editorial introduction to the interview reported that, as early as 1980, Tsipko wrote a book, entitled *Sotsialism: zhizn' obshchestva i cheloveka* (Socialism: The Life of Society and Man), in which he referred to the negative consequences of all revolutions, including the October Revolution of 1917. He complained that revolutions, especially those followed by civil wars, as was the case in Russia, accustom people to violence, murder, and cruelty. The editorial introduction added that Tsipko got into trouble with the authorities on account of his 1980 book. It seems that Tsipko's criticism of Marx and Lenin has had a strong effect on some rank-and-file members of the Communist Party. For example, the bulletin of the Lithuanian Restructuring Movement, *Soglasie* (No. 3), published a statement by a Lithuanian who had been a member of the CPSU since February, 1974, informing the Central Committee of the Communist Party of Lithuania of his wish to leave a Party that had committed so many crimes. The disillusioned Lithuanian wrote that he used to think that Stalin had deviated from Lenin's line and that this was the reason for Stalin's cruel policies. Current critiques of Marxism-Leninism, how-

Philosopher Repeats His Criticism of Marxism

ever, adopt the stance that Stalin only developed further the "antihuman" ideology of class struggle expounded by Lenin.

Perestroika Influences Film Industry

Soviet filmmaker Leonid Gurevich said about 90 percent of Soviet documentary films released now would not have been made before *perestroika*. Gurevich spoke at a Washington preview of a Soviet documentary film festival that is starting a tour of the United States. The twenty-two films in the festival tackle the Chernobyl' nuclear disaster, the Armenian protests, the war in Afghanistan, and the repressions of the Stalin era (*USIS*, March 28).

Gorbachev on Election of Politburo Members

On March 27, *Pravda* and *Izvestia* published a TASS interview with Gorbachev on the elections. Asked to comment on the 12 [out of 641 participants in the recent Central Committee Plenum] who voted against him, Gorbachev said: "Too few. I would have been disappointed if there had been no critical remarks at all," adding that he also regarded the pace of *perestroika* as too slow. Gorbachev declined to speculate why 12 percent of those voting voted against Ligachev and 9 percent against Yakovlev.

Tuesday, March 28

Election Results

According to *Izvestia*, voter turnout for the elections on March 26 was about 80–85 percent in most regions, a level that *Izvestia* considered "convincing enough by any international standards."

In Ukraine, Vladimir Shcherbitsky, who had run unopposed in Dnepropetrovsk, Ukrainian Supreme Soviet Chairman Valentina Shevchenko, and Chairman of the Ukrainian Council of Ministers Vitalii Masol were elected. The first secretary of the Kazakh Communist Party, Gennadii Kolbin, received 97 percent of the vote. The first and second secretaries of the Moldavian Communist Party also won, together with the chairman of the Supreme Soviet and the chairman of the Council of Ministers. Vazgen I, the Armenian Catholicos, was elected, as was Vitalii Vorotnikov (who received 84.6 percent of the vote in Voronezh and who, it will be remembered, chose not to run against Boris El'tsin in Moscow).

In Moscow, Leningrad, Kiev, Minsk, and Kishinev—to name but a few cities—local Party officials were defeated, as were five regional Party secretaries in Ukraine

178

(*TASS*, March 27–29, and *Central Television*, March 28). According to Soviet Foreign Ministry spokesman Gennadii Gerasimov, about 20 percent of the Communist Party candidates who were nominated did not win (*AP, Reuters*, March 28).

In the Baltic republics, the results of elections to the new parliament offered an impressive demonstration of public support for the popular movements there. The most striking results were scored in Lithuania, where "Sajudis," the movement for restructuring, won 31 of the republic's 42 seats by a sizable majority, averaging some 70 percent of the vote. In Latvia, 25 of the 29 candidates supported by the Popular Front were elected, according to the movement's spokeswoman. On March 27, Estonian radio said that Popular Front candidates won 15 of Estonia's 21 seats in the new body.

On March 29, *Pravda* praised the elections as a victory for reform efforts, saying that, unlike past elections, these allowed the voter to make a real choice based on his preference for the candidate whose platform suited him best. On March 31, *Pravda* devoted its editorial to the elections. The editorial discussed the defeat of Party officials in various regions of the USSR.

Save-the-Aral Contest Announced

TASS announced a contest organized by Central Television for the best project to save the Aral Sea. Kirgiz writer Chingiz Aitmatov commented in the course of a televised round-table discussion (March 28, 1745) that the Aral disaster is not a local, Central Asian phenomenon, but attests to the monopolistic and self-interested actions of various organizations, particularly the USSR Ministry of Land Reclamation and Water Resources. Environmentalists had cause for some rejoicing last week with the announcement of the retirement of Nikolai F. Vasil'ev as minister of land reclamation and water resources (*Radio Moscow-1*, 1900, March 25). Vasil'ev, who was one of the most vocal proponents of the northern and Siberian river diversion schemes, has been heavily criticized by environmentally-conscious intellectuals in terms similar to those used by Aitmatov against Vasil'ev's ministry.

Soviet Germans Set Up Interest Group

DPA reported on a conference of Soviet Germans opening on March 29 in Moscow. The conference is to set up a society representing the interests of all Soviet Germans. More than 100 participants in the conference have gathered from all over the USSR. According to one participant, the new society hopes to press for "a correct solution" to the problem of the Soviet Germans before the CPSU Central Committee plenum on interethnic relations convenes later this year. The DPA's informant insisted that "the correct solution" involves reestablishment of a republic for ethnic Germans on the Volga. On March 29, TASS reported on the conference's opening. The same day, the "Vremya" news program reported that the possibility of setting up a German Autonomous Republic on the Volga river was indeed on the agenda of the conference.

USSR Loses Contact with Second Mars Probe

TASS said that Soviet controllers had lost contact with *Phobos-2*, the unmanned spacecraft that has been circling Mars for the past two months. TASS said the radio link to the spacecraft was lost on March 27 after it was maneuvered into position to take pictures of the Martian moon Phobos. It said Soviet controllers were trying to find out why the link was lost and how to reestablish it. The Soviet Mars program started with two *Phobos* spacecraft, but controllers lost contact with *Phobos-1* last September when they sent an incorrect computer command. On March 29, TASS and *Izvestia* quoted the director of the Soviet space agency, Aleksandr Dunaev, as saying experts have a week to decide what can be done about the loss of contact with *Phobos-2*.

Moscow Reports Unpublished Food Import Figures

Radio Moscow-1 (1900) reported figures for last year's Soviet food imports, which, it said, had never been published before. The radio listed large imports of grain, sugar, meat, butter, potatoes, fresh fruit, and eggs costing in all more than 10,000 million rubles last year and asked how many much-needed machines that would have paid for. It quoted the Soviet trade journal *Vneshnyaya torgovlya* as the source for the figures.

Wednesday, March 29 —————————————————————

Gorbachev Meets Media Executives

TASS reported that Mikhail Gorbachev had met representatives of the Soviet media to discuss the results of the elections to the Congress of People's Deputies. TASS said other top officials at the meeting included Politburo members Egor Ligachev and Vadim Medvedev. Gorbachev also talked about the results of this month's Central Committee plenum on agriculture. After the meeting, the chief editor of *Ogonek* Vitalii Korotich gave Western reporters some information on the meeting. He said that Gorbachev described the defeat of some Communist Party candidates at the elections as a natural part of the democratic process and not a cause for alarm (*Reuters*, March 30). Gorbachev was quoted elsewhere as saying that the election results proved the Soviet Union did not need a multiparty system (*AP, UPI,* March 30). The full text of Gorbachev's speech was released by TASS on March 30.

In an interview with the chief editor of *Izvestia*, Ivan Laptev, British Prime Minister Margaret Thatcher said that having the right leaders in the right place at the right time had helped ease world tensions. She told Laptev she thought that, with Mikhail Gorbachev and Ronald Reagan, she had helped create conditions for improved East-West relations. She praised Gorbachev as a leader of vision with ideas on how to carry out programs and to motivate people to exercise their talents and their responsibilities (*Izvestia*, March 29). A lengthy interview with Thatcher was also published in *Ogonek* (No. 11).

Thatcher Interviewed by *Izvestia*

The Soviet ambassador to the United Nations, Aleksandr Belonogov, repeated allegations that forces from Pakistan are fighting in Afghanistan. During a news conference at the United Nations, Belonogov said Pakistani tribal militia were fighting alongside the resistance. He also blamed the United Nations in part for the situation in Afghanistan and said it should arrange "a true dialogue" between the government and the resistance (*AFP*, March 29).

USSR Renews Criticism of Pakistan over Afghanistan

A leading USSR junior chess player defected to the United States. US chess officials said fourteen-year-old Gata Kamsky and his father, Rustam, went into hiding in the New York area last week. They had come to the United States the previous week as part of a Soviet chess delegation attending an international tournament in New York. An official of the American Chess Foundation, Allen Kaufman, said the Kamskys approached him during the tournament and asked for help in seeking political asylum (*Reuters, AP*, March 29).

Soviet Chess Player and His Father Defect to US

Radio Moscow-1 (1400) reported the replacement of Pavel Gilashvili as chairman of the Presidium of the Georgian Supreme Soviet. The report said that he had retired; he is seventy years old. Gilashvili was replaced by Prime Minister Otar Cherkezia, who has just been elected

Georgia Gets New President, Prime Minister

a deputy to the new Soviet parliament. Zurab Chkheidze, who had been first deputy prime minister, was appointed the new prime minister.

Pravda Warns of Continued Protests in Moldavia

Pravda warned of the possible consequences of "nationalist" activities in Moldavia, saying that a tragedy might occur if such activities continue. Recent protests in the Moldavian republic have called for the Latin alphabet to replace the Cyrillic and for Moldavian to replace Russian as the official language of the republic. *Pravda* said that demonstrators who had gathered in Kishinev on March 19 carried signs reading "Down with the Government." On March 31, Radio Kishinev, in Moldavian, reported that a law had been drafted that would make Moldavian the state language of the republic.

Four Russian Hunger Strikers Demand Return of Church

Four women demanding the return of a Russian Orthodox church to believers have been on a hunger strike for the past week in the central Russian city of Ivanovo, *Izvestia* reported. Local authorities closed the church and turned it into a state archive in the 1930s.

Gorbachev on Protection of Socialist Countries

Gorbachev said that every measure should be taken to protect Communist countries from outside interference. Hungary's MTI news agency quoted Hungarian Party General Secretary Karoly Grosz as saying that Gorbachev made the statement during last week's talks with Grosz with reference to the events of 1956 and 1968 when the Hungarian revolution and the Prague Spring were suppressed by Soviet troops (*MTI*, in English, *Reuters*, *AP*, March 29).

Thursday, March 30 ───

Students to Be Freed from Military Duty during Study

A Soviet official said rules were being changed to exempt university students from military service during their period of study. The deputy chairman of the Soviet State Committee for Public Education, Gennadii Kutsev, said in *Komsomol'skaya pravda* that the change in the rules would take effect this fall with the start of the new academic year. Kutsev said compulsory military education courses would continue at all universities except those teaching medicine; the courses would, however, be updated and shortened.

Soviet Defense Minister Dmitrii Yazov met in Damascus with President Hafez Assad after a two-day tour of Syrian military installations. TASS said that they discussed the situation in the Middle East and "the growing dynamism" of relations between Syria and the USSR. Yazov arrived in Syria on March 27 and spent March 28 and 29 at a Syrian naval base and visiting Syrian ground forces. The USSR supplies most of Syria's weapons (*AP, TASS,* March 30).

Yazov Meets with Assad, Heads for Home

The Ukrainian Writers' Union has posthumously readmitted Soviet writer Viktor Nekrasov, who was stripped of his citizenship after emigrating to the West (*TASS,* March 30). Nekrasov came under official criticism in the 1960s for his writings about travels to the West and for his human-rights activities. He emigrated to the West in 1974 after being expelled from the Party and from the Writers' Union. He died in Paris in 1987. Just before Nekrasov's death, *Moscow News* published an article that praised Nekrasov's works. Since then, several Soviet periodicals have written positively about Nekrasov's work, including his broadcasts for Radio Liberty.

Nekrasov's Membership in Ukrainian Writers Union Restored

More than 30,000 people are now reported homeless as a result of recent landslides in the Chechen-Ingush Autonomous Republic. TASS said the landslides had been set in motion by melting snow in mountain areas of the republic. It said no casualties had been reported.

Landslides in Chechen-Ingush Republic

A number of Soviet and US companies have signed an agreement defining financial and administrative rules for future joint ventures in the Soviet Union. TASS said that the agreement, signed in Moscow, involves a trade consortium of six major US companies and a group of about thirty Soviet foreign trade enterprises. The American side includes companies dealing in oil, pharmaceutical and health-care products, and consumer goods. TASS said there are plans to set up twenty-five joint enterprises in the USSR over the coming months in agriculture, the oil industry, medicine, and other areas.

US and Soviet Firms Sign Agreement on Joint Ventures

Latvia's creative unions began two days of talks on human rights and ethnic issues arising from the final document of the Vienna conference. TASS said that guests from other Soviet republics and from Moscow, as well as foreign experts on international law, are attending. The Latvian

Human Rights and Ethnic Issues Discussed in Riga

Writers' Union first secretary, Janis Peters, told the meeting that unions want to make a contribution to improving the political situation and ethnic relations in Latvia.

Iran's Foreign Minister in Moscow

Iran's Foreign Minister Ali Akbar Velayati arrived in Moscow amid what Western correspondents describe as improving relations between Iran and the USSR. TASS said Velayati was making a brief working visit at the invitation of Eduard Shevardnadze. Velayati told reporters before leaving Teheran that Iran had always favored the expansion of ties with the USSR (*AP*, *Reuters*, March 30). On March 31, Velayati met with Gorbachev. Reporting on the talks, TASS said the situation in Afghanistan, the Middle East, and the Iran-Iraq war were discussed. The agency also quoted Gorbachev as saying the USSR regards Iran as "a desirable partner" for economic and cultural ties and political dialogue. The same day, Velayati had talks with Shevardnadze (*TASS*, in English, March 31).

Soviet Spokesman Raps Baker's Ideas on Eastern Europe

Soviet Foreign Ministry spokesman Vadim Perfil'ev said a proposal on Eastern Europe by US Secretary of State James Baker was an attempt to interfere in the internal development of East European countries. Baker proposes an agreement by which the Soviet Union would relax its controls in Eastern Europe in return for a NATO pledge not to use this to endanger the USSR. Perfil'ev told reporters in Moscow that such proposals were an attempt to misuse other countries' difficulties and "are devoid of prospects" (*AFP*, *TASS*, March 30).

Hijack Attempt in Baku

An attempt to hijack a Soviet airliner to Pakistan was foiled by KGB commandos who stormed the plane after it landed at Baku airport in Azerbaijan and overpowered the would-be hijacker. A Foreign Ministry spokesman, Vadim Perfil'ev, said the man had threatened to blow up the plane unless he was given half a million pounds sterling and flown to Pakistan. Perfil'ev said none of the passengers or crew being held was hurt (*TASS*, March 31).

Friday, March 31 _____

Psychiatric Abuses in USSR

Amnesty International said that the Soviet Union still commits sane dissidents to psychiatric clinics but that the numbers of such cases have fallen following Western criticism of the practice. The human-rights group said that reforms of Soviet psychiatry appear not to have been implemented effectively. In Spain, the Executive Committee of the World Psychiatric Association recommended readmitting the official Soviet Psychiatric Society into the WPA. Reuters and AP reported that this move has drawn criticism from some members of the WPA who say that the Soviet organization does not yet deserve readmission. The official readmission of the Soviet Union to the WPA requires the approval of the full membership in a vote scheduled for October.

The memoirs of former Soviet leader Nikita Khrushchev, published in the West after he was ousted in 1964, are being excerpted for the first time in the Soviet press. The weekly *Argumenty i fakty* began publishing the excerpts in its latest issue, which went on sale in Moscow on March 31 (*AP*, March 31).

Argumenty i fakty Starts Publishing Khrushchev's Memoirs

Egor Ligachev said all restrictions should be removed on private family farms and gardens because they produce so much of the country's food. He said on Soviet television that private farmers should be given all the land and resources they need. Ligachev also said the country's food problem must be alleviated quickly and solved by 1995. (On April 1, *Pravda* printed a resolution of the recent Central Committee plenum on agriculture.)

Ligachev Comments on Agricultural Issues

Soviet Deputy Foreign Minister Anatolii Adamishin said South Africa's system of apartheid could be dismantled peacefully. But he said the South African government and the African National Congress must be ready to compromise. Speaking in Zimbabwe at the end of a tour of southern Africa, Adamishin said South Africa should stop what he called state violence and show its readiness for talks (*AP, Reuters*, March 31).

Foreign Ministry Official on South Africa

A powerful earthquake in the Spitak region of Armenia was reported. TASS said there were no human casualties but that cattle were killed and that buildings weakened by last December's earthquake were destroyed.

Strong Earthquake Strikes Spitak Region of Armenia

The Month of April

Police Remove Fasting Women in Ivanovo

Reuters and *AP* quoted a religious rights activist, Aleksandr Ogorodnikov, as saying police had removed four women on a hunger strike outside a former church in the Russian town of Ivanovo. Ogorodnikov said the women were taken to a hospital. They had been fasting since March 20 in support of their demand to have the church returned to the Orthodox community. It has housed state archives since the 1930s. (The hunger strike was reported by *Izvestia* on March 29.) On April 11, *AP* quoted unofficial religious sources as saying the women had ended their fast after the head of the local government, Lev Dubov, visited them in the hospital. He promised the women that the question of the church's future would be decided within a month.

Journal Publishes Story on Atrocities of Cheka

The journal *Sibirskie ogni* (No. 2) published a story entitled "Shchepka" ("The Chip") by writer Vladimir Zazubrin, a victim of Stalin's purges. The story was written in 1923 but was immediately banned by Soviet censors. It gives a horrifying account of the atrocities committed by the Cheka in the early 1920s, including executions of clergymen, White Army officers, and other "alien class elements." *Moscow News* (No. 14) carried a letter written to the Council of People's Commissars by a Social-Democrat lawyer, Vladimir Zhdanov, in July, 1918, condemning the Cheka's uncontrolled activities.

Georgians Protest against Abkhaz Demands

Georgian activist Zviad Gamsakhurdia told AFP that some 10,000 Georgians had protested in Sukhumi against Abkhaz demands for Union-republican status for Abkhazia. According to Gamsakhurdia, there were also violent clashes on April 1 in the town of Lesselidze, where some 2,000 Georgians demonstrating against Abkhaz demands were attacked by Abkhaz who threw stones and fired shots at the demonstrators. A number of Georgians were injured. Gamsakhurdia added that Georgian nationalists had been holding mass meetings in Tbilisi since March 25 to discuss the Abkhaz issue. On April 6, it was reported that the Party first secretary in Abkhazia, Boris Adleiba, had been removed from office (*TASS*, April 6).

Demonstration in Vilnius

Members of the Lithuanian Restructuring Movement "Sajudis" told RFE/RL by telephone from Vilnius that about 5,000 people had demonstrated in the Lithuanian capital in support of demands that Lithuanians be allowed to do their military service in Lithuania or in other Baltic republics. The demonstrators also protested against what they called the harassment and brutal treatment of recruits in the Soviet Armed Forces.

Gromyko Interviewed

In an interview published in *The Observer*, veteran Soviet politician Andrei Gromyko talked about his years in top Soviet political circles. Discussing Stalin, Gromyko insisted that, although he met Stalin many times, he did not know about the dictator's mass repressions. He said Nikita Khrushchev had extraordinary intelligence but lacked a solid education, while Leonid Brezhnev had no new ideas and had a drinking problem. Gromyko described Mikhail Gorbachev as dynamic and as a man of sharp and profound mind.

Archbishop and Apostolic Administrators Installed in Lithuania

Lithuanian Roman Catholic Cardinal Vincentas Sladkevicius was officially installed as Archbishop of Kaunas. Thousands of people gathered in the cathedral in Kaunas to witness the installation ceremonies. Three other bishops were also installed as apostolic administrators in other parts of Lithuania. All four men were named to their new posts last month by the pope. For the first time in decades, fully empowered episcopal-rank officials now lead all of Lithuania's dioceses (*Reuters*, April 3).

Journalists Criticize Restrictions on Reporters' Activities

Moscow News (No. 14) published a protest against the new regulations adopted in January of this year requiring journalists to obtain special passes to gain access to the scene of accidents and other emergencies and to large rallies. The protest was signed by the three leading Soviet reporters on foreign affairs, Aleksandr Bovin, Vladimir Pozner, and Vladimir Tsvetov. *Ogonek* (No. 13) carried a letter by two well-known Soviet writers, the Strugatsky brothers, who condemned the regulations as an attack on *glasnost'*.

Gorbachev Visits Cuba

Gorbachev arrived in Cuba on April 2 and was met by President Fidel Castro and tens of thousands of cheering Cubans. Shortly afterwards Gorbachev gave an impromptu news conference at which he said friendship between the two countries "has sometimes gone through difficult times, but it is tried and tested and we all know where we stand" (*Reuters*, April 3, *Pravda*, April 4).

On April 3, Gorbachev began formal talks with Castro. The key topic of the talks was reported to be the estimated 6 billion dollars of aid that the Soviet Union provides to Cuba annually (*UPI*, April 3). The same day, *Pravda* reported on Gorbachev's visit, saying his talks with Castro would include "discussion of sometimes difficult problems." It did not elaborate, however.

On April 4, Gorbachev spoke on Soviet television from Havana. He said "new thinking" and its implications for the world were the central theme of his talks with Castro. Gorbachev said the international political climate was improving, and Socialist countries were making a big contribution to this (*TASS*, April 4; *Pravda*, April 5). The same day, Gorbachev continued talks with Castro and also addressed Cuba's National Assembly (*Reuters*, *UPI*, April 4). Gorbachev told the assembly that he opposed any theories or doctrines that seek to justify the export of revolution or counterrevolution. (On April 5, the United States said Gorbachev's words about not exporting revolution were not matched by the Soviet Union's deeds in Nicaragua [*Reuters*, April 5].) Gorbachev also restated his offer to stop the delivery of Soviet arms to Central America if the United States ceased supplying the Nicaraguan *contras*. (The United States had earlier rejected this offer [*Reuters*, April 4].)

At a news conference following his address to the assembly, Gorbachev said he was willing to write off Cuba's estimated 10 billion-dollar debt to the Soviet Union but he said more talks were necessary with Castro before "taking concrete steps" to cancel the debt (*UPI*, April 4). Castro, who also gave a press conference, emphatically denounced Soviet-style *perestroika* while answering questions from reporters. He rejected as "madness" the possibility of a similar reform drive for Cuba, citing as the reason geographical and demographic differences between the Soviet Union and Cuba (*UPI*, April 4). On April 5, Gorbachev left Havana for London (*TASS*, April 5, *Pravda* April 6).

French Defense Minister Jean-Pierre Chevenement held talks in Moscow with Soviet Defense Minister, Army General Dmitrii Yazov. Reports said the talks included a discussion of nuclear weapons and the potential danger of nuclear power. Reports also said Chevenement defended France's maintenance of a nuclear arsenal separate from NATO's (*AP*, *AFP*, April 3). TASS said Chevenement also met with Prime Minister Nikolai Ryzhkov, who stressed that Soviet military doctrine had been "radically revised" and had become more defensive.

French Defense Minister Meets Yazov

Soviet economists are discussing the possibility of introducing a second currency—a convertible ruble—that would be used in foreign trade. Academician Abel Aganbegyan told reporters in Moscow that a two-ruble system, if implemented, would be used only temporarily as a step towards establishing a fully convertible currency, which he said the USSR needs in order to compete on the world market. He said a second, convertible ruble could be used in the meantime in the special economic zones that are being set up in the Soviet Union to attract foreign investment. He also said the use of a second ruble is opposed by some Soviet economists (*Reuters*, April 3).

Soviet Economists Discuss Introduction of "Second Ruble"

Abel Aganbegyan said the drop in world oil prices in recent years had cost the Soviet Union 40 billion dollars annually. According to TASS, Aganbegyan also told journalists in Moscow the Soviet Union had been getting up to 75 percent of its hard currency from oil exports. He said that the USSR has no possibility of increasing oil exports in the next few years and that therefore major attention is being devoted to processing oil and gas into products worth five to ten times as much as oil on the world market. *Izvestia* (April 3) said a group of Soviet scientists is opposing a plan to build five major oil and gas chemical complexes in Western Siberia. The group is headed by Academicians Boris Laskorin, Nikita Moiseev, and Mikhail Styrikovits. The newspaper said the plan calls for US and Japanese companies to participate in the West Siberian project. It quoted the opponents as saying the plants should be built in other areas where chemical production centers already exist. *Izvestia* also published a letter from leaders of the oil and gas industries defending the West Siberian projects. The newspaper said there should be broad discussion of the plans because an issue affecting millions of people should not be decided without their knowledge.

Economist Says USSR Losing Huge Sums on Oil

Party Officials Comment on Elections

In Leningrad, oblast and city Party officials met to discuss the results of the elections to the Congress of People's Deputies. Senior Leningrad Party officials were defeated at the polls. (In a front-page interview in *Leningradskaya pravda* on March 31, Leningrad Oblast Party First Secretary Yurii Solov'ev blamed his defeat on "the unusual psychological and emotional circumstances" created in Leningrad by food shortages and other economic problems.) TASS said the Leningrad leadership had characterized the elections as "a serious political lesson." Responding in a telephone interview from Riga to a question from RFE/RL, the Latvian Party secretary in charge of ideology, Ivars Kezbers, said the Party had fared badly in the recent elections to the Congress because Party members had been held responsible for many negative phenomena. (The Popular Front of Latvia scored major election successes against Party candidates.)

Soviet PEN Center Set Up in Moscow

A group of leading Soviet writers was reported to have formed a chapter of the international writers' organization PEN. Western agencies and TASS reported that the group's first action was to defend British author Salman Rushdie against death threats from Ayatollah Khomeini. The Leningrad writer Daniil Granin, who is reported to have been elected president of Soviet PEN, appears to have been the first Soviet author to demand in print that the USSR Writers' Union be disbanded. Subsequently, Granin's call was echoed by other prominent writers who also joined the new PEN chapter. On April 6, Granin gave a telephone interview to RFE/RL. He said one of the PEN center's next actions would be to protest against the imprisonment of Czechoslovak playwright Vaclav Havel.

Voinovich Reinstated in USSR Writers' Union

Emigré Soviet writer Vladimir Voinovich, now on a visit to the USSR, said he had accepted the decision of the USSR Writers' Union to reinstate his membership in the union. He said he hoped that as a member of the union he would be able to contribute to *perestroika* within the organization. Voinovich, forced to emigrate from the USSR in 1980, is in Moscow to discuss the production of a film based on one of his novels. He was expelled from the union in the 1970s because of his human-rights activities (*RFE/RL Special*, April 4). On April 3, Voinovich commented on Soviet television on the union's decision to reinstate him.

Soviet refusednik Georgii Samoilovich was given permission to go to London for cancer treatment. Samoilovich's son and wife were allowed to accompany him on the trip. Britain has pushed for the resolution of Samoilovich's case, and Samoilovich said the decision to let him leave was undoubtedly connected with Gorbachev's visit to Britain. According to figures just released, Jewish emigration from the USSR has risen to its highest level in ten years. A spokeswoman for the Geneva-based Intergovernmental Committee for Migration said 8,735 Soviet Jews had arrived at the Vienna transit center in the first three months of 1989 (*UPI, AP*, April 4).

Samoilovich Allowed to Emigrate

Wednesday, April 5

On the eve of Gorbachev's visit to Britain, more than 200 British parliamentarians welcomed efforts by the Soviet Union to improve the human-rights situation in the country but said abuses still continued. In a full-page advertisement in *The Times*, the parliamentarians called, among other things, for freedom for Soviet citizens to emigrate and for the release of prisoners of conscience. (On April 3, AP reported that about forty Jews denied permission to emigrate from the USSR had demonstrated outside the British embassy in Moscow.) The same day, the British Foreign Office said it had been told the Soviet Union had freed nine prisoners of conscience and would give travel visas to fourteen refuseoniks. The news came only a few hours before Gorbachev arrived in London from Havana (*Reuters*, April 5). On April 5, *Pravda* criticized Margaret Thatcher for wanting to keep nuclear weapons. The same day, Soviet television interviewed Thatcher. *Moscow News* (No. 15) carried a review of Anglo-Soviet relations since World War II. (*Reuters, AP*, April 5).

In connection with Gorbachev's visit to London, several protest demonstrations were held. Agencies reported that some demonstrators demanded exit visas for Soviet Jews and others a just solution to the Nagorno-Karabakh dispute. On April 5, Gorbachev and Thatcher held preliminary talks on several issues, including Afghanistan, Namibia, and Mozambique, and Gorbachev talked about the recent elections to the Congress of People's Deputies (*Reuters, AP*, April 5; *Pravda*, April 6). On April 6, the talks continued, with discussions on human rights, arms control, and Afghanistan. The same day, Soviet Foreign Minister Eduard Shevardnadze and British Foreign Secretary Sir Geoffrey Howe met for talks and prepared three agree-

Gorbachev's Visit to Britain

ments for signing by Gorbachev and Thatcher—an agreement on protecting foreign investment, an agreement in principle for Britain to build a school in Armenia, and a memorandum on new provisions to speed up business visas (*Reuters*, April 6).

Speaking to reporters after the talks with Thatcher, Gorbachev said his dialogue with Britain had reached a stage that showed the degree of mutual understanding was increasing. A spokesman for Thatcher told reporters that she and Gorbachev had disagreements over arms-control issues, including the reduction of nuclear and chemical weapons (*Reuters, AP*, April 6). During the talks with Thatcher, Gorbachev said the policy review being conducted by the new US administration was threatening the momentum of arms talks (*TASS*, April 6). Thatcher raised the question of human-rights abuses in Romania and political developments in Hungary and Poland. Gorbachev presented Thatcher with a detailed review of the domestic situation in the USSR. He said the reform process in his country was entering a difficult period, when a lot of concrete steps should be taken. The same day, Thatcher held a dinner in honor of Gorbachev during which she praised the Soviet leader for conducting "a peaceful revolution" (*Reuters, AP*, April 6, *Pravda*, April 7).

On April 7, Gorbachev spoke before British politicians at London's Guildhall. In the speech, he reaffirmed his opposition to NATO's modernization of its short-range nuclear missiles in Europe. He said East and West should work towards the complete elimination of all nuclear weapons. He also said the USSR was prepared to resume negotiations on reducing long-range strategic nuclear forces whenever the US was ready. He announced that the USSR would stop producing weapons-grade uranium, saying this was "yet another step towards the wrapping up of production of fissionable materials for use in nuclear weapons" (Western agencies, *TASS*, and *Central Television*, which broadcast Gorbachev's speech live). Thatcher spoke after Gorbachev and praised his political boldness. The same day, Gorbachev visited Queen Elizabeth II at Windsor Castle and invited her to visit the Soviet Union (*AP*, April 7). She accepted the invitation in principle. The same day, Gorbachev left London for Moscow (Western agencies, *TASS*, April 7; *Pravda*, April 8).

Khrushchev's 1956 Speech and Excerpts from Memoirs Published in USSR

Radio Moscow-1 (1840) reported that *Izvestiya TsK KPSS* (No.3) had been published and was being sent to subscribers. The issue contains the full text of the speech on Stalin's personality cult delivered by Nikita Khrushchev at the Twentieth Party Congress in 1956. It is the first time the text of the speech has appeared in the open press in the USSR. *Argumenty i fakty* (Nos. 13 and 14) carried an excerpt from Khrushchev's memoirs.

The public prosecutor of Lithuania is investigating virulent anti-Lithuanian leaflets signed by a group representing the republic's Russian minority, a journalist said. Algis Cekuolis, editor of the Lithuanian-language weekly *Gimtasis Krastas*, told Reuters the investigation was prompted by the reproduction of a leaflet in his magazine last week that said "the only good Lithuanian is a dead Lithuanian." The leaflet, which Cekuolis said had been sent to him in the post, was signed "Edinstvo," a group representing Russians in Lithuania that has fought moves to restore Lithuanian as the official language of the republic.

Row in Lithuania over Anti-Lithuanian Leaflets

Deputy Chairman of the State Commission for Air Traffic Safety Rudolf Teimurazov said that 115 people had been killed and 93 injured in sixteen Soviet air crashes last year. According to *Izvestia*, Teimurazov said 154 accidents took place last year, costing Aeroflot 10 million rubles.

Official Gives Figures on Air Crashes in 1988

An agreement has been signed in the United States creating the Soviet Union's first university graduate degree program in business administration. The agreement, signed in Oregon by Portland State University and representatives of the Soviet authorities in Khabarovsk Krai, will establish the program at the Khabarovsk Institute of National Economy (*RFE/RL Special*, April 5).

Agreement Creating Soviet Business School Signed

_____ *Thursday, April 6*

In an article in *Sotsialisticheskaya industriya*, economic journalist Vasilii Selyunin said that the national economy would perform worse than ever this year and that no real progress can be made until central planning is abandoned. Selyunin, whose earlier articles attracted considerable attention among the Soviet public, urged immediate economic reforms to remove shortages, in particular ending ministries' control over production. Selyunin said real reforms would be constantly delayed unless centrally controlled economic structures are dismantled. Endorsing the line advocated by economist Nikolai Shmelev,

Soviet Economist Says Economic Prospects Gloomy

Selyunin also proposed imports of some consumer goods to ease shortages. (Other economists, backed in this instance by Gorbachev, are against increasing imports of consumer goods.)

Soviet Muslim Leader on Rushdie Death Threat

A Muslim religious leader in Soviet Central Asia said the furor over the book *The Satanic Verses* should be a warning to atheists in the Soviet Union that they need to be more sensitive to the feelings of believers. Muslim leader Mukhammadsadyk Mamayusupov said Rushdie's book does insult Moslems, but he said he did not support Ayatollah Khomeini in his demand that Rushdie be killed for writing the book. Mamayusupov's comments appeared in *Moscow News* (No. 15).

Ligachev Says He Does Not Oppose Soviet Reforms

In a rare interview with the Italian newspaper *Corriere della Sera*, Politburo member Egor Ligachev said he does not oppose reforms in the USSR but wants to know where they will lead. He also said he did not think that the defeat of some top Party officials in the elections to the Congress of People's Deputies on March 26 was a vote of no confidence in the Party.

Ligachev Reaffirms Support for Collective Farming

Egor Ligachev insisted that kolkhozes and sovkhozes were the mainstay of Soviet agriculture. He was attending a seminar on family farming and rural cooperatives in the Belorussian city of Brest. At a similar meeting last week in Omsk, he called for the removal of all restrictions on family farms because they produce so much of the country's food. Today, however, he said that his remarks in support of private farming should not lead anybody to think he was dropping support for kolkhozes and sovkhozes. He said close cooperation between family farms and kolkhozes and sovkhozes was the best way to link private and public interest (*Central Television,* "Vremya," *TASS,* April 6).

Hunger Strike in Georgia

Scores of Georgian nationalists demanding independence for their republic are staging a hunger strike in front of the main government buildings in Tbilisi. AP quoted activist Georgii (Gia) Chanturia, who is chairman of a group calling itself the National Democratic Party of Georgia, as saying that 158 Georgians began a hunger strike on April 4 and plan to continue it until April 14, the anniversary of a demonstration for ethnic rights in 1978.

A Soviet nuclear-powered submarine caught fire and sank in the Arctic, about 500 kilometers off Norway's northern coast. Forty-two people died in the accident, and twenty-seven were rescued and immediately hospitalized. Norwegian Foreign Minister Thorvald Stoltenberg said Soviet officials had assured Norway there was "absolutely no danger" of any radiation leaking from the stricken submarine (*TASS, Reuters, AP*, April 8). On April 10, TASS said air and water samples showed no signs of radiation contamination from the submarine. On April 17, it was reported that Soviet search teams had so far failed to locate the Soviet nuclear submarine. *Izvestia* said it was still too early to say whether the stricken submarine would be raised to the surface. On April 21, *Sotsialisticheskaya industriya* carried an article that included accounts by people who survived the accident. The survivors, who included the captain of the submarine, complained that the majority of the victims died not in the fire but because there was insufficient emergency safety equipment aboard the submarine.

Fire on Soviet Nuclear Submarine

Life expectancy in the world's industrialized countries is highest in Japan and lowest in the Soviet Union, according to the first ever complete survey on mortality in developed countries. The World Health Organization, which published the survey in its weekly Epidemiological Record, said official statistics supplied by the USSR now made it possible to prepare an overall assessment of health conditions in the thirty-three countries.

Soviet Life Expectancy Lowest among Industrialized Nations

Izvestia published an article discussing the situation of the small nations of the Soviet North. The newspaper said there were serious ecological problems as well as a degeneration of the traditional life style of the peoples of the North.

***Izvestia* on Problems of Peoples of Soviet North**

The Soviet and Afghan governments criticized a United States decision to appoint an ambassador-level envoy to the interim government set up by the resistance. Spokesmen for Kabul and for the Soviet Foreign Ministry said the United States move would serve to prolong the war. (*Reuters, TASS*, in English, April 7).

USSR Criticizes US Move on Afghanistan

195

Saturday, April 8 ───────────────────────────────

Supreme Soviet Approves
Farm Leasing Plan

The USSR Supreme Soviet passed a decree allowing long-term private leasing of property, including farmland and equipment. TASS carried the announcement on April 8 and Soviet newspapers on April 9. TASS said the decree reflects reforms made at a Central Committee plenum on agriculture last month. It permits leases for fifty years and longer of land, natural resources, buildings, cattle, farm machinery, and other equipment. It covers collective as well as private and family leasing.

Government Minister
Negotiates End to
Miners' Strike

TASS said miners in Siberia had agreed to end a five-day sit-in at their mine after talks with a government minister. TASS said Minister of Nonferrous Metallurgy Vladimir Durasov flew to the city of Norilsk in the Soviet Far North to examine demands by miners over various pay-related issues. TASS said Durasov worked out a deal, but it collapsed when the strike leaders issued a new demand for a 30-percent pay rise. It said the issue was ultimately resolved, however, and that the miners had returned to work today. It was the second such end to a Soviet labor dispute in a month. Last month, Minister of the Coal Industry Mikhail Shchadov flew to the northern city of Vorkuta in the Urals to work out a pay arrangement to settle a miners' strike there.

Sunday, April 9 ───────────────────────────────

Violence Used against
Demonstrators in Georgia

Soviet security troops attacked a crowd of demonstrators in the Georgian capital of Tbilisi, killing a number of people. TASS immediately laid the blame for the violence on "national elements" who were intent on "fanning interethnic discord."

The violence came on the sixth day of demonstrations that began on April 4, when members of the unofficial Georgian National Democratic Party embarked on a hunger strike in front of the local government building to press demands for Georgian independence. Strikes and street demonstrations continued on April 8 in defiance of a televised appeal for calm by Georgian Party First Secretary Dzhumber Patiashvili. The demands voiced by the demonstrators were said to have ranged from greater political and economic autonomy to "independence," secession, and the withdrawal of the Russian presence from Georgia. A comparable but much smaller demonstration took place in Kutaisi, the second-largest city in Georgia (*AP*, April 8).

In the wake of the violence on April 9, a number of leading Georgian dissidents were arrested, including Zviad Gamsakhurdia, Merab Kostava, and Georgii (Gia) Chanturia, and an 11 P.M.–6 A.M. curfew was imposed (*RFE/RL Special*, April 9).

In an interview on the Soviet television evening news program "Vremya" on April 10, Patiashvili called the events "our common grief, for which we are all responsible." He said innocent people had died while "extremist" leaders had escaped uninjured. He said foreign tourists were being asked to leave Georgia "since it is not the best place for tourists to be." Western journalists were also barred from the republic.

On April 10, there were reports of some strikes in Tbilisi, apparently in response to a call by the Georgian Popular Front, and residents told reporters by telephone that black flags of mourning were flying from homes (*Reuters*, April 10). Soviet Foreign Minister Eduard Shevardnadze canceled a trip to East Germany and flew to Georgia together with Politburo member Georgii Razumovsky for consultations on the situation with local Party leaders (*TASS*, April 10; *Pravda*, April 11).

On April 11, an official day of mourning was held in Georgia for the victims of the clashes. Eduard Shevardnadze met in Tbilisi with Georgian intellectuals. He was reported to have told them that Sunday's violence against demonstrators was "a stab in the back for *perestroika*" (*RFE/RL Special*, April 11).

On April 12, Mikhail Gorbachev appealed for calm in Georgia (*TASS*, April 12; *Pravda*, April 13). RFE/RL was told in a telephone interview with Tbilisi that forty prominent Georgian writers had left the CPSU following the clashes (*RFE/RL Special*, April 12).

On April 13, the "Vremya" television news program carried a report saying the number of deaths from Sunday's clashes had risen to twenty.

On April 14, the Georgian Party Central Committee held a plenary meeting in Tbilisi. It accepted the resignation of Georgian Party First Secretary Patiashvili. Givi Gumbaridze, Georgia's KGB chairman, was nominated to replace him. Foreign Ministry spokesman Gennadii Gerasimov said the chairman of the republic's Supreme Soviet, Otar Cherkezia, and the chairman of the Georgian Council of Ministers, Zurab Chkheidze, had also resigned from the Buro of the Georgian Party Central Committee at the meeting. He said they had also offered to resign their state posts (*Reuters, TASS*, April 14). The meeting was addressed by Eduard Shevardnadze. He told the meeting that "nobody and nothing can justify the deaths of innocent people." Western agencies reported the same day that the Georgian youth newspaper *Molodezh' Gruzii* had prepared a story on April 13 about Sunday's clashes but that the issue of the newspaper was banned. The head of the newspaper's information department, Mikhail Eligulashvili, said soldiers armed with machine guns had forced their way into the newspaper's offices to confiscate the issue. He told RFE/RL that the ban was later reversed, although copies of the newspaper went only to subscribers in Tbilisi.

Runoff Election Results

Runoff elections were held in twelve districts on April 2 and sixty-four districts on April 9. The winners of the elections in Moscow on April 9 were: historian Roy Medvedev; design engineer Yurii Andreev; enterprise director Viktor Yaroshenko; rector of the Moscow Aviation Institute Yurii Ryzhov; factory worker Andrei Sibentsov; general director of the "Kvant" enterprise Yurii Skokov; historian Sergei Stankevich; and Central Television commentator Yurii Chernichenko (*Radio Moscow-1*, 1000, April 10). In Lithuania, "Sajudis" claimed victory in at least four of the eight runoff elections held there on April 9. A member of the "Sajudis" electoral commission also charged that there had been instances of electoral fraud (*RFE Lithuanian Service*, April 9).

On April 8, *Pravda* reported on a meeting of twenty top Kiev Party officials that turned into a clash between the supporters and opponents of the first secretary of Kiev's City Party Committee, Konstantin Masik, and the mayor of Kiev, Valentin Zgursky, both of whom lost their single-candidate races on March 26. Zgursky's supporters were reported to have accused *Pravda* reporters of intriguing against him, while his detractors called for his resignation.

New Deputy Defense Minister Appointed

Krasnaya zvezda identified Colonel General Yurii Yashin as deputy minister of defense and commander in chief of the Soviet Strategic Rocket Forces. Army General Yurii Maksimov, who had been commander in chief of the Strategic Rocket Forces since 1985, was reported to have retired at the age of sixty-five. Both Maksimov and Yashin were elected to the Congress of People's Deputies. Yashin, who is fifty-eight, had occupied the post of first deputy commander in chief of the Strategic

Rocket Forces since 1981. He entered army service in 1948 and became a Party member in 1957. In 1984, he was elected a deputy of the USSR Supreme Soviet and a member of the Youth Commission of the Council of the Union.

Police Demonstrate in Leningrad

AFP quoted unofficial sources as saying that some 500 Soviet policemen had mounted an unauthorized demonstration in Leningrad today. The policemen were demonstrating for the right to use their firearms more freely against criminals (*Pravda* reported in March that Soviet police are outgunned by the mafia.) They also protested against sending Leningrad police units into the Baltic republics "for the maintenance of law and order." This appears to be the first time that Soviet policemen have mounted an unauthorized demonstration.

Moscow News on Religion

Moscow News (No. 15) reported that the Council for Religious Affairs had canceled all the edicts it issued betweeen 1961 and 1983. These edicts banned various religious activities, from charity work to bell-ringing. The same issue of the newspaper included a report on what was done in 1988 to improve the situation of believers in the USSR. The measures reported by the newspaper include the opening of new churches and mosques, the registration of new religious societies, and plans to open new theological seminaries. The newspaper also carried statements by various religious officials who discussed the draft law on freedom of conscience that is due to be published in the USSR for public discussion.

Moscow News on Crimean Tatars

Moscow News (No. 15) carried an article on the deportation of Crimean Tatars in the 1940s on Stalin's orders. The article said that Crimean Tatars were still having difficulties in returning to their homeland. The article defended activists of the Crimean Tatar movement, who have been attacked in the Soviet press even under *glasnost'.*

Solzhenitsyn, Brodsky, and Galich among Most Popular Authors in USSR

Moscow News (No. 15) carried an article by an employee at the Institute of Books, Sergei Shvedov, who reported on the results of polls conducted by his institute on the level of popularity in the USSR of various writers and poets writing in Russian. Among the most popular were Aleksandr Solzhenitsyn, Joseph Brodsky, and Aleksandr Galich. The newspaper said that two other émigré writers, Sasha Sokolov and Aleksandr Zinov'ev, had also aroused great interest among Soviet readers. In addition, the youth journal *Sobesednik* (No. 15) published an interview with Natal'ya Reshetovskaya, Solzhenitsyn's first wife. In the interview, Reshetovskaya complained that a book she wrote about Solzhenitsyn in the 1970s, published by Novosti press agency, had been heavily censored, and she claimed that some passages had been inserted in the book by censors and were not written by herself. In the interview, Reshetovskaya also praised Solzhenitsyn and tried to show what a large role she had played in his life prior to their divorce.

Monday, April 10 ———————————————————————————

Sakharov Nominated by Academy of Sciences

It was reported that Academician Andrei Sakharov had been nominated for one of the USSR Academy of Sciences' seats in the Congress of People's Deputies. He was one of more than twenty-five candidates approved by the academy's Presidium. Academy employees, and some of its members protested against Sakharov's exclusion from the Presidium's original list of candidates and forced a new round of nominations and elections (*TASS*, April 10).

Rally Reported in Kishinev

More than 15,000 people gathered in the Moldavian capital of Kishinev demanding that Moldavian be made the official language of the republic and that the Latin alphabet be reintroduced. On April 10, Radio Kishinev said participants in the meeting, which had been sanctioned in advance, protested against the use of Russian as the official language of communication for the people of Moldavia. The radio said the Moldavian Council of Ministers had decided to abolish a decree issued in 1949 that provided for the deportation from Moldavia of families of kulaks, landowners, and rich tradesmen. It said these people had now been rehabilitated and could return home, provided that they had not collaborated with German or Romanian occupiers during World War II.

Tuesday, April 11 ———————————————————————————

Pravda Calls for More Actions against Nationalists

Pravda said Soviet law-enforcement bodies had slackened in carrying out of laws against anti-Sovietism, interethnic strife, and "arrant nationalism." The newspaper said this had resulted in small groups being able to use advocacy of *perestroika* as an excuse for violations of law and order. It said this had taken place in Armenia, Azerbaijan, the Baltic republics, Moldavia, and now in Georgia. The daily said the decree issued by the USSR Supreme Soviet on April 9 to strengthen existing laws against antistate activities could be expected to stabilize public order in the USSR.

Izvestia published the text of a decree issued on April 9 by the Presidium of the USSR Supreme Soviet on amendments to the USSR law of 1958 "On Criminal Liability for Crimes against the State." The decree is signed by Gorbachev. The amendments replace two articles of the old law on crimes against the state—the notorious Article 70 of the Criminal Code of the RSFSR dealing with "Anti-Soviet Agitation and Propaganda," and the former Article 74 of the Criminal Code of the RSFSR "On Violation of Equality of Rights of Nationalities and Races," or the articles numbered 7 and 11 in the all-Union law on crimes against the state.

Amendment to Law on Crimes against the State

In addition, two new articles, 7-1 and 11-1, have been introduced into the law. Article 11-1 seems to be replacing another law that was used in the Brezhnev era against political opponents of the Soviet regime—Article 190-1 of the RSFSR Criminal Code "On Knowingly False Dissemination of Fabrications Discrediting the Soviet Political and Social System."

The changes disappoint expectations that were aroused by Gorbachev's speech to the United Nations last December, in which he promised to put an end to the practice of imprisoning people for exercising free speech. Instead of prohibiting "Anti-Soviet Agitation and Propaganda," the new edition of Article 7 outlaws "Calls for the Overthrow or Change of the Soviet State and Social System." It covers public calls for changes in the political system by anticonstitutional methods, which may be acceptable by Western standards, but it also outlaws calls "for obstructing the execution of Soviet laws"—i. e., for actions of civil disobedience. According to Academician Vladimir Kudryavtsev, the head of the USSR Institute of State and Law, whose comments on the changes were broadcast on Soviet television on April 11, criticism of the Soviet system in private conversations or in entries in private diaries cannot be punished under the new law, in contrast with the application of the old Article 7.

The new Article 7-1 prohibits "Public Calls for the Betrayal of the Motherland or for the Commission of a Terrorist Act or Sabotage." It should be recalled that, in an interview published in *Moscow News* in January, Aleksandr Yakovlev, a scholar from the Institute of State and Law, who was responsible for drafting the new criminal laws, promised that the law on "Betrayal of the Motherland" that defines such crimes as "flight abroad" as "high treason," would be abolished entirely. Nonetheless, "Betrayal of the Motherland"—that is, Article 1 of the USSR law "On Criminal Liability for Crimes against the State"—is not amended by the present decree and, therefore, remains as it has been since the days of Stalin. On April 12, Western agencies reported that Yakovlev had criticized the new Article 11-1, which prohibits "insulting and defaming" Soviet government organizations and even officials. AP and Reuters quoted Yakovlev as saying the appearance of this article was an absolute surprise to him.

Sugar Rationing Anticipated for Moscow

Reports said sugar rationing would begin in Moscow in May. *Pravda* and *Vechernyaya Moskva* said each Moscow resident would be limited to two kilograms of sugar next month and to three kilograms in June and July.

Wednesday, April 12 ————————————————————————

Chairman of USSR Supreme Court Retires

Chairman of the USSR Supreme Court Vladimir Terebilov was reported to have retired at the age of seventy-three. He had held the post for the past five years. Earlier this year, Nikolai Ivanov, the deputy chief of the group investigating corruption among members of the Brezhnev clique, accused Terebilov of using his position to stop corrupt Uzbek officials from being exposed.

Abolition of Military Draft for Students

According to TASS, students of Soviet institutions of higher education and their teachers have won an important battle against the military with the publication today in *Krasnaya zvezda* and *Izvestia* of a government decree granting students the right to postpone their military service until the end of their studies. This right, however, applies only to day students under the age of twenty-seven. The practice of drafting students into active military service was one of the two main reasons for mass protests on university campuses all over the Soviet Union in the past two or three years. Another reason for the student protests was the excessive amount of time given to military training in the university curriculum. It is not clear from the TASS comment on the new decree whether the practice of training reserve officers at the expense of the professional education of all students would also be changed. Writing in *Krasnaya zvezda* on April 13, Soviet Defense Minister Dmitrii Yazov rejected suggestions to turn the Soviet Armed Forces into an all-volunteer force half its current size.

_____ *Thursday, April 13*

Krasnaya zvezda said Soviet soldiers sent to Vietnam in the 1960s took part in combat operations and often shot down US aircraft. The newspaper printed reminiscences of Soviet soldiers who served during the war in Vietnam, thereby acknowledging that Soviet soldiers, rather than advisers, fought alongside the North Vietnamese. The newspaper did not comment on the accounts.

Soviet Soldiers Say They Shot Down US Planes in Vietnam

A member of the USSR Academy of Sciences, Boris Chertok, has defended the Soviet government's spending on space research. He said the USSR last year got more back in satellite services, weather forecasting, and technology transfers than it spent on space research. Chertok told TASS that calls to cut space spending reflect ignorance about the benefits of space technology. Demands for cuts in the space program emerged during the recent Soviet election campaign (*TASS*, April 13).

Official Defends Spending on Space Research

TASS said a Jewish community had been registered in Lvov. TASS said the Lvov Jewish community planned to send a representative to the yeshiva, a school for advanced Jewish studies, at the main synagogue in Moscow. The agency said the Lvov community also maintained active contacts with Jews in other Soviet cities and in foreign countries and was recently visited by rabbis from the United States.

TASS Says Jewish Community Registered in Lvov

Prominent Soviet economist Leonid Abalkin said that meeting economic plan targets should no longer be obligatory for enterprises but that the targets should serve as goals. TASS reported that Abalkin discussed new models of five-year plans in *Kommunist* (No. 6). According to the report, Abalkin said that plan targets should no longer be used for the evaluation of economic activity and that planned economic changes should open the way to complete

Economist Says Plan Targets Should No Longer Be Obligatory

self-sufficiency of enterprises and should allow workers to become the real masters of production. Abalkin said the fate of *perestroika* depends to a large extent on the way the next five-year plan (1991–1995) is prepared.

Friday, April 14 ──────────────────────────────────────

Pravda Says Leningrad's Democratic Union Harmful

Pravda said the Leningrad unofficial group "The Democratic Union" was harmful to *perestroika*. The daily said the group wants to eliminate the CPSU from Soviet political life and completely change the social order of the country. The newspaper accused the union of radicalism and striving for power.

Draft Law Making Tajik Official Language Published

Draft legislation giving Tajik the status of a state language was published in the Tajikistan press for public discussion. TASS said the draft calls for Tajik to be used in government bodies and in economic, scientific, and cultural affairs in Tajikistan. The draft says the Russian language is to be used in contacts between Tajikistan and other Soviet republics. The draft also said other nationalities in the republic will be able to develop their own languages and cultures.

USSR to Put First British Astronaut into Space

Britain is to send its first astronaut into space on board a Soviet spacecraft. Under an agreement signed in Moscow, a British astronaut will spend two weeks on the space station *Mir* with Soviet cosmonauts during a mission planned to take place over the next two or three years. Radio Moscow's World Service said the USSR had signed similar agreements with Austria and Japan and was also negotiating a joint mission with West Germany.

Soviet Official Says More than Twenty POWs Freed

Soviet Deputy Foreign Minister Vladimir Petrovsky said the Foreign Ministry had helped arrange the release and return of more than twenty Soviet prisoners of war from Afghanistan. TASS said Petrovsky reported the information at a Foreign Ministry meeting on April 13 with representatives of the Soviet "People's Committee for the Release of Soviet Prisoners of War in Afghanistan." He did not say when the prisoners were released. TASS said those serving on the committee include journalists, writers, clergymen, cultural figures, Afghan war veterans, and relatives of Soviet POWs.

On April 15, a group of Moscow intellectuals, including Andrei Sakharov, blamed the clashes in Tbilisi on decrees adopted in July, 1988, to control demonstrations. The decrees gave broad rights to special MVD troops in dealing with protesters (*AP*, April 15).

On April 16, a mass demonstration took place in Moscow to demand that those responsible for the deaths of demonstrators in Tbilisi be punished. Sakharov addresssed the gathering (*Reuters, AFP*, April 16). The same day, the authorities in Tbilisi shortened the curfew by two hours and began pulling troops out of the city (*UPI*, April 16). On April 16, *Pravda* published the text of a speech delivered by Shevardnadze in Tbilisi on April 14. The newspaper quoted Shevardnadze as saying the decision to deploy the troops in Tbilisi had been taken by the republican Party leadership, who chose "to talk to the people from behind tanks." (Soviet activists questioned Shevardnadze's assertion, pointing out that it would be unusual for a republican-level leadership to take a decision to deploy troops without checking with Moscow.)

On April 17, students in Tbilisi ended protest boycotts and went back to their classes (*AP, Reuters*, April 17). The same day, the curfew in Tbilisi was lifted and on April 18, *TASS* reported that all troops had been withdrawn from Tbilisi.

On April 19, six deputies to the new Congress of People's Deputies were quoted as saying the violent dispersal by riot squads of the demonstration in Tbilisi on April 9 showed how reform could be cut short in the USSR. They charged that the authorities had imposed fierce censorship on reports from the Georgian capital and had issued a blatantly distorted official account. The deputies insisted that poison gas had been used against the demonstrators in Tbilisi. They said that a remark on the use of shovels and poison gas had been cut out of an interview conducted by Soviet television with Georgian Health Minister Irakly Menagharishvili. The statement of the deputies appeared in *Moscow News* (No. 17). The behavior of troops on April 9 in Tbilisi was also criticized at a meeting in the USSR Academy of Sciences (*AP*, April 19). The same day, *Pravda* commented on the use of chemicals in the April 9 clashes. It said MVD officials claimed that tear gas (not poison gas) had been used.

On April 21, a meeting took place at the Cinema Workers' Union in Moscow to discuss the situation in Georgia. Georgian filmmaker Eldar Shengelaya, who has

Use of Troops in Tbilisi Protested

been elected to the Congress of People's Deputies, told the meeting that the Soviet authorities had attempted a massive cover-up after troops killed at least twenty demonstrators in Tbilisi. The meeting was shown a clandestine video film that contradicted official accounts that troops in Tbilisi had used maximum restraint and only responded when they came under attack. The film showed clearly that the troops had attacked without provocation. Shengelaya told the meeting that the local authorities in Georgia would not have had sufficient authority to call in the troops without the go-ahead from Moscow (*Reuters*, April 21).

Printing Machine Meant for Christian Publisher Impounded

A printing machine taken to the Soviet Union as a gift for a publisher of Christian literature was reported to have been impounded by Soviet customs agents. A British clergyman, Reverend Dick Rodgers, had flown from London to Moscow with the machine to deliver it to Aleksandr Ogorodnikov. Ogorodnikov publishes the *Bulletin of the Christian Community*. Rodgers' wife said the Soviet customs agents had told Rodgers he did not have the proper documents (*AP*, April 15).

Agricultural Association Set Up in Latvia

Latvian farmers have set up an agricultural association to help improve the republic's food situation. TASS said the association's constituent congress began work in Riga today. The association already has 146,000 members. TASS said the association's program aims to increase agricultural output by using updated economic methods and various forms of farming—ranging from individual farms to the already existing sovkhozes and kolkhozes. TASS said the situation in agriculture in the republic is extremely unfavorable. It said that, while Latvia used to be famous for its high-quality bacon and fats on world markets, now it is unable to feed its own population. The agency also said one million hectares of arable land had been lost because of excessive industrial development (*TASS*, April 15).

USSR Gives Up *Phobos-2* Mars Probe

Soviet space agency officials have decided to abandon the *Phobos-2* Mars probe, with which contact was lost last month. A Soviet space official, Roald Kremnev, told a press conference near Moscow that no further attempts would be made to reestablish contact with the unmanned probe, which has been circling Mars for the past two months. He said it is not yet clear why the link was lost.

Last September the USSR lost contact with the *Phobos-1* Mars probe because of an incorrect computer command sent by a ground controller (*TASS*, April 15).

Britain's Prince Edward arrived in Moscow on a three-day visit. He was welcomed at the airport by USSR Deputy Minister of Culture Yurii Khilchevsky. The visit is linked to the staging in Moscow of T. S. Eliot's play *Murder in the Cathedral* by Britain's National Youth Theater, of which Prince Edward is a patron (*UPI, AP*, April 15).

Britain's Prince Edward Visits Moscow

―――――――――――――――――――――――――――――*Sunday, April 16*

Moscow News (No. 16) reported that a Soviet writer had uncovered the remains of the last Russian Tsar, Nicholas II, ten years ago but did not dare to say anything. The newspaper quoted Gelii Ryabov as saying he uncovered the bodies of Nicholas and his family by a swamp near present-day Sverdlovsk in the Urals in 1979. Sverdlovsk was formerly called Ekaterinburg, the place where Nicholas and his family were shot in July, 1918. Ryabov said he identified the remains by the number of bodies, the teeth, the wounds, and the shards of pots of acid nearby. It had previously been maintained that the bodies were destroyed and all traces removed by acid after the execution. Ryabov said the authorities tried to conceal the place where the bodies were to prevent it from becoming a shrine. Ryabov is a former MVD official and the author of stories about Chekists.

Soviet Writer Says He Found Tsar's Remains

Soviet workers will be subject to a new progressive tax system with a top rate of 50 percent, according to a draft law carried by TASS. Under the draft law, the new rates will affect people earning more than 700 rubles a month, who will pay 15 percent. According to the draft, the rate will rise to 20 percent on earnings over 900 rubles a month, 30 percent on 1,100 rubles, 40 percent on 1,400 rubles, and 50 percent on 1,500 rubles and above. People earning less that 700 rubles a month will continue to pay the current flat rate of 13 percent, which is levied on all incomes over 80 rubles a month. (The average salary is 234 rubles a month.) Observers believe that the new system is aimed at workers in the cooperative sector, whose wages are often higher than the average, but workers in the state sector who qualify for productiv-

New Soviet Law Provides for Progressive Income Tax System

ity bonuses could also be affected. The government proposed a progressive income tax last year on cooperative earnings, with a top tax bracket of 90 percent. That proposal was withdrawn following criticism that it would stifle the cooperative movement.

Khrushchev Hailed in Moscow as Godfather of Gorbachev Reform

Nikita Khrushchev was hailed at a mass meeting in Moscow as the man who sowed the seeds for Gorbachev's restructuring drive. "None of us in [Stalin's] labor camps believed that out of the gang around Stalin there would emerge one who would storm the evil citadel of Stalinism out of moral conviction, but Khrushchev did," said writer and former prisoner Lev Razgon. Historian Roy Medvedev, who also spoke at the meeting, said that Khrushchev's fall in 1964 had provided a lesson that "dark forces" constantly fight to prevent genuine change. The meeting marked the ninety-fifth anniversary of Khrushchev's birth (*AP*, April 17; *Izvestia*, April 19).

Yazov Agrees to Some Lithuanian Demands on Military Service

Radio Vilnius said USSR Minister of Defense Dmitrii Yazov had agreed to allow Lithuanians to perform their military service in or near Lithuania when not posted abroad. The radio said Yazov had agreed to the proposal at a meeting in Moscow with Lithuanian Party First Secretary Algirdas Brazauskas. On April 19, *Pravda* criticized demands that Soviet military conscripts be allowed to serve in locally raised units in their home republics. The author of the article, Lieutenant Colonel M. Zakharchik, said no republic is capable of raising and maintaining its own army. He said unofficial groups in the Baltic republics are naïve in demanding that conscripts serve at home.

May Day Slogan Urges Rejection of Nationalism

The Soviet leadership, facing an upsurge of national sentiment and unrest in many of the Soviet Union's republics, called on the country to reject nationalism and reinforce "Soviet patriotism." The appeal against nationalism appeared among slogans from the Party Central Committee issued in advance of the May Day holiday— an annual practice. Their formulation signals what Moscow sees as its key policy concerns. One slogan read: "People of the USSR! Preserve and develop the traditions of Socialist internationalism and Soviet patriotism! Deal a decisive rebuff to manifestations of nationalism and chauvinism!" (*Pravda*, April 16).

Ogonek (No. 16) gave details of a missile disaster in the USSR in 1960, when a fully fueled intercontinental ballistic missile exploded on the launch pad, killing a number of people, including the head of Soviet Rocket Forces at that time, Marshal of Artillery Mitrofan Nedelin. The magazine blamed the accident on the USSR's rush to catch up with the United States in the missile race and on the flouting of safety rules to which this led. It did not say how many died.

Details Given of Soviet Missile Disaster in 1960

Monday, April 17

Czechoslovak Party General Secretary Milos Jakes arrived in Moscow for an official visit. Speaking on Soviet television on April 16, Jakes said Czechoslovakia was devoting "very great attention" to *glasnost'* as a means of furthering democracy. On April 18, Jakes met in Moscow with Mikhail Gorbachev (*TASS*, April 18, *Pravda*, April 19).

Jakes Begins Soviet Visit

An international symposium on law and psychiatry opened in Moscow. TASS said the Ministry of Health's chief psychiatric expert, Aleksandr Karpov, told the opening session that the Soviet authorities had abused the rights of mental patients. He said this practice must stop. Among those attending the Moscow meeting were representatives from the United States, Bulgaria, Hungary, Czechoslovakia, and Poland. Two members of the recently created Soviet Association of Independent Psychiatrists, Viktor Lanovoi and Konstantin Karmanov, appeared uninvited at the opening session. Lanovoi told RFE/RL by telephone that he and Karmanov were formally introduced to the forum. He said he told the gathering that psychiatrists and neurologists who were not involved in the abuse of psychiatry for political purposes could join his organization.

International Psychiatric Symposium Opens in Moscow

The chief editor of *Ogonek*, Vitalii Korotich, was named international editor of the year by the New York-based magazine *World Press Review*. The *World Press Review* said in making the award that Korotich had in three years turned the publication from "a banal coffee-table magazine into a glossy publication resembling *Life* magazine and read by more than three million subscribers" (*AP*, April 18).

Korotich Named International Editor of the Year

Soviet Military Planes to Deliver Vegetables

A Soviet Air Force commander said military transport planes would begin delivering vegetables to various parts of the USSR in the next few days. Colonel General Vyacheslav Efanov said in *Izvestia* that military cargo planes would transport at least 50,000 tons of goods and equipment this year. Efanov said this was in keeping with plans for Soviet Air Force pilots to take part in large-scale transport operations for civilian purposes. Defense Minister Dmitrii Yazov said last week that military transport planes should do more to help the national economy.

Controversy over AIDS in USSR

Yurii Fedorov, the deputy director of the Main Epidemiological Administration of the USSR Ministry of Health, told *Sel'skaya zhizn'* that 570 HIV carriers had been identified in the Soviet Union. He said that 378 of these were foreigners who had been expelled from the country and that the other 192 were Soviet citizens. (Deputy Minister of Health Aleksandr Kondrusev told reporters at an international conference in Moscow last month that 176 Soviet citizens had been identified as HIV carriers.) Fedorov said that there had been seven officially registered cases of the disease in the USSR, four of them Soviet citizens, and that three of these had died and the fourth was an invalid. Despite these disturbing figures, Fedorov said that "we [the USSR] do not yet have an [AIDS] epidemic in the true sense of that word." This statement was challenged by Vadim Pokrovsky, president of the Soviet Association for the Struggle against AIDS, who told the newspaper that "the fact that 192 Soviet citizens are infected with the human immunodeficiency virus and over fifty of them are children means that an epidemic has started." Pokrovsky emphasized that it is impossible to say exactly how quickly the disease will spread in the USSR: "we do not have basic data on how many homosexuals, drug addicts, and prostitutes there are in this country." He predicted, however, that it would spread quickly, "and not only in the big cities."

Opinion Poll on Political Sympathies

The magazine *Vek XX i mir* (No. 3) published the results of a poll into the attitude of different sectors of the Soviet population to political and economic reforms. Those polled were asked, among other things, to rate on a five-point scale the popularity of the following people: Tsar Nicholas II, Lenin, Stalin, Nikita Khrushchev, Yurii An-

210

dropov, Leonid Brezhnev, Mikhail Gorbachev, Boris El'tsin, Egor Ligachev, Aleksandr Yakovlev, Andrei Sakharov, Fidel Castro, Ronald Reagan, and Deng Xiaoping. Brezhnev got the lowest rating from all the groups, Lenin, the highest; Gorbachev came second, and El'tsin third. The poll was conducted in Moscow in November and December, 1988, by the Soviet Sociological Association. Those who conducted the poll divided the respondents, who totaled 1,231, into six groups according to their political preferences and, specifically, according to their ideas about the kind of *perestroika* they would like to see. These groups were (1) "pragmatic-Westernizers"; (2) "renewers" (supporters of "social justice"); (3) "*gosudarstven-niki*" (disciplinarians, or supporters of a strong state); (4) "Greens"; (5) "patriots"; and (6) "*obyvateli*" (those holding consumerist values). Groups (1) and (2) supported Gorbachev's policies, while group (6) was apolitical and had little interest in *perestroika*.

Farmers' Attitudes towards Land Leasing

Pravda reported on an opinion poll of 176 kolkhoz chairmen in Kursk Oblast. Nearly 60 percent of the respondents evaluated the new system of land leasing positively, though only 20 percent gave an unequivocal "yes" when asked whether they thought it was the best way of improving Soviet agriculture. Just under 50 percent expressed some doubts about the new system, while 20 percent expressed a firmly negative attitude, saying they thought leasing would aggravate an already complicated situation. Fifty percent said they saw land leasing as a step towards the restoration of capitalism, while 4 percent called it "a concession to capitalism." Many of the kolkhoz farm chairmen polled said they based their own negative attitudes on the reluctance of the members of their collective farms to embark on a new undertaking.

_____*Wednesday, April 19*

Academician Apologizes to Sakharov

The USSR Academy of Sciences began a two-day conference to elect deputies for its twelve unfilled seats in the Congress of People's Deputies. At the meeting, one of the academicians, Sergei Vonsovsky, took the floor to apologize to Academician Andrei Sakharov, who is one of the nominees, for signing letters attacking him during the hate campaign against Sakharov in the Soviet press in the 1970s. "I acted very badly," Vonsovsky said in front of hundreds of top Soviet scientists. "I am offering a profound apology" (*AP*, April 19). Vonsovsky is a physicist and specialist in magnetism. He signed several letters condemning Sakharov, including one published in *Pravda* on August 29, 1973, that said Sakharov had stopped his scientific activities and was devoting himself entirely to anti-Sovietism. He also signed a letter written by many members of the Academy protesting against the awarding of the Nobel Prize for Peace to Sakharov in 1975 (*Izvestia*, October 26, 1975).

Soviet Prosecutor Criticizes Churbanov Trial

Tel'man Gdlyan, the chief of the inquiry group appointed to investigate corruption in the USSR Public Prosecutor's Office, was quoted by Radio Kiev as saying there were irregularities in the trial of Yurii Churbanov, son-in-law of the late Leonid Brezhnev. Gdlyan said there was evidence of connections between bribe-takers in Uzbekistan and representatives of the Public Prosecutor's Office, the court, and the Ministry of Internal Affairs. He did not elaborate. (Churbanov was sentenced to serve twelve years' deprivation of freedom on corruption charges in December, 1988.) The same day, *Sotsialisticheskaya industriya* carried a report on the conditions under which Churbanov was serving his sentence. The newspaper's reporter, who visited the camp where Churbanov is serving his term, said Churbanov appeared to have an easier time than the other prisoners.

Turkey Agrees to Credit Deal with USSR

TASS said Turkey had agreed to extend 150 million dollars worth of credits to the Soviet Union. TASS said the deal was signed in Ankara on April 18. The agency reported on April 19 that most of the credits would be used to buy Turkish consumer goods.

Editor Discusses His Journal's Problems with Censorship

A Soviet editor, Gleb Pavlovsky, commented on his journal's problems with censorship in an interview with RFE/RL. Pavlovsky works for the Soviet Peace Committee monthly *Vek XX i mir*. The monthly recently published Aleksandr Solzhenitsyn's "Live Not by Lies!" (In an earlier interview with RFE/RL, the chief editor of *Vek XX i mir* said that he had published Solzhenitsyn without asking the permission of the USSR's main censorship body, Glavlit.) Pavlovsky said the monthly had been involved in "a dispute" with "some circles of the apparatus," whom he identified as "Party bureaucrats" and "some circles of the KGB." He said those circles had been putting pressure on the leadership of the Soviet Peace Committee, demanding the removal of "this or that material from the issue." In its turn, the leadership of the committee had passed on these demands to the monthly's editorial board. Pavlovksy said the conflict had reached "a very critical stage" before a meeting on April 18 between members of the editorial board of the monthly and the leadership of the committee. He said it had now been decided to seek a peaceful solution to the conflict. Pavlovsky named two items in the April issue of *Vek XX i mir* that had aroused criticism. One was a letter from a Ukrainian reader demanding public control over the KGB. The other was an article examining various alternatives for the future development of the USSR and possible forms of Western assistance. Pavlovsky said censorship is still a problem not only for his journal but for the Soviet press as a whole.

―――――――――――――――――――― *Thursday, April 20*

At the end of a two-day meeting of the USSR Academy of Sciences, TASS reported the preliminary results of voting by the academy for its twelve unfilled seats in the Congress of People's Deputies. Academicians Andrei Sakharov and Roald Sagdeev were reported to have been elected, together with other members and employees of the academy known for their reformist stands. Sakharov received 806 and Sagdeev 739 of the 1,101 votes cast. Reform-minded economist Nikolai Shmelev received the most votes—869. (Three other reformist economists—Nikolai Petrakov, Pavel Bunich, and Gennadii Lisichkin—were also elected). Another successful candidate was Academician Georgii Arbatov, an expert on the United States. His candidacy drew some protests at the election meeting because of his association with Brezhnev. Also elected was corresponding member Sergei Averintsev, a specialist in the history of Christianity, who can be expected to do a lot in the Congress to defend the rights of religious believers in the USSR. Two other elected deputies, a specialist in social sciencies, Yurii Karyakin, and philologist Vyacheslav Ivanov, have had serious conflicts with the authorities in the past. Academician Vitalii Ginzburg, who also won election, has attracted a lot of attention for his articles in the Soviet press criticizing bureaucracy within the academy. Another elected deputy, Doctor of Law Aleksandr Yakovlev, is a leading figure in the current campaign to improve the Soviet legal system. The television evening news program "Vremya" carried a commentary on the elections in the academy.

Elections of Congress Deputies in Academy of Sciences

Corresponding member A. Yablokov said the whole story of the nomination of candidates and election of deputies to the Congress demonstrated that the academy is very disorganized. (The academy's Presidium provoked an outcry in January when it rejected Sakharov and other reformist academicians as candidates. At elections last month, only eight of the twenty-three candidates nominated for the academy's twenty seats won a sufficient number of votes.) Yablokov proposed to organize an association called "The Union of Scientists" that would be independent from the Academy of Sciences.

Construction of Two Reactors at Chernobyl' Canceled

The Soviet government has abandoned plans to build two new reactors at the Chernobyl' nuclear power plant. The decision by the USSR Council of Ministers was announced six days before the third anniversary of the Chernobyl' disaster. TASS quoted First Deputy Chief of the Council's Fuel and Energy Bureau, Vladimir Marin, as saying the Council of Ministers had also ordered a halt to the construction of a fourth reactor at the Smolensk power plant and a sixth reactor at the Kursk plant.

Soviet Embassy in Kabul Damaged

The Soviet embassy in Kabul was damaged by a rocket fired by the Afghan resistance. No one in the complex was reported hurt. Heavy fighting was reported on April 20 at the Kabul end of the Salang highway, which links the capital with the Soviet border and is the main route for supply convoys (*Reuters, UPI*, April 20). On April 21, Foreign Ministry spokesman Gennadii Gerasimov threatened Soviet retaliation for the rocket attack on the Soviet embassy (*Reuters*, April 21).

Lithuanians Send Resolution on Economic Reform to Moscow

Lithuanian delegates to the Congress of People's Deputies have appealed to the central Soviet authorities to allow Lithuania to carry out its own plan for economic self-rule. Professor Kazimieras Antanavicius, a member of the council of "Sajudis" and a delegate to the new Congress, told RFE/RL that a resolution to this effect was passed overwhelmingly at a meeting of the Lithuanian delegates in Vilnius on April 19. According to Antanavicius, the resolution said the draft program for economic self-management adopted last month was superficial. It said more far-reaching reforms were needed. The resolution demands that Lithuania be allowed to implement its own plan for economic self-rule beginning next year (*RFE/RL Special*, April 20).

More than fifty people were killed in Georgia after a landslide caused a river to flood. TASS said the disaster struck the village of Tsablana in the Adzharia region of the republic, but it did not say when. TASS said over 2,000 families had been evacuated from the region in recent days following a series of landslides, snowslides, and spring floods.

Dozens Feared Killed in Georgian Landslide

Friday, April 21

A special meeting was held in the Kremlin to mark the anniversary of Lenin's birth. The main speech was delivered by Politburo member Vadim Medvedev. In his speech, Medvedev said that recent elections to the Congress of People's Deputies had been a major victory for *perestroika*. He added, however, that more work is needed to continue Gorbachev's reform drive. He complained that there were some people who, under the flag of "street democracy," pursued extremist goals. He said extremism and nationalism were not the way to solve major problems (*Central Television, TASS*, April 21; *Pravda*, April 22).

Medvedev Speaks at Celebrations of Lenin's Birthday

Soviet television broadcast a special program devoted to the first meeting in March of the newly created committee "*Aprel'. Pisateli v podderzhku perestroiki*" ("April": Writers in Support of *Perestroika*). Many of the speakers at the meeting demanded the abolition of the USSR Writers' Union, which they said had completely discredited itself.

Soviet Television Quotes Writers Demanding Abolition of Writers' Union

---

Saturday, April 22

On April 23, *Sovetskaya Rossiya* accused "nationalists" in Georgia of orchestrating mass gatherings in Tbilisi and suggested they were largely to blame for the deaths of people in the clash on April 9. A group of Western journalists was permitted to travel to Georgia for the first time since April 9. Correspondents for Reuters and AFP reported that thousands of people kept vigil today for those killed in the clash.

On April 24, the newly appointed Georgian Party chief, Givi Gumbaridze, told reporters in Tbilisi that some victims of the April 9 clash had died of gas poisoning (*AP*, April 24).

Situation in Georgia

On April 25, AP quoted Georgian pro-independence activists as saying they had canceled a demonstration scheduled for today after being told it could spark another bloody confrontation with soldiers. The same day, speaking at a press conference after the CPSU Central Committee plenum, Vadim Medvedev and Georgii Razumovsky said that the authorities in Moscow had not known about the decision to send in troops to break up the demonstration in Tbilisi (*TASS*, April 25). At least 3,000 people gathered in Tbilisi's main square to honor once again the victims of the April 9 clash and to demand the release of detained Georgian activists. Western reporters said the police did not interfere (*Reuters*, April 26)

On April 26, Foreign Ministry spokesman Vadim Perfil'ev announced at a press conference in Moscow that a criminal investigation had been started in connection with the use of poisonous gas in Tbilisi (*TASS*, in English, April 26). In his speech to the CPSU Central Committee plenum, Mikhail Gorbachev said everything must be done to prevent anything like the April 9 clash from happening again (*Pravda*, April 26).

On April 27, it was reported that this year's traditional May Day parade had been canceled in Tbilisi. The decision was taken by the Georgian Party Central Committee. USSR Deputy Prosecutor General Aleksandr Katusev said four Georgian activists detained after the violence on April 9 had been charged with violating the public order (*AP, Reuters*, April 28).

On April 28, an official of the USSR Ministry of Internal Affairs defended actions by ministry troops during the clash with demonstrators on April 9. A. I. Grienko, chief of the ministry's Political Department, told Soviet television that MVD troops exercise great professionalism in all their actions in order to avoid casualties. But he said they do not always manage to achieve this, because "two sides are involved" (*Central Television*, April 28).

Operation "Law and Order"—
A Police Raid in Moscow

Radio Moscow-1 (2200) said 160 people had been arrested for criminal offenses and over 8,000 others for various minor infringements in a twenty-four-hour police raid in Moscow on April 21. The radio said over 25,000 policemen and some 10,000 members of the people's militia and Komsomol cooperative units had been deployed in the operation, called "Law and Order." The radio said the raid was intended to strengthen law enforcement in the struggle against criminality, drunkenness, hooliganism, drug addiction, parasitism, speculation, and violations of passport regulations.

Komsomol'skaya pravda reported that police had used clubs to break up a march through the provincial town of Tambov by young people chanting "Long Live Soviet Power" and "Beat Up the Fascists" and that seventy-seven demonstrators had been detained. The newspaper said the young demonstrators, many of them drunk, had gathered in Tambov on April 20 after hearing rumors that neo-Nazis were planning to meet on the hundredth anniversary of Hitler's birth. Although the neo-Nazis did not appear, the demonstrators rejected appeals from a local police chief to go home and instead marched through the center of town.

Police Break Up Demonstration in Tambov

Minister of Defense Dmitrii Yazov said the USSR had begun the withdrawal of troops and tanks from Eastern Europe. Reports quoted Yazov as saying one paratroop battalion each from East Germany and Czechoslovakia and 700 tanks had been recalled to the USSR. He said the withdrawals were part of the unilateral force reductions announced by Gorbachev last year. (*Reuters*, April 22). On April 25, the Soviet Union began the first stage of a partial withdrawal of its forces from Hungary. About 10,000 of an estimated 62,000 Soviet troops in Hungary are to leave by next June (*AFP, DPA*, April 25).

USSR Begins Withdrawing Troops from Eastern Europe

Sunday, April 23

Pravda carried the Goskomstat report on plan fulfillment for the first quarter of this year. It shows considerable disequilibrium in the economy. Compared with the first quarter of last year, officially reported growth in output is somewhat below plan targets (GNP is up by 5 percent, national income produced by 4 percent, and gross industrial output by 3.2 percent). Wage payments continue to run ahead of the plan by some 8 percent, while investment completions and housing construction are reported down. Sales of alcohol are reported to have increased, with sales of vodka up 39 percent on the first quarter of 1988 and sales of cognac up 38 percent. A figure of 2.7 million for people engaged in cooperative and individual labor activity is given—presumably as of April 1, 1989. This is said to exclude 1.6 million people holding both a state and a nonstate job. If the latter are reckoned as half-timers in the nonstate sector, that brings the total number of full-time equivalents in the nonstate sector to 3.5 million, or just under 3 percent of the labor force.

First Quarter Plan Results

217

Leningrad Party Boss Attacks Gorbachev's Policy

Leaders of the Leningrad Party organization who were defeated in the elections to the Congress of People's Deputies on March 26 attacked the Gorbachev administration for inconsistencies in conducting *perestroika*. In an interview published in *Izvestia*, the first secretary of the Leningrad City Party Committee, Anatolii Gerasimov, complained that a number of important Politburo decisions were "hasty and half-baked." Gerasimov said that the Leningrad Party bosses had criticized the Moscow leadership during a recent meeting of the local Party organization. He singled out the Kremlin's reversal of its drive against alcoholism and the creation of Gosagroprom as examples of Gorbachev's inconsistencies. Gerasimov also challenged Gorbachev to name the authors of these various "ill-considered high-level decisions." Gerasimov said the Nineteenth Party Conference last year did not examine some issues that are now of special importance, including the idea of a multiparty system. Gerasimov said the Leningrad Party had got used to the comfort of one-party conditions and had therefore been unprepared for the elections to the Congress of People's Deputies.

Monday, April 24 _____

Armenians Mark Anniversary of 1915 Massacre

Western reports said hundreds of thousands of Armenians had marked the anniversary of the massacre of their countrymen in Turkey in 1915. Crowds honored the victims of the massacre at a monument outside Erevan. Western reporters quoted witnesses as saying many marchers also demanded the release of fourteen Armenian activists arrested following last year's ethnic unrest (*Reuters, AFP*, April 24). TASS, in English, also reported the Armenian march.

USSR Tightens AIDS Rules for Foreigners

Foreign Ministry spokesman Gennadii Gerasimov announced that, starting on May 1, all foreigners who leave the Soviet Union for more than a month must submit to an AIDS test on their return if they plan to stay in the USSR for more than three months (*Reuters, DPA*, April 24). Foreigners who test positive for the AIDS virus must leave the Soviet Union or face expulsion. In an apparent concession to concerns about the low level of hygiene in Soviet medical establishments, the latest rule permits foreigners to be tested using their own syringes and needles; it also allows blood samples to be taken by embassy medical staff.

218

Nedelya (Nos. 13 and 14) carried a two-part article by its correspondent Eduard Polyanovsky, in which members of the so-called first wave of emigration from Russia in the postrevolutionary years are described in very favorable terms. Polyanovsky even finds good words for White Army leaders and officers who left Russia after the Civil War. He also points out that, contrary to earlier Soviet propaganda claims that first-wave émigrés had collaborated with Hitler, in fact many émigrés were anti-Nazi, and some even perished as active participants in the French Resistance.

Nedelya Praises Russian Emigrés

A Soviet legal expert said that Moscow plans to sign an accord allowing Soviet citizens to take human-rights complaints directly to international investigators. The legal expert, who spoke on condition of anonymity, said Moscow would sign the optional protocol to the International Covenant on Civil and Political Rights later this year or early next year. Official Soviet acceptance of that protocol would give Soviet citizens the right to appeal to the UN-affiliated human-rights committee in cases involving emigration, torture, forced labor, arbitrary arrest or detention, and freedom of thought, conscience, and peaceful assembly, among other rights (*AP*, April 24).

USSR Plans to Allow Outside Judgment of Rights Cases

TASS reported that foreign specialists had questioned a Soviet diagnosis that children in the Ukranian city of Chernovtsy lost their hair as a result of thallium poisoning. Dr. Gerar De Groot of the Toxicological Center in the Netherlands told TASS the amounts of thallium found in the patients could not have caused such serious symptoms. But he and other experts, including one from the Geneva-based World Health Organization, were unable to determine what caused more than 160 children to have lost their hair since last fall.

Foreign Experts Question Soviet Diagnosis of "Chernovtsy Disease"

Tuesday, April 25

A plenary meeting of the Central Committee of the CPSU was held in Moscow and accepted the resignation of 110 members of the Central Committee and the Central Auditing Commission. Among those who resigned were former Foreign Minister Andrei Gromyko, Central Committee Secretary Boris Ponomarev, former Chief of General Staff Marshal Nikolai Ogarkov, and disgraced former

CPSU Central Committee Plenum

Politburo member Geidar Aliev. The plenum also promoted twenty-four people to full membership in the Central Committee. Among those promoted were head of the CPSU's International Department Valentin Falin, Soviet Ambassador to West Germany Yulii Kvitsinsky, and Gorbachev's advisers Evgenii Primakov and Evgenii Velikhov (*TASS*, April 25). The plenum was addressed by Mikhail Gorbachev, who criticized the state of the Soviet economy. TASS quoted him as telling the plenum that "the state's financial position is grave." (*Pravda* carried the text of Gorbachev's speech on April 26.)

Many of the speakers at the plenum were sharply critical of Gorbachev and his policies, expressing concern that "the leading role of the Party" was coming under threat. Several speakers, including Leningrad Party boss Yurii Solov'ev, who failed to win election last month to the Congress of People's Deputies, accused the Soviet media of sensationalism and said "extremist" informal groups were abusing the new freedoms to challenge the authority of the Party. Others accused the Party leadership (specifically, Central Committee Secretaries Aleksandr Yakovlev and Vadim Medvedev) of failing to give a clear lead in ideological matters. *Pravda* carried a lengthy account of the proceedings at the plenum on April 27. This was followed by an editorial in the newspaper on April 28 saying that many Party officials were unprepared or unwilling to accept the rapid changes brought about by *perestroika*. It said many officials were lapsing "into old thinking, nostalgia for authoritarian leadership, and panicky attempts to check grass-roots initiatives under the pretext of protecting socialism."

Rogachev Says Yalta Agreement Gave Kuriles to USSR

Soviet Deputy Foreign Minister Igor Rogachev said the Yalta agreement of 1945 gave the Southern Kurile Islands to the USSR. Writing in *Izvestia*, Rogachev criticized Japan for repeatedly raising the issue of ownership of the islands. He said that the islands historically belonged to the Soviet Union and that Japan should stop trying "to revise the results of World War II." Japan refuses to sign a peace treaty with the USSR until the issue of the islands has been resolved.

Two Soviet Citizens Defect during Border Ceremony

US immigration officials said two members of a Soviet friendship delegation had defected and were seeking asylum in the United States. The officials said the two had approached an Alaska national guard and asked for asylum just hours before the signing of a protocol on

April 23 aimed at easing travel restrictions between Alaska and Siberia (*UPI*, April 25). AP reported the same day that a Soviet seaman had jumped ship off the Danish coast and asked for political asylum in Denmark.

Another Antidrug Operation in Turkmenistan

The authorities in Turkmenistan have started another antidrug operation. Radio Moscow-1 (0800) said it was aimed at cutting off supply channels and destroying plants, such as poppies, that are used to make illegal substances. The radio said an operation last year uncovered dozens of places where such plants were grown, despite assertions that Turkmenistan did not have the raw material base for producing drugs. The radio said such plants were also sometimes grown on private plots at sovkhozes and kolkhozes.

Prison Siege Ends in Convict's Death

TASS said the MVD and the KGB used force to end a hostage-taking at a labor camp in the Soviet Far East, killing one convict and freeing the four hostages unharmed. The agency said the incident occurred on April 24 and was revealed at a news conference at the Ministry of Internal Affairs on April 25. TASS said the briefing was the first of a new kind of press conference held by the MVD to brief reporters on events in the USSR over the preceding twenty-four hours.

Wednesday, April 26

New Restrictions on Reporting on Accidents

In an article marking the third anniversary of the Chernobyl' accident, *Izvestia* said it had been given a copy of a new directive barring the Soviet media from revealing details of certain incidents. The directive, signed by Anatolii Maiorets, minister of energy and electrification, covers reports of accidents and breakdowns leading to material damage, casualties, and "noncatastrophic" environmental contamination. The directive prevents, among other things, the revealing in nonclassified documents of information on radiation levels and other kinds of contamination after accidents. Commenting on the regulations, *Izvestia* asked "how long the interested parties will be able to define the borders of *glasnost'*." Earlier this year, the MVD and the Union of Soviet Journalists signed an agreement in accordance with which Soviet journalists can gain access to places of emergency, including accidents, only after receiving a special pass from the MVD.

Many journalists protested against this regulation on the grounds that it limits their freedom in reporting. *Moscow News* (No. 18) included an article on how the authorities attempted to suppress information about the Chernobyl' accident. *Moscow News* said that the administration of the Chernobyl' plant had not allowed people to measure radiation levels after the accident and had doctored data that it passed on to higher bodies. Last week, Nikolai Mashchenko, a film producer who made a film about Chernobyl', said that the ministries of atomic energy and health had ordered him to cut sequences showing the doses of radiation suffered by Chernobyl' workers (*Reuters*, April 26).

Krasnaya zvezda Discusses Prevention of Air Piracy

Krasnaya zvezda said more than fifty hijackings of airplanes had been prevented on Soviet domestic routes since 1973. The daily said Aeroflot was now taking extra technical measures at airports and was improving training of personnel in order to step up security. But it said it was necessary to improve coordination with other Soviet authorities and with foreign countries. It noted that last year Israel handed over to the USSR Soviet citizens who had hijacked a Soviet plane. It said Iran, Finland, and some other countries had acted in a similar way. On April 27, the newspaper *Leninskoe znamya* complained about the lack of security at Moscow's Domodedovo Airport.

Over 200 Bodies Found in Ukrainian Mass Grave

Literaturnaya gazeta said over 200 bodies had been found in a mass grave near the Ukrainian capital of Kiev. The newspaper said the mass grave in Bykovnya contained the remains of Soviet men and women, as well as foreign servicemen and civilians. Earlier this year, the Soviet media reported that the Ukrainian public believed those buried in Bykovnya had been killed by NKVD troops. The newspaper said reburials in 1944, 1971, and 1987 were used by several generations of bureaucrats in Kiev to cover up Stalinist crimes. The Kiev authorities are reported to have pledged to look into claims that hundreds of thousands of Stalin-era victims may be buried in a mass grave near Bykovnya.

Yunost' on Suppression of Popular Front in Kuibyshev

Yunost' (No. 4) contains a long article on the attitude of local officials in the city of Kuibyshev towards the activities of informal groups. In October, 1988, the creation of a Kuibyshev Popular Front was announced. (According to documents issued by the front that were published in the

Soviet press, the organization supports the introduction of a market economy in the USSR and the democratization of the country's political and social life.) The *Yunost'* account describes the measures taken by local Party officials to suppress the organization. These include breaking up meetings of the front and the detention and harassment of its members. The *Yunost'* article says that the authorities made clear to representatives of the Popular Front that membership in it was incompatible with membership in the CPSU and that front members found themselves expelled from the Party.

Soviet Envoy Meets Egyptian Officials

Gennadii Tarasov, a deputy chief of the Soviet Foreign Ministry's Middle Eastern Countries Administration, again expressed Soviet support for an international Middle East peace conference. He told reporters in Cairo that Moscow believed the time was right for a United Nations-sponsored Middle East peace conference with the participation of the five permanent members of the UN Security Council. Tarasov is on a Middle East tour (*AP*, April 26).

Soviet Official Arrives in South Africa for Namibia Talks

Special Soviet envoy Vyacheslav Ustinov arrived in Cape Town for talks on Namibia. Cuba, Angola, South Africa, and the United States are also involved in the talks. Along with the USSR, all are members of a commission set up to monitor withdrawal of Cuban and South African troops from Angola and independence for Namibia. Ustinov is an African specialist in the USSR Foreign Ministry. He told a news conference his only mission was to assist in implementing the peace plan. He ruled out the possibility of talks with South Africa on other subjects. Two weeks ago, Western reporters said Soviet Deputy Foreign Minister Anatolii Adamishin had secretly visited South Africa in late March or early April. He was the highest ranking Soviet official to go there since the two countries broke off relations thirty-three years ago (*Reuters*, April 26).

Moscow Rally Condemning Violence in Georgia Broken Up

TASS said fifty-nine people had been punished with fines and administrative arrests for taking part in a demonstration on Pushkin Square in Moscow on April 23 to protest against the massacre in Tbilisi on April 9. The demonstration was organized by the Democratic Union. TASS also said seventy-one people had been detained. TASS quoted Moscow police official Major General Lev Belyansky as telling a press conference in Moscow that some of those detained were fined up to 1,000 rubles.

Moscow News Editor Discusses International Journal

The chief editor of *Moscow News*, Egor Yakovlev, said he was discussing publication of a monthly international journal in cooperation with Western publishers. He was speaking at the London Information Forum. He said the monthly would deal with universal human values and current problems, such as environmental pollution. He said discussions are under way with leading newspapers in France (*Le Monde*), Spain (*El País*) and Italy (*La Repubblica*). Commenting on the problems of the Soviet press, he stressed its limited access to modern information technology. But he said the Soviet media were catching up in the use of computers and other equipment. He said *Moscow News* had a satellite link facility in Pushkin Square to ensure transmissions to its foreign editions in Athens, Budapest, Cologne, and London. A French edition is to be published in Paris starting in June (*RFE/RL Special*, April 27). At the London Information Forum, the Soviet delegation also proposed setting up a Pan-European Information Council. According to a statement issued by the delegation, its purpose would be "to facilitate the broader and freer flow of all forms of information" and promote interpersonal dialogue. It would also aim at improving working conditions for foreign journalists in the USSR (*RFE/RL Special*, April 27).

Scandal over Suggestion to Remove Lenin's Body

A noted Moscow stage director, Mark Zakharov, caused a furor reaching all the way to the CPSU Central Committee by suggesting on the television program "Vzglyad," broadcast live on April 21, that Lenin's body be removed from its mausoleum and buried. In the program Zakharov compared keeping Lenin's body in a mausoleum to a pagan cult practice, and he proposed that the mausoleum be turned into a monument to the founder of the Soviet state. The program was shown only hours after Soviet television had transmitted a Kremlin ceremony marking the 119th anniversary of Lenin's birth. On April 27, the Soviet press carried speeches delivered by some Party officials at the plenum of the CPSU Central Committee on April 25, attacking Zakharov's suggestion. The Party leader of Vladimir Oblast, Ratmir Bobovikov, called it "immoral." He said that literally the next morning people had begun calling the Party committee and asking in disbelief, "How are we supposed to understand this? Whose point of view is this?" Georgii Zhukov, a candidate member of the Central Committee, who retired at the plenum, demanded, "Why does our television—state, Party television—permit such statements?" Aleksandr Aksenov, director of Gosteleradio said that "Vzglyad" was a live broadcast and that no one had expected such comments. He indicated that the editors of the show faced disciplinary action for the broadcast (*Pravda*, *Izvestia*, April 27).

PEN Club President Hails Soviet Intention to Join

Francis King, President of the International PEN club, welcomed the desire of a group of Soviet writers to join his organization. He told a Moscow press conference that Russian literature is one of the greatest in the world and that it is paradoxical that Soviet writers are not represented in the international PEN club. TASS said King was visiting the USSR at the invitation of the USSR Writers' Union. A chapter of the international PEN club was set up in the Soviet Union this month on a provisional basis. There is, however, a controversy in the Soviet Union about who should be a member of the Soviet chapter of PEN. Some writers, such as Tat'yana Tolstaya, have protested against the inclusion of the head of the USSR Writers' Union, Lev Karpov, who is known to have participated in repressions against writers in the past. Tolstaya discussed the issue on the television program "Vzglyad" on April 14.

Rallies in Ukraine and Belorussia to Mark Chernobyl' Anniversary

TASS said 40,000 people took part in a rally in Kiev to mark the third anniversary of the Chernobyl' disaster. TASS said the rally was sponsored by the Ukrainian "Green World" organization, a branch of the republic's Committee for the Defense of Peace. TASS said speakers at the rally urged the Ukrainian government to consider shutting down the Chernobyl' nuclear power station and called for a referendum on the further development of nuclear power in Ukraine. Meetings also took place in Belorussia, which was also heavily affected by the fallout from the Chernobyl' accident.

Soviet Jewish Association Publishes Newspaper in Moscow

A Jewish Cultural Association has begun publishing a newspaper in Moscow, using the printing facilities of the newspaper *Izvestia*. The first issue of the four-page paper, dated April 26, was distributed in Moscow on April 27 (*Reuters*, April 27). The newspaper, which is called *Herald of Soviet Jewish Culture*, said in its editorial that it aims to promote Jewish culture and history. The publication of the newspaper demonstrates the recent improvement in the official attitude towards Jews in the USSR.

Mir Cosmonauts Return to Earth

The three-man crew of the Soviet space station, *Mir*, returned to earth, landing in Kazakhstan. The crew's commander, Volkov, commented on the landing on Soviet television, saying it "was not one of the softest." Volkov said the spacecraft landed, then turned over several times before coming to a stop. A television report also said the spacecraft landed several kilometers from the normal site because of stormy winds (*TASS, Central Television*, April 27).

Friday, April 28 ───────────────────────────

Roy Medvedev Readmitted to the CPSU

TASS said the CPSU had restored membership to dissident historian Roy Medvedev, whose writings about Stalin's personality cult prompted his expulsion in 1969. The agency said that Medvedev had asked for his membership to be restored and that the Central Committee's Control Committee had granted the request, saying his expulsion had been "groundless." AP, however, quoted Medvedev as saying the Party had approached him and asked whether he would object to reinstatement. AP quoted Medvedev as saying he had reacted "positively" to the move. He said that his views had not changed but that there had been a turnabout in the Party. Medvedev won a seat in the new Congress of People's Deputies earlier this month. His writings are also appearing in the Soviet press again following a lengthy ban.

Gorbachev and Jaruzelski Agree to Speed Clarification of "Blank Spots"

Mikhail Gorbachev said the USSR is not proud of everything in its long history of relations with Poland. He said detailed attention is now being given to the dark pages in bilateral relations. Gorbachev was speaking at the end of two days of talks in Moscow with Polish President Wojciech Jaruzelski. Moscow television said a Soviet-Polish historians' commission studying "blank spots" in the history of bilateral relations would soon publish a joint document. Polish television said Gorbachev and Jaruzelski had decided the commission should speed clarification of all issues of interest to both nations. It said this applies above all to the Katyn massacre of Polish officers. The USSR has traditionally blamed the massacre on the Nazis, saying it took place in the fall of 1941. Western historians and Polish émigrés believe that the crime was committed by NKVD troops in the spring of 1940. Earlier this year, the official Polish press published documents showing that the murder was committed in 1940, before the Nazis occupied the area. On February 20, Radio Moscow broadcast a commentary by its Warsaw correspondent on the Polish revelations, but there has yet to be any official Soviet reaction to them. At a press conference on April 26, Soviet Foreign Ministry spokesman Vadim Perfil'ev said that "new facts" had been uncovered about the Katyn massacre, and he promised that the Soviet Union would soon issue an official statement on the issue (*UPI*, April 26). Meanwhile, Polish film director Andrzej Wajda is working on a film devoted to Katyn. On April 23, Reuters reported that he had had to delay a trip to the USSR to film at the site of the massacre because the Soviet authorities had claimed there were no hotel rooms available in the Smolensk area.

USSR Releases Preliminary Census Figures

The population of the Soviet Union reached 286.7 million in January, according to preliminary census statistics released today. TASS said this figure represented an increase of 24.3 million people, or 9.3 percent, since the last census in 1979. TASS said women outnumber men in the Soviet Union by 15.7 million. The report said the highest population growth rates in the Soviet Union—between 22 and 34 percent—were registered in the Central Asian republics. The results also showed that the RSFSR now accounts for 51 percent of the total Soviet population, down from 56 percent in 1959.

State to Return Kishinev Cathedral to Orthodox Church

TASS said the authorities in Kishinev had decided to return the city's former Russian Orthodox cathedral to the Church. The cathedral had been used as an exhibition hall for the past twenty-five years. TASS said the move to restore the cathedral to the Church came in response to a request by the metropolitan of Kishinev and Moldavia, Serapion. TASS quoted a representative of the USSR Council for Religious Affairs, Ivan Vichku, as saying more than 300 religious communities have been registered in Moldavia in response to applications from believers. Vichku also said the building of new churches was being allowed.

USSR and Sweden Sign Treaty on Pollution

Sweden and the Soviet Union signed a treaty aimed at reducing pollution in the Baltic area. The treaty was signed in Stockholm by Fedor Morgun, chairman of the USSR State Committee for Environmental Protection, and Swedish Environment Minister Birgitta Dahl. Morgun told reporters the Soviet Union plans to halve air and water pollution in the Baltic area and the Kola Peninsula by 1992–93. He said the building of sewage treatment plants in the Baltic states and Leningrad will be given top priority. Morgun said the Soviet Union needs to create the kind of environmental protection systems that have existed in Western countries for at least fifteen years (*AP, Reuters,* April 28). The same day, Soviet delegates to a UN-sponsored conference on the atmosphere said the Soviet Union was prepared to sign an agreement on a total ban on ozone-depleting gases, providing alternatives to these gases can be developed (*AP,* April 28).

Saturday, April 29 _____

Rodionov Says MVD, Not Army, Used Gas against Georgian Demonstrators

The military commander of the Transcaucasus said in a television interview that people are wrongly blaming army soldiers for the use of gas against demonstrators in Tbilisi on April 9. Lieutenant General Igor Rodionov said units of the Ministry of Internal Affairs (MVD), not army units, had used the gas. He said people could not tell the difference, because both forces wear the same uniform, and he suggested that MVD troops should have special uniforms in order to avoid confusion. Rodionov also said he had opposed having his troops take part in the action of April 9. Valerii Voloshin, the military correspondent who interviewed Rodionov, said members of the families of soldiers in Tbilisi had been beaten up by local people and apartments had been stoned (*Central Television,* 1900–1930, April 29). On May 1, Georgia's Minister of Internal Affairs, Shota Gorgodze, rejected the report that soldiers and their families had been harassed by Tbilisi citizens. He told *Pravda* that a few accounts of attacks on servicemen had been recorded but that upon investigation all had turned out to be false.

Soviet General Says NATO Seeking Military Supremacy

Krasnaya zvezda carried a statement by Army General Vladimir Lobov, charging that it is NATO, not the Warsaw Pact, that seeks military supremacy and claiming that the Western alliance is expanding its potential for surprise attack. Lobov, who is chief of staff of the Warsaw Pact forces, was commenting on talks between NATO and the Warsaw Pact on reducing conventional forces in Europe that resume in Vienna on May 5. NATO says that there are far more Warsaw Pact conventional forces than NATO forces and that the strength of the Warsaw Pact forces exceeds defense requirements.

Komsomol'skaya pravda said at least two children in the border town of Termez had died after playing with live ammunition given to them by Soviet troops returning home from Afghanistan. The newspaper said the soldiers had given bullets, grenades, and even mortar shells to children in the town. It said two boys, aged around ten and fourteen, died on April 11 after throwing the tip of a heavy artillery shell into a fire. The newspaper said a document from the boys' school, dated just under a week earlier, recorded that fifty-eight cartridges, one grenade, and six magazines for Kalashnikov rifles had been confiscated from pupils.

Children Die in Border Town after Playing with Weapons

A plenum of the Moscow Oblast Party Committee complained that farmers are not willing to lease land or to take risks and responsibility. As reported by Radio Moscow (1700), speakers at the plenum said there had been no breakthrough yet in the agrarian sector in the region. The radio report said administrative methods had over the years formed a certain type of worker who is used to carrying out orders. New Soviet laws give individual farmers the right to take long-term leases on state land. The move is aimed at giving a major boost to Soviet farm production.

Moscow Farmers Unwilling to Lease Land

Sunday, April 30

In an interview with *Zarya Vostoka*, the chief toxicologist at the Georgian Ministry of Health, Mikhail Vashkidze, said he had identified the poisonous gas that troops used to help disperse demonstrators in Tbilisi on April 9. He said the gas was used twice by the German Army during World War I but had not been used since. He named its toxic agent as chloroacetophenone or phenacyl chloride. *Zarya Vostoka* said that, since April 9, a total of seventy children who live near the site of the demonstration had been hospitalized suffering from symptoms of poisoning. It said their condition was now improving.

Opinions Conflict over Identification of Tbilisi Gas

The first secretary of the Kiev Oblast Party Committee, Grigorii Revenko, said decontamination work in the area around the Chernobyl' nuclear power plant had not yet brought "the required results." Writing in *Pravda*, Revenko said this puts a question mark on the future of the region. He said there was no alternative to the

Kiev Party Chief Complains about Insufficient Decontamination

Chernobyl' plant as an energy source, but he said safety questions are no longer given top priority there. He complained that not enough qualified workers were being sent to the plant and that it was difficult to get proper equipment. Revenko said many people were calling for the plant's closure. "We have no right to ignore public opinion," he wrote.

Chazov Says AIDS Spreading Quickly, Outlines Countermeasures

USSR Minister of Health Evgenii Chazov was quoted by *Pravda* as saying that the AIDS virus is spreading quickly in the Soviet Union. Chazov said there are now 198 Soviet carriers of the disease—nearly double the total last year. Four citizens have already died of the disease. He said that, although these numbers are not large, they show the virus is spreading quickly. Chazov outlined measures against the disease, including the import of equipment for the manufacture of one billion disposable syringes a year. The reuse of dirty syringes is known to have been responsible for infecting a number of people with AIDS in the USSR. Chazov also said regional AIDS prevention centers would be set up to carry out mass medical checkups on the population and to inform the public on how to avoid contracting the disease. On May 5, TASS reported that ten children in a Volgograd hospital had been found to be infected with AIDS. TASS said that the virus had been spread through infected syringes and that a commission was investigating.

Pasternak's Anti-Revolution Poem Published

Novyi mir (No. 4) carried a previously unknown poem by Boris Pasternak, entitled "Russkaya Revolyutsiya" (The Russian Revolution). The poem, said to have been written in 1918, leaves no doubt that the poet welcomed the February Revolution but was horrified and alienated by the Bolshevik terror. In this poem, Pasternak professes his sympathy for Christian socialism; it is a clear political declaration—something most unusual for Pasternak. His son Evgenii, who wrote the accompanying commentary, explained that the manuscript of the poem had survived in the family archive for more than sixty years only because his father had forgotten its existence.

The Month of May

**Methods of Soviet
Investigator Questioned**

Tel'man Gdlyan, the Soviet Union's leading investigator of official corruption, said senior Party and KGB officials were trying to stop his probe of corruption among top Soviet officials. He said he and his staff had been the targets of crude KGB provocations and what he called a dirty political deal designed to protect "Moscow bribe-takers." Gdlyan rose to prominence through his investigation of corruption in Uzbekistan, which led to the conviction of many prominent officials, among them Brezhnev's son-in-law Yurii Churbanov. Complaints about Gdlyan appeared in *Pravda* on April 30. A lawyer said Gdlyan had arrested the families of bribe-takers and held people in jail for years without trial. The chairman of the Party Control Committee, Boris Pugo, said Gdlyan had been reprimanded for incorrect conduct once and had overstepped the limits of his authority on another occasion (*AP*, *AFP*, May 1).

**May Day Celebrations
Canceled in Erevan
and Tbilisi**

The Soviet Union celebrated May Day with the traditional parade through Moscow's Red Square, but officially sanctioned marches normally staged in republican capitals were canceled in Erevan and Tbilisi, where residents were still mourning the victims of the Armenian earthquake and of political violence. A massive unauthorized but peaceful demonstration was staged in Erevan, where marchers waved banners thanking other nations for their provision of earthquake relief and demanding freedom for jailed members of the Karabakh Committee. *Izvestia*, which reported the Erevan demonstration, also said young people had stayed away from celebrations in Kishinev, the capital of Moldavia, where student activists were refused their own column in the parade. In Lithuania, the traditional parade in Vilnius was replaced by a more informal gathering. A Radio Stockholm reporter said there were no speeches about the international workers' movement. Instead, there was talk of the need for harmony between Lithuanians, Poles, and Russians in the Lithuanian SSR (*AP*, *Reuters*, May 1).

231

Students Rampage in Ashkhabad

Some 200 students celebrated the May 1 holiday by attacking stores, stalls, and restaurants and smashing windows and damaging cars, according to *Pravda* of May 2. The head of the Political Department of Turkmenistan's Ministry of Internal Affairs told *Pravda* at least 100 people had been arrested. The republican minister of internal affairs, Vasilii Grinin, said those detained described their actions as a protest against high prices charged by cooperatives for low-quality goods and services.

Protests in Western Ukraine

According to reports received by RL's Ukrainian Service, large-scale patriotic demonstrations took place in at least two Western Ukrainian cities during the official May Day celebrations. In Lvov, several hundred members of the city's informal groups, many of them carrying the Ukrainian national flag, formed their own column in the official procession. The police tried to disperse them but eventually let the group march through the city. A similar demonstration was reported to have taken place in the nearby city of Chervonograd. In Lvov tensions are reported to be running high because the local authorities have been attempting to block popular figures from standing for the runoff elections to the new Congress of People's Deputies scheduled for May 14. Renewed demonstrations in Lvov, held to protest against alleged manipulations of the elections, were reported on May 4.

Tuesday, May 2

Greenpeace Warns of Lasting Damage from Sunken Soviet Submarine

The environmental group Greenpeace said a Soviet nuclear-powered submarine that sank off Norway on April 7 could harm marine and human health for tens of thousands of years. A Greenpeace study said if the submarine's reactors were not retrieved from the sea they could eventually release up to 20 million curies of radioactivity into the ocean and into marine food chains. The report said this would be equivalent to one third of the radiation released by the Chernobyl' nuclear accident. Norwegian officials have not detected any radiation so far from the Mike class submarine. Oslo says it will continue monitoring the area, probably for years to come (*Reuters*, May 2). On May 3, TASS said the USSR Academy of Sciences was planning to conduct a comprehensive survey of the area where the submarine sank. It said that a research ship would check radiation levels in the area this month in order to give a better ecological assessment and that results would be regularly reported to the Soviet and international public. The same day, leading Soviet economist Gavriil Popov demanded a full account of the sinking of the submarine from the Ministry of Defense. In a letter to *Literaturnaya gazeta* he paid tribute to the courage of the survivors and those involved in rescue efforts but also asked "what our high command was doing during those hours."

Group Says Record Number of Soviet Jews Left USSR in April

The National Conference on Soviet Jewry in the United States said 4,557 Jews had left the Soviet Union in April, the highest monthly figure since October, 1979. The conference said the April figure represented an increase of almost 7.5 percent over March, when about 4,200 Jews had emigrated to the West. The conference said about 14,000 Jews had left the Soviet Union during the first four months of this year. The figure for the corresponding period last year was about 3,000 (*RFE/RL Special*, May 2).

Uzbekistan Halts Operations at Some Chemical Plants

Environmental protection authorities in Uzbekistan have ordered a halt to operations at several industrial plants. Radio Moscow (0600) named three plants it said had been badly polluting the environment in the eastern part of Fergana Oblast. It did not say whether they were being closed down. The Uzbek Supreme Soviet last year rejected the republic's economic development plan for 1989, and tens of millions of rubles were ordered diverted from construction of new industrial enterprises in Uzbekistan to environmental and social programs.

Wednesday, May 3

Report Says Leningrad Police Demand Free Unions

A group of Leningrad police were reported to have demanded the creation of independent police trade unions. *Sotsialisticheskaya industriya* said the demands had been made at an unauthorized rally by police on April 9 in Leningrad's Palace Square. It quoted witnesses as saying some 300 to 400 people attended. The report said seventy members of the Leningrad police force had signed the demands, which also dealt with wage, housing, and supply issues. The report also said Nikolai Arzhannikov, a deputy police commander for political affairs who was among those who addressed the rally, had been dismissed two days after the rally for his participation in it. On May 5, General Mikhail Mikhailov, deputy chief of the

Main Internal Affairs Administration, said in *Pravda* that many police complaints were justified. The report said a Leningrad police officer had been murdered while on duty on March 30, and it said there had been an increasing amount of crime, particularly organized crime, in the city.

Estonians Polled on Free Election

A Finnish newspaper published the results of a public opinion poll conducted in Estonia on how people would vote in a free election. The poll, published in the newspaper *Ilta Sanomat*, was carried out by an Estonian polling organization and, the newspaper said, was done with Estonian government permission. The results showed that, if a free election were held now, the Estonian Popular Front would win the most votes, followed by the environmentalist "Greens." The Communist Party would come in third (*UPI*, May 3).

No Movement on Kuriles in Soviet-Japanese Talks

A Japanese Foreign Ministry spokesman said the Soviet Union had made no move to settle the Kurile Islands dispute with Japan during high-level talks today in Moscow. Soviet Foreign Minister Eduard Shevardnadze and Japanese Foreign Minister Sosuke Uno discussed Japan's claim to the Soviet-occupied islands, but Japan's spokesman said the Soviet side insisted there is no dispute. The USSR has occupied the four islands in the Kurile chain since the end of World War II. Until the dispute is resolved Japan refuses to sign a treaty with the Soviet Union to formally end hostilities (*AP, TASS*, in English, *DPA*, May 3). On May 5, Uno had talks with Gorbachev. At the end of the talks neither side reported any progress on the Kurile Islands dispute. Gorbachev suggested that Japan was applying a double standard in its relations with Moscow. TASS said Gorbachev wanted to know why Japan considers the dispute an obstacle to relations with the USSR but does not view similar claims against China and South Korea in such a manner. He suggested that any talks about his visiting Japan be left until next year (*TASS*, in English, *Reuters*, May 5, *Pravda*, May 6).

Affiliate of Radical Party Formed in USSR

A branch of the Rome-based Radical Party has been formed in the USSR, members of the group said. Aleksandr Rubchenko, a spokesman for the newly formed group of about seventy members named the Transnational Radical Party, said they would campaign for elimination of nuclear weapons, for more political freedom, and for protection of the environment (*AP*, May 3).

TASS said Kazakhstan television had begun broadcasting a weekly German-language program for the more than one million ethnic Germans who live in the republic. It said the first German-language program had showed, among other things, the tragic events of 1941, when the population of the German Autonomous Republic was forcibly resettled in other regions of the Soviet Union.

Ethnic Germans in Kazakhstan Get First Television Program

Officials in the Crimea were reported to have sent the Soviet government a petition calling for a halt to construction work on a local nuclear power plant. Radio Moscow (1200) said over 300,000 people had signed the petition organized by members of the Crimean Oblast Soviet, who want Soviet legislation on health resorts to be extended to the Crimean Peninsula. The petition says that pollution on the peninsula is getting worse and that a nuclear power station would aggravate the situation.

Soviet Government Asked to Halt Work on Crimean Nuclear Power Plant

_____*Thursday, May 4*

Radio Moscow (1300) said human-rights activist Andrei Sakharov, space scientist Roald Sagdeev, and literary scholar Dmitrii Likhachev are to help investigate the Tbilisi clashes on April 9 in which twenty people died. All three are members of the USSR Academy of Sciences, which previously called for them to help investigators and also denounced the troop attack in Tbilisi. All three have also been elected to the new Congress of People's Deputies.

Sakharov Named to Help Investigate Tbilisi Incident

Izvestia carried an article saying that Soviet troops had helped to storm the presidential palace in Kabul in 1979 to overthrow the government of former Marxist President Hafizullah Amin. Today's article conflicts with the previous official version of events. Previously, Soviet officials have said the Afghan government requested assistance to counter outside aggression. Amin was killed on the night of December 27, 1979, after the presidential palace had been stormed. The article says Soviet troops first arrived in Kabul on December 24—while Amin was still in power. The article says that doubts were expressed among the upper levels of the Soviet leadership about sending troops to Afghanistan but that Leonid Brezhnev made the final decision to send in troops.

Report Says Soviet Forces Helped Overthrow Afghan Government in 1979

New KGB Chief in Georgia

Zarya Vostoka reported that a deputy prime minister of Georgia, Tariel Lordkipanidze, had been appointed the new KGB chief in the republic. He replaces Givi Gumbaridze, who was appointed Party chief in Georgia following clashes in Tbilisi on April 9 between demonstrators and troops. Lordkipanidze, who is fifty-one, has been a Party member since 1971 (*AFP*, May 4).

Estonian Party Condemns Unconstitutional Activities

An Estonian Party plenum condemned attempts to create alternative power bodies and any activities incompatible with the republic's constitution. TASS said the plenum also warned Communists that Party statutes and programs are above those of any public movement in which members are participating. In addition, plenum speakers said it was important not to allow a split within the republic because of ethnic problems.

Soviet Writer Venyamin Kaverin Dies

TASS said Soviet writer Venyamin Kaverin, who is known for supporting his unjustly persecuted colleagues, had died at the age of eighty-eight. Kaverin's novels include *Fulfilled Wishes*, *Two Captains*, and *An Open Book*. For an obituary, see *Pravda*, May 5.

Growing Tension in Soviet Prisons

Krasnaya zvezda carried a lengthy article that discussed what it called "the sharp growth of aggression among inmates" of jails and labor camps. The newspaper expressed concern about the growing number of cases in which prisoners took prison staff hostage in their attempts to force the administration of penal institutions to meet their demands. The newspaper put the number of cases of hostage-taking in Soviet penal institutions during 1988 at sixty-six.

Soviet Hockey Player Decides to Stay in Stockholm

A Soviet ice hockey player, Aleksandr Mogilnyi, has chosen to remain in Sweden and not return home with the Soviet team. Soviet television and TASS reported the development but did not say that Mogilnyi had sought asylum or defected. His team returned to Moscow without him today after winning the world championship in Stockholm. The main coach of the team, Viktor Tikhonov, told TASS the twenty-year-old player's decision only provokes disgust. On May 5, Mogilnyi arrived in the United States (*Reuters*, May 5).

The Latvian Supreme Soviet passed a controversial law making Latvian, rather than Russian, the language of business and government in the republic. TASS said Russian workers had staged the latest in a series of rallies against the planned law on May 3 and threatened "countermeasures" if it were adopted. TASS said the law would take effect in three years.

Latvian Supreme Soviet Passes Controversial Language Law

KGB head Vladimir Kryuchkov said the KGB was lifting the traditional veil of secrecy over its work in the Soviet Union. In an article published in *Izvestia*, Kryuchkov said the KGB had adopted a resolution called "The State Security Committee and *Glasnost'*." He said that from now on the KGB would report to the public about its major operations. Kryuchkov said the KGB was now paying special attention to ensuring that its personnel act within the framework of Soviet law. On May 6, the KGB collegium met in Moscow to discuss ways to promote *glasnost'* within its ranks. TASS said the meeting called for a mechanism to make the KGB more accountable to the people and the state. Soviet television said the collegium criticized the way some KGB officials try to avoid meeting the public, and it urged more frequent contacts (see *Pravda*, May 7).

KGB Announces New Policy of Openness

Reports from Nagorno-Karabakh said there were widespread strikes in the capital Stepanakert this week. The strikes were reported to have affected industries, transportation, and other sectors, with only essential services continuing operations. Radio Baku reported that one of the objectives of the strikers was the dissolution of the special commission that is administering the region. The same day, the military commandant of the Armenian capital, Erevan, warned that the authorities would not continue to tolerate unauthorized meetings or demonstrations (*Radio Erevan*, 1800).

Strikes Reported in Nagorno-Karabakh

The Soviet Union has set a record by buying 19.3 million tons of grain from the United States this year. The US Department of Agriculture said the USSR had taken advantage of US President George Bush's offer of an additional 1.5 million tons of wheat under a subsidy program making the wheat available at prices lower than world prices.

USSR Breaks Previous Record of Buying US Grain

Nine Outages at Soviet Nuclear Plants in April

A report in *Izvestia* said Soviet nuclear power stations had broken down nine times last month but with no threat to safety. Starting what it said would be regular reports on the atomic energy industry, the newspaper said there had been no increase in radiation levels at any of the country's forty-four nuclear power plants. The report appeared aimed partly at countering the fear of nuclear energy that has grown in the USSR since the Chernobyl' accident.

West German Military Chief Says Moscow Visit Helps Ties

West German Armed Forces Chief of Staff Dieter Wellershoff said his visit to the Soviet Union this week had been a step towards better relations between Bonn and Moscow but that many differences remained. Speaking at a press conference in Moscow, Admiral Wellershoff repeated Bonn's opposition to modernizing short-range nuclear weapons. He dismissed as a distant goal, however, Soviet proposals for the complete elimination of nuclear weapons. Wellershoff, who met Soviet Defense Minister Dmitrii Yazov and Soviet Chief of Staff Mikhail Moiseev during his visit, said that the two sides had agreed to strengthen cooperation in a number of military areas but that this could not happen overnight (*Reuters, DPA*, May 5).

Saturday, May 6 ───────────────────────────────

Party Officials Say No Improvement in Nagorno-Karabakh

The Nagorno-Karabakh Oblast newspaper *Sovetsky Karabakh* (May 5) printed an open letter to Gorbachev signed by the Party first secretaries of five of the oblast's seven raions, the chairmen of the respective raion soviets, and former Oblast Party First Secretary Genrikh Pogosyan. The signatories profess their understanding of the Soviet leadership's decision in January of this year to impose "special status" on Nagorno-Karabakh, but they charge that this has not led to the anticipated improvement in the situation in the region. Specifically, they claim that, in contravention of the terms of the joint Party and government resolution adopted last year on the socioeconomic development of Nagorno-Karabakh, construction of new roads, housing, and industrial and social projects is confined exclusively to the Azerbaijani villages of the region. The signatories further express concern about statements by the Party first secretary in Azerbaijan, Abdul-Rakhman Vezirov, to the effect that the Nagorno-Karabakh question has been definitively resolved once and for all; about the absence of any political evaluation of the Sumgait massacre; about what they term "the anti-Soviet slogans"

voiced during last December's unsanctioned mass meetings in Baku; and about the continued detention of members of the Karabakh Committee. In the name of "the overwhelming majority" of the population of Nagorno-
Karabakh they demand the removal of the oblast from
Azerbaijan, arguing that "the most correct and just solution" would be its annexation to Armenia. On May 9, TASS
gave more information on a disturbance that occurred in
Nagorno-Karabakh on May 5. TASS said about 200 people
were involved in a clash between Armenians and Azerbaijanis in which seven people had been injured. The
security forces fired warning shots to restore order in the
settlement of Kirkidzhan where the disturbance took
place. The authorities lengthened an overnight curfew in
the oblast capital.

Demonstrations in Armenia

AFP reported that some 200,000 Armenians had defied
an official ban and staged a three-hour demonstration
near the republican Central Committee headquarters in
Erevan. One of the participants told AFP by telephone that
the demonstrators had called for the resignation of the
Armenian government and the release of members of the
Karabakh Committee, who have been held in a Moscow
prison for five months without being charged. One member of the committee is reported to have been allowed to
return to Erevan, where he is under house arrest. The
military commander in Erevan warned residents of the
city in broadcasts on local television that the demonstration did not have official approval but that force had not
been used against the demonstrators. On May 12, AP and
AFP reported that another unauthorized demonstration in
Armenia took place on May 11. Unofficial demonstrations
were also reported from Georgia (*AP*, May 12).

**Resolution in Latvia
on Farming**

The Latvian Supreme Soviet has passed a law on farming
that increases the rights of individual farmers. TASS said
the law would allow individual farmers to use state land
allotted to them for an unlimited period of time and to
pass it on to their descendants. Individual farmers would
also be able to get bank credits and to dispose of their
produce as they wish. They would also be able to buy
technology, fertilizers, seeds, and livestock at state prices.

**Files of Pushkin's
Tormentors Declassified**

Voprosy istorii KPSS (No. 4) contained an article devoted
to archive materials that have been declassified thanks to
glasnost'. The article revealed that some important docu-

ments that were considered "secret" and therefore not available to scholars date back to the early nineteenth century. Among them are documents relating to the appointment of Count Aleksandr Benkendorff to head the gendarmerie of Tsar Nicholas I and also papers concerning the head of the tsar's Third Section (the secret police), L. V. Dubelt. In their capacities as police officials both Benkendorff and Dubelt played important roles in the life and death of Russian poet Aleksandr Pushkin. The reason why these archive documents have remained locked in secret files until the late 1980s remains a mystery.

Sunday, May 7

Moscow News Reports New Opinion Polls

Moscow News (No. 19) carried the results of two opinion polls conducted in September, 1988, and February, 1989, by the weekly's sociological service on the attitudes of Muscovites towards twenty-three different organizations, ministries, and departments (*vedomstva*). Those polled were asked to evaluate the activities of these organizations on a five-point scale, with five the best possible mark. *Moscow News* said the fact that both polls showed similar results proved that they were an accurate representation of opinion. Those polled evaluated the press highest (it received an average grade of 4.3 in September, 1988, and 4.2 in February, 1989). Radio and television came in second. Third place went to the CPSU Central Committee, whose average grade was 4.0 in both polls. The worst grades (lower than 3.0) were given to Aeroflot, the Ministry of Transportation, the Ministry of Finance, Gosplan, the Central Committee of the Komsomol, cooperatives, Gosagroprom, the Ministry of Health, the State Committee on Prices, and the Ministry of Trade (which had an average grade of 2.3 in September, 1988, and 2.2 in February, 1989). *Moscow News* said the majority of the organizations received a grading of less than 3.0 and that 46 percent of those polled in 1988 and 53 percent in 1989 had refused to give an evaluation of the KGB.

Shevardnadze Says USSR Does Not Want to Split NATO

The USSR is not trying to split NATO by persuading West Germany to push for negotiations on short-range nuclear missiles, Eduard Shevardnadze said in an interview published in *Time* magazine. In the interview, Shevardnadze rejected US Defense Secretary Dick Cheney's speculation that the failure of *perestroika* may lead to the replacement of Gorbachev with a leader less friendly to the West.

240

The USSR in May, 1989

On May 7, *Pravda* published the text of a resolution of the USSR Supreme Court passed down at a plenum of the court on April 25. The resolution announced the rehabilitation of Estonian scientist I. Hint. A well-known Estonian scientist, engineer, and inventor, Hint was arrested in 1982 and sentenced on charges of embezzlement and bribe-taking in 1983. Hint died in prison. His arrest provoked an outcry in Estonia. Now the USSR Supreme Court has announced that the charges against Hint were fabricated and that the investigation "violated Socialist legality." The investigation into the Hint case was supervised by Tel'man Gdlyan, who, as the investigator for especially important cases at the USSR State Prosecutor's Office, has become very well known for his inquiries into corruption among high-ranking Soviet government and Party officials, especially in Uzbekistan. The resolution of the USSR Supreme Court states that, because of errors and violations of legality committed by Gdlyan in the Hint case, Gdlyan should not be used further in such an important capacity.

Pravda Reports Rehabilitation of Hint, Demands Ouster of Gdlyan

---

Monday, May 8

Pravda published a detailed account of what Soviet intelligence knew about German plans to invade the USSR on the eve of World War II and said Stalin had ignored the warnings. The author of the *Pravda* article, Professor of History A. Baidakov, quoted from the reports of intelligence agents, some of whom had infiltrated the Gestapo, the German aviation industry, and the German coding service. Baidakov blamed the USSR's ministries of state security and defense for not convincing Stalin of the gravity of the German threat. He also blamed "the Soviet political leadership of the period"—i.e., Stalin—for failing to heed the warnings.

Pravda Attacks Stalin's Policy on Eve of World War II

The Soviet Union indicated that it would respond to any decision by NATO to modernize its short-range nuclear weapons by updating its own arsenal. In a commentary on the NATO dispute over the future of tactical nuclear arms in Europe, *Pravda* reaffirmed the Soviet call for negotiations to reduce and eventually eliminate these weapons. *Pravda* said a NATO decision to modernize short-range nuclear arms, which have a range of up to 500 kilometers, would increase the threat to the security of West European countries by provoking a Soviet response. Such a decision would also have a negative effect on the

Moscow Says It Will Respond to NATO Arms Modernization

241

Vienna talks to reduce conventional arms in Europe, the newspaper said. NATO is sharply divided over a Soviet proposal to negotiate cuts in short-range nuclear weapons. The United States and Britain favor modernizing NATO's short-range missiles and oppose talks to reduce them, but West Germany wants to postpone modernization until at least 1991 and is pushing for early East-West negotiations to reduce the missiles. *Pravda* said the US and British stance on the issue was motivated not by military concerns but by a political desire to maintain their influence in the alliance. On May 12, the NATO allies welcomed the Soviet offer to withdraw nuclear warheads on 500 short-range missiles but described it as "a rather modest step" (*Reuters, AP, UPI,* May 12).

Moscow Authorities Agree to Return Synagogue

The Moscow authorities have agreed to return the city's main synagogue and the building adjoining it to the Jewish community. The synagogue has been used as a clinic since World War II. A US Rabbi, Arthur Schneier, said it was the first time property taken from the Jewish community had been returned under Gorbachev's policy of greater tolerance of religion. Schneier said negotiations are under way for restitution of the synagogue in Lvov (*Reuters,* May 8).

Tuesday, May 9

Soviet Arms Experts Testify before Congress

A group of Soviet arms experts told a US Congressional Committee in Washington that NATO's proposed modernization of short-range nuclear missiles would threaten military stability in Western Europe. The Soviet experts said an updated arsenal of short-range missiles would increase NATO's offensive capability and violate "the commonly agreed principles" on the military build-up in Europe. Aleksandr Konovalov, head of a department that deals with conventional arms control at the USA and Canada Institute, said the USSR was currently cutting its armed forces and was making "substantial" changes in the production of military hardware. The four Soviet experts were speaking before the US House of Representatives' Armed Services Committee, which had invited them to discuss US-Soviet relations (*RFE/RL Special,* May 9). On May 10, Soviet Ambassador to West Germany Yulii Kvitsinsky told *Stern* magazine that NATO's plan to modernize its short-range nuclear arsenal could ruin the basis the INF treaty had agreed on earlier (*Reuters,* May 10).

In an interview with Radio Moscow, USSR Minister of Defense Dmitrii Yazov said a special working group is drafting a new law on defense. Yazov gave no details of the projected law but said the working group consists of representatives of the General Staff, the Main Political Administration of the Soviet Army and Navy, several main and central administrations of the USSR Ministry of Defense, and leading military academies. According to Yazov, the draft will be completed by 1990 and will then be published for general discussion. The legislation now in force dealing with the armed forces is the Law on Compulsory Military Duty.

Law on Defense in Preparation

In the wake of the much-publicized and ultimately successful hunger strike by parishioners in Ivanovo seeking the return of a local Russian Orthodox church, a group of believers from Krasnodar began a second week of picketing at the Moscow residence of Patriarch Pimen. They are demanding the return of Archbishop Vladimir to the Krasnodar eparchy. The picketers claim that Vladimir was transferred by the Church from Krasnodar to Pskov because he tried to stop thefts from the Krasnodar cathedral. See *Argumenty i fakty* (No. 16).

Believers Demand Return of Archbishop

An official of Soviet television said the USSR would start receiving US Cable Network News satellite television programs at the beginning of next year. Eduard Sagalaev, head of news for Soviet television, was speaking at Brown University in the US city of Providence, Rhode Island. He said Soviet citizens would see the European version of CNN programming, for which a special fee would probably be payable (*Reuters*, May 10).

Official Says USSR Will Start Receiving US Television Programs

Wednesday, May 10

US Secretary of State James Baker arrived in Moscow from Helsinki for talks with Soviet officials, including Mikhail Gorbachev. He began his visit with talks with Foreign Minister Eduard Shevardnadze (*TASS, UPI, AP,* May 10). TASS reported that during their first session Baker and Shevardnadze discussed regional issues, including Central America, the Middle East, and Afghanistan and that working groups to discuss other US-Soviet areas of concern were set up. Baker also met with members of the new Congress of People's Deputies and

US Secretary of State Baker in Moscow

told them that Washington believed there were real changes taking place in the USSR (*TASS, AP, AFP,* May 10, *Pravda,* May 11).

On May 11, Baker met Gorbachev for talks in the Kremlin after discussions lasting an hour with Shevardnadze during which the issue of short-range missiles was raised (*Reuters,* May 10). Shevardnadze and Baker also signed an agreement stipulating that the United States and the USSR would help each other with pollution emergencies in the ocean between Siberia and Alaska. TASS said the agreement provides for regular bilateral consultation and joint exercises to combat ocean pollution.

During the talks between Baker and Gorbachev, the Soviet leader proposed that the USSR and the United States negotiate on their differences over NATO plans to improve short-range nuclear-missile forces in Europe, but Baker rejected the offer. This was disclosed by Baker at a press conference in Moscow (*AP,* May 11). Shevardnadze also gave a press conference, at which he reiterated his criticism of the US stand on short-range missiles. He said that the administration of US President George Bush had taken "a very negative position" on the missile issue and that this "seriously concerns" Moscow. Shevardnadze also disclosed that, during the talks with Baker, Gorbachev had offered to reduce unilaterally short-range nuclear weapons and had made other offers to reduce conventional forces in Europe (*TASS,* May 11). (In a later report that day, TASS revealed that Gorbachev had proposed the USSR unilaterally withdraw 500 warheads on short-range nuclear weapons in Europe. TASS said that Moscow was also prepared to withdraw all nuclear weapons from the territory of its Warsaw Pact allies by 1991, if the United States were to take an analogous step.) Both Baker and Shevardnadze assessed positively the two days of talks, saying that they had made progress on the full range of US-Soviet issues and new areas of global concern. (*Reuters, AP,* May 11).

Medvedev Criticizes Soviet Broadcasting

The Politburo member in charge of ideology, Vadim Medvedev, said during a meeting with Soviet television officials that Soviet broadcasting was often inexact and lacked credibility, especially on such issues as economic reforms and nationalities relations. He discussed ways of making broadcasting more informative and interesting. He said more program makers and more competition between channels were needed. The "Vremya" television news program, which reported Medvedev's speech, quoted him as praising the editors of the popular television youth program "Vzglyad" for their open and critical approach but also as telling them to treat themes in a more balanced and thorough way. (See *Pravda*, May 11).

PEN Approves Chapters in Moscow and Lithuania

The international writers' organization PEN approved chapters in Moscow and Lithuania. The decision was taken during PEN's international congress in the Netherlands. A report from the group's Writers in Prison Committee listed twenty Soviet writers who had recently been released from prison, but it said four others were still being detained (*AP*, May 10). Soviet novelist Anatolii Rybakov addressed the PEN congress and later disclosed to reporters the possibility of opening chapters of PEN in Estonia, Latvia, Georgia, Ukraine, and Armenia (*RFE/RL Special*, May 11).

Estonian Agrarian Union Set Up

TASS said in a report from Tallinn that an agrarian union had been set up in Estonia. The Soviet news agency said the new social organization was aimed at coordinating the efforts of farm workers to boost agricultural production in the republic. The decision to form the agrarian union was taken recently at a congress of cooperative farmers and state-farm workers, representatives of trade and the food-processing industry, and Estonian agricultural officials. TASS said the agrarian union's status is such that it envisages putting forward its own candidates in elections to local soviets and to Estonia's Supreme Soviet.

Jewish Demonstration in Moscow

Western reports from Moscow said Soviet security forces had dispersed about three dozen Jewish demonstrators seeking permission to emigrate. The demonstration came as US Secretary of State James Baker had his first day of talks with Soviet officials. The demonstrators also urged the United States not to give most-favored-nation tariff status to the USSR until Moscow adopts a more liberal law on emigration (*AP*, May 10).

Gerasimov on Afghan War Prisoners

Foreign Ministry spokesman Gennadii Gerasimov said efforts to locate and return Soviet servicemen captured in Afghanistan had "rescued twenty-five people." Gerasimov was briefing reporters in Moscow on talks between Shevardnadze and James Baker. Gerasimov said that the soldiers had been rescued through the efforts of the Soviet Foreign Ministry and other organizations, not only in Pakistan and resistance-controlled parts of Afghanistan but also in the United States, Canada, and some West European countries. He gave no details but said that contacts with the resistance were also being used in the search for missing Soviet servicemen (*TASS*, May 10). The USSR lists more than 300 soldiers as missing in Afghanistan.

Soviet Expert Hopes for Truth on Psychiatric Abuse

A Soviet legal expert on psychiatry, Aleksandr Rudyakov, has expressed hope that the full truth about Soviet abuse of psychiatry for political purposes will be revealed. Rudyakov is in charge of the legal consultation department under the chief psychiatrist of Moscow Oblast. He spoke to RFE/RL by telephone from Moscow about psychiatric abuse and about a widely publicized article he coauthored in the February issue of the Party Central Committee journal *Kommunist*. Rudyakov attributes much of the abuse of psychiatry for political purposes to the Serbsky Institute of Forensic Psychiatry in Moscow and said that he hoped the institute's files would be opened for examination (*RFE/RL Special*, May 10). On May 11, the USSR's chief psychiatrist, Aleksandr Churkin, admitted abuses in the Soviet Union took place but denied that there was a government policy to use psychiatry for political purposes (*RFE/RL Special*, May 11, 1989). Churkin was attending a symposium in San Francisco sponsored by the American Psychiatric Association.

Armenians Hospitalized after Gas Poisoning

TASS said seventy-eight people had been hospitalized after toxic gas escaped from a factory in the Armenian city of Alaverdi, near the border with Georgia. It said the victims, who included women and children, were in satisfactory condition. The gas came from a metallurgical enterprise and, following the emission, several people began a hunger strike in front of the factory, demanding that production be stopped immediately. According to TASS, the accident happened over the weekend while repair work was being done; an increased emission of gas had been expected, but the engineer on duty failed to prevent it becoming what TASS called an "extraordinary" emission. TASS said the council of workers' collective of the enterprise had decided to stop production as of July 1.

Economist Urges Caution on Ruble Convertibility

Soviet economist G. Matyukhin said in *Pravda* that the Soviet ruble should be convertible but should not be floated until the economy is strong enough to take the consequences: "The convertibility of the ruble is a necessary condition for the integration of our economy into world markets." While agreeing that foreign-trade operations, enterprise self-financing, and joint ventures would all benefit from a convertible ruble, he warned that the Soviet economy was not yet ready for the convertible ruble. Matyukhin added that the Soviet Union had no experience of fluctuating bank rates and that the state bank, Gosbank, had no infrastructure to enable it to deal with other countries' central banks on foreign exchange markets. "So if ruble convertibility is introduced, there could be a real danger of the Soviet economy finding itself subject to the extreme influence of the moods of the international hard-currency market," he said.

Thursday, May 11

Soviet TV Reports on Protests in Moldavia

The Soviet television news program "Vremya" showed a film of a big protest rally in the Moldavian capital, Kishinev, and reported on demands made by the protesters. The national tricolor could be seen displayed at the rally. "Vremya" reported that such protest rallies are being held every Sunday in Kishinev. It also said that the Gagauz minority in southern Moldavia is holding meetings to demand autonomy.

Soviet Official Critical of Some Independent Journals

The chief Soviet delegate at the London Information Forum, Boris Pyadyshev, criticized some *samizdat* journals in the USSR. At a press briefing, Pyadyshev said that editors of some *samizdat* journals were not prepared to obey Soviet laws and sought to attract attention to themselves by any means. Pyadyshev had been asked to comment on the future of independent press organizations such as the Siberian independent press service, whose members were being harassed. The questioner also mentioned the *Byulleten' Khristianskoi obshchestvennosti* (Bulletin of the Christian Community), which has been unable to take possession of a copying machine sent from Britain. (Pyadyshev is editor of the journal *Mezhdunarodnaya zhizn'*, which is sponsored by the Soviet Foreign Ministry.)

Lithuanian Cardinal Critical of Draft Law on Religion

Lithuanian Cardinal Vincentas Sladkevicius described the draft Soviet law on religion as an important but inadequate step towards more democratic Church-state relations. He is quoted as saying in the youth weekly *Sobesednik* that the draft law retains passages from the existing conservative law on religion. The cardinal said that he saw no need for an all-Union law on religion and that the republics should be allowed to draft their own law according to local needs (*TASS*, May 11).

Friday, May 12 _____

Shevardnadze Visits Bonn

West German Chancellor Helmut Kohl and Soviet Foreign Minister Eduard Shevardnadze met in Bonn and discussed new Soviet arms proposals and next month's visit to West Germany by Mikhail Gorbachev. Kohl was quoted as saying that the Soviet proposals were a step in the right direction but did not amount to effective reductions. He said that it was not realistic to eliminate all nuclear weapons from Europe in the face of the Warsaw Pact's superiority in conventional arms. (*AP, Reuters*, May 12). On May 13, Shevardnadze held talks with West German Foreign Minister Hans-Dietrich Genscher. They signed a protocol on West German aid for the area affected by the Armenian earthquake last December. Officials said West Germany would provide 2,000 breeding cattle worth 4 million marks to restock herds lost in the quake. They said it would also build an orthopedic center in the region to help those who had lost limbs (*RFE/RL Special*, May 13). Speaking to reporters after the talks with Genscher, Shevardnadze said that if NATO modernized its short-range nuclear missiles, the Soviet Union would have to reconsider whether to destroy its SS-23 missiles as it has pledged to do under the INF treaty.

Ukrainian Catholic Priest Reported Arrested

The Rome-based Press Bureau of the Ukrainian Catholic Synod reported the arrest of a Ukrainian Catholic priest in Lvov. The bureau quoted "underground Ukrainian Catholic Church sources" in Ukraine, but there was no independent confirmation of the report. The report said Father Mikhailo Havriliv was arrested on May 11 at the Lvov machine plant where he works. He was reported to have been arrested for the holding of Easter services in several Ukrainian villages on April 30 (*RFE/RL Special*, May 12).

Clashes in Turkmenistan Reported

The Soviet media reported that fifteen police officers had been injured during clashes in the Turkmenistan city of Nebit-Dag. *Pravda* reported that demonstrators had set fire to shops and thrown rocks at police at the end of a holiday on May 9 to commemorate the German surrender at the end of World War II. The newspaper described the demonstrators as hooligans dissatisfied with the quality of private cooperatives. *Komsomol'skaya pravda* said the demonstrators had shouted nationalist slogans and denounced public institutions. Pravda of May 2 reported a similar disturbance that took place on May Day in Turkmenistan's capital of Ashkhabad.

Soviet television carried parts of a documentary film entitled "Svidetel'" (Witness) that attempted to show Stalin's mistakes on the eve of World War II cost the USSR millions of lives. The film traced how the USSR under Stalin's leadership signed a nonagression pact with Hitler's Germany in August, 1939, only to be betrayed by Hitler less than two years later when Germany attacked the USSR in June, 1941. The documentary included a commentary by Valentin Berezhkov, a Soviet diplomat who served as Stalin's interpreter. Berezhkov recalled that Stalin had praised Hitler for the executions in 1934 of the leaders of the Sturmabteilung—his former right-hand man Ernst Röhm among them. According to a story Berezhkov heard from Anastas Mikoyan, Stalin praised Hitler's action before members of the Politburo, many of whom were themselves executed in Stalin's purges later in the 1930s.

Stalin's Interpreter Compares the Dictator with Hitler

Saturday, May 13

AP reported the creation of an informal group in Leningrad whose aim is to oust the city's Party first secretary, Yurii Solov'ev. It quoted Petr Filipov, a Communist Party member and the leader of the new group, as saying that he and several other reform-minded Communists were working at bringing about Solov'ev's replacement. Solov'ev was defeated in the elections in March to the Congress of People's Deputies.

Informal Group Campaigns for Solov'ev's Ouster

The USSR's top corruption investigator Nikolai Ivanov, who is a candidate in repeat elections to the Congress of People's Deputies, indicated during debates on Leningrad television on May 12 that the name of conservative Politburo member Egor Ligachev had figured in materials concerning corruption among top government and Party officials. He said the names of former Leningrad leader Grigorii Romanov, former Politburo member Mikhail Solomentsev, and former head of the USSR Supreme

Investigator Says Ligachev Figures in Corruption Probe

Court Vladimir Terebilov were also to be found in the investigation materials. Ivanov gave no details of the investigation and stressed that he was not saying that any of the top Party officials he mentioned was guilty.

On May 13, *Pravda* carried a statement by the Presidium of the USSR Supreme Soviet saying that Ivanov and Tel'man Gdlyan, another prominent investigator, had been making "provocative statements" on radio and television about alleged law-breaking by Soviet political leaders. (Earlier this month Gdlyan accused senior Party officials and the KGB of trying to stop his probe of corruption among top Soviet officials.) On April 25, the USSR Supreme Court issued a resolution proposing that Gdlyan be removed from his position as an investigator of especially important cases. The reason given was that in 1982–83 Gdlyan became a leading figure in the fabrication of charges against a well-known Estonian scientist, I. Hint, who was arrested on trumped-up charges of embezzlement. *Pravda* of May 13 also quoted the Presidium of the USSR Supreme Soviet as saying a special commission had been set up to look into violations of legality that Ivanov and Gdlyan are alleged to have perpetrated while conducting various investigations.

On May 16, Ligachev denied allegations that he was involved in a corruption case under investigation by Ivanov. *Novosti* press agency said Ligachev made his denial in a message to the special commission investigating Ivanov and Gdlyan's methods. Ligachev called Ivanov's statement slanderous and said it was made for political purposes. Ligachev demanded a full investigation and a public report (*AP, UPI*, May 16). On May 18, Solomentsev also denied allegations of his involvement in corrupt circles. He said he had been discredited by Ivanov and Gdlyan, and he called for the matter to be investigated.

On May 19, more than 3,000 people were reported to have demonstrated in Moscow in support of Ivanov and Gdlyan (*TASS*, in English, May 19 and 20). The demonstration took place after Soviet television (May 19) quoted the specially appointed commission of the USSR Supreme Soviet as saying Ivanov and Gdlyan had seriously violated the law. The commission said the two had used illegal methods to obtain evidence in the Uzbekistan corruption affair that involved Yurii Churbanov, the late Leonid Brezhnev's son-in-law. See RL 282/89.

Representatives of Baltic Movements Meet in Tallinn

Representatives of the independent reform movements in Lithuania, Estonia, and Latvia met in Tallinn to discuss efforts to gain greater political and economic autonomy from Moscow for their republics. Reuters said that speakers at the "Baltic Assembly" had called for the republics to be given control of their own economies. The assembly is sponsored by the Popular Fronts of Estonia and Latvia and the Lithuanian Restructuring Movement "Sajudis" (*AP*, *Radio Stockholm*, May 13). Western agencies reported that participants criticized the annexation of the Baltic states by the USSR in 1940. They called on the international community to consider the legal status of the region (*Reuters*, *AP*, *Radio Stockholm*, May 14). They also called for a conference with the Moscow authorities over the future development of the Baltic republics. The call came in the form of a draft resolution issued by the assembly (*RFE Lithuanian Service*, May 14).

Soviet Troop Withdrawal from Czechoslovakia Begins

The first of about 80,000 Soviet forces stationed in Czechoslovakia began to withdraw as part of a partial pull-out of Soviet troops from Eastern Europe announced by Gorbachev last December. Withdrawals have also begun from Hungary and East Germany. Czechoslovak Chief of Staff Colonel General Miroslav Vacek said about 1,500 Soviet troops would leave his country this year and more than 5,000 next year (*TASS*, *Radio Prague*, May 13).

Sunday, May 14

Gorbachev's Visit to China

On May 14, Gorbachev left Moscow for China to attend the first Sino-Soviet summit in thirty years. He made a stopover in the Siberian city of Irkutsk. Speaking to a crowd in the city, Gorbachev said that production of consumer goods was improving and that there were more goods gradually reaching the market. He said, however, that some "hot-heads" wanted to speed up economic reforms and let the market balance supply and demand. But Gorbachev said this would cause price fluctuations. He said he favored gradual price reforms (*Central Television*, May 14, *Pravda*, May 15).

On May 15, Gorbachev arrived in Beijing. He was accompanied by senior Soviet Party and government officials. In a last-minute change, formal welcoming ceremonies for Gorbachev were switched to the airport from Tiananmen Square because of continuing demonstrations there by tens of thousands of Chinese students (*Reuters*, *AP*, May 15). Speaking the same day at a banquet in Beijing, Gorbachev said he believed China and the USSR could jointly help solve global problems and strengthen peace and security in Asia (*TASS, Reuters,* May 15, *Pravda,* May 16). Soviet television devoted a thirty-minute report to Gorbachev's arrival in Beijing. It reported the formal greetings and also included a film clip of the mass student demonstrations on Tiananmen Square. The report did not explain, however, that the students were demonstrating for a more democratic society in China.

On May 16, Gorbachev began talks with Chinese leader Deng Xiaoping in Beijing's Great Hall of the People. A wreath-laying ceremony in Tiananmen Square was canceled because of continuing student demonstrations there. During the talks, which lasted two and a half hours, Deng said relations between China and the Soviet Union had been normalized. Deng said the crucial issue in the world today was relations between the USSR and the United States. He said he thought US-Soviet ties were changing from confrontation to dialogue. Later the same day, Gorbachev had talks with Chinese Prime Minister Li Peng. Soviet Foreign Ministry spokesman Gennadii Gerasimov said they had discussed the issue of border troops. Chinese television quoted Li as saying Gorbachev also expressed willingness to discuss an eventual total withdrawal of Soviet troops from Mongolia. Gorbachev also met with Chinese Party General Secretary Zhao Ziyang (*Xinhua,* in English, Western agencies, May 16).

On May 17, Gorbachev gave a major televised address to representatives of the Chinese public in the Great Hall of the People. He called for the demilitarization of the Chinese-Soviet border and said it should be turned into a frontier of peace. He also gave fuller details of deep cuts Moscow plans to make in its Far East forces. He said twelve army divisions would be slashed, eleven air regiments disbanded, and sixteen warships removed from the Pacific fleet. He said that by 1990 Soviet troop levels along the Soviet-Chinese border would be cut by 120,000 men. He called the summit a milestone in Sino-Soviet ties and said he believed both sides had learned from past mistakes and wanted never to repeat them. He also said the international community should take a more vigorous stand on the Afghan conflict and that a settlement on Cambodia was "gradually taking on a realistic shape" (*TASS,* in English, *Xinhua,* in English, *Reuters, AP, AFP,* May 16 and 17).

Following his speech, Gorbachev told a news conference that a very important stage had begun in Sino-Soviet ties. He called the Beijing summit a watershed event. As he spoke, more than a million pro-democracy marchers surged through central Beijing. Gorbachev told the news conference, which was delayed because of the demonstrations, that he would not judge the protests. But he said he would use political methods if such events occurred in Moscow. Gorbachev defended Socialist countries experiencing unrest as they try to reform. He said such problems only proved that the changes under way are profound. He said anyone who thought this road would lead socialism "to the ash heap of history" would be disappointed (*TASS*, in English, *AP*, *Reuters*, *UPI*, May 17, *Pravda*, May 18).

In a live interview on Chinese television the same day, Gorbachev said he had received a letter from Chinese students expressing support for reform. He said "this is something that brings our two people even closer" (*Reuters*, May 17).

Soviet media coverage of the summit stressed the normalization of relations between China and the Soviet Union. The media carried only brief reports on the student demonstrations, however, and *Pravda* suggested that many Chinese disapproved of the protests. All the major newspapers said the students welcomed Gorbachev and hailed his policy of *perestroika*. On May 18, the Soviet television news program "Vremya" carried a film of the student protests, also showing those on a hunger strike.

On May 18, Gorbachev ended his visit to China in Shanghai. As Gorbachev arrived in Shanghai, students stepped up pro-democracy demonstrations there. Tens of thousands of students were said to be taking part. TASS said the authorities had "practically lost control" over the demonstrations in Beijing, and it reported the demonstrators' demands for the resignation of several Chinese leaders. A joint communiqué issued at the end of Gorbachev's visit called for a further improvement in Sino-Soviet relations and said "neither side would seek hegemony of any form" in any part of the world. The document also called for an international conference on the Cambodian war as soon as possible. It urged that arms shipments to Cambodia's warring factions be reduced and eventually end when Vietnamese troops withdraw (*TASS*, in English, *Xinhua*, in English, *Reuters*, May 18, *Pravda*, May 19).

Repeat Elections of Congress of People's Deputies

Repeat elections to the Congress of People's Deputies took place in the Soviet Union today. Among the winners were *Ogonek* editor Vitalii Korotich, who received 84 percent of the vote in a race against nine other candidates, and criminal investigator Nikolai Ivanov, who defeated twenty-seven other contestants to win 60 percent of the vote. Both men were opposed by local Party officials. Other victors included the recently appointed head of the Muslim Religious Board for Central Asia and Kazakhstan,

Mukhammadsadyk Mamayusupov. According to officials of the People's Front of Latvia, its candidates won five of six contested seats. In Estonia's single runoff election, Klara Hallik, who was endorsed by the People's Front of Estonia, won over 50 percent of the vote. The conservative editor of *Molodaya gvardiya*, Anatolii Ivanov, was defeated, as was reform-minded playwright Mikhail Shatrov (*TASS, Radio Moscow-1, AP*, May 15). It was reported on May 16 that the poet Evgenii Evtushenko had won a seat in the congress from a constituency in Kharkov. Reuters quoted Evtushenko's wife as saying that he had won the seat against eight other candidates, including the city's mayor. Evtushenko is a vocal supporter of *perestroika* but earlier failed to gain nomination to the congress as a Writers' Union candidate (*Reuters*, May 16).

Sakharov Says Soviet Economic Reforms Going Too Slowly

Speaking to a congress of the Italian Socialist Party in Milan, Academician Andrei Sakharov said the Soviet reform process was moving too slowly. He said the USSR was "on the brink of economic catastrophe." Sakharov said that although Gorbachev's reforms were a move in the right direction, their slow pace was causing "profound distress." Sakharov said there had been a need to dismantle the old centralized system. But he said people were demoralized because the old system "is not being replaced by anything else" (*Reuters*, May 14).

142 AIDS Carriers Reported in Ukraine

Ukrainian Deputy Health Minister Yurii Spizhenko said 142 carriers of the AIDS virus had been recorded in Ukraine. He described this fact as alarming. Spizhenko, who heads a Ukrainian AIDS commission, was quoted by TASS as saying that twenty-seven of the identified AIDS carriers were Soviet citizens, while 115 were foreigners.

Monday, May 15

Pravda Defends Kadar against Hungarian Opposition

Pravda defended Hungary's former Party head, Janos Kadar, against criticism from the Hungarian opposition. The newspaper called Kadar "a prominent and influential leader." *Pravda* said the Hungarian opposition was acting against Hungarian interests by making "insulting and unfair remarks" about Kadar and the Hungarian Communist Party. (Kadar led the Hungarian Party for thirty-two years after the Soviet invasion in 1956.)

Radio Moscow said citizens of the city of Cheboksary on the Volga River had won a victory over the authorities by blocking plans to increase the water level of the city's reservoir. The radio said the USSR State Planning Committee had decided to stop the project after scientists and experts had advised against it. It said Cheboksary citizens gathered tens of thousands of signatures for a petition opposing the plan on the grounds it would endanger the ecological situation and the fish reserves and lead to flooding. The radio said the foundations of many buildings in the city were below the present water level of the reservoir.

Victory for Ecologists in Cheboksary

TASS said jurists from East and West opened an international conference on human rights in Moscow. The four-day conference is organized by the Soviet Jurists' Association and the International Commission of Jurists. The topics of discussion at the conference included Gorbachev's *perestroika*, human rights, the independence of judges and lawyers, the reform of criminal legislation, and the correlation between international agreements and domestic law on human rights.

International Human-Rights Conference Opens in Moscow

Nuclear power plant operators from around the world gathered in Moscow to launch a new association designed to prevent a repetition of accidents like the Chernobyl' disaster in 1986. Representatives of more than 300 power-generating stations in thirty countries, including the United States, the USSR, France, and Britain, signed a charter inaugurating the World Association of Nuclear Operators. AP said the organization's charter stated that its mission "is to maximize the safety and reliability of the operation of nuclear power plants by exchanging information and encouraging comparison, emulation, and communication among its members."

International Association of Nuclear Operators Formed

The USSR began a planned partial withdrawal of its military forces from Mongolia. It is to withdraw 75 percent of its troops from Mongolia by the end of next year. Moscow says that will mean a pullout of 50,000 troops plus a large number of tanks, combat vehicles, and aircraft. The withdrawal coincided with Gorbachev's arrival in China, which has long demanded a cut in Soviet forces in Mongolia. A Soviet official said in Moscow, however, that the coincidence was unintentional (*TASS, RFE/RL Special*, May 15).

USSR Begins Withdrawal of Troops from Mongolia

USSR Allows Japanese to Visit Vladivostok

Some 240 Japanese tourists from the city of Niigata left by ship for Vladivostok today after the USSR agreed to allow Japanese to tour the Far East port city for the first time since World War II. The mayor of Niigata, Genki Wakasugi, who was among the group, said that during the visit he would discuss with Soviet officials the possibility of establishing sister city relations and economic and cultural exchanges between Niigata and Vladivostok (*AP*, May 15).

National Center for Soviet Germans Created

TASS reported that a national center to represent the interests of Soviet Germans had been created in Orenburg. At the center's opening session, emphasis was laid on finding a solution to the more pressing problems besetting the Soviet German population, such as the deterioration of the role and status of the German language and the loss of national customs and traditions. (In 1979, only 57 percent of the 1,963,000 Soviet Germans considered German their mother tongue.) It was noted at the session that it is these problems that have prompted mass emigration to West Germany.

Tuesday, May 16

Jewish Activist Says Many Jews Still Waiting to Emigrate

Soviet Jewish activist Yulii Kosharovsky said that despite great increases in Jewish emigration from the USSR there are still many Soviet Jews "stuck in refusal." He told reporters in Washington that thousands of Soviet Jews are "still fighting for freedom." Kosharovsky arrived in the West in March after waiting seventeen years for an exit visa. Kosharovsky said he supports President Bush's call for the Soviet Union to codify its emigration practices in accordance with international law and the Helsinki accords (*RFE/RL Special*, May 16).

New Gosteleradio Chief Appointed

Radio Moscow (2000) reported that Mikhail Nenashev had been appointed head of the USSR State Committee for Television and Radio Broadcasting. He replaces Aleksandr Aksenov, who is retiring. The move was made by the Presidium of the USSR Supreme Soviet. Nenashev was former chairman of the State Committee for Publishing Houses, Printing Plants, and the Book Trade. It seems that the last straw that led to the replacement of Aksenov was a statement made on Leningrad television on May 12 by corruption investigator Nikolai Ivanov about the involvement of Egor Ligachev and other officials in corruption.

Reports quoting unidentified government officials in Washington said Gorbachev had informed President Bush in a letter this month that all Soviet weapons deliveries to Nicaragua had been halted at the end of last year. The officials said the letter was received shortly before US Secretary of State James Baker visited Moscow, where he was given reconfirmation of the halt in weapons deliveries. They stressed that Gorbachev's assurances did not cover delivery of other forms of military assistance, such as vehicles and supplies. The United States has been seeking to persuade the USSR to cease its arms supplies to Nicaragua for some time (*AP*, *AFP*, May 16).

USSR Said to Have Stopped Arms Supplies to Nicaragua

Richard Schifter, US assistant secretary of state for human rights and humanitarian affairs, said there has been a big increase in the number of emigration permits issued in the Soviet Union so far this year. Schifter said 57,000 emigration permits were issued during the first four months. He said 27,000 permits were for ethnic Germans and 21,000 for Jews and Pentecostalists (*USIS*, May 16).

Schifter Cites Increase in Emigration Permits

The head of the Soviet space center, Aleksandr Dunaev, said there would be no flight of the space shuttle *Buran* this year. Dunaev told a press conference in Moscow that the decision was in no way connected with any technical deficiencies. He said that *Buran* was ready to fly and that the next flight would be made when there was a payload to pay at least part of the cost (*TASS*, May 16). Shuttle pilot Igor Volk said in New York two weeks ago that there were technical problems with the shuttle's flight control system and that it might not fly again until 1992. *Buran* made its only flight, unmanned, last November 15. It flew two earth orbits before landing near the launch site at Baikonur.

No Soviet Shuttle Flight This Year

Wednesday, May 17

A leading Soviet space expert said half the equipment aboard the orbiting *Mir* space station does not work. Former cosmonaut Vladimir Shatalov said crews have "wasted a great deal of time" on technical repair work. Shatalov, who is chief of cosmonaut training, was quoted in *Izvestia*. He said the Soviet Union should create a special agency that would "put space to use for the economy." He said the lack of such a controlling body has led to decisions made without regard for cost.

Soviet Space Expert Criticizes *Mir* Space Station

257

Writer Asks If Chernobyl'
Clouds Were Seeded to
Avoid Moscow

Komsomol'skaya pravda published a letter by Ales Adamovich, a prominent author and a member of the Congress of People's Deputies, in which he asked whether clouds loaded with radiation from the Chernobyl' nuclear accident were seeded to make them rain before they could reach Moscow. In the letter, addressed to Deputy Prime Minister Boris Shcherbina, head of the commission in charge of the Chernobyl' cleanup, Adamovich speaks of fears expressed by people in the Mogilev and Bryansk Oblasts that they were sacrificed in order to spare Moscow from radiation. He says serious scientists also believe the clouds were seeded, but he offers no evidence and does not name the scientists. TASS reported today that eleven villages near Bryansk are to be evacuated because of persistently high levels of radiation. On May 18, the British science magazine *Nature* quoted Vitalii Starodumov, director of the group that is working on the cleanup around Chernobyl', as saying that decontamination of the most radioactive land around the power plant is almost complete. Starodumov told *Nature* that there was virtually no radioactive dust being spread by the wind, because contaminated top soil had been removed and the land recultivated and treated with chemicals (*Reuters*, May 17).

Thursday, May 18 ⸻

Lithuania and Estonia Adopt
Legislation on Sovereignty

The Supreme Soviets of Lithuania and Estonia passed legislation giving their republics more autonomy. The Lithuanian Supreme Soviet adopted a declaration of sovereignty for the republic and approved amendments to the republic's constitution. One amendment said Soviet laws are valid in Lithuania only if approved by the Lithuanian Supreme Soviet. In Estonia, the Supreme Soviet approved a plan for economic self-management that includes limited ownership of private property (*AP*, *RFE Estonian and Lithuanian Services*, May 18). The same day, the Lithuanian Supreme Soviet issued a resolution calling on the new USSR Supreme Soviet to condemn and abrogate the Molotov-Ribbentrop Pact of 1939. The Estonian Supreme Soviet also passed a resolution condemning the use of troops and poison gas to suppress a demonstration in Tbilisi last month (*RFE Estonian Service*, *TASS*, May 19).

Heads of Warsaw Pact and
NATO Meet for First Time

The commander in chief of the Warsaw Pact forces, Soviet General Petr Lushev, met and shook hands with the supreme commander of Allied Forces in Europe, US

General John Galvin. Reuters said this was the first such encounter between the top military men of the two alliances. It took place at a conference in London on defense matters. In a speech to the conference, Lushev reiterated Soviet opposition to modernization of NATO's short-range nuclear missiles. Later Lushev told reporters he hoped the informal encounter with Galvin would be followed by official meetings.

Israeli Foreign Minister Moshe Arens said he expects a majority of the more than 1.5 million Soviet Jews to emigrate in the next few years. Arens said his belief stems from assurances by Soviet Foreign Minister Eduard Shevardnadze to US Secretary of State James Baker in Moscow last week that all barriers to Jewish emigration will be lifted (*The New York Times*, May 18).

Arens Said He Expects Majority of Soviet Jews to Emigrate

The Soviet Union formally offered proposals for reducing NATO and Warsaw Pact forces to equal ceilings by the end of the century. The proposals were made by Soviet delegate Oleg Grinevsky at today's session of the twenty-three nation Vienna conference on cutting conventional forces. The figures are not new. Mikhail Gorbachev described them to James Baker in Moscow last week. NATO diplomats welcomed the move as a help to negotiations but said some of the Warsaw Pact figures are too high (*RFE/RL Special*, May 18).

USSR Makes Formal Proposals at Conventional Arms Talks

An interview with Mikhail Gorbachev published in the journal *Izvestia TsK KPSS* (No. 5) said Gorbachev works virtually round the clock and relaxes by taking walks in the forest. The interview contained reminiscences about Gorbachev's childhood and youth in Stavropol. Gorbachev also said his 1,200-ruble salary is no higher than that of any other Politburo member. He says he has the use of a private country house but has never owned one himself (*TASS*, in English, May 18).

Gorbachev Interview Focuses on Private Life

Radio Moscow (2100) said a Soviet commission had recommended reducing the number and size of nuclear tests conducted underground at the Semipalatinsk site in Kazakhstan. The report said the state commission acted after investigating a leak of radioactive gases following an underground test on February 12. It said the gases spread to a small town but were not a danger to residents.

Commission Recommends Fewer Nuclear Tests at Semipalatinsk

Ukrainian Clergymen Stage Hunger Strike to Press Demands

Three bishops and three priests of the Ukrainian Catholic Church were reported to be staging a hunger strike in Moscow to press demands for the relegalization of their church. The Ukrainian Catholic Church has been banned since 1946 when Stalin ordered it absorbed by the Russian Orthodox Church. The six clergymen traveled to Moscow from Ukraine on May 16 to seek talks with Soviet officials. Reports said the delegation had begun the hunger strike while waiting at the Kremlin to meet a member of the Presidium of the USSR Supreme Soviet (*RFE/RL Special*, May 18). It was reported on May 19 that Ukrainian Catholics in Lvov had joined the hunger strikers in Moscow (*RFE/RL Special*, May 19). Later the same day, the press office of the Ukrainian Catholic Synod in Rome said the hunger strike by the Ukrainian Catholics had ended after six churchmen had met with a member of the Supreme Soviet. The press office said the meeting had produced no immediate results, but another meeting was promised, and the Supreme Soviet official said he would try to intervene with the local authorities to ease persecution of the church. It was reported on May 30, however, that a group of Ukrainian Catholics had resumed a hunger strike in Moscow to urge legal recognition of their church. The Ukrainian Catholic Synod's press bureau in Rome said a core group of about thirty Church members among the 200 fasters planned to continue the strike "indefinitely." The bureau said it had been informed of the plan on May 29. (*RFE/RL Special*, May 30).

Soviet Television Shows Film of Polish Protesters

Soviet television showed short scenes from demonstrations in the Polish city of Cracow held this week to protest against the presence of Soviet troops. The "Vremya" news program showed demonstrators marching in front of the Soviet consulate carrying a poster and chanting "Soviets go home." It also showed them raising barricades and throwing stones at police armored cars.

Lithuanians and Latvians Hold Rallies in Support of Crimean Tatars

Solidarity rallies were held in the capitals of Riga and Vilnius to mark the forty-fifth anniversary of the deportation of the Crimean Tatars. Radio Riga said Tatars and representatives of the Popular Front of Latvia had spoken at the Riga rally and expressed the hope that the next USSR Supreme Soviet would allow the Tatars to return to their homeland. The radio said the rally in Vilnius was organized by the "Rebirth of Culture" society of Tatars living in Lithuania (*Radio Riga*, in Latvian, 2200, May 18).

Interviews with Boris El'tsin were published in *Paris Match* and *The Washington Post* on May 18 and 19 respectively. In *Paris Match* El'tsin warned that the Soviet people would not wait much longer for better living standards. He also said that, to be successful, *perestroika* required the election of a new Party Central Committee. He proposed that a special Party congress be called to do this. El'tsin said he and Gorbachev shared a joint strategy but had differences over tactics. Asked in the interview whether he would run for the office of president against Gorbachev, El'tsin replied, "Why Not?" In his interview with *The Washington Post* El'tsin expressed concern that officials were trying to "neutralize" evidence of high-level corruption and were putting pressure on witnesses to retract statements given to prosecutors. Referring to the mention of Ligachev's name in connection with the corruption scandal, El'tsin said that the investigator Nikolai Ivanov must have evidence linking Ligachev and others to corruption cases, that otherwise Ivanov would not have dared to say anything.

El'tsin Interviewed by *Paris Match* and *Washington Post*

—————— Friday, May 19

Soviet biologist Aleksei Yablokov, who is a corresponding member of the USSR Academy of Sciences, criticized Soviet Prime Minister Nikolai Ryzhkov's record on protecting the environment. At a news conference in Moscow, Yablokov called Ryzhkov "an illiterate" on ecological issues. He said the Congress of People's Deputies should consider whether Ryzhkov ought to be replaced, but he stopped short of actually calling for Ryzhkov's ouster. Yablokov has been elected to the Congress. He specifically criticized Ryzhkov's support for a plan for developing the chemical industry in Western Siberia (*Reuters, AFP,* May 19).

Ryzhkov Criticized as Ecologically "Illiterate"

A four-hour strike by more than 200 bus drivers in Frunze resulted in a promise from the Kirgiz government of more pay and better social conditions. TASS said the strike had taken place on May 16. It said the drivers had long demanded a change of the labor organization and pay system. It said the Kirgiz government had decided to increase the drivers' wages, modernize the buses, allot land for the construction of apartments, and introduce breaks for the bus drivers along their routes. TASS said the measures would go into effect on June 2.

Frunze Bus Drivers Get Wage Increase after Strike

Number of AIDS Carriers in Elista and Volgograd Rises

More children and adults have contracted AIDS at two places in the RSFSR where the disease was spread earlier this year through the use of unsterilized syringes. Soviet television said in the news program "Vremya" that fifty-eight children and nine adults had been infected in Elista in the Kalmyk Autonomous Republic and that twenty-three children and one adult had contracted the virus in Volgograd. The same day, Deputy Prime Minister of the RSFSR Nikolai Trublin told Soviet television that a wide network of laboratories would be set up in the RSFSR to diagnose AIDS cases. He said that an RSFSR AIDS center would open in Moscow within one and a half months.

Demonstration in Tbilisi

Thousands of people took part in a march in the Georgian capital of Tbilisi to mourn the victims of last month's clashes between demonstrators and security forces. Soviet television in its evening news program "Vremya" said people from all over Georgia, including some Armenians, had participated.

Saturday, May 20 ——————————————————————

Wounded Soviet Pilot Lands in Turkey

A Soviet pilot wounded in the arm landed a two-engine military plane at the airport of Trabzon on Turkey's Black Sea coast, a spokesman of the Turkish Foreign Ministry said. Spokesman Inal Batu said it appeared that the plane had been fired on as it took off from the Soviet Union (*AP*, May 20). On May 22, the Soviet media gave more details of the incident. *Pravda* said Soviet fighter jets had been sent to intercept the MiG but had failed to catch it before it crossed the Soviet-Turkish border. *Izvestia* said the MiG pilot, whom it identified as Aleksandr Zuev, had wounded an airfield sentry with a pistol before climbing into the aircraft. The same day the Turkish authorities reported that Zuev had been taken to the hospital and had asked for political asylum in the United States (*Reuters, AP*, May 22). On May 23, the pilot met with Soviet officials in Turkey. He was quoted as telling them that he had no plans to return to the USSR (*Reuters, AP*, May 23). Moscow called for Zuev's extradition, but the Turkish authorities said they had no legal obligation to send Zuev back and that the decision over asylum lay with the United States (*Reuters, AP*, May 24). Meanwhile, the USSR started a legal case against Zuev on charges of violating international flight regulations, attempted murder, theft of firearms, hijacking a plane, and desertion (*TASS*, in English, May 24).

Soviet television commentator D. Kiselev said the findings of a commission of the Presidium of the USSR Supreme Soviet concerning the investigators of the USSR Public Prosecutor's Office, Nikolai Ivanov and Tel'man Gdlyan, were only of "a preliminary character." The commission said there was evidence that Ivanov and Gdlyan had "grossly violated" the law while conducting their investigation of corruption in Uzbekistan. Kiselev said the commission is an "extrajudicial" body and that the issue of guilt can only be determined by a court "in accordance with the law."

On May 21, *Izvestia* carried a damning account of Gdlyan's and Ivanov's work by Aleksei Buturlin, who was the republican prosecutor in Uzbekistan from October, 1984, to December, 1987. Buturlin said that their methods were reminiscent of the Stalin purges. On May 22, Egor Ligachev read out a statement at the Central Committee plenum, again rejecting Ivanov's claim that he (Ligachev) might have been implicated in a corruption case. It was also announced that the case against Viktor Smirnov, the former second secretary of the Moldavian Party Central Committee, who was arrested in January on bribery charges, had been dropped for lack of evidence and that the State Prosecutor's Office had apologized to him. Gdlyan had accused Smirnov of being implicated in "the Uzbek affair" while he was head of the Central Asian section of the Organizational Party Work Department of the CPSU Central Committee, prior to his transfer to Moldavia in 1984 (*TASS*, May 22).

At large rallies in Moscow on May 20 and 21, crowds of people expressed their disapproval of the commission's findings and their support for Gdlyan and Ivanov, who were recently elected to the Congress of People's Deputies by large majorities on the strength of their image as fighters against "the Uzbek mafia." Both Gdlyan and Ivanov addressed a large rally at the Moscow Luzhniki stadium, at which Andrei Sakharov proposed that the Congress create a commission to get to the bottom of the accusations against the two investigators (*TASS, Reuters*, May 21). On May 21, Soviet Justice Minister Boris Kravtsov said the case against Ivanov and Gdlyan was not yet closed. Kravtsov said in *Pravda* that "no one is talking about any final conclusion. . . . All the facts are still being studied."

On May 21, *Moscow News* (No. 21) carried an article by Egor Yakovlev on the Gdlyan-Ivanov affair. Yakovlev expressed concern that Soviet people demonstrating in support of the two investigators did not want to acknowl-

Gdlyan and Ivanov Affair

edge the fact that the law had indeed been broken by them, as for instance in the case of Estonian scientist I. Hint, who was arrested on trumped-up charges in the early 1980s. Yakovlev stressed, however, that the wrong-doings of Gdlyan and Ivanov should not be investigated separately from other violations occurring all the time in the Soviet legal system, of which Gdlyan and Ivanov were just elements.

On May 24, a member of the USSR Supreme Soviet's special commission on the case, said there would be another independent investigation. Lawyer Yurii Kalmykov told Moscow Television that a commission of the new Congress of People's Deputies should conduct its own investigation. The same day, Gdlyan and Ivanov turned down an offer by *Pravda* to discuss their case on the pages of the newspaper. *Pravda* reported their refusal and said the offer remained open. On May 25, *Sovetskaya Rossiya* attacked Gdlyan, saying he had employed Stalinist methods in obtaining testimony from jailed people.

On May 31, Novosti carried an interview with Colonel Aleksandr Dukhanin, head of the KGB Department of Investigations, concerning the case of Gdlyan and Ivanov. Dukhanin said Uzbekistan's former Party secretary for ideology, Rano Abdullaeva, who was arrested for corruption by Gdlyan's group, had claimed that Gdlyan and Ivanov had put pressure on her to confess that she had given bribes to Politburo members Aleksandr Yakovlev and Grigorii Razumovsky. Dukhanin added that the investigators had allegedly also asked Abdullaeva to incriminate *Pravda*'s chief editor, Viktor Afanas'ev, and USSR Minister of Culture Vasilii Zakharov. Meanwhile, *Moscow News* (No. 23) reported that, in addition to the official inquiry into the methods of Gdlyan and Ivanov that has already been announced, a criminal case had been opened against them. This information was reported to have been provided by USSR Public Prosecutor Aleksandr Sukharev.

Mass Food Poisoning in Uzbekistan

TASS said two people had died and 147 others had been affected by mass food poisoning in eastern Uzbekistan. A TASS report from Turakurgan said 50 percent of the sick had been diagnosed as having paratyphoid-B. It said many of them were in a serious condition. TASS said the source of the poisoning was fish from a market at the "Uzbekistan" kolkhoz. It quoted a deputy health minister of the republic as saying elementary hygiene regulations had been violated at the market.

At a three-hour rally on May 21 called by representatives of a dozen independent political groups, tens of thousands of Muscovites cheered as deputies to the Congress promised to fight the attempts of Party bureaucrats to reduce the powers of the Congress and the Supreme Soviet it will elect. Addressing a cheering and chanting crowd, Boris El'tsin told his audience, "If, at this historic moment, we capitulate to the apparatus as we have so many times in the past, we will not advance but will sink back into the swamp from which we are only beginning to extricate ourselves." El'tsin proposed that the date for the Twenty-eighth Party Congress be earlier than 1991. He also proposed that the deputies first listen to Gorbachev's opening report and then decide whether he should be elected president. Deputy Aleksandr Tolstoukhov's proposal that "we should vote for true people's power with a true people's president, Boris El'tsin" was met with loud cheers. Andrei Sakharov also addressed the rally, arguing that the Congress, not the Supreme Soviet, should be the supreme legislative authority, rather than "a preparatory organ." "Deputies who have the people's mandate cannot give it away to one-fifth of their number," he said, criticizing the new system whereby the 2,250 deputies will elect 542 of their number to serve in the Supreme Soviet, which will draft legislation (*AP*, May 21; *The Baltimore Sun, The Los Angeles Times*, May 22).

Lead-Up to First Session of Congress of People's Deputies

Soviet First Deputy Foreign Minister Yulii Vorontsov met with leaders of the eight-party Afghan resistance coalition based in Iran. In an interview with the Iranian news agency IRNA, Vorontsov said he had "a long and very good meeting" with the representatives. He said the atmosphere and quality of today's meeting differed from previous meetings with resistance leaders before the Soviet withdrawal from Afghanistan, but he did not say how (*Radio Teheran*, May 21).

Vorontsov Meets with Iran-Based Afghan Resistance

Ogonek (No. 21) carried an article about the execution of the last Russian Tsar, Nicholas II, and his entire family on the night of July 16, 1918, by a group of Chekists. The five-page article is based on an account of the execution written by Yakov Yurovsky—who was in charge of the operation—that has been preserved in Soviet archives. The article in *Ogonek* said the account shows that all the

Ogonek on Execution of Tsar's Family

members of the family were shot and that "all the stories . . . of a miraculous escape by one of the tsar's daughters, Anastasia," are false. The article in *Ogonek* follows a recent article in *Moscow News* by writer and former MVD official Gelii Ryabov, who said that in 1979 he had found the skull of Nicholas II and the remains of other members of the family near the city of Sverdlovsk (formerly Ekaterinburg), where the execution took place. On May 19, Ryabov gave a lengthy interview on his findings on the television news program "Vremya."

Glasnost' Emerges in Soviet Coverage of Chinese Protests

Soviet media coverage of the unrest in China, minimal during last week's visit to Peking by Mikhail Gorbachev, has become more detailed since his return. Radio Moscow reported today that over one million demonstrators were on the streets of Peking and said this number was growing. Previous media reports on the protests generally avoided crowd estimates.

Dead and Injured in Kazakhstan Rail Crash

TASS reported that an unspecified number of people were killed and injured in Alma-Ata in Kazakhstan on May 20 after two freight trains collided. The agency said the collision occurred as the two trains—one of them carrying propane—were being switched from one track to another on the approach to the Alma-Ata-2 station. TASS said the collision caused a "huge" fire that produced "a powerful explosion that claimed human lives." TASS said the fire devastated thirteen buildings, including houses. A special commission has been set up to investigate the accident.

Moscow News Points to NKVD Responsibility for Katyn

Moscow News (No. 21) carried an article by Aleksandr Akulichev and Aleksei Pamyatnykh, who listed for the first time in the Soviet press facts that suggest that NKVD troops, not the Nazis, were responsible for the massacre of Polish officers in Katyn forest near Smolensk. The authors noted that available information showed that the tragedy occurred in the spring of 1940, not in the fall of 1941, as the Soviet official version has so far maintained. The material in the *Moscow News* article was made public in the Polish official press earlier this year. Akulichev and Pamyatnykh make clear, however, that they did not want to draw any final conclusions on the Katyn issue. They said the new official position of the Soviet Union concerning the Katyn massacre would be given by the Soviet side of the joint Soviet-Polish commission set up in 1987 to clarify "blank spots" in Soviet-Polish relations.

Moscow News (No. 21) carried an article by Belorussian writer Ales' Adamovich who defended Academician Andrei Sakharov against a rude attack on him in the newspaper of the Azerbaijani Academy of Sciences on April 15 of this year. The attack was leveled by Academician Z. Buniyatov, who also carries the title Hero of the Soviet Union. Buniyatov was displeased with Sakharov's stand on the conflict between Armenians and Azerbaijanis over the Nagorno-Karabakh issue. Buniyatov apparently regarded Sakharov's position as pro-Armenian. Buniyatov did not attempt to argue with Sakharov over the Nagorno-Karabakh issue, however, but instead made insulting remarks about Sakharov and his wife Elena Bonner. Buniyatov said that Sakharov had stopped being a scientist and "had turned into an ordinary pensioner, who gets his money for doing nothing but indulging in empty twaddle." Buniyatov asserted that Sakharov sends material abroad with his wife that is characterized by "infamy and triteness" and aimed "against everything Soviet." Buniyatov said that in "the good old days" Sakharov would have been justly prosecuted for what he has allowed himself to say. In his commentary on the article, Adamovich expressed surprise that the Azerbaijani press had published such material. He also expressed concern that the Azerbaijani intelligentsia had so far failed to respond to Buniyatov's outburst, just as it failed to say anything about the massacre of Armenians in Sumgait last year.

Moscow News **Defends Sakharov against Azerbaijani Academician**

Moscow News (No. 21) reported that the first steps had been taken to set up a Russian People's Academy of Sciences. The decision to set up such an academy was taken at a scientific conference in Moscow, the newspaper disclosed. The new academy, according to *Moscow News*, has as its main goal the better utilization of the RSFSR's scientific potential. It will also be concerned with ecological problems in the RSFSR. An organizational committee was set up to prepare the rules of the new body and its inaugural meeting. *Moscow News* did not say who the members of the organizational committee are but only that they include scientists, writers, and public figures. It disclosed that the chairman of the commission is Candidate of Military Sciences Petr Ivankov. Previous reports on plans to create a Russian Academy of Sciences have indicated that the initiators of the project are conservatives. The choice of a military specialist to head the organizational committee seems to confirm this.

Moscow News **on Creation of Russian Academy of Sciences**

**Moscow Orders Out
British Citizens**

Britain said the Soviet Union had ordered eight British diplomats and three journalists to leave the USSR. A further three diplomats currently outside the USSR have been declared *persona non grata*. The British officials said the move was in retaliation for the unannounced expulsion from Britain on May 19 of a group of Soviet citizens. The Foreign Office spokesman said the Soviet citizens had engaged in activities incompatible with their status—a diplomatic euphemism for spying (*Reuters, AFP*, May 21).

On May 22, Soviet Foreign Ministry spokesman Gennadii Gerasimov announced that Britain would have to cut the number of British nationals working in the USSR from 375 to 205 to match the number of Soviet citizens working in Britain (*AP, Reuters*, May 22). British Foreign Secretary Sir Geoffrey Howe said Soviet reprisals for Britain's expulsion of Soviet spies showed how far Moscow still has to go to match normal Western standards of behavior (*AP, Reuters*, May 22). The same day, the International Press Institute protested against the USSR's expulsion of three British journalists from Moscow (*AP*, May 22). On May 24, Gerasimov said the USSR was willing to lift its quota on the number of people in British institutions in the USSR if Britain responded in kind. Gerasimov made the comment in response to the British request that the USSR reconsider its decision (*TASS*, May 24).

On May 28, British Foreign Office Minister William Waldegrave said there were "grounds for optimism" in the dispute with the USSR over the expulsions of the diplomats and journalists. In an interview with the BBC, Waldegrave said that both sides had a great interest in maintaining the recent improvement in bilateral relations and that there were signs that "wiser counsel" was prevailing in the Soviet government (*AP*, May 28). At a press conference on May 30, Gennadii Gerasimov clarified who is covered by the USSR's new quota on employees of British institutions in Moscow. Gerasimov said the quota of 205 applies to British and Soviet nationals working at the embassy and in diplomats' households. Gerasimov said it does not include British businessmen and teachers, or Soviet personnel at British firms, banks, and journalists' offices in the Soviet Union (*TASS*, May 30).

Monday, May 22 ———————————————————————————————

**Soviet Military Historian on
His Biography of Trotsky**

The Soviet military historian and philosopher General Dmitrii Volkogonov said his biography of Leon Trotsky would be ready by the end of next year. Volkogonov said he was writing on the basis of documents he had found in Moscow, London, and at Harvard University in the United States. Volkogonov discussed the Trotsky biography in the Bulgarian Defense Ministry's daily *Narodna Armiya*. (Volkogonov's biography of Stalin has already been published in the USSR.)

Space specialist Academician Roald Sagdeev said growing strife between scientists and industry officials threatens future Soviet plans for the unmanned exploration of Mars. Sagdeev said this strife also contributed to the failure of the Soviet attempt to explore the Martian moon Phobos this year. Contact was lost with the two craft sent on that mission. Sagdeev said scientists did not have enough say in designing those spacecraft and must demand a larger role in designing future craft. He made his comments in an interview with this week's edition of the US magazine *Aviation Week and Space Technology*. Sagdeev said there is also growing concern in the USSR about the cost of the space program and skepticism about its benefits. He said "there is a kind of space phobia developing in our country."

Soviet Space Expert Sees Strife Hurting Space Program

The USSR Supreme Court said last month's decree on crimes against the state does not mean people will be jailed for criticizing officials or the government. It said the decree aims to protect officials and state bodies from deliberate circulation of slanderous allegations and false information. It said criticism of shortcomings of officials or of the state is not viewed as a crime. Soviet television also reported that during a recent session the Supreme Court rehabilitated over fifty people jailed or executed under Stalin on charges of crimes against the state.

Supreme Court Clarifies Changes in Law on Antistate Crimes

Pravda said popular fronts in the Baltic republics were going too far in their demands for greater independence and in backing programs that amount to complete secession from the Soviet Union. *Pravda* called the demands issued by grass-roots groups in Estonia, Latvia, and Lithuania "extremist and nationalist." Referring to resolutions passed at a mid-May assembly of Baltic popular movements held in Tallinn, *Pravda* said that "in total, although no one talks about this directly, they [the resolutions] make sense only if their authors have in mind the complete secession of the three republics from the Soviet Union."

Pravda Accuses Baltic Fronts of Going Overboard

Commissions Urge State-Language Status for Uzbek

Three commissions of Uzbekistan's Supreme Soviet are reported to have recommended Uzbek be given the status of a state language. Radio Moscow said the commissions had made the recommendation after discussing the Party's draft law on language at a meeting with experts. It said the meeting had also stressed the importance of the Russian language for communication among different nationalities. It said the commissions had then forwarded the draft law on language to the Presidium of Uzbekistan's Supreme Soviet for adoption (*Radio Moscow-2*, 0800, May 22). In March, an unofficial demonstration was staged in Tashkent to press demands for the use of Uzbek as the republic's state language.

Soviet Jewish Groups Meet in Latvia

Representatives of Jewish clubs and communities from thirty Soviet cities met in Riga. TASS said the group had discussed a wide range of issues related to the revival of Jewish culture and education, including the teaching of Yiddish and Hebrew. AFP quoted the secretary of the European Jewish Congress as saying the group had set up a federation of Soviet Jewish organizations. He said they demanded freedom to emigrate, the right to a distinct cultural identity, the right to form community associations, and the enactment of a law on anti-Semitism.

Tuesday, May 23 ————————————————————————————

Reformist Deputies Interviewed on Television

As part of its coverage of the Congress of People's Deputies, Soviet television began broadcasting a new program this week called "All Power to the Soviets," immediately following the "Vremya" evening news program. Today's program included interviews with Igor Shamshev, a leader of the Popular Front in Yaroslavl; Vitalii Korotich, the editor of *Ogonek*; economist Nikolai Shmelev; and Sergei Ambartsumov, rector of Erevan State University. Shamshev called for a reform of the political system, including direct elections by secret ballot of the president by the Soviet population. Korotich's most interesting remark was the observation that the Soviet people must not fear the leadership any longer and that, in fact, the leadership should be in awe of the people. "Vremya" also interviewed several deputies, including CPSU General Secretary Mikhail Gorbachev, chief ideologist Vadim Medvedev, historian Roy Medvedev, economist Gavriil Popov, and writer Daniil Granin, in connection with its coverage of a meeting of deputies to the Congress who are members of the CPSU. Gorbachev said that their meeting was extremely "useful" and revealed that Belorussian writer Ales Adamovich, elected as a delegate by the USSR Cinema Workers' Union, had addressed the CPSU deputies on behalf of the non-Party deputies who have been elected to the Congress. Both Roy Medvedev and Daniil Granin observed that there would undoubtedly be factions in the new Congress. Vadim Medvedev made it clear that the Party considers the disputes and radical proposals that have been voiced in advance of the first session of the Congress a normal part of the development of democracy. Popov said that if the Congress failed to work out and adopt "radical measures" with regard to the economy, *perestroika* would be stopped in its tracks.

El'tsin Sweeps Elections among Soviet Voters Living Abroad

Byulletin' ministerstva inostrannykh del (No. 7) carried a breakdown of the votes cast by 133,995 Soviet voters living abroad in elections to the Congress of People's Deputies. Among those entitled to vote in Moscow's national-territorial district (which included Soviet citizens living in West Germany, Mozambique, Algiers, Norway, and Egypt, among others), the overwhelming majority voted for Boris El'tsin. Soviet voters residing in the United States cast 1,353 votes for El'tsin and only 179 for his opponent, Evgenii Brakov.

Another Member of the Karabakh Committee Released

Following the release of Karabakh Committee member Aleksandr Akopyan in late April, a second person associated with the Karabakh movement, Armenian SSR Supreme Soviet deputy and Chairman of the unofficial Armenian Charitable Society Hachik Stambultsyan was reported to have been released from prison in Moscow (*AFP*, May 23). Up to 200,000 people are reported to have participated in demonstrations in Erevan last week to demand the release of the dozen Karabakh Committee members arrested in December and January.

Soviet Official Defends Cost of Space Program

Soviet space center chief Aleksandr Dunaev said the USSR had spent 2,350 million dollars during the past three years on the *Mir* space station. Dunaev told a Moscow press conference that commercial sales of products and services directly related to the *Mir* program had only recovered about a quarter of the costs. Responding to criticisms of the cost of the space program raised by candidates in the recent Soviet election campaign, Dunaev insisted that such criticism was based on "insufficient knowledge."

271

Dunaev said criticism of the space program had focused too much on cost and had not taken into account that benefits such as medical research cannot be measured in hard currency revenues (*Reuters, AP*, May 23).

"Memorial" Stages Rally in Moscow

A rally organized by the anti-Stalinist group "Memorial" in Moscow's Gorky park drew a crowd of some 3,000 people who cheered a succession of speakers calling for greater freedom of expression. "Memorial" member and former political prisoner archivist Arsenii Roginsky complained that the official de-Stalinization campaign had not gone far enough. He said "millions of people still had not been rehabilitated." He called for the publication of Aleksandr Solzhenitsyn's *Gulag Archipelago* (*Reuters*, May 23).

Supreme Soviet Presidium Restores Yurii Lyubimov's Citizenship

Radio Moscow reported that the Presidium of the USSR Supreme Soviet had restored Soviet citizenship to theater director Yurii Lyubimov. Lyubimov was stripped of his Soviet citizenship while working in the West in the early 1980s. He has returned to Moscow twice since then, most recently in February of this year when he directed two plays at the Taganka Theater.

Interior Minister Suggests Police Cooperatives

Minister of Internal Affairs Vadim Bakatin suggested creating cooperatives of policemen who would provide private guard services for other cooperatives. He said the cooperatives would be controlled by the local police headquarters but paid by the businesses they guard. TASS said Bakatin had made the suggestion at a round-table discussion on crime that was published in *Izvestia*.

Decree Sets Tougher Penalties for Traffic Offenses

A Soviet official said a new decree on traffic offenses due to take effect next week provides for tougher punishment for traffic violations. Major General Valerian Ishutin of the Ministry of Internal Affairs told reporters that as many as 47,000 people had died in road accidents in the USSR last year and that 300,000 had been injured. He said drivers were to blame for over 80 percent of the accidents. Ishutin said stricter penalties would be administered for drunken driving, not using seat belts, and for traffic offenses by pedestrians, cyclists, and groups of people on motorcycles. He said the new decree reduces the number of offenses carrying fines. He said more than half the 35 million people fined for violating traffic regulations last year had committed minor offenses (*TASS*, May 23).

TASS said the Soviet nuclear submarine that caught fire and sank in the Norwegian Sea on April 7 had been located. TASS said the submarine was found by so-called deep-sea *Mir* vehicles sent down from a Soviet research ship. TASS said latest checks show no abnormal radiation levels in the area where the submarine went down.

Soviet Vessels Locate Sunken Nuclear Submarine

Novoe vremya (No. 16) contains several articles on "the free flow of information." The first article, by Vladislav Kurochkin, points out that the USSR is the country with the largest volume of broadcasting to the outside world and notes that satellite communication is becoming the technical basis for international broadcasting. Kurochkin goes on to argue that jamming foreign broadcasts or destroying satellites is both unreasonable and dangerous. He claims that, in the future, transnational forms of control over international broadcasting will be unnecessary because public opinion in every country will play the role of a "natural" censor. A second article, by *Washington Post* correspondent F. Havlicek, describes the effects of the cessation of jamming of Radio Liberty and Radio Free Europe, pointing out that American opposition to jamming was based not only on the right of the Soviet population to listen but also on the desire of Americans to be heard. The third article, by Vladimir Ostrogorsky, argues that foreign radio stations broadcasting to the USSR do not engage in slander, defamation, or incitement, nor do they employ former Nazi collaborators. Rather, at every opportunity they have employed first-rate Soviet literary figures who were forced to leave the USSR. Ostrogorsky suggested that instead of trying to cover events in the Soviet Union, Western broadcasters would perform a greater service by providing information about their own countries' experience in various fields.

***Novoe vremya* Calls on Western Radios for Cooperation**

_____*Wednesday, May 24*

The president of the Georgian Academy of Sciences, Albertas Tavchedlidze, has criticized an official report on last month's clashes in Tbilisi, which claimed at least twenty lives. According to a reporter from the information agency of "Sajudis," the Lithuanian Restructuring Movement, who is visiting Tbilisi, the president has sent an appeal to the Congress of People's Deputies saying the report is incompetent and tendentious and does not reflect the facts and circumstances. He said the report's

Preliminary Report on Tbilisi Events Criticized

"incorrect and unobjective" conclusions can only aggravate the situation in Georgia. Tavchedlidze blamed the chairman of the special commission that drafted the report, Georgii Tarazevich, for the shortcomings of the report. Tarazevich is chairman of the presidium of the Belorussian Supreme Soviet. The information about the criticism of the report was provided by a representative of "Sajudis" in a telephone interview with RFE's Lithuanian Service. (On May 12, *Zarya Vostoka* reported that the Georgian Public Prosecutor's Office had started a criminal case against "specific military men" who killed people in Tbilisi. The office has also instituted proceedings against leaders of informal groups in Georgia who are believed to be the organizers of the unofficial demonstrations in Tbilisi that led to the clashes.) In the city of Borzhomi in Georgia, voters have asked the Central Electoral Commission to recall Colonel General Igor Rodionov, elected to the Congress of People's Deputies on March 26, in protest against the killing of demonstrators in Tbilisi on April 9 (*AP*, May 19, 1989; *Reuters*, May 21).

French Physicians on Toxic Gas Used in Tbilisi

A French-Belgian medical organization said it had identified a toxic gas that was used against demonstrators in Georgia last month and caused deaths. The organization said the toxic gas chloropicrin was only one of the gases used when Soviet troops broke up the demonstration in Tbilisi. The Georgian government asked "Médecins Sans Frontièrs" (Physicians without Borders) to investigate the deaths. Spokespeople for the organization said their conclusions were based on medical inquiries in Georgia and autopsies on sixteen of the victims. Their findings support those reported by the Georgian authorities earlier (*Reuters*, May 24).

Soviet Ideologist Speaks about Multiparty System

Vadim Medvedev, Politburo member in charge of ideology, was quoted as saying there was no contradiction between a multiparty system and a Socialist state. Medvedev told the French newspaper *Le Monde*, however, that the time for establishing such a system in the USSR had not yet arrived. Medvedev told the newspaper it was necessary "to maintain the force for integration that the Party represents in the present state of development, in the extreme complexity and diversity of *perestroika.*" Medvedev was quoted as saying that "efforts to weaken" the Party "by putting other political forces and organizations [i.e. informal groups] up against it" were aimed at "blocking *perestroika.*"

Pravda said a key mandate of the new Congress of People's Deputies is to improve living standards. *Pravda* made clear that the economy is the Soviet Union's main problem at present, and it suggested that this should not hamper the current process of democratization in the Soviet Union.

Key Mandate of New Congress Is Improving Living Standards

A column of 120 tanks, together with fresh supplies of artillery and other military equipment, arrived in Kabul from the USSR. Afghan Defense Minister Lieutenant General Shahnawaz Tanai told TASS that the deliveries would help Afghan government forces increase their defense capability around the Afghan capital of Kabul. Tanai said the resistance intended to strengthen military operations around the besieged Eastern cities of Jalalabad and Khost, and around other cities. He said the resistance also planned to concentrate its forces for a siege of Kabul (*TASS*, May 24).

Soviet Tanks and Artillery Arrive in Kabul

Thursday, May 25

The new Congress of People's Deputies opened its inaugural session in the Kremlin. One of the first speakers was Academician Andrei Sakharov. In his speech Sakharov criticized the idea of electing a new Supreme Soviet and a president before the Congress had debated a wide range of issues. Sakharov said that after the debate he would support Mikhail Gorbachev for the presidential post because he does not see anybody else who could do the job. A vote was taken on whether the election of the president and the Supreme Soviet should be the first item on the agenda, and it was decided that the elections should come before the debates.

Congress of People's Deputies Convenes

The morning's proceedings included a demand by a deputy from Riga that last month's events in Georgia be accounted for. The deputy said his constituents wanted to know who gave the order for troops to attack peaceful demonstrators in Tbilisi. In response to this proposal, the Congress decided to launch an investigation into the use of troops in Tbilisi. Summing up the heated exchanges at the morning session of the Congress, a Radio Moscow commentator said the session was "absolutely different from anything we have ever had in the Soviet Union."

During the afternoon session, the Congress discussed nominations for the post of president. Boris El'tsin was nominated. He turned down the nomination, however, leaving Gorbachev as the only remaining candidate. After being nominated, he stressed his commitment to *perestroika* and *glasnost'*. Before the voting started, Gorbachev underwent tough questioning from deputies about his private life, the recent clashes in Georgia, and his handling of domestic affairs. On the evening of May 25, in a widely expected move, Gorbachev was elected as the country's new president. Radio Moscow said 87 of the 2,000 deputies present voted against him. The Congress was well covered by Soviet television and radio.

On May 26, the Congress continued its work. At the opening of the afternoon session, Congress chairman Anatolii Luk'yanov announced several concessions to the Moscow group of deputies, who have argued that the Congress, not the Supreme Soviet, should be the supreme legislative body. First, deputies not elected to the Supreme Soviet or its commissions or committees will have the right to attend all sessions of these bodies and to vote at them. Further, they will have full access to the same information. The Congress will also have the right to annul any decisions that are passed by the Supreme Soviet (*Radio Moscow, Soviet Television*, May 26).

At the morning session on May 27, the results of the elections to the USSR Supreme Soviet were announced. Boris El'tsin was among twelve candidates running for the eleven seats in the Council of Nationalities assigned to the RSFSR. Although there were more votes for him than against him, his vote total was the lowest of the twelve nominees, and he thus did not win a seat. Coming in ahead of El'tsin to win the eleventh seat was Politburo member Vitalii Vorotnikov. Among others elected to the Council of Nationalities were Estonian pro-reform economist Mikhail Bronshtein, Latvian Popular Front member Janis Peters, Estonian Popular Front leader Marju Lauristin, and Estonian President Arnold Ruutel. Among the reformists who lost in the elections to the Supreme Soviet were the sociologist Academician Tat'yana Zaslavskaya, the economist Gavriil Popov, the agricultural specialist Professor Vladimir Tikhonov, the historian Sergei Stankevich, and the journalist Yurii Chernichenko. The results of the elections were criticized by reformers. The same day, the Congress declared void the results of the vote for the two seats in the Council of Nationalities representing the Nagorno-Karabakh. A dispute over the oblast's representation began on May 26 when a Congress deputy from the region complained that Azerbaijan had nominated Nagorno-Karabakh's candidates for the Council of Nationalities. He said each area had the right to field its own candidates (*Radio Moscow*, May 27).

At the afternoon session on May 27, the Congress decided to establish commissions to investigate last month's clashes in Tbilisi and the Gdlyan-Ivanov affair. The Congress then adjourned until May 29. The same day, AP reported that several thousand people had gathered in Moscow to protest against the rejection of reformist candidates in the elections to the Supreme Soviet.

On May 28, Western agencies reported that at least 8,000 people had rallied in Moscow to protest against the exclusion of El'tsin and other reformists from the Supreme Soviet. Andrei Sakharov was one of the speakers who criticized the composition of the new Supreme Soviet (*Reuters, DPA*, May 28).

On May 29, heated debates continued while the deputies discussed Anatolii Luk'yanov's qualifications to become first deputy chairman of the new Supreme Soviet. In the course of the discussion, Luk'yanov promised that the controversial government decree of April 8, 1989, which prohibits "discrediting state officials," would be amended. Luk'yanov also promised that the congressional commission investigating the activities of investigators (and deputies) Tel'man Gdlyan and Nikolai Ivanov would be fair. Both Gdlyan and Ivanov questioned Luk'yanov during the morning session on May 29, and Ivanov asked whether all Politburo members shared Ligachev's conservative opinions. Without naming Ligachev, historian Roy Medvedev made a speech depicting the zigzags of Soviet policy every time Gorbachev and Yakovlev have gone abroad in the last four years leaving Ligachev in charge at home. (On May 27, writer Ales' Adamovich also criticized Ligachev's conservative stand on agriculture.) At the end of the morning session on May 29, Luk'yanov was elected first deputy chairman of the Supreme Soviet by the overwhelming majority of the deputies; there were 179 votes against him and 137 abstentions (*Radio Moscow*, May 29).

At the afternoon session on May 29, El'tsin won a seat in the Supreme Soviet after Aleksei Kazannik resigned his seat in the Council of Nationalities so El'tsin could take it. (Kazannik is a university lecturer from Omsk.)

On May 30, Mikhail Gorbachev delivered a report to the Congress on the major directions of Soviet domestic and foreign policy (*Soviet Television*, May 30). In his opening remarks, Gorbachev praised the Congress as an important event for the Soviet people and said a new mechanism was being formed. He also spoke of the need to solve the shortage of consumer goods and reduce the rising budget deficit. He said reforming the wage and price mechanism was a key issue. In the report, Gorbachev also said that the Soviet Union spends 77.3 billion rubles a year on defense, which is almost four times more than the official figure of 20.2 billion rubles (see *RL* 185/89).

The sessions of May 30 also heard heated debates over the events in Tbilisi. Academician Tomaz Gamkrelidze, director of the Institute for Oriental Studies of the Georgian Academy of Sciences, questioned the institution of republican "second Party secretaries," whom he termed "satraps sent from Moscow" who do not represent the national interests of the republics where they serve and know nothing of the national customs of these republics. According to Gamkrelidze, neither the second secretary of the Georgian Communist Party, Boris Nikolsky, nor Igor Rodionov, the army general responsible for breaking up the Tbilisi demonstrations on April 9, has the right to represent Georgia in the Congress of People's Deputies. In response to Gamkrelidze's suggestion that General Rodionov should not be Georgia's representative at the Congress, Rodionov delivered his own speech, trying to defend the actions of the Army and MVD troops in breaking up the demonstration in Tbilisi on April 9. Rodionov tried to put the blame for the tragedy on the leaders of informal groups (*Radio Moscow*, May 30). The Congress was also addressed by former Georgian Party First Secretary Dzhumber Patiashvili, who revealed that he did not order Rodionov to use troops against the demonstrators but that, on the contrary, the day before the clashes he was visited by Rodionov and Deputy Defense Minister Konstantin Kochetov who told him that Rodionov had been given command of all troops in Georgia. Patiashvili said he did not ask who had given this order. In summing up the debates over the clashes in Tbilisi, Gorbachev said the clashes were "a political and global issue." He told the Congress that information on the events in Tbilisi was contradictory and time was needed to sort it out (*Radio Moscow*, May 30).

On May 31, the Congress fell further behind schedule as more deputies lined up to speak. Discussion of Gorbachev's report was scheduled for the morning session of May 31, but deputies raised other issues instead, including Nagorno-Karabakh. Armenian Party First Secretary Suren Arutyunyan said people in Nagorno-Karabakh should be allowed to decide their own future in a referendum. The results of the elections of the oblast's representatives to the Council of Nationalities were also announced. The winners were former oblast Party First Secretary of the NKAO Genrikh Pogosyan (Armenian) and First Secretary of the Shusha Gorkom V. D. Dzhafarov (Azerbaijani).

The session was also addressed by Boris El'tsin. He said the pace of *perestroika* was too slow and attacked the privileges of what he termed the elite class that still exists in the USSR seventy years after the revolution. El'tsin called for the promulgation of a law to limit the power of the Party and for the establishment of a congressional commission to control the Party. He complained that the chairman of the Supreme Soviet—i.e., Gorbachev—has too much power. El'tsin proposed an annual referendum to test the confidence of the citizens of the USSR in their president (*Radio Moscow*, May 31).

The session on May 31 heard sharp criticism of the KGB. Speaking before the Congress, deputy Yurii Vlasov called for more information to be released about the operations of the KGB. (Earlier, other deputies voiced their dissatisfaction with the KGB.) In another speech, a Ukrainian deputy demanded closure of the Chernobyl' nuclear power plant.

For reports on the first seven days of the Congress of People's Deputies, see *Izvestia* May 26–June 2, 1989. The coverage of the Congress in *Izvestia* was more detailed than that in *Pravda*.

USSR Will Not Reduce Garrison on the Kurile Islands

Spokesman for the Soviet Armed Forces General Staff Oleg Lisov was quoted as saying the Soviet Army will not reduce its garrison on the Kurile Islands as part of overall force reductions in the Far East. Novosti press agency quoted Lisov as saying the Kurile garrison is currently just large enough for defense purposes. (Japan claims several of the southern Kurile Islands, which have been held by Soviet troops since the end of World War II.) Novosti quoted Lisov as saying that details of the Soviet military cutbacks in the Far East will be made public soon.

Prestigious Soviet Theater Producer Dies

TASS reported that Georgii Tovstonogov, one of the Soviet Union's leading stage directors had died at the age of seventy-three. Tovstonogov was chief director at Leningrad's Bolshoi Drama Theater.

Friday, May 26

Estonian President on *Perestroika* and Reform

Estonian President Arnold Ruutel said that, in order to promote economic development, Estonia needed "bold initiatives overstepping the rigid limits" of national law. But Ruutel, in an interview with Novosti, said this does not mean discarding the national constitution. He said a plan for self-management recently adopted by the Estonian Supreme Soviet would be sent to the USSR Supreme Soviet for consideration. Ruutel said that without the aid of central organizations the plan "is sure to flop."

Mass Rallies in Georgia

Mass rallies in Georgia marked the anniversary of the founding of independent Georgia in 1918. Reuters quoted dissident sources in Georgia as saying delegations from Lithuania, Armenia, Belorussia, and Ukraine attended. Leading Georgian activist Zviad Gamsakhurdia delivered a speech to the crowd, calling for Georgian independence. The rallies were tolerated by the authorities, and Soviet television reported on them in its evening news program "Vremya."

Saturday, May 27 ————————————————————————

US Considering New Immigration Rules for Soviet Jews

The United States is reported to be considering a change in immigration rules that would significantly cut the number of Soviet Jews allowed into the country. Reports quoting a senior government official say new rules are needed to cope with an increasing outflow of Jews from the USSR under the relaxed emigration policies of Mikhail Gorbachev. The reports said officials were considering a plan that calls for Soviet Jews to face the same restrictions as other refugees. A key restriction says that, if another country will take refugees, they will be refused admission to the United States. Israel has a standing policy of accepting all Jewish emigrants. In recent years, fewer than 10 percent of Jews emigrating from the Soviet Union have settled in Israel. Most go to the United States (*AP*, May 27).

Sunday, May 28 ————————————————————————

Independence Day Celebrated in Armenia

There were marches and rallies in Armenia to mark the republic's proclamation of independence seventy-one years ago. Reports from Erevan said several thousand people took part in a march and rally. Many waved placards demanding a solution to the dispute with Azerbaijan over Nagorno-Karabakh. It was the first time the anniversary celebration has been officially permitted (*Reuters, AP*, May 28). The Soviet news program "Vremya" reported the celebration.

280

_____ *Monday, May 29*

City officials, community leaders, and educational representatives from nearly 100 cities in the Soviet Union and the United States arrived in Tashkent for the two countries' first "sister cities" conference. In a message to the participants, Mikhail Gorbachev praised the "sister cities" movement as an effective way of destroying stereotypes inherited from the Cold War era. TASS said US President George Bush also sent a message saying the United States welcomed such opportunities for contact between the Soviet and American peoples.

US-Soviet "Sister Cities" Conference Opens in Tashkent

_____ *Tuesday, May 30*

Soviet Foreign Minister Eduard Shevardnadze welcomed US President George Bush's proposals for arms reductions. He called them a step in the right direction. Shevardnadze spoke to reporters on his arrival in Paris for a human-rights conference. He said time would be needed to examine the proposals in detail and finally determine what the position of the Soviet Union and the Warsaw Pact would be. In a statement on May 29, Bush called for an East-West agreement on conventional forces to be wrapped up within a year—with troop and weapons reductions to be completed by 1993 (*UPI, Reuters,* May 30). On May 31, Soviet Deputy Foreign Minister Viktor Karpov said Bush's proposals for cuts in conventional forces in Europe could lead to agreement on "a substantial deep cut" in those forces. TASS quoted Karpov as saying differences on many issues must still be overcome at the Vienna talks on conventional arms reductions.

Shevardnadze Welcomes Bush's Proposals on Arms Cuts

Soviet Prime Minister Nikolai Ryzhkov said loans offered by the West would not relieve the Soviet Union's difficult economic situation. He said running into debt would only cause problems for future generations of Soviet citizens. In an interview with *Komsomol'skaya pravda,* Ryzhkov argued the USSR must buy the technological equipment needed to produce goods and mentioned that steps had already been taken in this direction through the formation of joint ventures with the West. He said there are more than 400 joint enterprises already operating in the USSR, but, he added, "we need thousands of them."

Ryzhkov Says Western Loans Will Not Solve Economic Problems

281

Wednesday, May 31 ———————————————————————————————

Lithuanian Independence Union Issues Statement

The newly formed Union for the Independence of Lithuania issued a statement saying it seeks to unite Lithuanians at home and abroad for the reestablishment of an independent Lithuania. The movement is made up of seven informal Lithuanian groups and includes most of the independent organizations outside "Sajudis," the Lithuanian Restructuring Movement. Antanas Terleckas of the Lithuanian Freedom League, which is one of the seven groups, said the Lithuanian Independence Movement's statement of aims was signed at a meeting in Vilnius six days ago. Terleckas told RFE that the new umbrella organization urges Lithuanians to mark the forty-ninth anniversary of the Soviet occupation on June 15 and the fiftieth anniversary of the Molotov-Ribbentrop Pact on August 23 (*RFE Lithuanian Service*, May 31).

Karabakh Committee Members Released

The Soviet authorities were reported to have freed eleven Armenian activists who campaigned for the annexation of Nagorno-Karabakh from Azerbaijan. Reports quoted Ashot Aslibegyan, head of an unofficial youth group, as saying eleven members of the Karabakh Committee had been freed from jails in Moscow and flown to Erevan on May 31. The eleven were jailed in December. There have been many demonstrations in Armenia demanding their release (*RL Armenian Service*, June 1). On the evening of June 1, Radio Erevan confirmed that the eleven had been released.

The Month of June

Debates on June 1 started with a witty speech by prominent Moldavian writer Ion Drutse, who reminded the
deputies that Brezhnev's career had begun with Stalin's
decision to make him first secretary of the Moldavian
Communist Party; Drutse then called for an end to the
practice of appointing Moldavian leaders from Moscow.
The most outspoken speaker during the morning session
seems to have been Yurii Chernichenko, the prominent
campaigner for reforms in Soviet agriculture. Chernichenko said Party administration of agriculture was to
blame for the Soviet Union's pressing agrarian problems.
He named Egor Ligachev and asked rhetorically why such
an important sphere as agriculture was entrusted "to a
man who does not know anything about it, and was a total
flop at ideology too." The overwhelming majority of
speakers, however, belonged to the conservative camp.
Among them was former Politburo member Kirill Mazurov, who attacked "those who advocate introducing elements of the capitalist market economy and even a multiparty system in our country." The session ended with an
appeal by Estonian deputies for the establishment of a
commission to study the impact of the Molotov-Ribbentrop Pact of 1939. There was a heated discussion over this
point. While backing the establishment of the commission, Gorbachev called for cautious treatment of the issue
of the secret protocols attached to the pact. He reiterated
that the originals of the protocols have not been found in
Germany or the USSR (*Radio Moscow, TASS,* June 1).

The afternoon session on June 1 was also marked by
interesting speeches. Poet Evgenii Evtushenko proposed
annulling all trials of Soviet dissidents and returning
Soviet citizenship to those illegally deprived of it. The
session also approved a seventeen-member commission
to investigate the work of Gdlyan and Ivanov and
continued to discuss the situation in Georgia. Vice President Anatolii Luk'yanov read telegrams to the Congress
showing that Georgian leaders had taken the decision to
use troops against demonstrators in Tbilisi. TASS said the
telegrams were read because some Georgian deputies
had charged that the authorities in Moscow had ordered

**Congress of People's Deputies
Session Continues**

the use of troops. (Luk'yanov said the telegrams he read had been sent to Moscow by Georgian Party Leader Dzhumber Patiashvili. Luk'yanov quoted from a telegram received the night before the clash saying the situation was under control. He said the next telegram, after the clash, told Moscow what had happened.)

On June 2, the greatest sensation of the morning session of the Congress was the wave of outrage directed against Andrei Sakharov by conservative deputies for his criticism of the Afghan war earlier this year. The disturbance began when Sergei Chervonopisky, a Ukrainian Komsomol secretary and Afghan war veteran, attacked Sakharov for having said that Soviet helicopter gunships fired on surrounded Soviet units in order to prevent their being taken captive by the Afghan resistance. Sakharov's response to Chervonopisky provoked a long series of rebuttals by various deputies, among them veterans and a weeping mother of a fallen soldier, whose hysterical outbursts received a standing ovation. During the afternoon session Sakharov was defended by the prominent social scientist Yurii Karyakin, who also appealed to Gorbachev to restore Soviet citizenship to the exiled writer Aleksandr Solzhenitsyn.

On June 2, the Congress approved the membership of a commission to study the impact of the Molotov-Ribbentrop Pact of 1939. Gorbachev requested that Politburo member Aleksandr Yakovlev should chair the commission. The Congress also heard a speech by Kirgiz writer Chingiz Aitmatov, who discussed nationalities issues. TASS quoted him as saying he approved of the idea of full Socialist sovereignty for the Union republics. Also remarkable was a speech by KGB chief Vladimir Kryuchkov, who said he fully supported the idea of putting the KGB under the supervision of the USSR Supreme Soviet.

On June 3, one of the two chambers of the new USSR Supreme Soviet, the Council of the Union, held its first session in Moscow. The session was opened by Mikhail Gorbachev. There was also a joint session of the councils of elders of both chambers of the Supreme Soviet, at which the agenda and work of the Supreme Soviet were examined. Academician Evgenii Primakov was elected as chairman of the Council of the Union (TASS, June 3). Primakov, who is fifty-nine, was formerly head of the USSR Academy of Sciences Institute of World Economics and International Relations. At the morning session of the Congress of People's Deputies on June 5, Gorbachev proposed that the Congress adjourn for the day to mourn the victims of the gas explosion near Chelyabinsk. Before the Congress adjourned, however, Gorbachev read aloud an appeal signed by a group of deputies from Moscow, Leningrad, and the Baltic calling on various Soviet nationalities to refrain from violence and to air their grievances by peaceful means (*Radio Moscow*, June 5).

On the morning of June 6, the Congress approved almost unanimously a noncommittal declaration on the bloody events in Beijing. While acknowledging that "human casualties" had occurred, the declaration avoided specifics and stated that any attempt to interfere in China's internal affairs could hinder stabilization of the situation.

Of the twelve principal speakers at the morning session, only five presented what might be called reformist programs. Four of these were representatives of various nationalities who were seeking more rights and more independence for their peoples. The fifth, Academician Sergei Alekseev, put forward a substantive program of overdue legal and economic reforms. The academician characterized the four constitutions since 1918 as propaganda documents, and he called for the introduction of a real constitution. The other main speakers came out against reformist trends, particularly the developments in the Baltic republics and in the media. They rebuffed earlier critiques of the Soviet Army and the KGB aired by their reformist colleagues. Some condemned Yurii Karyakin's proposal to remove Lenin's body from the mausoleum, and three made speeches in defense of Egor Ligachev.

Ligachev's most outspoken champion proved to be Valentin Rasputin, who likened his liberal opponents to some liberal and Socialist figures who overthrew the Tsarist regime in 1917. He also defended Ligachev against the accusations arising from the Ivanov-Gdlyan affair. "The struggle for supreme power has been going on for a long time in our country," Rasputin claimed. "The first victim [Ligachev] is marked. There is no need to remind you of who will be the next," said Rasputin, clearly hinting at Gorbachev.

A Kazakh deputy compared the recent events in Tbilisi with the troubles in Alma-Ata of December, 1986, when, he claimed, a peaceful demonstration had been brutally broken up by soldiers using trenching tools. A woman deputy from the Far East who tried to defend Sakharov's criticism of the Afghan war was silenced by the chairman and requested to leave the rostrum.

On June 7, both houses of the USSR Supreme Soviet met to confirm appointments of officials. Deputies elected Gennadii Kolbin, who had been proposed by Gorbachev, as chairman of the People's Control Committee at a joint session of the Council of the Union and the Council of Nationalities. Against all expectations, this candidature encountered much greater resistance than that of Nikolai Ryzhkov, who was confirmed in his post as Soviet Prime Minister during the same session.

The afternoon session of the Supreme Soviet chose a new chairman of the Supreme Court. He is Evgenii Smolentsev, a Russian, who has been chairman of the RSFSR Supreme Court since 1987. He replaces seventy-three-year-old Vladimir Terebilov, who had held the post since March, 1984. The Supreme Soviet also elected a new chief arbiter. He is Yurii Matveev, a forty-nine-year-old Doctor of Law who has been chief arbiter of the Ukraine since 1987. He replaces Nikolai Mashakov, who was appointed in the summer of 1987. The Supreme Soviet also voted to retain Aleksandr Sukharev as general prosecutor (*Radio Moscow*, June 7).

On June 8, the Congress continued discussion of reports by Gorbachev and Ryzhkov. In his speech to the Congress on June 7, Ryzhkov provided a breakdown of the figure of 77.3 billion rubles for Soviet defense expenditure given by Gorbachev on May 30; he also said the USSR planned to reduce by one-third to one-half the relative share of defense expenditure in the national income by 1995. Ryzhkov supplied further details of the budgetary deficit and set improbably high targets for the agricultural sector through 1995 (an average annual output of 200 billion rubles worth of foodstuffs). See *Izvestia*, June 8.

On June 8, the first of the thirteen speakers at the Congress suggested calling a congress of Soviet blue-collar workers. Economist Nikolai Shmelev suggested some radical measures for cutting the Soviet budget deficit, which, he claimed, will reach 120 billion rubles this year. Among reasons for the present catastrophic state of the Soviet economy, Shmelev cited Soviet interference in Latin America—in particular, subsidizing the crippled Cuban economy. The measures suggested by Shmelev include ceasing all exports of industrial equipment and putting an end to "all building-sites of communism"—i.e., ambitious projects of questionable economic value. Shmelev said that the Soviet Central Bank should be subordinate only to the Congress of People's Deputies.

Aleksei Emel'yanov, head of the Department of Agronomy at Moscow State University, received a storm of applause when he sharply criticized the role of the Communist Party in Soviet society. The people are higher than the Party, Emel'yanov said, and thus a Congress of

People's Deputies must be higher than a Congress of the CPSU, and a Supreme Soviet higher than the CPSU Central Committee.

Georgian Party leader Givi Gumbaridze criticized the Soviet Army and General Igor Rodionov, the commander of the Transcaucasian Military District, for the army's role in breaking up the Tbilisi demonstration on April 9. While acknowledging that the demonstration was of a controversial political nature, Gumbaridze said the use of force against demonstrators was not justified. He suggested the police rather than the army be used on such occasions. Gumbaridze particularly criticized the military for its refusal to tell the truth about the use of poisonous gas against civilians and expressed gratitude to Gorbachev, Shevardnadze, and Razumovsky for their cooperation both in investigating the Tbilisi events and in bringing in physicians from Moscow and from abroad to provide medical treatment for the victims.

The tragic events in Tbilisi would not have happened if the Soviet public had learned the true nature of the student demonstrations of December, 1986, in Alma-Ata, said the Kazakh writer Olzhas Suleimenov. Suleimenov termed the Alma-Ata events of 1986 "the first unauthorized meeting in our country" and called on the gathering "to review them in the light of the new approach."

On the evening of June 8 there was a surprise closed session of the Congress of People's Deputies. Mikhail Gorbachev asked the press and guests to leave the hall before the session but gave no reason. Deputies later told Western news agencies that the closed session had discussed the recent violence in Uzbekistan, where more than seventy people have died in interethnic clashes since June 3. Gorbachev addressed the deputies at the session.

Addressing the Congress on June 9, Prime Minister Nikolai Ryzhkov said the Soviet Union owes the West the hard-currency equivalent of 34,000 million rubles. Western analysts say it is the first time that the Soviet Union has officially revealed the extent of its debt to the West. The same session was also addressed by Mikhail Gorbachev, who rejected suggestions that he was trying to concentrate power in his own hands by combining the posts of state and Party leader.

At the afternoon session voting took place on who should serve on the new Committee for Constitutional Compliance. Human-rights activist Andrei Sakharov was nominated by fellow academician Roald Sagdeev for a seat on the committee. Voting was blocked on June 8 when the Lithuanian delegation and some other Baltic deputies walked out of the hall to protest against the way the committee members were being chosen. They objected to the lack of information about deputies proposed as committee members and the vagueness of the powers of the committee, which is expected to decide whether laws are constitutional. Later the same day, TASS reported the results of voting on the committee's membership. The Congress of People's Deputies named Mikhail Gorbachev to head the committee. TASS said other members include Andrei Sakharov, Boris El'tsin, and public figures from all the republics.

The afternoon session was addressed by Andrei Sakharov, who spoke against the concentration of too much power in Gorbachev's hands. He also proposed that the length of military conscription be cut by half and said the Soviet Union did not need an army stronger than those of the United States and China together. When, however, Sakharov started discussing the USSR's nationalities problems, Gorbachev interrupted him on the grounds that Sakharov's speech was too long. At the same session, the Congress also voted for the abolition of a controversial decree that made it a crime to criticize public officials in the Soviet Union. (The decree was issued by the Presidium of the USSR Supreme Soviet on April 8.)

The Congress of People's Deputies ended its session in disagreement over what it had accomplished. Andrei Sakharov said the Congress had failed in its main task—namely, to provide a power structure that ensured that problems will be solved. Gorbachev, however, said that Sakharov's assessment sought to depreciate the role and significance of the Congress. Gorbachev said the Congress's first session had provided convincing evidence that compromises on crucial issues can be reached through democracy and openness (*Radio Moscow*, June 9). For reports on the last nine days of the Congress, see *Izvestia*, June 2–10.

TASS Cites Medical Problems in Nagorno-Karabakh

TASS said problems with medical care in Nagorno-Karabakh were being aggravated by strikes. The report told of an acute shortage of hospital beds for special treatment in the region, a shortage of physicians, and a high infant mortality rate. It also said 80 percent of the medical facilities were in "hardly suitable premises." TASS said continuing strikes in Nagorno-Karabakh make it hard for hospitals to get transportation, medicine, and food. It quoted a local medical official, Tat'yana Tovmasyan, as saying there had been attempts to force clinics to close. She said physicians had refused to do so.

288

Georgian Newspaper Rejects Rodionov's Criticism

The Georgian Komsomol newspaper *Molodezh' Gruzii* rejected criticism leveled against it by General Igor Rodionov in his speech to the Congress of People's Deputies. (Rodionov told the congress on May 30 that *Molodezh' Gruzii* had published "a new provocative lampoon, in which an attempt was made to shove the blame on the country's highest military command and political leadership." He called for an investigation of the newspaper's action by a commission of the USSR Supreme Soviet.) The newspaper's executive secretary, Besiko Urigashvili, told RFE/RL in a telephone interview that Rodionov, who commanded the operation against the demonstrators in Tbilisi, was apparently upset because the newspaper had reported a controversial remark he had made in an interview. The newspaper quoted Rodionov as telling a Georgian journalist that "Moscow knew . . . some of the military leaders were informed how the operation [against the demonstrators in Tbilisi] was going to be conducted." Urigashvili told RFE/RL that his newspaper had a tape of Rodionov's interview.

Soviet Judicial Official Insists Wallenberg Is Dead

An employee of the USSR Public Prosecutor's Office, Nikolai Andreev, told correspondents in Paris that Raoul Wallenberg died in a Soviet prison. Andreev described the Wallenberg case as "a dark page in our history" and promised that, if more information about Wallenberg's fate becomes known, the USSR would make it public. The chief Soviet negotiator at the Paris human-rights conference, Yurii Kashlev, linked Lavrentii Beria and former minister of state security, Viktor S. Abakumov to Wallenberg's death and claimed they had also destroyed the papers dealing with the Wallenberg case. The president of the US Wallenberg Committee promptly rejected the Soviet assertions (*Reuters*, June 1).

--- *Friday, June 2*

Ryzhkov Rejects Criticism against Ligachev

Soviet Prime Minister Nikolai Ryzhkov was quoted by TASS as saying at a meeting with Soviet and foreign reporters that the CPSU Politburo is convinced that allegations against Politburo member Egor Ligachev are untrue. Soviet investigator Nikolai Ivanov said last month Ligachev's name had come up during a corruption investigation. (On May 23, the Soviet press carried a letter by Egor Ligachev to the CPSU Central Committee, denying accusations leveled against him by Ivanov.)

Newspaper Gives Details of Deaths of Strikers in 1962

More details have emerged about an incident in which Soviet troops opened fire on strikers in Novocherkassk in Rostov Oblast twenty-seven years ago. One witness told *Komsomol'skaya pravda* more than twenty people were killed. Another said the authorities were unable to clean the blood from the square where the shooting took place and finally repaved it. The Rostov Oblast newspaper, *Komsomolets*, carried a story about the incident a year ago but did not say how many people had died.

Saturday, June 3 ———————————————————————————————

Ogonek Attacks Soviet Censorship

Ogonek (No. 22) published an article by Vyacheslav Kostikov strongly criticizing censorship of the press and the suppression of freedom of expression throughout the Soviet Union's history. Kostikov was particularly critical of the suppression of so-called bourgeois periodicals by Lenin's decree on the press adopted on October 27, 1917. The article showed how the revival of press censorship by the Bolsheviks (censorship was abolished by the February Revolution of 1917) eventually led to the closure of all non-Bolshevik periodicals. It went on to criticize the political crackdown that took place during the NEP period and strongly condemned the expulsion without trial (simply by an OGPU administrative decision) of a group of leading Russian philosophers in 1922. Among those expelled were Nikolai Berdyaev, Father Sergei Bulgakov, Semen Frank, and others whose works have only now started to be published in the Soviet Union.

USSR Accuses Britain of Planting Listening Devices

The Soviet Union accused Britain of planting listening devices in Soviet offices and diplomats' apartments in London. The British Foreign Office immediately denied the accusation. The accusations followed the expulsion from Britain two weeks ago of eight Soviet diplomats and three journalists for spying. In apparent retaliation, the Soviet Union expelled eight British diplomats and three journalists (*Reuters, TASS*, June 3).

Central Asian Military District Abolished

The Soviet Union's Central Asian Military District has been abolished. TASS said the district, which borders China, had been incorporated into the adjacent Turkestan Military District as of June 1. The agency quoted Lieutenant General Yurii Petrov, a deputy chief of the Armed Forces

General Staff, as saying the abolition of the Central Asian District is related to the reduction in the USSR's armed forces by 500,000 men.

———————————————————————————— *Sunday, June 4*

Ogonek (No. 23) carried Aleksandr Solzhenitsyn's "Matrenin dvor" (Matryona's Homestead), a short story about a decaying Russian village. It is the first work of fiction by Solzhenitsyn to be published in the USSR since well before his exile in 1974. On May 26, *Literaturnaya Rossiya* published an article by literary critic Vladimir Bondarenko analyzing Solzhenitsyn's prose. An introduction to the article said a collection of Solzhenitsyn's works would be published next year by the "Sovetskaya Rossiya" publishing house.

Ogonek Publishes Solzhenitsyn Short Story

The Soviet media said hundreds of people had been killed when a gas explosion wrecked two trains traveling on the Trans-Siberian railway between Chelyabinsk and Ufa in the Urals on the night of June 3. Soviet television and TASS said more than 1,200 people were aboard the two trains. Mikhail Gorbachev, who visited the scene of the tragedy, told a television interviewer it appeared that negligence and safety violations were to blame for the accident. On June 5, *Izvestia* said the gas leak that led to the fatal explosion had been noticed hours before the blast but nothing had been done to stop it. A special government commission was set up to investigate the accident. June 5 was declared a day of national mourning in the USSR for the victims of the disaster. (*TASS*, June 5). On June 6, it was reported that the Soviet Union had received international offers of help for burn victims of the explosion. A USSR Foreign Ministry spokesman compared the offers to the international response to the Armenian earthquake last December (*Reuters*, June 6). *Sotsialisticheskaya industriya* of June 6 reported that a gas pipeline had also exploded near a railroad in Moldavia on June 3 but that nobody was injured. On June 7, a mass funeral was held in Chelyabinsk for fifteen young victims of the disaster. On June 10, investigator Vladimir Lyseiko said shoddy construction and operation of a gas pipeline were to blame for last week's railway disaster in the Urals. The pipeline exploded as two trains passed nearby. The investigator said it was likely that an overhead spark from one of the trains or from a

Railway Disaster in the Urals

wheel ignited leaking gas. As a result of the accident, 607 people were killed and 334 were hospitalized (*Sotsialis- ticheskaya industriya*, June 14). On June 10, TASS report- ed another train accident. It said thirty-one people had been killed on June 9 when an express train collided with a bus in the southern RSFSR. On June 11, it was reported that a group of American burn-treatment experts and tons of medical supplies had been flown to Ufa to aid the victims of the explosion (*UPI, AP*, June 11).

Ogonek Depicts Torture in Stavropol Prison

An article in *Ogonek* (No. 23) described "a pressure cell" in Stavropol prison in which persons are held while under investigation. (In Soviet prisoners' slang, the term "pres- sure cell" refers to a cell in which selected criminals beat and torture other prisoners on the instructions of investi- gators or prison administrators in order to extort deposi- tions advantageous to the prosecution. Soviet prisoners believe that such "pressure cells" exist in all Soviet prisons.) According to Mikhail Korchagin, *Ogonek*'s cor- respondent in Stavropol, local prison officials provided the inmates of Cell No. 19 with drugs, causing them to become addicted. The prisoners' resulting dependence on the prison authorities was used to induce the inmates of this particular cell to extort confessions from their cell-mates on the orders of the administration. Korchagin describes acts of great cruelty committed in Cell No. 19 in order to force innocent people to confess to crimes that the local police were unable to solve. Several prisoners, Korchagin writes, died as a result of torture in "the pressure cell." Only one official, Major Viktor Lazarenko, the prison's former deputy chief for operational work, was prosecuted for use of "the pressure cell." The investigators, who had ordered the torture that took place in "the pressure cell" and therefore bore more responsi- bility than did Lazarenko, have not been punished.

Clashes in Uzbekistan

The Soviet media said there had been deaths as a result of violence between Uzbeks and Meskhetian Turks in the Fergana Oblast of eastern Uzbekistan on June 3 and 4. (The Meskhetians were deported to Central Asia from Georgia in November, 1944, on Stalin's orders.) A curfew was imposed in several cities in eastern Uzbekistan following the clashes. According to TASS, the clashes resulted from "armed hooliganism by youth groups." (Over the past twenty years many Meskhetians have lobbied persistently for permission to return to Georgia, and in the past five years some of them have been allowed to do so; others consider themselves Turks and have requested permission to emigrate to Turkey.)

On June 5, more details emerged of the scale of the violence in Fergana Oblast. Speaking on Soviet television, USSR Minister of Internal Affairs Vadim Bakatin disclosed that 6,000 MVD troops had been flown to the area where "dozens" of people had been killed and hundreds wounded in what was described as "bitter clashes of thousands of bestial people." Most of the dead were said to be Meskhetians, and most of the sixty-four persons arrested, Uzbeks. Oblast Party leaders were castigated for thinking primarily of their own safety and cordoning off Party headquarters with troops rather than engaging in dialogue with the people and taking measures to stabilize the situation. Telephone reports from Moscow indicate that the Uzbek authorities may be trying to pin blame for the clashes on the unofficial society "Birlik."

On June 6, "Vremya" reported that 1,000 members of the Meskhetian minority had been evacuated from the Fergana Valley. The same day, *Sotsialisticheskaya industriya* quoted Bakatin as saying more troops were on their way to Uzbekistan. Speaking at the Congress of People's Deputies on June 6, Gorbachev said that the situation in Uzbekistan was under control but that the atmosphere was still charged from the conflicts (*Radio Moscow*, June 7). A TASS report from the scene of the clashes in Fergana said shots were heard in parts of the city on the night of June 6. In its news program "Vremya," Soviet television reported more incidents in the Fergana area. In one town a police station was attacked, and in another there was an incident at an administrative building.

On June 9, the Uzbek Ministry of Internal Affairs said about eighty people were now known to have been killed and 800 others injured during the week of ethnic disturbances in Uzbekistan. As quoted by *Izvestia*, the ministry said hundreds of houses and vehicles had been destroyed in what it called pogroms. TASS said the situation was still tense in the town of Kokand, where the latest clashes took place. In its "Vremya" news program, Soviet television said that MVD troops had sealed off the center of Kokand and that more troops were being flown in to cope with the unrest.

On June 10, a curfew was imposed in the Uzbek town of Kokand, where there were also clashes between Uzbeks and Meskhetians (*TASS*, June 10). On June 12, *Pravda* reported on an incident at the weekend in which troops killed two men described as "extremists" who were among a group that tried to storm a camp holding Meskhetian refugees near Kokand. The newspaper said the trouble in Uzbekistan had gone beyond the scope of a local and merely ethnic conflict. It said "bandits" had been looting, killing, and committing arson regardless of national links. TASS also issued a report saying the situation in Uzbekistan was very tense. It said several hundred Uzbeks had converged on the railway station in Namangan on June 11, disrupting traffic and stoning police. Radio Moscow said that, as a result of the attack on the refugee camp at the weekend, the USSR Supreme Soviet had ordered the evacuation of thousands of Meskhetians from Uzbekistan to the RSFSR, where they were to receive shelter and jobs. By June 13, 4,500 had been evacuated. On June 12, Soviet Prime Minister Nikolai Ryzhkov and Politburo member Viktor Chebrikov flew to Fergana. The evening news program "Vremya" showed Ryzhkov touring burnt-out settlements in the Fergana Valley.

On June 13, TASS said citizens' self-defense groups were being formed in the Fergana Valley to counter armed gangs. The agency also reported that Ryzhkov had visited a refugee camp near Fergana for members of the Meskhetian community. While visiting the camp, Ryzhkov proposed the creation of a commission to study the possibility of returning Uzbekistan's minority Meskhetians to their original homeland in Georgia. The same day, Mikhail Gorbachev who was on a visit to West Germany, commented on the situation in Uzbekistan. He blamed the unrest on Moslem fundamentalism (*AP, DPA*, June 13). Also that day, Soviet MVD official, Lieutenant Colonel Aleksandr Gurov told a press conference in Moscow that criminal organizations were continuing to provoke interethnic conflicts, including the current unrest in Uzbekistan (*TASS*, June 13). TASS quoted Uzbek Party chief Rafik Nishanov as apologizing to the Meskhetians on behalf of the Uzbek people for the tragic events in Uzbekistan, and the local authorities in Fergana were accused of passivity during the unrest. The criticism came at a meeting between Ryzhkov and the Fergana Oblast leadership (*TASS*, June 13; *Pravda*, June 14).

On June 14, Radio Moscow reported that peace was gradually being restored to the Fergana Valley and that the situation there was being brought under control. *Pravda* (June 15) also quoted MVD General Anatolii Anikiev as reporting an improvement in the situation in Fergana. Anikiev said several hundred people had been arrested in Uzbekistan for participating in the unrest. *Moscow News* (No. 24) said other minorities living in Uzbekistan were afraid because of what had happened to the Meskhetians. The same day, another MVD official, Lieutenant General Vyacheslav Pankin, reiterated that the violence in Uzbekistan was not spontaneous but carefully planned by "anti-*perestroika* forces." "Vremya" quoted Ryzhkov as accusing some local Party and government officials in Uzbekistan of being involved in the violence between the Uzbeks and the Meskhetians.

On June 15, *Izvestia* reported a mass exodus of Meskhetians from Uzbekistan into the neighboring Central Asian republics because of fears of fresh outbreaks of violence. The same day, Ryzhkov and Chebrikov went to Tashkent, where they met with the republic's Party and government leadership. They discussed the possibilities for stabilizing the situation in Uzbekistan and returned to Moscow the same day (*TASS, Radio Moscow,* June 15).

On June 16, *Pravda* reported that almost 8,000 weapons, including firearms and incendiary devices, had been confiscated in the Fergana region. It said more than 1,000 buildings had been plundered and burned since the violence began nearly two weeks ago. The newspaper said two members of the Congress of People's Deputies had visited the area to gather information for an investigation. It quoted them as saying there would not have been so many casualties if the authorities had acted earlier. The same day, TASS quoted Colonel General Yurii Shatalin, head of the MVD troops in Uzbekistan, as saying his men had sometimes had to use firearms and had killed four people and wounded seven. Shatalin said in an interview with *Krasnaya zvezda* that 1,542 people had been detained, 364 of them for hooliganism, since the imposition of a curfew in the Fergana area. In Moscow, about 100 Meskhetians marched on the building of the Supreme Soviet demanding to see Mikhail Gorbachev. Among the crowd were survivors of the violence in Uzbekistan (*Reuters, AFP,* June 16).

On June 17, the Party first secretary in Uzbekistan's Fergana Oblast, Shavkat Yuldashev, said the local Party, government, MVD, and KGB were surprised by and unprepared for the outbreak of violence between Uzbeks and Meskhetians (*Radio Moscow, TASS,* June 17). *Izvestia* complained that some policemen in Uzbekistan had helped those who persecuted the Meskhetian minority there. The newspaper said the police had provided the addresses of Meskhetians whose houses were later destroyed.

On June 19, TASS and Western agencies reported that a group of about 100 Meskhetians had entered the building of the USSR Supreme Soviet in Moscow demanding to meet with Gorbachev. At the same time, a group of about fifty Meskhetians was reported to be demonstrating outside the Supreme Soviet building. (The demonstrators wanted Gorbachev's support in their campaign to return to Georgia, from where they were deported in 1944. See RL 286/89. At a session of the CPSU Politburo, severe punishment of those who took part in the ethnic riots in Uzbekistan was called for (*TASS*, June 20, 1989).

On June 20, Chief of the MVD Press Bureau Colonel Boris Mikhailov said law enforcement officers had stabilized the situation in the Fergana Valley. Mikhailov put the death toll from the violence there at ninety-nine, with more than 1,000 people injured. He said 35,000 "citizens of Turkish origin" had voluntarily left Uzbekistan as a result of the violence (*TASS*, June 20).

On June 21, General Eduard Didorenko, a deputy minister of internal affairs in Uzbekistan, blamed the recent violence there on the rise of "a pan-Islamic front" devoted to religious fundamentalism and to the expulsion of all non-Muslims from the region. Didorenko told *Krasnaya zvezda* that Uzbeks began killing the minority Meskhetians, who are also Muslims, because they had refused to join the front. Didorenko's explanation differs sharply from other accounts, which put the blame mainly on unemployment and poverty and on corrupt local leaders.

On June 22, *Sovetskaya Rossiya* quoted RSFSR First Deputy Prime Minister Fukrat Tabeev as saying that the more than 16,000 Meskhetians evacuated from Uzbekistan had been given free clothing and temporary shelter in central Russia. Tabeev said many Meskhetians had been asked to work on farms and had already been given farm and construction jobs.

On June 23, the Presidium of the USSR Supreme Soviet established a commission to deal with the problems of the Meskhetians in Uzbekistan. TASS said the commission would operate as part of the Council of Nationalities. On the clashes, see RL 271/89 and RL 301/89.

Soviet Television Shows Beijing Clashes

Film of the clashes between troops and protesters in Beijing was shown on "Vremya," the main Soviet television news program. The item, however, which used explicit footage from a Eurovision video film, came twenty-seven minutes into the program, following not only a report on the Urals train disaster but also several domestic news items of secondary interest and a film report on the Polish elections. The "Vremya" report on the events in Beijing quoted the official Chinese statement that the action was carried out "to maintain normal life in the capital," but the commentary also included references to foreign news reports that hundreds had been killed in

Tiananmen Square and that there was unrest in other Chinese cities. On June 5, Boris El'tsin told reporters in Moscow that the attacks by Chinese troops against civilians in Beijing were "a crime against the people" and he likened the incident to the clashes in Tbilisi. A comparison between the events in Beijing and Tbilisi was also drawn on June 5 in a broadcast of Radio Moscow's World Service in English (1810).

KGB Chairman on Organized Crime

Nedelya (No. 22) carried a memorandum by KGB Chairman Vladimir Kryuchkov in which he claimed that the state security organs were stepping up the struggle against organized crime. Kryuchkov's memo came in response to a letter from "a Moscow worker, Yu. Nikiforov," who suggested (in *Nedelya*, No. 14) that the KGB take a more active part in the fight against racketeering and other organized crime.

Monday, June 5

Soviet Media Coverage of Polish Election

From what was monitored in Munich, it would appear that the Soviet domestic media gave minimum coverage to the remarkable results of the Polish elections. "Vremya" devoted less than thirty seconds to the matter half an hour into the program, while Radio Moscow reported the results in a few lines. TASS, in Russian, quoted a Polish Communist Party spokesman as saying the Party had lost to "Solidarity," but it did not elaborate or comment.

Call for Moscow to Investigate Lithuanian Situation

The Russian-dominated "Edinstvo" (Unity) organization in Lithuania wants Moscow to establish a commission to investigate the situation in that republic. RFE's Lithuanian desk reported today that the organization held a meeting in Vilnius on June 4. Participants told RFE that the organization wants a commission to analyze the work of the latest session of the Lithuanian Supreme Soviet, which adopted resolutions on sovereignty, and to investigate the activities of the "Sajudis" reform movement and relations between nationalities in Lithuania. Several speakers even went so far as to say the Vilnius region should be transferred to the RSFSR. Earlier this year, the Russian-dominated International Front in Estonia put forward a similar proposal—namely, that the Tallinn region be transferred to the RSFSR. This invoked strong criticism from the Estonian Party leadership.

297

Lithuanian Komsomol Declares Independence from Moscow

The Lithuanian Komsomol was reported to have declared its independence from Moscow. TASS said the Twenty-second Congress of the Lithuanian Komsomol approved a resolution calling for relations with the USSR Komsomol to be based on partnership and mutual understanding. The resolution said political and organizational independence were essential for participation in *perestroika*.

Kuznetsov Proposes Talks with US on Emigration Delays

Speaking at the Paris human-rights conference, head of the Visa Department at the USSR Ministry of Internal Affairs Rudolf Kuznetsov proposed talks with the United States about the thousands of Soviet citizens with exit visas who cannot leave because of delays in US processing of their applications for immigration. The chief US delegate, Morris Abram, said 26,000 Soviet citizens were waiting for interviews with US immigration officials. He said the United States was taking steps to deal with the increase in applications (*RFE/RL Special*, June 5).

Tuesday, June 6 ————————————————————————————

MVD Reports Deaths in Prison Uprisings

TASS quoted the USSR Ministry of Internal Affairs as saying convicts had been shot dead during uprisings in Soviet penal camps this year. It did not say how many people were killed. It quoted Lieutenant General Ivan Katargin as saying the shootings had occurred to end incidents in which convicts took camp officials hostage. He was quoted as saying none of the hostages were killed.

Soviet Jewish Emigration Down in May

A total of 3,333 Jews emigrated from the Soviet Union in May, compared with 4,129 in April. The announcement was made in Geneva by the intergovernmental committee for migration. Altogether 16,197 Jews have left the Soviet Union in the first five months of this year. Soviet Jewish emigrants in 1988 totaled 20,082 (*AP, Reuters*, June 6).

Wednesday, June 7 ————————————————————————————

Soviet Officials in Paris Discuss Ukrainian Catholic Church

A Soviet law expert at the Paris human-rights conference said some Soviet citizens are hostile to the banned Ukrainian Catholic Church because they believe it supported the Nazis during World War II. But Professor Aleksandr Berkov, of the Institute of State and Law of the

USSR Academy of Sciences, said the issue of legalization must be considered in drawing up a new national law on religious freedom (*RFE/RL Special*, June 7).

A rally was held in Moscow on June 6 in support of Andrei Sakharov. AFP (June 7) said the rally drew about 20,000 people. Participants told RFE/RL by telephone that the number of people taking part was much higher. Speakers included Boris El'tsin. He called on the crowd to applaud Sakharov for having the courage to publicly criticize the Soviet intervention in Afghanistan. (On June 2, Sakharov was shouted down in the Congress of People's Deputies during a debate in which some deputies criticized him for having said in February that Soviet helicopters had fired at Soviet soldiers to prevent them from being captured.)

Pro-Sakharov Demonstration Held in Moscow

Academician Abel Aganbegyan said the USSR's inflation rate was between 8 and 9 percent last year. Deputy Finance Minister Vyacheslav Senchagov told reporters he felt Aganbegyan's estimate was basically correct, though somewhat high. But both said the USSR has trouble deciding what the inflation rate is because it is hard to get accurate statistics. The officials spoke at a Moscow conference aimed at exploring the possibilities and problems of Western investment in the USSR. Some 300 Western businessmen and financial experts are attending (*AP*, June 7).

Aganbegyan Estimates Inflation Was 8 to 9 Percent Last Year

Thursday, June 8

The deputy head of the CPSU Central Comittee's International Department, Andrei Grachev, said the Baltic problem resulting from the Molotov-Ribbentrop Pact of 1939 could undermine the future of the USSR. Speaking at a news conference in Bonn, Grachev also commented on the current situation in China, saying that both China and the USSR are undergoing reforms that are sometimes very sensitive and dramatic (*RFE/RL Special*, June 8).

Soviet Aide Says Baltic Problem Can Undermine Future

Friday, June 9

Soviet Foreign Minister Eduard Shevardnadze arrived in East Berlin for an official visit. Speaking at an official lunch in East Berlin, Shevardnadze said each nation has the right

Shevardnadze in East Berlin

299

to choose its own course. (East German leaders have said that the GDR does not need *perestroika*.) The same day, Shevardnadze started talks with East German officials. They discussed Gorbachev's visit to West Germany as well as the session of the Congress of People's Deputies in Moscow (*AP*, *Reuters*, June 9; *Pravda*, June 10).

Soviet Pilot Defector Receives Asylum in United States

The Turkish Foreign Ministry said a Soviet pilot who defected to Turkey in a MiG-29 fighter last month had been flown to the United States. A ministry spokesman said the United States had agreed to grant captain Aleksandr Zuev political asylum. Zuev landed his plane at an airport in Trabzon on the Black Sea coast on May 20. Turkey has rejected a Soviet request for Zuev's extradition (*AP*, June 9). On June 14, the USSR lodged a formal protest with Turkey over its refusal to extradite Zuev. The USSR said Zuev was guilty of hijacking a plane and of shooting a Soviet soldier (*TASS*, June 14).

Gerasimov on Situation in China

Soviet Foreign Ministry spokesman Gennadii Gerasimov said Soviet officials were extremely dismayed at the way the Chinese authorities had put down the pro-democracy demonstrations in Beijing. Gerasimov said in an interview with AP that the Soviet authorities had not expected the Beijing action.

USSR Seeks to Limit Damage after MiG Crash

The USSR sought to limit damage to its aviation reputation after a MiG-29 combat jet crashed on the first day of the Paris air show. Soviet officials held a news conference on board an Antonov-225 cargo aircraft, the world's biggest plane, which is being exhibited for the first time in the West. Soviet aviation official Petr Balabuev told reporters that MiG pilot Petr Kvorchur, who ejected from his plane two seconds before it crashed, was out of the hospital. Soviet aviation officials said it was now virtually certain that the MiG-29, one of the Soviet air force's most powerful fighters, blew its right engine as it flew a demonstration flight at Le Bourget Airport on June 8 (*Reuters*, June 9).

Saturday, June 10 ———————————————————————————

First Session of New Supreme Soviet

The newly elected USSR Supreme Soviet held its first session since the close of the USSR Congress of People's Deputies. El'tsin was elected new chairman of the

Supreme Soviet Standing Committee on Construction and Architecture. Radio Moscow said there were seven votes against him and five abstentions.

Addressing the session, Chairman of the USSR Council of Ministers Nikolai Ryzhkov outlined a substantial reorganization of the Council of Ministers. Ryzhkov characterized the current government as "unwieldy" and "hypertrophied," and, as a result, unable to move forward with economic reforms. The aim, he continued, is to make it "impossible" for any of the central administrative bodies to interfere in production. According to Ryzhkov, two basic principles were followed when setting up the new government. The first is the retention of certain executive-management functions for central government. These include "overall economic regulation" and overseeing the development of the social sphere, defense, and ecology. The second is the development of the material and technical base for production. Twenty-five all-Union committees and ministries will be responsible for the executive-management functions; thirty-two ministries and state committees will oversee material and technical development.

The shift is to be away from ministries with a very specific focus to ministries with a more general portfolio. For example, the ministries of ferrous and nonferrous metallurgy are to be combined into one Ministry of Metallurgy. Similar consolidations were proposed for the construction, energy, chemical, timber, and defense spheres. Two entirely new committees were created: one for dealing with natural and man-made disasters and one on economic reform (to be headed by economist Leonid Abalkin).

Ryzhkov emphasized in his speech that only ten members of the new government were appointed before 1984 and that over half of the current members are being retired. The Supreme Soviet will vote on Ryzhkov's recommendations at its next session, which will open on June 20 (*TASS*, in English, *AP*, June 10; *Pravda*, June 11).

Sunday, June 11

Soviet Officials Say Eastern Europe Free to Choose Its Own Path

Soviet officials in Bonn preparing for the visit of Mikhail Gorbachev told a news conference that Poland and other East European countries can choose their own paths. Georgii Arbatov, director of the Institute of the USA and Canada, said Moscow sees Eastern Europe's search for new paths as an effort to solve problems that have been building up for a long time. He declined to answer a question about whether Moscow would accept Communist parties in Poland and Hungary relinquishing power if they were voted out in elections. Nikolai Portugalov, consultant to the CPSU Central Committee International Department, told journalists Moscow is serious about allowing East European countries complete freedom (*RFE/RL Special*, June 11).

Moscow News Speaks in Neutral Tone about Ukrainian Catholics

Moscow News (No. 24) carried an article about members of the Ukrainian Catholic (Uniate) Church holding prayer meetings and gatherings on the Arbat in Moscow. The article was the first detailed coverage of these activities. The Ukrainian Catholics have gathered in Moscow to demand the legalization of their Church, which was banned in 1946. The newspaper quoted a member of the Committee in Defense of the Ukrainian Catholic Church as saying he thought his Church should be rehabilitated on the grounds that it was a victim of Stalin's repressions. The newspaper also revealed that, at one of a number of large gatherings organized by Moscow's informal groups at the Luzhniki stadium while the first session of the Congress of People's Deputies was in progress, Rev. Yaroslav Lesiv of the Ukrainian Catholic Church asked Congress deputies to support the legalization of the Ukrainian Catholics. The article in *Moscow News* seems to be the first balanced report on the Ukrainian Catholic Church to appear in the Soviet press, which in the past has always attacked the Church.

Moscow News Quotes Lakshin on Solzhenitsyn

Moscow News (No. 24) carried excerpts from a book by literary critic Vladimir Lakshin entitled *Otkrytaya dver* (Open Door), which is due to be published soon in the USSR. The excerpts published by *Moscow News* include Lakshin's recollections about how Aleksandr Solzhenitsyn first came to the editorial board of *Novyi mir* in 1962, when *One Day in the Life of Ivan Denisovich* was due to be published in the journal. (At the time Lakshin worked at *Novyi mir.*) In the introduction to Lakshin's book, *Moscow News* said the attitude towards Solzhenitsyn is changing in the USSR.

Soviet Citizens Skeptical about Congress

According to a public opinion poll featured on June 11 by the "Vremya" television newscast, the majority of Soviet citizens share Andrei Sakharov's skeptical attitude towards the results of the inaugural session of the Congress of People's Deputies rather than the optimistic appraisal of the congress given by Gorbachev. The poll, conducted by trade unions and the Institute for Studies of Public Opinion at the USSR State Committee for Labor, was held in nine large cities. "Vremya" said 90 percent of the Soviet population had regularly watched live coverage of the Congress of People's Deputies. Asked whether they believed the Congress resolutions would improve the economic, social, and political situation in the country, only 39 percent said "yes," while 42 percent replied "no." Even more interesting were respondents' views on the viability of the new USSR Supreme Soviet. Only 27 percent of those asked said they were sure the new legislature would succeed, whereas 43 percent said they were not optimistic. In their comments, these people pointed out that many progressive deputies had failed to be elected to the Supreme Soviet and that the body's first sessions had not been notable for their democratic spirit.

_____ *Monday, June 12*

On June 12, Mikhail Gorbachev began a four-day official visit to West Germany. He arrived in Bonn accompanied by his wife Raisa and an official delegation, including Foreign Minister Eduard Shevardnadze and CPSU Central Committee Secretary for International Affairs and Politburo member Aleksandr Yakovlev. Gorbachev was welcomed by West German President Richard von Weizsäcker at a formal ceremony (*DPA, Reuters*, June 12). The same day, Gorbachev started talks with West German Chancellor Helmut Kohl. The first round of talks focused on East-West issues. West German spokesman Hans Klein said the two men discussed the effect of Moscow's reforms on East and West. He said the talks also covered the issue of short-range nuclear weapons. In remarks prepared for a dinner on June 12, Kohl called on Gorbachev to unilaterally reduce short-range nuclear weapons, easing the way for negotiations to reduce such systems. In his speech, Gorbachev said NATO proposals gave him reason to believe an agreement to cut conventional forces in Europe could be reached quickly. Gorbachev expressed concern about Western intentions to maintain a nuclear deterrent, saying Europe needs to eliminate nuclear weapons (*Reuters, AP*, June 12; *Pravda*, June 13).

The same day, AP and AFP reported that the Soviet Union had released the names of 1,500 German soldiers who had died in Soviet prisoner-of-war camps. The list was presented to the West German Red Cross. West

Gorbachev Visits West Germany

German officials were quoted as saying it was the first time the USSR had provided a list of German soldiers still unaccounted for after World War II.

On June 13, Gorbachev met with West German Foreign Minister Hans-Dietrich Genscher over breakfast (*DPA*, June 13). The same day, Gorbachev and Kohl signed a joint declaration that emphasized the right of all states to self-determination, the need to prevent war, and the protection of the environment. The declaration said the two countries are determined to work towards overcoming the division of Europe by building a European peace order in which the United States and Canada also have their place. The documents said both sides seek to reduce armed forces to a stable balance at levels sufficient for defense but not for attack (*DPA*, June 13; *Pravda*, June 14).

The same day, Marshal Sergei Akhromeev, Gorbachev's senior military adviser, who is accompanying the Soviet leader on his trip to West Germany, met in Bonn with West German Defense Minister Gerhard Stoltenberg and leading officers of the West German Armed Forces (*DPA*, *AFP*, June 13).

On June 13, Gorbachev traveled to Cologne. Speaking to West German businessmen there, Gorbachev said the USSR was working on new foreign-trade laws. He asked for understanding that Western demands for a currency reform leading to a convertible ruble cannot be carried out in a hurry. He said a precondition is the stability of the financial situation and the competitiveness of Soviet exports (*DPA*, June 13; *Pravda*, June 14).

The same day, Gorbachev returned to Bonn. Speaking at a dinner given for him by von Weizsäcker, Gorbachev said cooperation between the USSR and West Germany can be a catalyst for new relations between East and West. Gorbachev called on the Federal Republic to spend money on economic development rather than on military confrontation and the arms race (Western agencies, June 13).

On June 14, Gorbachev traveled to Stuttgart. There he spoke with the prime minister of the state of Baden-Württemberg, Lothar Späth. (The state of Baden-Württemberg has built up close economic relations with the Soviet Union. Späth met Gorbachev in Moscow in February of last year.) He also met some 200 political, business, and public leaders at a reception. Before returning to Bonn, Gorbachev visited Stuttgart University to see advanced electronic equipment. The same day, the West German government issued a statement summing up the results of Gorbachev's visit to West Germany. The statement said the West German government remains ready, together with West German businessmen, to help Soviet economic reforms succeed. The statement specifically referred to the participation of West German firms in modernizing the Soviet food and consumer-goods industries (*DPA*, June 14; *Pravda*, June 15).

A joint statement issued on June 14 by the West German and Soviet Foreign Ministers Hans-Dietrich Genscher and Eduard Shevardnadze called for the early conclusion of a worldwide verifiable ban on chemical weapons. The Foreign Ministry in Bonn said Genscher and Shevardnadze expressed their intention to be among the first to sign such a ban (*DPA*, June 14). On June 14, Gorbachev returned to Bonn for another round of talks with Kohl. It was reported that the two leaders discussed the situation in East European countries.

On June 15, Gorbachev wrapped up his visit to West Germany with stops in Dortmund and Düsseldorf. Speaking at a steel plant in Dortmund, Gorbachev said his policy of *perestroika* is aimed at renewing socialism and not at renouncing its basic ideas. In Düsseldorf, Gorbachev held talks with North Rhine-Westphalian Prime Minister Johannes Rau. The same day, Gorbachev held a televised press conference in Bonn. Gorbachev said his visit to the Federal Republic was a great event not only for the USSR and West Germany but for all of Europe and the world. He said the new Soviet-West German declaration signed on June 13 "properly reflects new thinking" on both sides. At the press conference, Gorbachev also criticized NATO defense policies, saying their insistence on nuclear deterrence continues to reflect the spirit of the Cold War. At the press conference, Gorbachev was asked about the events in China. He said he was concerned about recent developments in that country and regretted some aspects of what had happened. The same day, Gorbachev left Bonn for the Soviet Union (Western agencies, June 15; *Pravda*, June 16).

Throughout his visit Gorbachev was given a jubilant reception by the West German people, who greeted him with cheers and shouts. Summing up the results of Gorbachev's visit, Western experts said it gave more hope for an improvement in Soviet-West German ties. They stressed, however, that Gorbachev's statements in the Federal Republic did not bring any of the dramatic political gestures that had drawn so much speculation for months in advance of his visit, such as a dramatic disarmament move or the dismantling of the Berlin Wall.

On June 16, West German Chancellor Helmut Kohl was quoted as saying Gorbachev's visit had been a great and important success. Speaking in the West German parliament, Kohl said the visit would make it possible to overcome the consequences of World War II, especially the division of Europe and Germany (*DPA*, *AFP*, June 16). See RL 276/89.

Latvian Government Rehabilitates Stalin's Victims

The Presidium of the Latvian Supreme Soviet has rehabilitated thousands of Latvians deported from their homeland in the 1940s and 1950s. Sources in Riga contacted by telephone by RFE/RL said the Presidium issued a decree last week rehabilitating an estimated 15,000 Latvians forcibly deported on the night of June 13, 1941, and thousands of others deported later in the 1940s and the 1950s. The sources said the Presidium had also issued a decree declaring June 14 a day of national mourning for Latvian victims of Stalinist policies.

El'tsin Speaks at Unofficial Gathering in Moscow

Boris El'tsin told tens of thousands of cheering supporters he was dissatisfied with the new Supreme Soviet, and he vowed to fight to achieve social justice. El'tsin said the authorities wanted to give the impression that the inaugural session of the Congress of People's Deputies, which ended last week, had fulfilled its objectives. "I cannot agree, I expected more," El'tsin told the crowd of at least 30,000 outside Moscow's largest stadium, Luzhniki. El'tsin also pledged to work hard following his nomination as chairman of the Committee for Construction and Architecture of the Supreme Soviet. In an interview with French television on June 14, El'tsin said he was still dissatisfied with what he called "the half-measures" taken by Gorbachev to introduce reforms in the USSR.

Other deputies of the Congress of People's Deputies spoke at the same gathering. Public Prosecutor Nikolai Ivanov who, together with Tel'man Gdlyan, is himself under investigation for allegedly violating the law while investigating corruption, urged the crowd to be on guard against attempts by conservatives to overturn Gorbachev's reforms. (In an article in *Literaturnaya gazeta* on May 24, Ol'ga Chaikovskaya, a journalist who specializes in law, condemned Ivanov and Gdlyan for serious misdeeds in investigating corruption in Uzbekistan. She also complained that Ivanov and Gdlyan use demagogy in appealing to the public for support.) Also speaking at Luzhniki was Professor of History Yurii Afanas'ev, who said the inaugural session of the Congress of People's Deputies was "morally very satisfactory but a political defeat" (*Reuters*, June 12).

El'tsin also commented on the inaugural session of the Congress of People's Deputies in an interview published this week by the magazine *Newsweek*. In the interview El'tsin stressed that the new congress has much to do if it is to become a force in Soviet politics.

Soviet Publisher Receives Freedom Award in US

Sergei Grigoryants, the chief editor of the unofficial journal *Glasnost'* and a former political prisoner, received the International Federation of Newspaper Publishers' "Golden Pen of Freedom" award for 1989. The award was created in 1961 to recognize the outstanding actions of an individual, group, or institution in promoting freedom of the press (*AP*, June 12).

Soviet Troops Withdraw from Austro-Hungarian Border

A Soviet military unit began pulling back from Hungary's border with Austria. The mechanized infantry regiment began withdrawing from the west Hungarian town of Szombathely, where it has been stationed since 1958 (*MTI*, in English, *Reuters*, June 12). The Soviet Union began a partial troop withdrawal from Hungary on April 25 as part of the cutback in Soviet forces announced by Gorbachev last December.

US Military Chief Arrives in Moscow

Admiral William Crowe, the chairman of the US Joint Chiefs of Staff, is in the Soviet Union at the start of an official visit. (*AFP*, June 12). On June 13, Crowe visited a Soviet strategic missile launch site and an air base southwest of Moscow. At Kubinka Air Base he sat behind the controls of the Soviet long-range bomber designated "Blackjack" by NATO. Later the same day, he addressed an audience at the Military Academy of the Soviet General Staff, near Moscow. In his speech he said the traditional Soviet system of military secrecy breeds suspicion and fuels the arms race. He also said that recent arms cuts by the Soviet Union only affect "the margin of its power" (*UPI*, June 13).

Tuesday, June 13

Soviet Officials Discuss Gangs, Crime Increase

A spokesman for the USSR Ministry of Internal Affairs, Aleksandr Gurov, said thousands of criminal gangs are operating in the USSR. Gurov said some groups have begun to form links with international organized crime to illegally import computers, antiques, and jewelry. A second spokesman for the ministry, Major General Anatolii Smirnov, said reported crime in the first five months of this year increased almost 32 percent over the same period last year (*Reuters*, June 13).

Soviet Refusedniks Attend Paris Meeting

The USSR has granted travel visas to two refusedniks to attend the Paris human-rights conference. Semen Akselrod arrived in Paris from Leningrad. He is sponsored by the USSR as a nongovernment guest at the conference. Delegates said the other refusednik, Aleksandr Lerner, is expected to come to Paris on June 15. Both will return to the USSR next week. Both have been denied permission to emigrate because of objections by family members. Soviet delegates said laws allowing relatives to block emigration are under review (*RFE/RL Special*, June 13).

Chinese Foreign Minister Meets Rogachev

During a stopover at Moscow on his way home from a foreign tour, Chinese Foreign Minister Qian Qichen met with Soviet Deputy Foreign Minister Igor Rogachev. It is the highest-level meeting reported between the two sides since the Chinese authorities used troops to repress massive pro-democracy demonstrations in Beijing. Radio Moscow said they discussed Sino-Soviet relations, but it did not say whether the internal situation in China came under discussion. On June 14, Novosti said there was internal and external pressure on Moscow to withdraw its ambassador from Beijing to protest against the repression of student demonstrators. Novosti said the sources of the pressure were sincere, naïve people who believe this is the way the USSR should show its disapproval of the Chinese action. The agency did not identify these "sources," however. Commenting on the situation in China, Novosti said "without democratic traditions" a move in the direction of democracy could take dangerous turns, and it pointed to the example of the disturbances in the Fergana Valley of Uzbekistan.

Wednesday, June 14 ———————————————————————

Katushev On Turkish Minority in Bulgaria

USSR Minister for Foreign Economic Relations Konstantin Katushev is quoted as saying he hopes Bulgaria approaches its current problem with Turkey carefully (*RFE/RL Special*, June 14). Katushev was in Ankara for talks and was asked by reporters about the problem of ethnic Turks in Bulgaria. He was quoted as saying interethnic relations are a sensitive matter that must be handled carefully. He said he hoped Bulgaria would solve the problem in a way that satisfies the interests of all residents of Bulgaria. (In the wake of the Turkish unrest that began in Bulgaria on May 6, the Bulgarian authorities have adopted an increasingly hard-line policy that has resulted in mass deportations of Turks from Bulgaria [*RFE/RL Special*, June 14].)

Explosion Releases Toxic Gas, Seventy Injured

Seventy people suffered gas poisoning after an explosion released chlorine in the Khabarovsk region of Siberia. TASS said that twenty-seven people were hospitalized and four of them had been in serious condition. TASS said the explosion took place on June 13 at the pumping station of the Khabarovsk waterworks and released some 800 kilograms of liquid chlorine.

USSR and US Oppose Forced Repatriation of Boat People

The United States and the Soviet Union have taken similar positions on the Vietnamese boat people. Both said the repatriation of the refugees should only take place on a voluntary basis. During a United Nations conference in Geneva, chief Soviet delegate Genrikh Kireev said raising living standards throughout Southeast Asia was the only permanent solution to the refugee problem. Kireev's remarks were similar to the US position expressed on June 13 by US Deputy Secretary of State Lawrence Eagleburger (*AP, UPI*, June 14).

Demonstrations in Baltic Republics

Thousands of people were reported to have attended observances in Latvia, Lithuania, and Estonia to commemorate the mass deportations of their countrymen to remote parts of the USSR. The observances marked the anniversary of the wave of mass deportations that began in 1941. In Washington, President George Bush proclaimed June 14 "Baltic Freedom Day" and called on the USSR to listen to the demands of the Baltic republics for freedom and self-determination (*Reuters*, June 14).

Thursday, June 15

Ogonek Carries Criticism of Andropov

Ogonek (No. 24) carried an article by former KGB Chairman Vladimir Semichastnyi criticizing Yurii Andropov. Andropov succeeded Semichastnyi as KGB chairman in 1967 and then served as Party general secretary from 1982 until his death in 1984. Semichastnyi accused Andropov of assisting in the conduct of purges in the late 1940s under Stalin and of ignoring corruption during the Brezhnev era. (Some leading Soviet reformists—for instance, Fedor Burlatsky—have praised Andropov in the Soviet press as Gorbachev's predecessor in the movement for reform.)

Friday, June 16 ————————————————————————————

Soviet Media on Nagy Reburial

On June 16, Radio Moscow-1 (0800) carried a report about the reburial in Budapest of Hungarian Prime Minister Imre Nagy, who was executed in 1958. Avoiding any comments of its own on the event, Radio Moscow quoted a statement by the Hungarian government that said "Imre Nagy understood the necessity of changing an earlier impracticable policy that had failed to take into account the national tradition of Hungarians." The report also included information on a mass demonstration in front of the Soviet embassy in Budapest held on June 15 to demand the immediate pullout of Soviet troops from Hungary. Radio Moscow described the demonstration as having been organized by "oppositional youth groups" who carried banners similar to those carried by "counter-revolutionaries in 1956." Until now, coverage in the Soviet press of the Hungarian reevaluation of the events of 1956 has avoided the use of the term "counterrevolutionaries." Later on June 16, Radio Moscow-2 (1030) carried a commentary on Nagy's reburial by its correspondent in Budapest, Vladimir Stefan. The commentary said the Supreme Procurator's Office of Hungary had concluded that the trial and capital punishment of Nagy and his followers were illegal. (On June 2, *New Times* quoted a Hungarian Party official as saying the execution of Nagy was a mistake.)

On the evening of June 16, a lengthy report on the reburial of Nagy and his associates was carried by TASS. The report complained that some speakers at the ceremony had made openly anti-Soviet speeches. It cited them as saying interference by the Soviet Union had triggered the 1956 revolution and put an end to Hungarians' hopes. The agency cited Sandor Racz, former chairman of "the so-called Workers' Council" of Budapest in 1956 as saying that the presence of Soviet troops in Hungary hampered the flowering of freedom in Hungary. TASS complained that Racz also said the Soviet presence was still overshadowing life in Hungary.

The Latvian newspaper *Sovetskaya molodezh'* attacked the central Soviet media for remaining silent about the extent of the death toll following the brutal suppression of student demonstrations by the authorities in China. The newspaper praised Western press coverage of the events in China. *Sovetskaya molodezh'* said foreign newspapers had published photographs of mass shootings by the Chinese army "in which only a blind person could fail to see dozens of corpses of ordinary citizens." "TASS appeared unable to do so and, to put it bluntly, consciously chose not to provide such 'eloquent' pictures for Soviet newspapers," it said. "We believe this fact does not require any special comment," *Sovetskaya molodezh'* concluded.

Latvian Newspaper Criticizes Media over Coverage of Events in China

The Soviet Union officially acknowledged for the first time that there was a powerful nuclear explosion at an atomic weapons plant in the Ural mountains in September, 1957. The accident, kept secret by the authorities until now, created a radioactive trail 105 kilometers long and 8–9 kilometers wide and forced the evacuation of more than 10,000 people, TASS reported. More than thirty years later, large areas around the town of Kasli, 100 kilometers north of the city of Chelyabinsk, were still contaminated and water reserves undrinkable, it said. Western experts have long suspected there was a serious nuclear accident in the area about that time.

Soviet Union Admits 1957 Nuclear Disaster in Urals

Ivan Ivanov, deputy chairman of the State Foreign Economic Commission, said three free economic zones are being formed in the USSR, one of which will begin to function by the end of this year. Ivanov told TASS his commission is preparing the zones. They will operate initially on an experimental basis. The zones are to be set up in Vyborg in the Leningrad Oblast, Nakhodka in the Far East, and Novgorod in the northern part of the RSFSR. Ivanov did not say which zone will start up first.

First Free Economic Zone to Function by End of 1989

A conference in the Kazakh capital of Alma-Ata is discussing the possibility of an early solution to the problems of Soviet ethnic Germans. Radio Moscow said the meeting began on June 16. The radio said it was attended by Party and state officials and a number of experts from the RSFSR, Ukraine, and the Central Asian republics. The participants are discussing the history and the current situation of Soviet Germans in the multinational structure

Solution to Problems of Soviet Germans Discussed in Alma-Ata

of the Soviet Union and their contribution to *perestroika*. The chairman of the Cultural Center of Germans in Kazakhstan, Gerold Belger, said last month the question of restoring the Autonomous Republic of Volga Germans must be resolved. The republic was abolished in 1941, and its German residents were scattered to Siberia and Central Asia.

Soviet Economists Predict Unrest and Famine without Early Radical Reform

The Soviet Union will face social and political unrest and even famine within the next two years without fast radical reform and a quick boost to living standards, top Soviet economists predicted. The economists, including Academician Leonid Abalkin, who has just been nominated deputy prime minister, issued their warnings at a news conference in Moscow. "Our studies show clearly that if the economy is not stabilized over the next one and a half to two years and the start of an improvement is not achieved, a rightward swing by society is inevitable," Abalkin told the news conference. In turn, agricultural scientist Academician Vladimir Tikhonov of VASKhNIL told the conference that if reforms giving peasant farmers full control over their land are not introduced and implemented quickly "we can expect famine in the very near future" (*Reuters*, June 16).

Saturday, June 17———————————————

Sakharov Says Events in China Could Be Repeated in USSR

Academician Andrei Sakharov said he did not rule out the possibility that events similar to those that recently occurred in China could happen in the USSR. Sakharov was speaking to reporters in the Dutch city of Groningen. Sakharov said that the Soviet people's confidence in their leadership had dropped dramatically and that the situation was not unlike that which preceded the 1917 Bolshevik Revolution. Sakharov said Mikhail Gorbachev must speed up the pace of economic and democratic reform in order to avoid a catastrophe (*UPI, Reuters*, June 17). In Groningen, the city's university conferred an honorary law degree on Sakharov. On June 18, he went to Britain to receive honorary degrees from Oxford University and the University of Sussex (*AP*, June 18). On June 19, Sakharov gave a press conference at Sussex, at which he disclosed that he had urged world leaders to press China to revoke death sentences passed on pro-democracy demonstrators in China. (The demonstrators had been sentenced to death in Beijing and Shanghai after being convicted the week before on charges including sabotage, rioting, and arson.) Sakharov said he had sent telegrams to George Bush, Mikhail Gorbachev, Margaret Thatcher, and Helmut Kohl urging them to do everything in their power to save those convicted (*UPI*, June 19).

Speaking on June 20 at the Royal Institute of International Affairs in London, Sakharov said the West underestimated the growing unpopularity of the leadership in the Soviet Union. He said that despite reforms the whole system of monolithic government remained. Sakharov said that the Soviet Union was perhaps the world's last great colonial power and that, if this problem were not solved in a constitutional, rational way, the destruction or downfall of his country was inevitable. He cautioned the West about giving help to the Soviet Union, saying it would be wrong to assume the country was already on the right path.

Komsomol Newspaper Calls for Reassessment of Soviet Role in 1956

Komsomol'skaya pravda carried an article calling for a reassessment of the role of the Soviet government and its allies in the suppression of the Hungarian uprising in 1956. In a commentary pegged to the reburial in Budapest on June 16 of former Hungarian Prime Minister Imre Nagy and his associates, who were executed for their part in the uprising, *Komsomol'skaya pravda* said Nagy shared the goals of the current Hungarian leadership and was not anti-Socialist. In a clear sign that the Soviet reappraisal of history still has its limits, however, the newspaper said Nagy's short-lived multiparty government was incapable of governing and let the country slide into chaos. On June 20, TASS criticized several statements made at Nagy's reburial—in particular, those that referred to "forty years of Soviet occupation of Hungary" and to "the Asiatic blind alley" into which Hungary was driven by the Soviet Union.

Soviet Delegation Flies to Islamabad

A Soviet delegation flew to Islamabad for talks with the Afghan resistance about the release of Soviet prisoners of war. Radio Moscow said the delegation was made up of members of the "People's Committee for the Release of Soviet Prisoners of War in Afghanistan" and was headed by writer Aleksandr Prokhanov. (Prokhanov, a conservative, has written several works supporting the Soviet intervention in Afghanistan.) Prokhanov told Radio Moscow the delegation would appeal to the mercy and humanity of members of the resistance. On June 18, TASS disclosed the inclusion in the Soviet delegation of the parents of four

Soviet soldiers missing in Afghanistan. On June 21 the delegation met with the interim president of the resistance, Sibghatullah Mojaddedi, and other resistance officials. They also met a former soldier from Minsk who said he had become a Muslim and did not want to go home (*RFE/RL Special*, June 21).

Ministers Warned of Personal Responsibility in Armenia

Ministers have been warned that they bear personal responsibility for delays in construction in rural areas of Armenia that were damaged by last December's earthquake. TASS said the warning was issued in Erevan by the special commission of the CPSU Central Committee Politburo sent to Armenia to supervise reconstruction. TASS said the commission found that the rate of construction work in rural Armenia is "far from satisfactory." On June 18, *Sotsialisticheskaya industriya* carried an article that said failure to observe building standards had contributed to the death toll in the Armenian earthquake.

Kommunist Says "Self-Determination" No More Than a Slogan

The CPSU Central Committee journal *Kommunist* (No. 9) carried an article saying that within the Soviet Union the principle of people's self-determination has never been implemented. The article, by a staff member of the Institute of Marxism-Leninism, Aleksandr Zharnikov, said national self-determination had been turned into a slogan nobody took seriously. He said the present state of interethnic relations in the USSR was the result of the collapse of a system that suppressed interethnic problems.

Disturbances in Kazakhstan

Radio Moscow reported disturbances in the town of Novyi Uzen' in Kazakhstan. It said the disturbances started with a fight in a discothèque between Kazakhs, Armenians, Georgians, and Azerbaijanis. This was followed by a crowd of youths rampaging through the streets. They destroyed shops and vehicles and tried to storm a city administration building. The report said shots were fired into the air to disperse them. On June 19, TASS acknowledged that deaths had occurred during the disturbances in Novyi Uzen' but did not give figures.

On June 20, TASS quoted an MVD spokesman as saying three people had been killed, fifty-three injured, and fifty-seven detained in the violence in Novyi Uzen'. The spokesman said two battalions of MVD troops had been sent to restore order and a curfew imposed in the city (*TASS*, June 20). That day, *Izvestia* carried a report on the violence stating that Kazakhs in Novyi Uzen' had demanded that non-Kazakhs be moved out of the city and that cooperatives run by people from the Caucasus region be closed. Radio Moscow (June 20) said MVD Colonel Boris Mikhailov had disclosed that toxic gas was used against youths in Novyi Uzen'.

On June 21, *Izvestia* reported a fourth death from the ethnic disturbances. Kazakh officials who visited Novyi Uzen' said that the situation was returning to normal but that 600 people had already left the area. Kazakh Party Central Committee Secretary Uzbekali Dzhanibekov, who also visited Novyi Uzen', told reporters that social and economic problems, not ethnic differences, were the main cause of the recent violence (*TASS*, in English, *AP*, *AFP*, *Reuters*, June 21).

On June 22, refugees were reported to be crowding Novyi Uzen' airport trying to flee the ethnic violence (*AP*, *AFP*, June 22). *Pravda* said the refugees feared threats by native Kazakhs who wanted settlers from the Caucasus expelled. *Pravda* said two more people were wounded by gunfire near Novyi Uzen' on June 21, but it gave no details. Radio Moscow (0615, June 22) said that tensions persisted in Novyi Uzen' and that local Party officials were not helping to ease the situation. The radio's correspondent at the scene said that there was another unsanctioned demonstration in the town on June 21 and that the situation in a nearby settlement was near the explosion point. He said Party officials were watching from their office windows instead of mixing with the crowds. The correspondent also said people from the Caucasus who live in Novyi Uzen' had formed a committee called "Solidarity," which called for unity and for joint efforts to bring peace to the town. He quoted the committee as saying there are forces behind the unrest that do not reflect the interests of Kazakhs.

On June 23, *Pravda* said there had been attempts to disrupt water and electricity supplies and seize gas facilities in Novyi Uzen'. It also said one quarter of all factory and office workers stayed away from their jobs on June 22. Kazakh Deputy Prime Minister Oktyabr Sheltikov said the lack of economic infrastructure was the major cause of rioting in Novyi Uzen'. TASS said Sheltikov headed a newly created government commission that had been set up to take immediate steps to remedy the economic situation in the area. See RL 297/89.

In a speech in Moscow to the All-Union Academy of Agricultural Sciences, published in *Pravda* on June 17, conservative Politburo Member Egor Ligachev empha-

Ligachev Says His Family Suffered under Stalin

sized (as he did at the Party Conference last summer) that the policy of *perestroika* was being guided by a hard core of politicians who entered the Politburo at the Central Committee plenum in April, 1985. Ligachev himself belongs to that inner circle. Asked about special investigator Ivanov's allegations that he was involved in corruption, Ligachev rejected the accusations and claimed that he had been instructed by the Politburo to lead the struggle against corruption after he became a member of that body. Ligachev said that members of his own family had been unjustly repressed in 1937 and 1949 under Stalin.

New Biographies of Military Officials Published

The military journal *Kommunist vooruzhennykh sil* (No. 10), published short biographies and photographs of all military personnel elected on March 26 to the Congress of People's Deputies. The collection included the full biography of the forty-five-year-old former commander of Soviet Forces in Afghanistan, Boris Gromov, who is the youngest colonel general in the military's top ranks. The biographies of Vladimir Osipov, Nikolai Popov, and Stanislav Postnikov did not mention their present positions as theater of military operations (TVD) commanders. Marshal Akhromeev was described as an adviser to the Soviet President and as a member of the Group of General Inspectors of the USSR Ministry of Defense.

Sunday, June 18

Moscow News on New Religious Periodicals

Moscow News (No. 25) carried a short article by Father Mark Smirnov, a regular contributor to the newspaper, reporting the publication of several new periodicals by various churches in the USSR. They included *Moskovsky tserkovnyi vestnik* (The Moscow Church Herald), a weekly bulletin of the Adventist Church called *Slovo primireniya* (The Word of Reconciliation), and a Lithuanian-language journal, *Kataliku tasaulis* (The Catholic World).

Russian People's Academy of Sciences Formed

TASS reported the formation in Moscow on June 17 of a Russian (*Rossiiskaya*) People's (*Narodnaya*) Academy of Sciences, which, according to TASS, is dedicated to "revealing more fully the scientific potential of Russia." TASS said the founders of the new academy believe that "bureaucratic principles" dominated the USSR Academy of Sciences and hampered the free development of scientific thought. It mentioned that the chairman of the organizing committee of the Russian academy was Candidate of Military Sciences Petr Ivankov. Among the persons reported by TASS to have spoken at the academy's inaugural meeting were several who are not to be found in the ranks of leading Soviet scholars. On May 21, *Moscow News* (No. 21) carried a report about plans to set up the new academy. In 1988 and earlier this year, several conservative Soviet literary figures, including writer Yurii Bondarev, complained that Russia was discriminated against because, unlike the other Union republics, it does not have its own academy of sciences.

Monday, June 19

Head of Youth Committee Says Komsomol Has No Right to Power

The chairman of the Supreme Soviet Committee on Youth said the Komsomol has no inherent right to leadership of the country's youth. Valerii Tsibukh said he believed the right to youth leadership must be earned by deeds in intellectual competition. In an interview with the Novosti press agency, Tsibukh said attempts had been made to give the Komsomol a higher status than the emerging independent youth groups under a new Soviet law on youth. He said this attempt had failed, but he gave no details. (Last year, a conservative draft law on youth was elaborated, but it was eventually dropped following criticism in the press.) Tsibukh is the former first secretary of the Ukrainian Komsomol. He told Novosti his committee would not be a Komsomol lobby in the Supreme Soviet even though some of its members are former Komsomol officials. He said the committee would try to serve all young people by making and defending laws, not ideology.

Pravda Criticizes Gdlyan and Ivanov

Pravda said corruption investigators Tel'man Gdlyan and Nikolai Ivanov were impeding the search for the truth about their work by criticizing the parliamentary commission that is investigating them. *Pravda* quoted the investigators as saying the formation of the investigative commission of the Supreme Soviet was an attempt to ruin the work they did to expose corrupt leaders in Uzbekistan and Moscow.

Draft Language Law Published in Uzbekistan

A draft law giving Uzbek the status of a state language has been published in Uzbekistan. TASS said the draft also proclaimed Russian to be the language of communication between nationalities and guaranteed the right of all citizens of the republic to use their mother tongue. Under the draft proposals, translations would have to be provided in all official and cultural contacts for those who do not speak Uzbek. The draft also says opportunities for teaching the old Uzbek script should be provided. The Uzbek alphabet was changed from Arabic to Latin and, later, from Latin to Cyrillic. The Uzbek Popular Front "Birlik" has for some time been pressing for the restoration of the Arabic script, in which the Uzbek classics are written.

Campaign for Legalization of Ukrainian Catholic Church Intensified

The Canadian delegation at the Paris human-rights conference asked the Russian Orthodox Church to help legalize the Ukrainian Catholic Church. Canadian delegate William Bauer made the appeal at today's session, which was attended by Metropolitan Pitirim of the Russian Orthodox Church. Bauer said he was addressing the appeal to Pitirim because Soviet officials sometimes say they are reluctant to lift restrictions on the Ukrainian Church owing to resistance by some sections of the Russian Orthodox Church (*RFE/RL Special*, June 19). Simultaneously, Ukrainian Catholic Bishop Platon Kornylyak asked the Moscow Patriarchate to begin "summit talks" on theological and practical problems connected with the legalization of the Ukrainian Catholic Church, according to *Ordinariats-Korrespondenz* (No. 21, June 15), the publication of the press office of the Archbishop of Munich. On June 19, AP reported that a crowd of Ukrainian Catholics, numbering perhaps as many as 70,000-100,000, had gathered on June 18 in Ivano-Frankovsk to hold a prayer service. Meanwhile, the leader of the Ukrainian Catholic Church, Cardinal Lubachivsky, who lives in Rome, is touring Western Europe urging support for the legalization of his Church in the USSR (*RFE/RL Special*, June 20).

German Religious Community Registered

The June issue of *Volk auf dem Weg*, the press organ of Germans from the USSR, reported that a new German religious community had been registered in the town of Marks on the Volga. It is unusual for German parishes to obtain registration. An accompanying photograph of the community's altar indicates that the group is Roman Catholic.

Statistics on Cruelty in Soviet Prisons

Nedelya (No. 23) carries an interview with Yurii Khitrin, a senior aide to the USSR Public Prosecutor in which a preliminary disclosure of statistics on cruelty in Soviet penal institutions seems to be made. Khitrin informs the weekly about the activities of the USSR in the UN Committee against Torture. Questioned by the interviewer about known cases of the violation of the rights of the accused or of convicts in Soviet prisons, Khitrin said 795 Soviet prison officials committed 831 violations of "Socialist legality" last year. These included four cases of forging material pertinent to an investigation, two cases of illegal arrest, and four cases of illegal detention. The remaining 821 are various cases of illegal cruel treatment of prisoners, but they include only the cases regarded as proven by the authorities.

Independent Journal to Hunt Criminals in USSR

An independent journal was founded in Moscow to publish political articles and help track down major criminals. A member of the editorial board, Evgenii Dodolev, said on Moscow television that the first issue of the journal, which is entitled *Sovershenno sekretno* (Top Secret), would be published later in June and would contain an interview with the director of the US FBI, William Sessions. Dodolev said the journal is not connected with the CPSU Central Committee or any of its departments. Dodolev said that the journal wants to work with the international police organization Interpol and that Soviet thriller writer Yulian Semenov is trying to arrange this. Dodolev specializes in reports on organized crime; last year, he wrote a major article for *Nedelya* on corruption under Brezhnev.

Tuesday, June 20

Iranian Parliamentary Speaker Visits Moscow

Iranian parliamentary speaker Hashemi Rafsanjani left Teheran for Moscow, accompanied by several senior government officials. He is the highest-ranking official to visit the Soviet Union since the 1979 Iranian Revolution (*Reuters*, June 20). Upon his arrival in Moscow, Rafsanjani was met by Vice President Anatolii Luk'yanov and Foreign Minister Eduard Shevardnadze. Rafsanjani started talks that day with Mikhail Gorbachev. TASS quoted Gorbachev as saying at the meeting with the Iranian officials that prospects for improved relations with Iran had never been better. On June 21, TASS quoted Rafsanjani as saying the Iranian people hold Gorbachev in high esteem. In a series of accords drafted during further talks between Gorbachev and Rafsanjani on June 22, the Soviet Union and Iran pledged to boost economic and political cooperation. The draft agreements included one on the development of good-neighborly relations as well as agreements on joint projects in such fields as atomic energy, gas processing, and space (*Reuters, TASS,* June 22; *Pravda* June 23). Concluding his two days of talks, Rafsanjani said "new horizons" had opened in Iranian-Soviet relations. In a joint declaration signed at the end of the talks, the Soviet Union pledged to help strengthen Iran's defenses and to foster religious contacts with the Muslim nation. It also said the two nations would work towards a better understanding of each other's culture and convictions (*AP, UPI, Reuters, TASS,* in English, June 22). It was announced on June 23, that Mikhail Gorbachev had accepted an invitation to visit Iran. US State Department spokeswoman Margaret Tutwiler said the United States was watching closely the evolution of the relationship between the USSR and Iran. She said that the United States and others found it difficult to understand Soviet efforts to move close "to a regime that continues to support international terrorism and hostage-taking" (*RFE/RL Special,* June 23).

Before returning to Iran on June 23, Rafsanjani traveled to Baku, the capital of Azerbaijan, after a day of sightseeing in Leningrad. In Baku, he attended prayers with the city's Shi'ite Muslims and met with the city's Muslim leaders and Party officials. A spokesman for the Muslim Religious Board for the Transcaucasus told Reuters of the board's hope that Rafsanjani's visit would increase Soviet Muslim ties with Iran. See *Pravda,* June 24.

Aral Sea Called Threat to Planet

Sotsialisticheskaya industriya said enviromental damage to the Aral Sea was so severe that it had become a threat to the entire planet. It said the sea was choked with salt, dust, and chemical waste. The newspaper said that most people who lived near the sea were sick and that the area had one of Asia's highest infant mortality rates. It said airborne materials from the sea were also causing increased pollution across the USSR. Yurii Kotov, a Soviet ecology professor and member of the Supreme Soviet, said on a joint US-USSR television program on June 19 that he advocated halving cotton production in the area. Rivers feeding the Aral have been diverted to irrigate cotton crops.

Soviet Cruise Ship Hits Iceberg

A Soviet cruise ship struck an iceberg in the Arctic, and there were fears it might founder. The ship, the *Maxim Gorky,* was carrying some 950 people, many of them elderly West German passengers. There were no casualties (*Reuters*, *TASS*, June 20). On June 21, a Norwegian naval officer said the ship was moving through fog at more than 30 kilometers an hour when it hit the ice. He said it was not safe to go much faster than 5 kilometers an hour under such conditions.

Dissidents in Moscow said police had detained a number of people in two separate incidents in the center of Moscow on June 19. Dissident Viktor Dovyatin said about twenty people were detained when police broke up a demonstration near the Lenin library by the independent rights group "Free Migration." Another dissident, Andrei Babitsky, said some members of an independent political group, the Democratic Union, were also detained on June 19 on Pushkin Square (*AP*, June 20).

Moscow Dissidents Detained after Incidents in Moscow

Following the example of their radical colleagues of "the Moscow Group" in the Congress of People's Deputies, a group of deputies representing Kiev announced their decision to create a similar alliance (*Radio Kiev-3*, 1900, June 20). The issues on which the Kiev club intends to focus, as explained by deputy Yurii Shcherbak, include "the concept of the structure of the Soviet Union" and the "concept of republican sovereignty and republican *khozraschet*."

"Kiev Deputies Club" Formed

Wednesday, June 21

Andrei Sakharov said the lack of "democratic mechanisms" in the USSR could lead to Mikhail Gorbachev losing power. Sakharov made his comments in an interview in *Literaturnaya gazeta*. Sakharov reiterated his opinion that Gorbachev's position would be stronger had he been elected president by direct popular vote as one of several candidates.

Sakharov Says Gorbachev Could Lose Power

USSR Minister of Health Evgenii Chazov said that registered carriers of the AIDS virus in the Soviet Union numbered 269—seventy more than had been reported by Chazov two months before. Chazov told Radio Moscow (1700) that eleven other people had actually contracted the disease. He said a special Politburo commission chaired by Politburo member Nikolai Slyunkov had been monitoring the spread of the disease in the USSR for the

Soviet Health Minister Gives New AIDS Figures

past two months. Chazov said a committee for AIDS research had also been set up under the State Committee for Science and Technology. On June 22, *Izvestia* reported that a ten-year-old boy in the city of Rostov had died of AIDS. The boy contracted the disease through the use of unsterilized syringes while being treated for a heart defect in a city hospital. Two other children in Rostov were reported seriously ill with AIDS.

START Talks Begin in Geneva

Detailed talks began in Geneva between the United States and the Soviet Union on reducing strategic nuclear weapons by half. The talks also involve space defense issues. Gorbachev said on June 20 that he believed disagreements were not insurmountable (*AP, UPI*, June 21).

Commissions Vote on Ministerial Candidates

Supreme Soviet parliamentary commissions voted to endorse or reject ministers for the streamlined cabinet proposed by Prime Minister Nikolai Ryzhkov. Radio Moscow (1700) said Leonid Abalkin was recommended to be deputy prime minister and to head a commission overseeing economic reform. It also said the commissions had recommended that Evgenii Chazov be retained as minister of health and Mikhail Nenashev as head of the State Committee for Radio and Television. Marat Gramov, head of the State Committee for Physical Culture and Sports, failed to win the commissions' approval. As predicted, many of the candidates were subjected to tough questioning by the the commissions. Yurii Maslyukov, the chairman of Gosplan, for example, was questioned for four hours before being confirmed in his post. Deputies also approved the nomination of Vitalii Doguzhiev as head of a newly created commission responsible for disaster prevention and emergency measures.

Roy Medvedev Criticizes *Pravda* over Gdlyan-Ivanov Story

Independent Soviet historian Roy Medvedev said members of the commission investigating the Gdlyan-Ivanov case, of which he is chairman, believed the Party daily *Pravda* was trying to influence their work. It was *Pravda* (June 21) itself that carried his comments. Medvedev complained that an article in *Pravda* of June 19 would "substantially complicate" the commission's work. (The article of June 19 criticized statements made by Gdlyan and Ivanov implicating high-level officials in Moscow in corruption.) Medvedev also complained about the article's suggestion that the commission would be quick to put an end to the matter. He said the investigation into the

Gdlyan-Ivanov case would be "quite a long process" and that the investigating commission would report to the next session of the Congress of People's Deputies.

_____ *Thursday, June 22*

Nursultan Nazarbaev, Kazakh prime minister since 1984, replaced Gennadii Kolbin, a Russian, who was elected chairman of the USSR People's Control Committee this month as party first secretary in Kazakhstan. Kolbin took over as Party first secretary in December, 1986, replacing a Kazakh. His appointment sparked rioting in Alma-Ata, which took two lives (*TASS*, in English, June 22). Soviet television reported that Soviet Politburo member and former KGB chairman Viktor Chebrikov attended the Kazakh Party plenum at which Nazarbaev was elected Party first secretary.

Party First Secretary in Kazakhstan Replaced by Kazakh

An article in *Pravda* blamed Stalin for the Red Army's initial defeats in 1941. The article appeared on the forty-eighth anniversary of the German invasion of the USSR. It said that Stalin and the Soviet leadership had been informed on more than one occasion Germany intended to attack on June 22 but that Stalin disregarded the warnings as "disinformation." As a result of these "gross mistakes," *Pravda* said, the Red Army was taken by surprise and placed in an extremely difficult position.

***Pravda* Blames Stalin for Soviet Defeats in 1941**

TASS denied allegations by *The Daily Telegraph* that the expulsion of Turks from Bulgaria was being carried out with the sanction of the Soviet Union. Moreover, it called Western reports that the Turks were being expelled or deported "biased and untrue." TASS claimed that the Turks in Bulgaria were simply taking advantage of new legislation on passports for foreign travel and were exercising their legal right to leave the country and return to it. In its issue for June 22, *The Daily Telegraph* quoted highly placed Turkish officials as saying they suspect the Soviet Union may be sanctioning the expulsions.

USSR Denies Involvement in Bulgarian "Expulsions"

TASS said the chairman of the Presidium of the Azerbaijani Supreme Soviet, Suleiman Tatliev, who publicly blamed Armenians for the bloodshed during ethnic unrest last year, had asked to be relieved of his duties at a session

President of Azerbaijan Resigns

of the republic's Supreme Soviet. Tatliev's replacement
was identified as Elmira Kafarova, previously a deputy
chairman of the Azerbaijani Council of Ministers.

"What Is the KGB Doing?"
Asks Soviet Citizen

In a letter to the editor of *Sovetskaya kul'tura*, a reader,
V. Vasil'ev of Penza, asked: "What is the KGB doing?" His
question was prompted by the recent riots in Uzbekistan,
where the law-enforcement agencies suddenly discovered that large numbers of the civilian population were
armed with automatic rifles and even heavy machine
guns. Vasil'ev questioned how so much weaponry could
have been secreted in the Soviet Union in peacetime,
adding: "Is it still fully preoccupied with tales of the
intelligentsia and with *samizdat?*" See RL 536/88.

Friday, June 23 ────────────────────────────────

Zhivkov in Moscow

Bulgarian State Council Chairman Todor Zhivkov arrived
in Moscow for talks with Mikhail Gorbachev. Zhivkov
later described the talks to reporters as fruitful, matter-of-
fact, and useful for the development of bilateral relations.
Reporting on the talks, TASS said Gorbachev had discussed Soviet problems in the social and economic
spheres and in interethnic relations. It said that Zhivkov
had briefed Gorbachev on Bulgaria's planned political reforms and that the two leaders had agreed no country
should imitate another without taking domestic conditions into consideration (*Pravda*, June 24).

USSR Approves Forty Family
Reunification Cases

The USSR told the United States that Moscow had approved forty longstanding family reunification requests.
The names were given to the US delegate at the Paris
human-rights conference, Morris Abram. Abram said it
was a positive move, but he reminded Soviet delegates
that they are required to resolve all outstanding family
reunification cases by July 15 under the terms of the
Vienna document signed in January of this year (*RFE/RL
Special*, June 23).

Soviet and Afghan Foreign
Ministers Meet

The Soviet and Afghan foreign ministers, Eduard Shevardnadze and Abdul Wakil, urged more international talks
towards settling the Afghan conflict. TASS said Shevardnadze and Wakil agreed at a meeting in Moscow that
participants in the talks should include the Soviet Union,

Pakistan, Iran, and "possibly other countries." TASS quoted Shevardnadze and Wakil as saying that, despite what they described as a massive onslaught by the Afghan resistance after the withdrawal of Soviet troops, the Kabul government's position was now stronger than ever before (*Pravda*, June 24).

Islam Karimov is the new first secretary of the Communist Party of Uzbekistan. Karimov had been first secretary of the Kashkadarya Oblast Party Committee since December, 1986. Radio Moscow said Karimov replaced Rafik Nishanov, who was elected chairman of the Council of Nationalities. Nishanov had been first secretary since January, 1988. See *Pravda*, June 24.

New Party First Secretary Chosen in Uzbekistan

Soviet human-rights activist Andrei Sakharov had a meeting in London with British Prime Minister Margaret Thatcher. A spokesman for Thatcher said they had mainly discussed internal events in the Soviet Union (*UPI*, June 23).

Sakharov Meets Thatcher

A society of Soviet Germans with the name "Revival" was established in the Kazakh capital of Alma-Ata. TASS said the society would chronicle events that concern Soviet Germans. TASS quoted the society's chairman, Adam Merts, as saying his organization would coordinate the activities of the recently established German socio-political clubs and act as a cultural center for Soviet Germans in Kazakhstan.

"Revival" Society of Soviet Germans Set Up in Kazakhstan

Saturday, June 24

In the first interview with USSR KGB Chairman Vladimir Kryuchkov to be broadcast on television, Soviet viewers were told that the KGB not only supported the creation of a Supreme Soviet committee to oversee the state security organs but that this idea had originated with the KGB itself. The prerecorded interview with Kryuchkov was screened on June 24 as part of the popular late-night program "Do i posle polunochi" (Before and After Midnight). In the course of the interview, Kryuchkov revealed some details of the present functions of his agency; he also answered public critics of the KGB and spoke about his own career and private life. Kryuchkov confirmed that the KGB was responsible only to the

First TV Interview with KGB Chairman

Politburo, but he said that his agency was fully accountable to the Party and the Supreme Soviet not only administratively but also financially. Discussing Yurii Vlasov's attacks on the KGB at the Congress of People's Deputies, Kryuchkov stated that, although he disagreed with Vlasov, he did understand his point of view. In Kryuchkov's view, Vlasov had spoken about the KGB as it was in the period between the 1930s and 1950s, not in 1989.

Yakovlev Interviewed on "Vremya"

The television news program "Vremya" screened an interview with Politburo member Aleksandr Yakovlev following his speech to the Soviet-American philosophical conference on the values of Western civilization. Yakovlev said Soviet economists had suggested that "the Socialist market" could not function in "an economy of shortages," adding that "some people need an economy of shortages" because the shortages give them power. "Any economy of shortages," Yakovlev explained, "creates a second, shadow economy." He implied that resistance to *perestroika* was a deliberate policy of certain influential forces, motivated by economic interests and a thirst for power. On June 27, TASS reported on another speech by Yakovlev. Addressing graduates of the CPSU Central Committee's Institute of Social Sciences in Moscow, he said that internal critics of the USSR had gone too far during the past four years. He said criticism of life in the Soviet Union was so harsh that it had frightened some within the country and some friends of the USSR abroad.

Gorbachev Protégé Rejected by Soviet Legislature

A legislative committee of the USSR Supreme Soviet rejected a protégé of Mikhail Gorbachev who had been nominated to head the government's food program, as well as two candidates for ministerial posts, the World Service of Radio Moscow reported. Vladimir Kalashnikov failed to win the Supreme Soviet Committee's endorsement to become first deputy prime minister after being nominated by Nikolai Ryzhkov, the chairman of the USSR Supreme Soviet, on June 10. Ryzhkov said Kalashnikov had vast experience of agriculture and should head a new government commission on food and purchases. The Supreme Soviet Committee also denied promotion to Polad Adzhievich from first deputy to minister of land reclamation and water resources. Vladimir Gribov was turned down for upgrading from his post as a department chief at Gosplan to chairmanship of the board of the USSR State Bank. Also rejected was the nomination of Vasilii

Zakharov to continue as culture minister, a post he had held for nearly three years. In a speech to the committee, Ryzhkov tried to explain why the Soviet Union was in "a very difficult situation." Ryzhkov said almost half the budget of 16 billion rubles in the present five-year plan had gone to pay debts. He said that these debts had accumulated since 1971 and that repayment had only started in the past year or two. He said some of the rest of the money (3 billion) had gone for nonplan items and that, to gain financial breathing space, the government had postponed some social programs (*TASS*, June 24; *Pravda*, June 25).

Resolution of Congress of People's Deputies

The Congress of People's Deputies issued a resolution saying work should begin without delay on a new constitution embodying "humane and democratic socialism" and recognizing the "inalienable human rights" to life, freedom, and self-determination (*Pravda* and *Izvestia*, June 25).

Armenian Supreme Soviet Sets Up Commission on Quake, Karabakh

The Armenian Supreme Soviet decided to form a deputies' commission to oversee work in the area hit by a devastating earthquake last December. The commission will also monitor implementation of Party and government decisions relating to the Nagorno-Karabakh Autonomous Oblast. At the session in Erevan, deputies demanded that members of unofficial organizations, such as the Karabakh Committee, be invited to take part in the Supreme Soviet discussion (*Radio Moscow-2*, 2200, June 24). Leaders of the committee, which is campaigning for the transfer of Nagorno-Karabakh to Armenia, were jailed in December and only released last month. Addressing the deputies, Armenian Party First Secretary Suren Arutyunyan said the Nagorno-Karabakh problem, along with the earthquake, had stripped the republic's economy bare and put extreme strains on society.

More Soviet Troops Leave Czechoslovakia

Radio Prague said more Soviet troops and military equipment had left Czechoslovakia for the Soviet Union. The radio reported the departure of a train carrying the last soldiers and vehicles of a battalion of engineers from the Moravian city of Olomouc for Belorussia. It said 1,500 Soviet soldiers along with 192 tanks and twenty fighter planes would be withdrawn from Czechoslovakia this year; two battalions have already returned to the Soviet Union from Olomouc alone.

Belorussian Popular Front Holds Founding Congress

Reports from Moscow said the Belorussian Popular Front had held its founding congress in the Lithuanian city of Vilnius over the weekend. DPA and AFP said more than 400 supporters of the front had met on June 23 and 24 and agreed on a platform based on political, economic, and cultural sovereignty for Belorussia. AFP said the meeting had elected a fifty-two-member committee to head the Belorussian Popular Front and agreed on plans to ask the Supreme Soviet for official recognition. Members elected include Belorussian writers, intellectuals, and representatives of youth organizations. Western correspondents in Moscow quoted a spokesman for the front as saying the meeting was held in Lithuania because it had not been possible to hold it in Belorussia. (The Belorussian authorities have been trying hard to suppress the informal group movement in the republic.)

Demonstration in Kishinev

A mass rally took place in Kishinev to mark the annexation of Moldavia by the USSR in June, 1940. Reuters and AFP reported that tens of thousands of people had taken part in the rally, at which some speakers denounced the incorporation of the territory that is now the Moldavian SSR into the USSR, demanded the resignation of the republic's leaders, and called for the restoration of territories ceded to the Ukrainian SSR. Others demanded that Moldavian be made a state language and be written in the Latin rather than the Cyrillic script.

Two Alternative Unofficial Groups Hold Congresses in Leningrad

Moscow News (No. 26) carried a report about the founding congress of the Leningrad Popular Front, which was held in the city beween June 17 and 18. The newspaper said that the congress was attended by 680 delegates elected from over 100 different unofficial pressure groups at factories, offices, and institutions in the city and oblast. Among leaders of the Leningrad Popular Front are liberal Leningrad intellectuals. More information on the front and its aims was given in the newspaper *Sovetskaya molodezh'* (June 22), which reported that among the informal groups that set up the Leningrad Popular Front were the "Memorial" and "*Perestroika*" societies as well as various ecological groups. The newspaper said that the Leningrad Popular Front was now the biggest unofficial organization in the RSFSR with about 7,000 members. *Sovetskaya molodezh'* disclosed that, in the coming elections to the local soviet in Leningrad, the city's popular front not only intended to support candidates with democratic platforms but also wanted to nominate its own. The newspaper indicated the popular front was concerned about the reactionary composition of the Leningrad Party organizations and intended to exert a positive influence on it through Communist members of the popular front.

Sovetskaya molodezh' also reported that a congress to found another unofficial group had been held in Leningrad. This new group is called the United Front of Workers. The newspaper said that, while the united front claimed that its aims were similar to those of the popular front, there were signs that caused worry. The congress of the United Front of Workers had as an honorary guest Nina Andreeva—author of the notorious "anti-*perestroika*" letter. (Support for reactionary groups, especially ones such as "Pamyat'" that draw on Russian nationalist sentiment, is very strong in Leningrad. *Leningradskaya pravda*, the organ of the Leningrad Party organization, has given a great deal of publicity to the United Front of Workers [*Leningradskaya pravda*, June 8 and 14].) On the formation of the two fronts, see also *Trud*, June 24.

The literary journal *Oktyabr'* published the late Vasilii Grossman's short novel *Vse techet* (All Is Flux), which was first written in 1963. The publication was a landmark for *glasnost'*—in his novel Grossman was very critical of Lenin's postrevolutionary policy, which he depicted as tyrannous. While criticism of Lenin has been permitted in the Soviet press since last year, the policies of the founder of the Soviet state still remain a very sensitive subject in the USSR. *Oktyabr'* announced its intention to publish the work last year (see RL 349/88).

Oktyabr' Publishes Grossman's Novel *Vse Techet*

Monday, June 26

On June 26, TASS quoted Vice President of the USSR Supreme Soviet Anatolii Luk'yanov as saying the live television and radio coverage of the proceedings of the Congress of People's Deputies resulted in a 20 percent fall in industrial output. According to an item in *Pravda* (June 23), it cost 40,000 rubles per hour to broadcast the proceedings of the Congress, with a total of 90 hours and 25 minutes of coverage broadcast. Consequently, live radio and television coverage of the Supreme Soviet's sessions from June 25 until August 4 was canceled.

Live Coverage of Supreme Soviet Canceled

According to TASS, some of "the most important meetings" would be recorded and broadcast in full outside working hours, and highlights of the proceedings would be broadcast during the evening news. This decision was made on June 25 by the Supreme Soviet deputies, several of whom complained that coverage of the Congress by "Vremya" had not been objective.

Composition of Committee to Oversee Army and KGB

On June 26, the Supreme Soviet approved the composition of a committee to oversee defense and state security, with Vladimir Lapygin as chairman (see RL 284/89). *The Baltimore Sun* (June 26) reported that the committee includes at least three top officials of the KGB: Ivan Gorelovsky and Veniamin Baluev, the chairmen of the republican state security committees of Kazakhstan and Belorussia, and V. Britvin, the chief of the Main Political Directorate of the Border Troops. In the course of the discussion, several deputies sharply criticized the makeup of the committee, complaining that it was dominated by defense-industry managers and military and KGB officers; despite the criticism, however, the proposed composition of the committee remained unchanged. Among the members whose names are known, Academician E. Velikhov and A. Gaponov-Grekhov both have close ties to the military-industrial complex. The membership also includes Gorbachev's chief military adviser, Marshal S. Akhromeev, Deputy Minister of Defense Genera V. Shabanov, and a model Afghan veteran, Colonel Ruslan Aushev. Even several of the workers on the committee are employed in the defense sector.

Chairman of Supreme Soviet Committee Backs Professional Army

Vladimir Lapygin, chairman of the newly created Committee on Defense and State Security of the USSR Supreme Soviet, said in an interview with *Izvestia* that he supported the idea of transforming the Soviet armed forces into a professional army. In Lapygin's opinion, such an army would be much better than the present one because recent generations of conscripts have been unable to cope with increasingly sophisticated military technology. Lapygin added that the cost of a professional army must be carefully studied. The high cost of a professional army was one of the main arguments advanced by the USSR's top military establishment for retaining conscription. A nationwide debate over reform in the armed forces was initiated last fall when journalist Artem Borovik urged viewers of the popular television program "Vzglyad" to discuss the matter. While giving general support to the idea of reforming the army, some top military command-ers who have participated in the debate have refrained from expressing their views on the subject of a profes-sional army, and others have opposed it. Several middle-level officers and a number of civilian political activists, however, have expressed their support for the idea (See *Vek XX i mir*, Nos. 9 and 10, 1988, and Nos. 1–4, 1989).

Gorbachev Criticized for Having Opposed Moscow Deputies

Tat'yana Ivanova took Gorbachev to task for his unkind treatment of Andrei Sakharov and other progressive Moscow intellectuals at the Congress of People's Depu-ties. In a long article entitled "The Intellect of the Nation?" published in *Knizhnoe obozrenie* (No. 24), the literary critic lambasted the "aggressively obedient majority" in the Congress of People's Deputies, as well as Gorbachev personally, who, she claimed, encouraged the illiberal voting of the majority.

Another Accident on Soviet Nuclear Submarine

A Soviet nuclear submarine caught fire in the early morning off the northern coast of Norway. Norwegian Defense Minister Johan Joergen Holst told state radio there was reason to believe that the submarine had nuclear weapons aboard (*Reuters, AP,* June 26). TASS quoted the submarine's commander as saying the vessel's reactor broke down and had to be shut off. AP quoted a spokesman for the Norwegian Northern Defense Com-mand as saying the command received a telex from Soviet authorities in Murmansk to say there was no danger of a radiation leak on board the submarine. TASS added that there were no casualties among the crew. Western agencies reported meanwhile that Norwegian officials had complained the USSR failed to notify them promptly of the submarine's accident. The Soviet authorities, however, were quick to allay fears. That evening, Soviet Defense Minister Dmitrii Yazov confirmed that the acci-dent on the Soviet nuclear submarine had caused no casualties and no radiation leak (*TASS,* June 26). Speaking on Soviet television, the commander in chief of the Soviet Navy, Vladimir Chernyavin, said the Soviet submarine was carrying both nuclear and conventional weapons. Chernyavin said the weapons were safe and were not connected with, or affected by, the accident (*Central Television,* June 26). On June 27, Admiral Kon-stantin Makarov claimed that there had been no fire aboard the Soviet submarine and that the clouds of smoke seen by Norwegian officials had been exhaust fumes (*TASS,* June 27).

Commission to Deal with Armenian and Azerbaijani Refugees

The Soviet government set up a special commission to deal with the return of Armenian and Azerbaijani refugees and possible compensation for their losses. Many thousands of Armenians living in Azerbaijan and Azerbaijanis resident in Armenia fled their homes during ethnic unrest over Nagorno-Karabakh. Radio Moscow said the commission was proposed by authorities in both republics.

Latvian Popular Front Member Says Secession Unrealistic

Andris Rucs, a member of the council of the independent Popular Front of Latvia, said it was unrealistic for Latvia to seek secession from the USSR. He said the real issue was to improve relations between individual republics and the central Soviet authorities. His remarks were published by *Pravda*, which said he was commenting on a recent appeal for front members to discuss whether their organization should seek Latvia's total political and economic independence. That appeal did not mention secession from the USSR.

Leading Economist Attacks *Pravda*

On June 26, *Izvestia* published an article by Academician Stanislav Shatalin that lambasted *Pravda* for its recent articles on the economy. Citing three articles that have appeared in *Pravda* since April 10, 1989, Shatalin accused the newspaper of having begun a crusade against *perestroika*. Shatalin also accused some contributors to *Pravda*—Academician V. Semenikhin, D. Valovoi and A. Chekalin—of participating in the current "witch hunt" against progressive economists, such as Leonid Abalkin, who was recently appointed USSR deputy prime minister with responsibility for economic reforms. The article was part of the continuing dispute between the editors of *Pravda* and *Izvestia*, with the latter appearing to be the victor.

Afghan Resistance Talks with USSR about War Prisoners

Soviet diplomats and Afghan resistance leaders meeting in Pakistan reported progress in talks on the release of prisoners captured during the Afghan war, but they disagreed on the extent of progress. AP and Reuters quoted resistance leaders as saying the Soviet representatives had agreed on a direct exchange of prisoners of war. A statement from the Soviet embassy in Islamabad, however, said only that progress was made and that the Soviet Union was committed to discussing the release of captured resistance forces with the Afghan government. The Soviet Union had previously said it was not responsible for prisoners of war held by the Afghan government.

Lithuanian Party First Secretary Algirdas Brazauskas arrived for three days of talks in Warsaw with Politburo member Jozef Czyrek. Brazauskas was invited to Poland by the Central Committee of the Polish Party (*Radio Warsaw*, June 26). PAP said on June 25 that Brazauskas' talks were to cover the Polish minority in Lithuania and the Lithuanian minority in Poland. Upon his arrival in Warsaw, Brazauskas told Radio Warsaw that Lithuania wanted to establish its own diplomatic representation in Poland.

Lithuanian Party First Secretary Holds Talks in Warsaw

A team of sixteen experts from the International Atomic Energy Agency said the design concept of the Gorky nuclear district heating plant was "sound." The Vienna-based agency said its review of the Gorky facility was being conducted at the request of Soviet authorities. The design concept was completed at the Kurchatov Institute in Moscow. A review of the plant's construction and preparation for operation is to take place in Gorky itself in August. The inspectors, including Western experts, said the review to date indicated that the basic design of the plant included the essential features required for safe operation (*RFE/RL Special*, June 26).

Inspectors Say Gorky Nuclear Plant Design Safe

―――――――――――――――――――――――――― *Tuesday, June 27*

Yurii Zhurkin, deputy minister of the USSR Ministry of Internal Affairs, stated at a press conference on June 27 (*TASS*, June 27) that many units of the MVD were still unable to operate effectively in the new conditions in which they found themselves—facing organized crime, corruption, and nationalist disturbances. Zhurkin stated that in future the training of rank-and-file policemen would last ten months instead of four. He added that special programs of action to cope with interethnic conflicts were being studied on refresher courses at the MVD Academy and in all the educational institutions under the ministry. In the republican MVD and internal affairs departments, efforts were being made to improve knowledge of the local language among the police.

MVD Introduces Training Program to Deal with Interethnic Conflicts

The USSR Supreme Soviet debated whether to endorse the cabinet proposed by Prime Minister Nikolai Ryzhkov. Six of his nominees had been turned down earlier by various committees of the Supreme Soviet. TASS disclosed that Ryzhkov decided not to insist on those nomi-

USSR Supreme Soviet Debates Ryzhkov's Nominations

nations but to propose new candidates instead. TASS said it was the first time in Soviet history that parliamentary deputies had turned down candidates for government posts. On June 28, the USSR Supreme Soviet confirmed economist Leonid Abalkin as a deputy prime minister and head of a new economic reform commission (*TASS*, June 28). Speaking the same day on Soviet television, Ryzhkov said he could not find anybody who wanted to be the USSR environmental protection minister—he had asked four people to take the job, and they had all refused. Ryzhkov said the head of the Soviet State Committee for Environmental Protection for the past fifteen months, Fedor Morgun, wanted to retire.

More Than 20,000 Troops Keeping Peace in Soviet Republics

Deputy chief of MVD Troops, Major General Yurii Alekseev, said more than 20,000 Soviet MVD troops were at present assigned to deal with outbreaks of unrest across the country, most of them in Uzbekistan. Alekseev told a news briefing in Moscow that several thousand troops were deployed in Armenia and Azerbaijan. He added that in the Fergana Valley of Uzbekistan about 12,000 troops were assigned to preventing a repetition of the riots in June in which 100 people died (*Reuters*, June 27).

Moscow Announces Death of KGB Agent

Krasnaya zvezda reported the sudden death the week before of a thirty-three-year-old man said to be a long-time KGB agent. It published an obituary issued by the Collegium of the KGB that identified the man as Mikhail Orlov. The FBI in Washington identified him as Glenn Michael Souther, who was dishonorably discharged from the US Navy in 1982. He disappeared in May, 1986, after graduating from a university in Virginia with a degree in Russian. Reports at the time said he was under investigation for espionage (*Reuters*, *AP*, June 27). KGB Chairman Vladimir Kryuchkov disclosed to reporters covering the Supreme Soviet session that Souther had committed suicide and had been buried on June 27 (see *The Guardian*, June 28).

Moscow Seeks Diplomatic Solution on Bulgaria's Ethnic Turks

According to the Soviet ambassador to Ankara, the Soviet Union sought a diplomatic solution to the dispute between Turkey and Bulgaria over the exodus of ethnic Turks from Bulgaria (*Reuters*, June 27). More than 72,000 ethnic Turks fled to Turkey this month to escape a forced assimilation campaign involving up to two million members of Bulgaria's mainly Muslim minority. Soviet Ambassador

Albert Chernyshev returned to Ankara on June 26 from a four-day visit to the USSR and Sofia, during which he met Bulgarian leader Todor Zhivkov.

Soviet Newspaper Says Mayor of Novyi Uzen' Replaced

The newspaper *Trud* reported the replacement of the mayor of the Kazakh town of Novyi Uzen', the scene of recent ethnic violence. The newspaper said that on June 24 the Novyi Uzen' City Soviet elected D. Zhumashev as the new chairman of the Soviet's executive committee, while a plenum of the Novyi Uzen' Party Committee elected a new first secretary, identified as R. Cherdabaev.

Chebrikov Urges Crackdown on Opposition Groups

Viktor Chebrikov, a member of the CPSU Politburo, said harsh measures should be taken against unofficial groups that try to discredit the CPSU. TASS said Chebrikov told a meeting of aviation workers in Moscow that, while some criticism of the Party was justified, various anti-Socialist groups were trying to discredit the Party and the idea of *perestroika*. Chebrikov said that it should be clear that the CPSU was the only force capable of leading the USSR out of the present crisis. In a lengthy article in *Kommunist* (No. 8) devoted to legal reforms in the USSR, Chebrikov developed a similar theme. He complained about the current "activation of forces [in the USSR] that do not conceal their animosity towards socialism and put themselves in opposition to the CPSU."

_____ *Wednesday, June 28*

Soviet Ambassador Quoted on Possible Socialist "Neutrality"

Hungary's MTI news agency quoted the Soviet ambassador to Budapest, Boris Stukalin, as saying neutrality was not appropriate to a Communist country as long as NATO and the Warsaw Pact existed. He was speaking at a forum in Budapest sponsored by the Hungarian Communist Party. There has been public discussion in both Hungary and the USSR about the possibility that Hungary might choose neutrality and still stay within the Warsaw Pact.

_____ *Thursday, June 29*

Ryzhkov on Poor State of Consumer Market

Soviet Prime Minister Nikolai Ryzhkov said he fully agreed with complaints about the poor state of the country's consumer market. Speaking on Radio Moscow, Ryzhkov said he was not happy to hear the government's performance come under criticism, but he said he agreed that the problems facing consumers were bad. He said the government had worked out a program to improve labor efficiency and the supply of consumer goods. Ryzhkov's comments were broadcast on the radio between sittings of the Supreme Soviet, where deputies have criticized many aspects of the government's work (*Radio Moscow World Service*, June 29).

Aganbegyan on Need to Improve Living Standards

Soviet economist Abel' Aganbegyan said that Soviet citizens deserved a better standard of living but that they would need to wait two to three years for better supplies of food and consumer goods. Aganbegyan, an adviser to Mikhail Gorbachev, told a Brussels seminar that *perestroika* had not yet produced the economic results expected, partly because of early mistakes. A similar point was made on June 28 by Leonid Abalkin, chairman of the Soviet State Committee on Economic Reform and a deputy prime minister (*TASS, Reuters*, June 29).

Vladimir Gusev Criticizes Soviet Medicine

Soviet Deputy Prime Minister Vladimir Gusev said it was shameful that the Soviet Union could provide only about 40 percent of the medicines it needed. Gusev was speaking to Radio Moscow following his confirmation by the Supreme Soviet as a deputy prime minister and head of the government Bureau for the Chemical and Timber Complex. He said prompt and proper development of the chemical industry was urgently needed. Apart from the "shameful" shortfall in medicines, he said the shortage of newsprint was a disgrace and also referred to shortages of furniture and paint (*Radio Moscow-2*, 1730, June 29).

Moscow Renames Troops Stationed in GDR

The Soviet Defense Ministry has decided to give a new title to Soviet forces stationed in East Germany. They will be called the "Western Group of Forces." Until now, they have been called the "Group of Soviet Forces in Germany." TASS said the new title would have no effect on obligations assumed under accords and decisions concluded during and after World War II by the USSR, United States, Britain, and France. Soviet troops in Poland are already called the "Northern Group of Forces," in Czechoslovakia—the "Central Group of Forces," and in Hungary—the "Southern Group of Forces."

Mehdi Mamedov, a scholar and a journalist on the staff of *Bakinsky rabochii*, reported the release from prison of Ne'mat Panahov and Muhammed Hatemi, who emerged as popular leaders during the large public meetings in Baku in November and December, 1988. According to reports made to Radio Liberty's Azerbaijani Service by telephone, the Azerbaijani State Prosecutor's Office was continuing its investigation of the activities of both men. Ne'mat Panakhov, a twenty-six-year-old blue-collar worker, had been in jail since he was arrested on December 8, 1988. Muhammed Hatemi, a historian at the Azerbaijani Academy of Sciences, was also arrested in December, 1988. Bakhtiyar Shakhverdiev, who made flags of independent Azerbaijan and took them to the Baku meetings, was released from jail a few days ago. He had been arrested in January, 1989.

Popular Leaders Released in Baku

Friday, June 30

Nikolai Ryzhkov said he was sure that the country's economic and social development would accelerate because of the work of the new Supreme Soviet. In an interview with *Izvestia*, he expressed hope for the future efficiency of the government now that there was a parliament ready to take responsibility for key decisions, and he said he believed there was an opportunity to agree on common positions that would lead the country on the road to social and economic development. On the final day of the joint session of the USSR Supreme Soviet before reconvening on July 3, Eduard Shevardnadze was unanimously confirmed as foreign minister and Vitalii Doguzhiev approved as a deputy prime minister and head of a new state commission for emergencies. Nikolai Laverov was approved as deputy prime minister in charge of science and technology. Mikhail Shkabardya became the Council of Ministers' business manager (*TASS*, June 30).

Ryzhkov Interviewed by *Izvestia*, Joint Session of Supreme Soviet Ends

Soviet television reported in its news program "Vremya" that Soviet scientists had formed an independent association called the Union of Scientists of the USSR. According to "Vremya," the new body's founding congress ended in Moscow on June 30. Speakers at the congress were quoted as saying the prestige of Soviet science had suffered because pressure from the authorities had produced a type of pseudoscientist who covered up decisions that caused harm to the public. One of the partici-

Independent Association of Soviet Scientists Formed

337

pants in the congress, A. M. Elyashevich, said the new association was not meant to be an alternative to the USSR Academy of Sciences but simply a new form for the organization of scholarly work. The plan to set up the Union of Scientists of the USSR was first disclosed in the Soviet media by corresponding member of the USSR Academy of Sciences Aleksei Yablokov when he spoke on Soviet television on April 20. He emphasized that the new organization should be independent of the USSR Academy of Sciences, whose leadership he saw as having discredited itself when it initially rejected Sakharov, Sagdeev, and other leading reformers as candidates for elections to the Congress of People's Deputies. In his remarks, Yablokov disclosed that he expected the Union of Scientists of the USSR to become the largest Soviet scientific organization (*Moscow News*, No. 23).

Estonian Miners' Strike Ends after Demands Met

TASS reported the ending of a miners' strike at an Estonian shale mine that began on June 29. TASS said the strike at the Ahtme pit of the Estonslanec enterprise ended after the workers' demand that one of the mine's nine sections be shut down was met. TASS said that workers of three sections of the pit went below ground on June 29 but refused to work. The miners said that they would not return to the surface until demands were met. The strikers were joined by miners of the morning workshift. The miners wanted closure of one of the pit's sections because of a lack of transport facilities inside the mine that left workers standing idle and unable to make normal earnings. TASS reported the resumption of normal work in the shale mine by that night.

KGB Deputy Chairman on Respect for Law

In an interview published by *Nedelya* (No. 26), Vladimir Pirozhkov, one of the deputies to USSR KGB Chairman Vladimir Kryuchkov, said that the KGB was putting a new emphasis on the legal training of its staff. Distancing the present state security organization from the atrocities of Stalin's NKVD, Pirozhkov claimed that in the KGB there was "not a single staffer who participated in the crimes of the Stalinist period." He also tried to stress the role of the KGB in the rehabilitation of the victims of the Stalinist terror. Pirozhkov, a member of the working group of the Politburo commission on rehabilitations, stated that during 1988 and the first quarter of 1989 the commission had rehabilitated 47,000 persons who suffered repressions under Stalin. The KGB is represented on the commission, which is chaired by senior Politburo member Aleksandr Yakovlev, and by present and former top officials such as Viktor Chebrikov, Vladimir Kryuchkov, and Boris Pugo.

Cooperatives Open First Congress, Urge Lower Taxes

The first national congress of cooperatives in the Soviet Union opened in Moscow, with speakers calling for lower taxes. The congress came one day before a new ruling on the taxation of the earnings of cooperatives took effect. A Supreme Soviet Presidium ruling published in February allowed republics to set their own tax rates for cooperatives. The Supreme Soviet last year rejected government proposals to impose taxes of up to 90 percent on cooperatives' profits. Private cooperatives were introduced under Gorbachev as a way of easing shortages of food and other goods and services. One delegate told the congress that over 100,000 cooperatives had already been set up in the USSR (*TASS*, June 30).

Tallinn Conference Evaluates 1939 Pacts

An international conference of scholars opened in the Estonian capital of Tallinn with the purpose of making a legal assessment of the treaties signed by Germany and the USSR in August and September, 1939. The treaties and their once secret protocols led to the division of Poland between the USSR and Nazi Germany and the annexation by the Soviet Union of the Baltic republics, Bessarabia, and Northern Bukovina. Scholars from Moscow, Estonia, Latvia, Lithuania, Ukraine, Poland, West Germany, and Finland attended the meeting.

USSR Backs Arab Peace Efforts on Lebanon

Pravda reported that Mikhail Gorbachev supported the Arab League's efforts to bring peace to Lebanon. According to *Pravda*, Gorbachev also indicated the USSR's willingness to discuss Lebanon with Syria and Iraq. The newspaper said Gorbachev met with Moroccan Foreign Minister Abdellatif Filali in Moscow on June 29. Filali, who represents an Arab League committee trying to end the conflict in Lebanon, appealed to Moscow to use its influence with Syria and Iraq to bring peace.

USSR and US Make Progress on Chemical Weapons Ban

A Soviet official said the United States and the Soviet Union had resolved months of disagreement over monitoring procedures for on-site inspections of chemical weapons sites. The official, who briefed reporters in Geneva on condition he remain anonymous, said the two sides had drafted a joint document setting out procedures for "challenge inspections." Max Friedersdorf, the chief US delegate, said, however, that the Soviet statements were "premature and exaggerated" and that, while the three-week talks had made some progress, "fundamental differences" remained. Friedersdorf cautioned that any bilateral agreement would be reviewed in Washington to decide whether it should be submitted to the forty-nation Geneva conference on disarmament, which is negotiating a global chemical weapons ban (*AP*, *DPA*, *Reuters*, June 30).

USSR and France Sign Managerial Training Agreement

The USSR and France signed an agreement on cooperation in the training of business managers. The French Foreign Ministry said the agreement covered the period 1989-90 and addressed the the granting of French scholarships in particular. France already has similar agreements with other Warsaw Pact countries, including Poland (*AFP*, June 30).

The Month of July

Mikhail Gorbachev went on national television to say the fate of the Soviet Union depended largely on solving the question of interethnic relations. He said no citizen could fail to be concerned about the intolerance, friction, and conflict that have arisen between various ethnic groups. He spoke of "the tremendous danger" of ethnic conflict and said the authorities had been obliged to take firm measures against those who provoke ethnic clashes, call for borders to be redrawn, or demand the expulsion of minorities (*Izvestia*, July 2).

Gorbachev Addresses the Nation on Nationalities Issue

An international conference in Tallinn to investigate the 1939 pact between the Soviet Union and Nazi Germany ended. According to TASS, the conference concluded that the Molotov-Ribbentrop Pact should be declared null and void. The conference also said the pact and its secret protocol were directed against third countries and their sovereignty, political independence, and territorial inviolability. The conclusions of the conference were forwarded to the commission on the Molotov-Ribbentrop Pact created by the Congress of People's Deputies. On the conference, see *Sovetskaya molodezh'*, July 5 and 7.

Tallinn Conference on 1939 Nazi-Soviet Pact Ends

On July 14, the Estonian Popular Front demanded that the Supreme Soviets of Estonia and the USSR declare the Molotov-Ribbentrop Pact invalid. A spokesman for the front in Tallinn told Reuters that a petition denouncing the secret protocol to the pact had been forwarded to Estonian deputies in the USSR Supreme Soviet and to the parliament as a whole. See RL 333/89.

MVD troops and extra police were deployed in parts of Georgia because of rising ethnic tensions. *Izvestia* said that lately relations between Georgians and Azerbaijanis in Georgia had become "complicated." The newspaper said more than 3,000 police and troops had been sent to the Marneuli, Bolnissi, and Dmanissi districts southwest of Tbilisi, where their duties were to patrol roads and keep order in towns and villages. The newspaper also reported

Forces Sent to Counter Georgian-Azerbaijani Ethnic Unrest

341

the confiscation of about 500 weapons by the police, adding that people wanted a quick end to the conflict and were helping the authorities.

Vorotnikov Speaks in Chelyabinsk

Speaking to local officials in Chelyabinsk, Politburo member Vitalii Vorotnikov said some people were using *perestroika* as a cloak to oppose socialism. He said that those who genuinely supported *perestroika* and far-reaching reforms were in the majority but that there were also "pseudodemocrats" who hid their anti-Socialist intentions behind the appearance of support for restructuring. He did not identify any particular groups or individuals, but he said their influence on society must not be underestimated (*TASS*, July 1; *Izvestia*, July 2).

Pravda Criticizes Leadership in Belorussia

Pravda fiercely criticized the Party and government of Belorussia for aloofness, intolerance, and lack of democracy, and it mentioned Party First Secretary Efrem Sokolov by name. The attack seems to have been prompted by the refusal of the Belorussian authorities to allow the Belorussian Popular Front to hold its founding congress in Minsk (the congress was held in Vilnius instead), a decision that *Pravda* considered symptomatic of the Belorussian leadership's inflexible approach to popular movements. The use of such "outdated methods," the article said, could lead to popular discontent. *Pravda* also condemned "the continuing crude attacks" on author Vasyl Bykov and said that, with respect to the Belorussian language question, "the Vatican has moved faster" than the republican government. The Vatican has already produced a Belorussian version of the Bible. This unusual dressing down in print of a republican Party leader appointed by Gorbachev may be seen as an indication of the urgency of Moscow's desire to eliminate sources of friction in the non-Russian republics.

Officials Ignored Safety Warnings about Urals Pipeline

The head of a criminal investigation into the fatal explosion of a gas pipeline in the Urals on June 4 said those in charge of the pipeline ignored safety warnings prior to the catastrophe. The blast east of the city of Ufa engulfed two passing trains, killing at least 500 people and injuring hundreds more. *Pravda* disclosed that the Tyumen Oblast prosecutor had warned the pipeline authorities about safety twice—the first time in August, 1988, and the second time only weeks before the explosion.

An article by liberal Soviet historian Evgenii Ambartsumov in _Moscow News_ (No. 27) said the Soviet Union and Nikita Khrushchev personally were "guilty" of the execution of former Hungarian Prime Minister Imre Nagy in 1958. Ambartsumov wrote that Khrushchev was "unable to overcome his ingrained Stalinism" and approved the execution. Ambartsumov also praised Nagy for refusing to betray his belief in "socialism with a human face," despite the prospect of death. Another attack on Khrushchev, this time from conservatives, appeared in _Sovetskaya Rossiya_. The article was written by Anatolii Ponomarev, a specialist in the history of the Moscow City Party organization and a deputy director of the Institute of the History of the Party attached to the Moscow City Party organization. Ponomarev's article implied that Khrushchev was no better than Stalin's other associates. Ponomarev described Khrushchev as part of a group loyal to Stalin who entered the leadership as a result of their active fight against rightists. Quoting previously inaccessible archive materials, Ponomarev said Khrushchev told a Moscow Party meeting in 1937 that the Party should "step over the dead bodies" of its enemies for the sake of the people.

Historian Indicts Khrushchev

Izvestia commentator Aleksandr Bovin said the Soviet Union should make sure it did not make the same mistakes that were made in China, where the army was used against students. Bovin said China tried economic reforms without enough political change whereas the USSR was making political changes without enough economic reform "and the results could be the same." He also said Western countries looked at what happened in China and thought twice about helping the USSR because of the fear that "today there is Gorbachev, but tomorrow there may be tanks." On July 6, a group of people staged a rally outside the Chinese embassy in Moscow to protest against the methods used against demonstrators in China (_Radio Moscow_, 1100, July 7).

Commentator Urges USSR to Learn from What Happened in China

Western reporters said the USSR Writers' Union had recommended that Aleksandr Solzhenitsyn's epic on the labor camps, _Gulag Archipelago_, be published in the USSR. Reuters and AP said the union's leadership had voted unanimously for publication at a meeting on

Writers Union Recommends Publication of _Gulag Archipelago_

June 30. The union also urged the authorities to rehabilitate Solzhenitsyn and restore his Soviet citizenship. Meanwhile, the Estonian literary journal *Looming* began publishing Solzhenitsyn's *Gulag Archipelago* (*Reuters*, *UPI*,
July 3. See also *Literaturnaya Rossiya*, July 7).

**Union of United
Cooperatives Formed**

The first national congress of cooperatives in the Soviet
Union concluded its work in Moscow and appealed to the
USSR Supreme Soviet to suspend a decree on progressive
taxation of cooperatives. TASS said the congress also
drew attention to the need to regulate relations between
cooperatives and the state and to assist the Ministry of
Internal Affairs in combating racketeering. A new all-
Union organization was founded whose main work will
be the development of an infrastructure for cooperatives.

**Gorbachev Attacks Those
Resisting New Agricultural
Policy**

Mikhail Gorbachev said officials at all levels who resisted
new agricultural policies could face "the appropriate personnel policy." Gorbachev made his remarks at a meeting
on agriculture held on June 30 by top Soviet officials immediately after an address by agricultural chief Egor Ligachev, who was quoted as saying he still believed in the
collective farm system as the backbone of Soviet agriculture (*TASS*, July 2; *Izvestia*, July 3). On previous occasions,
Ligachev has defended collective farms as preferable to
the leasing of land to those who farm it, which is
advocated by Gorbachev.

**Mass Grave of Victims of
Stalin's Purges Found
Near Leningrad**

Trud (July 2 and 5) published reports on the discovery, by
representatives of the Leningrad branch of the "Memorial"
society, of a mass grave of victims of Stalin's purges near
Leningrad. The mass grave is in the settlement of Levashovo close to Leningrad. *Trud* (July 2) reported that the
Leningrad authorities and the KGB had known about the
grave for a long time but had initially attempted to prevent
journalists and informal activists from inspecting the site.
Trud (July 5) said that the city Soviet, with its conservative
chairman Vladimir Khodyrev, had decided to take the
initiative in commemorating victims of Stalin's purges. In
an interview with *Trud* (July 5) Khodyrev said that a monument would be built on the site of the Levashovo mass
grave. In both reports the newspaper mentioned that
there are other (unidentified) mass graves of victims of
purges in the Leningrad Oblast. Leningrad was one of the
cities that suffered the most severe purges in the early
post-revolutionary years as well as during Stalin's time.

Andrei Gromyko Dies

The Soviet media reported the death of former Soviet Foreign Minister and President Andrei Gromyko in Moscow at the age of seventy-nine (_Pravda_, July 4). Gromyko's official obituary, signed by the Party and state leadership, was read on Soviet television. He was praised as a major political figure who served his country long and faithfully through a difficult stage in its development. On July 5, Gromyko was buried. RSFSR President Vitalii Vorotnikov was the highest-ranking Soviet official present and the only Politburo member to attend the funeral.

Yazov Reappointed as Defense Minister

Some Supreme Soviet deputies voiced disapproval of Defense Minister Dmitrii Yazov, but a majority confirmed his reappointment at the urging of Mikhail Gorbachev (_Pravda_, July 4). Gorbachev said that Yazov had played a considerable personal role in restructuring the Soviet armed forces and that he needed Yazov with him at the Warsaw Pact summit scheduled to meet in Bucharest on July 7. TASS said some deputies criticized Yazov for not paying enough attention to improving the living conditions of Soviet soldiers. See RL 315/89.

Radical to Chair Commission on Tbilisi Events

Reuters quoted a report in the Georgian daily _Zarya Vostoka_ as stating that Leningrad lawyer Anatolii Sobchak had been elected chairman of the commission set up by the Congress of People's Deputies to investigate the violence in Tbilisi on April 9. Sobchak was one of the most radical antiestablishment spokesmen during debates at the Congress and in the sessions of the USSR Supreme Soviet, of which he is also a member.

Yazov Excludes Possibility of Military Coup in USSR

Soviet defense minister Dmitrii Yazov said a military coup was out of the question in the USSR. He told Radio Moscow's World Service that the army was charged with defending the country and had "no intention whatsoever of staging a coup." Yazov said control of the military by the Defense Council made talk of a coup "irrelevant."

New Currency for Comecon Proposed

An article in _Pravda_ proposed that Comecon create a new currency for use in trade between Socialist countries. The proposal came from a Polish finance professor, Urszula Wojzechowska, and the Soviet economist Ninel Bautina.

They proposed that a new currency, the chervonets, be issued by the USSR State Bank and sold to Comecon countries for trade within Comecon. The original chervonets was a gold-backed currency used in the USSR in the 1920s.

Turkish Minister Discusses Trade, Credits in Moscow

Turkish and Soviet delegations met in Moscow to discuss increased bilateral trade and trade credits for the USSR (*Pravda*, July 4). TASS said the delegations agreed there should be an increase in bilateral trade based on the USSR trading oil for Turkish consumer goods. The Turkish delegation was headed by Finance Minister Ekrem Pakdemirli. On July 4, Pakdemirli went to Baku to discuss increasing direct trade ties with Azerbaijan (*TASS*, July 4). On July 7, the Anatolian news agency said Turkey and the USSR had signed an accord in Ankara on regulating border trade. The report said Pakdemirli and USSR Minister for Foreign Economic Relations Konstantin Katushev signed the accord. Katushev was quoted as saying the USSR is interested in trading Soviet heavy-industry products for light-industry goods from Turkey (*RFE/RL Special*, July 7).

Central Committee Criticizes Memorial Work for Stalin Victims

The CPSU Central Committee said not enough work was being done in some parts of the USSR to honor the victims of Stalinist repressions. TASS quoted a Central Committee resolution recommending that republican and oblast authorities speed up the work to honor the memory of Stalin's victims, including those who died in internal exile. The Central Committee called for the places where the victims were buried to be marked as official cemeteries and for memorials to be built there; see *Pravda*, July 4.

Shmelev on Soviet Economy

Soviet economist Nikolai Shmelev said the Soviet economy needed hard currency worth 30 billion dollars over the next two or three years to avoid a financial crisis. He said that the money should be put to use to modernize Soviet industry and reduce inflation and that the USSR could borrow the money or use its gold reserves and cut imports of meat and grain (*Reuters*, July 3).

Tuesday, July 4 ———————————————————————

Gorbachev's Visit to France

Mikhail Gorbachev began a three-day visit to France for talks with French President Francois Mitterrand (*Radio Moscow, Reuters, UPI*, July 4). At a dinner in Gorbachev's honor the same evening, Mitterrand endorsed Gorbachev's call for "a common European home" but said all people living in it had to be free. Outside the Soviet embassy, a crowd of at least 2,000 Armenian émigrés demanded that Gorbachev meet with them to discuss the conditions under which their compatriots are living in the Armenian SSR. French and Soviet officials signed the first eleven of a number of economic and scientific agreements (*TASS, AP*, July 4).

On July 5, Gorbachev spoke to French intellectuals and also had a brief meeting with conservative opposition leader Jacques Chirac (*Reuters, UPI*, July 5). In his speech at the Sorbonne, Gorbachev compared the impact of the French Revolution with changes going on in the Soviet Union. Regarding China, he said that the bloodshed in Tiananmen Square was very saddening and that he hoped the Chinese government would engage in dialogue with society. Gorbachev and Mitterrand also issued a joint statement calling for a cease-fire in Lebanon and for steps to effectively end arms supplies to all Lebanese groups involved in the civil war there (*Reuters*, July 5). At a joint press conference later, Gorbachev said *perestroika* carried the risk that someone might exploit the opportunity to destabilize the country. He called the situation in the USSR complex and fragile, referring too to the complexity of nationality problems, but he denied that reforms were a rejection of communism (Western agencies, July 5).

On July 6, Gorbachev delivered a speech at the Council of Europe in Strasbourg, during which he offered more unilateral cuts in Soviet short-range nuclear missiles in Europe if NATO agreed to talks on their complete elimination. He said the Soviet Union wanted total nuclear disarmament and also a radical reduction in conventional weapons. Expanding on this theme, he said the Soviet Union wanted to see the liquidation of all chemical arms, the withdrawal of all troops stationed in foreign countries, and the dismantling of military blocs. He declared that security issues were primary in his philosophy of "a common European home," which he said meant that the European community should stretch from the Atlantic to the Urals (*Reuters, AFP*, July 6). In response, NATO said its negotiating position on short-range nuclear weapons was unchanged by Gorbachev's latest proposal. NATO said its position was that a partial reduction in these weapons could be negotiated only when agreed cuts in conventional arms had started (*Reuters, AP*, July 6). On Gorbachev's visit, see *Pravda*, July 5–7.

Supreme Soviet Continues Debate on Cabinet Appointments

In the USSR Supreme Soviet, debate continued on the new government proposed by Prime Minister Nikolai Ryzhkov. TASS said discussion began with the nomination of Ivan Silaev for the last of the deputy prime ministerships. TASS said the decision to change the voting rules of the Supreme Soviet would have a positive influence on discussion of personnel issues. The new rules allow a minister to be confirmed by a majority of the deputies attending a session instead of a majority of all 542 members, which is difficult to achieve because many deputies have other duties. TASS blamed the old rule requiring a 272-vote majority for the failure of Vladimir Kamentsev to win confirmation last week as deputy prime minister; however, Kamentsev's nomination for the post of deputy prime minister and chairman of the State Foreign Economic Commission was again rejected today. TASS said there was tough debate before deputies rejected him. Some deputies said they doubted his ability to carry out radical changes in Soviet foreign-trade policy (*Pravda*, July 5).

On July 5, the Supreme Soviet approved another group of government ministers, including a cousin of Leonid Brezhnev, Vladimir Brezhnev. He was approved with eight other new ministers. The Supreme Soviet rejected a second nominee for the government of Nikolai Ryzhkov—the minister of railways, Nikolai Konarev, who failed to win reappointment after deputies heard criticism of the state of the USSR's railways, railroad safety, and the quality of passenger service (*TASS*, July 5). On July 6, at the request of Nikolai Ryzhkov, the USSR Supreme Soviet approved five more ministers after it had postponed consideration of the list of ministers for cabinet posts. Supreme Soviet deputies also criticized the USSR Supreme Court, accusing it of inconsistency. TASS reported that the deputies rejected the nomination of Sergei Gusev as first deputy chairman of the Supreme Court on the grounds that he had been a "conspicuous" figure in the judiciary before *perestroika* (*Pravda*, July 6).

On July 7, the Supreme Soviet confirmed Aleksei Vasil'ev as first deputy prosecutor general. TASS said Ivan Abramov, Janis Dzenitis, Vladimir Andreev, and Aleksandr Katusev were confirmed as deputy prosecutor generals (*Pravda*, July 8).

Minister Criticizes Bush's Call for Soviet Withdrawal from Poland

Soviet Foreign Minister Eduard Shevardnadze criticized a call by US President George Bush for Soviet troops to be withdrawn from Poland. Shevardnadze said in Paris that Bush's idea was neither original nor properly thought through. A limited number of the 40,000 Soviet troops in Poland are being withdrawn as part of a partial Soviet pullout from Eastern Europe. Bush said a full withdrawal could be a step towards the removal of all foreign forces from the continent. Shevardnadze told reporters he agreed that all foreign troops should go, but he asked why US soldiers should not leave the Philippines, South Korea, and West Germany (*Reuters, AFP*, July 4).

Law on Individual Farming Passed in Lithuania

TASS reported that the Lithuanian Supreme Soviet had passed a law guaranteeing farmers the right to manage farm holdings independently. Although the law stops short of permitting formal private ownership of land, it allows an individual farmer to use land permanently allotted to him by the state without lease payments and to pass the land on to his descendants. It also gives him the right to hire outside labor. The Lithuanian law differs in some ways from the similar law passed in Latvia in May of this year: Lithuanian independent farmers are explicitly restricted in the amount of land they can hold (50 hectares), whereas their Latvian counterparts are not. Other differences in the Lithuanian law are limits on the use of land (the Latvian law requires that it be used specifically for agricultural production), limits on hiring labor (the Latvian law only permits temporary hiring of outside labor at peak harvest time), and provision of legal protection for farmers' property.

Aeroflot to Get Competition

Soviet Civil Aviation Minister Aleksandr Volkov said he was going to set up a second government-run airline to end Aeroflot's monopoly. Volkov announced the plan during a debate in the Supreme Soviet but gave no details. Volkov was reappointed by the Supreme Soviet despite criticism from former Moscow City Party First Secretary Boris El'tsin. TASS quoted El'tsin as saying that the industry had done nothing to improve working conditions and repair facilities and was not providing adequate service to remote areas. Volkov promised a package of measures to improve Soviet air passenger service, including the early introduction of new planes. He blamed Aeroflot's current problems on shortages of modern planes and fuel and insufficient ground facilities (*Izvestia*, July 5).

List of Ethnic Groups Expanded to 400

TASS said a Soviet researcher had found far more ethnic groups in the USSR than did the census taken six months previously. The researcher identified 400 ethnic groups, whereas the last census counted only 128. The list of 400 groups was compiled for the Soviet Cultural Foundation by Fedor Klimchuk, an employee of the Belorussian Academy of Sciences. Klimchuk's extension of the list of ethnic groups was the result of a detailed study of dialects, traditions, and rites.

On Dispute over Nagorno-Karabakh

Continuing tensions were reported in the disputed Nagorno-Karabakh Autonomous Oblast. TASS said rallies were still being held in the oblast capital of Stepanakert to demand that control of Nagorno-Karabakh be transferred to Armenia. Reporting that Stepanakert had been paralyzed by a strike for two months, TASS said that industrial enterprises and construction projects in the region were standing idle and that public transport was only partially operating. The situation is further aggravated by drought, which threatens to inflict heavy damage on rural cooperatives. The agency said what was a bad situation was being made worse by conflicts between Armenians and Azerbaijanis, trouble in the streets, thoughtless articles and statements in the press by both sides, and unauthorized demonstrations.

On July 7, an exchange of gunfire was reported between Armenians and Azerbaijanis outside Stepanakert. TASS said the trouble coincided with the arrival in Stepanakert of a Soviet parliamentary group to examine the dispute over Nagorno-Karabakh.

On July 11, it was reported that a fresh outbreak of violence in Nagorno-Karabakh had left two people dead. TASS said two Azerbaijanis were shot dead in an ambush on the outskirts of Stepanakert, while a third was gravely wounded. It did not say who did the shooting. TASS said MVD troops and military reserves were in a state of "extreme readiness" to prevent further ethnic clashes and deaths. On July 13, TASS reported that an Armenian had been found shot dead on a country road on July 12. On July 14, Radio Moscow said the death toll from the violence had risen to four. The radio said the fourth victim was an Armenian but gave no details.

Soviet MiG Fighter Crashes

A Soviet-made MiG-23 fighter plane crashed in Belgium after flying across Western Europe without a pilot. The MiG came down in the west of Belgium, killing a young man on the ground. Belgian officials said the plane was not carrying nuclear weapons (*Reuters, AP,* July 4). On July 5, Defense Minister Dmitrii Yazov said a commission would fly to Belgium to discuss the case (*TASS,* July 5), and he also gave details of how the fighter began its pilotless flight. According to him, the MiG took off on a training flight in Poland, but the plane lost power and the pilot bailed out. Apparently, the plane then regained power and flew uncontrolled for 900 kilometers. Belgium said the USSR had agreed to pay full compensation for the accident (*Reuters*, July 5). Belgium's Defense Minister Guy Coeme said NATO and the Warsaw Pact should set up a permanently manned joint crisis center to warn each other of such incidents (Western agencies, July 5). The USSR Supreme Soviet was told that the Soviet Air Force had only discovered the ultimate fate of the strayed aircraft from Western news reports (*TASS*, July 5). On July 6, the first deputy commander of the Soviet Air Force said he was not happy with the performance of the Soviet Northern Group Command in this matter (*Reuters*, *AP*, July 6).

--*Wednesday, July 5*

Soviet Economist Says Joint Ventures May Threaten Environment

Writing in *Literaturnaya gazeta*, Soviet economist Valentin Katasonov accused international companies of exporting pollution to poorer countries and demanded a referendum on the desirability of joint industrial ventures in the Soviet Union. He said "international monopolies" sought to set up joint ventures in less-developed countries to evade tough pollution controls at home. He also urged a freeze on talks on industrial joint ventures at least until the Soviet parliament has passed new laws to protect the environment. "International monopolies follow a double standard on ecological policy," Katasonov said. "At home they meet the strictest demands for protection of the environment and people's health, but abroad, especially in countries lagging behind economically, they ignore elementary precautions." He complained that there is no central Soviet body to regulate the activities of the more than 500 registered joint ventures, especially with regard to air and water pollution. Katasonov singled out petro-chemical projects for closer scrunity, including the big Tengiz oil field project, led by a consortium of US, Japanese, and Italian firms, and Occidental Petroleum's proposed plastics plant in the Ukraine.

Medvedev Discusses Migration, 1939 Pact with Estonian Scholars

Soviet television said CPSU Politburo member Vadim Medvedev had met in Tallinn with Estonian scholars to discuss ethnic relations and sovereignty in Estonia and the 1939 Molotov-Ribbentrop Pact. In a report from Tallinn,

351

Soviet television said senior members of Estonia's Academy of Sciences complained to Medvedev that native Estonians were being outnumbered by immigrants. Medvedev and the scholars devoted much attention to the language issue in Estonia. The Estonians also criticized delays in giving the republics more economic independence. They were quoted as saying both Estonia and the central government would have to compromise. Also discussed was the Molotov-Ribbentrop Pact. On July 6, Medvedev held a meeting with Estonian journalists who complained that events in Estonia were inadequately reported in the Soviet central press (*Central Television*, July 6). It was disclosed on television that Estonian journalists had proposed an all-Union daily that would publish reports from journalists of each of the Union republics, but Medvedev's reaction to this proposal was not reported. On July 7, Medvedev met with representatives of Estonia's two largest informal groups, the Popular Front and the International Movement. Later in the day he talked to Estonian Party officials and told them tensions in the republic must be defused through dialogue and compromise (*Central Television*, "Vremya," July 7).

Turkmenistan Developing Border Trade with Iran

Turkmen First Deputy Prime Minister Khan Akhmedov said cross-border contacts between Iran and Turkmenistan were expanding again. TASS quoted Akhmedov as saying such contacts had stagnated for years but were growing once more. He linked this development to his recent visit to Iran, where he discussed trade with Iranian officials. Akhmedov said that a store selling Iranian goods would soon open in the Turkmen capital and that a similar Turkmen shop would open in Iran.

Declaration Signed by Soviet and Emigré Activists

Literaturnaya gazeta published an article by lawyer and journalist Arkadii Vaksberg, who gave details of a conference on *perestroika* held in Cologne at the end of June. The conference was attended by a Soviet delegation that included historian Natan Eidel'man, journalist Anatolii Strelyanyi, and Vaksberg. Among émigrés who attended the conference were figures still regarded as "anti-Soviet" by the Soviet press, such as writers Vladimir Maksimov and Aleksandr Zinov'ev. Vaksberg described favorably reports by the émigrés made at the conference. He stressed that all of them were concerned about the fate of the USSR. He also disclosed that a joint declaration was signed in Cologne by Soviet representatives as well as émigrés (except Zinov'ev). The declaration, which puts forward proposals to make the USSR more democratic, is the first joint political document signed by Soviet citizens together with politically active émigrés.

The head of the Moscow police, Deputy Minister of Internal Affairs Petr Bogdanov, said the number of serious crimes in the capital had doubled since last year. Bogdanov told a Moscow press conference that more than 3,000 of the 18,000 crimes recorded in Moscow this year had been serious crimes. He said crimes against property had risen by 80 percent. Bogdanov also said sending large numbers of police and troops to various parts of the USSR to deal with nationalist unrest had prompted local criminals to migrate to Moscow and other big cities. He added that the Moscow police force was short of about 4,000 staff and that low pay was one reason for this (*TASS*, in English, July 5). Bogdanov also told reporters that about 300 unauthorized meetings and demonstrations were held in Moscow in the first half of 1989.

Moscow Police Chief on Rising Crime

TASS published a report on the training and duties of an antiriot squad of the Moscow police, which it said was styled *Otryad moskovsky osobogo naznacheniya* (OMON for short) and was created in October, 1988. According to the report, OMON has been in action more than 600 times since its creation and has detained some 2,000 people. TASS said that a member of the special unit receives about 1,000 hours of training; that preference in the selection of personnel for the unit was given to former Soviet Army paratroopers; and that the average age of members of the unit is thirty-three. The length of the training period indicates that the unit actually must have been set up long before October, 1988, when it was used for the first time to break up a demonstration of the Democratic Union in Moscow. According to *samizdat* sources, similar units have been formed in other cities, including Leningrad, Novosibirsk, Kiev, and Minsk. According to TASS, the techniques and equipment used by OMON are similiar to those employed by Western antiriot squads; however, it appears that the Soviet antiriot squads are patterned more on the Polish antiriot police, ZOMO, which were the first such units in a European Communist country.

Details on Soviet Antiriot Squads Reported

A memorial was unveiled in a square in the Latvian capital of Riga where a permanent monument will be built to honor tens of thousands of Jews killed during the

Memorial for Latvian Jews in Riga

occupation of Latvia by Nazi Germany. The stone block memorial was dedicated at a mass rally on July 4. It stands on the site of a synagogue that the Nazis filled with Jews and burned down during the war. TASS said that the Latvian society of Jewish culture had begun to raise money for a permanent monument to replace the stone block eventually and that émigré sculptor Ernst Neizvestny, who recently visited the USSR, had already declared his readiness to work on the monument.

Official Says Crew of Crippled Submarine Healthy

A Soviet Defense Ministry official said radiation tests conducted after a Soviet submarine accident last week in the Norwegian sea showed that all crew members are well. TASS quoted Lieutenant General Igor Sinopalnikov as saying four crewmen who had been hospitalized with suspected radiation sickness were healthy and had no excessive radiation. Norwegian experts said small amounts of radioactivity were detected where the submarine was crippled. Sinopalnikov said the complete decontamination of the entire crew was carried out by June 28, two days after a pipe burst in the reactor of the submarine (*TASS*, July 5).

Weekly Says Moscow Wants Better Relations with Saudi Arabia

The Soviet weekly *Ekho planety* (No. 27) said the Soviet Union was ready to normalize relations with Saudi Arabia. TASS reported the weekly as saying that, although the Soviet Union had been one of the first countries to recognize the Saudi kingdom in 1926, current bilateral relations could not be considered normal. The two countries have had no diplomatic relations since 1938, when Saudi Arabia suspended ties with Moscow. High-level contacts between the two governments resumed last year.

Authorities Examine Possiblity of Homeland for Meskhetians

The Soviet authorities are to study ways to provide a homeland for the Meskhetians, the Muslim people who were deported from Georgia in 1944. Many lived in Uzbekistan until they became the target of ethnic violence there in June and were evacuated to central Russia. The chairman of the Council of Nationalities, Rafik Nishanov, told Radio Moscow that a special commission of the Supreme Soviet would study the problem. He said he was sure the commission would find a way to solve it gradually. On July 4, TASS reported the lifting of the curfew in most parts of Uzbekistan's Fergana Oblast and its limitation in the towns of Margilan, Fergana, Kokand, and Kuvasai. The curfew was imposed after the clashes between Uzbeks and Meskhetians in June. On July 6, Yurii Gremitskikh, a spokesman for the Soviet Foreign Ministry, said a Greek report about Meskhetians was false. TASS said the Greek magazine, *Ekonomikos Tachydromos*, had reported that the Soviet Union had an understanding with the Turkish Cypriot leadership about resettling Meskhetians in the north of Cyprus. When asked about this at a press briefing in Moscow, Gremitskikh said that the report was "a figment of the imagination" and that all Soviet Meskhetians were being settled in the USSR.

Thursday, July 6

Official Rally Honors Stalin's Victims in Moldavia

TASS reported on an official rally in Kishinev, the capital of Moldavia, to honor the victims of Stalinism. The agency said that the rally was sponsored by the Kishinev city soviet and that speeches were given by Moldavian leaders and members of the Congress of People's Deputies.

Kirgiz Schools to Begin Kirgiz Language-Teaching

Radio Moscow said many schools in Kirgizia would begin teaching the Kirgiz language to first-grade schoolchildren in September. It said a new textbook had recently been published for first-grade pupils, with a textbook for second-grade pupils and a teacher's manual due to follow. The decision followed lengthy debates in Kirgizia over whether Kirgiz language and literature should be made compulsory subjects at all schools in the republic, including Russian schools.

Soviet Commentator Hails Sakharov as Hero of Reform

Leading Soviet commentator, Stanislav Kondrashev, hailed Academician Andrei Sakharov as a hero whose political writings and struggle for human rights had helped prepare the way for Gorbachev's reforms. Reuters said Kondrashev's article would appear in *Moscow News* (No. 28). This article is the first detailed analysis to appear in the Soviet media of Sakharov's role as an exemplar for free thought during two decades of persecution.

Journal Says Soviet Troops in Mideast Clashes between 1969 and 1971

Soviet air force units and antiaircraft troops took part in armed clashes between Egypt and Israel from late 1969 to 1971 and shot down a number of Israeli planes, according to the weekly *Ekho planety* (No. 27). The first admission of Soviet military participation in the clashes came in an article in the journal *Sobesednik* several months ago.

Siberian Journalists Released from Jail, Summoned for Court Appearance

Two Siberian journalists jailed a few days ago during a hunger strike in the Siberian city of Novosibirsk were released. They and two colleagues were ordered to appear in court on July 7. The journalists, Aleksei Manannikov and Maksim Klimenko, work for the independent Siberian Information Agency. Fellow workers telephoned RFE/RL to report their release. Manannikov, Klimenko, and two other colleagues had been arrested in connection with the hunger strike in Novosibirsk, which is continuing. The hunger strikers are protesting over the confiscation a week ago of the press bulletin of the Siberian Information Agency by the authorities. The bulletin had been printed in Lithuania and flown to Novosibirsk, where it was confiscated at the airport by the police. Reports from Novosibirsk said a Supreme Soviet deputy, Stepan Sulakshin, had asked the first secretary of the local Party committee, Vladimir Kazarezov, for an explanation of the circumstances surrounding the hunger strike and confiscation of the bulletin (*RFE/RL Special*, July 6).

Friday, July 7 ———————————————————————————

Warsaw Pact Leaders Hold Summit

Warsaw Pact leaders opened a two-day summit in Bucharest with discussion expected to focus on European security and disarmament. TASS said key issues were moves to eliminate nuclear and chemical weapons, reductions in armed forces, efforts to stop the modernization of nuclear arsenals, and Mikhail Gorbachev's latest offer to make unilateral cuts in short-range nuclear weapons if NATO agrees to talks on eliminating those weapons from Europe. The agenda also called for discussion on improving cooperation among Socialist countries. Gorbachev used the opportunity to meet with Hungary's new Party chairman, Rezso Nyers, and prime minister, Miklos Nemeth. The two sides discussed ties between the Soviet and Hungarian Parties (*TASS*, July 7; *Pravda*, July 8). Gorbachev addressed a reception for the leaders attending the summit. He said each member of the Warsaw Pact is free to follow its own path to socialism. Gorbachev also spoke about positive changes in relations between the Warsaw Pact and NATO. On July 8, ending a two-day meeting in Bucharest, the leaders of the Warsaw Pact countries declared the right of each member to formulate its own policy, saying there cannot be only "one standard" for social organization. They also vowed to work for rapid accords with the West on conventional and nuclear arms and expressed optimism that an initial conventional arms accord could be reached as early as next year. The leaders made no new arms proposals, however, saying it was up to the West to match recent Soviet initiatives (*Izvestia*, *Pravda*, July 9). On July 9, TASS quoted Gorbachev as describing the final declaration of the summit as "realistic and constructive." The text of the declaration was published in *Pravda*, July 9.

Soviet Foreign Minister Eduard Shevardnadze said changes in the way Soviet foreign policy is made will prevent the kind of secret decision-making that sent Soviet troops into Afghanistan. Shevardnadze said practices now being adopted will protect the USSR against senseless expense. He said this would have been the case if the USSR had stopped chemical weapons production twenty years ago. His remarks appear in the weekly *New Times* (No. 28).

Shevardnadze on Changes in Drafting Soviet Foreign Policy

TASS said the Supreme Soviet discussed the rehabilitation of Soviet citizens who had been "unjustly condemned" in previous years. TASS said this included "so-called dissidents."

Supreme Soviet Discusses Dissidents

Reuters reported that Soviet novelist Anatolii Rybakov, who is the author of anti-Stalinist works, had been elected president of the new Russian PEN Center in the Soviet Union. The new group, called Russian Soviet PEN Center, was established along with a Lithuanian PEN branch at the organization's annual congress in the Netherlands in May.

Rybakov Elected President of New Russian PEN Center

A chemical plant in the Uzbek city of Kokand is to be closed because it was built on the largest underground fresh water source of the area—the Fergana Valley. Radio Moscow-1 (1700) said the location of the plant is now viewed as a grave mistake that will cost 120 million rubles. The prosecutor has opened investigations to determine responsibility. The radio said the Uzbek State Committee for Environmental Protection made the decision to close the plant. The plant will process the raw materials that are in its possession and then close permanently.

Chemical Plant to Be Closed Down in Kokand

***Pravda* Blames Stalinism and Centralization for Ethnic Tensions**	*Pravda* blamed Soviet ethnic disorders on the forced migration of minorities under Stalin and on the country's extreme centralization of power. The newspaper defended Gorbachev's *perestroika* policy and said some people wrongly blamed it for the troubles. The comment came a day after TASS reported fresh clashes between Armenians and Azerbaijanis in Nagorno-Karabakh.

Nuclear Test Conducted Near Semipalatinsk

The Soviet Union conducted a nuclear test at a site near Semipalatinsk in Kazakhstan. TASS said the 20-kiloton nuclear blast was carried out for the purpose of upgrading military hardware. It added that radiation levels at the test site and surrounding areas were normal.

Newspaper Details 1982 Soccer Stadium Tragedy

Sovetsky sport revealed details of a Moscow soccer stadium tragedy in 1982 in which up to 340 fans were crushed to death. The newspaper blamed the deaths on police incompetence. It said that fans leaving an international match at Luzhniki stadium were forced to exit through a single corridor and that the victims were crushed to death when a last-minute Soviet goal sent fans back towards the field. The newspaper said officials covered up the tragedy by cordoning off the stadium and withholding bodies for two weeks.

Procurator's Office Says 261,141 People Rehabilitated

Vladimir Andreev, a special aide to the general prosecutor of the USSR said 261,141 people "unjustly condemned" in earlier years have been rehabilitated. Andreev said the rehabilitations are the result of a Supreme Soviet decree issued in January calling for greater justice towards victims of repressions in the 1930s–1950s. (The decree stipulates the rehabilitation of people sentenced by the so-called *troiki* [courts of three] and *osobye soveshchaniya* [special assemblies].) Andreev spoke in Moscow on July 7 during the confirmation hearings by the USSR Supreme Soviet for nominees to the USSR Public Prosecutor' s Office (*Izvestia*, July 8).

Pipeline Blast Cut Soviet Gas Supply by 20 Percent

Last month's explosion of a major pipeline in the Ural mountains not only killed more than 600 people but also decreased the country's gas supply by 20 percent, forcing a drastic cut in gas exports and supplies to domestic factories and consumers, according to Gas Minister Viktor Chernomyrdin. He added that Soviet consumers should conserve gas used in kitchen stoves and be prepared for shortages of rubber and plastic goods made from the petroleum products the pipeline also carried (*Izvestia*, July 8).

Sunday, July 9

Soviet television reported on another mass rally in the Moldavian capital of Kishinev that developed into a confrontation between Moldavian and Russian groups. The report said the rally was prevented from "exploding" only because of steps taken by law-enforcement bodies. It did not say what steps were taken. According to Soviet television, protesters heckled a Moldavian representative to the Congress of People's Deputies who tried to speak. On July 10, RFE/RL reported that the Moldavian Popular Front was urging its members to write letters to the Chairman of the USSR State Committee for Television and Radio to protest about the television coverage of the Kishinev demonstration. The front said the television report's claim that law-enforcement bodies prevented an interethnic clash was inaccurate. Spokesmen for the Popular Front told RFE/RL that police were on hand during the demonstration but did not interfere. On July 11, Radio Moscow-1 (0840) said the demonstration on July 9 in Kishinev had pressed demands for the creation of two separate Autonomous republics in Moldavia. The radio's correspondent in Moldavia, Ivan Petrov, said there had been calls from the southeastern city of Tiraspol for the creation of a republic on the eastern side of the Dniester. There has been an influx of Russian-speaking peoples into the lands on the eastern side of the river. The radio reported that members of the Gagauz nationality had called for the setting up of an Autonomous republic in southern Moldavia.

Mass Rally in Kishinev Develops into Interethnic Confrontation

An unofficial Soviet delegation ended a visit to Pakistan designed to seek information on Soviet soldiers missing in the Afghan war. A member of the delegation, the journalist Iona Andronov, said on his return to Moscow that progress had been made on the issue. The delegation had talks with Afghan resistance leaders based in Pakistan and with Pakistani Prime Minister Benazir Bhutto. TASS said the delegation managed to get a more accurate list of

Soviet Delegation Ends Visit to Pakistan

Soviet prisoners of war held by the resistance. The resistance also promised that prisoners would be allowed to exchange more letters with their relatives. Another delegation member, Evgeniya Poplavskaya, said the delegation was acting as mediator between the Afghan resistance and the Soviet government. The Soviet delegation included relatives of the 311 Soviet soldiers listed as missing (*TASS*, July 9). On July 14, Gorbachev addressed members of the Soviet delegation. He said everything must be done to prevent a recurrence of the Soviet experience in Afghanistan (*TASS*, July 14).

More Criticism of Reconstruction Work in Armenia

There has been more criticism of the reconstruction work in parts of Armenia devastated by an earthquake last December. Radio Erevan said building and restoration work was moving at a "strikingly slow" pace in Leninakan, one of the towns worst affected by the earthquake. It reported on a three-day visit to the disaster area by Armenian Party First Secretary Suren Arutyunyan. The visit ended on July 8. On July 11, *Stroitel'naya gazeta* said the mass collapse of apartment houses during the earthquake in Armenia would result in court trials. The newspaper said the results of a government investigation had been turned over to the USSR Prosecutor's Office so judicial proceedings could be started. It quoted the chairman of the investigation committee, Colonel General Konstantin Vertelov, as saying "flagrant shortcomings" and poor-quality construction caused buildings in northern Armenia to collapse "almost instantly" during the quake. Vertelov is head of the Defense Ministry's Department for Expert Examinations and Inspections.

Americans Visit Soviet Laser-Testing Area

A group from the United States, including members of Congress and physicists, was taken on a visit to a laser research center in Kazakhstan. The Sary-Shagan testing area was described by the US Defense Department last year as housing a ground-based laser "with some capability for attacking US satellites." One of the congressmen, Jim Olin, said he believed lasers at the site did not represent any threat as weapons (*The New York Times*, July 9, and *The Washington Post*, July 10).

Lithuanian TV Begins Regular Broadcasts for Catholics

Lithuanian television broadcast what TASS said was the first religious program to be carried on local television in three decades. TASS said the broadcast was the first of a regular Sunday program for Catholics in Lithuania. It said the programs would include live broadcasts from churches on religious holidays and would provide information on major religious events.

**Expert Estimates
Third-World Debt to Moscow**

Izvestia carried an interview with E. Arefeeva on the USSR's relations with the Third World. Arefeeva, a staff member of the World Economics and International Relations Institute, repeated the figure for foreign debt owed the USSR given by Chairman of the State Foreign Economic Commission Vladimir Kamentsev during his unsuccessful confirmation hearings. Kamentsev put the total debt at 87.5 billion rubles, of which more than 20 billion was in "freely convertible currency" (*TASS*, June 30). Arefeeva confirmed that most of this total is owed by developing countries.

Monday, July 10

Chazov on Psychiatric Abuse

During his confirmation hearing at the USSR Supreme Soviet on July 9, USSR Minister of Health Evgenii Chazov was asked about "abuses in psychotherapy." According to the TASS version (July 10) of his testimony, Chazov avoided a direct answer. TASS quoted Chazov as reminding deputies of new legislation in this sphere precluding the detention of healthy people in lunatic asylums and as saying mental hospitals that used to be the responsibility of the Ministry of Internal Affairs had been handed over to the public health system. He pointed out at the same time that speculation on these problems continues and claimed that foreign delegations that have raised this question could not name one person kept in a hospital for political reasons. See also *Izvestia*, July 11.

**Internal Affairs Minister
Reveals Number of Prisoners
and MVD Forces**

Minister of Internal Affairs Vadim Bakatin revealed new figures on the size of the MVD forces and prison population in the Soviet Union (*TASS*, July 10). At his confirmation hearing before the Supreme Soviet, Bakatin said his ministry had responsibility for 700,000 "policemen," and 36,000 "troops." (In response to a question from Gorbachev, Bakatin noted that there was one policeman for every 588 people. This yields a figure of 486,400 policemen.) Bakatin also announced that the number of inmates in labor camps was 800,000, down from 1,600,000. (He did not specify to which years these figures applied.) As a comparison, in the United States at the end of 1987 there were 582,000 prisoners under the jurisdiction of state and federal correctional authorities. This appears to be the first time these Soviet figures have been officially released. In a plea for more funding, Bakatin added that crime in the Soviet Union had risen 40 percent in the first six months of 1989, with juvenile delinquency increasing by 22 percent. See RL 421/89 and RL 424/89.

MVD Believes Soviet "Mafia" after Western Market

In an article in *Nedelya* (No. 27), two leading authorities on organized crime support claims by investigators Tel'man Gdlyan and Nikolai Ivanov (without mentioning Gdlyan and Ivanov by name) that some top Soviet officials are involved in a Mafia-like criminal network. (Gdlyan and Ivanov were suspended from the investigation of organized crime after they publicly accused certain officials, including Politburo member Egor Ligachev, of involvement in the corruption case they were working on.) The authors of the *Nedelya* article, Vladimir Burykin and Aleksandr Gurov, insist that some political leaders are indeed involved in organized crime. They also share the concern over this problem that was expressed by Gdlyan, Ivanov, and their supporters during debates in the Congress of People's Deputies. According to Burykin and Gurov, robbery and other crimes are not the most important activities of the Soviet "Mafia"; they say its main goal is to penetrate "the organs of administration and power" through corruption. Burykin and Gurov seem to be certain that this "Mafia" directed the recent ethnic riots in the Fergana Valley. They are also convinced the situation will get worse. They claim that the godfathers of the Soviet "Mafia" have already established international connections, and they predict that these connections will be developed further. Soviet organized criminals, Burykin and Gurov claim, "are eager to conquer the Western market, utilizing the developing trade between Soviet and foreign firms."

Reappraisal of Left Socialist Revolutionaries

The three most recent issues of the weekly *Nedelya* have contained articles about the role of the last officially tolerated non-Communist political party in the USSR—the Left Socialist Revolutionaries. The latter sided with the Bolsheviks against other Russian Socialist and Liberal parties during the October Revolution and participated in the first Bolshevik government until July 6, 1918, when they staged an abortive coup d'état in protest against the Brest-Litovsk peace treaty with Germany. The Stalinist tradition of historiography that prevailed in Soviet history books until recently portrayed the Left Socialist Revolutionaries (along with the other Russian Socialist parties) in an even worse light than it did the monarchists. The articles in *Nedelya* follow the publication of materials dealing with the coup attempt by the Left Socialist Revolutionaries in the May issue of *Izvestiya TsK KPSS*, the Party Central Committee's monthly edited by Mikhail Gorbachev. In *Nedelya* (Nos. 24 and 25), prominent liberal historian Vladlen Sirotkin claimed that Left Socialist Revolutionaries as well as leftist Mensheviks in fact formed a common left-wing front together with the Bolsheviks and that many policies of the three parties, whether correct or not, were identical. *Nedelya* (No. 27) contains an article by Boris Ileshin on Mariya Spiridonova, the Left Socialist Revolutionary leader, that lionizes her heroic behavior both before and after the October Revolution. The current reappraisal of Russian Socialists in the Soviet media may be of some political importance in view of the relations between the CPSU and the parties of the modern Socialist International.

Nagorno-Karabakh Newspaper to Be Published in Erevan

Copies of the main newspaper of Nagorno-Karabakh are to be published in Armenia. Radio Erevan said the decision was made after subscribers in Armenia experienced difficulties and delays in getting their copies. The radio said the Armenian Communist Party will print 45,000 copies of the newspaper *Khorhrdayin Karabakh* in Erevan and have them distributed in Armenia the next day. The newspaper is published in Armenian, which is the language of the majority of Nagorno-Karabakh residents.

Supreme Soviet Continues Proceedings

Continuing its hearings of nominations for government posts, the Supreme Soviet rejected another ministerial nominee proposed by Nikolai Ryzhkov. TASS said deputies voted against Mikhail Busygin, who was nominated to continue as minister of the timber and wood processing industry. He has held this post since 1982. TASS said the deputies criticized him for neglecting ecological problems and allowing forests to be depleted with enormous losses to the industry (*Izvestia*, July 11). On July 11, the Supreme Soviet approved three more ministers: Erlen Pervyshin as communications minister; Kondrat Terekh as trade minister; and Yurii Semenov as minister of power and electrification. Lawyer Veniamin Yakovlev was appointed as justice minister. TASS said many deputies believed Yakovlev's lack of bureaucratic experience will be an advantage in his new post (*Radio Moscow, TASS*, July 11, *Izvestia*, July 12). There was lengthy criticism before Pervyshin and Terekh were finally reappointed.

Leningrad Residents Boycott Private Markets over Prices

TASS reported that many of Leningrad's residents followed an appeal to boycott the city's private fruit and vegetable markets over the weekend. TASS said people's deputy Aleksei Levashev called for the boycott to protest against the prohibitively high prices cooperative farmers charge for their produce. TASS said sovkhozes and kolkhozes prefer to sell their produce to cooperatives, which offer higher prices and are more efficient than state outlets at transporting the goods to market. TASS commented that the situation is aggravated by the fact that there is virtually nothing to buy in state stores at the height of the season. TASS said the Leningrad authorities supported the boycott by selling fruit and vegetables at sharply reduced prices from stalls and stands set up at entrances to the private markets.

Moscow Protesters Released after Four Hours

AP said police detained a group of demonstrators for four hours after allowing them to protest against the recent seizure of copies of the unofficial human-rights journal *Ekspress khronika* from a woman as she tried to distribute them on July 7. AP said that, at the start of the demonstration by sixteen people in Pushkin Square, uniformed police informed organizer Viktor Sergeev that the group did not have permission to assemble. AP said the demonstrators were allowed to protest for exactly thirty minutes while plainclothes police took photographs. It said dozens of people paused to read posters and argue with the protesters. AP said the demonstrators then formed a line and followed a uniformed officer to a police station.

***Pravda* Article Attacks Party Bureaucrats**

Pravda accused bureaucrats of stifling the initiative of the Party and leaving the country's dominant political institution in the most "wretched state" since it took power. *Pravda* said new blood was needed. The article by commentator Leon Onikov also attacked the system of "*nomenklatura*," the mechanism by which Party officials perpetuate power and award loyalty through appointments to key posts. Onikov said the Party is lagging badly in Gorbachev's *perestroika* drive and must open up its ranks.

Tuesday, July 11 _____

Gorbachev Visits Leningrad, Solov'ev Replaced

Mikhail Gorbachev arrived in Leningrad on a previously unannounced visit accompanied by Georgii Razumovsky, chairman of the Central Committee Commission on Party

Work and Cadres Policy. Prime Minister Nikolai Ryzhkov said Gorbachev's visit was aimed at dealing with a range of problems that had piled up in Leningrad. Ryzhkov noted that many of Leningrad's city and oblast leaders were defeated in elections to the Congress of People's Deputies and that the Party leadership was concerned about this. During the first day of his visit Gorbachev talked with workers at a factory and also toured the city, speaking to citizens about the work of cooperatives and about the housing shortage (*TASS*, July 11; *Pravda*, July 12). On July 12, Gorbachev attended a plenum of the Leningrad Oblast Party Committee, which released Leningrad Oblast Party First Secretary Yurii Solov'ev and replaced him with Boris Gidaspov, the chairman of a state industrial enterprise (*Pravda*, July 13). At the plenum, Gorbachev delivered a speech in which he said that the CPSU needs major reforms and that any Party member who does not have the strength for this task must step aside (*TASS*, July 13, *Pravda*, July 14).

On July 12, the television news program "Vremya" carried an interview with Gorbachev in which he said he had heard expressions of concern during his trip to Leningrad that *perestroika* was not going as well as it should. The program also included interviews with Solov'ev and Gidaspov that focused on the enstrangement of the Leningrad Party leadership from the city's population, especially young people and the intelligentsia. Gidaspov said the Leningrad Oblast Party Committee should open up a dialogue with non-Party members and independent groups, including environmental groups and the newly created Leningrad Popular Front.

Newspaper Reveals Alliance between Leningrad Leaders and Workers' Group

Sotsialisticheskaya industriya disclosed one of the reasons for the Leningrad Party leadership's favorable attitude towards the United Front of Workers—one of two informal groups created in Leningrad in June. (As its name suggests, theUnited Front of Workers draws its membership predominantly from the working class. From its very inception, the United Front of Workers has enjoyed the strong support of the conservative Leningrad Party leadership, while the other informal group, the Leningrad Popular Front, set up by liberal Leningrad intellectuals, has been bitterly opposed by local Party leaders.) The newspaper disclosed that immediately after its creation the United Front of Workers, with members of the Leningrad Party leadership in its ranks, put forward a proposal for changes in the election rules to local soviets. The proposed changes stipulated that two thirds of the deputies in the city's parliament, which is to be elected by next spring, should be chosen by workers at major factories and that all preelection debates should take place at these factories. According to the newspaper, members of the United Front of Workers have openly stated that such a practice would prevent representatives of the intelligentsia, including members of the Leningrad Popular Front, from being elected. *Sotsialisticheskaya industriya* even implied that the whole idea of proposing changes in the election rules was born within the Leningrad Party leadership and was given to theUnited Front for the purpose of promoting it. The Leningrad public also protested against the election changes proposed by the United Front. On July 13, hundreds of Leningraders queued in the center of the city to protest against what they saw as attempts to pack their city and oblast councils with conservatives (*Reuters*, July 13).

On July 21, the Leningrad United Front of Workers called for "serious adjustments" in the process of *perestroika*. Coordinators of the front met with the news media in Leningrad. They produced a charter and commentaries concerning the discontent of state workers with the orientation of some current reforms. They strongly attacked cooperatives. See RL 326/89.

Anniversary of French Revolution Marked in Moscow

A conference marking the 200th anniversary of the French Revolution was held in Moscow. Leading Soviet political figures as well as scholars and cultural figures attended the conference. Among those attending were Politburo member Aleksandr Yakovlev and Foreign Minister Eduard Shevardnadze. Yakovlev addressed the meeting. In his speech he drew parallels between the French Revolution and the October Revolution in Russia. Evaluating the October Revolution, Yakovlev echoed some of the more outspoken ideas expressed recently concerning Soviet history. He said that, in identifying the roots of Stalinism, "the idealization of revolutionary violence," which was first endorsed in the nineteenth century, should be looked at. He also said that the Marxist concept of "violence as a midwife of history" should be rejected (see *Sovetskaya kul'tura*, July 15.)

Problems with Nuclear Plants in USSR

Trud reported protests from residents of the southern Siberian city of Krasnoyarsk against plans to dump nuclear waste near the city. The newspaper said the protesters want to halt construction of a facility being built to handle the waste. On July 10, *Izvestia* reported an increase in unplanned shutdowns of Soviet nuclear plants in June and said most of them were necessitated by human error. The newspaper said most of the shutdowns were at the nuclear facilities in Smolensk and in Balakovo, which is on the Volga, southeast of Moscow. It said there had been an incident on June 26 at the nuclear plant in Kursk, south of Moscow, in which lightly contaminated water had leaked into the surrounding area and topsoil had to be removed. On July 11, *Krasnaya zvezda* reported on the environmental situation at the Soviet nuclear testing site at Semipalatinsk in Kazakhstan. The report said that about 300 tests had been conducted there so far but that the radiological situation in and around the test site was normal.

Forty Detained in Demonstration in Baku

Reports reaching the West from Azerbaijan said police broke up a demonstration in Baku on July 8 and detained about forty people. RFE/RL was told in a telephone interview that the demonstration was sponsored by the unofficial society "Birlik." It was reported that members of the society were among those detained. The demonstrators were said to have called on the Azerbaijan Party Central Committee to fulfill its promise to designate May 28 as independence day in Azerbaijan. TASS also reported that a group of Azerbaijanis went on an anti-Armenian rampage in the town of Shusha, injuring one man. Radio Moscow reported shooting between Azerbaijanis and Armenians in the village of Dashchibulak. TASS said the situation was particularly bad on roads in the region.

"Sajudis" to Publish Daily Newspaper in Lithuania

Lithuanian journalist Vitas Tomkus said the Lithuanian Restructuring Movement "Sajudis" had received official permission to publish its own daily newspaper in Lithuania. Tomkus said permission was granted after a long application process and after most of the staff of the newspaper had been chosen. Tomkus expects to be one of the editors. Tomkus told RFE/RL no final decision had been made on a name for the daily. See RL 342/89.

Students Freed from Soviet Military Service

The Supreme Soviet voted for an early discharge of approximately 175,000 students whose studies have been interrupted by military service. The move represented a sharp reversal for Defense Minister Dmitrii Yazov, who, during his confirmation process last week, explained carefully to deputies why such an action would be detrimental to the functioning of the Soviet military (*TASS,*

July 11; *Izvestia,* July 12). Despite Yazov's plea, the decision of the Supreme Soviet was opposed by only five delegates, with three abstaining. It called for the students to be released in August. According to Yazov, the 175,000 students in question constitute a highly trained and extremely important segment of the Soviet junior officer corps whose discharge would have a negative effect on the combat readiness of the armed forces.

New Soviet Periodical to Tell about "Blank Spots" in History

TASS said a new periodical now being published in the USSR will provide information about blank spots in Soviet, Russian, and foreign history. TASS said the new publication, the monthly *Sovershenno sekretno* (Top Secret), the inauguration of which was reported last month, is an international, nongovernmental monthly with an editorial board that includes lawyers, scientists, artists, and writers from various countries, including the United States. The first issue has twenty-four pages and appears in an edition of 100,000 copies. TASS said a larger edition is planned later. Chief editor Yulian Semenov, who is a writer of thrillers, said talks are being held about launching a German-language edition in West Germany.

Arms Control

USSR Deputy Foreign Minister Viktor Karpov was reported to have expressed conditional approval for some new US arms control proposals. In an interview published in *The Washington Post,* Karpov said the Soviet Union is still working out its formal response. But he said the US proposal for trial inspections of land-based missiles before a strategic arms treaty is signed is acceptable as long as it applies equally to both sides. He said it must also apply to bombers and air- and sea-launched cruise missiles.

Wednesday, July 12 ———————————————————————

Supreme Soviet Questions Izrael' on Radiation Danger

Supreme Soviet deputies quizzed a cabinet nominee about radiation danger from Chernobyl', Semipalatinsk, and Soviet submarine accidents. TASS quoted Chairman of the State Committee for Hydrometeorology Yurii Izrael' as saying there was no danger and as defending the information he has released previously about the effects of the Chernobyl' accident. Izrael' also said the destruction of Soviet short-range nuclear missiles has posed no environmental danger. His reappointment was approved.

Soviet Defense Minister Dmitrii Yazov said the Supreme Soviet must be systematically informed about military affairs so that it can deal with them competently. Yazov remarked that in the past many military affairs were kept secret and that decisions were made by a few people. He said this had made errors possible and had not promoted the democratic development of military thinking. TASS said Yazov declared that military *glasnost'* strengthens security because it allows a broad stratum of Soviet society to contribute to maintaining defense capability. Yazov's comments are to appear in *Moscow News* (No. 29).

Yazov Says Supreme Soviet Must Be Informed about Military Issues

Pravda expressed concern about the fate of the USSR in light of appeals by popular fronts for independence for the Baltic republics. It said Soviet citizens must be concerned about intensifying intolerance and interethnic conflicts in the Baltic. *Pravda* said only the USSR has full and unlimited sovereignty. It said that all Union and Autonomous republics should be given more economic rights but must not infringe on the sovereign rights of the USSR and that the upcoming Central Committee plenum would make important changes in the relationship between the central government and the republics.

Pravda Criticizes Baltic Republics

The authorities in the old Russian town of Zagorsk near Moscow turned down a proposal to return to using the town's historical name of Sergiev Posad. The fourteenth-century town was named Zagorsk in 1930 after the revolutionary figure Vladimir Zagorsky. (On June 30, *Literaturnaya Rossiya* said the Zagorsk executive committee planned to discuss the issue. The newspaper carried an appeal for people to send telegrams to the committee calling for the return of the town's historical name.) An editor of the weekly *Literaturnaya Rossiya*, Evgenii Nekrasov, told RFE/RL by telephone from Moscow today that the executive committee had decided the name would not be changed.

Zagorsk Authorities Turn Down Proposal to Rename City

Officials of the Soviet alliance of united cooperatives said state directives were undermining the activities of their enterprises. The chairman of the alliance, Academician Vladimir Tikhonov of VASKhNIL, told reporters in Moscow that "there is a nationwide tendency towards strangling the cooperative movement" (*TASS*, in English, *DPA*, July 12). Tikhonov said some localities in Ukraine and Belorussia had begun taxing cooperatives' revenues rather

Cooperative Leaders Complain about State Directives

than their profits at rates as high as 50 percent. The alliance is calling for a maximum tax of 20 percent on profits only.

Coal Miners Strike in Siberia

Several thousand coal miners in Mezhdurechensk in Siberia went on strike in support of demands for better food supplies and longer holidays. *Trud* said the strike began when the night shift at one mine refused to come to the surface. The strike action spread on July 11. Several thousand miners from four other Mezhdurechensk mines marched through the town center and staged a sit-in opposite the local Party headquarters. On July 14, TASS said miners had stopped work at the Kapital'naya mine in Osinniki. Strikes were also reported to have begun late on July 13 at mines in Novokuznetsk and Prokopevsk (*Central Television*, "Vremya," July 14; *Pravda*, July 14; and *Izvestia*, July 15).

On July 15, strikes were reported continuing at coal mines in nine cities in the Kuznetsk Basin (Kuzbass) of Western Siberia. *Pravda* and other Soviet newspapers said Minister of the Coal Industry Mikhail Shchadov was in the region meeting strike committees in various towns.

On July 16, *Trud* said 100,000 miners were now on strike in the Kuzbass. It said the strike had been joined by building workers, instrument makers, and coal industry drivers and processors. *Sovetskaya Rossiya* alleged that anti-*perestroika* forces had driven the working people of the Kuzbass to strike. It said people who had failed to listen to working people were to blame for the situation. Radio Moscow said a joint strike committee has been formed to coordinate the activities of the miners in the Kuzbass.

On July 17, Radio Moscow said that strikers in the Kuzbass were holding meetings almost around the clock and that the situation in the region was "extremely tense." The radio said people attending the meetings were trying to find out the truth about the situation in Kuzbass. It said much inaccurate information was being spread. The same day, *Pravda* said strikers in the town of Prokopevsk had decided to stop coal being shipped to users. It said this would affect steel production and disrupt the export of fuel. At the same time, *Pravda* reported that miners at another pit had decided to ensure supplies were not interrupted. On July 17, Politburo member Nikolai Slyun'kov flew to the area (*TASS*, July 17). Slyun'kov heads a high-level commission set up to deal with the strikes. In its news program "Vremya," Soviet television gave a very detailed description of the situation in

Kuzbass. It also reported that more than 2,000 miners had gone on strike in the Donets Basin (Donbass) in Ukraine. On July 18, the number of strikers in Kuzbass reached 150,000 (*Sovetskaya Rossiya*, July 18). TASS said the scale of the strike in Donbass had expanded considerably. The same day, Soviet television asked why the government of Ukraine had so far not taken part in efforts to settle the miners' strike in Donbass. It noted that no competent commission had been set up to negotiate with the miners and that this was complicating the situation. Reports from Siberia said local officials in Novokuznetsk had held a meeting on July 18 in the city center to condemn what they termed extremists among striking miners in the region (*RFE/RL Special*, July 19).

On July 19, the Soviet media said that, while the miners' strike in the Kuzbass region appeared to be winding down, strikes in the Donbass region were spreading. The same day, AP quoted *Moscow News* (No. 30) as comparing the Gdansk shipyard strikes of 1980 that gave rise to the Polish "Solidarity" movement with the strikes in the Kuzbass.

On July 20, Soviet television and TASS reported that strikes had spread to three more areas: Vorkuta in the Komi ASSR; a mine near the Ukrainian industrial center of Dnepropetrovsk; and a mine complex near Rostov-on-Don in the RSFSR. Later the same day, TASS said the strike had spread to the Karaganda basin of northern Kazakhstan. It said miners had walked out of four mines in the towns of Abai and Shakhtinsk. TASS said that local government and Party officials had talked with the miners but that their appeals had had no effect. TASS said the strikers' demands in these areas were similar to those made by striking miners in the Kuzbass and Donbass regions—i.e., better working and living conditions. Western agencies reported that miners in Upper Silesia in Poland had expressed their support for the striking Soviet miners. The same day, Soviet television carried commentaries by USSR Supreme Soviet deputies on the strikes. A deputy from Estonia, Mikhail Bronshtein, said that the miners' demands were justified and that the conditions that had caused them to strike existed to one degree or another right across the Soviet Union.

On July 19, in an address to the USSR Supreme Soviet, Mikhail Gorbachev commented on strikes by coal miners in Donbass and Kuzbass. He said that the strikes were causing serious political and economic problems and that, if the strikes continued, the country might need to consider what means should be used to stop the situation getting out of control. Gorbachev also said there was an attempt being made to call a strike of Soviet train drivers on August 1 (*Radio Moscow*, July 19; *Izvestia*, July 20).

On July 21, Radio Moscow said all coal mines and other enterprises had resumed work in the Kuzbass region. Radio Moscow said the government commission headed by Slyun'kov would be sent to the Donbass in Ukraine where more than 300,000 miners are on strike. The radio said the losses from the Kuzbass strike were "tremendous." TASS said 600,000 tons of coal production had been lost in the Donbass. The radio said the strike was also continuing in the Karaganda region of Kazakhstan, where miners are demanding the closure of the atomic test site at Semipalatinsk. Meanwhile, it was reported that striking coal miners in Western Ukraine had called for the creation of an independent trade union for mine workers. The Moscow press spokesman of the Ukrainian Helsinki Union, Anatolii Dotsenko, told Radio Liberty the strikers want the new union to be called "Solidarity." He said miners in Chervonograd, twenty kilometers from the Polish border, began walking out on July 20. Dotsenko said the miners were demanding genuinely democratic elections in Chervonograd (*RL Ukrainian Service*, July 21). Meanwhile, a leader of the Ukrainian Helsinki Union, Vyacheslav Chornovil, denied Soviet press reports (for instance, *TASS*, July 17) that the human-rights group was trying to stir up trouble among the striking miners in Donbass. The same day, the Soviet government agreed to a sweeping reorganization of the coal-mining industry, including full economic and legal autonomy for all mines. The changes are part of an agreement reached with striking coal miners in Kuzbass. As reported by TASS, the document said that, from August 1, all coal mines and related enterprises can sell any of their products that exceed the state targets to both domestic and foreign customers and can negotiate their own prices. The same day, the "Vremya" news program broadcast an interview with Boris El'tsin, who said that a Supreme Soviet resolution might convince the striking coal miners to return to work. He said the miners do not believe resolutions coming from the Central Committee of the CPSU or the government. The same day, *Izvestia* carried an article by Stanislav Kondrashev on the strikes. Kondrashev said the strikers are defending their rights against Party and government structures that have exploited them under the pretext of acting in the state's interest.

On July 23, Gorbachev gave an interview to Central Television on the coal miners' strikes. In the interview Gorbachev agreed that many of the strikers' demands were legitimate. He said people in other sectors of the

Soviet economy also had complaints about the progress of *perestroika*, and he emphasized that the Soviet people should resolve the situation collectively (*Pravda*, July 24). On July 26, TASS reported that virtually all the strikes in the Soviet coal fields were over after agreements had been reached in talks between strike envoys and the central authorities. TASS said strikers in Vorkuta in the Far North had agreed to suspend their action for ten days pending the adoption of an agreement between strike envoys and Prime Minister Nikolai Ryzhkov. The miners decided to send a delegation to Moscow to help work on the draft of the agreement. TASS said in the Donbass region of Ukraine the main concern was now a deep analysis of the strikes and their causes. It said energetic supporters of *perestroika* were already being elected to labor collective councils and trade-union bodies. On July 25, the USSR Supreme Soviet guaranteed new laws on radical labor and economic reform. A resolution appealed for an end to the strikes and also to ethnic unrest during what was termed "this difficult period in Soviet history." On the strikes, see RL 334/89.

Newspaper Says 50,000 Flee Ethnic Strife in Uzbekistan

Literaturnaya gazeta said more than 50,000 people had fled Uzbekistan last month after 100 people died in ethnic clashes. The newspaper said most of the refugees were members of the Meskhetian minority, who clashed with Uzbeks in several towns and cities of the Central Asian republic during ten days of violence in June.

***Literaturnaya gazeta* Interviews Afghan Veteran Who Attacked Sakharov**

Literaturnaya gazeta carried a lengthy interview with Sergei Chervonopisky, the Afghan war veteran who rudely attacked Andrei Sakharov at the Congress of People's Deputies over the Afghan war. In the interview, Chervonopisky persisted in his positive evaluation of Soviet activities in Afghanistan and said he had no intention of apologizing to Sakharov. Describing his general views and interests, Chervonopisky said he liked the journals *Nash sovremennik* and *Molodaya gvardiya*. He attacked the informal Popular Movement of Ukraine for *Perestroika* and defended Nina Andreeva, saying that in her infamous letter she had simply expressed her own point of view, which she had every right to do.

New Committee Chairman Questioned on Housing

The new chairman of the Soviet State Construction Committee said the government's goal of providing every Soviet family with its own home by the year 2000 is

373

feasible, provided two conditions are met. Valerii Serov said that state funding alone will not be enough for the program and that therefore the state must attract extra funds, such as personal savings, as well as help from enterprises and cooperatives. He said the program will also require a high level of organization and tough controls. Serov, a building engineer by training, was one of three state committee chairmen confirmed by the USSR Supreme Soviet on July 12. Deputies also approved Vadim Kirichenko as head of the State Committee for Statistics, and Vladimir Shcherbakov as head of the State Committee for Labor and Social Affairs (*Izvestia*, July 13).

Literaturnaya gazeta on Stolypin

Literaturnaya gazeta carried a lengthy interview with Arkadii Stolypin, the son of Petr Arkad'evich Stolypin, who was prime minister under the last Russian tsar. Arkadii Stolypin lives in France. In the interview Arkadii Stolypin naturally gave a very positive portrait of his father as a personality as well as a politician. Traditionally, Soviet historiography has presented Stolypin in a negative light, emphasizing his role in the suppression of the Russian revolutionary movement and executions of revolutionaries. In an article in *Novyi mir* (No. 5, 1988) discussing Stolypin's economic reforms, however, Vasilii Selyunin spoke of Stolypin in laudatory terms.

Thursday, July 13

Supreme Soviet Approves Further Nominations

The USSR Supreme Soviet approved another five nominations for the posts of chairmen of USSR state committees. Gennadii Yagodin was reappointed head of the Committee for Public Education after deputies had criticized the Soviet school system and urged radical changes in the content of the curriculum and educational methods. TASS said deputies had also approved Mikhail Nenashev as head of the State Committee for Radio and Television, Aleksandr Kamshalov as head of the State Committee for Cinematography, and Boris Tolstykh as chairman of the newly created Committee for Computer Science and Information Engineering (*Izvestia*, July 13–14).

Soviet Official Urges Improvement in Soviet Psychiatry

A Soviet Foreign Ministry official said Soviet psychiatrists support to a considerable decree the critical remarks made by US experts about psychiatry in the USSR. The official, Yurii Reshetov, said improvement is needed in both medical and legal practices involved in compulsory psychiatric treatment. But Reshetov told reporters in Moscow there was currently no basis for talking about political abuse of psychiatry in the USSR. Reshetov was responding to a report from US doctors who visited the Soviet Union earlier this year to examine several patients believed by the West to be victims of psychiatric abuse. The US psychiatrists said that they saw signs that Soviet practices are moving closer to those of the West but that some practices continue that reinforce concerns about psychiatric abuse (*Reuters*, *TASS*, July 13). Reshetov is head of the ministry's Section for International Humanitarian Cooperation and Human Rights.

Azerbaijani Popular Front Calls for Abolition of Committee

The Azerbaijani Popular Front was reported to have demanded the abolition of the special committee set up to administer the Autonomous Oblast of Nagorno-Karabakh. A front member, E. Mamedov, told RFE/RL by telephone from Baku that the front had issued a statement demanding the committee's abolition and the restoration of full Azerbaijani sovereignty over Nagorno-Karabakh. Mamedov said that acts of violence in the oblast are increasing. He said if Moscow does not meet the front's demands over Nagorno-Karabakh the front will struggle for the full political sovereignty of Azerbaijan and for its secession from the Soviet Union.

Nikolai Chervov on Arms Control

Colonel General Nikolai Chervov said the USSR would be willing to give up all nuclear cruise missiles deployed at sea if the United States would do the same. Chervov, chief of the Arms Control Directorate of the Soviet General Staff, made the proposal during an interview with *The Washington Post*. Reports have said developing a verification regime for this class of weapons is among the toughest questions at US-Soviet strategic weapons talks in Geneva. Washington says cheating would be too difficult to detect.

Friday, July 14

Supreme Soviet Confirms Kryuchkov as KGB Chief

The USSR Supreme Soviet confirmed Vladimir Kryuchkov as KGB chairman after hearing his testimony about the agency's operations. Responding to questions, Kryuchkov alleged that the KGB neither has a network of informers nor taps telephones. Deputy Boris El'tsin said, however, that the KGB maintains "an army" of informers (*TASS*, in English, July 14; *Izvestia*, July 15). Supreme Soviet deputies also reappointed Vadim Malyshev as head of the State Committee on Safety in Industry and the Nuclear Power Sector. They endorsed Lyudmila Davletova, a former secretary of the Kazakh Party Central Committee, to oversee consumer-goods production. She will hold ministerial rank (*TASS*, July 14; *Izvestia*, July 15).

Clash between Tajiks and Kirgiz Reported

TASS said there was a violent clash between Tajiks and Kirgiz on July 13 over water rights on the border of the two Central Asian republics. First reporting the clash late on July 14, TASS said that one person had died and that eighteen others had been hurt in the violence. About 1,000 people in three border villages were reported to be involved in the fighting, and a curfew was ordered.

On July 15, the situation on the border between the Tajik and Kirgiz republics was reported calm after the clash. Party officials in both republics said MVD troops had restored order in the area. TASS reported that top Party and government officials in the two republics had held separate meetings on the conflict. They decided to set up special government commissions to devise a plan of action to resolve the dispute (see *Pravda*, July 16).

Article on Foreign Aid Draws Attention to Soviet Budget Deficit

An article in *Argumenty i fakty* (No. 27) called for a reappraisal of the Soviet foreign-aid program and quoted foreign estimates of the scale of Soviet aid in the absence of authoritative Soviet data. The author, B. Sergeev, noted that "a majority of the recipients of Soviet credits are experiencing serious economic difficulties." On the subject of the USSR's capacity to extend aid, he drew attention to the state budget deficit, saying, "this constitutes 11–14 percent of the GNP, according to various estimates." (The projected budgetary deficit for 1989 of 120 billion rubles amounts to over 13 percent of the projected GNP, which will be about 905 billion rubles at current prices). For comparison, Sergeev cites the US budget deficit, which represents some 3 percent of the US GNP.

Glavlit Official Reports on Liberalization of Soviet Censorship

Argumenty i fakty (No. 27) carried an interview with the chairman of the Department for Control over Foreign Literature, B. Skorokhodov, who spoke about liberalization in the work of the main Soviet censorship body, Glavlit. As examples of the easing of restrictions on the distribution of printed materials in the Soviet Union,

Skorokhodov cited the appearance of some Western newspapers on open sale in the country. The number of copies of Western periodicals sold in the USSR is, however, very low. Skorokhodov said there are 1,000 copies of each issue of *The Times* on sale, 600 copies of the *The International Herald Tribune*, and 600 copies of *Die Zeit*. Skorokhodov also pointed out that works by many Soviet émigré writers, such as Vladimir Voinovich, Joseph Brodsky, Vladimir Maksimov, and some others are now on open shelves in Soviet libraries.

Saturday, July 15

Retired KGB Colonel Publishes Memoir

In a pioneering memoir that exonerated virtually every dissident persecuted in the last thirty-five years, a retired KGB colonel expressed shame about his organization's work. Ya. Karpovich also said in the memoir, published in *Ogonek* (No. 29), that the KGB had not adapted to Gorbachev's policy of *glasnost*'. Karpovich said the very idea of a secret police force accountable to no one is repulsive to him now. "Every state should have security organs but not a secret police," he asserted.

TASS Reports Oil Leak into Ukrainian River

TASS said 4,000 cubic meters of oil leaked into the Nuren River in Ukraine this week after a pipeline accident. TASS said a bulldozer bucket accidentally struck the Druzhba pipeline near the village of Malye Moshki. TASS said the leak was capped within fifteen minutes. The report said the oil caught fire and burned for five hours after someone threw a lighted cigarette into the water.

Criticism of Soviet Psychiatry

In Vienna, the president of the Independent Association of Soviet Psychiatrists, Viktor Lanovoi, said doctors who previously sent political dissidents to mental hospitals are still in charge of Soviet psychiatry. He said that the Soviet Union would not clear itself of charges of abusing psychiatry while such doctors remained in control (*RFE/RL Special*, July 15). The Soviet Union is currently seeking readmission to the World Psychiatric Association. On July 17, the WPA said opposition to Soviet readmission to the organization was growing. It said that more cases of psychiatric abuse had come to light and that earlier optimism about an improvement in Soviet psychiatric practices had decreased (*RFE/RL Special*, July 17). See RL 498/89 and RL 499/89.

Gorbachev Sends Letter to Mitterrand

Mikhail Gorbachev said in a letter to the Paris economic summit that *perestroika* is inseparable from full Soviet participation in the world economy. He also called for more multilateral East-West cooperation on global economic problems. Gorbachev's letter to French President Francois Mitterrand was made public today. Gorbachev said that the world can only gain from the opening of Soviet markets to the world economy (*AP, DPA, AFP,* July 15).

Sunday, July 16 ————————————————————————

Disease in Kazakhstan Linked to Nuclear Tests

Maira Zhangelova, chairwoman of the Semipalatinsk Oblast Peace Committee, said a rising incidence of disease among residents of Semipalatinsk in Kazakhstan is directly related to nuclear tests conducted at the nearby underground test site. She was interviewed on the problem on Soviet television. She said preliminary results of a medical investigation show cases of disease to be in direct proportion to the time people have lived in the area and how close they are to the test site. Zhangelova said all the people tested had abnormalities in their blood and immune systems. She called for an immediate halt to all nuclear tests there. On July 17, Soviet antinuclear activists opened a conference in Semipalatinsk to discuss health problems linked to the nuclear-weapons testing site (*TASS,* July 17).

Situation in Georgia

TASS reported that eleven people had died on the weekend in ethnic clashes in Georgia. Quoting the official Georgian news agency Gruzinform, TASS said the fighting had occurred on July 15 in Sukhumi, the capital of the Autonomous Republic of Abkhazia. Clashes between Abkhaz and Georgians involved the use of firearms, knives, sticks, and stones, and 127 people were injured. The fighting was sparked by a dispute over the establishment in Sukhumi of a branch of Tbilisi State University. TASS said the situation was now under the control of MVD troops and the police. On July 17, *Izvestia* quoted USSR Minister of Internal Affairs Vadim Bakatin as saying the situation in Abkhazia was very serious following the clashes. He said there had been reports of disorder "virtually throughout the republic." Gruzinform reported on July 17 that three more people had died in Abkhazia, bringing the number of dead to fourteen. Bakatin, however, put the death toll at thirteen (*TASS,* July 17). The same day, the Popular Front of Georgia and various other informal groups in the republic appealed to Gorbachev to help put a stop to the violence (*RFE/RL Special*, July 17).

On July 18, the death toll in Abkhazia was reported to have risen to sixteen. Radio Moscow said the Soviet authorities had declared emergency measures for the Autonomous republic. Many people, most of them believed to be stranded vacationers, were said to have been evacuated from the area. A curfew was imposed. Soviet television said an armed group of about 300 people had attacked an MVD building in Chkhorotsu in Georgia to seize weapons. On July 19, TASS said eighteen people had been killed and 400 injured in the week's clashes. The agency said armed groups had attacked MVD troops. Georgian Party First Secretary Givi Gumbaridze appealed on local television for calm in Abkhazia (*TASS, AP*, July 19).

On July 20, TASS reported more ethnic clashes in Abkhazia. It said that firearms had been used in clashes in three areas, that thirty people had been detained for violating the curfew in Abkhazia, and that all vacation travel to the area has been halted. Later in the day, however, the agency said the situation in Sukhumi was gradually improving. It said that most stores in Sukhumi were open but that difficulties persisted with supplies of food and other essentials. *Izvestia* said the ethnic unrest in Abkhazia had severely affected southern railroads.

On July 21, TASS said there had been more attacks on law-enforcement organs in Abkhazia. Radio Moscow said most workers had failed to show up at their jobs because of the public transport shutdown in Sukhumi. It said that gunshots were heard in the Sukhumi area during the night and that an explosive device was thrown into a house. There were no casualties reported.

On July 22, several senior officials were replaced in the Autonomous Republic of Abkhazia. TASS said the Abkhaz Party Committee had dismissed secretaries Mikhail Tsuladze and Said Tarkil. Abkhazia's prime minister and first deputy prime minister were also replaced. An official of the USSR Ministry of Internal Affairs called the situation in Abkhazia "extremely tense" and said that both Georgians and Abkhazians had large numbers of weapons. TASS also reported that two policemen had been shot on July 21 as they tried to confiscate weapons and clear roadblocks. Another two law-enforcement officers were reported to have died on July 23 during an attempt to detain an armed group in Abkhazia.

On July 23, Colonel Yurii Shatalin, the commander of MVD troops, told Radio Moscow that unofficial self-defense units were being formed in Georgia, near the border with Abkhazia. Shatalin said that the leaders of informal groups were on hand where the units were being formed and that developments represented a great danger.

On July 24, Western agency reports said hundreds of people had demonstrated for independence in Tbilisi. They were also reported to be protesting against recent attacks on Georgians in Abkhazia. The demonstration coincided with a partial bus strike and a factory work stoppage. In Moscow, Mikhail Gorbachev said the situation in Georgia had become more critical, but he also expressed faith in the republican leaders' ability to end the crisis.

On July 26, Georgia's chief prosecutor, Vakhtang Razmadze, was quoted by *Izvestia* as saying some officials in Abkhazia and western Georgia were implicated in the ethnic violence in Abkhazia. He said some officials of the police and the prosecutor's office had personally handed out weapons to those involved in the disturbances. Razmadze also said the records of the Abkhazia Ministry of Internal Affairs for July 15, 16, and 17 had noted no crimes although "bloody fights were going on between Abkhazians and Georgians right in the center of Sukhumi and shots were ringing out."

TASS reported on July 26 that there had been three explosions in Sukhumi during the previous twenty-four hours. The report said there had been no casualties but gave no further details. It quoted the press center of the USSR Ministry of Internal Affairs as saying there had been unsanctioned rallies in the previous twenty-four hours in Tbilisi and in the Georgian cities of Chiatura and Akhaltsikhe. It said that the situation in Abkhazia was discussed at the rallies and that there were calls for strikes.

On July 27, the Soviet media reported that the unrest had claimed a further victim. They said a patrol of MVD troops had shot and killed a man who had fired at them. They did not say when or where the incident took place (*Central Television,* "Vremya," July 27).

On July 28, TASS said there had been further clashes between security forces and residents in Abkhazia. It said forty-seven people had been detained in the previous twenty-four hours, but it reported no casualties. The Soviet media said the death toll stemming from the unrest stood at twenty-two. The same day, the newspaper *Zarya Vostoka* revealed that Georgians had suffered two-thirds of the casualties in the recent ethnic unrest. The newspaper said 302 of the 448 injured were Georgian, including forty-nine of the sixty-two wounded by guns. Georgian activists claim that the rioting in Abkhazia was preceded by weeks of threats by Abkhazian activists and that during that time the latter acquired large numbers of arms. In a televised speech this week, Georgian Party chief Givi Gumbaridze promised an investigation into the source of the arms used on both sides (*AP*, July 28).

It was reported that the Soviet Union had imposed new restrictions on goods that can be taken out of the country. Radio Moscow said that, because of shortages on the domestic market, the export of building materials, household linen, and tableware is forbidden. In its report the radio said Soviet citizens and tourists to the Soviet Union have been taking goods out of the country. It said there has recently been evidence of the mass export of simple, cheap goods in everyday demand. The radio said the ban is temporary, like a similar ban imposed on the export of refrigerators and television sets that has been in force since the beginning of February.

USSR Forbids Export of Goods in Short Supply

Monday, July 17

The USSR Supreme Soviet approved the last of Prime Minister Nikolai Ryzhkov's nominees for posts in his new government. TASS reported that the Supreme Soviet had rejected Ryzhkov's attempts to resubmit the nominations of two candidates who had been rejected earlier by the parliament. (They are Polad-Zade for water resources minister and Vladimir Kamentsev for chairman of the Foreign Economic Commission.) Ryzhkov told the Supreme Soviet the debate on his slate of nominees had "laid bare" a cross-section of problems in Soviet society. He said some of the questions raised had already led the government to adopt new measures.

Supreme Soviet Approves Last Nominees for Government

USSR Minister of Internal Affairs Vadim Bakatin commented on the difficulties in dealing with a rising crime rate and an increase in ethnic disturbances. Interviewed in *Pravda*, Bakatin said that the MVD did not have enough troops for rapid deployment to areas of ethnic tension and that the 18,000 troops available were poorly equipped.

Bakatin Says MVD Needs More Money

Soviet Defense Minister Dmitrii Yazov said there was no accident aboard the Soviet nuclear-powered submarine spotted billowing smoke off Norway on July 16. Yazov said the smoke was exhaust fumes from the submarine's

Yazov Says There Was No Accident on Soviet Sub

diesel engines. He said the diesel engines were switched on following a short-circuit in the vessel's battery power system. Yazov said the submarine had returned to its base under its own power (*TASS*, July 17).

Pravda on Accident at Nuclear-Weapons Plant in 1957

Pravda said experience gained in the 1957 accident at the nuclear-weapons plant in the southern Urals could have been used in the clean-up after the Chernobyl' explosion; but, *Pravda* said, "departmental disunity" prevented this. A TASS summary of the article in the newspaper gave no specifics. The 1957 accident was a secret in the USSR until this year.

Memorial Ceremony Held for Tsar

A ceremony was held in a Moscow graveyard to honor the memory of the last Russian tsar and his family. It is the first public honor for the tsar since he and his family were executed seventy-one years ago. At least 150 people gathered to sing "God Save the Tsar" and participate in ceremonies conducted by four Orthodox priests. Western correspondents said police and Party functionaries had tried to interrupt the rites but were rebuffed and withdrew to observe (*AP*, *DPA*, July 17).

Azerbaijani Popular Front Founded

The founding conference of the Azerbaijani Popular Front was reported to have been held on July 16 in Baku. A member of the front's initiative group, E'tibar Mamedov, told RFE/RL by telephone from Baku that the conference elected Abulfaz Aliev, a historian, as chairman of the front. Mamedov said two officials from the Baku Party Committee attended the conference. Mamedov said a prominent Azeri poet, Bakhtiyar Vahabadze, sent greetings to the conference and called on everyone to support the new popular front.

Ecumenical Church Group Meets in Moscow

The Central Committee of the Ecumenical Council of Churches is meeting in Moscow. The council includes most of the world's Protestant and Orthodox Churches, but not the Roman Catholic Church. This is the first meeting in the Soviet Union for the organization, which is based in Geneva and represents about 400 million Christians. The meeting is expected to include a forum on *perestroika* at which the situation of the Russian Orthodox Church will be discussed. Other topics are expected to be genetic engineering and an initiative to speed the reunification of the two Koreas (*DPA*, July 17).

Mikhail Gorbachev said the next Party congress—scheduled for 1991—should be moved up to the fall of next year. Gorbachev made the proposal at a meeting of the Party Central Committee. Gorbachev said that the advance of *perestroika* in the Party was lagging behind Soviet society and that the Party could lose its leading role as a result. (Informal groups, such as the Belorussian Popular Front, and now the striking coal miners in Kuzbass have demanded the abolition of Article 6 of the Soviet Constitution on the leading role of the CPSU in Soviet society.) In another speech, Gorbachev proposed to donate 30 percent of the CPSU's budget—500 million rubles—to help the country's poor (*Pravda*, July 21).

Gorbachev Addresses CPSU CC

Politburo member Egor Ligachev said a multiparty system would be "fatal" for the USSR because the CPSU is the only politically unifying force in the country. Ligachev was speaking at a meeting of Party officials in Moscow. His speech was published in *Pravda* on July 21. In it Ligachev said there are examples of Party bodies in Moscow and in the provinces who fail to carry out Party policy. He referred to Mikhail Gorbachev's call for ethnic calm and said it was answered in some regions with "clashes and deaths."

Ligachev Says Multiparty System Would Be "Fatal" for USSR

Articles published in *Sotsialisticheskaya industriya* on July 14 and 18 laid the blame for the forcible resettlement of the Karachai in 1943 on Mikhail Suslov, Brezhnev's ideology chief. This episode in Suslov's life is not unknown to Soviet readers, because a number of Soviet newspapers have published Roy Medvedev's biography of Suslov, but the *Sotsialisticheskaya industriya* accounts contain many fresh details. The Karachai were accused of collaborating with the Nazi invaders in executing Jewish and Russian children who had been undergoing medical treatment at Teberda. According to *Sotsialisticheskaya industriya*, 42,000 of the 64,000 Karachai who were resettled died during the first two years of their internal exile. From 1939 to 1944, Suslov was Party chief of Stavropol Krai, which included the Karachai-Cherkess Autonomous Oblast and was the person primarily responsible for the anti-Karachai campaign in 1943.

Suslov's Part in Stalin's Crimes

Siberian Activist Given Jail Sentence

Siberian human-rights activist Aleksei Manannikov was detained in the Siberian city of Novosibirsk and sentenced to fifteen days in jail. RFE/RL was told by sources in Novosibirsk that he was jailed on charges of organizing an unsanctioned meeting in Novosibirsk two weeks ago (July 4). Manannikov did not have a defense lawyer at his trial, and no witnesses were called. Three months ago he spent ten days in jail on similar charges.

Metropolitan Visits Prison Camp

Filaret, Metropolitan of Kiev and Galicia, paid a visit to a strict-regime labor camp in the village of Buch near Kiev, according to *Literaturnaya gazeta*. Camp inmates were permitted to wear crosses, and the commandant of the camp promised that a Bible and New Testament given to the camp library by the metropolitan would be available to inmates without restrictions.

Arms Control

The USSR Foreign Ministry said the latest round of US-Soviet talks on chemical weapons was among the "most useful" rounds. The ministry's spokesman Gennadii Gerasimov told reporters that "considerable progress" had been made, and he cited progress on agreement about short-notice inspections of chemical weapons stocks and proposals to destroy existing stockpiles. In Washington, on July 18, State Department spokesman Richard Boucher said there had been progress on the wording of a draft treaty but no breakthroughs (*Reuters, DPA*, July 19).

Supreme Soviet to Set Up Press Center

The USSR Supreme Soviet has voted to set up a press center. A resolution passed by the body said the center would hold regular briefings for Soviet and foreign journalists and news conferences on the more important issues discussed at sessions of the Congress of People's Deputies and the Supreme Soviet. Soviet and foreign journalists who are accredited by the press center or who have invitations will be permitted to attend meetings of the chambers of the Supreme Soviet and of committees and commissions (*TASS*, July 19).

Afghan Veterans Say Soldiers Fired On by Own Side

Two Soviet veterans said that it was true Soviet soldiers in Afghanistan had been fired on by their own side several times during the war but that this was by mistake. The veterans' account, carried in *Moscow News* (No. 30), supports to some extent Academician Andrei Sakharov's assertions. Sakharov was jeered and shouted down by fellow deputies when he spoke of such incidents at the Congress of People's Deputies. The veterans, Valerii Abramov and Ruslan Umiev, gave eyewitness descriptions of two separate air attacks by Soviet helicopters on their own troops. They said the attacks were made by mistake.

Thursday, July 20

South African Foreign Minister Roelof "Pik" Botha called for the establishment of trade relations between his nation and the Soviet Union. TASS said Botha made the call in an interview in *New Times* (No. 30). TASS said it was the first time a South African cabinet member had given an interview to a Soviet publication.

South African Foreign Minister Interviewed by Soviet Weekly

A special investigation is being conducted into the riots in the Kazakh capital of Alma-Ata in December, 1986. Radio Alma-Ata said the commission was convened by the Kazakhstan Supreme Soviet "with a view to giving this matter full *glasnost*." The radio said the action was taken as a result of inquiries by deputies of the Kazakh Supreme Soviet and "appeals from citizens." It said the results of the investigation would be made public.

Investigative Commission Set Up in Kazakhstan

Friday, July 21

A Ministry of Internal Affairs official said violence and hostage-taking in Soviet prisons is on the rise. Ivan Katargin, head of the ministry's Department of Correctional Affairs, said crime in correctional institutions had increased by 28.8 percent in the first five months of this year. His comments appeared in *Nedelya* (No. 29). Katargin said that there have been forty-eight cases of hostage-taking this year—three times as many as last year—and that 114 guards have been subjected to violence, with fourteen wounded and one killed. He said that in the first five months of this year disciplinary or criminal charges had been brought against 263 inmates; that steps were being taken to reverse the trend, including increasing the number of visits by relatives; and that corrupt prison officials would be fired. See RL 421/89.

Violence on Rise in Soviet Prisons

Ukrainian Catholics Protest at Moscow Church Meeting

Ukrainian Catholics demanding the legalization of their Church demonstrated outside the building in which the World Council of Churches was holding a meeting in Moscow. DPA and Reuters said about thirty activists from the outlawed Church had participated in the protest.

USSR and Bulgarian-Turkish Conflict

The Soviet ambassador to Anakara, Albert Chernyshev, was reported to have traveled to Moscow for talks on the rift between Turkey and Bulgaria over Sofia's treatment of its ethnic Turkish minority. The Anatolian news agency quoted Chernishev as saying he might go to Sofia after his talks in Moscow. He said he will continue his efforts as long as both nations want Soviet mediation in the dispute (*RFE/RL Special*, July 21).

Akhromeev Speaks before House of Representatives

Soviet Marshal Sergei Akhromeev said talks on reducing naval forces are needed for a further improvement in US-Soviet relations. Akhromeev, chief military adviser to Gorbachev, spoke before the House of Representatives Armed Services Committee in Washington. He is the most senior Soviet military man ever to do so. Akhromeev said he is convinced the United States and its allies do not intend to start a war against the USSR and its allies. But he said the danger of war has not disappeared. He cited the US Strategic Defense Initiative and US reluctance to negotiate reductions in naval strength as points of contention. Akhromeev said Soviet tank production has been cut 40 percent this year, to 1,700. Committee chairman, Congressman Les Aspin, said this information was both completely new and encouraging (*Reuters, AP*, July 21).

New Council to Help Interethnic Relations

A new council attached to the Moscow journal *Friendship and Nationalities* is to help settle problems of interethnic relations in the Soviet Union. TASS said the council was made up of outstanding writers, scientists, and cultural figures of various nationalities. It said the council would invite to its sessions deputies of the Supreme Soviet and representatives of all strata of the population who want to contribute to the consolidation of interethnic relations. TASS said the journal, which has a circulation of over one million, will report on the activities of the council.

AIDS Increase Blamed on Infected Blood and Equipment

The head of the AIDS laboratory of the Central Epidemiology Unit in Moscow said there were 718 AIDS carriers in the USSR. The figure reported a month ago was 269.

Valentin Pokrovsky said infection often occurs through unsterilized medical equipment. He noted cases in Elista, Volgograd, and Rostov, most of which can be traced to the multiple use of unsterilized syringes. Pokrovsky said "an intolerably high percentage" of AIDS cases in the USSR were caused by the unwitting transfusion of infected blood during surgery. He said of the total number of carriers, about 40 percent have contracted the virus this way (*TASS*, July 21).

Russians Demonstrate in Tallinn

It was reported that about 10,000 Russians rallied in the Estonian capital of Tallinn to mark the anniversary of the 1940 annexation of the republic by the USSR. The reports said that Tallinn city officials had asked the predominantly Russian organization "Interfront" to delay its rally until the evening but that its leaders had insisted on gathering in the afternoon. Soviet television quoted a rally organizer as saying the gathering was held to defend the constitutional rights of Russians in Estonia. Reports quoted banners carried at the rally as saying "Down with the Estonian falsification of history," and condemning "Instigators of inter-ethnic hostility" (*Central Television*, "Vremya" July 22).

Deputy Calls for Restoration of Land Ownership

USSR Supreme Soviet deputy Vladimir Tikhonov called for a reform to restore land ownership in the Soviet Union. Tikhonov made the remarks during a meeting of the Supreme Soviet Committee for Agrarian and Food Issues. TASS quoted Tikhonov as saying land utilization should be replaced by full ownership of land by the farmer. He said this would give the farmer the right to profit from the sale of his products as well as choose customers and partners. According to TASS, many deputies said an existing draft law on land utilization lacks new approaches to problems of efficiency.

Saturday, July 22

Soviet Minister Attacks Shamir Plan

Soviet Deputy Foreign Minister Gennadii Tarasov said the Israeli government's election plan for the occupied lands was "a diabolic machination" out of touch with reality. Tarasov said the plan could not be put into effect, because it ignored the role of the Palestine Liberation Organization. He reiterated the Soviet position that an international Middle East Peace Conference is the way to settle the Middle East conflict. Tarasov spoke on his

387

departure from Tunis after talks with PLO chairman Yasser Arafat and Arab League Secretary General Chedli Klibi (*Reuters*, July 22).

Alternative Draft on Uzbek Language Published

An alternative draft law on granting Uzbek the status of a state language was published in the Uzbek Party daily *Pravda Vostoka*. The author of the draft was said to be the well-known Uzbek writer Sarvar Azimov. The official draft law on the Uzbek language was published by a team of specialists on June 19, and a two-month period was set for its discussion. The newspaper quoted Azimov as saying the sphere of interethnic relations needs "a truly Marxist approach and not an administrative-commanding cover." The newspaper said the alternative draft accurately defined the role of the Russian language as a means of interethnic communication.

Tajik Declared State Language

Tajikistan's Supreme Soviet made Tajik the state language of the republic. TASS said the new law stipulates that other nationalities in Tajikistan also have the right to use and develop their languages and cultures. In another development, TASS said a bilateral commission had been created to define the border between Tajikistan and Kirgizia at points where clashes have erupted. Thousands of Kirgiz and Tajiks fought at the border recently over land and water rights. At least one person was killed in the fighting.

USSR Cuts Number of Troops in Maneuvers in Hungary

Some 11,000 Soviet troops will take part in military exercises in Hungary in October rather than the planned 13,000. Radio Budapest (2200) quoted the Soviet Ministry of Defense as saying the move had been made within the framework of Soviet troop withdrawals from Hungary. The radio said the USSR will also cut the number of Soviet troops in military maneuvers to be held in the GDR, Czechoslovakia, and the Baltic. On July 23, Czechoslovak television carried a report saying some 13,000 Soviet troops would take part in military maneuvers in Czechoslovakia this fall, instead of 16,500 as originally planned.

Pravda Calls US Senate Resolution "Provocative"

Pravda described as "provocative" a US Senate resolution on the disputed oblast of Nagorno-Karabakh. Senators voted in favor of the nonbinding resolution, which urged Gorbachev to engage in meaningful talks with local representatives about demands that the oblast be transferred to Armenian control. In commenting on the resolution, *Pravda* said the situation in the Nargorno-Karabakh Autonomous Oblast was an entirely internal matter. It said outside interference only worsened the situation.

Kiev City First Secretary Replaced

The Party first secretary of the city of Kiev, Konstantin Masik, was reported to have been replaced. Masik is the second high-ranking Party official to be removed recently. Yurii Solov'ev, the Leningrad Oblast Party first secretary, was removed less than two weeks ago. Masik and Solov'ev were among several Party officials defeated in the March elections to the Congress of People's Deputies. The Soviet media said a plenum of the Kiev City Party Committee accepted Masik's resignation. They said he would be replaced by Anatolii Kornienko, formerly deputy head of the city's construction and personnel department (*Pravda*, July 22).

Ryzhkov Has Talks with Chinese Deputy Prime Minister

Soviet Prime Minister Nikolai Ryzhkov held talks in Moscow with Chinese Deputy Prime Minister Tian Jiyun. TASS said the two officials praised the developing links between Soviet and Chinese border areas (*Izvestia*, July 22). Ryzhkov and Tian also discussed the Soviet-Chinese Commission for Economic, Commercial, and Scientific-Technological Cooperation. They proposed cooperation in the fields of the power industry, including nuclear power, transport, electronics, consumer goods, timber, and farming. TASS said they noted that the USSR and China are going through a period of serious internal reforms that are aimed at "identifying reserves inherent in the Socialist system."

Yazov Urges More Attention to Individuals in Military

Soviet Defense Minister Dmitrii Yazov said political awareness needs to be improved in the armed services to ensure the success of *perestroika*. *Krasnaya zvezda* reported Yazov's remarks from a speech he made last week to chiefs of the military's political divisions. Yazov said more attention needs to be paid to individuals in the Soviet armed forces, adding that political workers do not always know how to work well with individuals. He also said the ideals of honor and dignity need to be nurtured in officers. Yazov called for new approaches but at the same time warned against "nationalist manifestations, abstract pacifism, and attempts to discredit the armed forces." He also said a broad package of measures is envisaged for strengthening the officer corps "in connection with ongoing military reductions."

Sunday, July 23 ────────────────────────────────────

Soviet Daily Says Chernobyl' Plant Should Be Closed Down

Komsomol'skaya pravda said the Chernobyl' nuclear power plant should be closed down. The newspaper said that contaminated soil around the plant would make the area unfit for human habitation for decades and that soldiers at the power plant are needlessly performing life-threatening duties. It added that the boundaries of the present closed zone around Chernobyl' must be made to correspond to the "real" radiation situation.

Falin Finally Confirms Existence of Secret Protocols

The head of the CPSU Central Committee's International Department and a member of the Congress of People's Deputies commission set up to evaluate the Molotov-Ribbentrop Pact, Valentin Falin, has confirmed the existence of the secret protocols attached to the Molotov-Ribbentrop pact. Falin acknowledged the existence of the protocols in an interview with West German television (*DPA*, July 23). Previously, Falin maintained that, because the originals of the secret protocols cannot be found, it was impossible to decide whether they had really existed. On July 27, Western reports said the commission had recommended that the Soviet Union officially acknowledge the existence of the protocols. The reports said the commission had also recommended that the pact and the secret protocols be annulled (*AP, DPA*, July 27).

Party Official Links Suicides and Disease to Nuclear Tests

A local Party official in Kazakhstan said cancer among young people, suicides, and mental retardation in his district were the result of forty years of testing of Soviet nuclear weapons at the Semipalatinsk test site. Abay Raion Party First Secretary Kh. Motaev spoke at a three-day meeting of scientists, antinuclear activists, and Party and local government officials. Soviet television reported that the delegates voted unanimously for the closure of the test site.

Monday, July 24 ────────────────────────────────────

Soviet Official Says US Afraid of Verification Schemes

A Soviet arms control official said the United States is afraid of verification schemes for naval atomic weapons. The official, Colonel General Nikolai Chervov, is the chief of the arms control directorate of the Soviet General Staff. In a letter to *The Boston Globe* he said the unresolved issue of cutting sea-based nuclear cruise missiles stands in the way of proposed cuts of Soviet and US strategic nuclear weapons. Chervov said the United States should consider Soviet proposals rather than contending that verification cannot be effective. Chervov's letter was a response to an interview with the US chief of naval operations, Admiral Carlisle Trost, which the newspaper published last week. Trost said a Soviet offer to ban all naval nuclear cruise missiles if the United States does the same was impracticable because such a ban could not be verified, short of intrusive shipboard inspection (*AP*, July 24).

Official Says Veterans and Disabled Persons Living in Misery

The chairman of the USSR Supreme Soviet Committee for Veterans and Disabled Persons, Nikolai Bosenko, said many millions of Soviet veterans and disabled persons are living in miserable conditions. Writing in *Izvestia*, Bosenko said 22 million people have pensions of no more than sixty rubles a month. Bosenko said these people have performed their obligations and done honest work. He said it has become evident that the government must act to correct the social injustice done to them.

Deputies on Situation in Estonia

A member of the Congress of People's Deputies said nationalism in Estonia could lead to a mass exodus of refugees. The deputy, Evgenii Kogan, told the Supreme Soviet that the situation in the Baltic republics, particularly in Estonia, is more serious than the strikes in the USSR's coal fields. (Kogan is a leader of "Interdvizhenie," a movement consisting of non-Estonians that is opposed to the current Estonian national revival.) Kogan said that there is now a strong movement in Estonia for complete independence from the USSR and that proposed changes in Estonia's election law will deprive tens of thousands of people of voting rights. The Estonian Supreme Soviet began a meeting on July 24 to discuss the changes in the law (*TASS, RadioMoscow,* July 24). Later that day, the "Vremya" television news program reported that the Estonian Supreme Soviet had postponed a vote on procedures for elections to local soviets. The draft law includes residency requirements for those who wish to vote in such elections or who wish to run in them. Radio Tallinn said the postponement came at the request of Russian-speaking delegates after non-Estonian workers opposed to the draft law had staged protest strikes (*AP, Reuters,* July 25).

Strikes by non-Estonian workers continued on July 26 and 27. By July 27 some twenty-three enterprises were reported to have closed down. TASS said Aeroflot workers had also joined the strike. Estonian Communist Party Ideological Secretary Mikk Titma said a number of Russian factory directors were locking out employees to protest against a proposal to grant the republic economic independence. On July 28, Estonian Radio said the republic's Russian workers had gone back to work after the Estonian government had agreed to form a commission to hear their complaints (*RFE Estonian Service, AP*, July 28).

Some Speeches Left Out of TV Coverage of Supreme Soviet

Radio Moscow said some speeches are being left out intentionally in Soviet television coverage of meetings of the USSR Supreme Soviet. Vice President Anatolii Luk'yanov said the speeches not being broadcast deal primarily with "clashes between the deputies themselves," especially on interethnic issues. He said such speeches are often emotional and "could cause an outburst" in the regions concerned. He insisted that failure to broadcast the speeches was not a violation of *glasnost'*.

Tuesday, July 25

Supreme Soviet Adopts Appeal to Soviet People

The USSR Supreme Soviet adopted unanimously an appeal to the Soviet people about recent ethnic violence and strikes in the country. TASS said the appeal states that these troubles show that *perestroika* is going through "an acute and difficult period." The appeal said a situation is being created that demands maximum unity of all forces to advance the causes of radical economic reform, democratization, and openness. The appeal said the Supreme Soviet "guarantees" that during its current session and one scheduled for autumn, a number of laws will be adopted to further this end (*TASS*, July 25). The draft of the appeal was presented to the Supreme Soviet by political commentator Fedor Burlatsky who said it was very important for the Supreme Soviet to take all responsibility for the situation in the USSR.

Yazov Visits Britain

Soviet Defense Minister Dmitrii Yazov headed a military delegation on a four-day visit to Britain. TASS (July 24) quoted Yazov as saying the visit would help to promote trust between Britain and the USSR. A spokesman for the British Defense Ministry said Yazov is the most senior Soviet defense official ever to visit Britain. On July 25, Yazov met with British Prime Minister Margaret Thatcher and with British Defense Secretary George Younger. During their meeting an agreement was reached to step up military contacts at all levels as a way of boosting mutual confidence. Yazov told a news conference: "The Cold War is behind us due to the efforts of the Soviet, British, and American peoples" (*RFE/RL Special*, July 25). On July 26, Yazov watched an air display by Britains's most advanced jet fighters at a Royal Air Force base in Scotland. He said his presence at the base reflected an easing of East-West tensions (*AP*, July 26). On July 28, Yazov said in London that NATO's plans to replace its shorter-range lance missile with a new, longer-range version could violate the INF treaty and that this might force the Soviet Union to resume production of SS-23s (*RFE/RL Special, Reuters*, July 28). See *Pravda* July 25–29.

Seventy Soviet citizens may lose their state awards because they have committed serious crimes. *Izvestia* said the Deputies' Commission on State Awards had approved a draft decree and had sent a seventy-name list to the Presidium of the USSR Supreme Soviet for discussion and approval. *Izvestia* said many of those on the list had taken bribes, including Yurii Churbanov, a former Soviet first deputy minister of internal affairs and son-in-law of Leonid Brezhnev. *Izvestia* noted that Brezhnev's widow had returned to the state "absolutely all" her husband's awards, both Soviet and foreign ones (*RFE/RL Special*, July 25).

Seventy Citizens May Lose State Awards

The leader of a US group concerned with Soviet Jews said the Soviet Union has failed to meet its obligations on emigration under the Helsinki follow-up process. Shoshna Cardin, chairwoman of the National Conference on Soviet Jewry, cited poor Soviet performance in the resolution of long-term refusednik cases. She noted that a key commitment of the concluding document of the Vienna follow-up meeting last January, which was signed by the Soviet Union, was to resolve outstanding cases within six months (*RFE/RL Special*, July 25).

USSR Accused of Failing to Meet Vienna Obligations

Mikhail Gorbachev said the CPSU must change itself from a commanding force into a genuine political vanguard and must learn to influence the masses by arguments. TASS said Gorbachev made the statements during a meeting in Moscow with visiting Hungarian Party leaders Rezso Nyers and Karoly Grosz. TASS said that during the

Gorbachev Meets Hungarian Party Leaders

meeting Gorbachev and the Hungarian officials also discussed the possibility of further reductions in Soviet troop strength in Hungary. It said they agreed that such cuts depend upon the general disarmament process in Europe and the troop reduction talks in Vienna.

Activist Says Armenian Leaders Back Karabakh Committee Goals

A founding member of the Karabakh Committee said Armenia's leaders support all but one of the committee's demands. Levon Ter-Petrossyan told *The International Herald Tribune* that the only goal not shared by the Armenian leadership is the formation of an Armenian army division. The committee's chief goal is the transfer of Nagorno-Karabakh from Azerbaijan to Armenia, but it also wants more cultural and economic sovereignty for Armenia.

Curfew in Novyi Uzen' Lifted

A curfew introduced in the town of Novyi Uzen' in western Kazakhstan following ethnic violence there last month has now been lifted. TASS said the Presidium of the Kazakhstan Supreme Soviet had decided to lift the curfew on July 24. It had been in force in the town since June 19 (*TASS*, July 25).

Bishop of Belorussia Named by Vatican

Western reports said that the Vatican had named Father Tadeusz Kondrusiewicz as apostolic administrator of Minsk and titular bishop of Ippona. The reports said this was the first such appointment—outside the Baltic and with the consent of the Soviet authorities—since the revolution and signaled an improvement in relations between Moscow and the Vatican (*RFE/RL Special*, July 26).

Radio Moscow Reports Problems of Bashkiria Oil Refineries

Radio Moscow (1700) said the oil refineries of Bashkiria are either shut down or nearly at a standstill while farm machinery elsewhere in the USSR is standing idle because of a lack of fuel. The radio said that the region's refineries are able to produce whatever diesel fuel is needed but that there is neither road nor river transportation available to deliver it to consumers. It said the Ufa refinery had been unable to deliver 3.6 million rubles worth of diesel fuel this month alone.

Police Disperse Latvian Environmentalists

Police dispersed environmentalists who staged an overnight demonstration in an attempt to close down a cellulose plant in the Latvian city of Skola. Six members of the Latvian Environmental Protection Club were detained when they refused to leave the area. The environmentalists have blamed the cellulose plant for pollution of the Lielupa River and the nearby beaches on the Gulf of Riga (*Radio Riga*, 2200, July 25).

Wednesday, July 26

Resistance Says Soviet Embassy Hit in Rocket Attacks

The resistance-run Afghan news agency said the *mujahidin* staged rocket attacks on the Soviet embassy in Kabul between July 3 and 17, killing a total of twenty-eight people. The pro-resistance Afghan Information Center quoted a resistance commander, Abdul Haq, as saying the attacks focused on the embassy complex, the Interior Ministry building, the airport, and the presidential palace and military installations.

Independent Journalist Freed from Jail

A journalist for the unofficial Soviet journal *Glasnost'*, Sergei Kuznetsov, was reported freed after seven months' detention. A spokesman for the opposition group Democratic Union, Yurii Mityunov, told Radio Liberty that a court in Sverdlovsk had released Kuznetsov on July 26. Mityunov said the court had freed Kuznetsov, who had been on a hunger strike, because of his physical and psychological condition.

Veterans Suggest Forming Volunteers' Division to Fight in Afghanistan

Moscow News (No. 31) was quoted as saying a group of Soviet veterans from the Afghan war had suggested forming a volunteers' division to resume the fight. The report added, however, that an unofficial reply from the USSR Ministry of Defense had dismissed the idea and mentioned, among other things, that Kabul had not asked for resumed Soviet intervention. The veterans said in their offer that a volunteers' division would not violate the Geneva accords governing the Soviet troop withdrawal. They also said it would help stabilize the region, saying that the conflict threatened to spill over into Uzbekistan.

China Increases Trade with USSR

A Chinese official said China's trade with the Soviet Union has risen more than 30 percent this year, but he denied that China is switching its business to the Soviet Union because of Western economic sanctions. Liu Xiangdong of the Ministry of Foreign Economic Relations and Trade told reporters in Beijing that normalization of relations and improved trading conditions account for the increased trade (*Reuters, UPI*, July 26).

IAEA Circulates Soviet Report about Kyshtym Accident

The International Atomic Energy Agency (IAEA) is circulating to its member states a Soviet technical report about a major release of radioactive waste from a nuclear weapons plant at Kyshtym in the southern Urals in 1957. IAEA sources say this is the first official Soviet disclosure to the IAEA of what happened. Moscow kept silent about the accident for thirty-two years until last month when some details were made public by TASS. The IAEA said the Soviet report shows that radioactivity was released after the failure of a cooling system for a storage tank containing "high-level radioactive nitrate acetate waste." This resulted in a chemical explosion. The report said the radioactivity affected an area 300 kilometers long and 8–9 kilometers wide. It said that, although people were exposed to radiation, there were no fatalities as a result of the accident; nor, it said, had there been any "observable changes in mortality or morbidity rates in those exposed." It added that no one suffered congenital defects as a result of exposure to radiation.

Moscow Buys More Sugar on World Market

A Soviet official was quoted as saying the USSR had bought 250,000 tons of white sugar on the world market in the past week. Aleksandr Krivenko, the chief of the Soviet procurement agency, said the purchases had been ordered because of a plentiful Soviet fruit harvest that increased the demand for sugar for home jam-making. He said the purchases are also part of a government program to increase food supplies in state stores. Sugar has been rationed in many areas of the USSR until recently (*Reuters*, July 27).

Rise in Crime in USSR

USSR Minister of Internal Affairs Vadim Bakatin said in an interview that crime in the USSR rose 32 percent in the first six months of this year compared with the same period last year. He said 1.1 million crimes were committed between January and June. Bakatin also said about 170,000 crimes were listed as serious, nearly 40 percent more than in the first six months of last year. He complained about an increase in organized crime and said this must be countered with force based on law (*TASS*, July 26).

USSR Deputy Foreign Minister Anatolii Adamishin said more than 22,000 Soviet Jews had emigrated in the past five months. Adamishin said the Supreme Soviet is to consider codifying emigration laws. He also said Moscow is reviewing long-term refusednik cases individually in an attempt to solve as many as possible. Adamishin made the remarks during a meeting with officials of major American Jewish organizations at the headquarters of the National Conference on Soviet Jewry in New York (*RFE/RL Special*, July 27).

Soviet Deputy Foreign Minister Meets American Jewish Leaders

_____ *Thursday, July 27*

The USSR Supreme Soviet voted for major economic changes in the three Baltic republics. Deputies approved a resolution granting self-financing to all three republics starting January 1 (*Izvestia*, July 28). This will give the republics control over the profits and investments of local industries. The deputies also approved a resolution granting economic independence to Lithuania and Estonia. Details are to be worked out by Supreme Soviet commissions. Moscow deputy Fedor Burlatsky told the USSR Supreme Soviet that the action "is the beginning of a movement in the direction of real radical structural reform" for the entire country. The approval of the resolutions came a day after the Supreme Soviet had failed to approve a draft law on economic autonomy for Lithuania and Estonia. TASS said the debate over the draft law was heated, with many deputies saying they opposed taking "rash decisions that were most likely to be followed by all Union republics." On July 26, thousands of Latvians staged a demonstration in Riga demanding that Latvia be included in plans for economic independence for the Baltic republics (*TASS*, July 26 and 27). On July 27, Radio Riga said the Latvian Supreme Soviet had adopted a law granting the republic economic independence.

Supreme Soviet Votes for Major Economic Changes in Baltic

RSFSR Prime Minister Aleksandr Vlasov said a mounting shortage of consumer goods is causing "a public outcry" in the Soviet Union. Vlasov told the RSFSR Supreme Soviet that Soviet citizens have some 35,000–40,000 million rubles available to buy goods that do not exist. He said this has led to inflation. TASS said Vlasov spoke at the opening of an RSFSR Supreme Soviet debate on how to improve the quantity and quality of consumer goods. On July 28, Vlasov said the cost-accounting methods being adopted

Vlasov Reports "Public Outcry" over Goods Shortages

by the Baltic republics are also the future path of the RSFSR. He added, however, that the transition to a system of profit and loss must be carefully handled. He also called for an increase in the republic's sovereignty. In a debate during the same session on speeding up local elections, RSFSR President Vitalii Vorotnikov reminded Soviet voters that they can recall local soviets and officials who fail to implement *perestroika* (*TASS*, in English, July 28).

Soviet and US Scientists to Publish Arms Control Magazine

US and Soviet scientists said they had begun a cooperative effort to publish a magazine devoted to the scientific aspects of arms control. The magazine is called *Science and Global Security*. The cochairmen of the magazine's editorial board are Director of the Soviet Space Research Institute Academician Roald Sagdeev and Frank von Hippel, a prominent US physicist from Princeton University. Sagdeev told reporters in Boston that politicians want to know what independent scientists think about the technical aspects of arms control (*RFE/RL Special*, July 28).

Figures Show Economic Growth behind Target

Official Soviet statistics for the first half of this year show the country's economic growth is running well behind target. The figures were released in Moscow by Nikolai Belov, chairman of the USSR State Committee for Statistics. Belov said the overall gross national product rose 3.5 percent compared with the same period last year. The target is 6 percent. He said the current inflation rate was 2.2 percent. Belov said national income rose 2.5 percent, well short of the target of 6 percent (*TASS*, July 27; *Izvestia*, July 28).

New First Deputy Prime Minister Appointed

The USSR Supreme Soviet appointed Vladilen Nikitin as a USSR first deputy prime minister and chairman of the State Commission of Food and Procurement. TASS said Nikitin had served as first deputy chief of the State Agroindustrial Committee of the RSFSR. The Supreme Soviet also appointed Vyacheslav Senchagov as chairman of the USSR State Committee on Prices (*Izvestia*, July 28).

Almost 200,000 Citizens Emigrate in Eighteen Months

The head of the Soviet visa registration office (OVIR), Rudolf Kuznetsov, said almost 200,000 Soviet citizens had emigrated from the USSR over the past eighteen months. TASS quoted Kuznetsov as saying that, since the Helsinki review conference accords were signed in January, more than 1,500 Soviet citizens had received visas to leave the country permanently or temporarily. Kuznetsov said the cases of about 300 other people cannot be resolved at present. He said most of these involved people who have had access to classified information.

New Chairman of Council of Ministers in Kazakhstan

TASS reported that Uzakbai Karamanov had been appointed chairman of the Council of Ministers in Kazakhstan. He replaces Nursultan Nazarbaev, who was elected to head the republican Party organization in June. To judge from the TASS report, Karamanov, who had headed Kazakhstan's State Committee for Material and Technical Supply since April, 1987, has drawn attention to himself through his role in Kazakhstan's "Housing '91" program, one of the more successful social programs instituted by former republican Party chief Gennadii Kolbin. Karamanov is also identified as one of the authors of a new concept of regional *khozraschet* for Kazakhstan, which has been actively promoted by Nazarbaev.

Friday, July 28

Nina Andreeva Writes Another Letter

Leningrad teacher Nina Andreeva was reported to have written another letter defending Stalin, saying attacks on him and other past leaders are a prelude to attacks on Lenin and the October Revolution. The letter appears in the July issue of the journal *Molodaya gvardiya*. Andreeva's first letter in defense of Stalin, which was published in *Sovetskaya Rossiya* in March, 1988, prompted a big controversy, with *Pravda* calling it a manifesto for opponents of *perestroika*. The new letter says anti-Socialist forces "at the heart of *perestroika*" are creating a situation similar to Hungary in 1956 or Czechoslovakia in 1968. It also says popular movements springing up around the country are aggravating ethnic tensions and fueling secessionism. She criticizes some prominent advocates of *perestroika* by name, including Roy Medvedev and Yurii Afanas'ev.

Akhromeev Visits White House

Marshal Sergei Akhromeev was received for an hour at the White House by US President George Bush and other senior members of the US government. A White House spokesman said Bush and Akhromeev "exchanged views on a wide range of topics, including the status of arms control negotiations." Akhromeev is a special adviser to Gorbachev on security and arms control. The spokesman said that *perestroika* had also been discussed and that

Bush reiterated his support for Gorbachev's reforms. Akhromeev said he was confident that the USSR's economic and labor problems would be resolved (*RFE/RL Special*, July 28; *Reuters, UPI*, July 29). At a press conference earlier in the day, Akhromeev said every country has the right to change its political system, including the right to become a neutral state. Asked if the USSR had renounced "the Brezhnev Doctrine," he said "force should be excluded from mutual relations that one might have with independent countries" (*RFE/RL Special, DPA*, July 28).

USSR Makes Large Purchases of Consumer Goods from Britain

Soviet Deputy Prime Minister Aleksandra Biryukova gave details of big consumer-goods purchases from Britain. She said she had ordered 50 million pairs of panty hose and 1.7 million pairs of women's shoes during a visit to Britain this week. Biryukova and four other ministers ended a five-day trip to Britain yesterday. She told reporters the Soviet delegation had spent 165 million dollars on consumer goods and medical supplies during the visit. Biryukova said her purchases were part of an emergency program to increase the supply of consumer goods in the Soviet Union. She said she had also placed large orders for coffee, cassette tapes, razor blades, soap, toothpaste, and other toiletries (*RFE/RL Special, Reuters*, July 28).

New Chairman of Belorussian Supreme Soviet

The Presidium of the Belorussian Supreme Soviet elected N. I. Dementei to replace Georgii Tarazevich as its chairman. Tarazevich has been elected chief of the Permanent Commission on Nationality Policy and International Relations of the Council of Nationalities of the USSR Supreme Soviet (*Radio Moscow*, 1700, July 28).

Novyi mir Says Gorbachev Losing Popularity at Home

A commentary in the July issue of *Novyi mir* said Mikhail Gorbachev is losing popularity at home. The commentary, by A. Migranyan, said Gorbachev was much more popular during his first two years in power when he first launched his reform drive. It said his popularity had dropped since then because of the failure of *perestroika* to bring concrete results. It also said his standing was hampered by his dual role as Party leader and reformer. The commentary said that, as head of the Party, Gorbachev personifies the existing Party structure in the public's mind even as he calls for major changes in that structure. It added that, if Gorbachev's support continues to decline, he could be challenged by other political forces on the right or left.

Argumenty i fakty (No. 29) carried a report on a briefing at the Soviet Foreign Ministry in Moscow on the situation in Soviet psychiatry. Among the speakers was Aleksandr Churkin, chief psychiatrist of the USSR Ministry of Health. Earlier this year, Churkin had admitted on Leningrad television that there had in the past been instances of the abuse of psychiatry for political purposes in the USSR. Asked what the current situation was regarding this matter, Churkin said there were still instances of people being sent to psychiatric hospitals following conflicts with managers at factories and enterprises where they work. "If these instances are to be regarded as political abuses, they still take place," Churkin said. He reported that in Karelia a man was recently confined in a psychiatric clinic for starting an unsanctioned election campaign [to the Congress of People's Deputies]. Churkin stressed that such abuses of psychiatry are usually the result of a local intitiative and that they are opposed by Moscow.

Situation in Soviet Psychiatry Discussed

——————————————————Saturday, July 29

About 250 radical members of the Congress of People's Deputies opened a two-day meeting at Dom Kino in Moscow to form an Interregional Group to press for further reforms. A TASS correspondent said the meeting was regarded by some analysts as "the emergence of a Soviet opposition." Economist Gavriil Popov, who opened the meeting, said, however, that the group's purpose was not to counterpose itself to the Supreme Soviet but to impel it to do fully what the electorate demands. Historian Yurii Afanas'ev said *perestroika* in its present form is "a deformed hybrid" preventing the USSR from moving ahead. He said Mikhail Gorbachev is rightly regarded as the man who launched reform but is no longer its only leader. Boris El'tsin told the meeting that "the Party aristocracy" had become a class in itself. He said that the workers' movement was directed against this class and that strike committees formed during the recent coal miners' strike were "the embryos of real people's power" (*AP, Reuters, TASS*, July 29).

On July 30, the group elected a five-man collective leadership consisting of El'tsin, Afanas'ev, Popov, Estonian Academician Viktor Palm, and Academician Andrei Sakharov. Early reports said El'tsin had been chosen as the leadership's "prime chairman," but it was later announced that deputies had rejected this idea in favor of a collective leadership. El'tsin was quoted as saying he thought this

Congress Deputies Meet to Form Radical Group

was the best outcome. He said: "the idea of a supreme leader has eaten deep into our minds in this country, and we find it difficult to break with it." El'tsin later told a press conference that the creation of the group showed the people's democratic consciousness had "come of age" (*AP*, *Reuters*, July 30 and 31).

In an interview with Hungarian television on July 31, El'tsin called the new group "a movement stemming from below" and said it could not be stopped. The interviewer asked for El'tsin's opinion of Politburo member Egor Ligachev, who, during a recent visit to Hungary, criticized El'tsin as irresponsible and vain. El'tsin said Ligachev was "ripe for retirement" and would have left already if not for his "lack of conscience and minimal sense of Party ethics."

Latvia Declares Itself Sovereign

The Latvian Supreme Soviet declared Latvia sovereign and said Soviet laws will take effect in Latvia only after it has ratified them. The declaration also denounced Stalinism, saying it had "deformed interethnic relations" for decades. Latvia is the third Baltic republic to declare itself sovereign. The Estonian Supreme Soviet made a similar declaration last November, and Lithuania followed in May. The Latvian Supreme Soviet also set up a commission to assess the consequences of the Molotov-Ribbentrop Pact (*TASS*, July 29).

Shevardnadze and Baker Hold Talks

Soviet Foreign Minister Eduard Shevardnadze and US Secretary of State James Baker spoke to reporters after meeting for more than three hours in Paris. The two men discussed arms control, Afghanistan, the Middle East, and Cambodia. They also discussed the situation of Bulgaria's ethnic minority. Soviet spokesman Vitalii Churkin said Shevardnadze accused the United States of encouraging extremist elements in Afghanistan. He said Shevardnadze told Baker that events in Afghanistan in the past several months had shown that attempts to force a military solution in Afghanistan were futile (*TASS*, *AP*, *UPI*, *RFE/RL Special*, July 29).

Investigator Replies to Report of Moscow Soccer Disaster

The chief investigator of a soccer tragedy that occurred in Moscow in 1982 told the newspaper *Sovetsky sport* that it was "impossible to imagine that 280 corpses disappeared in Moscow," and he insisted that only sixty-six people died in the crush at the Lenin central stadium. The death toll cited by chief investigator Aleksandr Shpeer was the first casualty figure released by the government in the nearly seven years since the disaster in October, 1982. In an exposé published three weeks ago, *Sovetsky sport* quoted parents of young people who had died in the tragedy as saying that 340 people lost their lives when they were crushed against a locked gate as they tried to leave the stadium. Relatives' accounts were confirmed by doctors who treated those injured in the crush.

Authorities Now Say 106,000 Should Be Evacuated to Avoid Radiation

Deputies of the Belorussian Supreme Soviet said 106,000 more people should be evacuated from areas still contaminated from the Chernobyl' nuclear disaster. The republic's Supreme Soviet was told on July 28 that some 11,600 people needed to be moved. The higher figures came from experts and deputies speaking to the Supreme Soviet in Minsk. TASS said the cost of such an evacuation could reach 10 billion rubles, a sum Belorussia cannot afford to pay. It said the entire country must participate in healing the wounds of the disaster. On July 31, *Izvestia* carried a letter from 600 people who live near the Chernobyl' nuclear plant expressing fears about the future. They said they were concerned that they and their children were still at risk from nuclear radiation in the area.

New President Elected in Moldavia

Soviet television said Mircea Snegur was elected the new chairman of the Presidium of the Moldavian Supreme Soviet at a regular session of the Presidium in Kishinev. He had been working in the Secretariat of the Moldavian Central Committee and replaces Alexander Mokanu. Mokanu had held the post since 1985. He was released from his post today in connection with his recent election as a deputy chairman of one of the chambers of the Soviet parliament (*Sovetskaya Moldavia*, July 30).

Uzbeks Dissatisfied with Draft Law on Language

Uzbekistan's Popular Front "Birlik" criticized a draft law granting Uzbek the status of a state language in the republic. A "Birlik" representative told RFE/RL in a telephone interview from Tashkent that, if the draft law is accepted in its present form, the Uzbek language will remain inferior to Russian. He said this was stated at a meeting organized by "Birlik" last week and attended by thousands of people. The spokesman said many of them carried banners disputing the need for two official languages. The draft law was published in June, and a two-month period was set for its discussion. TASS says the draft accurately defines the role of the Russian language as a means of interethnic communication.

Navy Chief Says Three Nuclear Submarines Lost in Twenty-Five Years

The head of the Soviet navy, Admiral Vladimir Chernavin, said three Soviet nuclear submarines had sunk in accidents during the past twenty-five years. In an interview with TASS, Chernavin said there had been a general decline in Soviet technological and production discipline, which had also affected the shipbuilding industry. He expressed "great regret" over this situation. Chernavin gave no details of the accidents. The most recent such accident known in the West was the sinking of an experimental Soviet nuclear submarine near Norway on April 7 after a fire broke out on board. Forty-two sailors were killed in the incident.

Sunday, July 30

Pravda Warns of Serious Consequences of a Rail Strike

Pravda expressed concern about the possibility of a rail strike in the Soviet Union, saying such a strike would plunge the country into chaos. *Pravda* spoke of debates now going on among rail workers and of calls for a strike. It said railmen were complaining that they do not have enough time to eat during shifts and that there are unjust differences in pay rates. In a speech earlier this month, Soviet President Mikhail Gorbachev referred to plans for a rail strike to start on August 1. He warned workers against such a strike, saying it could threaten the whole reform program. On July 31, Soviet television said acting USSR Minister of Railways Nikolai Konarev had met rail officials from all over the country to discuss improving working and living conditions for railway workers. On August 1, *AP* said the rail strike appeared to have been averted. It quoted a spokesman for the railways ministry as saying trains were running normally.

Soviet Deputy Sees Solzhenitsyn Returning to USSR

A leading Soviet publicist said he soes not rule out that Aleksandr Solzhenitsyn will return home to the USSR, become a member of parliament, and "live several happy years here." Yurii Chernichenko, a deputy of the Congress of People's Deputies told UPI Solzhenitsyn's sole condition for return was the publication of his works in the Soviet Union.

Protest Reported in Ukraine

A number of informal groups were reported to have held a protest in Kiev. A representative of the Ukrainian Helsinki Union told RFE/RL by telephone from Kiev that the protesters had called for the legalization of the

Ukrainian national symbols, the flag and trident emblem. The spokesman said the demonstrators gathered on July 29 outside the Ukrainian Supreme Soviet building. He said MVD troops tried to confiscate some national symbols held by demonstrators. Some protesters were injured. The troops later withdrew and the protest ended on the evening of July 30.

Shevardnadze Calls for Cambodian Cease-Fire

At the international peace conference being held in Paris, Soviet Foreign Minister Eduard Shevardnadze called for a Cambodian cease-fire to take effect before Vietnam withdraws its troops from that country in September. He called for a world body to monitor Vietnamese troop withdrawals and for measures to prevent military assistance to the country's warring factions. He said, however, that the USSR is against asking the United Nations to monitor Cambodia's transition to peace. He criticized the work of the UN-sponsored control mechanism in Afghanistan (*Reuters*, *AP*, July 30).

Thousands Threaten Strike over Language Rights in Moldavia

Thousands of Moldavians staged a demonstration in Kishinev and threatened a general strike if local leaders failed to meet their demands for language concessions. Some 30,000 people gathered in the main square of the capital to mark the fortieth anniversary of the creation of the Moldavian republic, according to Yurii Roshka, a member of the Moldavian Popular Front. There was no independent confirmation of the numbers involved (*Reuters*, July 30). A number of protests have been held in Moldavia this year calling for Moldavian to be declared the republic's official language and for the reintroduction of the Latin alphabet to replace the Cyrillic.

More Than 100,000 Sign Protest against Nuclear Plant

Radio Moscow said more than 100,000 residents of the city of Gorky had signed a petition protesting against the construction of a nuclear-powered heating plant near city recreation facilities. It said the project had already cost 200 million rubles. The radio said experts had suggested alternatives to the nuclear plant that would be both less costly and safer. One option calls for converting the project into a heating station that burns natural gas.

Sakharov Calls for Dismantling of Soviet Empire

In a lengthy interview with *Ogonek* (No. 31), Academician Andrei Sakharov called for the dismantling of the Soviet Union's "empire-like" structure built on oppression and for its replacement by a voluntary confederation. He told *Ogonek* that he believes the country is on the verge of an economic catastrophe and that he considers a military or right-wing coup a possibility. Sakharov said the Soviet Union must abandon its centrally controlled system and start all over again. He said the fifteen Soviet republics and other homelands set aside for ethnic groups "should receive independence to the maximum degree." "Their sovereignty should have the minimal limits of common defense, foreign policy, transport, and communications," he added.

Monday, July 31 ──

Soviet Newspaper Publishes US Interview with Solzhenitsyn

The weekly *Za rubezhem* published a translation of an interview that Aleksandr Solzhenitsyn gave to the US magazine *Time* earlier this month. In the interview, Solzhenitsyn says Lenin was "uncommonly evil" with "an absence of any humanity in his approach to people, the masses, to anyone who did not follow him precisely." A commentary signed by historian A. M. Sorokin accompanying the text of the interview says, however, that Solzhenitsyn must have "defective sight" to ascribe such characteristics to Lenin. He charged Solzhenitsyn with writing about Lenin and the Bolshevik Revolution "in a spirit of prejudice and intolerance."

USSR Lifts Curbs on Imports of Religious Material and Banned Authors

New customs regulations outlined at a press conference in Moscow say Bibles, Korans, and other religious works may be imported into the Soviet Union free of any restrictions as of August 15. The regulations also lift restrictions on importing the works of émigré authors, including the works of Aleksandr Solzhenitsyn, Aleksandr Galich, and Vasilii Aksenov. The new regulations bar only pornography and publications that advocate the overthrow of the state (*AP, DPA, TASS,* August 1).

Supreme Soviet Adopts Decree on Crimes against State

The USSR Supreme Soviet adopted a decree containing changes in Soviet law on criminal responsibility for crimes against the state. TASS said the new decree was an important step along the road to democratization of the USSR's Criminal Codes. TASS confirmed that anti-Soviet agitation and propaganda had been removed from the official list of criminal offenses. The agency said severe punishment for unofficial publishing had also been removed from the text of the new decree. On August 4, TASS reported that the new decree tightened the definition of the crime of sedition. An earlier version of the law approved in April outlawed public calls to overthrow the Soviet state. The new decree outlaws calls for the use of violence to overthrow the state. The same day, the Supreme Soviet passed a resolution on fighting crime in the USSR. President Mikhail Gorbachev said it was needed because criminals have become "brazen." The resolution calls for the death penalty for murderers of policemen. It also calls for an increase in the number of MVD troops to be used in "cases of mass disobedience by criminal elements."

USSR and South Korea Discuss Business

Soviet and South Korean officials met in Moscow to discuss business cooperation between the two countries. TASS said the two sides reviewed ways of establishing links between enterprises of both countries, of increasing trade, and of finding new forms of economic cooperation, including the setting up of joint ventures. South Korea and the USSR have no diplomatic relations, but the South Korean Corporation for Trade Development opened a permanent representation in Moscow earlier this month. On August 2, the head of the Korean delegation, Chung Ju-Yung, told a news conference in Seoul that the two sides were not yet ready for joint ventures. He said he stressed to Soviet officials that improved government relations would be needed before there can be full economic cooperation (*Reuters, UPI*, August 2).

US-Soviet Talks on Afghanistan Begin

US and Soviet officials started two days of talks on Afghanistan. The talks opened in Stockholm, with US Assistant Secretary of State John Kelly and Soviet Ambassador-at-Large Nikolai Kozyrev heading the delegations. Soviet Foreign Ministry spokesman Gennadii Gerasimov said the talks would focus solely on ways to end the Afghan conflict. The USSR has complained about continued US arms shipments to the Afghan resistance. The United States says there can be no political solution while President Najibullah remains in power (*AP*, July 31). On August 1, Kelly reported that there had been no progress in the talks (*Reuters, AP*, August 1).

USSR and West Germany Open New Consulates

The Soviet Union and West Germany opened new consulates-general in Munich and Kiev respectively. The Foreign Ministry in Bonn said such expansion of the consular network reflects the growing demand for West German-Soviet exchanges in the fields of economics, culture, and tourism (Western agencies, July 31).

USSR and Switzerland Set Up Management School in Kiev

The Ukrainian Academy of Sciences and the Swiss International Management Institute announced that they had set up a joint venture to run a management school in Kiev. The announcement said the school and a research center would open in October and provide research and consulting services to Soviet firms and schools (*AP*, July 31).

The Month of August

In a speech to the Supreme Soviet Mikhail Gorbachev discussed relations among Socialist countries. He said that there was no universal Socialist model and that no one had a monopoly on the truth. He also said the Warsaw Pact should be transformed from a military-political into a political-military organization. In his view, this would pave the way for the eventual dissolution of the Warsaw Pact and NATO, but he said conditions for such a dissolution were not yet ripe. Commenting on US President George Bush's recent visit to Eastern Europe, Gorbachev said Bush should overcome the temptation to take advantage of the complex reform processes going on in Eastern Europe. He said there would be "definite negative consequences for the whole of Europe" if Bush tried to divert countries from the paths they have chosen. Gorbachev's speech was carried by _Pravda_ on August 2.

Gorbachev Addresses Supreme Soviet

TASS reported fresh violence in Nagorno-Karabakh and adjacent areas of Azerbaijan. It said twenty-three people had been injured, including three MVD soldiers. It said the injuries occurred on July 31 when 300 people attacked a convoy of trucks carrying building materials from Armenia to Nagorno-Karabakh. TASS said that the situation in the area continued to be tense and that the commander of MVD troops had visited the region to see what could be done. In a separate report, Radio Baku said some railworkers in western Armenia had refused to go to work because of frequent attacks on passenger and freight trains.

New Clashes Reported in Nagorno-Karabakh and Azerbaijan

Soviet Prime Minister Nikolai Ryzhkov met with members of miners' strike committees from around the USSR. The Soviet media said miners from the Donbass region of Ukraine complained about the lack of suitable technology for deep mining. They also said state enterprises ignored miners' needs and often supplied equipment that was unreliable and inefficient. The miners again complained of poor working and living conditions, particularly hous-

Ryzhkov Meets Strike Committees

ing. An official Soviet report just issued said more than one million working days were lost through strikes last month in the RSFSR (*TASS*, in English, *Central Television*, "Vremya," August 1).

Shevardnadze in Iran for Talks

Soviet Foreign Minister Eduard Shevardnadze opened talks with Iranian officials in Teheran. TASS said Shevardnadze had discussed Afghanistan, bilateral relations, and other issues with Foreign Minister Ali Akbar Velayati. It said the two ministers had agreed that putting a stop to the bloodshed in Afghanistan was a priority task and that a government should be formed that would represent the interests of the various sectors of the Afghan population. TASS said Shevardnadze had also met with Iran's new president, Hashemi Rafsanjani (*Pravda*, August 2).

Report Says Soviet Weapons Sales to Third World Down in 1988

A report by the US Congressional Research Service said Soviet arms sales to Third-World countries dropped by almost half in 1988. The report said Soviet arms transfers to the Third World fell from 19,400 million dollars in 1987 to 9,900 million dollars last year. It called the decline "an aberration" caused by a short-term decline in demand from major Soviet clients (*RFE/RL Special*, August 1).

Law Adopted to Increase Pensions

The USSR Supreme Soviet adopted a law to improve pensions and social services for people on low incomes. TASS said the law provides for a rise in pensions and allowances that will improve living standards for about 30 million people. TASS said the law would go into effect on October 1, three months earlier than planned (*Izvestia*, August 4). A recent study by the USSR State Committee for Labor and Social Problems said about 105 million Soviet citizens are living in poverty—i.e., they have an income of 100–110 rubles a month or less. See RL 373/89.

United States Asks USSR to Help Secure Release of Hostages

The United States was reported to have asked the Soviet Union to help get Western hostages in Lebanon freed. The US request was made during talks on Afghanistan between US and Soviet officials. US delegation head John Kelly said he had asked if the USSR would use its influence with the Iranian government to win the hostages' release. The hostages are being held by a pro-Iranian group (*AP*, August 1). On his return from Iran on August 1, Shevardnadze was reported to have expressed "serious concern" about the reported killing of US Lieutenant Colonel

William Higgins by pro-Iranian extremists in Lebanon. Shevardnadze said Iranian President Rafsanjani voiced deep regret about what had happened but said Iran was not involved in the incident (*UPI*, August 2). The same day TASS called for restraint in connection with the events in Lebanon and urged the immediate release of all hostages and kidnapped people, wherever they were. It warned that violence generates violence.

An exhibition on Nikita Khrushchev's years as Soviet leader opened in Moscow. TASS said the display of photos, documents, and other items was intended particularly for young people, who, it said, know little about Khrushchev. Reuters said Khrushchev's son Sergei addressed the opening of the exhibition. It quoted him as saying that officials had recently tried to block publication of his father's memoirs in Soviet journals but that editors had opposed the censorship and the objections were dropped. Economist Gavriil Popov also addressed the opening. He was quoted as saying deep thanks were owed Khrushchev "for his brave bid to create something new by dismantling the system of rule by dictate that we are now seeking to destroy."

Khrushchev Exhibition Opens in Moscow

Wednesday, August 2

The USSR Ministry of Internal Affairs said about a ton of explosives had been collected in Georgia since ethnic unrest began there nearly three weeks ago. TASS quoted the ministry as saying more than 1,500 firearms, including three machine guns, had also been collected. It said some of the weapons were confiscated and some turned in voluntarily. According to TASS, criminal proceedings have been started against seventy-two people suspected of being involved in the disorders or of spreading rumors. See RL 536/88.

Ton of Explosives Confiscated in Georgia

A draft law specifying who will be allowed to strike in the USSR and under what circumstances was presented to the USSR Supreme Soviet by trade-union leader Stepan Shalaev. The draft has been in preparation, under conditions of strict secrecy, since 1986, but the drafting process was rushed through as a result of the coal miners' strikes in July. TASS said the law allows strikes only after two separate conciliation bodies have failed to resolve workers'

Strike Law Debated in Supreme Soviet

grievances and bans strikes that "threaten lives and health," endanger national defense, or threaten "the normal life of the population"—i.e., workers in transport, the health service, and the defense industry are likely to be excluded from the law's provisions. TASS said the deputies approved the bill in principle (*Pravda*, August 3). The draft law was published in *Izvestia* on August 16.

Miners' Leader Calls for Independent Trade Unions

The leader of last month's coal miners' strike in the Kuzbass said the USSR needs independent trade unions because the official unions are powerless. In an interview with *Moscow News*, Teimuraz Avaliani said official Soviet trade unions merely agree to decisions that have already been made by the government. He said this is the reason why "fundamentally new trade unions" must be created. He also said that further strikes could not be ruled out and that they would be inevitable if the government does not change its economic policies soon. Avaliani is a former trade-union official who lost his job in the 1970s after writing a letter to Brezhnev urging him to resign. He is now a member of the Congress of People's Deputies.

Estonian Commission Expels Reporters from Its Meetings

A commission appointed by the Estonian Supreme Soviet was reported to have expelled Estonian radio and television reporters from its meetings. Radio Tallinn reported the expulsion and apologized to its listeners for not being allowed to tell them what is happening at meetings of the commission. The commission has been meeting to hear the complaints of Russian workers who went on strike at plants in Estonia last week to protest about what they see as discrimination against them in Estonia. Radio Tallinn said representatives of the Russian organization "Interdvizhenie" protested at a meeting of the commission on August 1 that the Estonian media were presenting an unobjective picture of their cause. The radio said they specifically objected to a television broadcast that called the demands of "Interdvizhenie" demagoguery.

Soviet Newspaper Reports Murder of Young Journalist

Literaturnaya gazeta reported the murder of a young journalist involved in investigating corruption in the USSR. The newspaper said the twenty-six-year-old journalist, Vladimir Glotov, had assembled material on Mafia-like groups in the Transcaucasus and in Uzbekistan. The reports said that the crime took place several days ago in Moscow and that Glotov had previously been beaten up by a hired gang.

412

Moscow News (No. 32) accused the USSR of double standards in its foreign policy, citing the Kremlin's refusal to take stands on China or on Iran's death order against British writer Salman Rushdie. It quoted Soviet Foreign Minister Eduard Shevardnadze as saying recently that foreign policy that is not directed at human goals is amoral and that Soviet foreign policy is "deeply moral." Economist Aleksei Izyumov and historian Andrei Kortunov argued: "The principles the minister described have certainly been proclaimed. But to say that they have been implemented . . . is at present out of the question." They were particularly critical of the Soviet media's failure to present any alternative point of view on these issues.

Newspaper Accuses Moscow of Double Standards in Foreign Policy

CPSU Politburo member Egor Ligachev said one-third of the Soviet Union's grain-producing lands are suffering from a severe drought. He said the drought has afflicted the grain fields of the Urals, Western Siberia, and Kazakhstan. He said, however, that the harvest in the European part of the USSR would be higher than ever before this year. (*Central Television*, "Vremya," August 2).

Ligachev Says Severe Drought Afflicting Grain Fields

Thursday, August 3

The USSR Supreme Soviet heard a report on the country's economic development plan for 1990, which calls for "emergency measures." The chairman of Gosplan, Yurii Maslyukov, said the plan will address such problems as the huge national debt, the state budget deficit, and wages, which are rising faster than the production of consumer goods. The Supreme Soviet also approved amendments to the law on state enterprises. These include measures that would allow enterprises to choose their own managers, raise capital, and independently establish relations with foreign partners (*Pravda*, August 4). On August 5, *Pravda* carried the text of Maslyukov's speech.

Report Calls for "Emergency Measures" for Economy

The USSR Supreme Soviet elected Nikolai Vorontsov, a doctor of biological sciences and a senior researcher at the N. K. Kol'tsov Institute of Developmental Biology of the USSR Academy of Sciences, to serve as chairman of the USSR State Committee for Environmental Protection (*TASS*, August 3; *Pravda*, August 4). Vorontsov is the first non-Party member to hold an all-Union ministerial post (*Central Television*, "Vremya," August 2). The Supreme

Non-Communist Appointed Environment Minister

413

Soviet also elected Leonid Filimonov as minister of the oil and gas industry, Vladimir Mel'nikov as minister of the timber industry, Nikolai Rusak as chairman of the USSR State Committee for Physical Culture and Sports, and Viktor Gerashchenko as chairman of the board of the USSR State Bank (*TASS*, August 3, *Pravda*, August 4). On August 4, Nikolai Konarev was confirmed as minister of railways (*Pravda*, August 5).

Supreme Soviet Reports on Nagorno-Karabakh

A special commission of the USSR Supreme Soviet on Nagorno-Karabakh said the situation there had "gone beyond the degree of aggravation that could be described as explosive." Borys Oliinyk, a member of the commission, said that efforts to normalize the situation had not worked and that alienation between Azerbaijanis and Armenians in the region had "taken on exceptionally severe forms." He said the commission would continue working with residents to find solutions to Nagorno-Karabakh's problems (*Moscow Television*, August 3).

Study Released on Ruble Convertibility

Economic and currency experts from the Soviet Union, the United States, France, and Canada have devised a plan for making the Soviet ruble convertible into foreign currencies. The experts released the plan after it had been formulated by the private Geonomics Institute in Middlebury, Vermont. The experts said the plan would require far-reaching reforms of the Soviet economic and pricing systems and could cause high inflation, more shortages, and unemployment (*UPI*, *AP*, August 3).

Sakharov Calls for Faster Pace of Reform

Andrei Sakharov called for a faster pace of reform in the Soviet Union. He said if *perestroika* is not speeded up the Soviet Union could be threatened with chaos. Sakharov was speaking to an academic audience at Harvard University. He said Gorbachev's gradual approach to change may ultimately be doomed by political and economic problems (*The Boston Globe*, *AP*, August 5).

Friday, August 4

Gorbachev Concludes Supreme Soviet Session with Speech

At the conclusion of the first forty-day session of the new USSR Supreme Soviet, Mikhail Gorbachev praised the new body as "a powerful parliament of high working ability." He said political decisions that affect the fate of the Soviet people will now be "taken publicly, not by a narrow circle of people." Speaking about recent ethnic and worker unrest throughout the Soviet Union, he denied that panic is sweeping the Kremlin. Rather, he said, "this is what we call *perestroika*." He said that he believed the Soviet Union had reached the point of no return and that *perestroika* was irreversible (*TASS, Radio Moscow*, in English, August 4; *Pravda*, August 5).

El'tsin Says He's an Optimist about *Perestroika*

Supreme Soviet Deputy Boris El'tsin said there is a possibility of a return to authoritarian methods of leadership and a totalitarian state in the Soviet Union. El'tsin said this is possible because *perestroika* is being imposed from above and bureaucrats oppose it for infringing on their interests. He said, however, that he is an optimist and hopes that no matter how hard it may be "*perestroika* will be victorious." El'tsin was interviewed by Moscow television (1730).

Commission Says *Maxim Gorky* Was Moving Too Fast

A Soviet commission of inquiry has concluded that the captain of the cruise ship *Maxim Gorky* was allowing the ship to travel too fast when it struck an iceberg in the Arctic Ocean in June. The commission's findings, reported in *Izvestia*, also said Captain Marat Galimov had violated international and company regulations on traveling in ice-packed waters. *Izvestia* said the Soviet Association of Merchant Marine Captains had proposed revoking the captain's license, but the group opposed taking any criminal proceedings against him.

Trade Union Created for Cooperatives

TASS said a new Soviet trade union had been created to protect the interests of workers employed by cooperatives. The agency quoted Vladimir Ivanov, head of the organizational department of the Central Council of Trade Unions, as saying the new union will monitor working conditions and enforce safety regulations already in force at state enterprises. TASS said the cooperatives' boards often allow violations of labor legislation designed to protect workers' rights. Ivanov said the new union would give protection to two million workers employed in 180,000 cooperative businesses throughout the Soviet Union.

Coal Miners' Strike

On August 5, TASS reported that the coal miners in Vorkuta had suspended their strike after receiving government documents that TASS said satisfied their demands.

On August 6, First Secretary of the Kemerovo Oblast Party Committee (Western Siberia), Aleksandr Mel'nikov, said there could be a new outbreak of strikes in the region's coal mines. Mel'nikov complained that managers were being slow in carrying out promises to improve miners' pay and conditions and that workers were becoming restless. Reuters quoted him as saying in an interview that the coal ministry was clinging to its old authoritarian methods.

On August 7, Soviet television said new trade-union and other representative bodies were being elected in the Kuzbass. The report said workers had expressed no confidence in twenty-two trade union committees and were electing groups with new leaders who enjoy the workers' confidence. It also said a special plenum of the regional trade-union council had instructed the trade unions to set up a working group to prepare alternative proposals to Soviet draft laws on strikes and on the rights of trade unions. The same day, it was reported by Radio Moscow that the director general of the coal mine complex "Karaganda-Ugol" in Kazakhstan had been forced to quit his post after miners three times voted no confidence in him.

On August 9, the oblast Party committee in Kemerovo supported a moratorium on strikes. Soviet television said the Kemerovo Party's decision backed a proposal made by a group of people's deputies for a moratorium until the strike law is put into effect.

Budgetary Matters

Izvestia carried the text of a speech delivered by the chairman of Gosplan, Yurii Maslyukov, on the final day of the Supreme Soviet session. Maslyukov put the size of the national debt at 312 billion rubles. In an interview with Radio Moscow-1 (0430), USSR Minister of Finance Valentin Pavlov put the additional annual cost of the enhanced package for pensioners and handicapped persons at 6.6 billion rubles. In an interview with the *Financial Times* published on August 4, Pavlov said the increased expenditure would bring the pension bill up to 25–27 billion rubles a year and the cost of child allowances up to 20 billion rubles, while cuts in defense expenditure were likely to save some 9 billion rubles a year. Pavlov also told the *Financial Times* that the reform of retail prices is now scheduled for 1991.

Gorbachev on Prospects for Restructuring

Mikhail Gorbachev said the CPSU and the Supreme Soviet are "destined to succeed" in restructuring the country. If they fail, Gorbachev said, "this country might find itself in the ditch next to the highway of historical progress." That, he said, would affect not only the Soviet Union but also the rest of the world. Gorbachev's remarks came in an interview with Radio Moscow World Service (1610) in which he commented on the Supreme Soviet session that ended on August 4.

Gorbachev Donates 350,000 Dollars to Irkutsk Medical Center

TASS said Mikhail Gorbachev had donated 350,000 US dollars towards the construction of a children's medical center in the city of Irkutsk. TASS said the money came from royalties from the publication abroad of Gorbachev's book *Perestroika: New Thinking for Our Country and the World*. TASS said Gorbachev chose the Irkutsk center because the need for medical facilities, particularly for children, is greater in Siberia than in the European part of the USSR. It said an Irkutsk hospital was being renovated to provide the children's medical center.

KGB Chief Says Ideology Enforcement Department Abolished

KGB chairman Vladimir Kryuchkov said his committee had abolished the department that investigated ideological crimes in the USSR. Instead, Kryuchkov said, the KGB is organizing "a department for protecting constitutional rights." He linked the move to a change in Soviet law, which, he said, no longer punishes "expressing an opinion on Soviet power, no matter how negative." Kryuchkov discussed the changes in an interview broadcast by Radio Moscow International in Slovak.

CPSU to Reorganize Its Publications

The CPSU has decided to reorganize its publications because some of them have failed to measure up to the needs of *perestroika*. TASS said the changes were made public by the CPSU Central Committee, which issued a communiqué on the matter. It said the changes, which are scheduled for next year, are needed because some Party journals have concentrated on criticism instead of constructive work. One major change involves combining the newspapers *Stroitel'naya gazeta* and *Sotsialisticheskaya industriya* into a new Party daily to be called *Rabochaya tribuna.* Another would abolish the political journals *Agitator* and *Politicheskoe obrazovanie* and create a new Party sociopolitical journal called *Dialog.* TASS said the changes are designed to make the contents of Party publications "more relevant" and turn them into mass periodicals addressed to the widest possible readership.

Situation in Abkhazia

Pravda said the situation in the Abkhazian ASSR was gradually returning to normal. It said that MVD troops patrolled the streets of Sukhumi on August 4 without firearms and that in Georgia generally the situation was under control. Radio Moscow-1 (2200) reported, however, that in the Abkhazian city of Tkvarcheli, enterprises, mines, and transport facilities were not operating.

On August 12, dozens of strikes were reported to be continuing in Abkhazia. Radio Moscow carried a report saying the republic remained "tense." It said that in the Ochamchirsky Raion, thirty-eight enterprises, organizations, and sovkhozes and kolkhozes were not working. Twenty people in the village of Iloria were reported to be in the fourth day of a hunger strike.

On August 26, the USSR Ministry of Internal Affairs said 166 people had been detained overnight for curfew violations in Abkhazia (*TASS*, November 26).

***Komsomol'skaya pravda* Starts Series on Nationalities Issues**

Komsomol'skaya pravda started a new series called "The Nationalities Question." Radio Moscow said the series would be devoted to interethnic problems that have accumulated over the decades and would cover not only problems of language and history, culture, and ecology but also the human tragedies that have been the result of recent interethnic strife.

Managers Fired for Not Halting Dam Project

Officials in Western Siberia have been fired for not halting a hydroelectric project that was opposed by the coal miners of the Kuzbass region. Moscow television said the "irresponsible" managers were fired by the Kemerovo Oblast Party leadership and the construction stopped as promised. Miners at seventeen Kuzbass pits staged a two-hour strike two days ago to support their demand for a halt to the project to dam the Tom River. Moscow television said the Kemerovo Party leadership had also taken other steps, including opening for public use a clinic that had been reserved for "a narrow circle of senior personages" and ordering a tailor's shop to stop making clothes exclusively for the wives of "highly placed customers."

418

Thousands of people rallied in the Azerbaijani capital of Baku to demand official recognition for the Azerbaijani Popular Front. Historian Mehdi Mamedov told RFE/RL by telephone from Baku that more than 50,000 people had attended the rally. He said Popular Front speakers demanded more political and economic sovereignty for Azerbaijan (*RL Azerbaijani Service*, August 6).

Unofficial Rally in Baku

————————————————————————————————————— *Sunday, August 6*

Moscow News (No. 32) carried an article by its correspondent Gennadii Zhavoronovkov stating plainly that the NKVD was responsible for the massacre of Polish officers in the Katyn Forest near Smolensk and reporting that during the 1930s the Katyn Forest was the site of NKVD executions of Soviet victims of Stalin's purges. (Earlier this year, *Moscow News* [No. 21] went so far as to say that evidence pointed to NKVD culpability for the massacre of the Polish officers, but it refrained from drawing conclusions.) Zhavoronovkov's article, which contains information obtained from local residents who recalled mass executions in Katyn in the 1930s, ends with a proposal to create a large cemetery in Katyn to commemorate "Russians, Jews, Poles, and Latvians . . . victims of a crime, the like of which the world has never seen." Zhavoronovkov's article is another step towards official Soviet recognition by the Soviet Union that the massacre of Polish officers in Katyn was conducted not by the Nazis but by NKVD troops. See RL 112/89 and RL 274/89.

Moscow News Stresses Not Only Poles Were Executed in Katyn

Moscow News (No. 32) carried a brief memoir by lawyer Sofiya Kalistratova, a member of the Moscow Helsinki group, against whom charges of slandering the Soviet state were dropped only in December, 1988. Beginning in the 1960s, Kalistratova acted as defense counsel for many imprisoned members of the Soviet human-rights movement. Because of her membership in the group, Kalistratova had her apartment searched five times, was interrogated by the KGB, and subjected to other harassment. In 1981, a criminal process was started against her under Article 190-1 of the RSFSR Criminal Code although she has never been arrested, presumably because of her very advanced age. Kalistratova describes all of these events in her memoir in *Moscow News*, which she ends with a plea for the rehabilitation of all members of the Soviet dissident movement who have been persecuted since the 1960s.

Moscow News Publishes Memoirs of Dissident Lawyer

El'tsin and Mamedov Interviewed about Interregional Group

Moscow News (No. 32) carried interviews with two deputies of the Congress of People's Deputies—first secretary of a raion Party committee in Baku Veli Mamedov and Chairman of the USSR Supreme Soviet Committee for Civil Construction and Architecture Boris El'tsin. The deputies spoke about the Interregional Group of the USSR Supreme Soviet—formed by the radical deputies on July 29–30 to accelerate the pace of reform. (On the group, see *Literaturnaya gazeta*, August 2.) While Mamedov was not enthusiastic about the group, El'tsin, who is one of its leading members, defended its creation. He revealed that the group had received many letters from Soviet citizens supporting the radical reformist proposals put forward by the group. El'tsin also said that the group plans to publish a newspaper called *Narodnyi deputat* (People's Deputy) and that many people are already asking for subscriptions to it. El'tsin said it would be "the first independent newspaper in our country." Meanwhile, *Sobesednik* (No. 32) carried a lengthy interview with El'tsin, in which he discussed in detail the activities of the Congress of the People's Deputies and the USSR Supreme Soviet. On August 5, DPA reported that the West German journal *Der Spiegel* carred an interview with Professor of History Yurii Afanas'ev, who is also a member of the Interregional Group. Afanas'ev said the group either is or could become an opposition movement. He denied that the group seeks to split the nation. He said the split existed in the Supreme Soviet and the Congress of People's Deputies before the Interregional Group was formed.

On August 8, the first deputy chairman of the USSR Supreme Soviet, Anatolii Luk'yanov, welcomed the establishment of the Interregional Group (*TASS*, August 8). He said it was important to have alternative opinions when working out solutions to problems. On August 10, the group was criticized by historian Roy Medvedev, who said that the group's members—in particular El'tsin and Sakharov—lacked sufficient political caution (*Reuters*, August 10). For a detailed analysis of the Interregional Group, see RL 489/89.

Leningrad Police Force Apologizes for Sacking Members

Moscow News (No. 43) reported that Nikolai Arzhannikov, who was expelled from the Leningrad police force in April of this year for leading an unofficial demonstration in the city, had received an apology from the Leningrad MVD and been offered his job back. He turned down the offer, however, because he already has another job and, furthermore, has become a member of the coordinating council of the Leningrad Popular Front. The newspaper revealed that the Leningrad MVD was forced to to review its decision on Arzhannikov under pressure from people's deputies.

Vadim Borisov Interviewed on Solzhenitsyn

Sobesednik (No. 32) carried an interview on Aleksandr Solzhenitsyn with historian Vadim Borisov, chief of the publications department of *Novyi mir*. Solzhenitsyn has given Borisov the right to deal with all matters concerning publication of his works in the USSR. In the interview, Borisov described in detail plans to publish works by Solzhenitysn in the USSR in the near future. He rejected charges against Solzhenitsyn of anti-Semitism and monarchism. Asked about the possibility of Solzhenitsyn returning to the USSR, Borisov quoted Solzhenitsyn as saying: "The country that publishes my books would not be the same country as that from which I was expelled. And to this country I will certainly return."

Shevardnadze in Kabul

Soviet Foreign Minister Eduard Shevardnadze arrived in Kabul on a working visit. Shevardnadze met with Afghan President Najibullah and discussed a number of issues including efforts to win the release of Soviet prisoners of war held by the Afghan resistance (*TASS, Reuters, UPI,* August 6). On August 7, before ending his Kabul visit, Shevardnadze gave an interview to the Afghan Bakhtar news agency. The Soviet Foreign Ministry released the text of the interview at a press conference in Moscow. In the interview, Shevardnadze said that Iran had adopted a new approach to the Afghan war and that this encouraged hopes of a political settlement. Shevardnadze said Iran now favors a representative Afghan government of all political elements, including the Communist Party (*Reuters, Central Television, Radio Moscow,* August 7).

***Ogonek* Condemns Bolsheviks for Banning Other Political Parties**

Ogonek (No. 32) featured another attack on Bolshevik policies after the October Revolution. Writing in the journal, Vyacheslav Kostikov said the Bolsheviks' decision to ban all other parties soon after the revolution had lost them popular support and set in motion the terrible repressions under Stalin. Kostikov said the abolition of the first freely elected constituent assembly on January 5, 1918—where the Bolsheviks won only 24 percent of the vote—had crushed all future hopes for democracy. Without directly blaming Lenin, Kostikov made clear that under his leadership the Bolshevik Party turned the revolution against the people.

Regional Official Defends Party against Criticism

A CPSU official dismissed suggestions that the Party is lagging behind changes in society. Writing in *Sotsialisticheskaya industriya*, Ulyanovsk Oblast Party Committee Secretary O. Kazarov said the overwhelming majority of Party forums were proceeding just as "sharply" as the Congress of People's Deputies. But he said they were doing so "without walkouts from the auditorium and without the wish to create factions." Kazarov said in many cases the candidate who became a people's deputy was "not the one with the most constructive platform but the one who made the best job of bad-mouthing reality, was most extreme in criticizing the Party, and made the biggest promises." He said the prestige of the Party was "declining catastrophically in conditions where moral and material incentives are lacking." He said there were many questions regarding *perestroika* in the Party. But he said the Party remained the vanguard of society and was not lagging behind anyone. The CPSU has been accused on several occasions recently of lagging behind changes in society. Those making the accusations have included members of the top Party leadership, including Gorbachev.

Ambassador Says USSR Playing Active Role in Hostage Release

Soviet ambassador to Lebanon Vasilii Kolotusha said Moscow was playing an active role in efforts to win the release of Western hostages in Lebanon. He said Moscow had, at the request of the United States, contacted "regional parties" to help resolve the crisis (*Reuters, UPI*, August 6).

Newspaper Reports Details of Antidrug Operation in Moscow

Krasnaya zvezda published details of an antidrug operation in Moscow last month. It said that on the day the operation was mounted (July 1) MVD forces detained over 2,500 drug addicts. The newspaper said the operation was aimed at suppressing drug trafficking in the Soviet capital. Earlier this year, Novosti said that there were 120,000 drug addicts in the Soviet Union and that most of them were under twenty-five years of age.

Preliminary Report on Cause of April Submarine Accident

A USSR government commission said a fire on board a Soviet nuclear submarine that sank in the Norwegian Sea on April 7 was "most probably" caused by faults in the vessel's electrical equipment. This was reported by *Izvestia* in an interview with Central Committee Secretary Oleg Baklanov. He said experts had found "a number of technical imperfections in various systems of the submarine" that might have caused the accident. Forty-two crew members died in the accident.

An Azerbaijani government spokesman said that two Armenians had been killed in renewed fighting in Baku. Musa Mamedov, spokesman for the republic's foreign ministry, told Western news agencies a number of other people had been injured in the clash. An AFP report said the clash between Armenians and Azerbaijanis took place on August 3.

Two Armenians Killed in Baku

Soviet Foreign Ministry spokesman Vadim Perfil'ev announced the rehabilitation of 101 Soviet diplomatic or consular officials who were purged under Stalin. TASS quoted Perfil'ev as saying those rehabilitated were employees of the People's Commissariat for Foreign Affairs. Perfil'ev said a Foreign Ministry commission had determined the names and titles of 113 commissariat officials who had been purged. He said they included seven "deputies of the people's commissar" and forty-eight ambassadors. Perfil'ev said the commission was studying archive documents to prepare proposals on the rehabilitation of "other Foreign Ministry officials." He said the commission had decided to commemorate the purged diplomats by putting up a memorial plaque in the Foreign Ministry building (*TASS*, August 7).

Purged Soviet Diplomats Rehabilitated

Radio Moscow said draft laws on changes in Ukraine's Constitution and on the election of people's deputies to republican- and local-level Soviets had been published for public review. The draft law said the Ukrainian Congress of People's Deputies would be Ukraine's supreme state authority. It is proposed that a total of 600 deputies be elected to the congress, including 150 deputies from public organizations.

Ukraine Drafts Laws on Constitutional Changes, People's Deputies

Academician Roald Sagdeev said the Soviet Union could do a better job of explaining the benefits of its space program to Soviet citizens. In an interview with RFE/RL's Washington studio, Sagdeev said he has proposed that Soviet officials give a full account of all aspects of the space program, both civilian and military. Sagdeev is the former director of the USSR Academy of Science's Institute for Space Research and is now a member of the Congress of People's Deputies. He said the space program is being criticized because of its costs. Sagdeev said this is an

Sagdeev Says USSR Needs to Explain Space Program Better

emotional but understandable reaction because for years the Soviet people knew very little about their country's space activities. Sagdeev said space research consumes only a small percentage of the national budget, but he added that many of its benefits may not be seen until the twenty-first century.

Soviet Anti-AIDS Committee Wants Foreign Currency

The Soviet Health Ministry's anti-AIDS committee wants to be allocated foreign currency so it can import equipment from abroad. An appeal to this effect, addressed to the authorities and to public organizations, was published in *Pravda*. The newspaper quoted Deputy Health Minister of the Soviet Union Aleksandr Kondrusev as saying that the Soviet health system is "catastrophically" poorly equipped to prevent the spread of AIDS. Kondrusev said the disease had been registered in eight of the fifteen Soviet republics.

Scientist Warns against Change in Soviet Federal System

A Soviet scientist writing in *Pravda* said turning the Soviet Union into a confederation would be a step backwards. Academician Yulian Bromlei said the individual parts of the Soviet Union are connected by millions of ties developed in the years of Soviet power. He said recent strikes show how the Soviet system is endangered when these ties are violated.

Jewish Activists Set Up Zionist Organization in USSR

A group of Soviet Jewish activists have set up a Zionist organization in the USSR. One of the founders, Lev Gorodetsky, told RFE/RL by telephone from Moscow that between thirty and forty activists from fifteen cities gathered in Moscow last week to declare the establishment of the new Soviet chapter of the World Zionist Organization. Gorodetsky said the chairman of the World Zionist Movement, Simcha Dinitz, telephoned from Israel during the meeting to express his support. Gorodetsky said the meeting adopted a manifesto, a program, and a charter. One of the charter's main aims is to rehabilitate the word "Zionism," which Gorodetsky complained is equated by some in the USSR with "fascism." On August 8, TASS said the official Soviet anti-Zionist Committee had criticized the new Soviet chapter of the World Zionist Organization. TASS quoted the presidium of the anti-Zionist Committee as accusing the Soviet chapter of trying to woo Soviet Jews away from *perestroika*. According to TASS, the anti-Zionist group also accused the new organization of trying to aggravate ethnic tensions.

The Soviet Union has formally accepted international accords aimed at protecting civilians during internal and international armed conflicts. The International Committee of the Red Cross said Moscow had ratified the two 1977 protocols to the Geneva convention on international humanitarian law. The committee said it was extremely gratified by the decision. Moscow ratified the two protocols unconditionally (*AP, DPA*, August 8).

Moscow Ratifies Two International Accords

Despite the protests of deputies representing the Russian-speaking population of the republic, the Estonian Supreme Soviet approved a new election law requiring two years of residence in Estonia for voters in local elections and five years of residence for candidates. The law was passed by a majority of more than four to one. The thirty-six Russian-speaking deputies then refused to participate further in the work of the parliament (*RFE Estonian Service*, August 8; *Pravda*, August 10).

New Estonian Election Law Provokes Strikes

On August 9, nineteen industrial enterprises in Estonia with Russian-speaking workers on their staffs started strikes to protest about the adoption of the law (*TASS*, August 9). On August 10, the Soviet central authorities promised to set up a government commission to investigate the demands of the striking workers (*Reuters, AFP*, August 10). The same day, *Pravda* quoted the chairman of the strike committee, Mikhail Lysenko, as saying the new law was undemocratic. The same day, the Presidium of the Estonian Supreme Soviet ordered an end to the strikes in the republic and told the Estonian government to carry out the order. *Izvestia* reported that alienation was growing between Estonians and nonnative residents of the republic. On August 11, *Izvestia* said the strikes were affecting forty-one enterprises in Tallinn and Kokhtla-Yarve and involved 40,000 workers. The same day, Soviet Justice Minister Veniamin Yakovlev said Estonia's new election law violates the USSR Constitution by discriminating against residents who are not native Estonians (*TASS*, August 11).

On August 12, protest strikes by non-Estonian workers in Estonia were reported to be affecting the work of other enterprises not previously involved in the strike action (*TASS*, August 12).

On August 14, Justice Minister Veniamin Yakovlev said it was "highly advisable and legally correct" for the Estonian Supreme Soviet to reinstate laws giving equal electoral rights to all citizens. In an interview with *Izvestia*, he reiterated that the new law violates the Soviet Constitution. The same day, TASS reported that a resolution of the Presidium of the Estonian Supreme Soviet ordering an end to the strikes had not been enforced. In a separate report, the agency quoted Estonian Party First Secretary Vaino Valjas as saying that the republican authorities had made a mistake by not listening to the views of the republic's minorities and that the mistake should be corrected. Speaking on Estonian television, Valjas said Estonia's Supreme Soviet had set up a commission to consider all the proposals of the minority.

On August 15, Estonia's largest public organization issued a statement saying Estonians refused to back down in the face of strikes and threats from Moscow. The statement came from the Union of Estonian Work Collectives, which said it represented 400,000 Estonians. The statement said Estonians were worried by "the tense situation" in the republic and were asking whether Estonia could solve its problems while remaining part of a large state like the USSR (*RFE Estonian Service*, August 15). The same day, a delegation from Moscow arrived in Tallinn to attempt to settle disputes between Estonians and non-Estonian residents (*TASS*, August 15). Estonian radio reported that Estonia's Supreme Soviet had rescinded a back-to-work order to the striking workers. *Pravda* condemned what it called growing "nationalist hysteria" in the Baltic region and blamed extremists for the labor unrest. In an unsigned commentary, the newspaper criticized the new Estonian election law, saying that its discriminatory passages had had an extremely destabilizing influence on the political situation in the republic.

On August 16, TASS, *Izvestia*, and *Pravda* said strikes had left thousands of freight cars waiting for unloading at railway stations around Tallinn. The same day, the All-Union Central Council of Trade Unions called on the Estonian Supreme Soviet Presidium to reconsider the republic's election law (*TASS*, August 16), and the USSR Supreme Soviet met in Moscow to discuss the situation in Estonia. TASS said Estonian President Arnold Ruutel and others spoke at the session, but it did not quote them. It was reiterated at the session that the new Estonian law violates the Soviet Constitution. TASS said a resolution on the new laws had been passed by the USSR Supreme Soviet and would soon be published in the press. That evening Soviet television showed Arnold Ruutel telling the USSR Supreme Soviet that he had agreed to a plan that would remove the controversial voter residence requirements from the new Estonian law. Ruutel said he had worked out this arrangement with Vice President Anatolii Luk'yanov.

On August 17, TASS said the action by the Presidium of the USSR Supreme Soviet condemning the Estonian election law as unconstitutional and demanding that it be changed had not satisfied Russian strikers in Estonia. TASS said the strike committee wanted additional guarantees before it ended the strikes. The same day, Estonian President Arnold Ruutel, Prime Minister Indrek Toome, and other republican officials met with strike leaders to hear their grievances. TASS said the meeting was attended by a delegation of the USSR Supreme Soviet.

On August 18, the striking workers went back to work. Strike committee spokesmen in Tallinn told Western reporters the strike had been suspended after a late-night meeting of the strike committee and factory representatives. The spokesmen said the strike could be resumed if the Estonian authorities fail to meet strikers' demands by October 1 (*Reuters, AP*, August 18). In addition, more talks were held between government officials and representatives of the striking workers. The officials were quoted by TASS as promising that those who took part in the strikes would not be punished.

More Churches Reopened in RSFSR

TASS reported that the Gorky Oblast Soviet had agreed to reopen the Spassky Cathedral in the city of Gorky, along with twenty-nine other churches in the region, for religious services. The nineteenth-century cathedral, built by the same architect who designed St. Isaac's Cathedral in Leningrad, has been closed since 1929. The reopening of churches in the USSR has been hailed as a sign of improved relations between Church and state, but legislation has still not been passed to facilitate this procedure. Indeed, there have been complaints that local authorities have refused believers' requests to register new parishes. On June 26, *Vechernyi Novosibirsk* reported that the Novosibirsk city soviet had decided not to return the Aleksander Nevsky Cathedral to Russian Orthodox believers, even though poll results read out at a meeting of the city soviet indicated that 96 percent of the city's population favored such a move.

MVD Discusses Problems of Ex-Prisoners

At a briefing, MVD officials discussed measures being taken to help former prisoners reassimilate into Soviet society (*TASS, Radio Moscow*, August 8). In 1988, approximately 450,000 prisoners were released from Soviet prisons, thereby halving the size of the prison population. This process was part of an effort to make the Soviet legal system more humane. Minister of Internal Affairs Vadim Bakatin has admitted, however, that a large proportion of these "lucky" former prisoners are now faced with homelessness and unemployment, which induces many to turn to crime. According to the MVD, 30,000 former prisoners cannot return to their homes, because regulations in force in seventy Soviet cities prevent ex-convicts from receiving a residence permit (*propiska*). Former prisoners are also prohibited from living in border zones and special closed (*rezhimnye*) areas. Without a residence permit, a person cannot get a job; and even in areas without residency restrictions, finding a job can be difficult because enterprises are reluctant to hire former prisoners, especially since the shift to self-financing. See RL 421/89 and RL 424/89.

People in Area Contaminated by Chernobyl' Wait for Resettlement

TASS said people living in an area contaminated by the Chernobyl' nuclear disaster are still waiting to be resettled. It said more than 3,000 people in the Bryansk region in the RSFSR, north of Chernobyl', are still living in the area that TASS called highly contaminated. In another report, TASS quoted the head of the Ukrainian Academy of Sciences, Boris Paton, as saying all construction of nuclear power plants in Ukraine should be stopped until new types of reactors are developed.

El'tsin Says Gorbachev and Ryzhkov Withhold Economic Strategy

Boris El'tsin criticized Mikhail Gorbachev and Nikolai Ryzhkov for failing to outline how they plan to restore the Soviet economy. In an article in the Swedish daily *Dagens Nyheter*, El'tsin criticized speeches made by Gorbachev and Ryzhkov at the Congress of People's Deputies. El'tsin said the speeches failed to address problems such as the USSR's foreign debt and its low standard of living (*Reuters, AFP*, August 8).

Committee Rejects Uzbek Economic Plan

The Aral Committee, a grass-roots movement affiliated with the Uzbek Writers' Union, has rejected the draft of Uzbekistan's 1991–95 economic recovery plan. A member of the Uzbek popular front "Birlik" told RFE/RL by telephone from Tashkent that the committee had described the plan, prepared by the Uzbekistan government, as unsuitable for the Uzbek people. He said members of the Uzbek Party Central Committee and ministry representatives were among those attending the meeting.

The Soviet finance minister said the USSR has far too much money circulating and not enough for people to spend it on. Valentin Pavlov told *Trud* there is only eighteen kopecks worth of goods on the market for every ruble in the hands of consumers. He said this is a "completely abnormal" situation and is the result of the USSR living in debt for the past fifteen years. He said the USSR is consuming more than it earns, natural resources are being destroyed, and the state is spending 5 billion rubles a year to support 8,000 loss-making enterprises.

Finance Minister Says Too Much Money Chasing Too Few Goods

The Estonian Supreme Soviet criticized an article entitled "Great Russian Nationalism" by Tiit Made, a professor from Tallinn. TASS said the parliament acted at the request of Estonian members of the Congress of People's Deputies. Made is also a deputy. The article was published in the Swedish daily *Svenska Dagbladet* on July 24 and reprinted by *Sovetskaya Rossiya* on August 5. Made said "for us Estonians, and this is consoling, there is no such thing as an eternal empire, and the Russian empire can hardly be any such thing." He also said the Russians like to be better than others and to dictate their style of life. The Estonian people's deputies said Made had insulted the Russian people (*RFE Estonian Service*, August 8).

Estonian People's Deputies Condemn Article by Professor

At a meeting of heads of the central mass media at the CPSU Central Committee, Central Committee Secretary Viktor Chebrikov reported on preparations for the forthcoming plenum on interethnic relations. Warning that there were "careerists and irresponsible people trying to play on national feelings for their own ends," he called on journalists to be firm and adopt a genuinely Party approach in their treatment of interethnic problems. CPSU Central Committee secretary Nikolai Slyun'kov, who presided at the meeting, also spoke about the nationalities question, stressing "the increased responsibility of the mass media in implementing the Central Committee's ideas on overcoming difficulties in interethnic relations" (*TASS*, August 9; *Pravda*, August 10).

Meeting of Media Officials at CPSU CC

Wednesday, August 9

TASS quoted *Moscow News* (No. 33) as saying investigators had now ruled that the decision to use troops to break up a demonstration in Tbilisi in April was unlawful. The

Moscow News on April Events in Tbilisi

newspaper said the investigators from a special group set up by Georgia's Supreme Soviet had demanded that officials in the republic's leadership and in the armed forces be called to account. The investigators said that the rally had been peaceful and that there had been no reason to call in troops to end it.

Cosmonaut Says *Buran* Space Shuttle Too Expensive

There has been more criticism of the cost of the Soviet space shuttle *Buran*, this time from a cosmonaut. TASS quoted cosmonaut Konstantin Feoktistov as saying the cost of using the shuttle as a transport craft to orbital space stations will be ten to forty times higher than using the existing *Progress* spacecraft. TASS said Feoktisov was speaking at a meeting on Soviet space problems. *Buran* has not flown since making an unmanned flight in November, 1988. The chief of the Soviet space training center, Vladimir Shatalov, said in June he was unable to announce the date for the next flight. The cost of the *Buran* program has been repeatedly criticized, and the authorities have announced a series of cost-cutting measures.

Soviet Spokesman Denies Report on Kuriles-for-Money Offer

Soviet Foreign Ministry spokesman Vadim Perfil'ev denied a report of a Soviet offer to hand back four islands claimed by Japan in return for big Japanese investments in the Soviet economy. The report in the US magazine *US News and World Report* said the offer came in a secret Soviet message to the Japanese government. Perfil'ev described the report as unfounded. He told a Moscow press briefing there had not been, and could not be, any such message. Soviet forces seized the four islands in the Kurile chain off Japan's northern coast at the end of World War II. Japan has long said there can be no peace treaty formally ending hostilities until Moscow returns the islands (*TASS*, August 9).

Azerbaijani Raion Wants to Join Nagorno-Karabakh

The soviet of an Azerbaijani raion is reported to have asked to be incorporated in the republic's strife-torn Nagorno-Karabakh Oblast. The Armenian news agency Armenpress said the decision was made by the Shaumyanovsk Raion Soviet by a vote of fifty-three to zero with eight abstentions. Armenpress said the decision was based on "the unanimous wish" of the Armenians in the Shaumyanovsk Raion following "numerous appeals and demands." It did not say when the action was taken. Armenpress said the Shaumyanovsk Raion Soviet also asked the USSR Supreme Soviet to place the raion under its protection because some officials had said "the people's security cannot be guaranteed" (*Armenpress International*, August 9).

TASS revealed that a Supreme Soviet commission for problems of Soviet Germans has received a proposal to reestablish a Volga German Autonomous Republic. TASS said the proposal, put forward before the commission by the "Vozrozhdenie" (Rebirth) society of Soviet Germans, provides for the reestablishment of the republic at its former location along the middle reaches of the Volga River. TASS quoted Heinrich Groth, secretary of the Supreme Soviet commission, as saying the proposal, together with some other suggestions put forward before the commission, will be examined. He said he believes the process of reestablishing the Autonomous republic for Soviet Germans will take at least three years. The ethnic Germans were deported to Siberia and Central Asia in 1941, and their republic was abolished.

TASS Reports Proposal on Reestablishment of German Republic

Thursday, August 10

Pravda said Party bodies are being too passive at a time when current changes in the Soviet Union require that the Party present its position more forcefully in the press. The editorial said there were signs of incompetence in Soviet press reports on complicated issues concerning new forms of social life. *Pravda* said some Party committees give journals regular information, take care in guiding them, and make sure press criticism is effective. It said this is the correct approach. The editorial comes after a Central Committee resolution ordered a reorganization of Party publications because some of them failed to measure up to the demands of *perestroika*. *Pravda* said journalists must firmly follow Leninist principles of Party spirit and ideology.

***Pravda* Urges Stronger Party Role in the Press**

The president of the RSFSR, Vitalii Vorotnikov, said Autonomous republics located within the federation should be given much greater powers. In an interview with *Sovetskaya Rossiya*, Vorotnikov said the Autonomous republics must have the right to take independent decisions on a range of social, economic, cultural, and political issues currently handled by the federation. He demanded

Vorotnikov Urges More Powers for Autonomous Republics

that the federation have the same administrative structure as other Soviet republics. On August 9, Vorotnikov chaired a session of the Presidium of the RSFSR Supreme Soviet, which discussed proposed changes to the federation's constitution and draft laws on elections.

USSR Expresses Concern over Austria EC Application

The Soviet Union sent a message to Austria saying it was concerned about Austria's application to join the European Community. The message was handed to Austrian Chancellor Franz Vranitzky by Soviet Ambassador Gennadii Shikin in Vienna. It said Moscow understands Austria's economic reasons for the move but believes it would jeopardize Austria's neutrality (*Reuters*, August 10).

TASS Quotes Latvian Party Chief on *Perestroika*

Latvian Communist Party First Secretary Janis Vagris was quoted as saying the Latvian Party rejects all political structures that threaten *perestroika* or the constitutional basis of Soviet society. TASS said Vagris spoke at a meeting of the Latvian Party Central Committee in Riga, where he gave a detailed address on the political situation in the republic and called for the consolidation of all forces in Latvia to implement restructuring. TASS said more than 400 representatives of political and social forces in the republic had been invited to the plenum, including representatives of the People's Front of Latvia and "Interfront."

Protest Meeting in Tashkent

Uzbekistan media officials held a protest in Tashkent. The officials were protesting against a report in the Soviet journal *Ogonek* (No. 29) about the ethnic clashes in the Fergana Valley in June. They alleged that *Ogonek* reported the clashes in a distorted and unobjective manner. An Uzbek journalist reported the protest in a telephone conversation with RFE/RL. The article in *Ogonek* was written by journalist Anatolii Golovkov, and it contains some anti-Muslim remarks.

Soviet Farmers to Be Paid Partially in Foreign Currency

The Soviet government said it would start paying state and collective farmers partially in foreign currency in an attempt to stimulate crop production and reduce imports. TASS said such payments would be made to producers of wheat and some other commodities for amounts they produce above levels reached earlier in the 1980s. Money for the payments will be diverted from that for foreign purchases of food products.

Soviet Minister of Internal Affairs Vadim Bakatin said he has "precise information" about links between criminal elements and ethnic unrest in the USSR. Bakatin said "organized crime and the second economy" had an undeniable interest in mass ethnic incidents. He also linked the incidents to "all kinds of clans taking over the right of Socialist property." Bakatin listed the disturbances in Alma-Ata in 1986 and the more recent strife in Abkhazia, the Fergana Valley of Uzbekistan, and Nagorno-Karabakh as examples of unrest in which criminals were involved. (An article in *Ogonek* [No. 29] stressed that only a very small percentage of those participating directly in the riots in the Fergana Valley had a criminal record.)

Bakatin Links Criminals to Ethnic Disorders

The Soviet journal *World Economy and International Relations* said the USSR was still not ready for full membership in the General Agreement on Tariffs and Trade (GATT). The journal said the USSR understands it is not ready to assume the obligations connected with full membership in GATT but it would like observer status. Key GATT requirements are "open markets and fair competition." A Soviet move to join the UN-related body three years ago was rejected (*TASS*, August 10).

Journal on Soviet Moves to Join GATT

Friday, August 11

Soviet foreign-trade official Ivan Ivanov said two free economic zones are to be set up in the Soviet Union. One will be in Vyborg, northwest of Leningrad, the other in the Far East Nakhodka region. Ivanov said the zones will provide mainly for the domestic market. He said foreign investors and Soviet enterprises operating in the free economic zones will get preferential treatment. Ivanov said in January that republics and regions that have free economic zones on their territory will supply the zones with essential materials and have the right to expect a share of the profits (*TASS*, August 11).

Foreign Trade Official on Free Economic Zones

TASS said two US congressmen who believe they met political prisoners at a Soviet labor camp were mistaken. Congressmen Frank Wolf and Christopher Smith visited Perm Labor Camp No. 35 on August 10 and talked to inmates. They said afterwards they believed that some of the prisoners were being held solely because of their political beliefs. They singled out three prisoners—

TASS Contradicts Congressmen on Prisoners

Leonid Lubman, Valerii Smirnov, and Mikhail Kazachkov. TASS quoted the USSR Ministry of Internal Affairs as saying all three prisoners had been convicted of passing information to foreign agents. The agency said two of them, Lubman and Kazachkov, were alleged to have worked for the CIA. TASS said it was understandable that the congressmen spoke in favor of the prisoners, because they had spied for the United States.

Sweden Expels Soviet Diplomat for Spying

Sweden was reported to have expelled a Soviet consular official for industrial espionage. A Swedish Foreign Ministry spokesman said the Soviet official had tried to get information about Swedish and foreign technology. The Foreign Ministry said the official had worked for the Soviet consular mission in the port of Göteborg. It did not reveal his name or position. The ministry said the official had left Sweden (*Reuters*, August 11).

Saturday, August 12 ────────────────────────────────

Knizhnoe obozrenie Publishes Solzhenitsyn Short Story

Knizhnoe obozrenie (No. 32) carried a short story by Aleksandr Solzhenitsyn entitled "Pravaya kist'" (The Right Hand). In a short postscript the periodical noted that Solzhenitsyn's story, which is autobiographical, was written in 1960 and submitted by the author to the editorial boards of several Soviet journals. At that time they all rejected it for publication.

Official Comments on New Payment for Farmers

Oleg Klimov, general director of the Soviet foreign-trade association Exportkhleb, said the new plan to pay Soviet farmers foreign currency for part of their harvest will not have much effect on production this year but "may bring tangible results" next year (*TASS*, in English, August 12). The plan will allow sovkhozes and kolkhozes that increase their marketed output to sell grain to the state for foreign currency. US Agriculture Secretary Clayton Yeutter praised the plan as "innovative and creative."

TASS Says Reactor Producing Weapons-Grade Plutonium Shut Down

TASS said a reactor producing weapons-grade plutonium at a defense factory in the Chelyabinsk region had been shut down. It is the third Soviet reactor to be shut down since 1987. In April, Mikhail Gorbachev announced that the Soviet Union had stopped producing plutonium at two of fourteen reactors. TASS said a further two reactors

434

are to be phased out next year. It said closing these nuclear facilities is in line with Soviet policy to cut back production of fissionable material for nuclear weapons.

Tens of thousands of people demonstrated in the Azerbaijani capital of Baku to demand autonomy and new parliamentary elections. E'tibar Mamedov, a leader of the Azerbaijani Popular Front, which organized the rally, said a general strike would be called for August 14 if protesters' demands were not met. The demands include restoring Azerbaijani control over Nagorno-Karabakh. Other demands are the release of jailed members of the Azerbaijani pro-independence "Birlik" society and new parliamentary elections. Speakers at the rally said elections held last spring were manipulated by Party officials (*Reuters, RL Azerbaijani Service*, August 12). On August 14, Ismail Agaev, head of the Information Department of the Azerbaijani Foreign Ministry, told AP that no strike was evident in Azerbaijan. In a conflicting report, the Azerbaijani Popular Front told RFE/RL that strikes had started at thirty-six enterprises in Baku. On August 15, a spokesman for the Azerbaijani Popular Front said the Azerbaijani authorities had released all jailed members of "Birlik." He said they had also agreed to call a special session of the Azerbaijani Supreme Soviet to discuss Nagorno-Karabakh (*RL Azerbaijani Service*, August 15).

On August 19, reports said at least 600,000 people demonstrated in Baku (*Reuters, AFP, RL Azerbaijani Service*, August 19). On August 21 and 22, workers held strikes at a number of enterprises in Baku and Sumgait. Popular Front leader Mehdi Mamedov said they affected 60 percent of the industrial plants in the two cities. On August 22, the front held a rally in Baku to discuss the strikes and other ways of putting pressure on local authorities (*Reuters, AP, RL Azerbaijani Service*, August 22). Sources reported that half a million people had taken part in the rally. RFE/RL quoted Mamedov as saying in a telephone interview that it had been decided at the rally to stage a general stike in Azerbaijan in September. On August 23, TASS reported the end of the strikes. The same day, RFE/RL was informed that two members of the Azerbaijani Popular Front had been detained in Baku. On August 25, about 200 supporters and members of the Azerbaijani Popular Front were reported to be picketing in front of the MVD headquarters in Baku. A report from the scene said the pickets were protesting over the continued detention of Djanbakhysh Umudov, a member of the Popular Front's governing board.

Unauthorized Demonstration in Baku

Azerbaijani Trains Protected while Passing through Armenia

Special MVD units have been assigned to protect Azerbaijani trains running into and through southern Armenia. *Izvestia* said the guards were there to prevent further attacks on the trains. Earlier attacks halted traffic on one rail line for a week. In a front-page article, *Izvestia* quoted Major General V. Zelensky of the Ministry of Internal Affairs as saying a special investigative unit had also been formed to find the people who had been attacking trains and destroying railroad tracks. On August 18, TASS reported that a man had died in an attempt to blow up a railroad track connecting Armenia and Azerbaijan. It quoted the daily *Gudok* as saying the man was a kolkhoz worker from Ali-Darya in Azerbaijan.

Latvian Party Plenum Cites Crisis of Confidence

Latvia's Party Central Committee ended a two-day plenum during which it said there was a crisis of confidence in the Party and trends towards a split based on national feelings. TASS said the plenum, which was held in Riga, unanimously approved a call for further democratic development in Latvia. TASS said the plenum also discussed issues of national sovereignty and of the Latvian Party's relations with the Communist Parties of other Soviet republics.

New Official Report Released on Fergana Valley Unrest

The USSR Ministry of Internal Affairs released a new report on deaths and damage resulting from ethnic clashes in Uzbekistan's Fergana region in June. Moscow television quoted the report as saying a total of 105 people had been killed in the unrest and 1,011 injured. The previous official death toll was 103. The June violence involved clashes between Fergana's majority Uzbek population and its Meskhetian minority.

On August 31, an Uzbek villager was sentenced to twelve years' deprivation of freedom for his part in the violence between Uzbeks and Meshkhetians. This is the first announced conviction stemming from the violence (*TASS*, August 31).

New First Secretary in Chelyabinsk

Nikolai Shvyrev resigned "at his own request" as first secretary of the Chelyabinsk Oblast Party Committee, a post he had held since June, 1986. According to *Pravda* of August 14, Shvyrev was forced to leave his job mainly because of his failure "to make *perestroika* a success." His successor is Aleksei Litovchenko, a fifty-one-year-old Ukrainian, who has been the second secretary in Chelyabinsk since March, 1989. Prior to that, Litovchenko served as a Party committee secretary in the Magnito-gorsk Metallurgical Factory. Politburo member Vladimir Nikonov oversaw the change in leadership in Chelyabinsk. In a departure from previous practices, thirteen candidates were nominated for Shvyrev's vacated post, of whom three were included on the ballot for a secret vote.

USSR to Import Medicine

Soviet Health Minister Evgenii Chazov announced that the Soviet Union plans to import medicines worth a total of 500 million rubles. In an article in *Izvestia*, Chazov said the USSR needs to spend 1,500 million rubles to procure medicine in short supply. He said the Soviet Union will be importing medicines from West Germany, Britain, the United States, India, Switzerland, Yugo-slavia, and Turkey. He said that the first supplies will arrive next month and that shipments could be completed by November.

Independent Psychiatric Association Fails to Gain Admission to WPA

The Executive Committee of the World Psychiatric Asso-ciation has decided not to grant associate membership to an independent group of Soviet psychiatrists. At a meet-ing in Athens the committee said the group had failed to file its application for membership on time but that it would instruct its secretary general to ask the inde-pendent Soviet psychiatrists for more information about themselves. Konstantin Karmanov, a spokesman for the group of independent psychiatrists, said he was disap-pointed his group had not been granted membership in the WPA (*RFE/RL Special*, August 12).

--- *Sunday, August 13*

RSFSR's Draft Election Laws Published

Draft laws on the election of people's deputies from the RSFSR were published in *Sovetskaya Rossiya*. A TASS report on the laws said that the number of candidates in elections for republican-level and local soviets would not be limited. It was evident from the report that the republic's draft law, in contrast with the all-Union law, does not envisage the election of deputies by public organizations. The draft law limits the practice of holding district election meetings. Such meetings are to be held only in cases when more than ten candidates are running in a district. (Such meetings were mandatory during national elections of people's deputies.)

Radio Reports on Aftereffects of Donbass Coal Strike

Radio Moscow said major changes had taken place in the running of the Donbass coalfield in Ukraine since a miners' strike ended there late last month. The radio said the changes included extra payment for miners performing night and evening shifts and the granting of paid leave to women to enable them to look after small children. It also said "a number" of mine officials who did not have the confidence of workers had been replaced. It added, however, that mines in the region are not yet meeting daily production targets or making up losses incurred during the strike.

Wave of Strikes Continues in Azerbaijan and Nagorno-Karabakh

A spokesman for the Azerbaijani Popular Front said Azerbaijanis in Nagorno-Karabakh had been on strike since August 11. The spokesman said in a telephone interview with RFE/RL that people in Azerbaijan's Autonomous Republic of Nakhichevan are also striking to protest over what they say is negligence by Azerbaijan's leaders in handling the Nagorno-Karabakh situation. On August 14, Soviet television reported that more lives had been claimed by violence in Nagorno-Karabakh. It gave no figures, however. On August 16, TASS reported that part of the railroad in Nagorno-Karabkh had been damaged by an explosive device over the weekend. It said the explosion damaged the line between Stepanakert and the town of Agdam, which is outside the oblast. Meanwhile, senior officials of the USSR Ministry of Internal Affairs are in Stepanakert to help deal with the troubles there (*TASS*, August 15).

Trud on Writers Repressed under Stalin

Trud published an article about the hardships experienced by writers and poets in Stalin's labor camps. The article was written by V. Murav'ev, who is a member of the All-Union Commission on the Literary Heritage of Writers Who Fell Victim to Stalinist Repressions. Murav'ev himself served a term in a labor camp under Stalin. The article quoted Murav'ev as saying 2,000 writers who were victims of repression have now been identified.

Monday, August 14 ————————————————————————————

Government Says Economic Situation Is Serious

The USSR Council of Ministers said that some negative trends in the USSR economy have seriously complicated the situation in the country. TASS said the Council of Ministers met in Moscow to discuss next year's drafts of the plan and the budget and devoted special attention to the problem of the food supply. TASS said next year's plan and budget drafts contain special measures to "prevent a further worsening of the economic situation" and to significantly improve the domestic market. It said the Council of Ministers plans several steps to improve the financial situation, including cutting centralized capital investments in industry by almost one-third. Spending is also to be substantially cut for defense, administration, and imports of equipment and materials for heavy industry (*Izvestia*, August 15).

Soviet Reaction to Creation of New Government in Poland

Pravda criticized Poland's "Solidarity" leaders for attempting to form a coalition with two small Communist-allied parties. The newspaper said that, in approaching the United Peasants' Party and the Democratic Party before Prime Minister Czeslaw Kiszczak had formed a government, "Solidarity" had acted "against the accepted principles of parliamentary democracy." It said further that such actions do not facilitate Kiszczak's "difficult mission" or promote the relaxation of political tensions in Poland. The newspaper said it was necessary for Poland to form a government that unites all forces, including the Communists, and has the confidence of the people. The same day, Soviet Foreign Ministry spokesman Yurii Gremitskikh said Poland's political situation had been complicated by what he called the political maneuvers of "Solidarity." Reuters said Gremitskikh was responding to questions about criticism of "Solidarity" in *Pravda*. Gremitskikh emphasized, however, that the formation of the next Polish government was an internal Polish matter.

Nature Reserve to Be Set Up in Chernobyl' Contamination Area

A nature reserve is to be set up on part of the area contaminated by radiation from the Chernobyl' nuclear disaster. TASS said the reserve will cover three regions in the Belorussian republic from which the population was evacuated after the disaster. The agency said scientists will use the reserve to study how nuclear radiation has affected wildlife and plants.

Three Military Plants to Switch to Civilian Production

Deputy Prime Minister Igor Belousov today identified three military-industrial facilities that will switch over fully to civilian production by 1992. TASS quoted Belousov as saying the change is to be made at the shipbuilding yard in Kiev and at land-forces production facilities in Yoshkar Ola, east of Gorky, and at Yuryuzan, in the Urals.

Belousov said the production facilities would be used to build civilian ships and planes as well as higher-quality farm and light-industry equipment. He said money would have to be found to pay the resultant wage losses of plant employees and to retrain them. RL 261/89.

Tuesday, August 15

Discussion of Molotov-Ribbentrop Pact

On the eve of the fiftieth anniversary of the signing of the Molotov-Ribbentrop Pact, the discussion of the event intensified in the Soviet press. The conservative *Sovetskaya Rossiya* (August 6) said recent criticism of the pact was intolerable. Writing in the newspaper, historian Yurii Emel'yanov said moves to declare the pact void were weakening the USSR's unity and international position. On August 11, *Pravda* carried a discussion among Soviet historians who acknowledged the existence of the secret protocols to the pact. (The text of the secret protocols was simultaneously published in *Argumenty i fakty*, No. 32. The Baltic press published the text of the protocols last year.) *Argumenty i fakty* said the Congress of People's Deputies' commission on the Molotov-Ribbentrop pact had concluded that the existing copies of the protocols were authentic. On August 15, the Soviet government made clear that its long-awaited acknowledgment of the secret protocols attached to the Molotov-Ribbentrop Pact dividing up spheres of interest between the USSR and Nazi Germany does not mean the USSR is admitting the Baltic States were forced to join the Soviet Union. The latest statement on the issue came in a Foreign Ministry press conference with nine historians and a ministry spokesman. They said it was perfectly logical for the Baltic States to have invited the Red Army onto their territory after the Nazis invaded Poland (*Reuters*, August 15). It was stated at the conference that the USSR had had no choice but to sign the Molotov-Ribbentrop Pact. This cautious approach contrasts with what was said by some participants in a round-table discussion on the origins of World War II published in *Voprosy istorii* (No. 6). Speaking at the round-table, M. I. Semiryaga of the Institute of the International Workers' Movement of the USSR Academy of Sciences stressed that the conclusion by the USSR of the pact with Nazi Germany on August 23, 1939, "was a big political mistake on the part of the Soviet leadership," adding that the USSR could have done far more at the time to reach an agreement with Britain and France. Semiryaga said the pact secured rear

440

support for Hitler in the East thereby freeing him to concentrate on the invasion of Western Europe. In fact, Semiryaga stressed, this increased the political isolation of the USSR in the international arena and relaxed Stalin's vigilance on the eve of the Nazi invasion of the USSR. Semiryaga also strongly condemned the USSR's invasion of eastern Poland in September, 1939. Nevertheless, even Semiryaga avoided discussion of the USSR's annexation of the Baltic States. On August 17, *Izvestia* published an article by observer Vikentii Matveev, who said claims that the Baltic States joined the Soviet Union only as a result of the Nazi-Soviet pact disregarded popular support for the Soviet Union that he claimed existed in these states at the time.

On August 18, in an interview published in *Pravda*, Politburo member Aleksandr Yakovlev admitted the existence of the secret protocols attached to the Molotov-Ribbentrop Pact and condemned both the protocols and the pact. He denied, however, that the pact and its secret protocols had any legal impact on the Baltic republics' current status as members of the Soviet Union. He said it was "far-fetched to seek some kind of relation between the present status of the three republics and the non-aggression treaty." He insisted that it was a vote by each of the republic's legislatures in July, 1940, that led to the incorporation of Estonia, Lithuania, and Latvia into the USSR. See RL 333/89 and RL 387/89.

Moldavian Party Official Criticizes Party Actions

The Moldavian Communist Party secretary for ideology, Ion Gutsu, said Party reaction to public initiatives in Moldavia in the past had been "harebrained." The Moldavian Party Central Committee last November criticized public actions seeking restoration of the Moldavian language. The result was what Novosti called "a vicious press campaign" against the public organizations. Novosti quoted Gutsu as saying the Party made many propaganda blunders and failed to keep people informed. On August 16, TASS reported strikes in Tiraspol, Bendery, and Rybnitsa staged to protest against draft laws on language issued in Moldavia.

Senior Israeli Officials Talk to Soviet Media

Senior Israeli officials talked to the Soviet media about Israeli-Soviet relations. Israeli Prime Minister Yitzhak Shamir, interviewed in *Ogonek* (No. 33) called for the normalization of those relations. Radio Israel said Foreign Minister Moshe Arens had said on Soviet television that, since it was the USSR that had severed relations with

Israel, it was up to Moscow to renew them. On August 17, the Israeli media reported that the Israeli industry and commerce minister, Ariel Sharon, had been officially invited to visit the USSR (*Reuters*, August 17). Sharon's visit would be the first official visit by an Israeli minister to the USSR since 1967.

Wednesday, August 16 _____

New Estimates of Unemployed and Homeless

In an interview on Radio Moscow-1 (1900), Aleksei Lebedev, chairman of the International Association for Studying Unemployment and Homelessness, gave details of that body's work. Lebedev cited 4.5 million as his estimate of the total unemployed in the USSR; this is close to the 2–3 percent rate previously estimated by Western and Soviet economists. He also reckoned that there are some 1.5 million homeless or *bomzhi* in the Soviet Union. This is about 300,000 more than his earlier estimate, aired on "Vzglyad" in March. See RL 384/89.

Volga River around Kuibyshev Polluted by Mercury

Valerii Tsykalo, head of the Department for Water Resources and Environmental Protection in the Kuibyshev Oblast, said that the Volga River near Kuibyshev is polluted with mercury and that fish there have been found to contain carcinogens. Tsykalo said 70 percent of the fish tested in that part of the river were found to contain toxic substances. Tsykalo blamed this situation on chemical sustances used in agriculture that seeped from the ground into the river (*TASS*, August 16).

Reformists Call for Authoritarian Rule in USSR

Literaturnaya gazeta carried a discussion conducted by the newspaper's observer Georgii Tselms with two employees of the Institute of Economics of the World Socialist System of the USSR Academy of Sciences, Igor Klyamkin and Andranik Migranyan. Both Klyamkin and Migranyan are well known for their outspoken articles in the Soviet press (see *Novyi mir*, No.2, No. 7, 1989), and both have been regarded as pro-Gorbachev reformers. In their discussion with Tselms, Klyamkin and Migranyan paint a gloomy picture of the Soviet Union descending gradually into anarchy. They state that the USSR is in a deep crisis, with its economy falling apart, a catastrophic social situation, and insoluble interethnic problems. They argue further that it is impossible to move directly from totalitarianism to democracy, as the Soviet Union is trying to do now, and that therefore the country should pass through a stage of authoritarianism. Arguing that the Congress of People's Deputies did little but destabilize the situation even more, Migranyan states that the congress should have given Gorbachev emergency powers, set up a Committee to Save the People, and temporarily suspended the activities of all other institutions of power. Nevertheless, both Klyamkin and Migranyan suggest that some elements of democracy, including freedom of expression, should be allowed under the authoritarian system they propose.

Soviet television carried a program about exiled Russian writer Aleksandr Solzhenitsyn that praised both the author and his writing. The program gave a detailed account of his life and work in the Soviet Union and abroad after he was expelled in 1974. The program reported at length on Solzhenitsyn's major study of the Soviet labor-camp system, *Gulag Archipelago*, and on plans to publish it in the USSR. The program quoted Solzhenitsyn as having said he would return to the country that published *Gulag Archipelago* because it would not be the same country that expelled him.

Soviet Television Shows Program on Solzhenitsyn

The youth journal *Sobesednik* (No. 34) carried a lengthy interview with the director of Radio Liberty's Russian Service, Vladimir Matusevich. The journal left uncensored Matusevich's praise for the work of Radio Liberty, including his insistence that the radio is not involved in broadcasting primitive anti-Soviet propaganda.

***Sobesednik* Interviews Director of RL Russian Service**

Thursday, August 17

Pravda published the CPSU's proposals for "improving interethnic relations in the USSR and renewing nationalities policy." The document is entitled "The Party's Nationalities Policy under Contemporary Conditions (Platform of the CPSU)," and focuses on six general areas: (1) transformations in the Soviet federation and its investment with real political and economic content; (2) the expansion of the rights and potential of all forms and types of national autonomous entity; (3) the safeguarding of equal rights for every people and the satisfaction of the specific interests of every nationality; (4) the creation of conditions for the free development of national cultures

CPSU's Platform on the National Question

443

and languages; (5) the strengthening of guarantees to rule out the infringement of citizens' rights on the grounds of nationality; and (6) the renewal of all ideological, political, and educational work in the sphere of nationality relations. By far the greatest attention is devoted to the restructuring of the Soviet federation, which the document characterizes in terms of "a renewed federation" based on Gorbachev's slogan of a strong Union and strong republics. In this connection, there are a number of interesting proposals concerning the transformation of the RSFSR into a "normal" republic—i.e., creating various institutions that the Russian republic has been lacking but that exist in other republics. Such demands have been repeatedly raised by Russian patriots and, more recently, by Vitalli Vorotnikov, the chairman of the Presidium of the RSFSR Supreme Soviet. The document also revives the idea of creating a Central Committee Secretariat (Bureau) within the CPSU Central Committee "for the direct operational leadership of the RSFSR's Party organizations." The platform is to be submitted for examination to the Congress of People's Deputies and to the USSR Supreme Soviet for the adoption of the requisite legislation.

In an interview with *Pravda* on August 19, Politburo member and head of the Central Committee Commission on Legal Policy Viktor Chebrikov said the platform laid the foundation for better interethnic relations but did not offer any detailed solution of problems. He said the way out of any crisis was national reconciliation and compromise, not redrawing frontiers.

New Data on Soviet Losses in Afghanistan

Pravda carried a short article by Colonel V. Izgarshev revealing new figures on Soviet deaths in Afghanistan. Attributed to the General Staff of the Soviet Armed Forces, the figures are broken down by year and differentiate between total losses, combat deaths, and losses among officers. By aggregating Izgarshev's data, the following figures emerge. Total Soviet losses in Afghanistan between 1979 and 1989 were 13,833. Of these deaths, 11,381, or 82 percent, were combat fatalities. The remainder, according to Izgarshev, died through careless handling of their weapons or as a result of wounds and illness. Deaths of officers in this period amounted to 1,979, or 14 percent of total losses. Of this number, 1,755 died in combat. Izgarshev's figures indicate that Soviet losses peaked in 1984, when total deaths numbered 2,343, including 305 officers. The lowest full-year figure was 759, in 1988. If Izgarshev's figures are accurate, then Soviet losses during the last phase of the withdrawal, in January and February of 1989, were exceedingly low. He lists fifty-three dead, including ten officers.

Soviet Defense Minister Dmitrii Yazov said the number of Soviet troops in the Baltic republics will not be increased, despite the current strikes and unrest there. Yazov, who is visiting Finland, told reporters that the situation in the Baltic is a consequence of the policies of *glasnost'* and *perestroika* and that the results of those policies are not always positive. Yazov today met Finnish President Mauno Koivisto and is to end his visit on August 18 (*Reuters*, August 17).

Yazov Rejects Increase in Soviet Troops in Baltic Republics

Soviet trade-union chairman Stepan Shalaev said the recent strikes in various parts of the USSR were justified in most cases. Shalaev said in the majority of cases the strikers had serious cause for dissatisfaction. He said many enterprises had still not received the autonomy promised to them and remained without economic or legal rights and unable to control the use of the profits they earn. Shalaev was quoted in an interview published in *Pravda*.

Shalaev Says Workers Were Right to Strike

Izvestia said a former church in the central Russian city of Ivanovo will be returned to believers for religious use. The dispute over the use of the church prompted four members of a group of Orthodox Christians to stage a hunger strike in Ivanovo in late March and early April. The dispute began when the believers asked to use the former church but local authorities refused. The believers then appealed to the USSR Council on Religious Affairs, which recommended that local authorities release the building.

Church in Ivanovo to Be Returned to Believers

There was a meeting in Moscow between KGB officials and representatives of a recently created association of groups campaigning for the rehabilitation of victims of Stalin's repressions. Radio Moscow said the representatives were told that all Stalin-era cases against so-called enemies of the people are being reexamined. It said the KGB officials (unidentified) were questioned for two and a half hours. It said they assured the association's representatives that everything possible would be done to restore the good name of innocent victims of Stalin's repressions.

Representatives of Stalin Victims Meet KGB Officials

Friday, August 18 —————————————————————————

Trotsky Articles Published in the USSR for First Time in Sixty Years	The journal of the Komsomol, *Molodoi Kommunist* (No.8), printed a series of articles by Leon Trotsky. This was the first time that articles by Trotsky had been published in full in the Soviet Union since he was forced into exile sixty years ago. (Earlier this year, some excerpts from Trotsky's writings were published; see *Ogonek*, No. 17, *Kommunist*, No. 10, *Argumenty i fakty*, No. 34, and *Rodina*, No. 7, 1989.) The series of articles, called "The New Course," first appeared in *Pravda* in 1923. They criticized, among other things, the excessive strengthening of the Party apparatus. Trotsky remains the only leading associate of Lenin's at the time of the October Revolution not to have been officially rehabilitated in the Soviet Union. *Sobesednik* (No. 33) published an interview with Leningrad historian Vladimir Billik, who gave the most sympathetic treatment of Trotsky's views to appear so far in the Soviet press. See RL 397/89.

Saturday, August 19 —————————————————————————

Emergency Party Meeting Opens in Leningrad	Leningrad's Oblast Party organization began an emergency public meeting to promote *perestroika*. TASS said Leningrad Oblast Party First Secretary Boris Gidaspov warned the 1,500 delegates that the Party would lose its authority in Leningrad if it did not lead the movement for *perestroika* and if *perestroika* failed to improve everyday life. TASS called the meeting unprecedented and said it had been prompted by urgent social and economic problems as well as by "diverse public movements, which are on the rise" in Leningrad. TASS said the meeting was being televised live, and viewers could call in to ask questions and state their opinions. On August 21, *Pravda* carried a report on the meeting. The newspaper said the Leningrad Party organization needed to change its style of work. It also commented on general problems in the city, citing organized crime, inflation, poor protection of citizens against arbitrary treatment, ecological problems, and the uncontrolled activities of informal groups as among the chief evils.
Soviet Officials Comment on 1968 Invasion	Former Soviet Politburo member Kirill Mazurov told *Izvestia* he would not now agree to conduct an operation like the Soviet-led invasion of Czechoslovakia in 1968. He

added, however, that in 1968 he had acted in accordance with his convictions. Mazurov said that during the invasion he was in Prague under the name of "General Trofimov." Also interviewed in *Izvestia* was Ivan Pavlovsky, then a deputy defense minister and commander of the invasion troops. Pavlovsky said his view of the invasion had not changed. *Izvestia* said in an accompanying commentary that there must not be a repeat of the past and that Soviet and Czechoslovak historians should reexamine the events of 1968 in order to end discrepancies over the invasion. On August 21, a Soviet Foreign Ministry spokesman, Yurii Gremitskikh, said it was up to Czechoslovakia to analyze the events of 1968. Gremitskikh refused to say whether the Soviet Union believed the invasion was justified, but he told reporters in Moscow that the present Soviet government rejects the use of force, or the threat of force, to solve problems. Gremitskikh added that the events of 1968 in Czechoslovakia must be seen in the political context of the time (*Reuters*, August 21).

Curfew Lifted in Part of Tajikistan

TASS said a curfew imposed in part of Tajikistan last month, after ethnic clashes between Kirgiz and Tajiks, had been lifted. The dispute centered on water and land rights along the border between the two republics. It said water supplies, which had been affected by the turmoil, were being delivered to Kirgiz and Tajik farm cooperatives. TASS said that a bilateral commission had defined the border more precisely and that both sides had agreed to submit unresolved issues to the USSR Supreme Soviet.

Sunday, August 20

Moscow News Attacks New Draft Law on Informal Groups

Moscow News (No. 34) carried an article by Nina Belyaeva, reporting that yet another draft law on informal groups drawn up by the authorities has been severely criticized by the Institute of State and Law of the USSR Academy of Sciences. Quoting from a review of the draft presented by the institute, Belyaeva pointed out that the draft puts informal groups under the overwhelming control of the government. The review emphasizes that the draft takes no account of the current situation in the Soviet Union—namely, that new informal groups are appearing almost every day regardless of the government's attitude towards them. Belyaeva reminds readers that the draft under review is already the second to have been drawn up in the period of *perestroika*. The first draft was rejected in 1987 as too conservative. Belyaeva makes clear that the second draft is not much better and, in the opinion of lawyers from the Institute of State and Law, cannot be improved but should be rewritten from scratch.

Moscow News on Situation in Estonia

Moscow News (No. 34) carried two analyses of the situation in Estonia. Both articles, one by the newspaper's special correspondent in Tallinn and another by the poet David Samoilov, who lives in Estonia, supported the demands of the Estonians and criticized the position of "Interdvizhenie," which consists mostly of Russians and other non-Estonian workers. Both the newspaper's correspondent and Samoilov thought that the Estonian language law, which requires the non-Estonian population to learn Estonian and introduces franchise laws based on the length of residency in the republic, were entirely justified.

Luk'yanov on Confederation Concept

Soviet Vice President Anatolii Luk'yanov said "it would be a step backwards" to transform the USSR from a federal state into a confederation, as has been suggested by some Soviet radicals, including Andrei Sakharov. In an interview broadcast by Radio Moscow, Luk'yanov said the authorities believe the reform process now under way in the USSR will strengthen the Union, not weaken it. Luk'yanov said he and Mikhail Gorbachev work together closely in the daily running of the country. He said that Gorbachev successfully combines Party and state work but that Gorbachev's workload should be eased.

National Council Set Up in Nagorno-Karabakh

Armenians in the disputed oblast of Nagorno-Karabakh have set up a national council to try to solve the region's problems. Radio Erevan said the council was established on August 16 in Stepanakert by representatives of the Congress of People's Deputies. The representatives complained that the special committee that is administering Nagorno-Karabakh from Moscow in the wake of widespread ethnic unrest is not capable of reversing the current critical situation. The council also called for the unification of Nagorno-Karabakh with Armenia. The radio said the representatives expressed regret that Azerbaijani delegates of the Congress of People's Deputies had declined to sit on the council. On August 25, Radio Erevan reported that an attempt by the national council to end nearly four months of strikes in Stepanakert, the capital of Nagorno-Karabakh, had failed. TASS reported

on August 24 that work had resumed at several enter-
prises in the city. On August 27, the Azerbaijani Supreme
Soviet declared the national council in Nagorno-
Karabakh illegal (*RL Azerbaijani Service*, August 27).

TASS reported that a group of environmentalists in the
Tajik town of Rogun had staged a protest over the
construction of a dam in the Pamir Mountains. TASS said
the environmentalists fear that the dam's large storage
lake will flood the sites of many historical and architectural monuments and thousands of hectares of cultivated
farmland. It said the group wants the height of the dam
to be reduced by half. TASS said that the environmentalists had drawn up a memorandum outlining their concerns about the dam and that thousands of local residents
had signed it. The agency said the group will send
the memorandum to the autumn session of the USSR
Supreme Soviet.

**Tajik Environmentalists
Protest over Dam
Construction**

——— Monday, August 21

On August 21, Estonia's Komsomol daily *Noorte Haal*
gave details of plans for a major protest on August 22 and
23 to mark the fiftieth anniversary of the Molotov-
Ribbentrop Pact. *Izvestia* carried an article by Chief of
the CPSU Central Committee's International Department
Valentin Falin, who said the post-World War II boundaries in Europe could not be redrawn without causing
another conflict. Falin, who is a member of the Congress
of People's Deputies Commission on the Molotov-
Ribbentrop Pact, said that "to present the Soviet-German
nonaggression pact as the collusion of two aggressors to
divide Europe into spheres of influence" would cast a
shadow on "the legality of the territorial structure in
Eastern Europe."

On August 22, a commission of the Lithuanian
Supreme Soviet declared the Hitler-Stalin treaties of 1939
and their secret protocols invalid. The commission's
findings were printed in the Lithuanian Party daily *Tiesa*
(August 22). The commission said the treaties had led to
Lithuania's forced incorporation into the Soviet Union,
and it called the Soviet Army's entry into Lithuania in 1940
an act of aggression. The same day, AP said the popular
fronts in all three Baltic republics had issued a joint
statement calling for the Hitler-Stalin treaties to be declared null and void. See RL 428/89. On August 22, the

**Fiftieth Anniversary of
Molotov-Ribbentrop Pact
Marked**

449

Politburo of the Polish United Workers' Party condemned the Molotov-Ribbentrop Pact and its secret protocols. The Politburo said the pact and the protocols violated universally approved principles of international law (*Reuters*, August 22).

On August 23, Western correspondents obtained the text of the Congress commission's draft conclusions on the pact and its secret protocols The draft conclusions state that the secret protocols to both the pact and the subsequent border and friendship treaty between the USSR and Nazi Germany should be declared "null and void." The text of the document appeared in *Noorte Haal* on August 22. The document said that, with the treaties and protocols abolished, links between the USSR and the Baltic States should be governed by the 1920 treaties under which Soviet Russia guaranteed the territorial integrity of the Baltic States.

The draft conclusions were reported to have been signed by fourteen of the commission's twenty-six members. Those who signed the document include historian and rector of Moscow's Institute of Historical Archives Yurii Afanas'ev; Belorussian writer Vasyl Bykov; and an Armenian, Ludmilla Arutyunyan, as well as the Baltic members of the commission. Those who did not sign include the chairman of the commission, Politburo member Aleksandr Yakovlev, Central Committee member Valentin Falin, and other non-Baltic members of the commission (*RFE Baltic Services*, August 23). Mavriks Vulfsons, a Latvian member of the Congress commission on the pact, told a press conference in Bonn that Yakovlev and Falin wanted to consider the conclusions of the commission further and to consult lawyers at the Foreign Ministry.

A committee of the Estonian Academy of Sciences said the elections of July, 1940, that led to the incorporation of Estonia into the USSR were illegal (*RFE Estonian Service*, August 23). It said this means that the incorporation "must be considered an enforced annexation" under international law. To mark the fiftieth anniversary of the pact, activists in Latvia, Lithuania, and Estonia organized a human chain stretching 600 kilometers from Tallinn to Riga and Vilnius. In other events marking the anniversary, Estonian and Latvian Popular Front leaders met at the border between their republics to light symbolic bonfires. In Vilnius, several thousand people gathered near the cathedral to honor Stalin's victims and attend a rally of various groups demanding Lithuanian independence (*Reuters*, *UPI*, August 23). In Moscow, the independent opposition group Democratic Union staged a demonstration to condemn the pact. Reuters said that several hundred people had joined the rally near Pushkin Square and that police had attacked the demonstrators. TASS, insisting that the police acted "correctly," revealed that seventy-five people had been detained. Western agencies also reported that at least 10,000 people in Moldavia gathered to mark the pact's anniversary. (Most of what is Moldavia today was annexed by the Soviet Union a year after the pact and its secret protocols had been signed.)

On August 23, Radio Latvia broadcast a speech made by Dainis Ivans, chairman of the Popular Front of Latvia, as the human chain was formed. Ivans called the chain a united Baltic road for freedom and independence. There were other demonstrations held in the Baltic republics to mark the anniversary of the pact (*Reuters*, August 24).

The central Soviet press provided detailed coverage of the demonstrations in the Baltic republics. The coverage was mainly negative on August 23. *Pravda* and the evening news program "Vremya" criticized the independent political movements in the Baltic republics, calling them "naïve," "dangerous," and "hypocritical." Clearly demonstrating Moscow's great concern over the situation in the Baltic, *Pravda* published a lengthy attack on "Sajudis." It accused some of its leaders of maintaining contacts with Lithuanian émigrés who had cooperated with the Nazis.

On August 24, *Pravda* admitted that "the mood of 'division'" and calls for state independence were becoming an active factor of political life in the Baltic republics. It called for Balts to try to work with the rest of the USSR in implementing the Party program for restructuring the Soviet federation, which the newspaper presented as an alternative to separatist tendencies.

On August 25, the central Soviet media renewed their attack on independence activists in the Baltic. *Pravda* accused independence campaigners in Lithuania of waging a campaign of "moral and physical terror," and it warned that if Lithuania were to secede from the USSR the consequences would be "unpredictable." *Sovetskaya Rossiya* published a statement by local Party members in Moscow appealing to their counterparts in Estonia to defend the rights of Estonia's Russian-speaking citizens. They called the new election laws in Estonia "discriminatory."

TASS Reports KGB Meeting on Problems of Crime and Drugs

TASS said the board of the KGB had met in Moscow to discuss ways of stepping up the fight against smuggling and currency violations. TASS said that smuggling and currency violations were becoming part of organized crime and that there had been an increase in drug trafficking through Soviet territory to other countries and in the import of drugs to the USSR. On August 23, Chairman of the KGB Vladimir Kryuchkov said in *Izvestia* that measures taken so far to fight organized crime, smuggling, and drug trafficking in the USSR were inadequate.

Tuesday, August 22 ————————————————————————

Radiobiological Congress Opens in Moscow

Radio Moscow-1 (1500) announced that over 700 Soviet scientists had gathered in Moscow for the first All-Union Radiobiological Congress. The chief topic of discussion at the congress was the lingering effects of the disaster at Chernobyl'. This conference comes in the wake of a statement by Vladimir Evtukh, first deputy chairman of the Belorussian Council of Ministers, that it will cost more than 10 billion rubles to carry out a new cleanup and evacuation plan (*Sovetskaya Belorussiya*, July 29).

MVD Discusses Emigration and Travel Abroad

The USSR Ministry of Internal Affairs (MVD) has released data on emigration and travel abroad from the USSR in 1989. Speaking at an MVD briefing, Rudolf Kuznetsov, chief of OVIR, said that this agency had already granted 107,000 emigration visas this year and that, by July 1, 91,000 Soviet citizens had left (*TASS, AP*, August 22; see also *Moscow News*, August 6). According to Kuznetsov, 108,000 people emigrated from the USSR in 1988. Of this number, 41,000 were granted visas for emigration to West Germany and 35,000 for Israel. Ninety percent of those with visas for Israel, however, ultimately chose to reside in the United States. At the time of the signing of agreements in Vienna on January 19 aimed at facilitating international travel, there were 1,855 travel and emigration visa requests that had remained unresolved for a significant period of time. According to Kuznetsov, 84 percent of those requests have now been approved. The remaining 299 cases are being held up because of security regulations or because of objections by applicants' relatives or places of work. Kuznetsov also revealed that in the first half of 1989, OVIR received 1.7 million applications for tourist visas, a threefold increase over 1987. According to the OVIR chief, only 0.15 percent of these applications were rejected. Kuznetsov attributed the increase to a recent simplification of the documentation process and a lifting of restrictions on the frequency of an individual's travels abroad. See RL 458/89.

V. P. Ivanov, a deputy minister of the chemical- and petroleum-refining industry, was fired on August 22. Ivanov was charged with taking "an irresponsible attitude" towards improving "the satisfaction of people's demands" with regard to detergents (*Radio Moscow-1*, 2120). The ministry itself is new—the result of a merger of the Ministry of the Chemical Industry (Minkhimprom) and the Ministry of the Petroleum-Refining and Petrochemical Industry (Minneftekhimprom). It is headed by Nikolai Lemaev, who had been the minister of Minneftekhimprom since October, 1985. See RL 319/89.

Deputy Minister Fired for Detergent Shortage

Supreme Soviet deputy Boris El'tsin said the Soviet Union is in a crisis situation. In an interview with the Polish monthly magazine *Reporter*, El'tsin said the economy, the Party, the social situation, culture, and morality are in a critical state. He predicted that in a year to eighteen months a grass-roots revolution would start in the Soviet Union. He also said a civil war could break out but that this should be prevented. El'tsin said a new and attractive model of socialism must be created, and he suggested convening an extraordinary Party congress. In addition, he said a new Central Committee should be elected because the present one is too conservative. He also said a new Politburo should be elected.

El'tsin Says USSR in Crisis Situation

The first trial of a participant in last June's interethnic clashes in the Fergana Valley opened in the Uzbek city of Kokand. More than 100 people, mostly Meskhetians, died in clashes involving Uzbeks and Meskhetians. Tens of thousands of Meskhetians were then evacuated from Uzbekistan. TASS said twenty-year-old Khabibullo Abdurakhmanov was accused of organizing mass riots, theft of firearms and ammunition, and the attempted murder of policemen. It said the maximum punishment for those crimes is fifteen years' imprisonment. TASS said that the indictment had been read and that the defendant, witnesses, and experts would be heard in the coming days. TASS quoted a prosecution official as saying that twenty similar cases, including murder, had been prepared by courts as a result of the June violence. He said thirty-five people would be tried.

First Trial after Fergana Violence Begins in Kokand

Mikhail Gorbachev and head of the Polish United Workers Party Mieczyslaw Rakowski agreed in a telephone conversation that solving Poland's problems is "impos-

Gorbachev and Rakowski Say PUWP Necessary

sible" without the Communist Party. The conversation was announced by Party spokesman Jan Bisztyga at a news conference in Warsaw (*AP*, August 22). It came as Prime Minister-Designate Tadeusz Mazowiecki of "Solidarity" held intensive talks on forming the East Bloc's first non-Communist government.

Non-Moldavians Strike over Language Law

TASS said factories in the Moldavian city of Tiraspol were at a standstill after non-Moldavian workers stopped work to protest against laws that would make Moldavian the official language in the republic. The protest follows a short warning strike in Tiraspol last week. TASS did not say how widespread that stoppage was. On August 23, more strikes were reported in Tiraspol. TASS said at least ten factories and enterprises had joined the twenty enterprises already on strike in the city. On August 24, it was reported that more than fifty enterprises and plants had joined the strike (*TASS*, August 24). TASS said a republic-wide strike resolution was adopted on August 23 in Kishinev by the Union of Moldavian Working People. It said strikers wanted the draft language law to be adopted only after further discussion of it by the Moldavian Supreme Soviet this fall.

On August 25, the Presidium of the Moldavian Supreme Soviet issued a resolution condemning the continuing strikes in Moldavia. The resolution said the strikes were causing social and political destabilization and damaging the economy. It also said irresponsible appeals and incitement of interethnic differences had been allowed at public meetings. The resolution came as the Soviet media reported that more factories had joined strikes already under way in at least eighty enterprises (*Radio Moscow*, 2000, August 25). A member of the Moldavian Popular Front told RFE/RL that Moldavian workers had set up committees to keep factories operating during the strikes. He said that, as of August 25, Moldavian workers were doing the work normally performed by the strikers.

On August 28, *Pravda* criticized Party and government officials in Moldavia for not countering "nationalistic sentiments" in the republic. Between 250,000 and 300,000 people were said to have rallied in Kishinev on August 27 to back moves to upgrade the status of the Moldavian language. (Moldavian-speakers want Moldavian to be the official language of the republic and of communication between nationalities. Non-Moldavian-speakers—36 percent of the population—want Russian to remain the interethnic language.) In a separate article, *Pravda* called the rally "national blindness" and said participants had been "brainwashed" by nationalist-minded ideologists in the Moldavian Popular Front. In response to *Pravda*'s attacks, seventeen people's deputies from Moldavia and two Moldavian Supreme Soviet deputies sent a letter of protest to the editor calling the articles "tendentious and insulting."

In its issue for August 29, *Izvestia* accused Popular Front representatives from the Baltic republics and Georgia of stirring up trouble in Moldavia. It said that, at the rally in Kishinev on August 27, they had called for the formation of "a front of enslaved people." Radio Moscow (1730) said the Baltic representatives were trying to get Moldavia to secede from the USSR. It also said strikes by Russian-speaking workers were going on in more than a hundred enterprises in Moldavia.

On August 29, Moldavia's Supreme Soviet began a special session to consider the controversial language laws. Opening the session, Moldavian President Mircea Snegur urged the Supreme Soviet to endorse the draft language law, which would make Moldavian the language of interethnic communication. Several hundred people were reported to have gathered near the building where the session was being held (*AP*, August 29). The same day *Pravda* again criticized developments in the republic saying they were the result of "national intolerance, bitterness, and interethnic hostility."

The session continued on August 30. A leader of the Russian-speakers' group "Edinstvo" told AP that "life won't be quiet" in the republic if the law is adopted. Representatives of the Moldavian Popular Front told RFE/RL that Moldavian Communist Party First Secretary Semen Grossu made a speech to the session proposing the law should be amended to make Russian the language of interethnic communication. Grossu, an ethnic Moldavian, reportedly spoke in Russian, except for one sentence in Moldavian appealing to the Moldavian people to be calm and reasonable. He was also reported to have said that he had received an overnight phone call from Mikhail Gorbachev. Reports said Grossu quoted Gorbachev as saying that he is confident Moldavia can solve its own problems without assistance from the outside.

The front spokesmen also told RFE/RL that Moldavian writer Ion Drutse, who is a member of the USSR Congress of People's Deputies, had proposed a compromise on the language issue. They said Drutse proposed that Moldavian become the state language and that no language be designated for interethnic communication. He said that, in the case of a dispute between a citizen and a public official over which language to use, the citizen should be allowed to choose.

On August 31, Moldavia's Supreme Soviet voted to restore Moldavian as the state language and to bring back the Latin alphabet for writing it. The legislature also approved a compromise making both Russian and Moldavian the official languages for communication between different nationalities. Reuters quoted a popular front spokesman as saying the front was not pleased with the compromise. He said the front would continue pressing to have Moldavian made the republic's only official interethnic language. AP reported that thousands of Moldavians poured into the streets of Kishinev to protest against the compromise decision. Strikes by Russian-speaking workers were reported to be continuing. See RL 438/89.

Parts of Western Siberia Declared Disaster Zone

Several areas of Western Siberia have been declared a disaster zone because of severe drought. The radio's English-language service said the drought had destroyed grain crops on 300,000 hectares and had dried up small lakes and rivers. The report said emergency fodder supplies were being sent to farms in the drought areas.

Fuel Problem in Armenia

A spokeswoman for Armenia's official Armenpress news agency was quoted as saying there was practically no fuel left in Armenia. Reuters quoted the spokeswoman in Erevan as saying recent unrest in neighboring Georgia had forced the diversion of fuel trains through Azerbaijan. There have been frequent reports of attacks on trains and truck convoys in Azerbaijan and Armenia in the past month. *Komsomol'skaya pravda* said today that rail transport was paralyzed in Armenia and that the republic was suffering from a resulting shortage of fuel and building materials. It said railworkers in Armenia refuse to move trains for fear of attacks by "hooligans."

Memorial to "Erna" Restored in Estonia

TASS said a memorial to Estonian volunteers who fought against the Red Army had been restored in the Estonian town of Kautla. TASS said there was a memorial to the Estonian volunteer organization known as "Erna" at the same spot during the German occupation. "Erna" volunteers fought against the Red Army in the Soviet-Finnish war of 1939. They later parachuted into Estonia and joined the partisans fighting against Soviet rule. TASS called them "bandits" directed by "Hitlerites." TASS said about 500 people attended the unveiling ceremony for the new memorial in Kautla recently. TASS complained that at the ceremony one former "Erna" member called on Estonians to follow the example of "Erna" and "free Estonia of the Reds."

Andropov Is Criticized in Soviet Newspaper

Komsomol'skaya pravda leveled the strongest criticism of the late Yurii Andropov to appear so far in the Soviet press. The newspaper called Andropov the "last Stalinist" boss in the Soviet Union. It also said Andropov was "the most enigmatic figure" of the Brezhnev era. (Andropov was KGB chief for fifteen years under Brezhnev.) The newspaper also said that during Andropov's time as general secretary "constitutional norms were violated, and human rights were openly trampled upon."

Wallenberg's Case Discussed in USSR

Soviet Ambassador to Stockholm Boris Pankin acknowledged his country's responsibility for the fate of missing Swedish diplomat Raoul Wallenberg and apologized. His apology appeared in an article written for _Moscow News_ (No. 35) and was republished in the Swedish daily _Expressen_. Pankin insisted, however, that Wallenberg was dead. The secretary of the Raoul Wallenberg association, Sonja Sonnenfeld, called Pankin's article the most explicit public statement ever given by the Soviet authorities on the Wallenberg case but said she believed Wallenberg was still alive after forty-four years in Soviet prisons (_AP_, August 23). The newspaper _Komsomol'skaya pravda_ recently carried a series of articles on Wallenberg (June 4, July 11, and August 9). In the article that appeared on August 9, the newspaper emphasized that Wallenberg's relatives believe that he is still alive and reject the Soviet claim that Wallenberg died in 1947 in the Lubyanka prison. The newspaper informed Soviet readers that, since 1947, there have been a number of people who claimed that they had seen Wallenberg alive in the Soviet camps. _Komsomol'skaya pravda_ called on anyone who had any information on Wallenberg's fate to share their information with the editorial board of the newspaper. It promised further discussion of Wallenberg's case.

On August 30, Elena Bonner said she and her husband Andrei Sakharov tried for years without success to track down Raoul Wallenberg. Bonner said in an interview with UPI that she and Sakharov began their quest in 1972. She said that their investigations eventually led them to a camp for war prisoners in Torzhok, northwest of Moscow but that they had not been allowed to enter. She said she and Sakharov had not publicly discussed Wallenberg's case before, because "we tried to convince the Swedes to carry out the investigation through diplomatic channels."

Thursday, August 24 ───────────────────────────────

Soviet-Vatican Relations

TASS said Mikhail Gorbachev was ready to discuss the further development of Soviet-Vatican relations. Yurii Karlov, a personal representative of Soviet Foreign Minister Eduard Shevardnadze, delivered Gorbachev's message to Pope John Paul II in a meeting at the pope's summer residence outside Rome. TASS said Gorbachev's message also addressed "pressing issues of the present," including the elimination of the nuclear threat and safeguarding basic human values. The message is apparently a reply to a papal memorandum sent to Gorbachev fourteen months ago concerning Catholics in the USSR. On August 25, the pope had talks with three high-ranking Russian Orthodox churchmen. According to Vatican officials, the size and rank of the delegation made it unprecedented. The churchmen were reported eager to discuss problems between churches in the USSR, such as the forced assimilation of Byzantine-rite Catholics in Ukraine into the Orthodox Church (*RFE/RL Special*, August 25).

Sevastopol Party Committee Calls for Referendum on Crimean Tatars

The Party committee of the Crimean city of Sevastopol said there should be a referendum on whether the Crimean Tatars should be allowed to return to the Crimea. According to a report in *Izvestia*, the Sevastopol leadership also wants a vote on whether an Autonomous republic should be reestablished for the Crimean Tatars. The daily said the Party leaders made the suggestion "in connection with the exacerbation of national problems in Ukraine and the Crimea." It gave no specifics, but it seems that the leaders were referring to the opposition by the population of the Crimea to the repatriation of the Crimean Tatars. *Izvestia* said the Sevastopol Party Committee also wanted a referendum on the study and use of the Ukrainian language.

Slayings of Armenian Shepherds Reported

The Armenian Party daily *Kommunist* said two Armenian shepherds had been killed and their flocks stolen by raiders coming from Azerbaijani territory. It said one shepherd was killed at a sovkhoz in the Sisiansky Raion six days ago and another at a kolkhoz in the Gorissky Raion recently. Both raions are in the strip of southern Armenia that separates Azerbaijan from its Autonomous Republic of Nakhichevan. The daily also said there had been large-scale thefts of sheep and other farm animals in the area. It said there was a mass rally in the town of Sisian on August 20 to protest against the raids. It said participants asked for urgent measures to protect the population and called upon Azerbaijan to start criminal proceedings against the raiders.

A draft language law has been published in Kirgizia making Kirgiz the republic's official language. TASS said that the draft also stipulates that Russian will be used as the language of communication between nationalities and that the introduction of Kirgiz as the official language would be a gradual process stretching over ten years.

Draft Language Law Published in Kirgizia

On August 29, Chingiz Aitmatov, the head of the Kirgiz Writers' Union, praised the draft law. In a telephone interview with RFE/RL, Aitmatov said the draft is well-balanced because it takes into consideration the interests of other ethnic groups in Kirgizia.

Residents of the Kuibyshev Oblast are protesting over the siting in the oblast of a Soviet facility for the destruction of chemical weapons. Radio Moscow (0800) said a movement had been formed in the oblast to prevent the facility at Chapaevsk from being put into operation. The radio said one of the reasons for the protests is that the facility was built by the military under strict secrecy in the middle of a densely populated area.

Residents Protest over Plant for Destruction of Chemical Weapons

On August 28, Radio Moscow (1200) said a government commission had recommended that the Soviet Union should not use the Chapaevsk facility for the destruction of chemical weapons. The radio said the commission was headed by Nikolai Laverov, chairman of the USSR State Committee for Science and Technology. It said the commission proposes adapting the facility to be used as a study and training center for devising methods of destroying poisonous substances. The radio report did not say where the chemical weapons would be destroyed if not at Chapaevsk. On August 30, TASS said local residents had collected 60,000 signatures on a protest against the facility. It also said protest rallies were being staged frequently throughout the region.

Friday, August 25

Mazowiecki Interviewed by *Izvestia*

Poland's new prime minister Tadeusz Mazowiecki said Poland was watching Soviet *perestroika* closely. In an interview in *Izvestia* he said changes in the USSR were helping Poland's own reforms and creating a common climate of creativity. He said that Poland wishes the Soviet people success and that "we hope you wish us the same." He also stressed that Poland will honor its obligations as a Warsaw Pact member. Asked whether he sees himself as a Socialist or a Social Democrat, Mazowiecki said he is a Christian who follows the social teachings of the Catholic Church issued by the pope. On August 24, Soviet television showed Mazowiecki's election as prime minister by the Sejm. On August 24, the USSR Council of Ministers sent a message of congratuations to Mazowiecki upon his election (*TASS*, August 24). Talking to reporters in Moscow, Soviet Foreign Ministry spokesman Yurii Gremitskikh said the USSR considers Mazowiecki a partner in bilateral relations (*Reuters*, August 24). The conservative *Sovetskaya Rossiya* (August 24) also carried a commentary on Mazowiecki's election. The daily said Polish Communists had become complacent during their long years of monopoly of power while "Solidarity" had built up "an excellent command of the methodology of political struggle" as an underground organization. It added that Mazowiecki faces inflation, strikes, shortages of consumer goods, and a decline in productivity.

Interview Gives Glimpse of Gorbachev's Management Style

A senior aide to Mikhail Gorbachev offered a rare inside glimpse of the Soviet president's management style in an interview published in the monthly journal *Gorizont*. Georgii Shakhnazarov, a member of the Academy of Sciences' Department of Philosophy and Law, described round-table arguments that take place in the Kremlin preceding major policy decisions and in which Gorbachev listens to everyone, regardless of rank, but voices his own views with determination and conviction. Shakhnazarov said that Gorbachev was always careful to avoid offending anyone and that he eschews "rigid hierarchic discipline" (*Los Angeles Times*, August 26).

Cargo Craft Docks with *Mir* Space Station

A new type of unmanned Soviet space cargo craft docked with the *Mir* space station. TASS said the docking was controlled by automatic systems aboard *Mir* and the

Progress-M cargo ship. It said *Progress-M* was carrying fuel, water, equipment, and scientific instruments. TASS said the *Progress-M* is an improvement in the *Progress* series of spacecraft that have supplied *Mir* until now because it has more maneuverability and can carry larger loads. It said the craft's equipment had been redesigned so that docking requires less fuel.

Soviet envoy Gennadii Tarasov said the conflict in Lebanon cannot be solved by military means and that only a political solution can end the fighting. Radio Lebanon carried Tarasov's statement, made after talks near Beirut with Christian leaders. Earlier in the week Tarasov met Syrian leaders and Lebanon's acting prime minister. The Soviet Foreign Ministry today denied a French radio report that a Soviet battle cruiser was heading for the coast of Lebanon.

    On August 29, Tarasov went to Amman to discuss ways of ending the Lebanese conflict with Jordanian officials. In Amman, Tarasov met Foreign Minister Marwan Kasim. Tarasov told reporters he wanted to stress the danger of the Lebanese conflict to the entire region (*AP, UPI*, August 27). On August 28, Tarasov met with Iraqi Deputy Prime Minister Tariq Aziz in Baghdad. TASS said Tarasov delivered a message from Mikhail Gorbachev for Iraqi President Saddam Hussein, but it was not made public. While in Baghdad, Tarasov also had talks with PLO chairman Yasser Arafat (*TASS, Reuters*, August 30).

Soviet Envoy Says Lebanese Problem Cannot Be Solved by Military Means

Saturday, August 26

Soviet KGB Chairman Vladimir Kryuchkov said the USSR need not worry about political changes taking place in Poland. Kryuchkov spoke to reporters in Warsaw after meeting new Polish Prime Minister Tadeusz Mazowiecki. He described Mazowiecki as a man of principles. Kryuchkov earlier met Polish President Wojciech Jaruzelski and former Minister of Internal Affairs Czeslaw Kiszczak (*Reuters, DPA, Radio Warsaw-B*, 1600, August 26).

Kryuchkov Says USSR Should Not Worry about Changes in Poland

Pravda called for a crackdown on unofficial publications that attack the CPSU and its leadership. The article, by commentator Yurii Zhukov, denounced Sergei Grigoryants and Lev Timofeev, the publishers of the unofficial

***Pravda* Calls for Crackdown on Unofficial Publications**

journal *Glasnost'*, and also criticized an independent Siberian news agency and a newspaper published by the Democratic Union. Zhukov condemned cooperation between unofficial journals and Western news media. He said the foreign support makes them the equivalent of foreign publications on Soviet territory.

Soviet Official Says Radioactive Lake to Be Filled In

A Soviet official said radioactive Karachai Lake in the Chelyabinsk Oblast in the Urals will be filled in. The lake is near the site of an accidental nuclear waste explosion that contaminated much of the region in 1957. TASS quoted Soviet Deputy Prime Minister Lev Ryabev as saying the project will take three to four years and cost about 60 million rubles. Ryabev heads the Bureau of the USSR Council of Ministers for the Fuel and Energy Complex.

***Trud* Publishes Transcripts of Beria Trial**

Trud published excerpts from previously unreleased transcripts of Lavrentii Beria's closed-court trial in 1953 for his massive crimes as head of the NKVD under Stalin. Beria and a number of his former aides were sentenced to death in December, 1953. "All of them over many years had held high posts" in the secret police, *Trud* said. "All of them were responsible for thousands of ruined lives and deaths." During six days of testimony, Beria's former subordinates described his cruelty in carrying out brutal purges in Georgia in 1937 and 1938. "The investigation confirmed that Beria killed prisoners with his own hands," *Trud* said. "For this purpose various instruments of torture were stored in his waiting room."

US to Help Restore Fire-Damaged Leningrad Books

The US Library of Congress said it had received a grant from *Reader's Digest* magazine to help restore fire- and water-damaged books at the USSR Academy of Sciences library in Leningrad. Four million books were damaged or destroyed in a nineteen-hour fire at the Academy in February, 1988. The US Library of Congress is a leader in developing techniques to rescue books threatened by decay or disaster (*AP*, August 26).

Soviet Prosecutors Accused of Blocking Investigation

A Soviet official heading a probe into the activities of investigators Tel'man Gdlyan and Nikolai Ivanov accused state prosecutors of obstructing the investigation. In an interview with *Argumenty i fakty* (No. 34), Igor Sorokin said the Prosecutor's Office had refused to hand over details of cases of convicted officials from Uzbekistan and of a corruption case against a former Party second secretary in Moldavia, Viktor Smirnov. He said independent lawyers supervised by parliament should take over the investigation both in Uzbekistan and Moscow. Gdlyan and Ivanov played a major part in uncovering a web of corruption stretching from Uzbek officials to former First Deputy Minister of Internal Affairs Yurii Churbanov, who was convicted last December. They were taken off the case in May, however, soon after Ivanov had alleged that the name of Egor Ligachev "had come up" in corruption-probe materials. The authorities accused Gdlyan and Ivanov of using unscrupulous methods to extract confessions August 27).

Sunday, August 27

The CPSU Central Committee sharply criticized recent developments in the Baltic republics and accused leaders there of failing to stop negative trends. It also warned of impending disaster if these trends continue. The criticism came in a Central Committee statement on events marking the fiftieth anniversary of the Molotov-Ribbentrop Pact. The statement said "extremist, nationalist groups" had taken advantage of democracy and openness and steered events towards "an alienation of the Baltic republics from the rest of the country." It said that in some places there was a real threat of civil conflict and street clashes (*TASS, Central Television,* "Vremya," 1900, *Pravda,* August 27).

On August 27, a candidate member of Estonia's Communist Party Buro, Enn Poldroos, rejected the statement, saying "it in no way reflects the current situation" in Estonia. He said all the processes happening in Estonia were taking place peacefully and democratically. Estonian Popular Front activists said on August 26 that the statement would not divert them from their goals. A member of the executive board of the Popular Front of Latvia, Eduards Berklavs, said the CPSU was trying to frighten the Baltic popular movements into submission. The chairman of the Lithuanian Restructuring Movement "Sajudis," Vytautas Landsbergis, said it "creates a menacing atmosphere of psychological warfare" (*RFE Estonian, Lithuanian,* and *Latvian Services,* August 27). On August 28, a group of Lithuanian members of the USSR Congress of People's Deputies sent a telegram to Gorbachev attacking the Central Committee statement. Gorbachev was quoted as telling Lithuanian Party officials that

Moscow Condemns Baltic Developments

Lithuanians had "gone too far" in their campaign for independence. Officials of the Latvian Communist Party and the Popular Front of Latvia also sent a telegram to Gorbachev protesting the statement, but the Latvian Party Buro issued a statement saying the Central Committee statement should be the basis for normalizing the situation in Latvia (*AP*, *Reuters*, August 28).

The same day, CPSU Central Committee member Georgii Arbatov said he ruled out the possibility that Soviet President Mikhail Gorbachev, who was on vacation when the statement was prepared, did not know about the Central Committee statement criticizing developments in the Baltic. In Helsinki, Arbatov said he did not know how closely Gorbachev was involved in drafting the statement. Arbatov said there was official approval for many of the national aspirations of the Baltic states, but he said extremism would harm *perestroika* (*Helsinki Radio*, in Finnish, August 28).

On August 30, a group of Estonian people's deputies sent Gorbachev a message expressing their "perplexity" over the Central Committee statement. A copy of the message reached the West. In it, the deputies said there was no danger in Estonia of the conflicts and mass clashes referred to in the Soviet statement.

The same day, Latvian Communist Party First Secretary Janis Vagris said that there was a chance that new political parties would emerge in Latvia as democratization continues. He said there had been calls for Latvia to secede from the USSR and for the Latvian Party to leave the CPSU. He said he believed both ideas were devoid of prospects. Vagris was speaking on Soviet television. "Sajudis" Chairman Landsbergis also gave a television address in which he said the Central Committee statement had produced uncertainty, excitement, and speculation.

On August 31, a joint meeting of the popular fronts in the Baltic republics denounced the Central Committee's criticism. Western news agencies quoted a statement issued by the popular fronts as saying the criticism was the most dangerous document since the days of Stalin (*TASS*, *Reuters*, August 31). They said it only united them more firmly in favor of independence. The popular fronts also issued an appeal to the United Nations to investigate and publicly discuss the situation in the Baltic states. In a letter to UN Secretary General Javier Perez de Cuellar, the popular front leaders said the Baltic peoples felt threatened by the leadership in Moscow (*AFP*, *RFE Estonian Service*, September 1).

TASS said the shutdown of the Armenian nuclear power plant had led to a sharp cut in energy production in Armenia. Radio Moscow said "a harsh regime" of energy conservation had been introduced, causing all enterprises and organizations to lower their peak consumption by 15 to 20 percent. The report said plans were being worked out to convert the former nuclear power plant into a thermal power station using natural gas. It also said the development of hydroelectric power was being accelerated. The nuclear plant was shut down completely in March because of safety concerns following last December's devastating earthquake in Armenia. The plant was not damaged in the earthquake, but it lies only 40 kilometers from Erevan in a seismic zone.

Armenian Plant Closure Causes Power Shortages

The chairman of the USSR State Committee for Protection of the Environment, Nikolai Vorontsov, said "ecological *glasnost'* is under way" in the Soviet Union. In an interview with the West German magazine *Der Spiegel*, Vorontsov said ecology had become the Soviet Union's most important problem. Vorontsov said he will wage a tough fight against state ministries that continue to destroy the Soviet Union's environment. He said ministers must learn that ecology is just as important as economics, and he warned that ministers who ignore his advice will regret it. Vorontsov noted that he is the first non-Communist government minister in Soviet history and said he will not be the last.

Vorontsov Says Ecological *Glasnost'* under Way in USSR

Pravda criticized attempts to close the Russian-language newspaper of the Latvian Communist Party, *Sovetskaya Latviya*, saying that to do so would be "a manifestation of nationalism" and of discrimination against Russian speakers. It said that the Lativan Party Central Committee had heard proposals to close the daily and that these had been supported by the Latvian ideological secretary, Ivars Kezbers. *Pravda* printed a letter signed by nine readers of *Sovetskaya Latviya* criticizing a plan to publish the Latvian-language daily *Cina* in both languages as the sole Party daily newspaper. The Latvian Party now publishes both *Cina* and *Sovetskaya Latviya*.

Pravda Reports Attempts to Close Latvian Newspaper

Novy mir **Begins Publication**
of *Gulag Achipelago*

Novyi mir (No. 8) began publication of Solzhenitsyn's epic work on the Soviet labor camps, *Gulag Archipelago*. On August 25, TASS quoted the chief editor of the Leningrad literary journal *Neva* as saying that next year his journal will begin publication of the "March, 1917" section of Solzhenitsyn's cycle *The Red Wheel.*

Drug Crackdown in
Tajikistan

Special teams have been set up in Tajikistan to combat narcotics production and trafficking, according to *Sel'skaya zhizn'*. It said the teams are made up of MVD officials, lawyers, farming experts, and members of the public. The newspaper said mobile groups have checked for illegal crops on all private farm plots as well as at most kolkhozes and sovkhozes.

MVD Discusses
Counterfeiting Activity
in USSR

The USSR Ministry of Internal Affairs (MVD) devoted its weekly press conference to the problem of counterfeit money trade in the USSR (*Radio Moscow-1*, 1900). According to statistics released by the MVD, 329 crimes involving counterfeit money were uncovered in the 1986–88 period and 104 persons and 24 "groups" implicated in these crimes. During this period, the authorities removed from circulation 16,000 counterfeit rubles and 233,000 counterfeit US dollars. The source of the counterfeit money is unclear. The MVD cites the recent increase in Soviet contacts abroad as contributing to the problem. It also pointed out that 7,000 printing houses in the Soviet Union were now equipped with modern copying equipment.

Draft Ukrainian Language
Law Approved

Radio Kiev announced that the Presidium of the Supreme Soviet of the Ukrainian SSR had approved a draft law to make Ukrainian the state language. The draft, which also "guarantees the free use of the Russian language as the language of interethnic communication," will be made public in early September for discussion (see also *Izvestia*, August 30).

Wednesday, August 30 ─────────────────────────────

Soviet Historian Says
Redivision of Europe
Impossible

Soviet historian Valentin Berezhkov, who served as an interpreter in the talks leading to the pact between the Soviet Union and Nazi Germany, said it would be impossible to change the map of Europe to its pre-1939 status. Berezhkov was speaking to a youth group from the Evangelical Church in West Berlin. He said many European borders would need to be substantially redrawn if restored to their pre-pact status and cited the Lithuanian capital of Vilnius as an example, saying it would belong to Poland instead of the Soviet Union (*TASS*, in English, August 30).

United States and USSR Agree on Key Chemical Weapons Measures

The chief US negotiator on chemical weapons said the United States and the USSR have approved key elements for a proposed treaty to ban chemical weapons. Ambassador Max Friedersdorf told Reuters the United States and the USSR have agreed on how to make inspections of chemical weapons at short notice so countries cannot cheat. He said the technical details involved have been worked out. These include deciding which chemicals should be destroyed first (*Reuters, DPA, AFP*, August 30).

Up to 20 Million Alcoholics in USSR

According to *Sovetskaya Rossiya*, there are an estimated 15-20 million alcoholics in the USSR. The newspaper said there are also between 35 and 40 million heavy drinkers in the USSR. This estimate, if accurate, is much higher than the earlier official figure of 4.5 million (*Vestnik statistiki*, No. 6, and *Central Television*, "Vremya," April 17, 1989). The *Sovetskaya Rossiya* article also quoted a Goskomstat report that the volume of *samogon* production in the Soviet Union now equals the volume of vodka produced in the state sector. As a result of the antialcohol campaign begun in 1985, the official production of alcohol and other spirits is currently running at about 50 percent of the volume produced in 1984 (*Vestnik statistiki*, No. 6). This implies that, contrary to the government's assertions that alcohol consumption has declined significantly as a result of the antialcohol campaign, consumption has remained at earlier levels, thanks to the efforts of the *samogonshchiki*.

MVD Says No Political Prisoners in USSR

The USSR Ministry of Internal Affairs said there are no more political prisoners in the Soviet Union. Radio Moscow (0900) quoted a ministry spokesman as saying the last political convicts were set free in January when the Soviet Union signed the final document of the Helsinki review conference in Vienna. The spokesman denied Western reports that some people are still jailed for their beliefs. He said individuals mentioned in the reports had been convicted of treason of drug smuggling. Two US

467

Congressmen who visited a Soviet labor camp and talked with inmates earlier this month said there was overwhelming evidence the USSR is still holding some political prisoners.

Thursday, August 31

Party Leaders from Armenia and Azerbaijan Meet in Moscow

Leading Communists from Armenia and Azerbaijan met in Moscow to discuss the interethnic problems in the two republics. TASS said "profound anxiety" was expressed at the meeting because Armenian-Azerbaijani relations have "assumed a dangerous character." TASS did not report who said this. It said that the meeting was held at the CPSU Central Committee headquarters in Moscow and that two Politburo members—Viktor Chebrikov and Nikolai Slyun'kov—attended. The TASS report said arrangements had been made to conduct a dialogue between organizations in both republics at all levels in order "to restore traditional ties" between Armenia and Azerbaijan and "to ensure the safety of every person."

Soviet Historian Says World War II Could Have Been Prevented

Soviet historian Dmitrii Volkogonov said World War II might have been prevented if the Western powers and the Soviet Union had succeeded in creating a collective security system for Europe. Volkogonov is director of the Soviet Institute of Military History. He told TASS the war was triggered in part by the failure of the 1939 tripartite collective security talks between the USSR, Britain, and France. He said Western powers at the talks tried to "spearhead German aggression eastwards," but he said Stalinist policies were also to blame for the failure of the talks. He said those policies led to an atmosphere in which Western leaders naturally worried about the possibility of "an export of revolution" to their countries.

General Opposes Army Units in the Baltic Republics

Pravda carried an article in which First Deputy Chief of the Baltic Military District's Political Administration Major General Vladimir Sein attacked the military programs of various Baltic reform groups. Sein focused particularly on the demand by these groups that young Balts be allowed to perform their military service in their home republics in national or territorial units. He claimed that the establishment of such units would lower national defense capability. He also rejected proposals for a transition to a volunteer army and for a shortening of the term of military service. He dismissed these proposals as part of a broader campaign to portray the military as an enemy of *perestroika*.

Soviet Legislators Visit US Congress

Three Soviet legislators said in Washington that they want to introduce practices used by the US Congress into the USSR Supreme Soviet. The legislators are in Washington studying the Congress, as well as state government in the United States. The Soviet delegates said the Supreme Soviet should establish an intelligence oversight committee and an information service to serve legislators. They also said it should consider electronic voting (*Reuters*, *USIS*, September 1).

Causes of Miners' Strike Reviewed

Kommunist (No. 12) carried an article by its deputy editor, economist Otto Latsis, who argued that, while the unprecedented debates at the first Congress of People's Deputies clearly played a role in emboldening Soviet miners to call their strike in July, they clearly did not consider the Congress adequate to their needs. Latsis said many declarations made at the Congress failed to ring true in the ears of the general population, while the economic reforms put forward by the government are plainly, he believes, inadequate to solve the problems the country faces. In his commentary, Latsis joins other reform-minded Soviet economists in warning that the populations's patience is running out and that reforms that might have been sufficient a few years ago will not prove effective today. "Clearly," he writes, "we need not only a law on strikes but a whole array of democratic procedures." And he takes the government of Nikolai Ryzhkov to task for the way it appeased the striking coal miners in July. A decision of such importance, Latsis says, should surely have been taken not by the government but by the Supreme Soviet. For while it is known, he argues, how much the government had to promise the miners to get them back to work, no one knows where that money is going to come from—i.e., which sections of society are going to be made to pay for the miners' gains.

469

The Month of September

Reaction Continues to Moscow's Criticism of Baltic Developments

On September 1, the Communist Party Central Committees in the three Baltic republics each met to discuss the CPSU Central Committee statement. The Estonian committee issued a statement saying it is vital not to allow instability and tensions to escalate. The same day, CPSU Politburo member Viktor Chebrikov defended the CPSU Central Committee's criticism of the Baltic republics. In a speech at the Academy of Social Sciences, he said tough measures were needed to deal with people who use national sentiment to engender hostility. He said "murderers and bandits" must be punished no matter what flags they raise or what "brightly colored costumes" they wear (*Pravda*, September 2).

On September 2, *Pravda* carried an article by veteran commentator Yurii Zhukov, who alleged that Western radio stations were trying to incite armed struggle in the Baltic republics. On September 3, *Krasnaya zvezda* criticized the popular fronts in the Baltic republics. The newspaper said popular front leaders who had rejected criticism by the CPSU Central Committee were trying "to present a simplistic picture of the situation" in the region. It said they were also trying to conceal from the public negative processes for which they themselves were responsible. An assembly of "Sajudis" said on September 5 that the march towards independence in Lithuania "can only be halted by physical force and only temporarily." The assembly issued an appeal to the Lithuanian nation saying that Lithuanians seek independence "by peaceful democratic means" (*Reuters*, September 5).

US Says Soviet Involvement in Afghanistan Increasing

A senior US diplomat said Soviet military advisers are returning to Afghanistan. Peter Tomsen, the US special envoy to the Afghan resistance, told reporters in Islamabad that the USSR has sent more than 2,500 planeloads of military supplies into Kabul. He said that there are now more than 300 military advisers in Afghanistan and that Soviet advisers supervise the firing of missiles from Kabul. He said the USSR is spending 7 million dollars a day on the war. (*RFE/RL Special*, September 1).

470

A letter from thirty-four Estonian members of the USSR Congress of People's Deputies calling for the removal from the Soviet Constitution of the article that stipulates the leading role of the CPSU was published in Estonia. The letter stated that the article on the Party's role was the basis for totalitarianism and should be dropped. The letter urged the Congress to adopt real guarantees for the self-determination of peoples and also to adopt legislation that would make the Soviet Union a federation of sovereign, equal, and voluntarily united republics (*RFE Estonian Service*, September 1).

Estonian Deputies Want to Scrap Clause on Leading Role of CPSU

Soviet Foreign Ministry spokesman Vadim Perfil'ev said the Soviet Union views the Bulgarian-Turkish rift over Bulgarian Muslims with "serious concern." TASS quoted Perfil'ev as saying the Soviet Union is trying to promote dialogue between the two countries and a political settlement of their dispute. The Soviet Union has previously sought to mediate in the dispute, but no result has been made public. Perfil'ev was quoted as saying the Soviet Union opposes attempts to bring the issue of the Bulgarian Muslims before international forums with the aim of bringing pressure on one of the parties. He said this could only hamper reaching an agreement.

USSR Voices "Serious Concern" over Bulgarian-Turkish Rift

Soviet President Mikhail Gorbachev said mutual respect and freedom of choice are among the foundations on which to build a secure future for Europe. In a message to Polish President Wojciech Jaruzelski marking the fiftieth anniversary of the start of World War II, Gorbachev said such foundations were not present in 1939. He said the war was triggered by the failure of states threatened "by fascism and militarism" to create a system of common security (*PAP*, in English, September 1; *Pravda*, September 2).

Gorbachev Sends Message to Jaruzelski on War Anniversary

The journal of the USSR Ministry of Internal Affairs, *Sovetskaya militsiya*, is offering subscriptions to the public for the first time. TASS said the sixty-eight-year-old journal plans to look into the problems of organized crime and publish material from the archives of the KGB. TASS said senior law-enforcement officials, including the minister of internal affairs, will answer readers' questions.

First Public Subscription to MVD Journal

471

El'tsin Discusses Disputed Dam Construction in Tajikistan

Boris El'tsin discussed the planned construction of a dam in Tajikistan at a meeting with several thousand people in Komsomolabad. The planned 335-meter-high dam for the hydroelectric power station at Rogun would be the largest in the world. The Soviet media have reported that the plan is opposed by environmentalists and local residents, who say a dam of this size would flood historical and architectural monuments along with thousands of hectares of farmland. They favor a lower dam. El'tsin told Radio Moscow the meeting in Komsomolabad showed that a compromise can be found to solve the dispute. El'tsin, who heads the Supreme Soviet Committee for Civil Construction and Architecture, was invited to the area by Tajikistan government leaders. El'tsin also told the radio that social problems in Tajikistan have been aggravated because they have been ignored for many years. He said that there was a lack of schools and kindergartens and that many more apartments could be built than are now being constructed (*Radio Moscow-2*, September 2, 1900).

Ligachev Speaks on Soviet Television

Politburo member Egor Ligachev called for political steps to prevent further attacks on Soviet institutions and leaders. In an interview on Soviet television, Ligachev said measures were needed to strengthen the unity of the Party and increase contacts between the Party and the masses. Ligachev did not specify how he proposed to do this but said he was not advocating repressive or dictatorial measures. Ligachev went on to say the Party Central Committee's recent warning of "impending disaster" in the Baltic republics had been wrongly portrayed as the work of only some members of the Politburo and as an attack on *perestroika*. But he said the statement was, in fact, designed precisely to create the most favorable conditions for *perestroika*.

Leningrad Society to Support Independence Campaigns in Republics

The third issue of the Tartu unofficial journal *Kur'er* reported the founding in Leningrad of a Russian (*Rossiiskoe*) Anticolonial Society favoring independence for the Union republics. *Kur'er* quoted members of the society as condemning what they call "imperial ambitions" on the part of many Russians. They stressed Russia will only benefit if the republics that want independence are allowed to have it. (This year Leningrad has become one of the main centers of activity by informal groups in the USSR.)

The USSR Supreme Soviet has set up a commission to study the sociopolitical situation in Moldavia at first hand. TASS reported that the commission had been established at the urging of the Moldavian strike committee, which was formed by Russian-speaking workers who want Russian designated the official language for interethnic communication in Moldavia. (On September 1, the Moldavian Supreme Soviet adopted a language law making Moldavian the official language of the republic and both Moldavian and Russian the languages of interethnic communication [*Pravda*, September 3].) TASS quoted the strike committee as saying work stoppages over the issue were continuing in Kishinev, Tiraspol, and many other cities in Moldavia. On September 4, TASS said about 200 enterprises in Moldavia had decided to continue the strikes. The same day, Soviet television complained that the strikes were causing serious economic difficulties.

On September 5, Radio Moscow World Service reported that leaders of the strike committees in Moldavia had met leading officials of the republic to discuss Moldavia's language law. The radio said the meeting had failed to produce any positive results. On September 6, TASS said striking workers at enterprises in Moldavia had still not gone back to work. On September 7, the Soviet media reported that strikes at major enterprises in Kishinev had been suspended but that strikes were continuing in Tiraspol, Bendery, and Rybnitsa (*Radio Moscow-2*, 1900, September 7; *Izvestia*, September 8).

On September 7, Radio Vilnius said a group of Lithuanian members of the USSR Supreme Soviet had sent a telegram to Mikhail Gorbachev saying they had been surprised to hear a TASS report on the establishment of a USSR Supreme Soviet commission to study the situation in Moldavia. The telegram said the deputies had not been informed that the Supreme Soviet was convening and had therefore not participated in forming the commission.

On September 10, the chairman of the USSR Supreme Soviet commission studying the situation in Moldavia, Erkin Auelbekov, called for an end to the strikes in the republic.

On September 11, *Pravda* listed the Moldavian strike committee among those calling for an end to the strikes. The same day, however, a member of the committee, Dmitrii Kondratovich, denied that the strike committee had called for a return to work. On September 15, the Moldavian Party leadership said that strikes in the republic were costing the Soviet economy "tens of millions of rubles." TASS said the Party Buro described the situation in Moldavia as "complex" and condemned what it called

USSR Supreme Soviet Sets Up Commission on Moldavia

nationalist and chauvinist statements of both "anti-Russian and anti-Moldavian character."

On September 25, TASS said the strikes in the Moldavian towns of Tiraspol and Bendery had been suspended. It said workers in nearly 100 enterprises in the two cities had returned to work after a break of more than one month. TASS said the strike committees that had called and controlled the strikes remain in operation.

Rally in Ukraine to Protest against Draft Law on Elections

Thousands of people rallied in Kiev to protest against the Ukrainian draft law on elections. A spokesman for the Ukrainian Helsinki Union, Anatolii Dotsenko, said the proposed law grants 25 percent of the seats in the Ukrainian Supreme Soviet to deputies chosen by organizations loyal to the Communist Party. An alternative draft will be submitted on September 4 to the Presidium of the Ukrainian Supreme Soviet. Meanwhile, the Popular Front of Belorussia is circulating its own draft law on elections, a copy of which has reached Munich. Signed by Vyachaslav Zhybul, the front's alternative law would eliminate public organizations' 25-percent share of the seats, render single-candidate elections invalid, and prevent high-ranking officials in the KGB, military, or executive, judicial, and internal affairs organs from standing for election. See RL 430/89.

Rules for Soviet Business Delegations Simplified

The USSR Council of Ministers is introducing simpler procedures for sending Soviet delegations and individuals on business trips abroad. Permission for such trips has in the past been left to the discretion of top-level Soviet government bodies. TASS said, however, that under the new procedures, such decisions can be made in some cases by lower-ranking central or republican bodies or even by executives of enterprises dealing with foreign partners.

USSR Sets Off Nuclear Explosion

The Soviet Union carried out another nuclear test at the Semipalatinsk test site in Kazakhstan. TASS said the purpose of the test was to refine military hardware.

Free Economic Zone Being Created Near Finnish Border

TASS said preparations were under way in the northwestern RSFSR for the creation of a free economic zone bordering on Finland. TASS said the zone would include the cities of Vyborg, Svetogorsk, Kamennogorsk, and Sovetsky, where large-scale construction sites and production facilities already exist. The news agency quoted a local official, Nikolai Smirnov, as saying there were already forty-three protocols of intent from firms in Europe, Asia, and the United States to set up joint enterprises in fields including high technology, pulp and paper mills, shipbuilding, and wood-processing.

_____ *Sunday, September 3*

Arkadii Vol'sky, the head of the special committee administering Nagorno-Karabakh, was quoted as saying the situation in the oblast was close to "internecine war." He told *Krasnaya zvezda* that tension between ethnic Armenians and Azerbaijanis had reached its peak and that there was an extreme danger of people taking ill-considered steps with unpredictable consequences. He also said attacks continued to take place on the MVD troops stationed in Nagorno-Karabakh to maintain order there.

Nagorno-Karabakh Said to Be Close to "Internecine War"

Argumenty i fakty (No. 35) said Soviet inflation in 1988 averaged between 8 and 9 percent. The weekly said about 5 percent resulted from official price increases and the rest from too much money chasing too few goods. *Argumenty i fakty* noted that the average monthly salary increased from 215 rubles in the first six months of 1988 to 236 rubles in the same period this year—i.e., about 10 percent. It said that the index of retail prices rose 2.2 percent and that food prices increased by 3 percent.

On September 10, *Izvestia* described the inflation situation in the USSR as "very stormy." The newspaper said that, in the first six months of 1989, almost 9 billion rubles of new currency had been put into circulation. The radio said this was an increase of one-third over the same period last year. Echoing what was said in *Izvestia*, Academician Abel Aganbegyan, who is on a visit to the United States, said inflation in the Soviet Union was at least 9 percent last year and had risen further in the first six months of this year (*RFE/RL Special*, September 12).

Soviet Press on Inflation in the USSR

Thousands of people in the Baltic republics took part in a seaside demonstration to protest against pollution of the Baltic Sea, AP reported. The agency quoted popular front members and activists in Latvia, Estonia, and Lithuania as saying the demonstrators joined hands in a line along the beach. A member of the Popular Front of Latvia, Askolds Rodins, said the demonstration was meant to draw

Beach Protest against Pollution Staged in Baltic

attention to the fact that the Baltic Sea is dying because of high pollution levels. AP said the protest was organized by the "Greens" environmental movement.

MVD Official Accuses Local Authorities of Conniving at "Extremists"

An official of the USSR Ministry of Internal Affairs has criticized local authorities in the Union republics for failing to control or punish people who promote what he termed "nationalist violence." Anatolii Anikiev, head of the ministry's political department, wrote in *Pravda* that the authorities in some republics have "essentially connived at" the statements of "extremists of the lowest sort." He said nationalist leaders in some republics had made public statements full of anti-Sovietism, racism, and Russophobia and had done so with "total impunity." Anikiev said "prosecutors seem to be deaf when these utterances are made; the courts are silent."

Vorotnikov Says RSFSR Should Have Its Own MVD

Chairman of the RSFSR Supreme Soviet Vitalii Vorotnikov said the RSFSR needed to have its own ministry of internal affairs. The RSFSR is the only republic that has no such ministry. Vorotnikov's comments appeared in *Sovetskaya Rossiya*. He also said that regular conferences should be held to resolve issues involving the RSFSR. Vorotnikov said that the creation of informal groups and popular fronts in the USSR had on the whole been positive but that some of them had taken on an anti-Socialist character.

Reappraisal of Former Dissidents Continues

Ogonek (No. 35) carried a long article reappraising the activities of Professor Yurii Orlov, leader of the Moscow Helsinki group. The article included many *samizdat* documents by Orlov and also some of those written in defense of Orlov by members of the Soviet intelligentsia. Echoing the opinion that prevailed in the West in the late 1970s, the journal calls the trial of Orlov in 1978 "a travesty of justice." Because of his role in the human-rights movement, Orlov was sentenced in 1978 to seven years' imprisonment and five years' internal exile under the provisions of Article 70 of the RSFSR Criminal Code, which at that time outlawed "anti-Soviet agitation and propaganda." After serving his sentence, Orlov was deported to the United States in 1986. This year, however, Orlov visited Moscow and is quoted in *Ogonek* as being very impressed by the changes in the country's political climate. *Moscow News* (No. 36) published an article by Valerii Chalidze, who, together with Andrei Sakharov, founded the first Soviet human-rights committee prior to his emigration to

476

the United States in the mid-1970s. In his article, Chalidze analyzed the first session of the Congress of People's Deputies. In his view, the liberal Moscow deputies, including Sakharov, erred by behaving like dissidents of pre-Gorbachev times at the Congress. In Chalidze's opinion, they should have exercised more restraint and more willingness to cooperate with the Gorbachev leadership.

Moscow News (No. 36) printed the stormy debates that arose over an article by Professor Vyacheslav Dashichev, a specialist in military history, that appeared in issue No. 35 of the weekly. Dashichev said that Western democratic countries (England and France) had undertaken serious attempts in 1939 to achieve agreement with the USSR and that it was the Molotov-Ribbentrop Pact, signed in August of that year, that frustrated these attempts. Dashichev also suggested that Stalin had an interest in bringing about World War II because he hoped in this way "to fan the flames of world revolution in Europe." In addition to criticism of Dashichev's views expressed in letters to *Moscow News* from historians, a special statement of protest against the publication of the article was issued by Novosti press agency, to which *Moscow News* is subordinate. The APN statement was first published in *Pravda* (August 26) and then reprinted in *Moscow News* (No. 36). In response to the statement, the editorial board of *Moscow News* argued that APN had simplified Dashichev's views and thereby distorted them. It also insisted that, under *glasnost'*, Dashichev should have the right to publish his views even if they do not coincide with the opinion currently dominating Soviet historiography.

Moscow News Publishes Controversy over Dashichev's Article

Monday, September 4

A general strike began in Baku, the capital of Azerbaijan, to press for greater independence for the republic from Moscow, for Azerbaijani control of Nagorno-Karabakh, and for legal recognition of the Azerbaijani Popular Front (*Reuters*, September 2 and 4). It was reported that some shops and the port were closed and that some bus and factory workers had not showed up at work. But the agency said that food shops, hospitals, schools, post offices, and government buildings remained open and that public transport was operating, even if at a reduced level of service. On September 5, the Party leader of Azerbaijan, Abdul-Rakhman Vezirov, called in an inter-

General Strike in Azerbaijan

view on Soviet television for an end to the current administrative subordination of Nagorno-Karabakh to Moscow. He also criticized the strike in Baku (*AP*, September 5). On September 5, Western agencies reported that some enterprises in Baku were closed but that many remained open despite the call for a work stoppage by the popular front (*Reuters*, September 5). On September 6, leader of the Azerbaijani Popular Front E'tibar Mamedov told a rally in Baku that the current strike would continue through September 8. He said if the demands were not met by that date, the front would ask for Gorbachev or an associate to visit Baku to discuss the situation (*RL Azerbaijani Service*, September 6).

On September 7, *Komsomol'skaya pravda* carried an article on the situation in Azerbaijan, saying it was tense. The same day Foreign Ministry spokesman Vadim Perfil'ev said the strikes in Azerbaijan were spreading. He said work had stopped at most major enterprises in Baku and also in Sumgait, Sheki, Kirovabad, and several other Azerbaijani cities. Perfil'ev denied reports that oil and power-generating enterprises had also shut down. (*TASS*, in English, *Reuters*, September 7). A spokesman for the Azerbaijani Popular Front told RFE/RL in a telephone interview from Baku, however, that pumping of oil was almost at a standstill. Perfil'ev said that police were patrolling the region but that the army had not been called in. The same day, a leading member of the Azerbaijani Popular Front Yusuf Samedoglu, told RFE/RL that Azerbaijani Party leader Vezirov had agreed to discuss the legalization of the front (*RL Azerbaijani Service*, September 7). On September 8, *Izvestia* reported that strikers were continuing to press their demands for Azerbaijani sovereignty. Radio Liberty's Azerbaijani service was informed that a meeting between Azerbaijani officials and leaders of the popular front had failed to find a solution.

On September 9 Western correspondents in Moscow quoted activists in Azerbaijan as saying a mass rally in Baku had called for the continuation of the general strike in the republic. The crowd demanded that the strike be prolonged because the authorities had not met the demands of the Azerbaijani Popular Front (*AP*, *Reuters*, September 9). In the meantime, Baku officials appealed for an end to the strike.

On September 10, direct, official talks began in Baku between front leaders and republican officials (*RL Azerbaijani Service*, September 10).

On September 11, a spokesman for the Azerbaijani Popular Front said the front had agreed to call off the general strike after the Azerbaijani authorities promised to recognize the front and to convene a session of the republican Supreme Soviet to discuss the situation in the republic and the question of Nagorno-Karabakh (*RL Azerbaijani Service*, September 11).

On September 13, a mass rally was held in Baku to announce details of the agreement between the republic's officials and the popular front (*AP*, September 12).

On September 15, the Azerbaijani Supreme Soviet met in emergency session to discuss the situation in the republic, the status of Nagorno-Karabakh, and other issues (*TASS*, September 15).

At its session on September 15 and 16, the Azerbaijani Supreme Soviet adopted a resolution proposed by the Azerbaijani Popular Front calling for the restoration of Nagorno-Karabakh to Azerbaijani control (*AP*, *TASS*, September 16).

USSR Condemns Rocket Attack on Kabul

The USSR sharply condemned a weekend rocket attack on Kabul by Afghan resistance forces. Reports said at least sixteen people were killed and more than fifty wounded on September 2 when resistance rockets hit Kabul airport and parts of the city. At a Moscow news conference on September 4, Soviet Foreign Ministry spokesman Vadim Perfil'ev said Moscow "cannot remain indifferent" to such acts (*TASS*, in English, September 4).

USSR Plans New Rights for AIDS Victims

The Soviet Union has decided to give new rights to people who have contracted or who are suspected of having AIDS. TASS quoted a draft law as saying a warrant issued by a prosecutor would be required before a person can be forced to take an AIDS test. It said that current law does not require a warrant, which has led to abuses by medical workers and law-enforcement officials. TASS said the draft law gives AIDS victims the right to medical and social assistance and permits criminal proceedings against medical workers who fail to render such assistance. According to TASS, the draft law also stipulates medical confidentiality for AIDS patients. The agency said the draft law is explained in *Izvestia* by the head of the health ministry's main epidemiological department, Mikhail Narkevich.

Official Describes Soviet Import Program

USSR Deputy Minister of Trade Suren Sarukhanov said the Soviet Union is spending billions of rubles on foreign goods to keep its promises to coal miners and make sure citizens have shoes for the winter. TASS quoted Sarukhanov as saying that spending on imports had already reached 43 billion rubles and that this was more than had been budgeted for the whole year. He said the goods being imported include detergents, coffee, baby food, and winter footwear.

Journals Says USSR Should Stop Spending Resources on Third World

Writing in the CPSU CC journal *Kommunist* (No. 13), Igor Malashenko said the USSR's past determination to keep up with the United States in levels of armaments had been a colossal burden on the Soviet economy. He also said material resources should not be used to gain "spheres of influence" in the Third World at a time when the USSR is in a difficult financial and economic situation. Malashenko put the USSR's standard of living today at between fiftieth and sixtieth in the world. He said that the Soviet Union's national interests are in danger and that resources that until now have been spent on the arms race should be used to improve the Soviet standard of living.

Tatar Writer Criticizes Policy towards Nationalities

Tatar playwright Tufan Minnullin criticized the Soviet Union's nationalities policy. Minnullin is head of the Board of the Writers' Union of the Tatar Autonomous Republic. He told Radio Moscow that current policy has created a four-class division of the country—with Union republics at the top, followed by Autonomous republics, Autonomous oblasts, and Autonomous okrugs. He said Union republics, for example, receive more per capita spending on cultural and social development than Autonomous republics, which in turn receive more than the oblasts and okrugs. Minnullin said eliminating the divisions would help the country solve its ethnic problems. Minnullin also said the Soviet Union should develop its national languages. He said that whole generations do not speak their native tongue and that a nation can only develop on the basis of its language.

Tuesday, September 5 ————————————————————————

Primakov on Republican Sovereignty

Evgenii Primakov, chairman of the Council of the Union of the USSR Supreme Soviet, said the USSR was trying to create a country in which the republics are "as sovereign and independent as possible." Speaking of the Baltic republics, he said, however, that it would not be in their interest or in that of the USSR for them to achieve complete independence. Primakov spoke in London at a press conference at the Soviet embassy (*AP*, September 5).

A Soyuz TM-8 spacecraft with two cosmonauts aboard took off bound for a linkup with the *Mir* space station. The craft lifted off from the Baikonur space center in Kazakhstan as planned. Cosmonauts Aleksandr Viktorenko and Aleksandr Serebrov will stay at the space station until February and carry out maintenance checks aboard *Mir* and its "Kvant" module and will oversee the attachment of two new modules to the station (*TASS, Reuters, UPI,* September 5). On September 8, the Soyuz capsule docked with the *Mir* space station (*Radio Moscow,* September 8).

Soyuz TM-8 Sent into Earth Orbit

The Presidium of the Ukrainian Supreme Soviet made public a draft on the status of languages in Ukraine. TASS said the draft proposes that Ukrainian become the state language and Russian the language of interethnic communication. TASS quoted Presidium Secretary Nikolai Khomenko as saying the authors of the draft took into account the fact that Ukraine is a multinational republic. Khomenko added that every child should have the right to be educated in the language of his nationality and that the draft provides for this.

Language Draft Published in Ukraine

Chairman of the All-Union Central Council of Trade Unions Stepan Shalaev said the unions will urge the government to freeze prices for basic foods and industrial goods until 1991. He told a plenum of the council that the unions want the price freeze because of a worsening situation on the consumer market. TASS also quoted Shalaev as saying that recent strikes show a crisis of confidence in the Soviet sociopolitical structure. He said workers had also lost confidence in their unions (*TASS,* September 5).

Unions to Urge Price Freeze

Izvestia published and criticized the state plan and budget for 1990. The daily complained that switching from military production to the production of consumer goods was causing "zones of incomplete employment" and that the state plan did not solve this problem. It said the plan also failed to resolve the issue of prices to be paid for cotton, although this question had been raised by the USSR Supreme Soviet. *Izvestia* also asked how the plan and budget would account for the 2 billion rubles it will cost to meet the demands of the coal miners and for the costs of closing plants that have been polluting the environment. For the first time, the budget reveals how much money the USSR plans to print during a budget

***Izvestia* Criticizes 1990 Budget**

period—10 billion rubles in 1990—but no comparison is made with previous years. The budget also calls for a reduction in the USSR budget deficit.

Wednesday, September 6

Unions Demand More Control over Wages, Labor Safety

The All-Union Central Council of Trade Unions approved a draft law providing for more union control over the observance of safety and wage laws. TASS said the Central Council had asked the trade-union Presidium to submit the draft law to the Supreme Soviet for approval. The council also urged central and local state bodies to take urgent measures against "secondhand dealers, speculators, and extortioners" in the cooperative movement. TASS said the council also adopted a resolution calling for the setting up of a unified nationwide system of price control (*Sovetskaya Rossiya*, September 6 and 7).

Former Uzbek Premier Sentenced to Nine Years in Labor Camp

TASS reported that the USSR Supreme Court had sentenced former Uzbek Prime Minister Narmakhonmadi Khudaiberdyev to nine years in a strict-regime labor camp. A report on the evening news program "Vremya" indicated that the court in its final statement had emphasized charges that Khudaiberdyev had given a bribe of 50,000 rubles to Yurii Churbanov, former USSR first deputy minister of internal affairs. Questioned by a "Vremya" correspondent after the sentence was pronounced, Khudaiberdyev said he was appealing. The court rejected retractions of statements made by Khudaiberdyev and various witnesses during the investigation; Khudaiberdyev and some of the witnesses claimed they had been put under pressure by the investigators. The Supreme Court's acceptance of the original statements, rather than the retractions, indicates that efforts to impeach the evidence gathered by the special investigations team headed by Tel'man Gdlyan have been unsuccessful (*Pravda*, September 7).

Trade Union of Russia to Be Established

A plenum of the All-Union Central Council of Trade Unions, which ended in Moscow, decided in favor of the establishment of a trade-union council for the RSFSR. TASS said the founding conference of the RSFSR Council of Trade Unions would be held in the first quarter of next year. An organizational committee will start work this month. TASS said that the RSFSR is the only Union republic whose trade unions are directly controlled by the Central Council of Trade Unions (*Sovetskaya Rossiya*, September 7).

Literaturnaya gazeta (No. 36) carried an article by Vladimir Abarinov on the Katyn massacre, pointing out that the Soviet side of the official Soviet-Polish commission of historians set up in 1987 to clarify "blank spots" in Soviet-Polish history is still not ready to agree with the Polish point of view on Katyn—namely, that the NKVD was responsible for the massacre. Abarinov included in his material a report written by the Polish army officer Jozef Czapski, who in 1942 traveled around Russia meeting with NKVD officials in order to discover the fate of a group of Polish officers imprisoned in the three Soviet camps of Starobel'sk, Ostashkovo, and Kozel'sk. (The officers had, of course, already been shot by then.) One of the NKVD generals Czapski met in 1942, Leonid Raikhman, is still alive. Raikhman's name is also listed in Soviet documents among those who prepared the Soviet testimony on Katyn for the Nuremberg trials. Abarinov wrote that when he interviewed Raikhman about Katyn, Raikhman not only said he knew nothing about Katyn but also claimed he had never heard of Czapski, and he denied having had anything to do with the Nuremberg trials. He claimed his name had appeared on the Soviet documents relating to the Nuremberg trials by mistake.

Newspaper Discusses Katyn Massacre

A report from Tashkent said the local authorities had allowed the leaders of the Uzbek Popular Front "Birlik" to appear on local television on September 6. An Uzbek journalist reported the television appearance in a telephone interview with Radio Liberty on September 8. He said the "Birlik" leaders had explained the goals and program of the front in a round-table discussion (*RL Uzbek Service*, September 8).

Popular Front Leaders in Uzbekistan Appear on Television

Thursday, September 7

A leading Soviet sociologist, Igor Bestuzhev-Lada, appealed to the USSR Public Prosecutor to bring a lawsuit against Stalin for crimes against the Soviet people. Bestuzhev-Lada said Stalin should be charged with premeditated murder, the persecution of innocent people, and genocide. The sociologist told Radio Moscow that the

Sociologist Calls for Stalin to Be Tried for Genocide

purpose of his request was to achieve "judicial verification" of Stalin's crimes. (Proposals were voiced in the Soviet Union earlier this year to hold a "symbolic" trial of Stalin.)

Moscow Meeting Urges Measures to Improve Food Supply

A meeting of Soviet Party and government officials in Moscow called for measures to improve the country's food supply. The meeting was presided over by Party Politburo member and Central Committee Secretary for Agriculture Viktor Nikonov. TASS said it was emphasized at the meeting that the food problem could not be tackled passively. It proposed better organization, an improvement in the utilization of funds, and increasing the contribution of cities to the food supply. TASS quoted participants in the meeting as saying many leading officials had been sluggish in implementing Party decisions concerning agriculture (*Pravda*, September 8).

General Rodionov Replaced

TASS reported that Colonel General Igor Rodionov, who was in charge of the troops who quashed the Tbilisi protest on April 9, had been replaced as commander of the Transcaucasian Military District. His successor is Colonel General Valerii Patrikeev. TASS said Soviet Foreign Minister Eduard Shevardnadze had met with Patrikeev while visiting Georgia. The agency said they had discussed how to restore confidence between the people and the military.

Strikes Continue in Abkhazia

Strikes were reported continuing in Georgia's Autonomous Republic of Abkhazia, the scene of ethnic tensions between Abkhaz and Georgians recently. Radio Moscow said strikes by Abkhaz were continuing in offices and enterprises in the towns of Tvarcheli and Gagra. It said about 1,500 people were involved. The radio said one of the strikers' demands is for Abkhazia to be placed under a special administration directly subordinate to the USSR Supreme Soviet.

Lithuanian Journalists on Media Disinformation

Radio Vilnius said the central Soviet media were distorting coverage of the situation in Lithuania. The radio said that, on September 6, the Secretariat of the Lithuanian Union of Journalists had issued a statement saying that from reading the Moscow-based media or watching Leningrad television "you get the impression that nearly all Lithuanians are nationalists, extremists, and hysterics." The statement said the coverage creates the impression that the

484

Lithuanians are just looking for ways to deceive Soviet society, to secede from the USSR, and to harm ethnic minorities who are allegedly the sole defenders of Soviet power and socialism. The statement noted that the Union republics have a constitutional right to secede from the federation. It asked why a discussion of constitutional provisions should cause such "fury" on the part of the central authorities (*Radio Vilnius*, in English, September 7).

Chairman of the Presidium of the Lithuanian Supreme Soviet Vytautas Astrauskas said he opposed plans to set up a Polish raion within Lithuania. On September 7, the local Soviet in the predominantly Polish Salcininkai Raion voted to declare the area an Autonomous Polish Raion. Soviet television said Astrauskas addressed the meeting before the decision was taken and urged deputies not to vote for the move, saying it would not benefit the local people.

Polish Districts in Lithuania Declare Themselves Autonomous Raions

On September 15, a second predominantly Polish raion in Lithuania declared itself an Autonomous raion. The decision was taken by deputies of the Vilnius Raion. The district adjoins but does not include the Lithuanian capital, Vilnius (*RFE Lithuanian Service*, September 16).

On September 16, "Sajudis" criticized the declaration of autonomy on September 15 by the Vilnius Raion. "Sajudis" Chairman Vytautas Landsbergis told RFE/RL by telephone that the move would only result in an increase in nationality tensions. A second "Sajudis" official, Virgilijus Cepaitis, said the aim is to create the impression that ethnic Poles are threatened by Lithuanian nationalist actions. On September 21, the Presidium of the Lithuanian Supreme Soviet annulled the decisions of the mainly Polish raions Salcininkai and Vilnius, to declare themselves Autonomous Polish Raions (*Radio Vilnius*, September 21).

It was announced on "Vremya" that Dmitrii Romanin, Party first secretary in Kaliningrad Oblast since January, 1984, had retired. His successor, Semenov, who previously held the post of Party second secretary in the oblast, was elected in a secret ballot in which ten candidates competed. The Kaliningrad Party leadership has come in for a good deal of criticism from Moscow during Romanin's incumbency. Early in 1987 it was criticized for failing to make adequate preparations when harsh winter weather caused interruptions in heating and public transport in the region. Later that year it was reprimanded for failing to

Party Leader Replaced in Kaliningrad

meet agricultural targets; Romanin himself was attacked for meddling in economic management. Last year he was criticized for stacking the Kaliningrad Oblast delegation to the Nineteenth Party Conference.

Friday, September 8 ————————————————————————————————————

Ukrainian Popular Front Assembles for Founding Congress

About 1,500 people gathered in Kiev for the founding congress of the Ukrainian Popular Front "Rukh." Reports said Polish "Solidarity" delegates were among those at the Congress, held at Kiev's Polytechnic Institute. Reuters said "Solidarity" adviser Adam Michnik was among the speakers. It was the first time a "Solidarity" leader had addressed such a large public gathering in the USSR. Reuters quoted Michnik as saying that he and the front's members were fighting for an end to Stalinist communism and national chauvinism. See RL 443/89. Reports said some members of the audience waved the Ukraine's blue and yellow national flag. TASS also reported the meeting.

On September 9, the founding congress of "Rukh" began. Accounts of the meeting from Western news agencies quoted Sergei Konev, a member of the Congress of People's Deputies, as saying *perestroika* could not succeed in Ukraine under the leadership of Vladimir Shcherbitsky. At least one speaker at the founding congress called for Ukraine to secede from the USSR (*Reuters*, September 9). Reuters quoted a Party ideology official, Leonid Kravchuk, who attended the congress, as saying "we are not against 'Rukh' . . . we are against those who do not make constructive suggestions." At the end of the session on September 9, the congress adopted statutes and a program. On September 10, a group of Ukrainian members of the USSR Congress of People's Deputies attending the congress issued a statement saying Shcherbitsky's conservative nature and inflexibility were increasing tension in Ukraine. The same day, "Rukh" elected poet Ivan Drach to head the movement (*Reuters*, *RL Ukrainian Service*, September 10). Western agencies reported that the program adopted by "Rukh" calls for economic and political reforms in the republic, for greater guarantees of environmental protection, and for guarantees of religious freedom and human rights. The organizers of the congress told reporters that the central aim of "Rukh" is economic independence for Ukraine (*UPI*, *Reuters*, September 10). On September 15, *Pravda* complained that anti-Soviet and anti-Socialist speeches had been made at the congress.

On September 16, the Kiev Party authorities organized a rally in the city's main sports stadium against "Rukh." Reports telephoned to RFE/RL said among those who denounced "Rukh" were Kiev city Party leader Anatolii Kornienko and Ukrainian ideology chief Yurii Elchenko. A member of "Rukh" who attempted to speak was drowned out by hecklers.

On September 23, "Rukh" held a mass meeting in Kiev. Radio Liberty was told that thousands of people took part. The leader of "Rukh," writer Ivan Drach, said the meeting had been called to make public the movement's platform. He said the Ukrainian Party authorities had been spreading lies to discredit the organization.

On September 26, the evening news program "Vremya" gave brief coverage to "Rukh." It interviewed passers-by on a Kiev street on their attitude towards the movement. Three of the four people interviewed by "Vremya" were hostile to the new organization. Also interviewed was one of the leaders of "Rukh," poet Dmytro Pavlychko, who denied that the organization's goal was the secession of Ukraine from the Soviet Union. See RL 441/89 and RL 515/89.

Reports of Large Shipments of Soviet Arms to Cambodia

A Thai Foreign Ministry spokesman said the Soviet Union was sending large quantities of arms and ammunition to Cambodia. It said the provision of such supplies was inconsistent with Soviet calls for an end to outside military assistance to the three Cambodian resistance groups. Cambodian peace talks ended in Paris last month without progress (*DPA*, September 8).

Soviet Generals Held Hostage by Azerbaijani Crowd

The New York Times correspondent in Moscow reported that three Soviet generals were held hostage by a crowd of Azerbaijanis for five hours last week in Nagorno-Karabakh. *The New York Times* quoted Vadim Bakatin, a spokesman for Moscow's special administration in Nagorno-Karabakh, as confirming the incident. The newspaper reported that the three generals were released in exchange for the transfer of two Azerbaijani prisoners in Nagorno-Karabakh to a prison in Azerbaijan. Other reports said that three Azerbaijani prisoners were involved and that they were set free in exchange for the generals (*RL Azerbaijani Service*, September 8). The newspaper said the hostage-taking occurred when the three generals, including the commander of the MVD troops in the region, Yurii Shatalin, went to Shusha to meet with local government and Party officials.

Solzhenitsyn's *Red Wheel* to Be Published Next Year

Nash sovremennik, the Russian nationalist monthly, is planning to start publishing *The Red Wheel* by Aleksandr Solzhenitsyn next year. The journal's editor, Stanislav Kunaev, told Radio Moscow he will start publishing the part "October 1916" with the writer's permission.

Saturday, September 9 _____

El'tsin Visits the United States

On September 9, USSR Supreme Soviet deputy Boris El'tsin arrived in New York for a series of lectures and meetings with prominent Americans. Upon his arrival, El'tsin said the USSR wants to see mutual arms reductions and more economic cooperation with the United States (*Reuters, AP, UPI*, September 9). On the eve of his trip, Radio Moscow broadcast an interview with El'tsin in which he said interethnic disturbances in the USSR would end if more independence were granted to the Union republics.

On September 10, speaking on US television, El'tsin said the Soviet Union was in crisis. He said his country must learn from other countries' experience, including that of the United States, and create a new model of socialism. He said Gorbachev had missed some opportunities to accelerate *perestroika* but had done a lot to bring about political democratization (*AP*, September 10). El'tsin also complained about the economic situation in the USSR at a press conference in New York. He told the news conference his impressions of the United States had changed "180 degrees" since his arrival. He said he was impressed by what he had seen so far (Western agencies, September 10).

On September 11, *Izvestia* carried an interview with El'tsin in which he said it was time for direct US business investment in the Soviet Union. El'tsin called for the construction of one million apartments in the USSR by US firms. He did not go into detail on the financing. In an interview with US television on September 11, El'tsin urged Gorbachev to speed up his reforms, saying that if *perestroika* failed to make progress the Soviet leadership would face "a revolution from below" (*Reuters*, September 11). Before leaving New York for Washington, El'tsin discussed the USSR's nationality problems. He said national dignity was constantly being crushed in the Soviet Union. Asked about the future of the Baltic republics, El'tsin suggested that whether the republics stay or secede "is up to them." On September 12, El'tsin met in Washington with US President George Bush. They talked for fifteen minutes. White House spokesman Marlin Fitzwater said Bush wanted to make it clear to El'tsin that the policy of the United States is to support Gorbachev's reforms. The same day, El'tsin met with US Secretary of State James Baker (Western agencies, *RFE/RL Special*, September 12).

On September 13, El'tsin went to Chicago. Speaking at the Chicago Council of Foreign Relations, El'tsin said Soviet republics should have the right to say whether they want to remain a part of the USSR or not (*Reuters, UPI,* September 13). He also called for more economic autonomy for the republics. On a visit to Philadelphia the same day, El'tsin said he believed *perestroika* needs rescuing. He said the euphoria Americans feel about the Soviet reforms is unrealistic. He said that the key problems facing the USSR—a bad economy and nationalist unrest—have not been tackled decisively and that the country is moving towards "an abyss" (*AP, Reuters*, September 13).

On September 14, El'tsin paid a courtesy call on former US President Reagan, who was recuperating from an operation. Speaking in Dallas on September 15, El'tsin called for the ouster of conservative Party leaders Egor Ligachev and Viktor Chebrikov (*UPI*, September 16).

On September 18, El'tsin ended his eight-day US tour by signing an agreement in Miami to use his lecture fees to buy disposable syringes to combat AIDS in the Soviet Union. El'tsin said the agreement should lead to the purchase of about 100,000 dollars worth of syringes (*RFE/RL*, September 18). El'tsin returned to Moscow earlier than initially scheduled to attend the CPSU Central Committee plenum on nationality issues.

Gorbachev Returns from Vacation, Makes TV Address

Gorbachev returned from vacation after an absence of several weeks and delivered a twenty-five minute television address. He said that attempts to discredit *perestroika* were being made by conservatives, "ultra-leftists," and anti-Socialists but that people must go forward along the path of reform that has been mapped out. Gorbachev said the Soviet government is drafting a program of emergency measures to improve the economy, especially the consumer market. Some of the measures, he warned, might be unpopular, harsh, and even painful. But, he added, they were necessary to bring the country out of its present situation (*Pravda*, September 10).

Politburo Criticizes Government Officials

The CPSU Politburo criticized three Soviet government officials for not ensuring steady supplies of everyday goods. TASS said the Politburo severely reprimanded

A. Ya. Efimov, a deputy chairman of the USSR State Planning Committee and said he should not continue to hold his post. It also criticized Vladimir Gusev, a Soviet deputy prime minister and chairman of the USSR Council of Ministers Bureau for the Chemical and Forestry Complex, and V. P. Lakhtin, first deputy chairman of the USSR Council of Ministers Bureau for Social Development (*Pravda*, September 10).

Bodies from Mass Graves Reburied in Chelyabinsk

The remains of 350 unidentified victims of Stalinist repressions were reburied near the south Urals city of Chelyabinsk. TASS said thousands of residents attended the reburial services on Zolotaya Gora hill. Clergymen, local government officials, and deputies of the Congress of People's Deputies, including Andrei Sakharov, also attended. Bodies were discovered in shafts of an abandoned gold mine on the hill where they were shot by the NKVD (See report in *Izvestia*, September 15). TASS said residents plan to build a monument to the victims. On September 12, Soviet television said the mass grave in Chelyabinsk was one of the biggest to have been found. It is reported to contain the remains of some 300,000 people (*Reuters*, September 12).

Sunday, September 10

Radio Moscow Criticizes Quayle for Interfering

Radio Moscow criticized US Vice President Dan Quayle for some comments he made about the independence movements in the Baltic republics. Radio Moscow said Quayle's comments were "a flagrant interference in the internal affairs of the Soviet Union" (*Radio Moscow-2*, 1400, September 10). Quayle said on US television (CNN) on September 9 that he hoped the Baltic republics would continue "in the direction they want to go." On September 11, Soviet Foreign Ministry spokesman Gennadii Gerasimov also criticized Quayle's remarks about the Baltic republics (*Reuters*, September 11).

Moscow News on Tbilisi Events

Moscow News (No. 37) devoted a full-page article to the role of Viktor Chebrikov in the massacre in Tbilisi on April 9. In a speech to the Congress of People's Deputies, former Georgian Party chief Dzhumber Patiashvili revealed that he had consulted Chebrikov and Georgii Razumovsky before taking the decision to call in the army to break up the nationalist demonstrations. The Soviet

490

media, however, have until now maintained that the names of those in Moscow who ordered the military action are unknown. *Moscow News* quotes Chebrikov as saying he views the tragic consequences of his decision as "everyone's mistake, including his own." The newspaper gives the major share of the blame to the military.

Monday, September 11

Latvia Wants More Independence for Communist Parties of Republics

The first secretary of the Latvian Communist Party, Janis Vagris, said the Communist Parties of the republics should have more independence from the CPSU. In an interview with Radio Moscow, Vagris said these Parties should have a new status. He said this was currently the subject of discussion in Latvia. He said the republican Parties should be able to take decisions on issues that concern their republics while taking all-Union interests into account (*Radio Moscow-1*, 1900, September 11).

Soviet Media on East German Refugees

Initially, Radio Moscow reported without comment the decision of the Hungarian government to allow East German refugees in Hungary to leave for the West (*Radio Moscow-1*, 1000, September 11) and made no mention of East Germany's protest against Hungary's decision. Early on September 12, Soviet television showed a short clip of East German citizens arriving in West Germany, and an announcer read out the text of a TASS statement attacking the West German media and "certain political circles" for using "the illegal departure abroad" of East German citizens as a pretext for "a tendentious campaign" against East Germany. This statement warmly defended East Germany as a worthy member of the European family of nations, but it did not condemn the refugees. On September 12, "Vremya" correspondent Vladimir Kondrat'ev reported from Bonn on the flow of East German refugees to West Germany. He accused West Germany of trying to undermine East Germany and to split the Socialist community with a view to achieving German reunification. On September 13, Foreign Ministry spokesman Gennadii Gerasimov said that the exodus of East Germans to the West via Hungary was not a Soviet problem but that the USSR was unhappy about it. He told the BBC the exodus was illegal because the East Germans were crossing borders without the consent of their government and because of West Germany's view that all Germans are West German citizens. Gerasimov said this was not the case.

Sino-Soviet Talks Held in Moscow

Official Soviet-Chinese talks were held in Moscow (*TASS*, *Radio Moscow*, September 11). Politburo member Aleksandr Yakovlev headed the Soviet side, while the Chinese delegation was headed by Zhu Liang, a senior foreign affairs specialist in the Central Committee of the Chinese Communist Party. During the talks, Mikhail Gorbachev invited Chinese Party General Secretary Jiang Zemin to visit the Soviet Union. Coverage of the talks by the Soviet media was minimal—the evening news program "Vremya" carried no report on the talks. The same day, a Soviet delegation led by Vice President Anatolii Luk'yanov left on an official visit to China (*TASS*, September 11). On September 12, Xinhua quoted Luk'yanov as telling Chinese officials upon his arrival in Beijing that potential exists for bilateral cooperation in several fields. On September 14, Luk'yanov held talks with Chinese State Council Vice Premier Tian Jiyun. TASS said the two discussed the growing importance of having exchanges on their experiences with *perestroika* (*Pravda*, September 13).

Suharto in Moscow

Indonesian President Suharto began an official visit to Moscow. Soviet Vice President Anatolii Luk'yanov was shown meeting Suharto at the airport, and Gorbachev and Shevardnadze were shown meeting with him in the Kremlin. At a dinner for Suharto, Gorbachev spoke about the Soviet Union's policy of sufficient defense. He emphasized that the reduction of Soviet forces in the Asian part of the USSR had already begun. Gorbachev welcomed what he said was growing opposition to militarization in the Asian-Pacific region. Earlier the same day, a joint Soviet-Indonesian communiqué was issued that said the Soviet Union and Indonesia had agreed to expand economic and political relations (*AFP*, September 11, *Pravda*, September 12, 13).

Prosecutor Says Charges against Ligachev Are False

In an interview with TASS, USSR Deputy Public Prosecutor Vladimir Kravtsev said corruption charges made against Politburo member Egor Ligachev were false. Kravtsev said the charges were an attempt to frame Ligachev (*Pravda*, September 12). The allegations surfaced in May, when an investigator in the Prosecutor's Office said Ligachev's name had come up in a probe of corruption in Uzbekistan. Kravtsev said the charges against Ligachev had been dropped. On September 16, Soviet investigator Tel'man Gdlyan, who was previously in charge of conducting corruption probes in Uzbekistan, commented on Kravtsev's statement in an interview with

RFE/RL. Gdlyan said the investigation that had just cleared Ligachev was a fiction and that some of the people who testified in support of Ligachev were also guilty of taking bribes (*RL Russian Service*, September 16).

_____ *Tuesday, September 12*

Ligachev in GDR

Politburo member Egor Ligachev began a three-day visit to the GDR, ostensibly to study the way agriculture is organized there (*Pravda*, September 13). The East German news agency ADN said Ligachev was also in the GDR to discuss "Warsaw Pact policies." ADN said Ligachev condemned what he called "the machinations" of "certain circles" in West Germany who seek to manipulate East Germans and persuade them to leave their country illegally. ADN added that Ligachev and SED Politburo member Werner Krolikowski accused these circles (which were not identified) of violating international law and employing "defamation, enticement, and lures" to get East Germans to leave the GDR. Ligachev was also quoted as saying the GDR is a true friend and ally of the USSR. He said all those who want to infringe on East German sovereignty and independence must know the USSR will honor its treaty obligations to the GDR. On September 14, ADN announced that Mikhail Gorbachev would attend ceremonies in East Berlin marking the fortieth anniversary of the founding of the East German state on October 7. ADN said the announcement of Gorbachev's visit "was received with thanks and joy."

Nishanov on Nagorno-Karabakh

The chairman of the Council of Nationalities of the USSR Supreme Soviet, Rafik Nishanov, said there must be neither winners nor losers in the solution of the Nagorno-Karabakh dispute. In an interview with *Izvestia*, Nishanov said that measures to ease the tensions in the oblast had not worked and that the alienation between Azerbaijanis and Armenians in the region "had gone too far." He said only calm, restraint, and rejection of violence could create the right atmosphere for "a sensible solution."

Reports on Economic Autonomy for Baltic Republics

Tunne Kelam, a founder of Estonia's National Independence Party, called for an international conference to discuss the issue of independence for the Baltic republics (*RFE/RL Special*, September 12). Speaking to US businessmen in Washington, Academician Abel Aganbegyan strongly supported economic autonomy for the Baltic republics. He said, however, that he thought they would find it hard economically to secede from the USSR (*RFE/RL Special*, September 12). On September 13, RFE's Lithuanian Service reported that, at a meeting organized by "Sajudis" in the Lithuanian town of Panevezys on September 8, it was announced that the Baltic republics were planning closer economic cooperation, with the goal of setting up a Baltic common market by 1993.

Wednesday, September 13

New Ambassador to Kabul Identified

The Soviet Union was reported to have appointed a new ambassador to Kabul. He is Boris Pastukhov, who has been Soviet ambassador to Denmark since April, 1986 (*AFP*, September 13). Pastukhov replaces Yulii Vorontsov, who has become Soviet first deputy foreign minister.

Pipe Crack Blamed for Soviet Submarine Accident

Krasnaya zvezda said a tiny crack in a pipe was probably the cause of a Soviet submarine accident north of Norway last June. The newspaper added, however, that the exact cause of the accident could still not be determined, because the radioactivity inside the submarine is still too high for experts to be able to investigate.

KGB Chief Calls for Cooperation among World's Intelligence Services

KGB Chairman Vladimir Kryuchkov called for increased cooperation among the world's intelligence services. He said international problems such as terrorism, smuggling, and illicit drug trafficking could be dealt with more effectively if the services worked together. Kryuchkov made the comment in a filmed interview shown to Western and Soviet journalists in Moscow. The journalists were also shown a new Soviet-made documentary about the KGB, entitled "The KGB Today" (*TASS*, in English, September 13).

Soviet Spokesman Wishes New Polish Government Success

Foreign Ministry spokesman Gennadii Gerasimov wished Poland's new "Solidarity"-led government success. TASS quoted Gerasimov as saying the Soviet Union noted "with satisfaction" Polish Prime Minister Tadeusz Mazowiecki's remarks about his government's intention to build relations with the USSR on principles of equality and sovereignty. On September 14, *Izvestia* gave Mazowiecki high marks for political acumen and for the composition of his

Cabinet. It said the new Cabinet was made up of people with "a high-level of competency and free-thinking." The newspaper praised Mazowiecki for resisting pressure "from various sides."

Sovetskaya Rossiya carried an article on the creation of a "United Front of Workers of Russia," which held a congress in Sverdlovsk last week. The congress was attended by 110 delegates from twenty-nine Russian cities, as well as by representatives of Russian groups in Moldavia, Tajikistan, and the Baltic republics. The delegates proclaimed as their goal the struggle against market-oriented economic reforms. They also oppose national movements in the non-Russian republics. The creation of yet another workers' front is a further step in the consolidation of antireform forces in the Soviet Union. The "United Front of Workers of Russia" will serve as an umbrella organization for local united workers' fronts that have been set up this summer in various Russian cities. It will apparently also have close contacts with Russian workers in the Union republics who have joined forces in various groups to stage strikes and other forms of protest against the increasing movement for sovereignty and even independence in the republics. On September 14, *Sovetskaya Rossiya* reported the formation of another new group—"the United Council of Russia," which represents more than twenty Russian patriotic and public organizations. The newspaper said the council's founding congress adopted a resolution offering support for strengthening Russia as the consolidating basis of the USSR as a multinational Socialist homeland. The newspaper said some of the speakers at the inaugural congress of the United Council expressed concern over attempts to introduce capitalist elements into the Soviet economy. See RL 449/89.

Creation of United Front of Workers of Russia

Mikhail Gorbachev was reported to have met in Moscow with the Party and government leaders of Estonia, Latvia, and Lithuania to discuss Soviet reforms. Reuters quoted Estonian Communist Party First Secretary Vaino Valjas as saying the talks covered moves by the Baltic republics towards economic independence and the issue of increasing the political rights of the Union republics. Valjas said he was pleased with how the talks had gone and said Gorbachev is on Estonia's side and understands its problems (*Reuters*, *RFE Estonian Service*, *Radio Tallinn-B*, 1900, September 13).

Gorbachev Holds Talks with Baltic Leaders

On September 15, TASS gave more details of Gorbachev's meeting with the Baltic leaders. The agency said Gorbachev emphasized that three points must be observed to protect the interests of the Soviet and Baltic peoples. He said the first is that all problems should be solved only within the framework of the Soviet federation; the second is the unity of the Communist Party; and the third is the equality of all nationalities. Gorbachev told the Baltic leaders that, within the federal framework, the republics can be given broad sovereignty (*Pravda*, September 16).

**Soviet Newsman Wins
Journalism Award**

Soviet journalist Aleksandr Pumpyansky received the 1989 Inter Press Service International Journalism Award for his contributions to *glasnost'*. Pumpyansky is currently deputy editor of *New Times* and was formerly a *Komsomol'skaya pravda* and *Moscow News* correspondent. He was received by UN Secretary General Javier Perez de Cuellar.

Thursday, September 14 ───────────────────────────

**Armenia under Economic
Blockade**

Pravda said Armenia was under a virtual economic blockade because of blocked railways in Azerbaijan. The newspaper said earthquake reconstruction and the ambulance service in Erevan were at a standstill. It said that 87 percent of Armenian supplies come by rail through Azerbaijan and that these have been disrupted by a series of strikes triggered by territorial disputes.

On September 17, the Armenian Supreme Soviet convened again to discuss the issue of Nagorno-Karabakh and ways of overcoming the blockade by Azerbaijan (*TASS*, September 17).

On September 22, the Armenian Supreme Soviet appealed to the USSR Supreme Soviet for help in overcoming the crippling blockade of transport routes by Azerbaijan. The appeal was reported by Radio Moscow and *Pravda*. The head of Azerbaijan's railroads confirmed that goods transport on the Azerbaijan-Armenia railroad was still running at less than half of its normal capacity (*Central Television*, "Vremya," September 22). The same day, *Pravda* reported that none of the newspapers in Armenia were published on September 21, because of a lack of paper caused by the Azerbaijani blockade. *Pravda* denounced the Azerbaijani action.

On September 23, Armenian Prime Minister Vladimir Markaryants said the blockade had caused an emergency situation in Armenia. Markaryants told the Armenian Supreme Soviet that economic pressure would not solve interethnic conflicts (*TASS*, September 23). On September 24, Armenian Party First Secretary Suren Arutyunyan expressed concern about the tense situation between his republic and Azerbaijan. He told Soviet television that the blockade had stopped a lot of the reconstruction work being done to repair the damage caused by last December's earthquake.

On September 25, speaking at a session of the USSR Supreme Soviet, Mikhail Gorbachev said he would propose extraordinary measures if the blockade were not lifted in the next two days (*TASS*, September 25). The same day, *Pravda* said a military airlift had started carrying vital supplies into blockaded Nagorno-Karabakh. On September 26, Radio Moscow quoted an Azerbaijani railway official as saying that Armenia had started receiving goods by rail from Azerbaijan. Deputy head of Azerbaijan's railways, Ali-Hussein Seidov, told the radio that rail transport would resume normal services that day. On September 27, however, there were conflicting reports on the blockade. While TASS reported that it was over, a spokesman for the Armenian Foreign Ministry told DPA that only a few rail cars containing fuel, gravel, and spoiled food had arrived. On September 29, Radio Moscow said that food and fuel destined for Armenia was not arriving from Azerbaijan and that rail lines between Armenia and Azerbaijan remained blocked by idled trains. See RL 476/89.

US Says Soviet Emigrés Will Not Be Turned Away

A US State Department official said the United States will not turn away any Soviet citizens who have already left their country and applied to enter the United States. The department's coordinator for refugee affairs, Jewel Lafontant, told a congressional hearing that all such applicants will be admitted to the United States either as refugees or under other programs. Another State Department official said Soviet citizens who apply next month to emigrate to the United States may have to wait more than a year for their cases to be considered because of a backlog of applications (*RFE/RL Special*, *AP*, September 14).

Solzhenitsyn again Praised on Soviet Television

On the television evening news program "Vremya," the editor of *Novyi mir* Sergei Zalygin said Aleksandr Solzhenitsyn was his top choice among writers being published by his journal. He said he admired Solzhenitsyn above all for his unflinching attitude. He said "there are moments in the life of a people and a country . . . when one must be unflinching." In August, *Novyi mir* started publishing excerpts from Solzhenitsyn's epic about the Soviet labor camps, *Gulag Archipelago.*

Economist Speaks on Measures to Improve Consumer-Goods Production

Pavel Bunich, deputy chairman of the USSR Supreme Soviet's Economic Reform Committee said a number of extraordinary measures are to be taken to ease the situation on the Soviet consumer market. TASS quoted Bunich as saying that some enterprises in heavy industry will be switched over to the production of consumer goods and that capital investments will be channeled into the development of agriculture. Because the effect of these measures will be temporary, Bunich said it will be necessary to get to work immediately to implement economic reform.

Friday, September 15

Two Men Sentenced in Connection with Clashes in Novyi Uzen'

A court in Gur'ev in Kazakhstan sentenced two men to labor-camp terms for offenses committed during inter-ethnic clashes in Novyi Uzen' in June in which five people died. TASS said that twenty-two-year-old E. Mamykov was sentenced to four years for looting a truck and breaking windows and that twenty-eight-year-old K. Bisenov was sentenced to three years for creating an atmosphere of open hostility and tension, shouting provocative slogans, insulting police, and throwing stones at them. The June clashes in Novyi Uzen' were between native Kazakhs and settlers from the Caucasus. Many Kazakhs had demanded that the settlers leave the region, and thousands of them did so shortly after the unrest.

Romanov Letter Denies Use of Palace and Tsar's Tableware

Pravda published a letter from former Politburo member Grigorii Romanov, who was once thought to be a challenger to Mikhail Gorbachev, denying that he celebrated his daughter's wedding in the Winter Palace in Leningrad and used the tsar's tableware. The letter was Romanov's first publication in the official press since he was retired from the Politburo in 1985. Romanov said in the letter that a commission of the Supreme Soviet of the RSFSR had investigated the allegations. He insisted that the wedding dinner was actually only for twelve people and was held in a small country house. "There was no tsarist tableware from the Hermitage," he wrote.

TASS reported that a three-day international protest meeting had started near the Semipalatinsk nuclear testing site in Kazakhstan. TASS said the meeting was organized by a section of the movement "Physicians of the World for the Prevention of Nuclear War" and the Alma-Ata branch of the international youth organization "Next Stop Soviet." TASS said medical scientists from several Soviet cities had been joined by scientists from Denmark, Norway, Sweden, and Finland. It said they adopted an appeal to the US and Soviet governments to ban testing of nuclear weapons and step up efforts to solve ecological problems.

Protest Meeting in Semipalatinsk

_____ *Saturday, September 16*

A Soviet report said 10,000 non-Tajik-speaking people left Dushanbe, the capital of Tajikistan, during the first half of this year. *Izvestia* said the recent decision by the republic's Supreme Soviet to make Tajik the official language was the main reason they gave for leaving. It said many non-Tajik-speaking people were concerned it would be impossible to live and work in Tajikistan if affairs there were conducted almost exclusively in Tajik. The newspaper said people feared the events taking place in the Baltic and Moldavia "may repeat themselves here, and they do not want to be involved in them." On September 23, the Tajikistan Supreme Soviet opened an extraordinary session. TASS said sharp debates broke out during talks on draft amendments to the Tajik Constitution, with a majority of deputies supporting provisions of the amendments that guarantee equal voting rights to all the republic's residents regardless of ethnic or religious affiliation or length of residence. The Supreme Soviet adopted an amendment to the republican penal code that makes the violation of equality of languages a punishable crime.

Language Law Causes Exodus from Tajikistan

The KGB is investigating an explosion on a bus in Azerbaijan that killed five people. TASS said the bus was traveling from Baku to Tbilisi when the explosion occurred near the town of Evlakh in Azerbaijan. On September 18, *Pravda* said the explosion had been caused by a time bomb that was planted under a seat.

KGB Investigating Fatal Bus Explosion in Azerbaijan

A three-day conference of Soviet democratic movements and organizations opened in Leningrad. TASS said the meeting was being attended by representatives of fifty-

Democratic Movements and Organizations Meet in Leningrad

one organizations from thirty-one Soviet cities. It said the groups included the Leningrad Popular Front and the Lithuanian Restructuring Movement "Sajudis." TASS said a deputy of the Congress of People's Deputies, Yurii Afanas'ev, opened the conference, representing the Inter-regional Group of reformers within the Congress of People's Deputies. In his speech, Afanas'ev said that the CPSU should shut down its main newspaper, *Pravda*, because it "lies and disinforms Soviet society." Afanas'ev also complained that conservative forces in the country's leadership, first and foremost the Politburo, were making "massive attacks on *perestroika* supporters." *Pravda* of September 17 carried Afanas'ev's speech with critical comments.

Lvov Demonstration to Mark Anniversary of USSR's Seizure of City

On September 16, a Radio Moscow correspondent in Ukraine criticized an unauthorized rally in Lvov. He said anyone who tried to address it in Russian was not allowed to speak. The rally marked the fiftieth anniversary of the Soviet occupation of the city at the start of World War II (*Radio Moscow-2*, 1900, September 16). On September 17, there was another demonstration in Lvov to mark the anniversary. Some 30,000 people were reported to have participated. The coverage of the September 17 demonstration in Lvov by the television news program "Vremya" was strikingly objective in contrast with Radio Moscow's treatment of the demonstration on September 16. Refraining from critical comments, "Vremya" showed film of marchers waving hundreds of still-outlawed Ukrainian nationalist blue-and-yellow flags.

Izvestia Carries Letters Condemning Invasion of Czechoslovakia

Izvestia published readers' letters condemning the Soviet-led invasion of Czechoslovakia in 1968. Among them was one from Jiri Hajek, who was Czech foreign minister at the time of the invasion. Hajek compared the Prague Spring with *perestroika* in the USSR. That comparison has also been made by Alexander Dubcek, who headed the Czechoslovak Party during the Prague Spring.

Sunday, September 17

Demonstration of Ukrainian Catholics in Lvov

More than 150,000 people took part in a march through the Western Ukrainian city of Lvov to call for the relegalization of the Ukrainian Catholic Church (*Reuters*, September 17). Soviet television reported the demonstration in its

"Vremya" news program, saying 100,000 people took part. "Vremya" said the rally adopted an appeal to Gorbachev calling for the rehabilitation of the Ukrainian Catholic Church and the granting of legal status to it.

The Sunday Times carried an interview with Leningrad KGB chief Lieutenant General Anatolii Kurkov, in which he claimed that "between 1937 and 1953, 60,000 people were unlawfully shot in Leningrad." Kurkov insisted that "these deaths are documented and that other figures are often little more than supposition, totally unsupported by any documentary evidence."

Leningrad KGB Chief Cites Number of Stalin's Victims

Monday, September 18

Pravda complained that the Party was being blamed for everything. It said that, after being considered the country's leading and guiding force for decades, the Party was now being blamed for everything that is wrong in the Soviet Union, including shortages of goods, increasing crime, and the poor situation of pensioners. It complained that both Communists and non-Communists were joining in the criticism.

***Pravda* Complains Party Is Blamed for Everything**

Pravda reprinted an article from the Italian newspaper *la Repubblica* that criticized El'tsin's conduct in the United States. Reprinted by *Pravda* in full and without comments, the article suggested that El'tsin spent too much money during the visit, demanded the use of a limousine, and drank too much. On September 19, El'tsin dismissed the accusations as slander (Western agencies, September 19). On September 20, Reuters and AP reported that *Moscow News* (No. 39) had criticized *Pravda* for reprinting the attack on El'tsin. *Moscow News* said the Party daily should have told its readers whether the Italian newspaper story was accurate. On September 21, *Pravda* apologized to El'tsin for reprinting the criticism of him without checking it. On September 22, the general director of TASS, Leonid Kravchenko, criticized *Pravda* for reprinting the article (*TASS*, September 22). The same day, *la Repubblica* complained that *Pravda* had reprinted its attack on El'tsin for political purposes (*AP*, September 22).
    On September 25, during the USSR Supreme Soviet session, a deputy from Yaroslavl, Igor Shamshev, urged the Soviet parliament to investigate why *Pravda* had

***Pravda* Prints Article Critical of El'tsin, Then Apologizes**

reprinted the article without checking its accuracy. TASS reported that Mikhail Gorbachev supported the idea of setting up a parliamentary commission to investigate the matter. On September 26, the Supreme Soviet set up a commission to examine the affair (*TASS*, September 26).

**Gerasimov Comments on
Anti-Soviet Demonstrations
in Poland**

Soviet Foreign Ministry spokesman Gennadii Gerasimov criticized anti-Soviet demonstrations in Poland held on September 17 to mark the fiftieth anniversary of the Soviet invasion of Poland. Gerasimov told reporters in Moscow some "extremist-minded" groups had taken part in the demonstrations. He said some of the slogans and banners were "insulting to the USSR." Gerasimov said "extremists" had taken a series of actions that "posed a threat to the safety of Soviet staffers" (*TASS*, September 18). The demonstrations were held at the Soviet embassy in Warsaw and at the Soviet consulate in Krakow.

**Illinois Signs Farming
Accord with RSFSR**

The US state of Illinois has signed an agreement to sell seed, farm equipment, and livestock to the RSFSR. At a news conference in Illinois, State Agriculture Director Larry Werries said the pact was signed last week during a visit by an Illinois trade mission to the USSR. Under the agreement, Illinois will establish an agricultural business consortium in Moscow in which Illinois firms can sell their products directly to Soviet buyers (*UPI*, September 18).

**Baltic Military Council
Addresses Baltic Residents**

The Council of the Baltic Military District said that many people in the Baltic republics viewed Soviet troops as a hostile occupation army and that this creates a difficult situation. The council made the comment in a statement addressed to the citizens of the Baltic republics. *Izvestia* reported the statement. The council said it was impossible to make assessments of the Soviet troops based on the past. The statement was signed by the commander of the Baltic Military District, Colonel General Fedor Kuzmin, and the Party first secretaries of Estonia, Latvia, and Lithuania.

**More Calls for Reform
of Party**

The controversial *Pravda* journalist Tat'yana Samolis published a review of readers' letters on the role of the CPSU. (An earlier article by Samolis, "Cleansing," caused a sensation when it appeared in *Pravda* in February, 1986, on the eve of the Twenty-Sixth Party Congress; it prompted a rebuke by Egor Ligachev from the Congress rostrum,

502

and Samolis barely kept her job.) Like its predecessor, Samolis' latest article uses quotations from readers' letters to call for a sweeping reform of the CPSU. She describes the Party as "in a state of siege" but says it has only itself to blame for this. She says its undemocratic organization means that the opinions of rank-and-file Communists count for nothing and that the general public has no control over Party decisions. She says many readers' letters raise the possibility of a multiparty system for the USSR.

The director of the Soviet grain import and export agency, Eksportkhleb, Oleg Klimov, said the USSR had stopped foreign purchases of grain while trying out a program that involves paying its own farmers hard currency. He told Reuters that the Soviet Union was starting to buy grain from its kolkhozes and sovkhozes for hard currency and that it might take as long as four months to complete the process. (Under the experiment, approved last month, kolkhozes and sovkhozes will be paid hard currency for grain they harvest above target.) Klimov said the USSR had met all its foreign commitments to buy grain in 1989. He declined to say how much had been purchased. The US Department of Agriculture said the USSR had bought nearly 2.2 million tons of grain in the past twelve months.

Soviet Grain Imports Suspended

Tuesday, September 19

A plenum of the CPSU Central Committeee on interethnic relations opened in Moscow with a report by Mikhail Gorbachev "On the Party's Nationalities Policy in Present-Day Conditions." While elaborating in his report on the need for profound changes in interethnic relations and for a strengthening of the political and economic autonomy of the Union republics, Gorbachev once again left the Baltic republics in no doubt that demands for independence and even some features of their concepts of economic autonomy are unacceptable to Moscow. As for such intractable problems as the dispute between Azerbaijan and Armenia over Nagorno-Karabakh, Gorbachev could offer only appeals to reason—with the threat of decisive action if reason did not prevail. In his speech, Gorbachev also proposed that the next Party Congress be brought forward five months to October, 1990. He said the solution of the problems of consumer-goods shortages cannot wait for the next Party Congress and that measures to put an end to the shortages should be taken

CPSU CC Plenum on Nationalities Issues

503

immediately. Gorbachev decisively opposed a federalization of the Party in connection with a reform of the Soviet federation (*Radio Moscow*, September 19; *Pravda*, September 20).

The plenum also heard other speeches. Kirgiz Party First Secretary Absamat Masaliev urged Gorbachev to take a firm stand on popular front activities in the Baltic republics. Masaliev told the plenum that many popular front activists were adopting undesirable positions (*Radio Moscow*, *TASS*, September 19). Speaking at the session, Lithuanian Party First Secretary Algirdas Brazauskas told the plenum that forces demanding Lithuanian secession should be considered, even though he believes secession would be "disastrous" (*Pravda*, September 21).

On September 20, the plenum was back in session with debates continuing on the main theme of the meeting—Party policy on nationalities and interethnic problems. One of the speakers at the session was Gosteleradio chief Mikhail Nenashev, who complained about the decline in the prestige of the CPSU. Uzbek Party First Secretary Islam Karimov said the proposal by some republics to set up a Soviet confederation was completely unacceptable. He told the plenum that a confederation would inevitably lead to an intensification of "localistic tendencies," the development of centrifugal forces, and a disintegration of the Soviet state (*TASS*, September 20). Soviet Defense Minister Dmitrii Yazov criticized the presence of "nationalistic, separatist, and extremist" forces in the Soviet military (*Radio Moscow-2*, 1600, September 20). Another speaker was conservative Politburo member Egor Ligachev. He said the main threat to *perestroika* comes from those who want to introduce capitalism in the USSR and from nationalists and those who play "democratic games" with them. Radio Moscow reported that the plenum unanimously approved the Party's platform on nationalities. In his closing speech to the plenum, Mikhail Gorbachev said the policy of reform must be continued, despite growing problems and skepticism among the population (*Central Television*, "Vremya," September 20; *Pravda*, September 22).

The plenum also made important changes in the composition of the Politburo. Three full members of the Politburo, Ukrainian Party First Secretary Vladimir Shcherbitsky, Chairman of the Central Committee Legal Policy Commission Viktor Chebrikov, and Deputy Chairman of the Central Committee Agriculture Commission Viktor Nikonov were retired. All three are regarded as conservatives. In a largely expected move, former First Secretary of the Leningrad Oblast Party Committee Yurii

Solov'ev retired as a candidate Politburo member. Another candidate Politburo member who retired was
Nikolai Talyzin, chairman of the USSR Council of Ministers Bureau on Social Policy. "Vremya" announced that
KGB chairman Vladimir Kryuchkov and Chairman of
Gosplan Yurii Maslyukov had been made full members of
the Politburo. Evgenii Primakov, chairman of the Council
of the Union of the USSR Supreme Soviet, and Boris Pugo,
chairman of the USSR Party Control Committee, were
made candidate members of the Politburo. National
activists in the Union republics expressed satisfaction
over the retirement at the plenum of the three conservative full members of the Politburo. The activists were not
sure, however, whether the move would have any
significant effect on the policies of the Soviet leadership
(*Reuters*, September 21; *Pravda*, September 22).

Academician Moiseev Proposes Reorganization of Academy of Sciences

TASS quoted Academician Nikita Moiseev as proposing
that the USSR Academy of Sciences be replaced by a union
of republican academies of sciences, equal in their rights.
Currently, the USSR Academy of Sciences is the supreme
scientific institution of the USSR and is much more
powerful and more prestigious than the academies of the
Union republics. Moiseev also reiterated the call for the
creation of a Russian Academy of Sciences for the RSFSR.
The RSFSR is the only Union republic that does not have
its own academy.

Ukrainian Elected Head of UN Assembly's Special Political Committee

Ambassador Gennadii Udovenko of Ukraine was elected
chairman of the UN General Assembly's special political
committee. He was proposed by Poland on behalf of a
group of East European states and elected by acclamation in the absence of other candidates (*RFE/RL
Special*, September 18). Udovenko has been Ukraine's
ambassador to the United Nations in New York since
1985. Before that, he served as Ukraine's deputy foreign
minister.

Turkey to Grant Asylum to Defecting Soviet Athlete

Champion Soviet weightlifter Hafiz Suleimanov and
his trainer Vitalii Stavrov defected at the Turkish embassy
in Athens. Turkey's ambassador to Greece, Gunduz
Aktan, said Greek officials had already been asked
to allow Suleimanov and Stavrov to leave for Turkey.
The Turkish Anatolian News Agency said Suleimanov
comes from Sumgait in Azerbaijan (*Reuters*, September 19).

Emigration from USSR

Yurii Reshetov, chairman of the Soviet Foreign Ministry's Humanitarian Affairs and Cultural Relations Department, said US classification of Soviet Jewish émigrés as "refugees" creates friction in US-Soviet relations. Reshetov said the USSR is portrayed as "some enemy of mankind from whom all the people are fleeing." Reshetov spoke in Washington at the National Conference on Soviet Jewry. The same day, US Deputy Secretary of State Lawrence Eagleburger told the conference that other Western democracies besides the United States have an obligation to help resettle Soviet Jews. He said the US quota of 50,000 Soviet Jews for the next fiscal year will not meet the demand, but he said the United States had no choice but to set "painful limits" (*AP*, September 19).

Trials in Fergana; Violence in Tashkent

TASS said twelve people accused of taking part in inter-ethnic clashes in Uzbekistan in June had gone on trial. TASS said the defendants, who are being tried in the Uzbek town of Fergana, are accused of hooliganism and complicity in murder. TASS also said there had been violence over the weekend in the Uzbek capital, Tashkent. The agency said rampaging youths disrupted a cultural festival, attacking passengers at a nearby subway station, overturning cars, and throwing stones. It said the youths became angry because they thought not enough Uzbek folksongs and dances were included in the program of the festival. On September 19, TASS said twenty-one people had been detained in Tashkent in connection with the disturbances. TASS said most of those detained were given jail sentences of between five and fifteen days and fined.

200 Tons of Radioactive Material Found Dumped near Moscow

Radio Moscow quoted *Moskovsky komsomolets* as saying somebody had dumped 200 tons of radioactive material at the Podolsk metal works south of Moscow. The newspaper said the authorities may never find out who did it. It said the material was discovered during a routine radiation check in the Moscow suburbs.

Wednesday, September 20 ───────────────────────────────

Sakharov Interviewed by French TV

In an interview shown on French television, Academician Andrei Sakharov said the greatest threat to Gorbachev arises out of the failure of his policies to produce results. Sakharov said Gorbachev is in a powerful position and is not threatened by members of his own entourage but rather by "the inconsequence of his own actions and hesitation between decisions of the right and of the left."

Soviet Foreign Ministry spokesman Gennadii Gerasimov said the USSR wanted US-Soviet relations to develop at a quicker pace. He said during a live interview from Moscow shown on US television that the Soviet feeling is that the Americans are "a little bit too slow" in developing relations. (His comments were made just before the start of Eduard Shevardnadze's visit to the United States.) Gerasimov also welcomed the US decision to drop its demand for a ban on strategic land-based mobile missiles. Gerasimov said the decision had removed a barrier to achieving an accord limiting strategic nuclear arms. The USSR has two mobile missile systems deployed. The United States has none, and until now it has sought a ban on these weapons. Secretary of State James Baker announced the new US position on September 19. Gerasimov urged the United States to put forward other constructive ideas (*Reuters, AFP*, September 20).

Gerasimov on US-Soviet Relations

Georgian newspapers published a draft plan for Georgia's economic sovereignty within the Soviet federation. Georgian First Deputy Prime Minister Otar Kvilitaya was quoted as saying the draft outlines various property relations, determines the lower ranks of economic management, points out ways of replenishing Georgia's state budget, and offers a new tax system. TASS said the draft was prepared by prominent Georgian economists. It said Georgia plans to switch to economic independence at the beginning of 1991.

Georgian Economic Sovereignty Plan Published

Literaturnaya gazeta carried an excerpt from Aleksandr Solzhenitsyn's *Red Wheel*, which includes a defense of Russian tsarist rule. The newspaper also carried a front-page photograph of Solzhenitsyn. The excerpt portrays left-wingers in the prerevolutionary parliament, the Duma, as working to seize power rather than help solve urgent problems.

Excerpt from Solzhenitsyn on Tsarist Rule Published in *Literaturnaya gazeta*

Three Estonian journalists are being drafted into the Soviet Army after having written on sensitive topics. All three have been called up for reserve duty on October 10. Another Estonian journalist, Sirge Endere, told RFE/RL

Leading Estonian Journalists Called Up for Army Reserve

that the drafting is "a clear attempt" to remove them from the scene. He said the three are among Estonia's best journalists. He said they are "noted for their outspokenness and willingness to write about sensitive topics."

USSR Proposes Summit on Environment

The Soviet Union proposed that a UN conference on the environment scheduled for 1992 should be held at the summit level. In a news conference at the United Nations, Soviet Deputy Foreign Minister Vladimir Petrovsky said holding the conference at the summit level would "give a strong push towards practical deeds in the environmental field." He said the conference, which is under preparation, should adopt some kind of code of environmental behavior (*Reuters*, September 20).

USSR to Accept UN Security Council Decisions as Legally Binding

Soviet Deputy Foreign Minister Vladimir Petrovsky said the USSR has decided to accept all future decisions of the UN Security Council as legally binding. He also said the USSR would try to "de-ideologize" the work of the United Nations and "depoliticize" its specialized agencies. Petrovsky said the Soviet Union will soon submit proposals for an agenda to the General Assembly. He said the Soviet delegation will be guided by the principle of nonintervention. (*RFE/RL Special*, September 20).

Pipeline Defects Found near Scene of Bashkiria Disaster

TASS said defects had been found in other sections of the gas pipeline that caused an explosion in Bashkiria on June 3, killing more than 500 people. The news agency said the defects had been found during examination of the pipeline one kilometer on each side of the disaster site. It said they included damage to insulation and scuffing and scratches on the pipe itself similar to defects found in the pipe at the scene of the explosion. TASS said investigators were trying to find out what caused the defects and who installed the pipeline.

USSR to Join IMF, World Bank

The USSR has decided to seek membership in the International Monetary Fund and the World Bank. Deputy Foreign Minister Vladimir Petrovsky told reporters at the United Nations the USSR would move gradually to join these organizations. The United States has objected to Soviet membership in the IMF and World Bank in recent years, arguing the Soviet political and economic system is not compatible with them (*AP*, September 20). Poland, Hungary, Romania, and China are already members.

Soviet Foreign Minister Eduard Shevardnadze arrived in the United States for talks with US leaders. Speaking at an impromptu press conference upon his arrival in Washington, Shevardnadze called for an acceleration of progress in improving superpower relations. Before going to the United States, Shevardnadze spoke on Soviet television. He disclosed that he would deliver a letter to US President George Bush from Mikhail Gorbachev. Shevardnadze said "the letter was a major political document" that sets out Soviet positions on the entire complex of arms control issues (_Reuters, DPA_, September 21). On September 21, Shevardnadze held talks with Bush. Shevardnadze told reporters afterwards that the talks took place in a very good atmosphere and were frank. Shevardnadze said the USSR and the United States both agreed that a summit meeting between Bush and Gorbachev was necessary (_Reuters_, September 21). It was reported that Bush and Shevardnadze also briefly discussed the current reforms in Poland and Hungary. The same day, Shevardnadze, together with US Secretary of State James Baker, flew to the Western state of Wyoming (_Pravda_, September 22).

On September 22, it was announced that on their way from Washington to Wyoming Shevardnadze and Baker discussed nationalities problems in the USSR. One of the main issues for discussion between the two foreign ministers in Wyoming is arms control. Shevardnadze brought with him a package of new proposals on reducing conventional armed forces. In his turn, Bush revived a US proposal that would allow each country to send unarmed surveillance flights over the territory of the other. On September 21, the Soviet Union officially welcomed this proposal (Western agencies, September 21 and 22; _Pravda_, September 23).

On September 23, Baker and Shevardnadze continued their talks in Wyoming. During the first day of talks, Moscow dropped a key demand that a strategic arms accord be linked to a treaty on space-based weapons (Western agencies, September 23).

The talks also focused on human rights. It was reported that Baker had raised concerns about the banned Ukrainian Catholic Church. The Soviet side gave no definite answer on the matter. Nationality issues, especially the situation in the Baltic, were also discussed. Shevardnadze and Baker also reviewed the cases of political prisoners. From a list of fifty-four names presented by the United States last May, twelve prisoners

Shevardnadze in United States

were reported to have been released, another twenty have been freed pending trial, while the rest remain unresolved (*RFE/RL Special*, September 23).

It was also reported that Baker and Shevardnadze had initialed six agreements in the course of their talks. The agreements include a memorandum of understanding on the exchange of chemical weapons data, provisions for advance notice of major strategic exercises and for the trial inspection of nuclear weapons, and an agreement on visa-free travel for Alaskan and Siberian Yupik Eskimos. Talking to reporters, Shevardnadze said that the United States and the Soviet Union had altered their positions on strategic arms reduction somewhat and that an agreement to cut strategic weapons by 50 percent "now appears to be quite a realistic prospect." Shevardnadze announced that the Soviet Union had agreed to dismantle its Krasnoyarsk radar station, which the United States maintains violates the Antiballistic Missile Treaty of 1972 (Western agencies, September 23 and 24).

Baker was quoted as telling reporters that he had "a frank and thoughtful" exchange of views with Shevardnadze on Afghanistan and other regional issues. A joint statement that was issued at the conclusion of the Baker-Shevardnadze talks said the two sides differed in their approach to achieving a political settlement in Afghanistan based on national reconciliation. US and Soviet officials said the talks had paved the way for further progress on arms control and other issues. US National Security Adviser Brent Scowcroft said the shift in the Soviet position on space-based defenses was "a step forward" (*Reuters, UPI*, September 24; *Pravda*, September 25). Speaking in Moscow on September 25, Soviet Foreign Ministry spokesman Vadim Perfil'ev said Soviet-US dialogue had reached a new stage. He said the two sides had finally completed a period of "mutual adaptation" (*AP*, September 25; *Pravda*, September 26).

On September 24, Shevardnadze and Baker flew to New York to attend the United Nations General Assembly. Speaking at the General Assembly on September 25, President Bush proposed a sharp reduction in US chemical weapons stockpiles if the USSR makes cuts to a similar level. Radio Moscow praised Bush's proposal as "a very serious and timely idea." On September 26, Shevardnadze proposed before the United Nations that the USSR work with the United States to reduce or eliminate both sides' chemical weapons. Shevardnadze's call was welcomed by the United States (*Reuters, UPI*, September 26; *Pravda, Izvestia*, September 27).

TASS revealed that the Moscow City Party Committee had been ordered "to consider the Party responsibility" of the two investigators, Tel'man Gdlyan and Nikolai Ivanov, who raised the question of whether Politburo member Egor Ligachev was involved in bribe-taking. TASS said that, in a resolution adopted on September 20 at the CPSU Central Committee plenum, the Central Committee noted that the USSR Public Prosecutor had found no basis for allegations that Ligachev may have taken bribes. The plenum told the Moscow City Party Committee to consider Gdlyan's and Ivanov's responsibility in the light of the public prosecutor's findings (*Pravda*, September 22).

Party Plenum on Controversy over Ligachev Allegations

The new Soviet ambassador to the European Community, Vladimir Shemyatenkov, said restructuring in the USSR is not going smoothly. He spoke at a seminar in Brussels. He said the USSR is seeking economic cooperation with industrialized countries in the form of joint ventures and training and in the financial services sector. He said the USSR is looking for ways to balance market efficiency with social priorities (*RFE/RL Special*, September 21).

New Soviet Ambassador to EC Speaks on Changes in USSR

Soviet Lieutenant General Frants Markovsky said the USSR has not sent any new tanks to East Germany, Hungary, Poland, or Czechoslovakia this year. Markovsky, deputy chief of the Main Administration of the Soviet Armed Forces General Staff, was interviewed by TASS. TASS said Markovsky rejected a statement by the NATO commander in chief that the USSR had removed some of its tanks in Central Europe and deployed new ones.

Soviet General Says No New Tanks Sent to Central Europe

The USSR Supreme Soviet Committee on *Glasnost'* and People's Rights, Suggestions, and Complaints criticized recent Soviet press stories that it said "insulted the honor and dignity of USSR people's deputies." TASS said the criticism came in a news release by the committee. It said the committee plans to investigate the circumstances under which some recent press articles were published. The committee specifically mentioned *Pravda*'s reprinting of an article from *la Repubblica* on Boris El'tsin. TASS quoted the committee as saying the *Pravda* action was tendentious and was "done in the manner of the gutter press." The committee also criticized a letter printed by *Sovetskaya Rossiya* that accused one of its members, Zita Slicite, of making anti-Soviet remarks at an unauthorized rally. Slicite denied even attending the rally.

Supreme Soviet Committee Denounces Press Articles on Deputies

511

**Kirgiz-Tajik Problems
Continue in Isfara Valley**

Soviet television reported that a dispute between people living on the border between Kirgizia and Tajikistan had not been resolved. The report quoted a local Tajik Party official as saying the USSR Supreme Soviet had been asked to intervene because the subject of the dispute— land and water rights—"is not worth the life of even one person." One person was killed and eighteen others injured in clashes between Tajiks and Kirgiz along the border in the Isfara River valley three months ago. The report said a commission subsequently set up by the Kirgiz and Tajik governments had failed to produce an agreement.

Friday, September 22 _____

**USSR Says It Did Not Approve
Hungary's Decision on
Refugees**

Soviet and Hungarian officials both said Moscow did not know about or approve in advance Hungary's decision to let East Germans go to the West. The Soviet Foreign Ministry denied US press reports that Moscow had known about Hungary's plan and had not objected. The ministry said the reports could mislead the world public. The Soviet statement was later supported by Hungarian parliamentary speaker Matyas Szuros (*Radio Budapest*, September 22).

**Police Detain Jewish
Refusedniks During
Demonstration**

Moscow police detained a group of Jewish refusedniks who demonstrated near the Kremlin to mark Shevardnadze's visit to the United States. One of the organizers of the demonstration, Aleksandr Rapoport, was sentenced to five days in jail (*AP*, September 22).

**Soviet Publication Reports
Foreign Debt**

Pravitel'stvennyi vestnik published the Soviet Union's foreign debt figure as it stood at the beginning of this year. TASS said the journal reported that the debt at that time totaled 33,600 million rubles, including 28,100 million rubles in hard currencies (*TASS*, September 22).

**Lithuanian Party Still Insists
on Independence**

The Lithuanian Communist Party reiterated its intention to become independent from the CPSU. TASS said the Lithuanian Party published a draft program on the issue as part of preparations for an extraordinary congress to be held at the end of the year. Vilnius newspapers printed the draft in Lithuanian, Polish, and Russian. TASS quoted the draft as saying that "in order to become a political force in the building of an independent Lithuanian state based on the rule of law, the Communist Party of Lithuania itself must become independent." The Lithuanian Party's intention conflicts with Mikhail Gorbachev's rejection of Party federalism. Gorbachev repeated his objections at this week's CPSU Central Committee plenum.

Supreme Soviet of Kazakhstan Adopts Reforms

The Supreme Soviet of Kazakhstan adopted a set of political reforms, including a new language law and changes in the future make-up of the Supreme Soviet. Kazakh was made the republic's official language, but Russian will be the language of interethnic communication and will be widely used alongside Kazakh. Another reform will make the Kazakh Supreme Soviet a full-time legislature. The number of deputies will be cut, and more than one candidate will be nominated to run for each seat (*TASS*, September 22, *Pravda*, September 23).

On September 23, *Izvestia* carried an article saying that the draft law on language in Kazakhstan had been considerably watered down by the time it was adopted. The revised draft submitted to the Kazakh Supreme Soviet stated that officials will be obliged to provide facilities for the public to communicate in either language by 1995 and that only by the year 2000 will they be required to know both Kazakh and Russian. Even this, however, provoked heated arguments, and it was only after the text was further amended that the law was adopted by a majority of votes. Evidently all deadlines were removed from the law, which now stipulates only that officials are to master Kazakh and Russian when the necessary conditions for learning them have been created. This is probably a realistic approach, given the large areas of the republic that are predominantly Russian-speaking and the almost total lack of facilities for non-Kazakhs to learn Kazakh, but it is, of course, an invitation to inaction.

USSR Aims to Cut Budget Deficit by Half Next Year

Vladimir Durasov, first deputy chairman of Gosplan, said the USSR intends to cut its budget deficit by 50 percent next year. He said extraordinary measures are needed to achieve this goal, such as a military spending cut and an increase in turnover taxes. Durasov said next year's draft economic plan provides for a reduction of 22 percent in capital investment in the production sphere. Agriculture and light industry, however, will not be affected. He said the draft provides for a threefold increase in expenditure to raise the standard of living of the population. TASS said Durasov made these comments in the journal *Pravitel'stvennyi vestnik*.

Saturday, September 23 ───────────────────────────────

Thatcher in Moscow

British Prime Minister Margaret Thatcher held talks with Mikhail Gorbachev in Moscow. Reuters quoted British officials as saying that there was no fixed agenda for the talks but that they covered internal Soviet developments, bilateral relations and trade, and human rights. The officials said considerable attention was also paid to developments in Eastern Europe, particularly in Hungary and Poland. Thatcher gave an interview to Soviet television in which she voiced strong backing for Gorbachev's reform program and praised the Soviet leader's vision, courage, and boldness. She urged the Soviet people to assist him in his economic reforms. Talking to reporters before leaving Moscow for London, Thatcher expressed optimism about Gorbachev's policies (*TASS, AP, Reuters*, September 23; *Pravda*, September 24).

Party Platform on Nationalities Published

The CPSU published its platform on nationalities policy, which was adopted on September 20 during the CPSU Central Committee plenum. The platform said the Party's major policy goal was to form better relations among ethnic groups. The document aims to broaden rights for Autonomous republics and boost the legal status of Autonomous raions and krais (*Pravda*, September 23).

Lithuanian Supreme Soviet Approves Economic Self-Management Plan

TASS said the Lithuanian Supreme Soviet had approved a plan for economic self-management. The project in its original form, due to take effect in January, provides for Lithuania to take over all enterprises on its territory, including those now controlled by Moscow. The CPSU Central Committee plenum on nationality issues criticized the provision. Gosplan chief Yurii Maslyukov called for the implementation of the plan in stages. He also said key industries should remain under Moscow's supervision for the present. The Lithuanian Supreme Soviet also adopted a resolution approving the findings of a republican parliamentary commission that condemned the incorporation of the republic into the USSR. (For the text of the findings, see the journal of the Lithuanian Communist Party Central Committee *Sobytiya i vremya*, No. 17.) On September 29, the Lithuanian Supreme Soviet voted to allow Soviet soldiers based in Lithuania to vote in local elections. Lithuanian activists have made longstanding demands that only Lithuanian citizens be allowed to vote in Lithuania (*RFE Lithuanian Service, DPA*, September 29).

514

Kirgizia's Supreme Soviet adopted a language law and a number of other bills. The law makes Kirgiz the official language of the republic and Russian the language of interethnic communication. TASS said the Supreme Soviet also adopted a law on elections of deputies to republican and local soviets and introduced amendments to the Kirgiz Constitution (*Pravda*, September 24).

Kirgiz Supreme Soviet Adopts Language Law

USSR Supreme Soviet deputy Boris El'tsin said Mikhail Gorbachev had shown greater resolve and self-confidence in last week's shake-up in the Party leadership. (Several conservative Politburo members were forced to retire at the CPSU Central Committee plenum.) El'tsin told Radio Moscow he hoped Gorbachev would be firm in the future, "passing from half-measures to strong and revolutionary actions." El'tsin also talked about his recent trip to the United States. He stressed the need for joint projects rather than direct aid to help speed up the Soviet reform process.

El'tsin Interviewed by Radio Moscow

On September 24, El'tsin delivered a speech in the town of Zelenograd near Moscow, where a demonstration took place in protest against an article in *Pravda* denouncing him. El'tsin told the crowd of 20,000 people about the wide variety of consumer goods he saw during his trip to the United States. AP quoted him as saying that at least 100 million Soviet citizens must pass through "the school of American supermarkets" to understand what they are missing and therefore change their own society. On September 25, Soviet television reported that El'tsin had delivered one million disposable syringes that he bought while in the United States as a contribution to combating AIDS in the Soviet Union.

Mintimer Shaimiev was named Party first secretary of the Tatar ASSR. Shaimiev replaces Gumer Usmanov, who has been elected a secretary to the CPSU Central Committee. TASS said Shaimiev had been elected at a plenum of the Tatar Party Committee. Shaimiev had been chairman of the Council of Ministers of the Tatar ASSR.

Tatar Party First Secretary Replaced

Ogonek (No. 38) carried an article by its correspondent Georgii Rozhkov, who presented what amounts to the strongest support of the banned Ukrainian Catholic Church yet to appear in the Soviet central press. Rozhkov said the ban on the Church violates the provision of the Soviet Constitution on freedom of conscience (Article 50). He noted with disapproval that Ukrainian Party officials,

***Ogonek* Supports Ukrainian Catholic Church**

as well as Orthodox Metropolitan of Kiev and Galicia Filaret, oppose the legalization of the Church. For the first time in the Soviet press, Rozhkov revealed details about the Church Synod held in Lvov in 1946 that merged the Ukrainian Catholic Church with the Russian Orthodox Church. Rozhkov insisted that the Synod was held in a way that violated Church canons. Citing documents, he showed that it was the Council of People's Commissars together with the NKVD that were mainly responsible for the Lvov Synod. He rejected as false official Soviet assertions that the incorporation of the Ukrainian Catholic Church into the Russian Orthodox Church was an expression of the will of Ukrainian Catholics. Finally, Rozhkov gave strong support to the Ukrainian Catholics' struggle for the legalization of their Church. See also *Moscow News* (No. 39), which reported that Ukrainian Catholics in Lvov had appealed to Gorbachev to legalize their Church.

Korotich to Publish Independent Magazine

Using the publishing resources at his disposal, *Ogonek* editor Vitalii Korotich is launching an independent magazine in Kharkov, the city he represents in the Congress of People's Deputies. The newspaper will be called *Kharkivs'ki profspilky* (Kharkov Trade Unions) and will initially appear once every two weeks. It will serve as a forum for residents to express their views to the local leadership. He told Radio Kiev-3 (2100, September 23) that he will take responsibility for compiling the material to ensure the magazine's independence from the Kharkov authorities.

Sunday, September 24

Popular Front Holds Demonstration in Tashkent

The Uzbek Popular Front held a demonstration in Tashkent. An Uzbek journalist told Radio Liberty by telephone that thousands of people took part. The demonstration was called to press for Uzbek to be made both the state language of Uzbekistan and the language for communication between national groups in the republic. It also called for the popular front to be officially recognized and a state commission to study the disturbances in Fergana in June.

Monday, September 25

Supreme Soviet Back in Session

The USSR Supreme Soviet began its fall session with a long agenda that included many economic issues. Mikhail

Gorbachev, who presided at the opening meeting, delivered a speech in which he said that the situation in the USSR had worsened since the deputies last met two months ago. Radio Moscow quoted the Soviet leader as saying supplies of consumer goods had worsened since July, that ethnic tensions were running high, and that the country's financial situation was in need of improvement (*Izvestia*, September 25).

The same day, plans for dealing with the USSR's economic difficulties were presented to the session. The deputies received the draft plan for next year's social and economic development and a draft of next year's state budget. USSR Minister of Finance Valentin Pavlov outlined the budget proposals for 1990. Adjectives used to describe the projected measures for next year included "emergency," "extraordinary," and "crisis" (*Izvestia*, September 27). In his introduction to the draft plan for 1990, First Deputy Prime Minister Lev Voronin portrayed the situation thus: "The dynamism of the economy in the current year has, in many of the most important directions, decreased month by month; social tension has increased; and the balance of the national economy has weakened" (*Pravda*, September 26). The meeting also heard comments on the USSR's military expenditure. Pavlov told the deputies that the USSR will cut its military expenditure to 70.9 billion rubles in 1990, which is significantly lower than the 77.3 billion rubles budgeted for 1989 (*TASS*, September 25; *Izvestia*, September 26).

On September 26, the USSR Supreme Soviet continued discussion of the draft economic plan and budget for 1990. One of the main themes of the discussion was the problem of cooperatives. Deputy Prime Minister Leonid Abalkin presented a draft program for amendments to the Law on Cooperatives, which had been approved by the Supreme Soviet in May and took effect in July. The impetus for the amendments is the large and growing body of negative public opinion concerning cooperatives. Abalkin outlined the three main points of his program, which will be published in the central press: (1) to firmly establish that the cooperative movement is a long-term program and not a temporary campaign; (2) to create equal conditions for cooperatives and state enterprises; and (3) to delegate more authority for dealing with the cooperative movement's affairs to local bodies. Another part of the program is the regulation of members' incomes. Abalkin was showered with questions, and there was a heated debate over his draft program, but it was finally approved on first reading and sent to a committee for further discussion and review (*Izvestia*, September 27).

517

Armenian Supreme Soviet Investigates 1921 Treaty

The Armenian Supreme Soviet has set up a committee to investigate the legality of the Russian-Turkish friendship treaty of March, 1921, that made the Nakhichevan Autonomous Republic a part of Azerbaijan, although it is separated from Azerbaijan by Armenia. Radio Erevan said the investigative committee was appointed by the Armenian Supreme Soviet two days ago. It said committee members include historians, Armenian Supreme Soviet deputies, and members of the USSR Congress of People's Deputies (*Radio Erevan*, September 24).

Tuesday, September 26

Sakharov Says Soviet Leadership Withdrawing from *Perestroika*

Academician Andrei Sakharov said in an interview with the French daily *Le Progres* that the Soviet leadership has started retreating from *perestroika*, especially on nationality issues. Sakharov said the Soviet leadership had shown itself extremely irresolute on the Nagorno-Karabakh issue. Sakharov was quoted as putting much of the blame for the outbreak of national passions in the USSR on the central government, which, he said, had been unable to take a precise and clear stand. He said Gorbachev's speech at the CPSU Central Committee plenum on nationalities issues amounted to a step backwards. He said the speech, as well as the CPSU platform on nationalities policy, failed to accept the principles of equality of peoples and of self-determination. In an interview with the French newspaper *Le Monde* (September 29), Sakharov also complained that Gorbachev's policy was indecisive.

Wednesday, September 27

Ministers Reprimanded for Shortages of Consumer Goods

The CPSU reprimanded a number of government officials for failing to provide Soviet consumers with basic goods, such as soap and toothpaste. *Pravda* quoted a report by the Party Control Committee as saying it had found that only thirty-three items on a list of 276 consumer goods could be found in sufficient supply in Soviet stores. The committee reprimanded First Deputy Prime Minister Vladimir Gusev for not taking measures to provide the goods. It said First Deputy Chairman of the Council of Ministers Bureau for Social Development Vladimir Lakhtin was reprimanded for failing to increase deliveries of consumer items. *Pravda* said a number of other lower-ranking officials had also received official reprimands.

The chairman of the USSR Supreme Soviet Subcommittee on Humanitarian Affairs, Fedor Burlatsky, criticized progress on draft legislation on various human-rights issues. TASS quoted Burlatsky as saying that the adoption of a human-rights bill is being delayed. TASS also quoted him as saying the draft press law was "half-hearted." It did not elaborate on his remarks.

Burlatsky Dissatisfied with Human-Rights Progress in USSR

Radio Moscow reported that Anatolii Saunin, a people's deputy from the Donbass mining region, told Gorbachev during a recent meeting that, unless the Supreme Soviet addresses the miners' concerns by October 1, the miners will call another strike. Several Soviet television reports have stated recently that the miners were unhappy that the authorities were failing to honor the agreements reached when the miners ended their strike in July.

Miners Threaten Another Strike

Thursday, September 28

TASS reported that Mikhail Gorbachev traveled to Kiev to attend a plenary session of the Ukrainian Party Central Committee. At the plenum Vladimir Shcherbitsky, who lost his seat in the Politburo at the latest CPSU Central Committee plenum, retired as Party first secretary of Ukraine. TASS said he was replaced by Ukrainian Party second secretary Vladimir Ivashko. TASS said Ivashko was elected in a secret ballot, winning against Stanislav Gurenko, a Party secretary. The plenum was addressed by Gorbachev, who said the time had come when no Communist could afford to take a wait-and-see position or adopt a pessimistic and defeatist attitude. In his speech, Gorbachev stressed the need for dialogue even with Party opponents. He said the Party must remain the leading political force but must open itself to other groups in order to advance _perestroika_ (_TASS_, September 28). The plenum was also addressed by Ivashko, who said the Party must press ahead with reform, relying on popular support and participation (_Pravda_, September 29. The text of Gorbachev's speech was carried in _Pravda_, September 30).

On September 30, _Pravda_ carried interviews with Ivashko, Gorbachev, and Shcherbitsky on the situation in Ukraine. Ivashko promised to tackle the problems of housing and food shortages in his republic. In turn, Gorbachev praised Shcherbitsky's seventeen years of leadership. He also praised Ivashko's "working ability and principled positions."

Gorbachev Attends Ukrainian Party Plenum, Shcherbitsky Retires

519

Shakhnazarov Says Party Will Drop "Leading Role" Provision

Academician Georgii Shakhnazarov, who is an aide to Mikhail Gorbachev, was quoted as saying the CPSU will drop its claim to "the leading role" in society. Instead, Shakhnazarov said, the Party would consider itself "the political vanguard" because that is a more appropriate role in a situation in which the Party must win power through elections. Shakhnazarov was interviewed by the Tokyo daily *Yomiuri Shimbun*. Shakhnazarov said the Soviet Constitution would have to be changed to eliminate the "leading role" phrasing. Asked whether this meant opening the way to a multiparty system in the USSR, Shakhnazarov said it did.

USSR Proposes Summit on Conventional Arms

The Soviet Union has proposed a big East-West summit next year to sign a conventional arms agreement. The proposal was made in Vienna by the Soviet Union's chief delegate to the conventional forces talks, Oleg Grinevsky. He said "a strategy of acceleration" would be needed if the talks were to produce an agreement by next year (*Reuters*, *AP*, September 28).

USSR Offers to Host Israel-PLO Talks

The Soviet Union has offered to host peace talks between Israel and the PLO. Eduard Shevardnadze made the offer in New York at a meeting with Israeli Foreign Minister Moshe Arens. There was no immediate response from Israel. In the past, Israel has always refused to talk to the PLO (*AP*, September 28).

Demonstration in Moscow on Nazi-Soviet Treaty Anniversary

About 100 Lithuanians, Latvians, and Estonians gathered in Moscow to commemorate the fiftieth anniversary of the second (border and friendship) treaty between the USSR and Nazi Germany. The treaty included a secret protocol that assigned Lithuania to the USSR's sphere of interest (*RFE Lithuanian Service*, September 28). On September 28, thousands of people demonstrated in Vilnius to protest against the treaty (*Radio Vilnius*, in English, 2400, September 28).

Post-Chernobyl' Decontamination Criticized

A Soviet government commission criticized shortcomings in decontaminating areas affected by the Chernobyl' nuclear accident more than three years ago. TASS quoted the commission that is reviewing progress on decontamination work as saying that there is a shortage of physicians in the affected region and that there have been interruptions in supplies of food and industrial goods. The commission also said the level of residents' exposure to radiation in the region in the period 1986–88 had not exceeded permissible levels. See RL 198/89, RL 238/89, and RL 466/89.

The late Soviet Party leader Leonid Brezhnev was stripped of the "Order of Victory" awarded to him in 1978. TASS said the decoration was rescinded by the Presidium of the USSR Supreme Soviet in an order signed by Gorbachev a week ago. The report said the award was canceled because it had been conferred on Brezhnev illegally. The Order of Victory is the Soviet Union's highest award for outstanding service in wartime; Brezhnev's service during World War II did not merit such a decoration.

Brezhnev Loses His "Order of Victory"

The Soviet Union opened its Plesetsk space center to foreign journalists for the first time and revealed that an accident there nine years ago had killed fifty workers. Lieutenant General Ivan Oliinyk reported the accident to reporters invited to the space center, which is located some 800 kilometers north of Moscow. He said that in March, 1980, the workers were killed by an explosion that occurred while a rocket was being fueled. Oleinik also said nine workers died in another fueling explosion at Plesetsk in June, 1973.

USSR Opens Space Center to Foreign Journalists

The television news program "Vremya" featured a report on a meeting of the USSR Supreme Soviet's Commission on Privileges. (Members of the commission include its chairman Evgenii Primakov, Gavriil Popov, Academician Vitalii Ginzburg, and newly elected Central Committee Secretary Yurii Manaenkov.) The commission discussed unjust and undeserved privileges, such as those relating to pensions, and also raised the question of transferring the financing of restricted-access hospitals and other health facilities from the Ministry of Health to the institutions that use them. (Presumably, this means that a hospital used exclusively by members of the Politburo would have to be financed with Party funds.) The commission also decided to retain the present health service "until a system of individual health insurance is introduced." *Moscow News* (No. 39) carried an article criticizing Party officials for attempting to retain their privileges. The newspaper quoted a member of the Supreme Soviet Commission on Priviliges, Yurii Tsavro, as complaining that, while Party officials have luxurious

Congressional Commission on Privileges Proposes Changes in Health System

sanitariums where they spend their vacations, Soviet children with serious diseases are treated in cramped conditions with inadequate care.

Friday, September 29 ————————————————————

Kremlin Criticized over Report on Nazi-Soviet Pact

Members of the commission of the Congress of People's Deputies set up to evaluate the Molotov-Ribbentrop Pact of 1939 criticized the Party leadership for delaying publication of the commission's findings. Deputies told a news conference in Moscow that the commission had concluded its work in July by denouncing the secret protocols to the Molotov-Ribbentrop Pact and the Border and Friendship Treaty that put Estonia, Latvia, and Lithuania in the Soviet sphere of influence. (The Estonian newspaper *Noorte Haal* carried the text of the findings of the commission on August 22.)

Speaking at a press conference, members of the commission complained that Politburo member Aleksandr Yakovlev, who chairs the commission, had prevented final approval of the findings and their publication in the central press. A member of the commission, historian Yurii Afanas'ev, condemned Yakovlev for saying in an interview in *Pravda* last month that the incorporation of the Baltic States into the USSR was not the result of the secret protocols but of parliamentary elections in the Baltic countries in which the Communists won. Afanas'ev called Yakovlev's statement "pure disinformation." Members of the commission said, however, that they still respected Yakovlev as the most liberal member of the Politburo. A commission member from Estonia, Igor Grazin, suggested that, in rejecting the findings of the commission, Yakovlev had acted "under pressure" from the Party apparatus (*Reuters*, September 29; *The Washington Post*, September 30).

Moscow News (No. 39) carried diplomatic documents on relations between the USSR and Nazi Germany in the period between August 23, 1939 (the signing of the nonaggression pact), and September 28, 1939 (the signing of the Border and Friendship Treaty.) These documents are known in the West, but this is the first time they have been published in the USSR.

Roy Medvedev on Gdlyan-Ivanov Case

Supreme Soviet deputy and historian Roy Medvedev told *Izvestia* that it took the intervention of Mikhail Gorbachev to convince Party officials to provide documents concerning the case of investigators Tel'man Gdlyan and Nikolai Ivanov. On the other hand, Medvedev said, the investigative commission of the Congress of People's Deputies had no trouble obtaining documents from the KGB on the matter. (Medvedev is chairman of the Congress of People's Deputies commission on the Gdlyan-Ivanov affair.)

Radio Moscow-2 announced that a plenum of the Board of the Union of Soviet Composers had decided to dissolve the union and replace it with a federated association of the country's composers' organizations, each of which will act in accordance with its own statutes. The Union of Soviet Composers and its chairman Tikhon Khrennikov (who has headed the union since it was created) have been subject to intense criticism in the Soviet media since the advent of *glasnost'*.

Composers' Union Reported Dissolved

At a session of the USSR Supreme Soviet Commission for Prices, Labor, and Social Policy, First Deputy Chairman of Gosplan Stepan Sitaryan stated that there are currently 1.2 million unemployed in the USSR (*Radio Moscow-1*, 1300, September 29). This figure is far below recent estimates by Soviet and Western economists. A careful assessment in *Soviet Studies* of July, 1989, for instance, puts the figure for "open unemployment" (i.e., frictional, regional, and localized) at 5.6 million, while the addition of the categories of concealed and indirect unemployment would bring the probable total to some 8.4 million, equivalent to 6.2 percent of the working population.

New Official Estimate of Unemployment

A US-Soviet panel met in California to discuss joint actions against terrorism. The actions were reported to call for US and Soviet intelligence to trade information about terrorists and to help one another investigate aircraft bombings and hostage-taking, restrict terrorists' movements, and to prevent them from acquiring weapons of mass destruction (*AP*, September 29).

US and Soviet Officials Discuss Terrorism

Krasnaya zvezda revealed that an atomic bomb was exploded as part of a Soviet military exercise in the Southern Urals in 1954. The newspaper said the purpose of the exercise was to find out how well troops could negotiate contaminated terrain. The newspaper said the soldiers "fulfilled their assigned tasks completely." It did not say whether there were any casualties.

USSR Reveals Atomic Bomb Was Exploded During Exercises in 1954

Saturday, September 30 ————————————————————————————

March in Kazan against Nuclear Power Plant

Radio Moscow said a protest against the construction of the Tatar nuclear power plant was staged in Kazan, the capital of the Tatar ASSR. The radio said construction of the plant had continued despite "authoritative" findings that the siting of the plant was "extremely unfortunate."

Thousands March through Minsk in Chernobyl' Protest

Reuters reported that thousands of people marched through Minsk to protest against the way the aftermath of the Chernobyl' nuclear disaster was handled. The dispatch said the police did not interfere with the marchers, who were defying a ban by local authorities. It also said that speakers addressing the rally demanded more measures be taken to clean up after the disaster and that they called for the evacuation of half a million people from contaminated zones. The march was organized by the Belorussian Popular Front. (On July 24, *Pravda* published an article on the disastrous effect the Chernobyl' accident had on Belorussia and the inadequate cleanup operation.) A book published by Politizdat praised the Soviet handling of the disaster and claimed that the increase in radiation resulting from the accident poses no threat to people's health. (For a review of the book, see *Sovetskaya molodezh'*, September 22).

Vlasov Discusses Elimination of Soviet Debt to Yugoslavia

RSFSR Prime Minister Aleksandr Vlasov has proposed ways to eliminate the Soviet debt to Yugoslavia, which amounts to some 2 billion dollars. Radio Moscow said Vlasov was on a five-day trip to the Yugoslav republics of Serbia and Montenegro. In Serbia, Vlasov proposed Soviet participation in the new construction or rebuilding of pipelines. In Montenegro, he discussed the possibility of joint ventures in construction, the aluminum industry, and shipbuilding (*Radio Moscow-1*, 1900, September 30).

Minister Claims Main Issues Raised by Coal Miners Resolved

USSR Minister of the Coal Industry Mikhail Shchadov said the main issues that led to strikes by coal miners this summer had been resolved. Shchadov announced on Moscow television that miners would receive improved benefits, including more pay for night- and evening-shift work, bigger pensions, and more housing (*TASS*, October 1). Miners have complained that an accord reached to settle their strike this summer has not been fully implemented.

The Month of October

Soviet Media Coverage of East German Decision on Refugees

Initial Soviet media coverage of the GDR's decision to let East German citizens travel to West Germany from Bonn's embassies in Prague and Warsaw through East German territory was very limited. The decision was reported only by the television news program "Vremya" and that without comment. The "Vremya" report quoted an East German representative as saying, "with this humane act, the East German authorities hope that the West German government will draw conclusions for normal operation of its embassies in accordance with international rules." On October 1, a spokesman for the West German Foreign Ministry, Jürgen Chrobog, revealed in an interview with *The Washington Post* that East Germany had agreed to let East German refugees in Prague go to the West after Soviet Foreign Minister Eduard Shevardnadze intervened. On October 2, the head of the CPSU Central Committee's International Relations Department, Valentin Falin, commented on the situation in an interview in the GDR's newspaper *Die Welt* (October 2). In the interview, Falin said East Germany had made the right decision in letting the East German refugees go to the West. On September 3, however, *Pravda* said West Germany's action in admitting East German refugees to its Warsaw and Prague embassies threatened European stability. The newspaper complained that the West German embassies in Prague and Warsaw had taken a course of action "that has nothing to do with normal diplomatic activity."

On October 19, Foreign Ministry spokesman Gennadii Gerasimov said the exodus of refugees from East Germany "unsettled us" in the Soviet Union. He said he hoped the new East German leadership would be able to cope with the exodus and with other problems. (*Radio Berlin*, October 19).

El'tsin Supporters Hold Rally

Some 10,000 supporters of Boris El'tsin rallied in Moscow. El'tsin did not appear at the rally, but he did address the crowd in a prerecorded message played over loudspeakers. The rally ended at about the same time that Soviet television started broadcasting an hour-long program

525

about El'tsin's recent trip to the United States. Most of the film came from US news programs (*Reuters, UPI*, October 1). The same day, Radio Moscow-2 broadcast an interview with El'tsin, in which he said *perestroika* must be given new impetus by the present session of the USSR Supreme Soviet.

Historian Says 9 Million Died in Famine

Soviet historian Stalinislav Kulchitsky was quoted by *Stroitel'naya gazeta* as saying over 9 million people had died during the famine that struck Ukraine and other areas of the Soviet Union in 1933. The daily quoted him as saying the famine was caused by Stalin's policies in agriculture. Kulchitsky's figure is the highest given in the Soviet press for the number of victims of the 1933 famine. Earlier this year, Roy Medvedev estimated that between 6 and 7 million people had died as a result of the famine. Academician Vladimir Tikhonov of VASKhNIL has said that about 10 million people were "repressed" during Stalin's collectivization.

Baltic Deputies Form Parliamentary Group

More than thirty Baltic deputies from the Congress of People's Deputies have formally founded an organization called "The Baltic Parliamentary Group." Their first meeting was in Riga on September 30. In its founding declaration, the group said it would work to reestablish the sovereignty of the Soviet Union's constituent republics and to promote a market economy. The group said it would defend national rights and is ready to work with groups within the Congress of People's Deputies that support similar principles (*RFE Latvian Service*, October 1).

Actions in Support of Legalization of Ukrainian Catholic Church

Several thousand people were reported to have rallied in the Western Ukrainian city of Ivano-Frankovsk to back appeals for the legalization of the Ukrainian Catholic Church. In an interview with RFE/RL, Ivan Hel, one of the organizers of the rally, said the demonstrators took part in an open-air mass and other religious services in the city center outside a church that has for many years been officially closed to worshipers. Speakers, who Hel said included two bishops, told the rally that the campaign for the legalization of the Church would go on. Hel said most of those who gathered in the city center then marched to another part of the city where a commemorative service was held for victims of Stalinist crimes (*RL Ukrainian Service*, October 1).

On October 1, *Moscow News* (No. 40) published an interview with Rostislav Bratun, a people's deputy from Lvov, in which he praised the Ukrainian Catholic Church for its role in preserving Ukrainian national traditions. Bratun also called on the authorities to discuss the legalization of the Ukrainian Autocephalous Orthodox Church.

On October 5, Pope John Paul II called on the Soviet Union to legalize the long-banned Ukrainian Catholic Church without delay. He was addressing Ukrainian Catholic bishops living outside the Ukraine, who were meeting in Rome (*AP, UPI*, October 5).

Moldavian Party Proposes Law on Rights of Minorities

The Moldavian Communist Party has proposed a draft law to guarantee the rights of minorities in Moldavia. TASS said a Party plenum on September 30 agreed to submit the new draft to the Moldavian Supreme Soviet and present the proposal for republic-wide discussion. TASS said the draft law would also endorse the idea of limited autonomy for the Gagauz minority. TASS said the plenum also supported a proposal to the republic's Supreme Soviet to make Russian the language of interethnic communication in Moldavia (*Pravda*, October 4).

_____ *Monday, October 2*

Economic Blockade of Nagorno-Karabakh

On October 2, the economic blockade of Nagorno-Karabakh organized by Azerbaijan was still causing shortages of food, fuel, and medical supplies. Deputy Head of the North Caucasus Railroad Network Vladimir Tutikov told Radio Moscow that the Azerbaijani Popular Front was preventing trains carrying food and fuel from leaving Azerbaijan for Armenia and Georgia. The day before, Radio Moscow quoted officials in Nagorno-Karabakh as saying the only supplies reaching the region were by air shipment.

In an interview with *Argumenty i fakty* (No. 39), an official in Nagorno-Karabakh, Valerii Sidorov, said there was a danger that the oblast would become another Lebanon. On October 3, Soviet First Deputy Foreign Minister Vasilii Trushin said the death toll from ethnic strife in Transcaucasia had reached 117 since February, 1988.

On October 5, AFP quoted *Moscow News* (No. 41) as saying unauthorized armed camps had been set up in the hills of Nagorno-Karabakh. The weekly said the camps had been spotted from the air by pilots flying supplies into

Nagorno-Karabakh. *Moscow News* said the camps held armed men who were undergoing military training. Radio Moscow reported that a man had been shot dead in the Shusha district of Nagorno-Karabakh.

On October 6, the Azerbaijani Popular Front announced the end of its rail blockade of Armenia in return for concessions that included lifting the curfew in Baku (*RL Azerbaijani Service*, October 6). TASS said that, as of 1800 on October 6, hundreds of rail cars loaded with cargo had passed in both directions between the republics, but the agency said the situation in the region remained tense, with the railroads still congested because of the backlog caused by the blockade.

On October 7, Radio Moscow reported that a river bridge had been blown up on the Agdam-Shusha highway in Nagorno-Karabakh. The same day, AFP and Reuters quoted the Armenian media as saying the railroad blockade of Armenia and Nagorno-Karabakh organized by the Azerbaijani Popular Front was not over. Radio Erevan said trains were still being attacked by supporters of the Azerbaijani Popular Front. *Izvestia* reported on October 9 that, as of the previous day, food and construction materials, but not fuel, were reaching Armenia by rail. Meanwhile, Nagorno-Karabakh remained virtually under a state of siege, with food and medical supplies being airlifted in by military aircraft (*TASS*, October 9).

On October 8, TASS reported that a virtual state of civil war between Azerbaijanis and Armenians had developed in and around Nagorno-Karabakh. On October 8, the official Women's Council of Armenia appealed to Gorbachev for help in facing the oncoming winter. Serious problems with gas and electricity supplies are expected in Armenia. The council also sent a telegram to Ryzhkov, asking why he was paying so little attention to the Azerbaijani blockade of Armenia (*Radio Erevan*, October 8).

On October 10, Radio Moscow said that the previous twenty-four hours had been "really stormy" in Nagorno-Karabakh. Radio Moscow said that there had been explosions and skirmishes and that cars had been stoned. It quoted Colonel Vladimir Skorobogatov as saying that a few trains had arrived early that day but that these carried only rotten goods or construction materials. The Supreme Soviet adopted a resolution that instructed the authorities in Armenia and Azerbaijan to take all necessary measures to restore the situation in the Transcaucasus to normal (*TASS*, October 10).

On October 11, the military commander in Nagorno-Karabakh, Major General Vladislav Safonov, said delaying a political solution for the area would bring the region to the brink of fratricidal war. In the same report, Radio Moscow said that murders and explosions were continuing in Nagorno-Karabakh and that road and rail shipments were being fired on. Reuters and AFP quoted a Soviet official as saying that one person had been killed and between five and twelve others hurt on October 10 in a clash between soldiers and civilians in Stepanakert. The official was reported to have said the clash began when civilians attacked troops with stones and hunting rifles. He said the soldiers fired in self-defense. Members of the Karabakh Committee, however, said the attack on the civilians was unprovoked. (A report on the clashes carried by *Komsomol'skaya pravda* on October 12 said two people had been killed.) TASS quoted Deputy Minister of Internal Affairs Stasis Lisauskas as saying there had been an attempt to cause an explosion on the Agdam-Fizuli highway, which runs through Nagorno-Karabakh. He also said that three MVD doctors had been taken hostage and that security forces had had to intervene to free them. Armenians were reported to have held a mass rally in Stepanakert on October 11, at which calls were made for people to organize their own self-defense groups. AFP said the rally was sponsored by the Karabakh Committee. In its news program "Vremya," Soviet television reported that the restoration of rail traffic between Azerbaijan and Nagorno-Karabakh did not mean safety for railroad workers. Two incidents were reported: one in which a freight train locomotive was fired on at the station in Karchivan and another in which an explosive device was discovered near railroad tracks in Nagorno-Karabakh. The report said trains from Azerbaijan were arriving without fuel or foodstuffs.

On October 12, USSR Minister of Railways Nikolai Konarev said Azerbaijani "nationalists" had extended the rail blockade to Georgia. Radio Moscow quoted Konarev as saying the "extremists" had asked Georgia's National Front to stop freight trains destined for Armenia. The front refused; the Azerbaijanis then blocked the flow of food and oil to Georgia itself. Konarev said the situation there was deteriorating. (On October 13, leaders of the Azerbaijani Popular Front denied that they had organized a blockade of Georgia [*RL Azerbaijani Service*, October 13].) The same day, leaders of the Armenian community in the United States called on the USSR to take immediate steps to end the blockade of Armenia and Nagorno-Karabakh by Azerbaijan (*RFE/RL Special*, October 12). On October 13, Radio Moscow quoted the Soviet Ministry of Internal Affairs as saying that in the past twenty-four hours five people had been killed and twelve injured.

On October 14, Radio Liberty's Azerbaijani Service quoted members of the Azerbaijani Popular Front as saying it had set October 24 as a deadline for the Soviet authorities to restore Azerbaijani control over Nagorno-Karabakh. The front said, if the issue was not settled by then, a rail blockade of Armenia and Nagorno-Karabakh would be reimposed. On October 14, *Izvestia* reported that law-enforcement officials from Armenia and Azerbaijan had met to discuss ways of easing tension between the two republics.

On October 15, *Izvestia* quoted Konarev as saying train traffic was now moving in the Transcaucasus but would take time to return to normal. On October 17, Soviet officials were quoted by Radio Moscow as saying that Nagorno-Karabakh was still having supply problems. See RL 476/89.

Deputy Suggests Special Powers for Gorbachev on Transport

Supreme Soviet deputy Viktor Kolesnikov has proposed that Mikhail Gorbachev be given special powers to ensure smooth commercial transport throughout the USSR. Kolesnikov, a member of the Supreme Soviet's transport commission, said in an interview broadcast by Radio Moscow that rail transport is now disrupted and disorganized in many regions of the country. He proposed a draft law on liability for disruption of rail transport that would apply both to individuals and enterprises. He also proposed that offenses linked to the disruption of rail transport should be regarded as terrorist acts, as they are in aviation. The same day, Gorbachev called on the USSR Supreme Soviet to approve a plan under which the USSR ministries of internal affairs, defense, and rail transport would place railroads in Azerbaijan and Armenia under "a special regime" immediately (*TASS*, October 2).

Ryzhkov Says No Need for Private Ownership of Land

The USSR Supreme Soviet convened in joint session to hear a report on economic changes from Prime Minister Nikolai Ryzhkov. TASS said the report would detail new laws on private ownership, land and leasing, and a universal tax system. *Pravda* said the Soviet countryside would start feeding the country only when "a true proprietor returns to the land and farms." In his report at the session, Ryzhkov said that land would remain state property and that there was no need for private ownership of land in the USSR. Ryzhkov said there should be changes in the way land is used but that improvements should not repudiate the principle of state ownership of the land (*Radio Moscow*, October 2; *Pravda*, October 3).

First Deputy Chairman of the USSR State Committee on Prices Anatolii Komin said in an article in *Pravda* that it was high time to tackle the problem of prices, incomes, and finances to make *perestroika* a success. Komin said prices and incomes are the key to the country's economic restructuring. He said that, without changes with respect to them, laws on cooperatives and economic independence for enterprises would not be successful. Komin said *perestroika* had produced only an insignificant rise in production efficiency in the past eighteen months. He said prices, incomes, pensions, finances, and the market must now be set right to successfully fight the ills of the present economic situation.

Economist Says Prices Problem Should Be Tackled

Mikhail Gorbachev was handed a complaint signed by forty Lithuanian members of the Congress of People's Deputies. The "Sajudis" Information Agency said the document objected to the tone and wording of a CPSU Central Committee statement on the situation in the Baltic. (The statement accused the Balts of extremism and nationalism and warned that action would be taken.) The statement provoked protests from activists in the Baltic republics and from liberal Moscow and Leningrad intellectuals. The complaint by the Lithuanian deputies noted that national consciousness is nothing new in the Baltic, since all three republics were once independent states (*RFE Lithuanian Service*, October 2).

Lithuanian Deputies Protest against CPSU Resolution

Two participants in what TASS described as "mass disorders" in the Kazakhstan city of Novyi Uzen' last June have been sentenced to prison terms. TASS said the two, named as Zh. Kuanbaev and B. Sugirov, took part in an attack on police near Shevchenko on June 22 and 23. Kuanbaev was sentenced to three years' imprisonment in an intensified-regime correctional labor colony. Sugirov received a suspended two-year term and will be required to work "in a designated locality."

Two Sentenced in Connection with Disturbances in Novyi Uzen'

Soviet police were reported to have clashed heavily with demonstrators in the Western Ukrainian city of Lvov (*RL Ukrainian Service*, October 2). Activists told RFE/RL that the trouble began when police moved to stop a large crowd of people carrying Ukrainian national flags from entering a stadium where a song festival was being held. The activists quoted eyewitnesses as saying the police confiscated flags and detained people. A number of

Security Forces Clash with Demonstrators in Lvov

people were reported to have been injured. On October 3, protests were made in Lvov against alleged police violence against demonstrators. The protests included a two-hour strike at a number of factories, shops, and schools, and a large demonstration (*RL Ukrainian Service*, October 4). On October 5, the Lvov City Party Executive Committee attacked those responsible for unauthorized demonstrations in the city as "extremists" and "nationalists" (*Radio Moscow-2*, 2200, October 6; and *Radio Kiev*, 2100, October 5). The situation in Lvov was described by *Ogonek*, No. 51.

Shevardnadze Calls for "New Deal" for Third World

Soviet Foreign Minister Eduard Shevardnadze called on industrialized nations to take radical steps to solve the developing world's debt crisis. He made the call in a speech to the Foreign Policy Association, which is based in New York. Shevardnadze said "radical new steps are needed, a kind of 'New Deal.'" The New Deal was the term used by former US President Franklin Roosevelt to embrace the far-reaching programs he initiated to try to rebuild the US economy during the depression of the 1930s. Shevardnadze proposed that the United States and the USSR share advanced technology with the developing world, and he said "some debt" should be written off (*Reuters*, October 2; *Pravda*, October 4).

Vadim Medvedev Says *Pravda* Was Not Directed to Print El'tsin Story

Politburo member Vadim Medvedev said no directives were given to *Pravda* to print an article critical of Supreme Soviet deputy Boris El'tsin. Speaking on Soviet television, Medvedev said "a negative attitude was expressed" when some newspapers asked about publishing the article. Medvedev did not specify how this attitude was expressed.

Yazov Visits the United States

Soviet Defense Minister Dmitrii Yazov said of his official visit to the United States that it should promote mutual trust in the military sphere. Yazov is the USSR's first defense minister to visit the United States. On October 2, Yazov met with US Secretary of Defense Dick Cheney with whom he discussed military strategies, defense spending, regional conflicts, and arms control negotiations (*UPI*, *AP*, October 2). On October 3, Yazov met with US President George Bush. Reuters and UPI reported that Bush and Yazov exchanged views on the full range of US-Soviet relations, including security and arms control. A White House statement said Bush expressed the desire to sign an agreement on conventional forces in Europe and on chemical weapons as soon as possible. He also said he hoped for progress in talks on reducing long-range nuclear weapons. Talking to reporters on October 4, Yazov said he wanted to increase exchange programs between US and Soviet armed forces. He also said he was optimistic about the chances for disarmament (*UPI*, October 4). On October 6, Yazov visited an air force base near Phoenix, Arizona; later, he toured an army base in North Carolina (*Reuters, UPI,* October 6). Before ending his visit to the United States, he told reporters that he was impressed with the dedication, discipline, and proficiency of the US armed forces (*AP, UPI, Reuters,* October 6).

On October 10, Yazov said talks during his recent visit to the United States had been frank and straight-forward. He told TASS Moscow and Washington had confirmed their readiness to further develop military contacts. He said that both sides had taken steps to meet each other halfway on disarmament matters and that this gave rise to hope that arms talks in Geneva and Vienna would make faster headway and produce positive results. See also an interview with Yazov in *Izvestia,* October 12.

Tuesday, October 3

Roy Medvedev Interviewed on Gdlyan-Ivanov Investigation

The television news program "Vremya" broadcast an interview with Roy Medvedev in which he talked about his background as a dissident political scientist and about his current role as chairman of the commission of the Congress of People's Deputies charged with examining the case of investigators Tel'man Gdlyan and Nikolai Ivanov. Medvedev said that, up to the time the interview was recorded, Gdlyan and Ivanov and their supporters had been the only party to the controversy that had re-fused to provide the commission with necessary materi-als. Meanwhile, *Argumenty i fakty* (No. 39) published an article stating that the commission inquiring into the Gdlyan-Ivanov case had not been allocated adequate premises in which to hold hearings. The meeting on Sep-tember 26 was cited as an example: the number of people who wanted to attend the hearing was too great for the venue, and the session was abandoned.

Measures Taken to Prevent Crimes Involving Foreigners

The USSR Ministry of Internal Affairs is taking measures to prevent crimes involving foreigners. Ministry officials told reporters in Moscow that the ministry's main criminal investigation department had set up a special section to combat such crimes. The officials said police units were being reinforced at international airports and hotels. The officials revealed that more than 2,000 crimes involving foreigners were committed in the USSR in the first seven months of this year. Most of the offenses had to do with purchasing foreign currency or clothing from foreigners (*TASS*, October 3).

Wednesday, October 4 ————————————————————————————————

TV Shows Anti-Cooperative Rally; Shmelev Attacks Trade Unions

"Vremya" showed thousands of people taking part in a Moscow rally against cooperatives and demanding a price freeze on basic goods. The rally was organized by the trade unions. Soviet television also broadcast an interview with reformist economist Nikolai Shmelev, who accused the unions of dodging complex issues and blaming all problems on the cooperatives.

Baker Suggests Stabilization of Ruble

US Secretary of State James Baker has suggested that the USSR consider using its sizable gold stocks to stabilize the ruble. During testimony before the US Senate Finance Committee, Baker made extensive remarks about Soviet political and economic reforms. He stressed the need to make the ruble convertible on international markets and said Soviet price reform could not proceed until the value of the ruble is stabilized. Baker also said the Soviet Union could get most-favored-nation trading status from the United States within a year if it passes and implements free emigration laws (*Reuters*, October 4).

US-Soviet Capital-Raising Fund Formed by Businessmen

US and Soviet businessmen have organized a venture capital fund to invest in high-technology joint-venture companies involving the USSR. The group said this will be the first capital-raising fund together with the USSR. The plan was announced in the US state of Vermont. The fund is being put together by the Soviet cooperative "Technology Innovations Production Company," a private US economic organization called the Geonomics Institute, and a US law firm (Pillsbury, Madison, and Sutro). The proposal is to raise 100 million dollars from Western investors to fund a Soviet high-technology project that can be sold worldwide by a joint venture company. The fund is similar to the Hungarian fund being organized with the participation of the World Bank (*RFE/RL Special*,

October 4). The same day, TASS announced that a foreign-funded bank designed to help Soviet industries operate independently on foreign markets was being formed in Moscow. TASS said the bank would be a stock company with 60 percent of its capital in foreign currency provided by banks in West Germany, Austria, Italy, Finland, and France. TASS said the "International Moscow Bank" will take over from the Soviet Bank for Foreign Trade the work of lending to Soviet industries seeking to operate on foreign markets.

_____ *Thursday, October 5*

Shevardnadze Visits Cuba for Talks with Castro

Eduard Shevardnadze arrived in Cuba for wide-ranging talks with Cuban President Fidel Castro. Cuba's acting foreign minister, José Viera, said Shevardnadze would discuss both international and bilateral relations. He said among the points expected to be raised will be Shevardnadze's recent visit to the United States. Shevardnadze arrived in Cuba after a two-day visit to Nicaragua, where he pledged to continue a freeze on Soviet arms shipments to Managua. Reuters and UPI also said Shevardnadze proposed a broad role for Moscow in Central America, offering to join the United States as a guarantor of a regional agreement on limiting armed forces in this part of the world. On October 5, Shevardnadze met privately with Castro. No details were given of the talks (*Reuters*, October 5; *Pravda*, October 7).

Three Soviet Divisions Withdrawn from Mongolia

TASS reported the completion of the first stage of a Soviet military withdrawal from Mongolia. TASS quoted Major General L. Maiorov, chief of Soviet Forces in Mongolia, who discussed the withdrawal at a press conference in Ulan Bator, as saying that two tank divisions and one air force division had already been withdrawn. TASS said fifty-two military settlements, including hundreds of houses, apartments, hospitals, and schools had been turned over to the Mongolians.

Azerbaijan Claims Greater Sovereignty, Right of Secession

Azerbaijan published a new constitutional law that asserts greater Azerbaijani sovereignty within the Soviet Union and reaffirms that Nagorno-Karabakh is part of Azerbaijan. TASS said the law states that Azerbaijan has an inviolable right to independent decisions on all political, economic, and sociocultural matters. It said this also applies to problems of territorial-administrative status. The law says Azerbaijan's authority will be restricted only where the republic voluntarily cedes powers to the Soviet federation. The law also says Azerbaijan could leave the Soviet Union if such a step were decided by a referendum. The new law was adopted by the Azerbaijani Supreme Soviet last month (*TASS*, October 5).

Estonian Parliament Turns Down Length-of-Residency Requirement for Voters

The Estonian Supreme Soviet voted not to put into effect a controversial residency requirement of two years for voting in local elections. The Estonian parliament voted against the enforcement of the requirement by 179 to sixty-two with seven abstentions. The proposal to introduce a residency requirement provoked strikes by Russian-speaking workers. The Presidium of the USSR Supreme Soviet told the Estonian parliament to abandon the law (*RFE Estonian Service*, October 5; *Sovetskaya Estonia*, October 6).

Government to End Controls on Copying Machines

The USSR Ministry of Internal Affairs has decided to give up trying to control the use of copying machines in the Soviet Union. *Izvestia* said the ministry was preparing the necessary documents to end the controls. It quoted a ministry official, V. Vashchenko, as saying the advent of computers and related printing equipment had made the controls on duplication of materials impossible.

Azerbaijani Popular Front Registered

A spokesman for the Azerbaijani Popular Front said the Azerbaijani Council of Ministers had registered the front as a legal organization. This has long been a major demand of the popular front. In an interview with RFE/RL on October 5, spokesman Mehdi Mamedov said the registration of the front was agreed to at a meeting of representatives of the front and Azerbaijani Communist Party officials in Baku on October 4.

State-Owned Shops Leased to Individuals

Some of Moscow's state-owned shops are being leased to individuals for the first time. TASS said the Moscow Production and Trade Association leased to interested individuals shops that sell consumer goods and foodstuffs that are currently unprofitable. TASS said lessees are to be granted economic independence to make deals with production associations and to participate in joint ventures.

Zarya Vostoka said a Georgian Supreme Soviet commission had found that Defense Minister Dmitrii Yazov and former KGB chief Viktor Chebrikov had approved a decision to use troops to disperse a rally in Georgia in April. The findings said that the operation had "the appearance of a pre-planned slaughter of innocent people, carried out with particular cruelty" and that, while the principal blame for the tragedy lay with the republic, the central organs of power also bore some responsibility.

Findings on Tbilisi Events Published

Friday, October 6

Mikhail Gorbachev was conspicuous among the dignitaries attending East Germany's fortieth anniversary ceremonies, which were accompanied by the flight of thousands of East Germans to the West. At the start of his visit, Gorbachev placed a wreath at the tomb of the Unknown Soldier. Addressing a crowd of East German citizens, Gorbachev talked about reforms and about allowing citizens to decide for themselves the fate of their country (*Reuters*, October 6). He said East Germany should be able to resolve its own problems by reaching out to all elements of society. He also said it should be understood in the West that matters affecting East Germany are decided in Berlin, not Moscow (*TASS*, October 6; *Pravda*, October 7).

On October 7, Gorbachev held talks with East German head of state Erich Honecker. Gorbachev was quoted as saying the most important thing was to recognize and meet the needs of the people before it is too late (*TASS*, October 7; *Pravda*, October 8). Meanwhile, at least 2,000 people marched to the Palace of the Republic in East Berlin, where Gorbachev and other leaders were attending a reception. Correspondents said there were also demonstrations in Leipzig and Potsdam. A cordon of police kept the crowd in East Berlin away from the palace. Demonstrators shouted "Gorby, help us!" and "Gorby, come out!" Police detained several demonstrators (Western agencies, October 7). The same day, Gorbachev returned home. In its coverage of the celebrations in the DDR, the Soviet domestic media failed to mention the protests by thousands of demonstrators demanding more democracy (*Central Television*, "Vremya," October 8).

Gorbachev at Anniversary Celebrations in East Berlin

The commission of the Congress of People's Deputies on the Gdlyan-Ivanov affair said the investigation of criminal charges against former Moldavian Party Second Secretary

Commission Says Smirnov Probe Halted Too Soon

537

Viktor Smirnov stopped too soon. According to *Izvestia*, the commission decided unanimously on October 4 that the investigation had been halted "prematurely and unjustifiably" by the USSR Prosecutor's Office. The newspaper said the commission had reached its conclusion after hearing the testimony of three KGB officers who particpated in recent investigations into bribery in Uzbekistan. *Izvestia* said most of their testimony concerned the Smirnov case. Smirnov was arrested last January on suspicion of accepting bribes. His case was prepared by investigators Gdlyan and Ivanov. Four months later, the USSR Prosecutor's Office cleared Smirnov, saying there was not enough evidence to charge him. Gdlyan and Ivanov were in turn accused of abuse of power in their conduct of the corruption probe.

Coal Miners Threaten Strike against Nuclear Test

Coal miners in Kazakhstan are reported to have threatened a series of warning strikes unless further nuclear tests at the republic's Semipalatinsk test range are called off. A spokesman for an antinuclear group in Alma-Ata, the republic's capital, told Reuters about the miners' warning.

British Human-Rights Team Cancels Visit to Soviet Union

The British government said a British human-rights delegation canceled a visit to the Soviet Union because Moscow refused to give a visa to one team member. Eleven government and private experts planned the visit at the invitation of the USSR to examine how the USSR is honoring promises to improve human rights. But a Foreign Office spokesman said Moscow refused Michael Bourdeaux a visa; he is head of a group that monitors religious freedom in the USSR and Eastern Europe. Soviet officials claimed Bourdeaux had made an unauthorized trip to the Baltic republics during a previous visit to the USSR, a claim that the Foreign Office spokesman denied (*AP, Reuters*, October 6).

***Argumenty i fakty* Carries Statistics on Special Settlements**

Argumenty i fakty (No. 39) published statistics on people confined to special settlements (*spetsposeleniya*) in Kazakhstan and Siberia under Stalin. The periodical quoted a historian at the Institute of History of the USSR of the Academy of Sciences, V. Zemskov, as saying that in January, 1953, there were 2,753,356 inmates of the special settlements. Almost half of them—1,224,931—were Germans. Others who were confined in special settlements included representatives of peoples deported on Stalin's orders from their native lands (Crimean Tatars, Meskhetians, Greeks, and peoples of the Northern Caucasus for example) and kulaks.

Saturday, October 7

Radio Moscow said the Soviet rail transport system was still experiencing serious difficulties. The radio said that for some reason 100,000 railroad cars were standing idle every day around the USSR while at the same time there was no transport available for imported goods waiting at Soviet ports. It said the imbalance was partly due to strikes in the Baltic republics, Moldavia, and the USSR's coal regions and also to the railroad blockade in the Transcaucasia. On October 11, Radio Moscow-2 (1700) carried the text of an appeal by the Presidium of the All-Union Central Council of Trade Unions to workers on rail and road transport, at sea and river ports, and in factories and enterprises to improve the supply of goods in the Soviet Union. The appeal described the transportation of goods as catastrophic, saying the USSR was inadequately prepared for the coming winter. On October 12, *Sovetskaya Rossiya* carried an article about mismanagement on the "October" Leningrad Railroad.

Soviet Rail Transport Still Not Functioning Properly

Prime Minister Nikolai Ryzhkov called for more effective measures to combat economic crime linked with the cooperative sector. TASS said Ryzhkov issued his call during a meeting with Cabinet ministers and other officials in the Kremlin on October 6. TASS said participants in the meeting expressed alarm about increasing speculation, embezzlement, and other crimes being committed in the cooperative sector. It said they also warned that the growing gap between the incomes of state employees and cooperative members was destabilizing the Soviet economy and society. Participants in the meeting included KGB chief and Politburo member Vladimir Kryuchkov.

Soviet Government to Step Up Fight against Economic Crime

The Soviet media marked Constitution Day with commentaries saying that the present Soviet constitution does not reflect the spirit of the country's social and economic restructuring processes. (The present constitution dates from 1977.) Writing in *Komsomol'skaya pravda*, Academician Andrei Sakharov said the constitution should specify that the USSR is "a voluntary union of sovereign

Deputies Say Soviet Constitution Not Consistent with *Perestroika*

republics based on a federal treaty and on the principle of the self-determination of peoples." Two deputies of the USSR Supreme Soviet, Fedor Burlatsky and Sergei Alekseev, marked the occasion by saying that in the constitution rights and freedoms are stated but not guaranteed (*TASS*, October 7).

Demonstration in Moscow in Support of El'tsin, Gdlyan, and Ivanov

Thousands of Soviet citizens demonstrated in Moscow in support of Supreme Soviet deputy Boris El'tsin and government corruption investigators Tel'man Gdlyan and Nikolai Ivanov. The demonstrators formed a human chain along Gorky Street and paraded near the Kremlin Wall and at other points in the Soviet capital. The demonstrators also called for a new Soviet constitution (*AP, AFP,* October 7).

Radio Moscow Says Dialogue with "Rukh" Should Continue

Radio Moscow criticized some activities of the Ukrainian Popular Movement for *Perestroika* ("Rukh") but said dialogue with this organization should continue. Radio Moscow said "Rukh" had been cooperating with what it called openly anti-Soviet informal groups such as the Ukrainian Helsinki Union and the Ukrainian Democratic Union. It said these and organizations of Ukrainians abroad were very dangerous allies. The radio said, however, that the authorities must maintain contact with "Rukh" and try to turn it into a truly national movement (*Radio Moscow-1*, 1200, October 7).

Sunday, October 8 ————————————————————

Popular Front of Latvia Adopts Program for Independence

At its second congress, which began in Riga on October 7, the Popular Front of Latvia adopted a program for achieving independence and a multiparty Latvian state. Reports quoted the program as saying "the last half century has seen the rule of an absurd economic system, the absence of human rights, and an administrative arbitrariness that has led Latvia to national, economic, and ecological catastrophe" (*Reuters, AP,* October 7 and 8; *Pravda*, October 10). AP said the program puts no timetable on the transition to full independence. Correspondents quoted popular front members as saying the program is a compromise aimed at avoiding confrontation with the central authorities. On October 4, *Literaturnaya gazeta* carried a lengthy article by émigré Soviet poet Naum Korzhavin, who urged the Balts not to

540

push for independence at the present stage of *pere-stroika*, because it would only jeopardize Gorbachev's reforms.

The Komsomol weekly *Sobesednik* (No. 41) carried an interview with Vladimir Kuptsov, the chief of the government department responsible for the teaching of social sciences in the USSR. According to Kuptsov, beginning this year, ideology courses for students will be removed from the curriculum of all Soviet institutions of higher education. These are dialectical and historial materialism, the history of the CPSU, and "scientific communism." They are to be replaced by courses on the social and political history of the twentieth century, on problems of the theory of modern socialism, and on general philosophy. He also revealed that the structure of courses will be much freer, allowing a teacher to devise a course together with students in order to emphasize the most important and interesting topics. Every institute of higher education now has the right to publish its own textbooks.

Courses on Marxism Reported Abolished in Higher Education Institutes

Monday, October 9

The USSR Supreme Soviet adopted a law on "collective labor disputes," popularly known as the law on strikes.

Before the adoption of the law, on October 3 the Supreme Soviet approved a resolution calling for an end to strikes in key areas of the economy and for an end to rail disruptions in Transcaucasia. The resolution called for a temporary ban on strikes in the transport, energy, raw materials, and metallurgy industries. Reporting on the resolution, TASS at the time said the ban would remain in effect until the strike law was adopted by the USSR Supreme Soviet. During the discussions at the Supreme Soviet, Mikhail Gorbachev called for a complete ban on strikes, but other deputies thought that only a partial ban should be enforced.

The new law bans strikes by workers in almost a dozen sectors but, for the first time, guarantees other Soviet workers the right to strike. The present law has been in preparation, under conditions of strict secrecy, since 1986, but the drafting process was accelerated in response to the wave of miners' strikes and work stoppages related to ethnic disputes that swept the USSR this summer. It was the first law to be adopted by the present session of the USSR Supreme Soviet. The new law sets up

Supreme Soviet Adopts Law on Strikes

a complex system of arbitration and conciliation procedures intended to defuse workplace conflicts before the
strike weapon is resorted to. Thus, the new law allows
strikes only after two separate conciliation bodies have
failed to resolve workers' conflicts. The new law specifically
bans strikes in certain essential public services, and it
prohibits strikes not only by state bodies responsible
for defense, law and order, and national security but also
all work stoppages that "threaten the lives and health"
of the population (*TASS*, October 9). For the text of the
law, see *Pravda*, October 14.

Poland's Janowski Visits Moscow

Polish Deputy Prime Minister Jan Janowski said Polish-
Soviet cooperation is becoming more frank and busi-
nesslike. He said that when Warsaw and Moscow used
to talk about mutual love and cooperation this was
nothing but a facade but that now the two allies speak
openly about problems in their relations and difficult
moments in their history. Janowski spoke on Central
Television on October 9 after arriving in Moscow as
head of a Polish delegation. He is the first representative of Poland's "Solidarity"-led government to visit
Moscow.

Ligachev Interviewed on Radio Moscow

In an interview with Radio Moscow, Politburo member
Egor Ligachev defended the privileges of the Party
apparatus, saying it was premature to think that the Soviet
economy can be removed from Party control, because a
ruling Party such as the CPSU cannot delegate responsibility for economic policy to "someone else." That statement contradicts Gorbachev's political strategy of transferring power from the Party to the soviets. To solve the
Soviet food crisis, Ligachev suggested not more private
plots or the encouragement of peasant initiative but an
increase in government financing of the ailing agricultural sector—just the opposite of what Gorbachev has
proposed.

Reaction to Changes in Hungary

Radio Moscow, *Pravda*, and *Izvestia* published reports
on the congress of the Hungarian Party at which the
decision was taken to disband the Party and create instead a Western-style Socialist party. A Moscow television commentary said the changes in Hungary and
Poland show that the postwar period is ending and
Europe is moving into an era of peace. The commentator,
Nikolai Shishlin, said that the process will take years

and may be painful but that it is inevitable. TASS said Mikhail Gorbachev had sent a message of congratulations to the president of the new Hungarian Socialist Party, Rezso Nyers. On October 11, the Soviet ambassador to Hungary, Boris Stuvalin, said the CPSU hoped to develop ties with the new Hungarian Socialist Party as the successor of the Hungarian Communist Party (*MTI,* in English, October 11).

Turkmenistan Officials Investigated for Drug Links

A Soviet investigator said officials in Turkmenistan may be involved in the drug business. Soviet television said three people accused of large-scale narcotics dealings had been sentenced in Turkmenistan to labor camp terms of six to eight years and their property confiscated. The chief investigator in the case, V. Boiko, said his team is now investigating possible links between the drug dealers and corrupt officials in the republic (*Central Television,* "Vremya," October 9).

Scientist Cites Disputes on Status of Turkmen Language

A professor of ethnography from Ashkhabad, Shamurat Annaklychev, said there had been heated disputes on giving Turkmen the status of a state language. Annaklychev said in an article in *Turkmenskaya iskra* that some people were campaigning for an immediate decision to make Turkmen the state language. But, he said, others had pointed out that such a decision would have adverse consequences for the republic's social and economic development. He apparently had in mind possible protests by the Russian-speaking population.

Scientists Confirm UFO Landing in Voronezh

TASS said Soviet scientists had confirmed that an unidentified flying object had landed in the Soviet city of Voronezh recently and that "aliens" had left the craft. TASS said witnesses described the "aliens" as human-like, three to four meters tall, with very small heads. TASS quoted Genrikh Silanov, the director of a geophysical laboratory in Voronezh, as saying his staff located the landing place and found traces of the "aliens," who were alleged to have walked in the park. He was quoted as saying that two unusual pieces of rock were also found at the site and that analysis showed they were of a substance "that cannot be found on earth." It was the first time that TASS had carried a story of this kind. On October 11, the "Vremya" news program broadcast interviews with Voronezh residents who claimed that they had seen the UFO.

Tuesday, October 10

Supreme Soviet Debates Price Controls

The USSR Supreme Soviet debated the question of runaway inflation and price controls. Two competing proposals were put before the deputies—one that had been prepared by the Committee of the Council of the Union on Questions of Labor, Prices, and Social Policy and one that had been prepared by the Soviet leadership. Radio Moscow described the draft proposal put forth by the leadership as containing measures to bring incomes into line with the supply of goods and services over time. This would attack the problem from both sides, attempting to retard the growth of money incomes and increase the supply of consumer goods (especially basic food and nonfood goods) while seeking to "control" the growth of prices for these products. The draft proposal prepared by the Committee for Questions of Labor, Prices, and Social Policy was reported to focus on a price freeze for those goods and services (wholesale as well as retail) that are now in greatest demand. The latter proposal was vigorously supported by Stepan Shalaev, chairman of the Central Council of Trade Unions, who proposed that the freeze take effect in the next ten days and last for fifteen months. Deputy Prime Minister Abalkin, however, supported the leadership's version, as did Prime Minister Ryzhkov, who noted that Soviet incomes had grown by 12.3 percent over the first nine months of 1989, as compared with the same period in 1988, and by 15.7 percent over the latest quarter (July–September). The parliamentary committee was instructed to work out a single document for presentation to the deputies at a later date (*Pravda*, October 11).

Belorussia Appeals for Help for Chernobyl' Victims

Belorussia appealed for equipment needed to cope with the aftermath of the Chernobyl' nuclear accident. The appeal was made by the Belorussian Peace Committee and read to the United Nations General Assembly by Belorussian Foreign Minister Anatolii Gurinovich. It said that over one billion rubles had already been spent on cleaning up areas that were affected by radiation but that the tragedy had turned out to be "much more serious than anyone could have expected." The committee said that there were "acute shortages" of radiation survey and measuring instruments and medical diagnostic equipment (*RFE/RL Special*, October 10).

Radio Warsaw said Mikhail Gorbachev met in Moscow with Polish Party First Secretary Mieczyslaw Rakowski. The radio quoted Gorbachev as telling journalists the Soviet leadership favors the development of relations with Poland. After meeting with Gorbachev, Rakowski said at a press conference that he believed the Polish Communist Party should change its name and program and that this would happen at the next Party congress. Rakowski said Gorbachev had no objection to the Communist Parties of Poland and Hungary changing their names and programs (_AP_, October 11).

Gorbachev Meets Rakowski in Moscow

In an interview with _Moscow News_ (No. 42), East Germany's Party ideology chief Kurt Hager urged reforms in the GDR. His comments were also reported by East German radio. In the interview, Hager urged greater participation of the people in solving the country's problems, more openness in society, and new concepts in the country's public information policy. Referring to the mass exodus of mostly young people from the country, Hager said "all of the obstacles have to be cleared away that have apparently prevented our youth from developing their full potential" (_AP_, _DPA_, October 11). On October 12, Kurt Hager arrived in Moscow with a Party delegation. TASS said he would attend the East German Cultural Days in Moscow. There had been no previous mention of Hager's visit.

East German Ideologist Urges Reforms in Interview with _Moscow News_

Protesters in Kazan, the capital of the Tatar ASSR, asked Prime Minister Nikolai Ryzhkov to stop construction of a nuclear power plant there. Radio Moscow said that the situation was "boiling" in Kazan and that there had been another march there to protest against construction of the plant. It did not say when. There were protests in Kazan and other Tatar cities on September 30 and October 1. Radio Moscow said participants in the latest rally appealed to Ryzhkov and also asked the USSR Public Prosecutor to prosecute those responsible for the project (_Radio Moscow-1_, 1200, October 11).

Kazan Citizens Ask Ryzhkov to Stop Construction of Nuclear Plant

Alan Greenspan, the chairman of the Board of the US Federal Reserve, met USSR Prime Minister Nikolai Ryzhkov in Moscow. TASS said the talks focused on developing

Greenspan Meets Ryzhkov

contacts and cooperation between the United States and the USSR on financial and credit matters. The agency quoted Ryzhkov as saying the use of US experience in those sectors may help normalize the Soviet economy and improve the socioeconomic situation in the country. TASS said Greenspan expressed "several practical ideas" on these issues, but it did not say what they were. Greenspan is on an unofficial visit to the Soviet Union.

Literaturnaya gazeta Carries Interview with Polish Prime Minister

Literaturnaya gazeta carried a lengthy interview with the new Polish Prime Minister, Tadeusz Mazowiecki. Mazowiecki said that, in order to overcome its present state of crisis, Poland should introduce a market economy and abandon the one-party system. He said Poland had not renounced ideas of socialism but added that at the present stage their realization looked impossible.

Thursday, October 12

Lithuanian Party Opens Plenum on Restructuring

The Lithuanian Party Central Committee opened a plenum to discuss preparations for the coming Party congress. The congress is to consider changing the Lithuanian Party's relationship with the CPSU. Lithuanian Party ideology secretary Valerijonas Baltrunas has previously said the Party cannot retain its present stagnant framework (*Radio Vilnius*, 1300, October 120; *Pravda*, October 14). On October 13, the RFE Lithuanian Service quoted sources in Vilnius as saying Gorbachev had personally urged the Lithuanian Communist Party to delay its decision on breaking with the CPSU. Lithuanian Communist Party First Secretary Algirdas Brazauskas told the Lithuanian Party Central Committee he had received a call from Gorbachev prior to the opening of the plenum. Brazauskas said Gorbachev had asked the Lithuanian Party to delay its congress. On October 13, however, the Lithuanian Party Central Committee decided to schedule its congress for December 19.

Former Kazakh Oblast Party Secretary on Trial

Former Party First Secretary of Chimkent Oblast in Kazakhstan Asanbei Askarov went on trial together with six other former Party, law-enforcement, and economic officials. Radio Moscow said the defendants were accused of giving and taking bribes. Askarov was first secretary in Chimkent Oblast from 1978 until 1985 when he was dismissed because of serious shortcomings in his work. He was also expelled from the Party for violations of social justice, nepotism, and using his office for personal gain.

Poland's Public Prosecutor called on the USSR Public Prosecutor to begin an investigation "into the murders at Katyn and other places" of Polish officers during World War II. Earlier this year, Polish officials said evidence showed that the Soviet NKVD was responsible for the massacre at Katyn. Warsaw television and radio also quoted the Polish prosecutor as calling for a rehabilitation hearing of members of Polish political groups who were sentenced in Moscow in 1945. Warsaw television said the rehabilitation procedure for Jan Stanislaw Jankowski, deputy premier of the Polish government in exile; General Leopold Okulicki, former commander in chief of the Home Army; and fourteen representatives of Polish political groups in the Council of National Unity cannot be held in Poland, since all the verdicts were pronounced by courts in the USSR.

Poland Asks USSR to Investigate Katyn

The US Agriculture Department said the Soviet grain harvest this year was larger than previously forecast. The department said the harvest is now estimated at 205 million tons—up five million tons from the previous forecast. The department said because of the better-than-expected production, its estimate of the amount of grain the Soviet Union will import has been reduced by two million tons. At the same time, the department announced that the USSR had bought an additional 100,000 tons of US corn (*AP*, *UPI*, October 13). A month ago, the USSR announced that it was suspending grain imports while it tried out a scheme that involved paying its own farmers in hard currency as an incentive to increase production. Since then, there had been much criticism of the scheme in the press, with calls for it to be abandoned because it was ineffective. See, for example, *Komsomol'skaya pravda*, October 3.

USSR Grain Harvest Higher Than Expected, USSR Buys More US Corn

A joint session of three Central Committee commissions was held in Moscow to determine the Party's strategy for the forthcoming elections to the local soviets. According to a Radio Moscow report on October 12, the meeting of the Central Committee Commissions on Party Organization and Cadres, Ideology, and Legal Policy was chaired by the head of the Ideological Commission, Vadim

Central Committee Commissions Meet to Discuss Elections

Medvedev. Speakers at the meeting criticized local Party organizations for failing to carry out the reform process. It was stated at the meeting that, following the forthcoming elections on the local level, the newly established soviets should become the real decision-making bodies. It was stressed that Party organizations should start a dialogue with all forces in Soviet society that support *perestroika* (*Pravda*, October 13).

Abalkin Discusses Economic Situation on Soviet Television

Deputy Prime Minister Leonid Abalkin was interviewed by Aleksandr Tikhomirov following the "Vremya" television news. Abalkin was asked to comment on a letter from a viewer who said, "We're always being told we work badly: let's conduct an experiment and give Siberia to the Japanese and the European parts of the USSR to the West Germans and see if that helps." In reply, Abalkin quoted Lenin's well-known words: "We Russians work badly." "It's painful and offensive," he added, "but it's true. Unless we become different, unless we change ourselves, no Japanese and no West Germans will do it for us." Abalkin said 20 percent of the Soviet population is living below the poverty line, and he called this a shameful figure for a civilized country, to say nothing of a Socialist one. He said he believes the Soviet government has fifteen months— until the end of next year—to achieve some improvement in living standards and to restore the faith of the population in their government.

Friday, October 13 ─────────────────────────────

Top MVD Official Calls for Public Support

In an article in *Kommunist* (No. 14), Lieutenant General Anatolii Anikiev, chief of the Main Political Administration of the USSR Ministry of Internal Affairs, calls for the creation of a public Social Defense Fund to help the Soviet police deal with social unrest and the rising crime rate by taking over some of the law-enforcement duties of the ministry. According to Anikiev, the fund should be a self-financing organization and should take over the voluntary police support forces. Anikiev claims that "nationalist and anti-Soviet elements of informal groups" are trying to discredit the police.

Conservative Writer Attacks Interregional Group

Literaturnaya Rossiya (No. 40) contains an article by conservative writer Anatolii Salutsky, who regularly contributes material criticizing Gorbachev's reforms to

Russian nationalist periodicals. In this article, Salutsky sharply attacks the Interregional Group of People's Deputies headed by Yurii Afanas'ev, Andrei Sakharov, and Boris El'tsin, and accuses the deputies of trying to suppress the United Front of Workers of Russia, which held its inaugural congress in Sverdlovsk in September. (The United Front includes in its ranks Party officials and workers whose privileges have been threatened by *perestroika*. The front condemns the current reforms as a step towards capitalism.) Salutsky claims that Sakharov and another deputy came to Sverdlovsk in September in order to keep the United Front from holding its congress. Salutsky alleges that the main goal of the reformist deputies is "not to allow the working class to participate in decision-making."

"Vzglyad" Censored because of Afghanistan Coverage

The popular television program "Vzglyad" was broadcast with considerable delay and in visibly censored form. Usually "Vzglyad" is broadcast live, but this time it was videotaped; during the broadcast a running line informed the audience that the program was not live "for reasons beyond the control of the editorial desk." In addition, the moderators of the program, Vladislav Mukusev and Aleksandr Polit'kovsky, complained that the telephone connection to the call-in studio had been interrupted by the Ministry of Communications. The final segment of the program (before its abrupt ending) dealt with the conditions set by the Afghan *mujahidin* for the release of Soviet prisoners of war being held in Pakistan. *Novoe vremya* journalist Irina Lagutina revealed previously unpublicized information about direct negotiations that have taken place between leaders of the Afghan resistance and the Soviet committee "Nadezhda," which is composed of mothers and wives of prisoners of war. According to Lagutina, who accompanied a "Nadezhda" delegation during its recent visits to Pakistan and Afghanistan, the leaders of the *mujahidin* told the Soviet delegation that they would release the prisoners of war in exchange for the halting of Soviet military supplies to the Kabul regime, the release of 40,000 people held in Kabul prisons, and a map of mine fields on the border between Afghanistan and Pakistan. The "Nadezhda" delegation then went to Kabul and managed to obtain permission from the government for the *mujahidin* to inspect Kabul prisons. Lagutina concluded that now the Soviet government must make a decision, hinting that the rest depends on Moscow. "Vzglyad" moderator Mukusev managed only to add that the Supreme Soviet must push the matter when the program was suddenly interrupted with unrelated video clips, and then the words "Good Night" flashed onto the screen, ending the program. This is not the first time the "Vzglyad" team has been in trouble for their coverage of Afghanistan: a similar episode took place in February. Last month, the "Vzglyad" moderators announced that in future they would publicize every instance of censorship of their program.

Prominent Georgian Dissident Killed in Car Crash

Reports from Georgia said prominent dissident Merab Kostava had been killed in an automobile accident early today. Reuters, AP, and the independent Moscow journal *Ekspress-khronika* said Kostava was in a car with two other Georgian activists when the accident occurred. It happened on a wet and deserted road between Tbilisi and Kutaisi. Kostava was a leading force in organizing Georgian pro-independence demonstrations. He was first arrested for political activity in 1956 and had served several prison sentences since. He was released from prison in 1987 under an amnesty that freed many political prisoners.

Prayers in Kremlin Cathedral, Top Patriarchs Canonized

Russian Orthodox churchmen prayed for peace and the prosperity of Russia in the first service held in the Kremlin's Uspensky Cathedral in more than seventy years. TASS said there was also a requiem for all deceased patriarchs of Moscow and all Orthodox believers in Russia. Special permission was given to use the cathedral as part of the celebration of the 400th anniversary of the Russian Patriarchate. The Uspensky Cathedral, once the scene of the coronation of the tsars, has been a museum since 1918. In connection with the 400th anniversary of the Russian Patriarchate, an Episcopal Council of the Russian Orthodox Church was held. TASS reported on October 11 that the Council had canonized Patriarchs Job and Tikhon. Metropolitan Job was elected the first all-Russian patriarch in 1589. Patriarch Tikhon anathematized Bolshevik rule in 1918. His testament, in which he called for cooperation with the Soviet regime, was signed only a very short time before his death in 1925.

Soviet Defense Minister Meets US Navy Chief

Soviet Defense Minister Dmitrii Yazov met in Moscow with visiting US Admiral Carlisle Trost, the US chief of naval operations. TASS said the two men discussed ways of improving US-Soviet relations on the military level. It gave no other details. On October 12, while in Leningrad,

Trost criticized Soviet proposals to limit US ability to protect US interests and deter aggression. Trost said the United States is dependent on overseas trade for its economic well-being, whereas seaborne trade for the Soviet Union is not crucial for national survival. Trost called his trip to the USSR a milestone in US-Soviet progress towards improving relations and easing tensions (*TASS*, October 13).

On October 14, Chief of General Staff of the Soviet Armed Forces, Army General Mikhail Moiseev, said he was bewildered by the US rejection of a Soviet proposal to limit naval power (*TASS*, October 14).

New Union of Soviet Managers Opens Founding Congress

A new organization of Soviet businessmen has been founded with the goal of combating bureaucracy. TASS said the three-day constituent congress of the USSR Union of Managers opened in Moscow on October 13. It said the 271 delegates included officials of large industrial enterprises, associations, and joint ventures. TASS said the director of the National Economy Institute in Moscow, Vladimir Groshev, told the opening session that the art of management should become part and parcel of Soviet intellectual potential. Groshev was later elected president of the union. TASS said the group will seek to rally public support for ideas aimed at accelerating socioeconomic progress. It will also organize public scrutiny of proposed legislation and in some cases may propose alternatives.

Gorbachev Criticizes Outspoken Periodicals

On October 17, *The Washington Post* carried a report on a meeting between Gorbachev and media officials that took place on October 13. The text of Gorbachev's speech did not appear in the Soviet press. *The Washington Post* quoted Gorbachev as criticizing the editors of *Ogonek*, *Izvestia*, and *Argumenty i fakty* and several parliamentary deputies for "irresponsible" and "inflammatory" statements and articles. *The Washington Post* said that, according to Vitalii Korotich, Gorbachev also condemned factional infighting between liberals and conservatives and attacked deputies of the USSR Supreme Soviet Yurii Afanas'ev and Gavriil Popov. Gorbachev reportedly questioned Afanas'ev's right to remain in the CPSU and make "anti-Socialist statements."

Gorbachev was especially displeased by the *Argumenty i fakty* (No. 40) survey of 15,000 letters from readers, suggesting that the most popular parliamentary deputy is Andrei Sakharov, followed by Gavriil Popov, Boris El'tsin, and Yurii Afanas'ev. See RL 490/89.

Gorbachev suggested that the chief editor of *Argumenty i fakty*, Vladislav Starkov, should leave his post. Breaking with past Soviet practice, however, Starkov refused to resign, and his colleagues supported him in his decision. AP, *The Baltimore Sun* (October 17), *The Washington Post* (October 19) and other Western sources have quoted Starkov as saying Gorbachev's demand was repeated at a private meeting between Starkov and the Party's chief ideologist, Vadim Medvedev, on October 16. Academician Andrei Sakharov called on journalists all over the world to rally behind Starkov and freedom of the press. A group of thirty-four parliamentary deputies were also reported to have signed a petition in support of Starkov. On October 18, however, Ukrainian legislator Nikolai Kutsenko was refused the floor by Gorbachev's deputy, Anatolii Luk'yanov, when he asked to read the text of the petition at a session of the USSR Supreme Soviet. Kutsenko was told that Starkov's case was a matter for the Party, not for parliament (*AP*, October 18).

Moscow News (No. 43) carried the only account of Gorbachev's speech of October 13. The newspaper's editor, Egor Yakovlev, gave a very cautious evaluation of the speech.

Argumenty i fakty Carries Survey and Other Controversial Materials

Argumenty i fakty (No. 40), whose popularity survey of Soviet politicians provoked Gorbachev's attack on the periodical at a meeting on October 13, also carried a number of other controversial items. One of them is the most detailed report to appear so far in the Soviet press about the creation of the first Soviet atomic bomb. The report was written on the basis of recollections by Academician Yu. Khariton, one of the fathers of the Soviet bomb. The issue also includes material on the Ukrainian Catholic Church, which is campaigning for legal status, saying there are some 4 to 5 million Catholics in Ukraine. Perhaps the most interesting item is a report about the work of the Supreme Soviet Commission on the Gdlyan-Ivanov affair, giving information about violations of the law by the USSR Public Prosecutor's Office and the KGB, which released the former head of a section of the CPSU Central Committee Department for Organizational Party Work, Viktor Smirnov, from custody in May of this year. The article in *Argumenty i fakty* claims that Smirnov was released despite evidence that he had accepted bribes. *Argumenty i fakty* quoted the head of the commission on the Gdlyan-Ivanov affair, Roy Medvedev, as saying the USSR Public Prosecutor's Office has so far failed to respond to the commission's request to resume the criminal case against Smirnov. On the work of the Gdlyan-Ivanov commission, see also *Moscow News* (No. 42).

_____ *Saturday, October 14*

Soviet Police Seek Advice on Fighting Crime

Soviet police are saying that, since *perestroika* began, crime has been rising in the Soviet Union. A Moscow police officer, Yurii Tomachev, told reporters that reforms had raised expectations about consumer goods that could not be met and that frustration had led to crime. He and other Soviet police officials were attending the European and North American Conference on Urban Safety and Crime Prevention that ended in Montreal on October 13. Last month, the United Nations signed an agreement with the USSR to give the Soviet police advice and training (*Reuters*, October 14).

EC and Comecon Open Meeting in Moscow

The European Community and Comecon opened a conference in Moscow devoted to ways of increasing cooperation. Radio Moscow said that "transition to real cooperation" between the two trading groups is a priority. The conference is also discussing how East-West relations will be affected by the EC's plans to create a single market in its twelve member-states from the beginning of 1993. Other topics will be Comecon's efforts to improve cooperation between its members and economic reforms in individual Comecon states (*Radio Moscow*, October 14).

Izvestia Says Soviet Invasion of Czechoslovakia Prolonged Stalinism

Izvestia described the Warsaw Pact invasion of Czechoslovakia in 1968 as an event that prolonged the domination of neo-Stalinism for almost two decades. The newspaper said that a really honest attitude towards the past required a reassessment of the events of August, 1968.

Report Says Many Casualties in 1954 Nuclear Training Blast

The deliberate detonation of an atomic bomb during a 1954 military exercise in the Ural Mountains killed and injured large numbers of servicemen, a report in *Izvestia* said. The newspaper published the account of an officer who took part in the exercise, but it gave no exact casualty toll. The officer said many survivors suffered long-term effects of exposure to radiation. The use of the bomb to test troops' battle-readiness was first disclosed last month by *Krasnaya zvezda*. That account said there were no injuries.

Soviet Television Provides Statistics on Childbirth Mortality

The Soviet television news program "Vremya" said more than three times as many women die in childbirth in the Soviet Union as in the United States and other developed countries. The program, quoting what it said were statistics never before released, revealed that mortality was thirty-five women for every 100,000 births. It said the comparable rate in the United States, Japan, and France was between ten and twelve, and as low as four in Scandinavian countries.

Moldavian Workers' Organization Founded

A new unofficial workers' organization has been established in Moldavia. Radio Moscow and TASS said the Union of Working People of Moldavia held its founding congress in the city of Bendery. TASS said the congress had adopted resolutions and a platform backing moves to broaden political and economic reforms in the USSR. Among other things, the congress called for real independence for enterprises, pluralism in forms of property ownership, and steps to combat inflation, the budget deficit, and "the shadow economy." (Bendery was one of the centers of last month's strikes by Russian-speaking workers in Moldavia, who downed tools to protest against a law making Moldavian the official state language.)

Commission Urges Reassessment of Party Personnel Policy

The CPSU Central Committee Commission on Party Development and Cadres Policy said there should be major changes in the way Soviet officials obtain their posts. One of the changes would end the practice of appointing Communists to Party positions solely on the grounds of appointments they already hold. This means that people such as senior military commanders and republican Party leaders would not, for instance, automatically become members of the Party Central Committee. Another change would require local Party secretaries to be elected directly by their constituents rather than indirectly through intermediary committees (*TASS*, October 14). On October 16, *Pravda* carried an article urging a thorough assessment of personnel policy in every Party committee. The article said that the political climate in the USSR had changed dramatically and that political leaders now needed qualities such as speaking ability, analytical thinking, and lively individuality.

Boris El'tsin again called for the removal of Egor Ligachev from the Politburo. El'tsin made the demand before a crowd of about 10,000 in Moscow. He also demanded the removal of two other Politburo members, Lev Zaikov and Vitalii Vorotnikov. In addition, El'tsin complained about a meeting on October 13 between top Party officials and media representatives at which Gorbachev sharply attacked outspoken periodicals and reform-minded people's deputies. El'tsin said the meeting was a setback for *perestroika* (*Reuters, AFP*, October 15).

El'tsin Reiterates Demand for Ligachev's Ouster

US Attorney General Richard Thornburgh arrived in Moscow for talks with Soviet officials. The aim of Thornburgh's visit is to study the Soviet legal and judicial system and to establish contacts between justice organs in the two countries (*AP*, October 15). On October 17, Thornburgh met with Prime Minister Nikolai Ryzhkov and KGB chief Vladimir Kryuchkov (*TASS*, October 17). Speaking at a news conference at the end of his visit on October 19, Thornburgh said the countries were laying the ground for cooperation on legal rights and law enforcement. He said US and Soviet officials had agreed to form seven working groups to discuss matters ranging from cooperation on fighting drug trafficking and terrorism to environmental protection (*Reuters*, October 19).

US Attorney General Arrives in Moscow

Leaders of the newly created United Front of Workers of Russia complained that workers are worse off under Mikhail Gorbachev's economic reforms, which they said are dividing Soviet society into rich and poor. Veniamin Yarin, cochairman of the United Front, spelled out his views in the trade-union newspaper *Trud*. He said there was widespread unhappiness over rising prices, inflation, and the black market.

New Russian Front Complains Workers Worse Off under Reform

At a session of the USSR Supreme Soviet, Mikhail Gorbachev suggested discussing reports circulating in Moscow that an assassination attempt had been made on Boris El'tsin (*TASS, Reuters*, October 16). In response to Gorbachev's proposal, USSR Minister of Internal Affairs

Controversy over Alleged Assassination Attempt on El'tsin

Vadim Bakatin told the Supreme Soviet that on September 29 El'tsin arrived at a police station in wet clothes and told police that unidentified persons had dragged him into a car outside Moscow, pulled a sack over his head, and thrown him off a bridge into the Moscow River. Bakatin said an investigation of the matter had, however, failed to confirm the story El'tsin told to the police. Bakatin also said El'tsin had asked the police not to report the incident anywhere. Following the minister's report, El'tsin took the floor and said there had been no attempt to kill him, but he made no further comment on Bakatin's statement. Winding up the discussion, Gorbachev said the reports by Bakatin and El'tsin clearly demonstrated that there had been no assassination attempt on El'tsin. Gorbachev also said El'tsin earlier told the leadership that he may have made a joke that was misunderstood by the police (*Izvestia*, October 17). Despite Gorbachev's statement, however, deputies were left wondering what had really happened. On October 18, Boris El'tsin distributed a statement, which was given to reporters, in which he accused Gorbachev of trying to purge him from Soviet political life. El'tsin said the public discussion of the allegations of an attempt on his life had included lies, but he did not elaborate (Western agencies, October 18).

On October 19, Bakatin held a press conference in Moscow to respond to criticism from El'tsin. He accused El'tsin of lying in his statement to reporters in order to boost his popularity (*AP*, October 19). The same day, El'tsin gave an interview to Radio Liberty in which he reiterated that Mikhail Gorbachev was promoting a campaign against him because of personal rivalry and also to compromise him politically.

Supreme Soviet Rejects Bill on Republican Economic Self-Management

The USSR Supreme Soviet refused to endorse the government bill on republican economic self-management after a Supreme Soviet commission said the plan did not go far enough in giving the republics real economic independence. Abalkin attempted to defend the bill, of which he is the chief author. Abalkin argued that the Soviet Union could not function as a federation without an economic basis in the form of all-Union property in key economic sectors (*Izvestia*, October 18). Abalkin's arguments were not accepted, however.

Changes in Legislation on Cooperatives Approved

A Supreme Soviet committee headed by liberal Leningrad lawyer Anatolii Sobchak introduced changes that will allow the state and local soviets to control prices charged

556

by cooperatives. TASS said the changes are expected to be approved by the Supreme Soviet as part of an overall law governing cooperatives. Sobchak was quoted as telling the Supreme Soviet that the proposed changes would make it possible to keep the cooperatives in business while preventing large profits. The changes are obviously a response to growing dissatisfaction among the population over the high prices charged by cooperatives for goods that are not always of a high quality. Some deputies attending the Supreme Soviet session called for the complete abolition of cooperatives (*Izvestia*, October 16; *Izvestia*, October 21). On October 17, the USSR Supreme Soviet passed another restriction on the activities of cooperatives. Reports said the move would ban cooperatives from buying goods in short supply from state agencies for later resale (*TASS*, October 17). In an interview with *Krasnaya zvezda* (October 17), the president of the Union of Cooperative Associations of the USSR described the new regulations as "unfair."

Kryuchkov on KGB Role in Making USSR Law-Governed State

KGB chairman Vladimir Kryuchkov said his agency was now taking an active role in helping to prepare legislation aimed at making the USSR a state ruled by law. In an interview broadcast by Radio Moscow's World Service, Kryuchkov said the KGB has a duty to defend human rights and act only in accordance with the law and in the interests of internal order. He also said the KGB was willing to do everything it could to ensure that "the lawlessness of the past" is never repeated. He said such lawlessness had brought grief and suffering to the country. In the same interview, Kryuchkov appealed to former KGB members who have defected to the West to return to the Soviet Union, and he said defectors can count on mercy from the Soviet authorities.

Gerasimov Says Wallenberg Arrest Was Tragic Mistake

Soviet Foreign Ministry spokesman Gennadii Gerasimov said the arrest of Raoul Wallenberg was "a tragic mistake." Gerasimov told a government news briefing that Wallenberg was caught up in "a maelstrom of repression." Meanwhile, Wallenberg's relatives arrived in the USSR to obtain more information from the Soviet authorities about Wallenberg's fate. AP and Reuters reported that Soviet officials today handed over to Wallenberg's relatives his identity cards and other personal belongings. On October 15, *Moscow News* (No. 42) carried a lengthy item on Wallenberg based on documents from the Swedish Ministry of Foreign Affairs.

AIDS Diagnosed among Children in Stavropol

Four children have been diagnosed as AIDS carriers in the city of Stavropol. *Izvestia* said the children had been moved to a special AIDS treatment center in Moscow. The newspaper said the USSR Ministry of Health had found that some medical institutions in Stavropol Krai had failed to install sterilization equipment and that medical personnel had "grossly violated" rules for the use of syringes and other instruments.

Poland Seeks Reparations from USSR for World War II

Poland is seeking to press claims for World War II reparations from the USSR. Polish Foreign Minister Krzysztof Skubiszewski told the Sejm that contacts had already been made with the Soviet government concerning reparations for the millions of Poles who were deported to the Soviet Union from 1939 onwards and used as forced labor (*DPA*, October 16).

Opinion Poll Shows Decline in Prestige of CPSU

Pravda carried an article summarizing the results of an all-Union opinion poll on people's attitudes towards the CPSU. The poll was conducted in June by the Academy of Social Sciences attached to the CPSU Central Committee. *Pravda* said the poll indicated that a critical attitude towards the CPSU was becoming increasingly prevalent adding that it was this poll that prompted the Party leadership to call a meeting of the Central Committee in July. According to *Pravda*, more than one-third of those polled were skeptical about the Party's ability to restructure itself and effectively "play a vanguard role" in society. The most disturbing fact, according to *Pravda*, was that those most critical of the CPSU were people of working age.

While the evaluation of the CPSU as a whole was negative enough, the attitude expressed by those polled towards Party members within their work collectives was even worse. More than half of workers, peasants, and white-collar workers evaluated the authority of Communists with whom they worked as low. *Pravda* also disclosed that Communists themselves, who were also polled, think that 73 percent of the Party apparatus consists of people with low professional qualifications.

*Tuesday, October 17*_____

USSR Readmitted to WPA

In a controversial move, the World Psychiatric Association conditionally readmitted the Soviet Union as a member. The decision was taken at the WPA's congress

558

in Athens. The conditions stress the association's right to check on Soviet psychiatric abuse for political purposes and to expel the USSR if such abuse continues. The Soviet Union left the association in 1983 when it faced expulsion over charges that Moscow confined sane dissidents to mental hospitals (*AP*, October 17 and 18). Former Soviet political prisoner and psychiatrist Anatolii Koryagin resigned as an honorary member of the World Psychiatric Association in protest against the readmission of the USSR to the body. The decision to readmit the USSR followed heated debates in Athens over the issue.

On October 16, official Soviet psychiatrists held a press conference at which they responded to tough questions from experts and Western journalists on psychiatric abuses in the USSR. AP quoted Petr Morozov, a secretary of the Society of Soviet Psychiatrists, as saying "it is clear that we regret our past, not only abuses but the whole system." *Moscow News* (No. 42) published an article on the situation in Soviet psychiatry, quoting Kovalev, an expert for the Administration on International Humanitarian Cooperation and Human Rights of the Ministry of Foreign Affairs, as saying the situation had improved a lot. It quoted a US official and independent Soviet psychiatrists, however, as saying there had been little improvement in Soviet psychiatry. See RL 498/89 and RL 499/89.

"Rukh" Figure Elected to Congress of People's Deputies

A leading figure in the Ukrainian Popular Movement "Rukh" has been elected a people's deputy. A report on Radio Kiev said poet Dmytro Pavlychko had defeated four other candidates in a by-election for the seat for the Kalush District in the Ivano-Frankovsk Oblast. Pavlychko is a member of the CPSU. He is also the chairman of the Taras Shevchenko Ukrainian Language Society, an informal group that is part of "Rukh."

Shevardnadze Meets Orthodox Church Leaders

Soviet Foreign Minister Eduard Shevardnadze discussed reforms in domestic and foreign policy with four leading figures of the Russian Orthodox Church. The Soviet media quoted Shevardnadze as telling four metropolitans that the Soviet government appreciated the Church's moral role in society. The reports said the Church leaders and Shevardnadze agreed to increase cooperation in building a Soviet state based on law and bringing humanitarian principles to international relations. The meeting was attended by Metropolitan of Kiev and Galicia Filaret, Metropolitan of Minsk and Belorussia Filaret, Metropolitan of Krutitsy and Kolomna Yuvenalii, and Metropolitan of Rostov and Novocherkassk Vladimir (*TASS, Central Television*, "Vremya, " October 17).

Draft Law on Ownership of Property Discussed

The Supreme Soviet resumed its session with discussion of a government draft of a law on ownership of property in the Soviet Union. The draft calls for multiple forms of ownership. Nikolai Ryzhkov said the issue of property ownership would shape developments in the USSR for years to come, and he suggested that the Soviet people should be asked whether they were in favor of private property (*Radio Moscow*, October 17; *Izvestia*, October 17).

Gorbachev Says Leadership Neglected Consumer Markets

Mikhail Gorbachev said that the Soviet leadership had neglected problems of consumer markets and that the result was "all our stores are empty." Gorbachev spoke during a tour on October 17 of a US commercial exhibit in Moscow, and his remarks were broadcast on Soviet television. Talking to US exhibitors at one of the stands, Gorbachev said the situation had reached the point where, when anything appears on the market, "people try to hoard as much as possible, and there is simply a shortage of goods" (*Central Television*, October 17; *Pravda*, October 18).

Wednesday, October 18 ———————————————————

Draft Law on Free Travel Abroad Discussed

Radio Moscow reported that the USSR Supreme Soviet's Committee on International Affairs had discussed a draft law that would give Soviet citizens the right to travel abroad freely. The report said the proposed law covers both emigration and travel and calls for the government to issue passports valid for five years for private travel abroad. Some deputies were reported to have suggested that the passports be valid for ten years. The only restrictions on free travel envisaged in the draft are for security reasons and cases of criminal liability, property obligations, or legal detention. The report said that requests for passports (which would be handled by the Ministry of Internal Affairs) would have to be answered within one month, and within three days in cases involving the illness or death of relatives abroad. The draft would also give citizens the right to appeal to a higher body if they were denied a passport. See RL 458/89.

TASS reported that the USSR Supreme Soviet had tentatively approved, on first reading, a bill that would give local soviets control over all income taxes paid by workers living on the territory controlled by the soviets. The bill also calls for local soviets to receive some of the revenue collected by the central government. The TASS report said the bill was overwhelmingly approved after deputies were told that local soviets in rural areas have little money allocated to them and that this has turned them into mere appendages of well-financed state farms (*Izvestia*, October 18 and 19).

First Reading of Bill on Financing of Local Soviets

TASS reported that the Lithuanian Supreme Soviet had issued a decree declaring December 25 a public holiday. According to a deputy of the republican Supreme Soviet who was quoted by TASS, this is the first time a religious celebration has been declared a legal holiday in Soviet Lithuania.

Christmas Declared Public Holiday in Lithuania

Academician Andrei Sakharov said at a session of the USSR Supreme Soviet that a multiparty system is possible in the Soviet Union. He said that constitutional changes were needed to accomplish this. He suggested that Article 6 of the Constitution asserting the leading role of the Party should be eliminated (*Radio Moscow*, October 18).

Sakharov Says Multiparty System Possible in USSR

A severe shortage of fuel is reported from Georgia. *Sotsialisticheskaya industriya* said that hundreds of cars are lined up at filling stations in Tbilisi and that a driver may have to wait in line for twenty-four hours for fuel. The report quoted an official of the Georgian State Committee for Fuel and Energy, T. Koyav, as saying that the republic has been on "starvation rations" of fuel for a month and that there is no improvement in sight. He blamed supply officials in Moscow and Azerbaijan and the problems on the Azerbaijani railroad.

Georgia Reported Suffering Severe Shortage of Fuel

_____ *Thursday, October 19*

The conservative editor of *Pravda*, Viktor Afanas'ev, was removed from his post and replaced by a political adviser to Gorbachev, Soviet television reported. The main evening news program said the Politburo had named Ivan Frolov as the new chief editor of *Pravda*. Before getting

Politburo Meeting Replaces *Pravda* Editor

his advisory post last year, Frolov was chief editor of the CPSU Central Committee journal *Kommunist*, which he transformed into a liberal periodical publishing controversial material. See RL 481/89.

Soviet Journal Says Imre Nagy Was Traitor

In contrast with other materials in the Soviet press, which have criticized the suppression of the uprising in Hungary in 1956, the military journal *Voenno-istorichesky zhurnal* said former Hungarian Prime Minister Imre Nagy was a traitor. The publication said Nagy played an active role in leading "the counterrevolution" of 1956. Hungary has fully rehabilitated Nagy, who was hanged in 1958 for his role in the 1956 uprising. *Voenno-istorichesky zhurnal* is a conservative journal that earlier this year carried materials approving Stalin's policies during World War II. It has come under strong attack by liberal Soviet periodicals.

Earthquake Reported Near Tatar Nuclear Plant Construction Site

Radio Moscow said there had been an earthquake in the area where a nuclear power plant is being built in the Tatar Autonomous Republic. The report did not say when the earthquake took place or how strong it was. It said there was another earthquake at the same place last April. Radio Moscow has previously quoted experts as saying the location of the plant in an earthquake-prone zone could be a disaster. There have been repeated protests in the Tatar republic against construction of the plant.

USSR Stops Construction of Two Chernobyl'-Type Reactors

A top Soviet nuclear official said construction of two Chernobyl'-type nuclear reactors had been stopped. The reactors are located at Kursk and Smolensk. In a telephone interview, Vice Chairman of the State Committee on Nuclear Safety Viktor Sidorenko told Reuters that authorities were also reconsidering the future of twelve other reactors. The halt to construction comes amid mounting public concern in the USSR over nuclear safety. See RL 461/89.

Rogachev in China for Border Talks

Soviet Deputy Foreign Minister Igor Rogachev arrived in Beijing for Sino-Soviet border talks. The two sides will discuss the boundary along China's far western region of Xinjiang. They reached a broad agreement on the eastern sector of their border at talks in Moscow a year ago (*Reuters*, October 19).

562

New Law to Allow Islamic Teaching in Mosques

A Moslem leader, Sheikh Abdulgani Abdulla, said a new law now being prepared will allow the teaching of the fundamentals of Islam and the Arabic language in mosques in the Soviet Union. Abdulla was quoted by Novosti as saying permission for the teaching "on a private basis" is included in a draft law on freedom of religion now being prepared. Novosti quoted him as saying the new law would also reduce by half, to ten, the number of people necessary to register a religious community and would give religious communities new legal rights.

Estonia to Partially Replace Ruble with New Currency

Estonia is planning to issue a new currency that will partially replace the ruble. TASS said that, starting in January, Estonians will get part of their income paid in the new currency. The report quoted Urbe Nou of the Estonian State Planning Committee as saying people would be able to use the new currency to buy scarce goods at special stores. He said the new currency could also be exchanged for rubles at a floating exchange rate. Nou said the system was a way of protecting Estonia's domestic market.

Radio Moscow Says Donbass Strike Leader Murdered

Radio Moscow said a member of the strike committee at the Donbass coal mines in Ukraine had been murdered. The radio said the victim had worked vigorously to expose corruption at his mine and had been receiving death threats. It said law-enforcement agencies in the Donbass are working on the case (*Radio Moscow World Service*, 1500, October 19).

Student Harvesters Poisoned by Pesticides

Radio Moscow-2 (0730) said nothing had changed at a state farm where nearly 100 students had suffered poisoning from uncontrolled use of pesticides during the harvest. It said pesticides continued to be improperly stored and transported on the Krasnoufimsk Sovkhoz in the Sverdlovsk Raion. The report said some high-school students and students from the Urals State University had worked at the farm this summer as harvesters. It said that nearly 100 of them had become ill and that it was found that chemical concentrations in the soil where they had been working were as much as 120 times the permitted norm. On October 19, *Sovetskaya Rossiya* quoted officials of the Krasnoufimsk Sovkhoz as insisting the students were simply overworked, despite the findings of a special commission that confirmed the poisonings.

Ryzhkov Says 1989 Most Difficult Year Yet for Economic Reorganization

In an interview with Soviet television, Soviet Prime Minister Nikolai Ryzhkov said this is the most difficult year so far in the reorganization of the country's economic system, but he added that the current path is both correct and necessary (*Soviet Television*, "Vremya," October 19). On October 20, TASS carried an official report on Soviet economic performance. The report said that economic growth had declined in the Soviet Union this year and that the output of consumer goods had also fallen in comparison with the first nine months of 1988. The report also said that incomes were increasing faster than the costs of goods and services and that the entire economic situation was "very tense, complicated, and contradictory." TASS quoted Vadim Kirichenko, the chairman of the State Committee for Statistics, as saying that restrictions on income and other drastic and unpopular measures are the only way to rectify "the otherwise unmanageable situation."

Soviet Psychiatrist Reports Doubling of Suicide Rate

A Soviet psychiatrist said the suicide rate in the Soviet Union today is nearly twice as high as it was in the 1920s. APN quoted Georgii Morozov as saying nineteen of every 100,000 Soviet citizens committed suicide during each of the past three years. Morozov was quoted as saying that the figure was only ten suicides per 100,000 when the last study was published in the 1920s. Morozov is the director of the USSR Ministry of Health Institute of General and Forensic Psychiatry in Moscow. He is quoted as saying the current suicide rate in the USSR is much higher than in Britain and the United States. See RL 69/89.

Pravda Opposes Extensive Development of Nuclear Power

Pravda said it opposed "extensive development" of nuclear power. The newspaper said that, in view of new technological developments, it was not known whether new nuclear power plants would be needed in the future. The article was prompted by a growing popular movement that opposes construction of a nuclear station to supply heat for the city of Voronezh. See RL 461/89.

Demonstrations at Induction Stations in Azerbaijan

A spokesman for the Azerbaijani Popular Front said demonstrations were being held in cities all over the republic to protest against the way Azerbaijani conscripts are treated in the Soviet army. Spokesman Alesker Siyabov told RFE/RL in a telephone interview that the demonstrations had started on October 17. Siyabov said most of the demonstrators were relatives of Azerbaijani conscripts who were anxious about the fate of the young men. The spokesman said the popular front had evidence of many cases of maltreatment of Azerbaijanis in the Soviet Army and evidence of some ninety deaths that had been the result of bad treatment (*Reuters, RL Azerbaijani Service*, October 20).

USSR Plans to Drastically Reduce Border Zones

KGB officials said the USSR plans a 90-percent reduction in the size of its border zones. TASS said KGB chairman Vladimir Kryuchkov told a parliamentary committee that the situation along the borders had changed and that there was no need to keep the present large border zones. KGB Deputy Chairman Vadim Matrosov told the committee there are also plans to simplify border-crossing procedures and to remove the barbed wire from many border areas (*TASS*, October 20). See also an interview with Kryuchkov in *Izvestia*, October 26. See RL 184/88.

Soviet Press Criticizes Yurii Afanas'ev

Following Gorbachev's attack on Rector of the Historical Archives Institute and People's Deputy Yurii Afanas'ev, several Soviet newspapers carried items critical of Afanas'ev. On October 20, *Pravda* carried an article attacking Afanas'ev for saying at a conference of informal democratic groups held in Leningrad last month that the Kurile Islands should be returned to Japan. *Pravda* said this makes Afanas'ev an ally of "bellicose Japanese nationalists" who lay groundless claim to the Kuriles. On October 21, *Moskovskaya pravda* reprinted an article from a local paper in Noginsk, just outside Moscow, accusing Afanas'ev of trying to discredit the Communist Party and remove it from the country's political life. On October 21, *Vechernaya Moskva* published two letters from readers saying Afanas'ev's criticism of the Party was not shared by his constituents and complaining that the historian's approach is not constructive at a time when the Party is trying to solve the country's problems. On November 22, *Vechernaya Moskva* published a letter by a group of people's deputies in defense of Afanas'ev. In an editorial note the board of the newspaper criticized those signing the letter.

Railroad Minister Promises to Rectify Import Jam

Radio Moscow-2 (0820) said USSR Minister of Railroads Nikolai Konarev had promised special steps within two weeks to move all imported goods piled up at Soviet ports and border points. The radio said 9,000 railroad cars with goods from East Germany, Bulgaria, Romania, Czechoslovakia, Hungary, and other countries were waiting for transshipment to Soviet cars at crossing points.

Saturday, October 21

Argumenty i fakty Publishes New Poll

Argumenty i fakty, which was attacked by Gorbachev for publishing an opinion poll ranking Andrei Sakharov as the most popular people's deputy, carried in its issue No. 42 another poll rating Gorbachev as the country's most authoritative politician. Reporting on the publication, TASS said the new survey polled people representing a cross-section of society and was more authoritative and scientific than the first, which was based on readers' letters.

Ligachev Interviewed by Argumenty i fakty

Politburo member Egor Ligachev was interviewed in *Argumenty i fakty* (No. 42). After Gorbachev attacked the periodical on October 13, Ligachev was reported to have called the editorial board of the periodical and expressed his support. In the interview, Ligachev denied that he was a rival of Gorbachev and alleged that he and Gorbachev were "of like mind." In the very same interview, however, Ligachev implicitly attacked Gorbachev's policy. Ligachev also defended collective farming as the main means of providing the country with food but said this did not preclude the need to create small peasant farms. He also warned that *perestroika* would take a long time to accomplish.

RSFSR Popular Fronts Hold Constituent Congress

A constituent congress of popular fronts of the RSFSR opened in the city of Yaroslavl. Radio Moscow said the congress was being attended by delegates from thirty-eight cities of the RSFSR representing popular fronts and other pro-democracy movements in the republic. The radio said the congress was discussing draft statutes and a program of action and electing working bodies (*Radio Moscow-2*, 1900, October 21). AP carried a more detailed report on the congress. It revealed that among the groups taking part in the congress were local popular fronts of various cities of the USSR, together with ecological, religious, and even monarchist groups. One of the demands of the congress was that the CPSU should give up its monopoly on power.

566

The Uzbek Supreme Soviet passed a controversial language law that sparked big demonstrations in Tashkent. According to TASS, the language law makes Uzbek the state language and "ensures the free and equal use of the Russian language as a language of interethnic communication." Opponents of the law wanted Uzbek to be both the state language and the language of interethnic communication. Sources said that 50,000 people demonstrated against the new law on October 19 and 20 in Tashkent and that more than 100 people were detained, including the leader of the Uzbek Popular Front (*AP, RL Uzbek Service*, October 21). TASS said the Supreme Soviet also appointed a new prime minister for the republic to replace Gairat Kadyrov, who, it said, had been relieved of his job and transferred to another post. Kadyrov was replaced by Irakhmat Mirkasymov, first secretary of the Tashkent Oblast Party Committee (*Pravda*, October 22).

Uzbek Supreme Soviet Passes Language Law

Western reports from Moscow said a group of Soviet military officers had met to form a military trade union. The group, known as "Shchit" (Shield), opened a founding congress in Moscow on October 21 that was attended by about 200 people. The group said it was concerned about the welfare of servicemen and their families. Several of those who attended gave accounts of corruption, nepotism, and abuse of recruits by higher-ranking personnel in the Soviet armed forces. The reports said the union had the support of the reformist Interregional Group of Deputies (*AP*, October 21).

Military Trade Union Set Up

Thousands of people demonstrated in Kazakhstan demanding an end to nuclear tests at the Semipalatinsk test site. The protests were held both in the Kazakh capital Alma-Ata and in the town of Semipalatinsk. An antinuclear group was formed in Kazakhstan in March to oppose testing and demand the closure of plants making nuclear materials for the military (*Reuters*, October 21).

Thousands Protest against Nuclear Tests in Kazakhstan

Lithuania was reported to be setting limits on tourism from Eastern Europe to stop tourists from buying up food and other consumer goods in local shops. TASS said that residents of Lithuania would be allowed to invite a given person from Eastern Europe to visit only once a year for preset dates. It also said a Lithuanian government order had reduced the number of Polish trains entering Lithuania and banned posting packages to Poland.

Lithuania Restricts Foreign Tourists to Prevent Buying Up of Goods

Special Measures Needed to Cope with Rail Problems in Transcaucasia

Grigorii Davydov, first deputy head of the Main Administration of Transport, said in an interview with Radio Moscow (1200) that extraordinary measures were needed to cope with continued problems with rail transport in Transcaucasia. Davydov said action was needed to deal with some 22,000 freight cars with various goods destined for Armenia. He said that there were at present only about 1,500–1,600 freight cars operating within Armenia and that steps should be taken to raise that number to 2,300–2,400 cars within twenty-four hours.

Sunday, October 22

Moscow News Says Tiananmen Crackdown Was Tragedy

Moscow News (No. 43) contained an article saying the crushing of Chinese student protests in Peking in June was "a tragedy." The article took a much more critical attitude towards the suppression of the protests in Peking than that taken by earlier reports in the Soviet media, which were very restrained.

Majority Untouched by Perestroika, Poll Says

Ogonek (No. 43) carried an opinion poll revealing that people are losing confidence in *perestroika*. *Ogonek* said 51 percent of those surveyed believe that the reform program will produce insignificant change or no change at all. Only 12 percent said they believe *perestroika* will lead to significant improvement, and 52 percent indicated that their standard of living had not improved in recent years.

Unauthorized Demonstration in Moldavia

An unauthorized demonstration of at least 20,000 people took place in Kishinev. The demonstrators demanded the legal registration of the Moldavian Popular Front, access by the front to the mass media, and the drafting of a law on Moldavian republican citizenship (*RFE Romanian Service*, October 24). TASS and Radio Moscow reported the demonstration on October 23, accusing the demonstrators of violating public order. On October 25, the Presidium of the Moldavian Supreme Soviet appointed a committee to prepare draft laws on guarantees for national groups. In a report on the appointment of the committee, Radio Moscow did not name any national group under consideration, but it seems that the Moldavian Popular Front is one of them. Radio Moscow also said the Supreme Soviet had set up a working group to prepare a draft law on the sovereignty of the Moldavian republic.

On October 26, a spokesman for the Moldavian Popular Front told RFE /RL that his organization had been granted legal status as "a mass public organization."

The trade-union newspaper *Trud* broke the Soviet media's silence on the turmoil in East Germany, saying problems had piled up there for years while the Party leadership spoke only of successes. The newspaper's correspondent in Berlin, V. Nikitin, said the exodus of tens of thousands of East German citizens to West Germany had done "great moral and material damage" to the country. The newspaper also said the East German mass media had "separated themselves from the realities of life with an impenetrable wall."

Trud on Situation in East Germany

The secretary of the parliamentary Commission on the Plan, Budget, and Finance told *Sotsialisticheskaya industriya* that the draft state plan and budget for 1990 were causing "deep concern" among deputies. TASS said Gennadii Filshin told the newspaper the drafts were nothing more than "a face-lift" of the old command-administrative system. Filshin said they effectively block transition to new economic methods. He urged ending regulation from above and giving more freedom to republics, regions, and enterprises.

Parliamentarian Criticizes Proposed State Plan and Budget

Soviet television said thousands of people in Western Siberia will have to be resettled because of danger caused by a poorly constructed pipeline carrying oil products. The pipeline runs from Western Siberia through the Urals to the Volga basin. Soviet television said a test on the pipeline in an uninhabited area near Tobolsk in Western Siberia had produced an explosion that could have wiped out a whole village. The report said the blast was caused by a build-up of heavy gases in the pipeline (*Central Television*, "Vremya," October 22).

People to Be Resettled Because of Danger from Pipeline

Pravda reported that over one million tons of undelivered goods had piled up at railroad stops and sidings, with about 185,000 containers delayed en route. The report mentioned consumer goods in short supply, such as sugar, cocoa, and detergents among the stalled cargoes. Czechoslovak television on October 21 said that about 1,000 wagonloads of goods bound for the Soviet Union were languishing on the border because of a shortage of

Railroad Freight Backlog Grows

railroad cars on the Soviet side (*Reuters*, October 21). On October 24, USSR Minister of Railways Nikolai Konarev said the USSR has serious problems with "a vast quantity" of freight accumulating in some areas. He told *Izvestia* that there are 176,000 containers of goods waiting to be shipped around the country and some 25,000 idle freight-cars. Konarev also said Soviet railways were not coping with freight arriving from abroad. On October 24, a USSR Deputy Minister of Railways told Soviet television that in Leningrad only 7 percent of containers were taken to their destinations every day and that in Moscow the figure was about 10 percent.

New Seminary in Tobolsk

TASS reported that a new Russian Orthodox seminary had been opened in Tobolsk in Western Siberia. This is the fifth Russian Orthodox seminary in the USSR. The fourth, in Kiev, was opened three weeks ago.

Monday, October 23 _____

Gorbachev Talks to *Pravda* Editors, Frolov Interviewed

On October 23, Gorbachev met with the editorial board of *Pravda* and introduced its members to Ivan Frolov, the newspaper's new chief editor. The remarks made by Gorbachev at the meeting confirmed the impression created by his speech to representatives of the mass media on October 13 that he is very concerned about the sharp criticism of the Soviet past and present that is appearing in the Soviet media. TASS and Soviet television quoted Gorbachev as telling the *Pravda* editorial staff that their most important task now is to keep radical slogans from gaining ground among the population. Gorbachev also insisted that the Soviet media should promote the humanitarian values of socialism among the population. On October 23, *Izvestia* carried an interview with Ivan Frolov, who spoke about his new job as *Pravda*'s chief editor. He echoed Gorbachev, saying everything that is published in *Pravda* should concentrate on the individual and the humanitarian values of socialism.

Supreme Soviet Votes on Draft Election Law

On October 23, the USSR Supreme Soviet began discussion of the draft law on changes and additions to the USSR Constitution with regard to the electoral system (*TASS*, October 23; *Pravda*, October 24). The changes concern elections to republican and local soviets, which are scheduled to take place in December or early next year.

The draft law will in effect sanction a one-tier republican parliament and also make the allocation of seats to public organizations optional. Gorbachev made plain, however, that he was not prepared—at least at present—to agree to the election of republican presidents by popular vote rather than by the republican legislatures. Gorbachev argued that having republican presidents directly elected could lead to the concentration of too much power in the hands of one person. He said the country did not need "saviors of the nation of the kind that we have already witnessed."

On October 24, after a heated debate, the USSR Supreme Soviet voted 254 to 85 in favor of removing from the USSR Constitution the provision for one-third of deputies to the all-Union and republican parliaments to be elected by public organizations (*TASS*, October 24; *Pravda*, October 25, 26; *Izvestia*, October 25).

The Supreme Soviet also approved an amendment permitting the republics to decide for themselves whether their presidents and the chairmen of local soviets should be elected by the parliament or by direct popular vote.

Meanwhile, on October 23, Lithuanian President Vytautas Astrauskas revealed at a meeting of the Presidium of the Lithuanian Supreme Soviet in Vilnius that Gorbachev had sent personal letters to the chairmen of the presidiums of all republican Supreme Soviets telling them that the laws approved by the republican Supreme Soviets must not be allowed to conflict with those that govern the USSR. The letter was quoted as criticizing laws and constitutional changes already made in the three Baltic republics and in Azerbaijan. The letter demanded that these actions be reversed (*RFE Lithuanian Service*, October 24).

Miners Strike Again

Coal miners in Western Siberia's Kuzbass staged a warning strike on October 23, and on October 25 miners at (at least) three pits in Vorkuta in the Soviet Far North were reported to have joined their action (four pits voted against strike action). In both areas, the miners are angry because they say the authorities have not honored pledges made at the end of their strike in July. One of the miners' demands that has evidently not been met is that the wholesale price of coal be raised to the world level. In general, the miners' demand for economic independence for their enterprises has been stymied by the failure of the Gorbachev leadership to institute a price reform and so make enterprise autonomy a real possibility. "Vremya" reported that, in the Mezhdurechensk area of the Kuzbass, between 15,000 and 20,000 coal miners staged a two-hour warning strike and were joined by other workers, including railroad workers. The miners were said to have given two days warning of their intention to strike. This does not appear to meet the requirements for advance notice and for arbitration and conciliation laid down in the law on labor disputes adopted by the USSR Supreme Soviet a fortnight ago. (For the text of the law, see *Pravda*, October 14.) In addition, that law explicitly forbids strikes by railway workers. The oblast Party first secretary, Aleksandr Mel'nikov, appeared on local television on October 23 and appealed to the miners to show "reason."

On October 24, *Izvestia* printed a letter from Gorbachev thanking workers at a Russian ore-processing plant for deciding to resist calls from colleagues to go on strike. He said this spared the country more convulsions.

On October 25, the chairman of the strike committee in the Vorkuta region, Valentin Kopasov, revealed that the miners' demands included the elimination of the constitutional provision on the leading role of the CPSU and the granting of official status to new committees formed to defend workers' rights (*Reuters, AP*, October 25).

On October 26, the strike undertaken by miners in Vorkuta was reported to have spread to include about 16,000 miners. Kopasov said local mine directors were trying to collect lists of strike participants and organizers apparently in anticipation of possible legal action (*AP*, October 26).

On October 27, miners at at least one pit in Vorkuta were reported to be continuing their strike, despite a court ruling against their walkout. The Supreme Court in the Komi Autonomous Oblast ruled that the strike at the Vorgashorskaya mine violated Soviet law. In a commentary, Radio Moscow said that many of the miners' demands were justified but that this was a bad time for them to go on strike, because there was already a shortage of fuel in many places (*TASS, Radio Moscow*, 0645, October 27).

Shevardnadze's Speech to the Supreme Soviet

In a speech to the USSR Supreme Soviet, Soviet Foreign Minister Eduard Shevardnadze said there are problems and difficulties, but no crisis, in the USSR's relations with other Socialist countries. He said the emergence of new political forces in some of these countries does not mean that these countries are no longer Soviet allies. He said, however, that it was no longer possible to act within old structures. The foreign minister declared his government is prepared to head towards the dissolution of military and political blocs in Europe (*TASS*, October 23). In his speech, Shevardnadze criticized both the Soviet decision to build a controversial radar station at Krasnoyarsk and the Soviet military intervention in Afghanistan. He told the Supreme Soviet that the radar complex violated the US-Soviet Antiballistic Missile Treaty of 1972. He also said the sending of Soviet troops into Afghanistan had involved "gross violations" of Soviet law, moral standards, and Party and civic norms. On October 24, the White House called Shevardnadze's acknowledgment that the Soviet Union had acted illegally in invading Afghanistan and in building the Krasnoyarsk radar complex "extraordinary" (*AP*, October 24; *Pravda*, October 24).

Baltic Republics Agree to Discuss Common Market

The prime ministers of Latvia, Lithuania, and Estonia agreed to discuss the formation of a Baltic common market and a gradual transition to local currencies. TASS said the agreement was contained in a communiqué issued following a meeting of the three Baltic prime ministers in Riga. The communiqué said there were plans to draft a treaty in December concerning cooperation between Latvia, Lithuania, and Estonia in 1990. The communiqué also said the transition to cost-accounting and self-management in the Baltic republics, set to start in January, will take place under "tense and difficult conditions," and it added that now was the time to draft the general principles and the structure of treaties concerning economic cooperation between the Baltic republics, the central government, and other Soviet republics.

Mass Grave of NKVD Victims Found near Irkutsk

Izvestia said a mass grave of people killed by the NKVD in 1937 and 1938 had been found near the airport in Irkutsk at the beginning of this month. The newspaper said that so far the remains of more than 300 people killed by the NKVD had been found.

Azerbaijani Party and Activists Discuss Nagorno-Karabakh

Azerbaijani Party officials met with representatives of the public and intellectuals in Baku to discuss a political solution to the Nagorno-Karabakh problem. Suggestions for a solution were drawn up on October 20 by the Presidium of the USSR Supreme Soviet, following a report by a parliamentary commission that studied the situation in the region. Soviet television said the Baku meeting was addressed by Azerbaijani Party First Secretary Abdul-Rakhman Vezirov. It gave no details of his speech.

Soviet Police and MVD Troops Hold Conference

Soviet police officers and MVD troops began a conference to discuss ways of dealing with interethnic conflicts and demonstrations. In its "Vremya" news program, Soviet television said recent violent incidents around the country had shown that those who were supposed to safeguard law and order often acted inappropriately. It said the consequences of this were too tragic to be ignored.

Tuesday, October 24

New Parliamentary Club Founded

"Vremya" reported that a new club had been founded to bring deputies and voters closer together. Called "Rossiya," the club is sponsored by the conservative newspapers *Sovetskaya Rossiya* and *Literaturnaya Rossiya* and the journals *Nash sovremennik* and *Molodaya gvardiya*. One of the founders of the new club, People's Deputy Veniamin Yarin, was interviewed by "Vremya." Yarin has recently made a name for himself as spokesman for a populist, Russian nationalist platform that opposes many aspects of Gorbachev's economic reform program. Yarin assured the viewers on October 24 that "Rossiya" "is not some kind of isolated, private club" but is open "to representatives of all republics and every nationality." Yarin said the sole aim of the club is to facilitate contacts between parliamentarians and the electorate. In fact voters' clubs have already been set up in Moscow, Leningrad, Kiev, and other cities on the initiative of the reformist Interregional Group of People's Deputies, so "Rossiya" would appear to be a rival organization.

Details on MVD Troops Revealed

The chief of the USSR's MVD troops, Colonel General Yurii Shatalin, said his troops will never be used to deal with workers' strikes in the Soviet Union. According to Reuters, on October 24 Shatalin revealed at a press conference in Moscow that 44 percent (16,000 out of 36,000) of MVD troops are deployed in southern Soviet republics hit by ethnic disturbances. He added that 5,500 of them are stationed in Nagorno-Karabakh and 4,500 in Georgia. Shatalin also told reporters that the number of MVD troops would be increased by 26,700 over the next two years. The MVD troops will apparently be staffed largely by members of the elite KGB border guards. According to KGB boss Vladimir Kryuchkov, the Soviet border zones will be cut to 10 percent of their present size, indicating that there will be no need to maintain the current border troop strength of 200,000.

Eduard Shevardnadze arrived in Warsaw for his first visit to Poland since "Solidarity" took over the Polish government. The same day, Shevardnadze started talks with Polish Foreign Minister Krzysztof Skubiszewski (*Reuters, UPI, AP,* October 24). It was reported that Shevardnadze pledged to keep up current Soviet fuel deliveries to Poland. Later he met for talks with Prime Minister Tadeusz Mazowiecki, which resulted in an agreement Mazowiecki would visit Moscow in November. "Blank spots" in Soviet-Polish relations were discussed, with Shevardnadze saying that the USSR is interested in finding out the truth. Speaking to reporters, he said the USSR will continue to study the issue of the massacre of Polish officers in Katyn. On the evening of October 24, Polish television reported on Gorbachev's visit. It revealed that Shevardnadze had told Skubiszewski that Moscow was not enchanted by the electoral defeat of Polish Communists but that "we do not see anything dangerous in it."

On October 25, Shevardnadze held talks with Polish Communist Party First Secretary Mieczyslaw Rakowski. Shevardnadze also talked to Adam Michnik, the former political prisoner who now edits the "Solidarity" daily *Gazeta wyborcza.* During the meetings, Shevardnadze was reported as saying the USSR wanted relations with Poland based on equality. Talking to reporters after the meetings, he again said the USSR was interested in filling in "blank spots" in Soviet-Polish relations (*DPA, AP,* October 25). The "Solidarity" leader in the Polish Sejm, Bronislaw Geremek, said that the elimination of "blank spots" in Polish-Soviet history was not going well. Geremek said that the Soviet side had given a verbal token of goodwill but that Poles were still waiting for this to be turned into deeds. Geremek's comments appeared in an interview with the West German newspaper *Die Welt* on October 26. On October 25, Shevardnadze met with Polish President Wojciech Jaruzelski (*TASS,* October 25).

Shevardnadze Visits Poland

Stepan Sitaryan, an Armenian, was nominated to become a Soviet deputy prime minister and chairman of the Council of Ministers' Foreign Economic Commission. TASS said Sitaryan's nomination is scheduled to be discussed later by the USSR Supreme Soviet. Sitaryan is an economist and has been deputy chairman of the State Planning Committee since December, 1986. The job he is supposed to fill has been vacant for about three months. In June and July, Ryzhkov twice nominated the incumbent, Vladimir Kamentsev, to keep the post, but Kamentsev was rejected by the USSR Supreme Soviet.

Ryzhkov Nominates New Deputy Prime Minister

575

"Sajudis" Drafts a Lithuanian Citizenship Law

The National Assembly of "Sajudis" wants a law establishing separate Lithuanian citizenship. The assembly approved a draft of such a law on October 24. Officials of "Sajudis" told RFE the draft is designed to make sure that accepting Lithuanian citizenship does not imply accepting Soviet citizenship. They said the draft also stipulates that accepting Lithuanian citizenship does not mean canceling citizenship of the pre-war Lithuanian republic (*RFE Lithuanian Service*, October 25).

Wednesday, October 25 ─────────────────────────

Gorbachev in Finland

Gorbachev arrived in Helsinki and opened talks with Finnish leaders. Gorbachev was accompanied on this trip by several Soviet officials, including Estonian Party First Secretary Vaino Valjas. Gorbachev met first with Finnish President Mauno Koivisto. At a welcoming ceremony at the president's residence, some demonstrators carried placards on the issue of the Karelian Peninsula, which Finland was forced to cede to the USSR in 1944 (*Reuters, AP*, October 25). Commenting on Gorbachev's visit, Finnish parliamentary speaker Kalevi Sorsa told *Izvestia* there is great interest in knowing what the USSR thinks about the Nordic countries' place in "the common European home." Speaking at a press conference in Moscow, Foreign Ministry spokesman Gennadii Gerasimov reported that Gorbachev had told his Finnish hosts that the USSR would not interfere with changes taking place in Eastern Europe (*TASS*, in English, October 25). Gorbachev also attended an official banquet in his honor at which he said that each stage of *perestroika* in the Soviet Union is proving to be more difficult than the previous one. He said the Soviet Union was now going through the most crucial stage. Gorbachev also paid tribute to "neutral Finland." He said Soviet-Finnish relations needed to adapt to the times but stressed that the basic ideas of the 1948 treaty—friendship, cooperation, and mutual assistance— were as relevant as they were then (*Reuters*, October 25; *Pravda*, October 26).

On October 26, Gorbachev met with Finland's leading businessmen and politicians to study ideas for capitalist projects in the USSR. Addressing the gathering, Gorbachev said the USSR was about to eliminate unilaterally certain classes of sea-launched nuclear missiles in the Baltic. He also revived an earlier proposal to declare the region a nuclear-free zone. (*Reuters, UPI*, October 26). On October 26, Gorbachev and Koivisto signed a bilateral economic agreement covering the period from 1991 to 1995. The agreement said Finland will import crude oil products and natural gas from the Soviet Union in exchange for Finnish machine tools, ships, and shipping equipment worth about 3.5 billion rubles. A protocol of intent for a joint venture to develop the Kola Peninsula was also signed. The project is designed to revitalize and develop the peninsula's industry (*AP, UPI*, October 26; *Pravda*, October 27). At a press conference the same day, Gorbachev said there were broad opportunities for direct political relations between Finland and the Baltic republics and other parts of the Soviet Union. Before returning to Moscow on October 27, Gorbachev toured a high-technology center located in the Arctic city of Oulu (*AP, Reuters, UPI*, October 27).

A TASS dispatch stated that, with effect from November 1, the official exchange rate for the ruble against freely convertible currencies for tourist and business travel purposes will be based on the rate of 6.26 rubles to the US dollar. On the face of it, this is a tenfold devaluation, lowering the official exchange rate of the ruble from about 1.61 dollars to about 16 cents, and bringing it much closer to the black-market rates of between 5 and 10 cents that have recently been quoted. On October 27, Deputy Chairman of the USSR State Bank Valerii Pekshev told a news conference that the devaluation of the ruble would help curb speculation in the Soviet currency (*Reuters, AP, TASS*, October 27).

New Exchange Rate for Ruble

The Supreme Soviet of the RSFSR discussed a draft law that would end the practice of reserving legislative seats for the Communist Party and other organizations (*Izvestia*, October 25). The draft presented to the RSFSR legislators makes all seats in a new Russian Congress of People's Deputies subject to elections from territorial districts (*TASS*, October 25). Speaking at the RSFSR Supreme Soviet session, the republican president, Vitalii Vorotnikov, said proposals to create constituencies within factories had been dismissed as unworkable. The idea of creating constituencies within factories was put forward by the conservative informal group the United Front of Workers of Russia. In the end, however, the RSFSR law on elections allowed "on experimental basis" the creation of constituencies within factories (*Sovetskaya Rossiya*, November 1). On October 27, the RSFSR

RSFSR Supreme Soviet Convenes

Supreme Soviet approved the creation of a Congress of People's Deputies for the republic and scheduled elections of its 1,068 deputies for March 4, 1990.

Chief of Staff Acknowledges Nationality Frictions

Armed Forces Chief of Staff General Mikhail Moiseev said nationality frictions in the Soviet armed forces required increased attention. Moiseev said in a TASS interview that the problems arise in the form of "national egoism and conceit" and "cliquishness." He dismissed talks of a "nationality-based" split in the armed forces as "ideological subversion," however.

New Commission to Study Conversion

TASS reported that, on the initiative of the USSR Academy of Sciences and the All-Union Central Council of Trade Unions, a new National Commission for Assistance in Converting War Industries to Civilian Production had been created. Its chairman is Vsevolod Avduevsky. Gennadii Yanaev, deputy chairman of the Central Council of Trade Unions, is also on the leadership roster. The first news conference of the group—held on October 25 at the USSR Foreign Ministry's press center—focused on the difficulties the Soviet Union is experiencing in the conversion process. The commission is preparing a special international conference to be held next July to study the issue in depth. The commission includes representatives of trade unions. This can be explained by the fact that when enterprises are switched to civilian production, they tend to receive lower earnings and profits and must therefore cut wages—something that is not well received by workers or their union representatives and has been an increasingly common theme in the Soviet literature on conversion. See RL 261/89 and RL 388/89.

Thursday, October 26 ————————————————————————

Member of Congress of People's Deputies Quits Party

A member of the Congress of People's Deputies left the CPSU to protest against what he called pressure against editors of several newspapers and journals. He is Yurii Vlasov, a former Olympic champion weightlifter. Vlasov attracted attention earlier this year when he delivered a speech at the Congress of People's Deputies, attacking the KGB. Vlasov was reported to have announced his decision to leave the Party at a meeting of voters in the Lyublino District of Moscow. Asked why he was quitting the Party, Vlasov said he had been considering the move for a long time. He said the last straw was the pressure being put on editors. He said that he felt this was extraordinary and that he would be considered a participant in this campaign if he remained a member of the Party (*RL Russian Service*, October 26). Vlasov was apparently referring to Gorbachev's attack on editors and contributors to outspoken reformist periodicals in his speech on October 13 and Gorbachev's demand for the ouster of Vladislav Starkov from the post of chief editor of *Argumenty i fakty*.

Protests against Nuclear Plant in Bashkiria Reported

Radio Moscow reported protests against construction of a nuclear power plant in the Bashkir Autonomous Republic. The radio said a protest meeting was held in Neftekamsk, about thirty kilometers from the plant site, but it did not say when. It said scientists, writers, and journalists had urged an immediate halt to construction of the plant. It said the meeting passed a resolution calling the nuclear plant "ecologically unfounded and economically unjustified."

Founding Congress of Kadet Party

Tanjug, in English, reported that the founding congress of an informal group whose members see themselves as the successors of the Kadet Party (Constitutional Democrats) had been held in Moscow. The Kadet Party, which included in its ranks representatives of the liberal Russian intelligentsia, played a visible role in Russian political life until the October Revolution. Many representatives of the Kadets were members of the Provisional Government. Tanjug said that the founding congress of the new Kadets was attended by ten delegates from ten Russian cities. One of the members of the new party said the organization's goals are to stimulate private enterprise and to promote private ownership, a multiparty system, and parliamentarianism in the Soviet Union.

Human-Rights Committee Founded in Belorussia

Reports reaching the West said the Belorussian Popular Front had created a committee to monitor human-rights developments in Belorussia. The committee, called "The Vienna Committee," is to monitor Belorussian compliance with the human-rights agreement signed last January in Vienna at the Conference on Security and Cooperation in Europe. The Vienna Committee has already issued a statement saying that the government of Belorussia is violating the accord (*RL Belorussian Service*, October 26).

*Friday, October 27*_____

Official Says Supreme Soviet Has Power to Curb Use of Military

Chairman of the Council of the Union of the USSR Supreme Soviet Evgenii Primakov said the Supreme Soviet is becoming an authoritative legislative body with the power to block use of the Soviet Union's armed forces at home and abroad. Primakov, who is heading a delegation of Soviet parliamentarians visiting the US Congress, said there could be no repetition of the Politburo's secret decision in 1979 to invade Afghanistan. Primakov was speaking to an audience of academics and journalists at the Brookings Institution, a private policy research organization in Washington. He said the domestic use of military force would in future be authorized through a declaration of martial law, which would have to be approved by the Congress of People's Deputies as well as the Supreme Soviet. He also said a new relationship is developing between the Soviet executive branch and the legislature. He said that, while the Politburo sets overall policy, the Supreme Soviet has developed into a truly legislative body making its own decisions. He added, however, that the CPSU still plays a central role in most things. Asked about reported attempts by the Soviet leadership to remove Vladimir Starkov from his post as editor of *Argumenty i fakty*, Primakov said the Party has the right "to criticize the views of Party members who occupy such posts" (*RFE/RL Special*, October 28).

Soviet Union Halts Construction of Nuclear Power Station

Izvestia reported that the USSR Council of Ministers has decided to halt construction of a nuclear plant in the Crimea and turn it into a nuclear research and training complex instead. *Izvestia* said the converted facilities will not threaten the environment. There has been strong public opposition to the Crimean plant mainly on the grounds that the area is prone to seismic activity. See RL 64/89 and RL 495/89.

Warsaw Pact Endorses Freedom of Political Choice

In a communiqué issued after a two-day meeting in Warsaw, members of the Warsaw Pact endorsed the principle of freedom of political choice for every nation. The communiqué said this principle was essential for a secure, peaceful, and indivisible Europe. It rejected the notion that military alliances are entitled to intervene in disputes between member states (*UPI, AFP, DPA, Radio Budapest*, 1830, October 27).

The Supreme Soviet of Belorussia approved a program to eliminate the consequences of the Chernobyl' nuclear accident. Radio Moscow said this was the second time the program had been submitted to the Belorussian parliament. The revised draft provides for measures costing about 17 billion rubles, which is 7 billion more than the republic's annual budget. Soviet television also reported the discussion at the Belorussian Supreme Soviet and revealed that further evacuations from the zones affected by the Chernobyl' accident were being prepared. It said that, according to preliminary data, over 100,000 people should be resettled. See RL 198/89, RL 322/89, and RL 324/89.

Belorussian Supreme Soviet Approves Chernobyl' Plan

A Soviet physician said the tomb of Lenin is being closed so that the leader's remains can be checked. Sergei Debov, the doctor who has been responsible for the remains since 1950, said the mausoleum will be closed from November 10 until January 15. Debov told *Pravda* that the body is in good condition and that people who call for the removal of Lenin's remains from the mausoleum "want to bury Leninism." In recent months there have been calls in the media and at the Congress of People's Deputies for the body to be removed and buried in a cemetery.

Lenin Tomb to Be Closed for Checks on Body

Soviet Foreign Minister Eduard Shevardnadze said the USSR respects the Czechoslovak Party and government view of the events that led to the Warsaw Pact invasion of Czechoslovakia. Shevardnadze's remarks came in an interview with Polish "Solidarity" editor Adam Michnik that was published in *Gazeta wyborcza*. Shevardnadze said that Prague's view of the events had not changed since 1968 and that Czechoslovakia had a right to evaluate its own history. Shevardnadze also said that the decision to use force in 1968 was made collectively by Warsaw Pact leaders and that a reevaluation of the decision could only be made by those leaders.

Shevardnadze Says USSR Respects Czechoslovak View of 1968 Events

The chief of the Soviet general staff, General Mikhail Moiseev, said the USSR plans to cut its Northwestern Group of Forces by 40,000 soldiers and 12,000 tanks by 1991. He said that big cuts would be made in artillery and that personnel in the Leningrad and Baltic areas would be reduced by a third. TASS said the USSR today destroyed the last of 957 nuclear missiles of the kind known in the West as the SS-23. They were banned under the medium-range nuclear missile treaty.

Cuts to Be Made in Northwestern Soviet Forces

Thirty-six Killed in Third Soviet Military Crash in One Week

The USSR Ministry of Defense said a military transport plane crashed in the Soviet Far East killing all thirty passengers and six crew members aboard. The plane was carrying both troops responsible for operating Soviet missile installations and the troops' families. A military official said the plane crashed into a mountain while trying to land with poor visibility. The crash was the third involving Soviet military aircraft in just over a week (*TASS*, in English, October 27).

Four Million Leave Komsomol in One Year

The head of the Soviet Komsomol, Viktor Mironenko, said 4 million members have quit the organization in the past year. Mironenko, who was delivering the main report to a plenary session of the organization in Moscow, said the organization had lost 10 million members in the past four years (*Central Television*, "Vremya," October 27).

Soviet Envoy Pledges Continued Support for Mengistu

USSR First Deputy Foreign Minister Yulii Vorontsov, who is visiting Addis Ababa, reaffirmed Moscow's continuing support for Ethiopia's Marxist government. "The Soviet Union will firmly support the Ethiopian revolution and will continue to provide both political and economic assistance for the prosperity and peace of the Ethiopean people," the official Ethiopian news agency ENA quoted him as saying. Ethiopia is the USSR's main ally in Africa, and Moscow has provided large amounts of sophisticated weaponry to help Mengistu in his war against the Eritrea and Tigré rebels (*Reuters*, October 27).

Saturday, October 28 ─────────────────────────────

Soviet Economy Worsens in Third Quarter

New figures on the Soviet economy indicate declining production and a worsening food supply. Figures released by the State Committee for Statistics for the first nine months of 1989 showed that industrial production was down significantly in the third quarter of the year. The committee noted an alarming situation in the coal industry, which was swept by strikes in July, and said production of oil and gas had also declined. It also revealed that, while food imports had increased, the supply of food to many areas had actually worsened. Commenting on the figures, TASS said they showed that policies for revitalizing the economy had not yet had tangible results (*Izvestia*, October 28).

The Ukrainian Supreme Soviet adopted a law making Ukrainian the official language of the republic. Russian is to be the language of interethnic communication and have equal status with all languages in Ukraine (*Radio Moscow*, 1600, October 28).

Ukrainian Approved as Official Language

TASS said that the crime rate rose more than 30 percent in the Soviet Union in the first nine months of this year and that serious crime is rising even faster than the overall crime rate. It said crime is rising practically everywhere with one crime in three remaining unsolved. A senior police official was quoted as saying the demand for private detective agencies poses threats to the legal rights of Soviet citizens, because private agencies would increase the possibility of bribery, blackmail, and illegal surveillance.

Crime Rate Soars in the Soviet Union

The Lithuanian Communist Party published a new draft platform based on the principle that the Party is independent and no longer part of the CPSU. Radio Vilnius said the ultimate goal of the Lithuanian Party is the reestablishment of a sovereign Lithuanian state. It said the new platform was worked out by a working group of the republic's Central Committee and the Lithuanian Academy of Sciences (*Sovetskaya Litva*, October 29). On October 31, Soviet television quoted Lithuanian Party chief Algirdas Brazauskas as saying, however, that his Party's leadership was using all means to avert a split with the CPSU. He said independence for the Lithuanian Party would not mean that all contacts with the center would be cut off.

Draft Platform Proposes Independence for Lithuanian Party

Sunday, October 29

Two Soviet officials said members of the Warsaw Pact are free to leave the alliance. Evgenii Primakov, chairman of the Council of the Union of the USSR Supreme Soviet, said the USSR would not prevent a Warsaw Pact nation from leaving. Nikolai Shishlin, a spokesman for the CPSU Central Committee, said the USSR would not be threatened if Hungary left the Warsaw Pact. He added, however, that Hungarian officials have said they want to remain in the pact for the moment. The comments of Primakov and Shishlin came during television interviews in the United States (*AP, UPI, Reuters*, October 30).

Soviet Officials Say Warsaw Pact Members Free to Leave Alliance

Many Young People Refusing to Serve in Armed Forces

In an interview in *Krasnaya zvezda*, a Soviet military, official said many young people were refusing to serve in the Soviet armed forces. Lieutenant General Norat Ter-Grigoryants, who is deputy chief of staff of Ground Forces, said refusal to serve in the armed forces was especially common in the Baltic and Transcaucasian republics. A TASS report on October 31 said Latvians of conscription age were refusing to do their military service on the grounds that this contravened a clause in the 1949 Geneva Convention barring service in an occupying army. An earlier report in *Krasnaya zvezda* (October 28) said Latvian nationalists had set up pickets at a conscription center and urged young men to refuse service "in the occupation army."

Soviet Party Apparatus Said Blocking New Line on Religion

In an interview with *Ogonek*(No. 44), Konstantin Kharchev, former head of the Council for Religious Affairs, claimed that Party bureaucrats are trying to block Mikhail Gorbachev's efforts to increase religious tolerance. Kharchev, who was ousted from his post earlier this year, said that the only change in the CPSU Central Committee's personnel responsible for religious affairs has been the appointment of even more conservative officials. Kharchev expressed his support for the legalization of the Ukrainian Catholic Church. On his dismissal, Kharchev said he had been forced to leave his post, which he had held since November, 1984, after being summoned twice for talks with an unnamed member of the Politburo.

Environmental Organizations Formed in Moldavia and Ukraine

Ecologists in Moldavia were reported to have formed an organization called "Green Action" (AVE). Moldavian writer and filmmaker Gheorghe Malarciuc was elected president of AVE. TASS reported that an environmental association in Ukraine called "Green World" held a constituent congress in Kiev today and elected USSR People's Deputy and writer Yurii Shcherbak as its chairman. At the congress, an initiative group was created to form a "Green Party" in Ukraine (*RL Ukrainian Service*, October 29).

Monday, October 30 ───────────────────────────────

Police Attack Demonstrators after Vigil at KGB Headquarters

Forty people were detained during a violent clash between riot police and demonstrators in Moscow. The Soviet media said the demonstrators were trying to march to Pushkin Square, where rallies are banned. Western correspondents said the police charged a section of the crowd, beating many with truncheons and dragging them to buses. Banners criticizing the Party and the KGB were ripped down. The trouble began after a peaceful vigil by at least 1,000 people organized by the anti-Stalin "Memorial" society. Participants in the vigil formed a human chain around KGB headquarters to commemorate the victims of political terror (*Radio Moscow*, 2000, *Reuters, DPA, AFP*, October 30).

New Editor of *Pravda* Promises More Information

At an unprecedented news conference for foreign reporters, *Pravda*'s new editor Ivan Frolov pledged that he would run an open newspaper dedicated to reform and free of bias to the left or right. "*Pravda* cannot be left or right, and it cannot be conservative or radical. What it must be is an honest, truthful newspaper," Frolov said. Frolov also revealed that the newspaper would be giving more detailed coverage of Central Committee and Politburo meetings and would carry interviews with Party leaders.

Pravda Says Police in Uzbekistan Granted Special Powers

Pravda said police in Uzbekistan had been granted special powers to try to keep order in the republic. It gave no details of the special powers but said they were needed because illegal demonstrations in Tashkent had led to "disorder, disruption of transport facilities, and vandalism." The newspaper was referring to demonstrations involving 50,000 people led by the Uzbek Popular Front to press demands for Uzbek to become both the state language and the language of interethnic communication in the republic. It said 100 policemen were injured in the clashes.

Leningrad TV Broadcasts Interview with Dubcek

Alexander Dubcek, leader of Czechoslovakia's "Prague Spring" movement, which was crushed by Soviet tanks in 1968, appeared for the first time on Soviet television defending his reforms and describing his arrest. Footage from a documentary film interview with Dubcek appeared on the popular Leningrad television program "Pyatoe koleso" (Fifth Wheel). According to AP, Dubcek said in the interview that his "Prague Spring" reforms were aimed at creating a society in which many different opinions could be expressed freely. He went on to describe how when he tried to call the then Soviet leader, Leonid Brezhnev, during the invasion, he was confronted by armed soldiers who ripped out the telephone wires. On November 3, Soviet Foreign Ministry spokesman

Vadim Perfil'ev told a news conference that Soviet officials had not known about the airing of the interview in advance (*AP*, November 4).

Polish Pilgrims Attend Mass at Katyn

About 460 Poles attended a Mass in the forest of Katyn where more than 4,000 Polish officers were killed in World War II. The Poles, mostly relatives of the murdered officers, traveled to the site near Smolensk in Belorussia. The Mass was celebrated in front of a wooden cross, and hundreds of candles were lit and wreaths laid at the grave-site. The issue of who killed the officers has been under investigation by a joint Soviet-Polish commission. The Poles have said the officers were killed by Stalin's NKVD, but the USSR has not yet formally admitted this. Soviet television carried film of the Mass (*AP, AFP*, October 30).

Umbrella Democratic Organization Established

An informal Soviet organization that supports peaceful reforms was reported to have held its founding meeting on the weekend and issued a manifesto. TASS said the Interregional Organization of Democratic Organizations, (MADO), was established at a meeting in Chelyabinsk. It reported that the meeting attracted several hundred delegates and guests from twelve Union republics who, it said, represent 92 informal movements and over 300,000 people. On MADO, see also *Sobesednik* (No. 49).

Tuesday, October 31 ─────────────────────────

Supreme Soviet Approves Budget and Plan for 1990

The USSR Supreme Soviet approved a budget for 1990 that could halve the Soviet Union's 120-billion-ruble budget deficit. The budget, which includes cuts in defense spending, was approved after legislators rejected a proposal to cut the budgets of TASS, Novosti, and state radio and television by 10 percent each. A proposal to raise the prices of beer, tobacco, and luxury foods was also rejected. Gorbachev said the budget was not satisfactory, "but we have to stop here." TASS said the final budget and economic plan calls for a sharp increase in the production of consumer goods and allocates 13.4 billion rubles to improve living standards (*AP*, October 31).

Renewed Protests Reported in Tbilisi

There were reports of renewed protests in Tbilisi. UPI said there was a mass rally in the city on October 30, and AP said a sit-down strike had started in front of the main government buildings. Both demonstrations were reported to have been staged to protest against the drafting of Georgians into the Soviet armed forces and the incorporation of Georgia into the USSR. A Georgian activist, David Nadiradze, told AP by telephone from Tbilisi that those taking part in the sit-down protest were surrounded by several thousand people trying to ensure their safety.

Two Sentenced to Death for Their Part in the Fergana Riots

TASS said two people had been sentenced to death for their part in the clashes between Uzbeks and Meskhetians in Fergana in Uzbekistan in June. It said ten other people had been given long prison sentences. TASS said the twelve sentenced today were almost all under thirty. It said they were found guilty of the murder of four Meskhetians and of robbery, hooliganism, and other crimes. According to TASS, another eighty-five cases arising from the disorder in Fergana were being examined.

***Pravda* Says 15–16 Million Jobless by 2005**

Pravda said that some 3 million Soviet citizens had lost their jobs since 1989 and that 15 to 16 million could be unemployed by 2005. The article said the estimate does not include those affected by planned reductions in the Soviet armed forces. *Pravda* said agencies now have job openings for 1.5 million people but most are in distant or undesirable locations. The report said that work has started on a law to guarantee employment but that a special fund, amounting to 2 billion rubles, would be needed to provide such a guarantee. See RL 384/89.

Shevardnadze Says Moscow Wants Cooperation, Not Aid

Soviet Foreign Minister Eduard Shevardnadze is asking the West to stop talking about economic aid to Moscow and instead focus on mutual cooperation. Shevardnadze told a Moscow news conference that talk of helping the USSR with its economic problems "offends our national pride." He made the remark after a US journalist asked if US aid would be a topic at the Mediterranean summit (*Reuters*, October 31).

Aitmatov Complains of Brain Drain

Supreme Soviet Deputy and writer Chingiz Aitmatov said the Soviet Union is losing many of its young intellectuals because of "a lack of value and respect" in Soviet society. A Soviet television report on Aitmatov's speech to the Supreme Soviet quoted him as saying many promising young scientists are emigrating to the West. Aitmatov also said the Soviet Union is losing many of its musicians, artists, writers, and dramatists. He said culture cannot develop fully without democracy (*Moscow Television*, November 1).

The Month of November

Miners on Strike Again

Miners in the Donets coal region of Ukraine staged a two-hour warning strike to press demands for better pensions and holidays. The action took place a day after miners' leaders in Ukraine decided against resuming the three-week strike that crippled the country's pits in July, but the results of a pit referendum revealed a deep split among miners. Reports from Vorkuta in the Soviet Far North said miners remained on strike at one of the area's thirteen mines for the eighth consecutive day in violation of the law (*Reuters*, November 1). By November 3, the strikes in Vorkuta were reported to have spread to twelve of the area's thirteen mines (*AP*, *Reuters*, November 3).

On November 4, warning strikes were held in some coal mines in the Donbass region. Soviet television said the strikes found support in all regional mines (*Central Television*, "Vremya," November 4). TASS reported the same day that the situation in Vorkuta remained tense, with eleven out of thirteen mines continuing to strike. It also reported an appeal by the Supreme Soviet of the Komi Autonomous Republic calling on the miners to return to work. On November 6, the strikes in Vorkuta were reported to be continuing despite attempts by Soviet Coal Minister Mikhail Shchadov to end the stoppage. TASS said the miners do not trust the government and want guarantees that it will implement their demands. It said the strikers are insisting that a government commission come to negotiate, saying that Shchadov lacks the necessary authority (*AP*, *AFP*, *DPA*, November 6). On November 9, a member of the strike committee in Vorkuta told RFE/RL that miners were voting on withdrawing from the official Soviet trade unions and setting up independent unions.

On November 13, it was revealed by TASS that striking miners in Vorkuta were planning to ask the USSR Supreme Court to overturn a local court decision that has ruled their strike illegal. The court said the strike contravenes a ban on strikes in the energy sector passed by the Soviet legislature last month. The strikers deny this. Because the strike was proclaimed illegal by the court, the strikers as well as leaders of the strike committee are not getting paid. (In the television program "Sem' dnei" on November 12, the Vorkuta strike leaders reported the cessation of payments to the strikers and rejected as a lie *Izvestia*'s recent report that the strike committee leaders currently draw very high salaries.)

On November 14, the RSFSR Supreme Court ruled that the miners' strike was illegal. Members of the Vorkuta strike committee still insisted, however, on the legality of the strike and said the miners would not return to work (*Reuters*, November 15). The same day, it was reported that coal miners at the striking Vargovskaya mine in Vorkuta had appealed to the US Labor Federation AFL-CIO to support their demands (*RFE/RL Special*, November 14). On November 15, the Soviet embassy in Washington assured US labor leaders that a US delegation would be allowed to go to the USSR to meet striking miners (*RFE/RL Special*, November 15). On November 16, the striking Vorkuta miners appealed for help to the International Labor Organization. This was revealed in a telephone interview between RFE/RL and representatives of the Vorkuta strike committee.

On November 16, the International Confederation of Free Trade Unions urged the Soviet authorities not to use force against the striking coal miners in Vorkuta (*Radio Moscow-2*, 2130, November 16).

On November 17, Nikolai Ryzhkov met in Moscow with miners' delegates from across the USSR. TASS said the talks proceeded in "a constructive atmosphere" but added that some "sharpness" was also noticeable. Ryzhkov was quoted as telling the miners that government promises to them were not specific enough and must be looked at again (*TASS, Central Television*, "Vremya," 2100, November 17).

On November 18, TASS said some striking miners in Vorkuta had returned to work after progress in talks between the government and the miners. TASS said work at most of the thirteen pits in Vorkuta had resumed. The Soviet government promised miners it would work out agreements on demands raised during the talks with Ryzhkov.

On November 19, it was reported that some of the striking miners were starting a hunger strike. Reuters said that one miner began fasting today and that another forty would join him on November 20. A strike committee spokesman said the hunger strike was to protest against a ruling of the Supreme Court in the Komi ASSR on November 17 that striking miners were liable to pay fines and compensation for losses resulting from their work stoppage (*Reuters*, November 19). On November 22, a leader of the strike committee told RFE/RL that the miners had ended their fast.

On November 21, reports from the Soviet Union said at least two of the thirteen mines remained on strike. A leader of the striking miners told RFE/RL by telephone that some miners were being penalized despite promises from Ryzhkov to the contrary.

On November 22, *Pravda* said that tensions were "white-hot" at the Vorgashorskaya coal mine—one of the two mines in the region still on strike. The newspaper complained that people had become hostages to strike leaders. It reported passions were being whipped up by various emissaries who, it said, were "flocking to the pit like flies to honey."

On November 28, TASS reported that miners at the Vorgashorskaya pit had decided to continue their strike. The agency said the miners wanted to use the strike to press for the implementation of government pledges made after last summer's work stoppages.

On November 30, the miners voted by secret ballot to return to work the following day. The same day, *Izvestia* published a critical commentary about the striking miners.

Krenz in Moscow

New East German Party General Secretary Egon Krenz paid a one-day visit to Moscow and spent three hours discussing his country's political unrest with Mikhail Gorbachev. Before flying home, Krenz told journalists the East German leadership will consider all demands put forward in the recent protests. He also said it was a good sign that many East Germans were calling for better socialism and a renewal of society. Krenz, who replaced Erich Honecker two weeks ago, said he favored letting East Germans travel freely and stated that the leadership would make proposals on election changes. In a report on the Moscow talks, TASS said Gorbachev had repeated that all East German issues are resolved in East Berlin and not in Moscow (*Reuters*, DPA, AP, TASS, November 1; *Pravda*, November 2).

Soviet Official Calls for End to Grain Imports

Deputy Prime Minister Stepan Sitaryan said he wants the USSR to stop importing grain by the end of next year. Sitaryan told the government periodical *Pravitel'stvenny vestnik* that grain imports are a burden on the economy. The Soviet Union last season imported 41 million tons of grain. Sitaryan said the foreign-trade situation was critical.

He said that exports were still not making up for hard-currency losses caused by the drop in oil prices on the world market and that the Soviet Union must improve its ability to export finished products (*TASS*, November 1).

Afanas'ev Says He Will Continue to Push for Change in CPSU

Soviet reformist Yurii Afanas'ev has responded to his critics by saying he intends to continue pushing for change in the CPSU. Over the past month, Afanas'ev has frequently been criticized in the Party press. Afanas'ev was quoted by Western agencies as saying that, since the attack on him by Mikhail Gorbachev on October 31, two commissions had begun investigations of his statements and conduct. Afanas'ev was also quoted by the agencies as criticizing Gorbachev personally. He said Gorbachev's concept of *perestroika* as a rejection of Stalinism and a return to Leninism is flawed (*Reuters*, November 2). In a telephone interview with RFE/RL on November 2, Afanas'ev said the type of socialism that has been built in the Soviet Union no longer works. He said the Party must renounce its leading role or face further social tension.

Soviet Officials Say Drug Abuse Increasing, Alcohol Still a Problem

Soviet officials said in the United States that drug abuse is increasing in the Soviet Union and that alcoholism remains a major problem. The officials spoke at the fifth General Chautauqua Conference on US-Soviet relations. Irina Anokhina, deputy director of the All-Union Scientific Center for the Medical and Biological Problems of Drug Addiction, said about 61,000 drug addicts and about 5 million alcoholics are being treated in the Soviet Union. She said officials have not determined how many others are addicted to drugs or alcohol. Another official said many young people had turned to drugs after alcohol production and sales decreased as a result of Gorbachev's antialcohol campaign launched in 1985 (*AP*, November 2).

Central Newspaper Criticizes Propaganda against Activists

Sotsialisticheskaya industriya defended independent groups in Ukraine against official propaganda attacks, saying peaceful demonstrations in Lvov and other cities had led to clashes with the police. It said the propaganda barrage against activists by the local Ukrainian media was only counterproductive. The newspaper said that striving for national rebirth is both legitimate and legal and that failure to acknowledge this ignores the underlying cause of tensions in Ukraine.

Reports said the Soviet Union has established its first banking presence in the United States by opening a New York office for Moscow's Bank for Foreign Economic Relations. A senior manager for the bank said that the Soviet Union will eventually consider offering Soviet bonds on US financial markets. The Soviet Union has already sold some bonds in Europe, but it is not allowed to sell bonds in the United States, because it has defaulted on hundreds of millions of dollars in earlier debts. Reports says US-Soviet negotiations are already under way to try to resolve the outstanding debts (*Reuters*, November 1).

USSR Opens Bank in New York with View towards Offering Bonds

Thursday, November 2

A leading US Jewish organization said more Jews had emigrated from the Soviet Union this year than in any previous year. The National Conference on Soviet Jewry said the emigration total this year now stood at 51,336, exceeding the previous high in 1979. It said 9,450 had emigrated in October alone. The chairman of the conference, Shoshana Cardin, said the organization was grateful for this increase but was still "deeply concerned" over the Soviet Union's refusal to let some long-term refuseniks and others emigrate (*RFE/RL Special*, November 3).

Soviet Jewish Emigration Reaches All-Time High

A group of KGB officers answered questions from the public in a seventy-five minute phone-in program shown live on Soviet television. Questions touched on the personal lives, salaries, and living conditions of KGB officers as well as on the secret service's activities both in and outside the Soviet Union. One questioner asked whether any KGB officers had been punished for hounding Andrei Sakharov and exiled Soviet writers Aleksandr Solzhenitsyn and Joseph Brodsky. Colonel Aleksandr Karbainov, who answered the question, said those actions had been determined by the law in force at that time and by the political situation. Asked whether a time would come when Soviet citizens could see their KGB file, Major General Gennadii Kilikh of the investigations department denied that the KGB has any personal files on Soviet citizens (*AP, DPA*, November 2).

KGB Officials Field Questions from Public in TV Phone-In

Izvestia said the Soviet government is buying less grain and sugar beet from farmers than last year because of persistent problems with transport, fuel, and processing

Government Buying Less from Farmers because of Transport Problems

593

in farming areas. It said that, despite a better harvest than last year, sales were lagging behind. In a separate report, the news program "Vremya" showed hundreds of bags of sugar beet lying at one farm and said there were no trucks to take them away (*Reuters*, November 2).

Medvedev on *Perestroika*

CPSU Politburo member Vadim Medvedev has repeated that *perestroika* is not to blame for the Soviet Union's difficulties. He said the problems are due to the country's lack of democracy. Medvedev was speaking to workers during a tour of a Moscow factory. His remarks were reported on Soviet television.

Soviet Scientist Says 300,000 Affected by Chernobyl'

Soviet Academician Aleksei Yablokov said radioactive fallout from the Chernobyl' accident was "at least several times" greater than has been officially reported. Yablokov told a press conference in New York a recent parliamentary hearing had established that about 300,000 people inhabited the area that was contaminated by high levels of radiation. Yablokov is deputy chairman of the Supreme Soviet's Committee on Ecology and the Rational Use of Natural Resources. He described Soviet environmental protection agencies as "extremely weak." He said the environmental situation around the Black Sea was "near to ecological catastrophe" (*RFE/RL Special*, November 2). See RL 198/89 and RL 466/89.

USSR to Let Iran Send Gas through USSR to Europe

Radio Teheran said the Soviet Union had agreed in principle to let Iran send natural gas through Soviet territory for sale in Europe. The radio said Iranian and Soviet officials would meet before the end of the year to decide on the volume of gas to be sent and other details. The agreement was announced after talks in Teheran between a team headed by Konstantin Katushev, the USSR minister of foreign economic relations, and Iranian Foreign Minister Ali Akbar Velayati (*Reuters*, November 2).

Soviet Official Says Ortega Erred on Cease-Fire Decision

CPSU Central Committee member Nikolai Shishlin said Nicaraguan President Daniel Ortega had erred in his decision to end the cease-fire in Nicaragua. Shishlin said that the decision was emotional and that its political consequences would be negative. Shishlin was speaking at the Chautauqua Conference in Pittsburgh (*RFE/RL Special*, November 2).

Supreme Soviet Approves Pension Draft in First Reading

The USSR Supreme Soviet approved a new draft pension bill after its first reading and will publish it for general discussion. Prime Minister Nikolai Ryzhkov said that the bill would increase pensions by an average of 40 percent and that length of service and skills would be taken into account in calculating retirement pay. Pensions will be granted to women at the age of fifty-five provided they have worked for a minimum of twenty years, while men will qualify for pensions at the age of sixty after at least twenty-five years of work. TASS said the bill upgrades the system of special pensions, in particular the benefits for coal miners and workers employed in the mining of other materials. The additional cost of the improved pensions was put at 29 billion rubles a year by Ryzhkov (*TASS, AP,* November 2).

Vol'sky Defends Need for Troops in Nagorno-Karabakh

Arkadii Vol'sky, the head of the commission appointed by Moscow to govern Nagorno-Karabakh, rejected calls for direct rule by Moscow to be abandoned and for MVD troops to be withdrawn. He warned that such an action would precipitate a new wave of bloodshed in the disputed oblast. He called, however, for the local government to be restored to share power with his special administrative committee. He also revealed that Azerbaijani nationalists had seized control of the local television relay station and were refusing to broadcast national programs, substituting in place of them "unruly and abusive texts and discussions." Vol'sky's comments were published in *Moscow News* (No. 45).

————— Friday, November 3

Lithuania Adopts Citizenship and Referendum Law

The Lithuanian Supreme Soviet passed legislation that could permit future referendums on important issues, including that of independence from the Soviet Union. A referendum can be called at the request of half the members of the republican Supreme Soviet or if supported by 300,000 signatures. The Lithuanian Supreme Soviet also adopted a law to establish separate Lithuanian citizenship for virtually everyone living in Lithuania. Soviet media reports said anyone permanently residing in Lithuania and holding a regular job on the day the law goes into force would be eligible to apply for Lithuanian citizenship. Western reports said future immigrants would have to wait ten years for citizenship (*Central Television,* "Vremya," *TASS, Reuters,* November 3).

El'tsin Attacks Gorbachev Again

Supreme Soviet Deputy Boris El'tsin attacked Mikhail Gorbachev again, saying he had replaced Egor Ligachev as the leadership's top conservative. El'tsin spoke in Moscow to about 1,000 people at a public forum organized by the Interregional Group of Deputies. He called Gorbachev "an eternal proponent" of half-measures and compromises. El'tsin said Gorbachev should decide whether he is with the Party apparatus or with the people and should stop trying to please both (*AP, AFP*, November 3).

United States and USSR Propose Joint UN Resolution

The United States and the Soviet Union jointly proposed a United Nations resolution calling on all countries to respect human rights and to promote peace and international cooperation. The proposal was presented at a press conference in New York held by US Assistant Secretary of State John Bolton and Soviet Deputy Foreign Minister Vladimir Petrovsky. In a joint statement, the two officials said the resolution marks the end of an era of confrontation and symbolizes "a new beginning at the United Nations—a new spirit of constructive cooperation" (*Reuters, AP, DPA, UPI*, November 3).

First Hard-Currency Auction in Moscow

The Soviet Union held its first hard-currency auction, designed to give more state-run businesses access to foreign equipment and services. TASS said the auction took place at the Bank for Foreign Economic Relations among enterprises buying and selling foreign currency. TASS said Soviet officials plan more such auctions. It said these will be a step towards a gradual transition to ruble convertibility.

On November 6, *The Financial Times* gave details of the auction. According to the newspaper, bidding enterprises offered between 15 and 13 rubles for one US dollar. This was more than twenty-two times the official exchange rate and represented an effective devaluation of more than 95 percent. The auction result showed that state enterprises were prepared to pay more than twice the special exchange rate just introduced for tourists, which values the dollar at 6.26 rubles. On the auction, see also *Ekonomicheskaya gazeta*, No. 46.

Ukrainian Catholics Occupy Russian Orthodox Church

Radio Moscow said a group of Ukrainian Catholics were occupying the Russian Orthodox Church of the Transfiguration in Lvov for the fifth day in succession to press demands that the government lift the official ban on their faith. The radio said the protest had roused strong objections by local Russian Orthodox clergy, who marched from St. George's Cathedral in Lvov to the captured church and later held a demonstration outside the city soviet building. The radio said officials were negotiating between the two sides and "trying to find a compromise."

On November 8, four Ukrainian Catholics were reported to have been charged with illegally seizing property in connection with the takeover of the Russian Orthodox Church. The report, from the Rome-based Ukrainian Catholic press bureau, identified the four as Ivan Hel, head of the Committee for the Defense of the Ukrainian Catholic Church in Ukraine, a Ukrainian Catholic priest named Antoi Maslyuk, and activists Stepan Khmara and Ivan Bilyk. The press bureau said virtually all the 10,000 parishioners of the Transfiguration Church signed a petition asking that it be recognized as Ukrainian Catholic rather than Russian Orthodox. The petition was handed to the state authorities (*RFE/RL Special*, November 8).

Saturday, November 4

Soviet-Iranian Gas Agreement

Under an agreement signed in Teheran, Iran will resume shipments of natural gas to the Soviet Union commencing on April 1, 1990. The volume of deliveries is scheduled to reach a rate of 2 billion cubic meters a year during the period 1991–2004 (*TASS*, November 4).

KGB Chief Gives Keynote Speech on Revolution Anniversary

KGB Chief Vladimir Kryuchkov gave the keynote speech at the Kremlin ceremony marking the seventy-second anniversary of the October Revolution. He is the third KGB man to be selected to speak on either the revolution anniversary or on Lenin's birthday since Gorbachev came to power. The section of Kryuchkov's address devoted to domestic affairs was very conservative and did not reflect the more benevolent image that he has been fostering of late. He acknowledged crimes committed by the NKVD under Stalin but overlooked KGB activities in the 1960s and 1970s. He rejected the idea that the Soviet Union is drifting away from socialism and criticized what he called excesses of *glasnost'* in the Soviet mass media. Kryuchkov's remarks on foreign policy displayed a more reformist approach. He welcomed the recent political changes in Poland and Hungary and said that the formation of Socialist structures and political institutions based on pluralism in these countries were "natural." While attacking liberal journalists for "falsifying the truth" when describing the Soviet past, Kryuchkov at the same time encouraged the mass media to report more on foreign policy because restrictions in this area have been removed. For the text of the speech, see *Pravda*, November 5.

Muscovites Stop Reading
Pravda

The number of subscribers to *Pravda* in Moscow dropped 43.2 percent in the first ten months of 1989, according to the November 4 issue of *Moskovskaya pravda*. Countrywide, the newspaper's circulation is known to have plummeted from a peak of 10.7 million copies in 1985. Soviet journalists said it had dipped briefly below 5 million earlier this year. The survey in *Moskovskaya pravda* showed that the conservative *Sovetskaya Rossiya* had done even worse, losing almost half of its Moscow subscribers, while more progressive papers like *Izvestia* retained virtually all their readers. *Moscow News* (No. 47) carried a short note on the decline in subscriptions for next year to many Soviet periodicals. The newspaper gave two reasons for the situation. First, it said, many Soviet citizens are gradually losing interest in sharp political debates and have stopped getting excited when controversial material appears in the press. Second, many subscribers have been discouraged by the limits of *glasnost'*. *Moscow News* complained that debates in the Soviet parliament as well as in many *samizdat* publications are more outspoken than in the official press. *Samizdat* publications are often in greater demand than official periodicals, *Moscow News* said.

Inaugural Congress of
Armenian Pan-National
Movement

The Armenian Pan-National Movement, founded on the basis of the Karabakh Committee and officially recognized by the Armenian authorities last June, held its inaugural congress in Erevan on November 4 and 5. The congress, attended by 900 delegates, including representatives of the diaspora, adopted a draft program calling for greater political and economic autonomy and religious freedom. Addressing the delegates, Armenian Party First Secretary Suren Arutyunyan reiterated earlier calls for cooperation between the Party and unofficial groups and for closer ties with the Armenian diaspora, including the Dashnak Party. According to AFP of November 7, Karabakh Committee activist Levon Ter-Petrossyan told the congress that Nagorno-Karabakh should be made a Union republic. This proposal can, however, be blocked by a provision in the new Azerbaijani Constitution precluding any territorial changes in that republic that have not been approved by a republican referendum (*Bakinsky rabochii*, September 17).

A Soviet parliamentarian argues in the current issue of *Argumenty i fakty* (No. 44) that the official Soviet death toll from the Afghan war is far too low. The Soviet authorities have claimed that 13,833 Soviet soldiers died there, but Eduard Gams said that the number must be higher, noting that Western analysts have put Soviet losses as high as 40,000.

Afghan War Death Toll Questioned

A senior Soviet trade official said the Soviet Union aims to freeze exports of raw materials at 1985 levels. Deputy Chairman of the Economic Commission Ivan Ivanov said the USSR would also like to double exports of manufactured or processed goods by the year 2000. Ivanov said 1,050 joint ventures with foreign partners have been established. He was speaking at the end of a two-day conference in Moscow on how to improve economic performance with respect to Soviet exports (*TASS*, in English, *Reuters*, November 4).

USSR Aims to Freeze Exports of Raw Materials

Argumenty i fakty (No. 44) said there had been great interest in a contest announced to find a solution to problems connected with the convertibility of the ruble. The weekly said more than 100 Soviet and foreign scientists and international organizations had entered the contest. It said the most entries were from the United States. *Argumenty i fakty* said the contest carried three prizes, ranging from 25,000 to 5,000 dollars. The deadline for entries is April 1, 1990.

Contest for Ruble Convertibility

Demonstrators outside the Soviet embassy in Budapest called for the immediate withdrawal of Soviet troops from Hungary. Radio Budapest said the Hungarian October Party and the Radical Party organized the demonstration. Members handed petitions to the embassy staff. Western reports said about 150 people took part. Today is the thirty-second anniversary of the Soviet invasion of Hungary that crushed the 1956 revolution. On November 3, the Hungarian government dissociated itself from the demonstration and said the call for withdrawal was harmful to Hungary's national interests (*Radio Budapest*, 1830, *DPA*, *AFP*, November 4).

Demonstrators in Budapest Call for Withdrawal of Soviet Troops

599

Infant Mortality Falls

USSR Deputy Minister of Health Aleksandr Baranov told TASS that infant mortality in the Soviet Union had fallen 8.8 percent in the first nine months of 1989, from 23.9 deaths per 1,000 live births to 21.8 per 1,000. (These figures are not directly comparable with Western ones, because the USSR uses a different methodology for compiling them.) He noted especially significant improvements in Central Asia; in Uzbekistan, the infant mortality rate was down 12.6 percent; in Kazakhstan, down 16.1 percent; and in Tajikistan, down 11.4 percent. Baranov attributed the fall in infant mortality in these areas to recent improvements in maternity and child care.

Sunday, November 5

Georgians to Hold Referendum on Independence

Thousands of Georgians ended an eight-day protest in front of government headquarters in Tbilisi when nationalist leaders announced that they had won the right to hold a referendum on independence for their republic. The referendum, which nationalists want to hold as early as December, would ask the United Nations to take up the cause of Georgian independence. The right to hold a referendum and other concessions were announced following negotiations between leaders of the newly formed Committee for National Salvation and members of the Georgian Communist Party and government. As part of the agreement, the government promised that none of the thousands of participants in the protest would be punished. It also promised clemency for hundreds of Georgian draft resisters who have rejected conscription into the Soviet army (*UPI*, November 5).

Akhromeev Interviewed by *Time*

Gorbachev's top military adviser, Marshal Sergei Akhromeev, said in an interview with *Time* magazine that military commanders will not accept orders from republican leaders any more. He said the Kremlin had "learned a lesson" from the events in Tbilisi last April 9. He asserted that military forces would in future be deployed only if the USSR Supreme Soviet demands it. He also said a faster pace for superpower disarmament depended on the United States. Akhromeev implied that Moscow would continue to make moves towards disarmament but said that the United States must not think it can exploit Soviet domestic difficulties to gain military concessions. He said the Soviet Union would not make any concession that endangered national security.

He added, however, that Moscow and its allies could see a day when there would be changes in the Warsaw Pact and NATO. "We and our allies are ready to sit down today and negotiate the simultaneous disbanding at least of the military aspects of the blocs," Akhromeev said.

Several Detained during Armenian Protest in Moscow

Police detained at least seven people during a demonstration in Moscow in support of exiled Armenian nationalist Paruir Airikyan. Western reports said some forty demonstrators—carrying banners calling for Airikyan's return—had gathered in front of the Lenin Library. According to AP, police prevented them from marching to Red Square. It said they pushed the protesters into the entrance of a subway station and tore down their banners. Airikyan, a former political prisoner, was arrested in Moscow last year and subsequently exiled to Ethiopia. He now lives in the United States (*AP, AFP*, November 5).

Monday, November 6

Gorbachev Says Public Fears Prevent Radical Economic Steps

According to a report published in *Pravda*, Mikhail Gorbachev has cautioned economic reformers to move slowly on sensitive issues because consumers will not tolerate more radical measures. Responding to economists who argue that imposition of a market economy could straighten out the country's consumer shortages in a short period of time, Gorbachev said: "I know only one thing, that after two weeks such a "market" would bring the whole nation out onto the streets and sweep out any government, even one declaring devotion to the people." *Pravda* reported the comments in a two-page report devoted to a recent conference that included Gorbachev and leading economists. It did not say when the conference had been held (*AP*, November 6).

French Doctors' Group Offers to Treat Kuznetsov

The Paris-based international humanitarian organization Doctors without Frontiers offered to send a French doctor to Moscow to treat dissident Soviet journalist Sergei Kuznetsov, who was seriously hurt in a fall last week. Kuznetsov suffered a fractured skull when guards dropped him down the steps of a Sverdlovsk courtroom in the Urals, where he was being tried for allegedly slandering the KGB. Kuznetsov, a writer for the independent magazine *Glasnost'*, had been on hunger strike since mid-October protesting against his arrest and was too weak to walk. He

601

was said to have refused Soviet medical attention and to have repeatedly called for the French to send a physician to treat him (*UPI*, November 6).

Tuesday, November 7

Alternative Demonstrations Staged on Revolution Anniversary

Unprecedented in Soviet history, serious counterdemonstrations took place in major cities on the anniversary of the revolution. In the only officially sanctioned alternative demonstration, some 10,000 people demonstrated in Moscow away from Red Square. An RFE/RL correspondent in Moscow reported that its participants were carrying placards supporting Boris El'tsin and calling for the ouster of Egor Ligachev. Other posters said "Down with the CPSU" and "Workers of the World Forgive Us." The meeting was addressed by members of the Interregional Group, who questioned the leading role of the Party. At the official parade in Red Square, Gorbachev gave an interview from atop the Mausoleum in which he acknowledged that the country's problems were "hanging like a sword of Damocles over us."

Outside Moscow, protests took place in Vorkuta, where striking miners carried their own slogans in the official parade, and in several republican capitals. In three republics—Moldavia, Kazakhstan, and Lithuania—demonstrators disrupted official parades. The most serious disruption took place in Kishinev, where thousands blocked the military part of the official parade, prompting the Moldavian leadership to leave the reviewing stands. In Armenia and Georgia, where official parades were canceled, local groups demonstrated against Soviet power. In Erevan, several thousand protesters called for an end to Communist rule, and several dozen youths burned the Soviet flag. In Tbilisi, tens of thousand of Georgians marched under slogans including "Down with the Soviet Empire" (RFE/RL correspondents' reports, Western agencies, November 7 and 8). The domestic Soviet media generally ignored or gave minimal coverage to the protests.

Soviet Dissent at Climate Conference

The Soviet Union joined Britain, the United States, and Japan as the lone dissenters as more than sixty nations at a global conference in the Netherlands on climatic change issued a call for the stabilization of carbon dioxide emissions by the year 2000 (*AP*, November 7). The US delegation said more study was needed, but Soviet objections probably arose from the size of the environmental cleanup Moscow would face if an agreement were reached.

Estonian Deputy Says Baltic Peoples Cannot Wait for Rest of USSR

A Supreme Soviet Deputy from Estonia said the Baltic peoples pushing for independence cannot wait for the rest of the Soviet Union to reach political maturity. Marju Lauristin, a member of the Popular Front and the dean of Journalism at Tartu University, said in Washington that the Soviet Union is like a big school where all the students are studying democracy. She said people in the Baltic republics cannot wait for the schooling to conclude "when all Soviet people . . . will have their degrees in democracy" (*RFE/RL Special*, November 8).

Soviet Union Opens Auschwitz "Death Books" to Red Cross

The international committee of the Red Cross said it now has access to new information in Moscow on those who died in the Nazi concentration camp at Auschwitz. The organization said the Soviet government had opened its central archives to the committee's international tracing service. It said in September representatives of the Red Cross had been shown the so-called death books containing the names of some 74,000 people who died in Auschwitz. The books were taken to Moscow in 1945 by the Soviet Army, which liberated Auschwitz (*RFE/RL Special*, November 8).

Grain Harvest Improves But Still Not Enough

The CPSU Politburo has been told the country's grain situation is slowly improving but that it is still not satisfactory. This was reported in *Pravda*, which said it was beginning detailed coverage of Politburo meetings. *Pravda* said Vladilen Nikitin, chairman of the State Commission for Food and Procurement, told the Politburo at its latest meeting on November 3 that further steps must be taken to improve the production and use of grain in order to reduce imports. The report said the Politburo discussed the possibility of raising prices paid to farmers for grain.

Zagladin Sees No Crisis in Eastern Europe

Soviet foreign policy adviser Vadim Zagladin said there is no need for talk about a crisis in Eastern Europe because of the changes taking place there. Zagladin said in an interview published in the Italian newspaper *la Repubblica* that such changes are normal and even necessary. He said the USSR wants East European countries to

603

remain friends and allies and does not object to their building a new socialism. Zagladin also said that Moscow and the Vatican share converging views on a number of issues and that this makes Moscow want to expand ties with the Vatican (*RFE/RL Special*, November 7).

Wednesday, November 8

Soviet Reaction to Changes in East Germany

TASS reported the sweeping changes in East Germany's Communist Party leadership and said the country was going through a difficult period. TASS issued periodic reports throughout the day on the dramatic events in East Berlin, but it did not comment on the composition of the new East German Politburo or the resignation of the old one. It said "the economy is facing serious problems. The flow of refugees to the West continues unabated, and mass demonstrations are being held in the country to demand more resolute measures from national leaders to renovate Socialist society." Soviet television carried an extensive report on the East German crisis in its evening news and showed East German leader Egon Krenz speaking to a crowd in front of Party headquarters. The newscaster read a list of protesters' demands, including calls for democratic elections and appeals to the Socialist Unity Party or SED, to relinquish its leading role.

Moscow News Says 250 Involved in Chernobyl' Accident Have Died

Moscow News (No. 46) said at least 250 people who were working at the Chernobyl' nuclear plant during the 1986 disaster or who helped clean up after it had died. The official death toll had been thirty-one. *Moscow News* did not give its sources and did not say how many of the deaths were the direct result of illnesses linked to the disaster. A spokesman for Kombinat, the organization handling the cleanup, confirmed the deaths but said some of the people had died of illnesses unrelated to radiation and that more study was needed on others.

Following the article in *Moscow News*, *Pravda* commented on the number of victims of the Chernobyl' disaster. The newspaper said on November 11 that nearly 150 people had suffered serious radiation sickness as a result of the Chernobyl' nuclear accident. The newspaper reported that fifty-six of these people had recovered, but it did not make clear whether the remainder had died or were still sick. "Of the fifty-six who recovered, sixteen are unable to work, while the rest are capable of resuming work, the newspaper added.

Argumenty i fakty (No. 44) released the results of a poll conducted by the All-Union Center for the Study of Public Opinion in September among residents of Armenia, Estonia, Latvia, Lithuania, the RSFSR, and Ukraine on attitudes towards draft laws on republican and local soviet elections. Between 80 and 90 percent of the respondents are in favor of at least two names on the ballot for each seat, while 60 to 80 percent are in favor of direct election of the chairman of the local soviet. Sixty-nine percent of the Armenian respondents also favor the direct election of the republican Supreme Soviet chairman, as opposed to only 46 percent of the RSFSR respondents. On the question of whether the same person should occupy the posts of Party committee leader and soviet chairman (as Gorbachev does at all-Union level), only some 7–17 percent of the respondents felt it was "essential," while some 25–30 percent deemed it impermissible.

Poll on Election Laws Released

Sovetskaya Rossiya announced plans in Leningrad to elect local deputies from factory-based districts in March, 1990. The approval for an experiment along these lines was given by the RSFSR Supreme Soviet at its session in October. On December 1, however, *Izvestia* reported that the Leningrad City Soviet had rejected the experiment by a vote of 385 to 16.

Egor Yakovlev, chief editor of *Moscow News* told an RFE/RL interviewer that he welcomes both conservative and radical opposition to *perestroika*. He praised Mikhail Gorbachev's "humanism" in creating what he called "a two-way street." He said that the formation of groups such as the rightist "Rossiya" faction in the Supreme Soviet or the reactionary "*Pamyat'*" society should be viewed calmly as a sign of "normal, political, life." Yakovlev argued that most people in the USSR do not understand the principle of pluralism, citing as evidence El'tsin's "inability to compromise and deal with political opposition." He concluded by saying he hopes to promote a new, more tolerant social consciousness in the USSR, while fighting for the goals of *perestroika*.

Egor Yakovlev Speaks in Favor of Pluralism

———————————————————————— Thursday, November 9

Soviet Foreign Ministry spokesman Gennadii Gerasimov said the USSR welcomes the changes in East Germany's Politburo. He told reporters in Moscow he is certain the changes "are for the better." He said East Germany is

Gerasimov Welcomes Politburo Changes in East Germany

605

moving towards *perestroika* on its own terms. Asked whether the USSR fears that East Germany will leave the Warsaw Pact, Gerasimov noted that Poland no longer has a Communist government but still remains a pact member. He said "governments may change but international obligations stay" (*AP, Reuters*, November 9).

Friendship of Peoples Monument Blown Up

Radio Moscow reported that two Armenians had been killed and a third seriously injured in an attempt to blow up a monument to the friendship of the Armenian, Azerbaijani, and Georgian peoples situated at the border between the three Transcaucasian republics. Radio Moscow's commentator linked the incident to the ongoing deadlock over Nagorno-Karabakh.

RSFSR to Revive Own Party Leadership

The RSFSR is to have its own Communist Party leadership for the first time in more than twenty years, a Party official disclosed. In an interview with *Pravda*, CPSU Central Committee Secretary Yurii Manaenkov said delegation of the republic's authority to central bodies had harmed its interests and those of the whole country. The main function of the new RSFSR Party Bureau will be to oversee the work of the regional Party organs and secretaries in the RSFSR. The bureau will remain a body of the CPSU Central Committee. Manaenkov rejected the notion of a separate Russian Communist Party (*Reuters*, November 9).

Food Rationing Reported in Many Parts of RSFSR

Radio Moscow said rationing of food products was in force in "many" parts of the RSFSR. The radio did not give details of what foods are being rationed or name the areas affected by shortages. It said its information came from a report of the RSFSR's statistical committee. It quoted the report as saying that the food situation in the RSFSR remained tense. The radio also reported that labor discipline had worsened and that more than 1 million working days had been lost due to strikes between January and September.

New Round of Talks on Conventional Arms

Negotiators from East and West began a new round of talks in Vienna aimed at reducing conventional forces in Europe. NATO proposals at this round will include some suggestions announced earlier, but Western delegates say they also include new provisions placing more emphasis on the obligations of individual countries (*Reuters, AP, DPA*, November 9).

Soviet nuclear power official Viktor Sidorenko said Soviet nuclear power plants lag behind foreign countries in automation and computing techniques and in other ways. *Izvestia* quoted Sidorenko as saying the nuclear power industry also lags behind in technological design and in the standards and reliability of electrotechnical equipment. *Izvestia* said there had been four unscheduled power drops and eleven unscheduled shutdowns at nuclear power plants in October. It said radiation did not exceed the normal limits and personnel were not overexposed to radiation.

Nuclear Power Official Criticizes Industry Standards

———— Friday, November 10

The USSR Supreme Soviet has adopted a state economic and social plan for 1990. Radio Moscow said the plan provides guidelines for the nation's domestic and foreign policy and outlines measures to stop negative trends in the economy. The report said the plan includes measures to stabilize the economy, improve the consumer market and social benefits for citizens on a low income, and expand construction of new housing substantially (*Radio Moscow*, November 10 and *Izvestia*, November 11).

Supreme Soviet Adopts State Plan for 1990

The Presidium of the USSR Supreme Soviet discussed a decree that would restore Soviet citizenship to those illegally deprived of it in the 1970s and 1980s, "while staying abroad," if any of them desire it (*Izvestia*, November 11). Such revocation of citizenship, begun with Stalin, was revived by the Brezhnev leadership in February, 1966, and its first victim was the writer Valerii Tarsis, who was punished for expressing anti-Communist views during a visit to the United Kingdom. Between 1966 and July, 1979, when the Brezhnev government adopted a new citizenship law providing a legal basis for such actions, Moscow stripped some twenty persons of their citizenship. Among them were Stalin's daughter Svetlana Allilueva (1969), human-rights scholar Valerii Chalidze (1972), biologist Zhores Medvedev (1973), writer Aleksandr Solzhenitsyn (1974), cellist Mstislav Rostropovich (1978), and several other prominent cultural figures. Since 1979, deprivation of Soviet citizenship has been one of Moscow's standard methods for dealing with political opponents of the Soviet government—even under Gorbachev. The most recent prominent victim was Armenian nationalist Paruir Airikyan, who lost his citizenship in April, 1988.

Decree on Restoration of Soviet Citizenship Discussed

607

Many individuals punished in this way have been rehabilitated by the media during the era of *glasnost*. At least one—theater director Yurii Lyubimov—has already regained his citizenship as the result of a public campaign.

Republics Instructed on Their Legislation

The Presidium of the USSR Supreme Soviet instructed the Presidiums of the Supreme Soviets of the three Baltic republics and of Azerbaijan to ensure that republican legislation is brought into line with the USSR Constitution (*Izvestia*, November 11 and 13). The Baltic declarations of sovereignty and the Azerbaijani law on sovereignty, amendments to the Baltic constitutions giving these republics the right to veto Soviet laws, and residence requirements for candidates standing in local and republic elections have provoked public dissension between republican and Union authorities. One deputy belonging to the Interregional Group told Reuters (November 10) that Gorbachev had also wanted the Presidium "to approve separate proposals curbing the republics' economic rights," but he was outvoted by, among others, Boris El'tsin. This is not the first time that the Presidium and Gorbachev himself have called on the Baltic republics to repeal recent republican legislation in conflict with the USSR Constitution, but these calls have had little if any effect.

Estonian and Latvian Supreme Soviet Sessions

The Estonian Supreme Soviet asked the Presidium to redraft a controversial bill on residency requirements for local elections. TASS said the Estonian parliament had also adopted a law on local self-government that enhances the powers of local organs (*Sovetskaya Estoniya*, November 11). In Latvia, Supreme Soviet deputies again discussed and upheld a proposal that requires five-year residency for candidates to local soviets and ten years for those to the republican Supreme Soviet. According to TASS, the Latvian deputies also voted against rushing to introduce a republican presidency (*Sovetskaya Latviya*, November 11). Gorbachev has voiced reservations about directly elected republican presidents, arguing that such a system would give too much power to a few people.

Ashkenazy Returns to His Native USSR

Soviet-born pianist Vladimir Ashkenazy returned to Moscow after an absence of twenty-six years. He arrived in the Soviet capital on November 9 to conduct two charity concerts with the London-based Royal Philharmonic Orchestra, of which he is musical director. He told a news conference in Moscow on November 10 that, by coming to the Soviet Union, he is endorsing what is happening in the country as a result of the reform movement of Mikhail Gorbachev (*Reuters*, November 10).

Nina Andreeva was interviewed on the November 10 broadcast of the television program "Vzglyad." She repeated the attacks on the Gorbachev leadership that won her notoriety last year, accusing the liberals of fostering a new class of Soviet bourgeoisie. Andreeva said she believes Boris El'tsin has never been a true Communist and hinted that El'tsin's political career may be finished.

Nina Andreeva Appears on "Vzglyad"

Izvestia said plans are at hand to form an independent Soviet airline to compete with Aeroflot on long-haul routes. The newspaper said the new airline, to be called "Asda," is being organized by a consortium of former Aeroflot pilots. It has received preliminary approval from a parliamentary commission and has until January, 1990, to present its final proposals. The newspaper said Asda plans to lease US-made Boeing 747 Jumbo jets, because of their greater fuel economy and range, but will switch to Soviet-made planes when a new generation of aircraft becomes available. Asda will fly long-distance domestic routes between Moscow and the Soviet Far North and Far East, as well as to destinations in the Western part of the Soviet Union. It also hopes to fly international routes. The state-run airline Aeroflot has often been criticized for its poor service and scheduling.

New Soviet Airline to Compete with Aeroflot

_____ *Saturday, November 11*

The USSR Public Prosecutor's Office announced that more than twenty former holders of office in Uzbekistan had been charged with taking large bribes in the 1970s and 1980s. Nineteen officials were named, and they included former Party First Secretary Inamzhon Usmankhodzhaev, two former secretaries of the Uzbek Central Committee (Erezhep Aitmuratov and Rano Abdullaeva), and the former first secretaries of six oblast Party committees. The list included two Slavs. Some of those named— e.g., Kallibek Kamalov, former first secretary of the Karakalpak Party organization—were removed from office as many as five years ago. The announcement also stated that the investigation of the former first secretary of the

Uzbek Officials Charged with Corruption

Kulyab Oblast Party Committee in Tajikistan for bribery was nearly complete and that investigations of other cases were continuing (*Radio Moscow*, 1900, November 11).

Latvian Supreme Soviet Designates New Public Holidays

On November 10, the Supreme Soviet of Latvia designated several new public holidays in the republic. They are Janis Day (summer solstice) on June 24; Christmas Day on December 25; and November 18, the day Latvia's independence was declared in 1918. November 11 will be a day of remembrance for Latvians who died fighting for independence (*Radio Moscow*, November 10).

Gorbachev's Message to Bush Expresses Support for GDR Reforms

The White House said Mikhail Gorbachev had sent a message to President George Bush expressing support for the reforms in East Germany. The White House press secretary described Gorbachev's message as important because in it the Soviet leader underscored the significance of the changes taking place in East Germany and expressed the hope that the situation would remain calm and peaceful (*UPI*, November 11).

TASS Hails "Virtual Destruction" of Berlin Wall

TASS hailed "the virtual destruction" of the Berlin Wall as a positive and important event, saying it was "perfectly obvious" that the Soviet Union supported the steps taken by East German leaders, who on November 9 opened the country's borders and the Berlin Wall. The article was signed by TASS political observer Yurii Kornilov.

Soviet General on Professional Army

In an article in the latest issue of *New Times*, Major General Vadim Makarevsky said the USSR would have to switch to a professional army if troop cuts proposed by the Warsaw Pact are approved at the Vienna conventional arms talks. Makarevsky said the proposals would reduce Soviet troop strength to 2,858,000 men, which is 1,400,000 fewer than at present. He said that under such conditions defense capability could be guaranteed only if servicemen were carefully chosen and served longer terms. Makarevksy said the draft should not be abandoned but applied more selectively.

Demonstrations, Strikes in Kishinev

On November 10, reports from the Moldavian capital, Kishinev, said police clashed with a crowd demanding the release of people arrested on November 7 during a parade to mark the seventy-second anniversary of the October

Revolution. The demonstration calling for the release of the detainees was organized by the Moldavian Popular Front. The demonstrators were reported to have attacked the MVD building. AP quoted a lecturer at Kishinev State University, Vladimir Solonar, as saying some people were injured in the clash.

On November 11, Moldavian Party and government officials passed an emergency resolution on measures to stabilize the situation in Kishinev. The measures include a ban on rallies and meetings. Reports from Kishinev also said MVD troops were being flown to the Moldavian capital. TASS said the resolution called actions by the Moldavian Popular Front a serious destabilizing factor.

On November 12, Moldavian Popular Front activists were reported to have called off a demonstration planned for November 12 (*Reuters, AP*, November 12). Meanwhile, an MVD official said 142 members of the security forces had been injured in the disturbances in Kishinev on November 10; he said four of them were in a very serious condition (*TASS*, November 12). The director of the Moldavian news agency told AP that forty-six protesters had been hurt in the disturbances.

On November 13, it was reported by TASS that, although activists had called off a demonstration on November 12, there were some gatherings in Kishinev that day in violation of the official ban. The Soviet media said the situation in Moldavia had become calmer. USSR Deputy Minister of Internal Affairs Ivan Shilov told Central Television on November 13 that the injury toll from the attack on the Ministry of Internal Affairs building in Kishinev stood at 215. Popular Front sources consider this figure to be too low, since it includes only the injured civilians who sought medical assistance in public health units; a substantial number of injured participants in the riots refrained from seeking assistance there.

On November 14, *Krasnaya zvezda* reported from Kishinev that, on November 12, members of the Popular Front of Moldavia had set up a citizens' committee, which announced that it would call a general strike in the republic within the next few days unless the republican leadership resigned. The committee cabled Gorbachev to seek his support in securing the prompt resignation of Moldavian Communist Party First Secretary Semen Grossu, Second Secretary Vyacheslav Pshenichnikov, Chairman of the Council of Ministers Ivan Kalin, and the republic's Chief Prosecutor Nikolai Demidenko. In telephone interviews from Kishinev, Moldavian Popular Front leaders confirmed the report, adding that the strike proposal had been voted down by the front's Council. The minority then went ahead with this initiative on its own. Although there is unity in the front's leadership with regard to the goal of securing the resignation of the republican leadership, there are differences over the best way of achieving this goal.

On November 15, a Moldavian Party Central Committee official, Ion Gutsu, said the authorities' attempts to normalize the situation in the republic had sometimes been ineffective and too late (*TASS*, November 15). See RL 525/89.

New Statistics on Gulag Deaths

Argumenty i fakty (No. 45) provided a report on the number of Stalin's victims by Soviet historian Viktor Zemskov. He reports that 963,766 persons died in Soviet labor camps between 1930 and 1947 because of inhuman conditions there. Zemskov reports that the number of camp inmates reached its peak in 1941, when the Gulag contained 1.56 million people; the highest annual death toll came the following year when 248,877 perished. Zemskov emphasized that his archival research vindicated many of Aleksandr Solzhenitsyn's claims. Zemskov's estimates of both inmates and deaths are lower than Western calculations.

Belorussian Exarchate Formed

TASS announced that the Russian Orthodox Church had established an exarchate to encompass Belorussia, with bishoprics in Mogilev, Pinsk, and Polotsk. Filaret's title will now be Metropolitan of Minsk and Grodno. There is reason to think that this step was taken in order to head off growing demands for Belorussian autocephaly—demands that would put the Belorussian Orthodox Church outside patriarchal authority.

Sunday, November 12 ───────────────────────────────────

Yakovlev Visits Japan

Politburo member Aleksandr Yakovlev arrived in Japan for a seven-day visit (*Reuters*, November 12). Upon his arrival Yakovlev said he hoped his visit would strengthen good-neighborliness and cooperation between the USSR and Japan (*TASS*, November 12). On Yakovlev's visit, see *Pravda*, November 13–18.

On November 13, Yakovlev started formal talks with Japanese leaders. TASS quoted him as saying during the talks that Moscow wants a peace treaty with Japan formally ending World War II. (There is no such treaty, because of the dispute over certain of the Kurile Islands.) As quoted by Reuters, Yakovlev did not discuss a solution to the Kurile problem beyond mentioning "a third way" as a compromise. Reuters said this was understood to mean future possible coadministration or the return of some of the islands. Reuters said Yakovlev mentioned this in talks with the head of the ruling Liberal Democratic Party, Ichiro Ozawa. It said Yakovlev did not elaborate or repeat the remark in meetings with government officials.

On November 14, Yakovlev met with Japanese Emperor Akihito. Yakovlev delivered a message from Mikhail Gorbachev calling for the two countries to cooperate on regional and global problems (*TASS*, November 14). Speaking at a news conference in Tokyo on November 15, Yakovlev said current changes in Eastern Europe were "healthy and normal." He said they did not threaten anyone and showed that "the democratic process is under way." Yakovlev rejected suggestions that East European events meant the death of socialism. He said they were actually a victory for socialism (*Reuters*, November 15). Yakovlev also indicated that his talks with Japanese leaders had failed to bring any significant change for the better in Soviet-Japanese ties. The Japanese were reported to have refused to discuss a Soviet request for help in developing Siberian resources until the issue of the Kurile Islands is resolved (*The Independent*, November 16). On November 18, Yakovlev left Tokyo (*TASS*, November 18).

Yazov Condemns Antimilitary Demonstration

A day after Moscow sent MVD troops to Moldavia, USSR Minister of Defense Dmitrii Yazov strongly condemned "nationalist, extremist, and separatist forces," which he said "were seeking to seize power" in the country. In an interview on November 12 with TASS, Yazov said that antimilitary sentiment and actions had gathered momentum in the Baltic, the Transcaucasus, Central Asia, and Moldavia. He ruled out any change in the Soviet call-up system, saying the draft "would continue according to the principles of extraterritoriality." In both the Baltic States and the Transcaucasian republics demands for local basing of military personnel are increasingly being raised. For Yazov's interview, see also *Pravda*, November 13.

New Weekly TV News Program

Central Television reported that every Sunday a new hour-long news program called "Sem' dnei" (Seven Days) would be featured instead of "Vremya." In its first broadcast, the program provided detailed coverage of the previously underreported unrest in Moldavia, the miners' strike in Vorkuta, the general situation in the country, and developments in East Germany. In his introductory comments, the moderator of "Sem' dnei," Eduard Sagalaev, said his show would present all kinds of information, including previously "unwanted" material, in order to gain the trust of viewers. The program also featured the alternative demonstration that was held in Moscow on November 7 organized by several informal groups to counter the official parade on Red Square. In his comments on the film, consultant to the International Department of the CPSU Aleksandr Tsipko, who gained repute as the author of a series of articles critical of Leninism, said he had not backed the demonstration and did not share "the hysterical mood" that, in his opinion, is engulfing the country. In his comments Tsipko also said he was dubious about the official Revolution Day parade and implied that the Soviet Union's current problems have their roots in the revolution itself.

The most interesting item on "Sem' dnei" was a live telebridge with the striking miners of Vorkuta. In response to Sagalaev's accusation that the miners were trying "to bring the country to its knees," a strike representative retorted that it was the Soviet leadership that had not allowed the country to rise from its knees over the past four years. The strikers also confirmed that they had turned to British miners for financial assistance. They also stated that they were happy to give information to Western news services because the Soviet media were spreading disinformation about the strike.

Gagauz Declare Autonomous Republic

"Sem' dnei" revealed that on November 12 the Gagauz minority in Moldavia had proclaimed part of southern Moldavia a Gagauz Autonomous Republic. This was confirmed by UPI on November 14, which cited a Radio Moscow report on the event. According to Radio Moscow, the proclamation, which was adopted at a congress of Gagauz, was immediately declared unconstitutional by the Moldavian parliament. The Gagauz have been demanding autonomy for several years now. A commission of the Presidium of the Moldavian Supreme Soviet was set up some time ago to look into the question of autonomy for the Gagauz, but it has not yet reported its findings.

Housing Auction in USSR

Stroitel'naya gazeta reported what was said to be the nation's first housing auction. A one-room apartment with a list price of 8,500 rubles went for 18,500 rubles, while a two-room apartment sold for 23,000 rubles and a three-room apartment for 34,000 rubles. The sale of Soviet housing to private individuals was announced in December, 1988 (see *Trud*, December 6, 1988, and *Pravda*, December 12, 1988). The decree enables tenants to purchase their apartments with a down payment of 50 percent of the state price and the balance to be paid over ten years. The auction goes much further and could represent the beginning of a real housing market.

The Estonian Supreme Soviet declared the incorporation of Estonia into the USSR in 1940 illegal. A declaration approved today described it as an act of aggression, military occupation, and annexation by the Stalinist leadership. The declaration also said, however, that this does not affect the republic's membership in the Soviet Union (*TASS*, November 12). A similar declaration was adopted earlier by the Lithuanian Supreme Soviet.

Estonia Declares Its Incorporation into USSR Illegal

Monday, November 13

A three-day conference tasked with finding solutions to problems plaguing the Soviet economy and with charting the course for long-term economic reform opened in Moscow. Some 1,300 economists, parliamentarians, government officials, and enterprise managers attended the highly publicized event organized by Gorbachev's chief economic adviser, Leonid Abalkin. A recently published draft program that calls for the introduction of private property and free markets and for a sharp reduction in governmental interference was the main issue under discussion. Opening the conference, Abalkin said that inflation for consumer goods was now running at more than 10 percent and that essential goods had become harder to find. He said tough, unpopular measures were needed soon to improve the economy. He also said that time was running out for reform and that people's expectations were being exhausted. Another speaker the same day was Politburo member Nikolai Slyun'kov, who said the Soviet economy cannot remain in a state of transition between two systems for very long. He said that the old administrative-command system had been undermined but that the new economic levers were not yet working properly (*TASS*, November 13). The conference closed on November 15. Speaking at the closing session, Abalkin warned that, if sweeping economic changes were not

Economic Reform Conference

adopted in the USSR, citizens might have to face further rationing (*Reuters*, November 15). TASS reported that 250 speeches were delivered during the conference but that it failed to reach any conclusions about the path of economic reforms in the USSR. The speeches will be sent to the CPSU Central Committee and the Soviet government for study (*Radio Moscow-1*, November 15). Speaking to reporters after the conference, Abalkin sounded a note of frustration over the fact that so many speeches at the conference had been delivered by conservatives who oppose radical economic reforms (*TASS*, November 15).

Liberalization of Travel Regulations

The USSR Supreme Soviet heard the first reading of a new bill on entering and leaving the USSR. The new law eliminates all existing restrictions for citizens wishing to emigrate or travel abroad. According to TASS, the bill permits emigration for virtually anyone who has an entry permit from another country, provided that he has no criminal charges against him or alimony obligations and no recent knowledge of state secrets. It sets a basic limit of five years on the length of time the right to emigrate may be withheld on the grounds of access to secrets. It also includes regulations providing for lump-sum payments or guarantees of continued remittances from abroad for would-be émigrés who are divorced and who have to pay alimony. Fedor Burlatsky, the chairman of the quasi-official Soviet human-rights committee and a supporter of the new bill, was quoted by Western agencies as predicting that as many as 500,000 to 600,000 Soviet citizens would emigrate from the Soviet Union within one year after its final reading. See RL 458/89.

Gorbachev Rejects Debate on Party's Leading Role

The USSR Supreme Soviet defeated by just three votes a motion to hold an open debate at the second session of the Congress of People's Deputies in December on Article 6 of the USSR Constitution, which states that the CPSU is the leading force in society (*Reuters*, November 13). Mikhail Gorbachev and Georgii Razumovsky both spoke out against the measure, which was proposed by Doctor of Physical Mathematics Sergei Ryabchenko, a deputy from Kiev. Ryabchenko justified his proposal by saying: "Article 6 inspires no confidence among the people but rather the suspicion that the Party seeks to hang on to power no matter what." It was time, he said, to debate the issue of whether the Party occupies its leading role by virtue of its authority or by force. Gorbachev called the proposal an attempt "under the cover of criticism, to debase the role of the Party." It would be, he added, "an error . . . that would cause unnecessary worry in the public mind." The vote followed the publication on November 13 in *Pravda* of an article flatly ruling out the introduction of a multiparty system in the Soviet Union.

The USSR Supreme Soviet adopted the new Principles of Judicial Organization of the USSR, which include two major innovations (*TASS*, November 13; *Izvestia*, November 13 and 16). For the first time since October, 1917, trial by jury will be provided in the Soviet Union, albeit only for those acccused of the most serious offenses—i.e., those punishable with imprisonment of up to fifteen years or with death. A second fundamental change in the Soviet legal system deals with the accused's right to defense. From now on, a defense counsel will be able to start working on a case as soon as charges are brought against his client instead of having to wait until the prosecution's case is complete. (This will make it more difficult for the police and investigator to extract false confessions from the accused by illegal methods.) Although these innovations in the Soviet legal system had hitherto been opposed by the Soviet law-enforcement establishment and, notably, by Chairman of the USSR Supreme Court Evgenii Smolentsev, the new Principles of Judicial Organization were adopted almost unanimously. As many as 391 of the deputies voted for introduction, no one against it, and only one person abstained from the vote.

Major Changes in Soviet Juridical System

TASS reported that the Supreme Soviet Commission on Nationalities Policy and Interethnic Relations had approved in the main a draft law "On the Free National Development of Citizens of the USSR Residing outside the Boundaries of Their National State Formations or Not Having Them on the Territory of the Country." According to TASS, the original draft was revised six or seven times and reduced to half its original length. The draft provides in particular for the formation of national raions, national settlements, and national rural soviets where the indigenous inhabitants constitute half or even somewhat under half the population.

Draft Law on Minorities Approved

The Baltic Council, an unofficial organization of representatives of the Latvian and Estonian Popular Fronts and the Lithuanian Restructuring Movement "Sajudis,"

Baltic Council Criticizes USSR Supreme Soviet

617

has criticized the work of the USSR Supreme Soviet. In telephone interviews with RFE/RL, a "Sajudis" spokesman said the council met on November 11 and issued a communiqué saying Baltic deputies in the USSR Supreme Soviet were no longer able to defend the interests of their republics. It called for a new voting rule under which the delegation of each republic would have an equal vote on fundamental laws concerning the sovereignty of the Union republics (*RFE Lithuanian Service*, November 13).

Some Russian Orthodox in Ukraine Switch Allegiance

On November 13, Radio Kiev said that some Russian Orthodox priests and parishes in the Lvov region had changed their allegiance to the banned Ukrainian Autocephalous Orthodox Church. The radio quoted a local representative as saying the Russian Orthodox Exarch in Ukraine, Metropolitan Filaret of Kiev and Galicia, had gone to Lvov to condemn the actions.

On November 14, TASS, in English, reported that the Russian Orthodox Church had decided to excommunicate a bishop who had proclaimed himself to be leader of the Ukrainian Autocephalous Church. The excommunicated clergyman is Bishop Ioann of Zhitomir. The agency said the decision on excommunication was taken by the Holy Synod of the Russian Orthodox Church.

New Chief Editor of *Pravda* Interviewed by APN

On November 13, Novosti press agency carried an interview with the new chief editor of *Pravda*, Academician Ivan Frolov. In the interview, Frolov revealed that Mikhail Gorbachev had orginally wanted to keep him as his consultant and had tried to find someone else for the post of chief editor of *Pravda*. Frolov said that, for him, working as an aide to the general secretary was more interesting than heading the Party daily. Frolov hinted that his appointment had been a kind of compromise, because otherwise a conservative would have taken the job. Asked about his plans to relaunch *Pravda*, Frolov said he intends to publish some unique material on Party policy, including details of the work of the Party apparatus and the Politburo. Frolov pointed out that, while the government newspaper *Izvestia* would concentrate on developments in the Supreme Soviet, materials on Party policy would be published exclusively by *Pravda*. On November 14, *Pravda* disclosed that subscriptions entered for 1990 are running at 6.5 million. This is nearly 3 million less than the figure for 1989.

Draft Law on Property

The USSR Supreme Soviet adopted the final draft of the law on property, which is to be published for nationwide discussion (*TASS*, November 14). The text of the draft was published in *Izvestia* on November 18. The bill was read aloud by Sergei Alekseev, the chairman of the Supreme Soviet's Committee on Legal Matters, and includes the theoretical innovations to be found in Alekseev's article in *Pravda* of November 10. Two major innovations in the new law are the rehabilitation of private property and the entitlement of a citizen to sue the state in order to defend his or her property rights. In order to reach a compromise between different forces in Soviet society, the lawmakers have introduced new terminology. One such novelty invented to pacify the orthodox Marxists is *trudovaya chastnaya sobstvennost'* (earned private property). There is also other new terminology identifying different forms of property. This terminology apparently aims not only to effect a compromise with Marxist theory and with the laws adopted by Lenin's government that are still extant but also reflects the fact that much of the property in the various Union republics was confiscated from private owners without any compensation and therefore cannot become the private property of other individuals. These new terms for "ownership" are *dostoyanie* (property) and *vladenie* (possession). The most important aspect of the new law is the provisions covering the property rights concerning land. The bill adopted by the Supreme Soviet deals with these questions in the following way: (1) the land is national property (*narodnoe dostoyanie*); (2) the land belongs to the nations living on its territory; (3) individuals have a lifetime lease on the land with the right to leave it to their heirs (*pozhiznennoe nasleduemoe vladenie*).

Declaration on Deported Peoples Adopted

The USSR Supreme Soviet adopted a "Declaration on Recognizing as Illegal and Criminal from the Very Beginning All Repressive Actions against Peoples Subjected to Forcible Deportation and on the Unconditional Restoration of Their Rights" (*TASS*, November 14). It completely exonerates the peoples deported under Stalin and unconditionally condemns the practice of forcible resettlement as a most serious crime contradicting the nature of socialism and the principles of democracy and law. Deputies sought to have included in the declaration a statement that the deported peoples should have the right to return to their homelands and also to be compensated. The final version does not refer to these matters. The text of the declaration was published in *Izvestia* on November 24.

Kazakh Supreme Soviet Calls for End to Tests at Semipalatinsk

The Kazakh Supreme Soviet unanimously adopted an appeal to the USSR Supreme Soviet, the USSR government, and people's deputies of the USSR for an end to nuclear testing in the Semipalatinsk area (*TASS*, November 14). Although the central authorities have to some extent coopted the anti-nuclear-testing movement in Kazakhstan that came into being in February this year for their own political purposes, there can be no doubt that nuclear testing is a very live issue locally. The Kazakh Communist Party has included a call for an end to nuclear testing in the republic in its draft political program for the forthcoming local and republican elections. On November 17, Nikolai Ryzhkov promised that no more nuclear tests will be carried out in Semipalatinsk this year. He also promised that, in the first quarter of next year, a government commission will examine demands for the permanent cessation of tests in the region (*TASS*, November 17).

Sharp Rise in Crime Rate

TASS reported that the crime rate during the first ten months of this year was 34.1 percent higher than in the same period of 1988. The number of crimes registered by the Ministry of Internal Affairs and the Public Prosecutor's Office totaled almost two million, with sharp increases in homicide, rape, and armed robbery. The statistics also showed a gradual increase in street crime and in crimes against personal, public, and state property. On November 15, Radio Moscow reported that MVD and KGB units had recently foiled several more hostage-taking attempts by prison inmates in the Chechen-Ingush Autonomous Republic, in Ivanovo, and in Khabarovsk Krai. The radio did not say exactly when the attempts had occurred (*Radio Moscow-1*, 2200, November 15).

Soviet Reaction to Leadership Changes in Eastern Europe

On November 14, Soviet Foreign Ministry spokesman Yurii Gremitskikh praised the changes in Bulgaria's leadership as necessary for the reform of socialism. He told reporters in Moscow the changes would help make socialism "more humane and democratic" (*AFP*, *Radio Sofia*, November 14). The same day, *Pravda* accused some sections of Western society of seeking to exploit current changes in Eastern Europe for their own ends. The commentary, signed by Vitalii Korionov, said some elements in the West, particularly West Germany, were trying to subvert "the natural process" of Socialist countries' choosing different paths of development. Gorbachev's adviser on relations with the United States, Georgii Arbatov, said the same day that sweeping changes in Eastern Europe threaten the existence of both NATO and the Warsaw Pact (*Reuters*, November 14). (On November 15, Gorbachev's military adviser, Marshal Sergei Akhromeev, was quoted by Reuters as saying Moscow was ready for the Warsaw Pact and NATO military alliances to be dissolved. Reuters said Akhromeev made his remarks in an interview with the West German weekly *Stern*.) On November 14, Gennadii Gerasimov again said at a press conference in Moscow that East Germany opened its borders to the West without first getting "a green light" from Moscow. Gerasimov said the decision was right. He also said German reunification would not please the USSR but that this was not now an issue (*TASS*, November 14). Gerasimov made similar statements in an interview with French radio on November 15. Speaking in Moscow to reporters before talks with French Foreign Minister Roland Dumas, Soviet Foreign Minister Eduard Shevardnadze said closer cooperation between East and West Germany was ideal for them and for Europe as a whole. Shevardnadze also said it was not important if others were further ahead with their reforms than the USSR. What was important, he added, was for all reforms to be aimed at making life more democratic (*Reuters*, *DPA*, November 14). Eastern Europe was also discussed during talks on November 14 between Gorbachev and Dumas. Speaking to reporters afterwards, Dumas said the Soviet leadership was not surprised that the Gorbachev-inspired reform movement was spreading. But, he said, the Soviet leadership seemed not to have anticipated that changes in Eastern Europe would happen so quickly (*Central Television*, "Vremya, " November 14).

Lithuanian Party Leadership Called to Moscow

Lithuanian Party leaders were called to Moscow for a meeting with the CPSU Politburo. AP said Soviet Foreign Ministry spokesman Yurii Gremitskikh was asked about the reported meeting. He said that he had no information but added that it was not unusual for a republic's entire Party leadership to attend a Politburo session. Western analysts said, however, that the action was unusual. On November 16, Reuters and Radio Vilnius, in English, reported that the CPSU Politburo was meeting with the leaders of the Lithuanian Communist Party in order to discuss a proposal of the Lithuanian Party to break with the CPSU. TASS and Soviet television said the Lithuanian Communist Party came under criticism by the Politburo. On November 17, Lithuanian Party First Secretary Algirdas Brazauskas said his Party would go ahead with a special congress as planned next month to discuss the possibility of becoming independent of the CPSU (*RFE Lithuanian Service*, November 17).

Wednesday, November 15

Gorbachev Outlines Party Stand on Marxism-Leninism

Speaking at a students' forum, Mikhail Gorbachev set forth his policies concerning Marxism-Leninism and the current reevaluation of postrevolutionary Soviet history. Gorbachev strongly condemned Soviet journalists who have criticized Lenin and the terror under Lenin. Gorbachev also condemned those who look for the origins of the Stalinist terror in "the origins and principles" of socialism. He was apparently referring to a series of articles by economic journalist Vasilii Selyunin entitled "Istoki" (Origins) and one by consultant to the CPSU Central Committee Aleksandr Tsipko entitled "Origins of Stalinism." The roots of all the USSR's problems, Gorbachev said, lie in the deformations of socialism in the Stalin and Brezhnev eras, not in Marx's ideas or Lenin's practice. Nonetheless, Gorbachev also criticized Party dogmatists who counter all attempts at reform with quotations from Marx, Engels, and Lenin; he pointed out these statements had often been purely polemical and applicable only to a specific occasion or period of history (*TASS*, in English, and *Central Television*, November 15; *Pravda*, November 16).

Despite the Soviet leadership's obvious annoyance over criticism of Marxism-Leninism, the Soviet press continues to debate the issue. For instance, on November 8 *Literaturnaya gazeta* carried a lengthy discussion under the title "Is Marxism Outdated?" between the director of the Institute of Marxism-Leninism, Academician Georgii Smirnov, and *Literaturnaya gazeta* observer Oleg Moroz. During the discussion Moroz posed tough questions, trying to force Smirnov to admit that Marxist teaching on socialism was utopian, that Marxism had failed to develop any viable ideas on the economic mechanism of Socialist society, and that the concepts of public and state ownership of the means of production together with central planning, which form the basis of Socialist society, had not worked in practice. Smirnov's efforts to defend

622

Marxism during the discussion were very weak. Commenting on current attempts to defend Marxism, including Smirnov's, Moroz noted sarcastically that these amount to such broad interpretations of Marxism that ideas opposite to Marx's main postulates are held to be Marxist. See RL 82/89, RL 482/89.

Supreme Soviet Gives First Reading to Laws on Nationalities

On November 15, the USSR Supreme Soviet gave the first reading to three bills concerned with nationality issues—the draft laws on the languages of the peoples of the USSR, on the status of minorities, and on Soviet citizenship. The first and third of these proved to be controversial. The most heated disputes over the draft language law concerned the article declaring Russian the means of all-state (*obshchegosudarstvennyi*) and interethnic communication, which it was felt would undermine the position of the native languages in the republics. Ukrainian deputy Borys Oliinyk, Latvian deputy Andris Plotnieks, and others stated that Russian should be given the status of "official" language and "language of federal communication," which would limit the sphere of its obligatory use to matters within the competence of the USSR. The chief point of disagreement as regards the law on citizenship was over the correlation of all-Union and republican citizenship. Deputies from Lithuania, which has already adopted a law restricting republican citizenship, were the most critical. They called for a halt to the discussion and for the publication of the draft law in the republics so that people could see how unacceptable it was, and they walked out when the draft law was put to a vote (*TASS* and *RFE Lithuanian Service*, November 15).

Thursday, November 16

Moldavian Party First Secretary Replaced

TASS reported that Semen Grossu had lost his post as Moldavian Party first secretary in the wake of violent antigovernment demonstrations. The report said that Grossu had been replaced by forty-nine-year-old Petru Lucinschi at a plenum of the republic's Party Central Committee. Lucinschi is a Moldavian who has spent the last three years as Party second secretary in Tajikistan. Grossu had held the post of first secretary since 1980. Speaking on Soviet television, Lucinschi said he wanted to cooperate with informal groups to solve the republic's problems (*Pravda*, December 17).

On November 19, Luchinsky said on local television that he rejected "the methods and approaches of the former era." Luchinsky said that every effort must be made to ensure such methods are never used again. In his television speech, Luchinsky said that the MVD troops flown into Moldavia after the demonstrations would be withdrawn on November 20 (*Reuters*, November 19). On November 20, TASS reported the withdrawal of a unit of MVD troops. The news agency did not specify, however, whether this represented the entire contingent sent in after the November 7 clashes.

West German and French Parliamentary Leaders in Moscow

The presidents of the West German Bundestag and of the French National Assembly, Rita Süssmuth and Laurent Fabius, began a two-day visit to Moscow at the invitation of Mikhail Gorbachev (*DPA*, November 16). The parliamentary leaders are accompanied by twenty-two young people from France and West Germany, who are to meet with Moscow schoolchildren during their visit to the Soviet capital. On November 17, Süssmuth and Fabius held talks with Gorbachev. They discussed changes in the USSR and Eastern Europe (*DPA, AFP, AP*, November 17).

Historian on Difficulties of Restoring Volga German Republic

Soviet historian Valentina Chebotareva said restoration of the Volga German republic is opposed by some of the population now living in that area of the USSR. Chebotareva was attending a two-day all-Union conference on problems of restoring autonomy for Soviet Germans. She told TASS that a decision on this complicated question should not be taken hastily. She said it was necessary to determine how many Soviet Germans wish to return to the territory of the former Volga republic and then to clarify the final standpoint of the local population. She added that, in her opinion, the best solution would be to set up an Autonomous republic for Soviet Germans in Kazakhstan, where the majority of them now live.

Friday, November 17

Gorbachev Answers Students' Questions

Pravda and *Izvestia* carried the text of Gorbachev's answers to questions put to him by participants in an all-Union students' forum that took place in Moscow on November 15. Many of Gorbachev's answers were marked by traditional Soviet rhetoric, which has of late figured more frequently in his official pronouncements. Thus,

Gorbachev insisted that all changes in the USSR should take place within the framework of socialism; he rejected the arguments of those who speak of the need to introduce Capitalist elements into the Soviet economy and insisted that the working class is the leading force in Soviet society and that it would not agree to the restoration of private ownership of the means of production. Gorbachev condemned those who seek to undermine the role and prestige of the CPSU and those who link current Soviet problems with the Bolsheviks' assumption of power in 1917. Regarding the possibility of the reunification of East and West Germany, Gorbachev replied, "we will see how things develop," implying that he has no plans to prevent this process. He added, however, that at present reunification is not on the agenda. On the fate of Article 6 of the Soviet Constitution on the leading role of the CPSU, Gorbachev said "any article of the constitution can be discussed, transformed, or even eliminated. This also applies to Article 6." (At a recent session of the USSR Supreme Soviet, Gorbachev had rejected a proposal to discuss the elimination of Article 6 from the constitution.) As regards private property, Gorbachev said that, although he "adheres to the position of *The Communist Manifesto*," which condemns private ownership of the means of production, he nevertheless supports cooperatives and leasing, which in practice make individuals "owners of the means of production."

Estonian Supreme Soviet Adopts New Election Law

The Estonian Supreme Soviet adopted a new election law that appears to be a compromise. The law, which governs elections to the Estonian Supreme Soviet, includes no residency requirement for voting but does require candidates for office to have been resident for ten years. Many ethnic Estonians wanted residency requirements for both voting and holding office, but many non-Estonians in the republic opposed having any residency requirements at all (*RFE Estonian Service*, November 17). The text of the law was published by *Sovetskaya Estoniya* on November 23. Meanwhile, on November 16, thousands of people rallied in Tallinn to protest alleged discrimination against the republic's ethnic minorities. The rally was organized by "Interdvizhenie," a group made up mostly of Russian speakers. Radio Tallinn put the crowd at 20,000, but an Estonian Foreign Ministry official said 10,000–12,000 took part. They repudiated a resolution by the Estonian Supreme Soviet that declared the joining of Estonia to the USSR in 1940 illegal. They called for a boycott of local elections on December 10 (*AFP*, November 16).

Turkmen Prime Minister Dismissed

The prime minister of Turkmenistan, Annamurad Khodzhamuradov, was relieved of his job by the republic's Supreme Soviet in Ashkhabad (*Pravda*, November 18). Khodzhamuradov had been prime minister since January, 1986. The Supreme Soviet said he had been transferred to other (unspecified) work. It said a new prime minister would be chosen in a multicandidate election when the Supreme Soviet meets again next month.

Katushev and Baker Meet in Washington

US Secretary of State James Baker met in Washington with USSR Minister of Foreign Economic Relations Konstantin Katushev. A State Department official said the two men had reviewed this week's meeting of the US-USSR commercial commission, which Katushev had cochaired, and had discussed ways to expand bilateral trade. The official said Baker had repeated that the Soviet Union would get most-favored-nation (MFN) trade status only after Moscow passed and implemented laws supporting liberalized emigration regulations. Another requirement for MFN is the negotiation of a bilateral trade accord. The joint commission set up a study group to prepare issues for eventual negotiations on a trade accord (*RFE/RL Special*, November 17).

Georgian Parliament Debates Sovereignty, Elects President

The Supreme Soviet of Georgia discussed republican sovereignty and unanimously elected Party First Secretary Givi Gumbaridze as chairman of its presidium. Gumbaridze succeeds Otar Cherkezia, who resigned last April. The deputies heard a report by Gumbaridze on constitutional amendments. They made proposals concerning Georgian sovereignty and formation of republican military units (*Central Television*, "Vremya," November 17).

Saturday, November 18 ————————————————————

Demonstration in Riga Urges Independence

The Popular Front of Latvia said half a million people had gathered in Riga to call for an independent Latvia. AP said the gathering had also commemorated Latvia's declaration of independence on November 18, 1918. On November 19, representatives of the popular fronts of Estonia, Latvia, and Lithuania asked for the future of the three Baltic States to be discussed at next month's US-Soviet summit. AP and Reuters said the representatives had sent their request in a letter to President Bush and Mikhail Gorbachev.

Pravda carried Shevardnadze's comments on Eastern Europe. The foreign minister welcomed the changes taking place there and said they were logical and historically justified. He described the changes as a renewal of socialism and the realization of people's right to a free choice.

Shevardnadze Comments on Eastern Europe

Activists in Azerbaijan said about 300,000 people took part in a mass rally in Baku. They said the event was called to celebrate the anniversary of the first mass rally in Baku last year. Activists said the 1988 gathering marked the start of the popular national movement in Azerbaijan (*Reuters*, November 18).

Baku Rally Celebrates Anniversary of Popular Movement

Radio Moscow World Service carried an interview with Egor Ligachev in which he commented on prospects for Soviet agriculture. Ligachev is a cochairman of the Central Committee Commission on Agriculture. In the interview, Ligachev said the Soviet Union would need years before it would be able to feed itself. But he said he was certain current problems could be eased in the near term. Ligachev said he did not entirely agree with the idea of giving land to farmers. He also called for more caution and discretion in advancing *perestroika*.

Ligachev on Prospects for Improving Agriculture

Soviet television ("Vremya") reported popular demands for reform in Bulgaria and Czechoslovakia but made only oblique references to violence in Prague. The program also showed at length the swearing in of East Germany's coalition government and described preparations for the Romanian Party Congress. A special news show broadcast at 0315 the same morning showed the demolition by Poles of the statue of the Cheka chief Feliks Dzerzhinsky in Warsaw.

Soviet TV on Eastern Europe

The Supreme Soviet of Georgia set up a commission on the region of South Ossetia (*Central Television*, "Vremya," November 18). In violation of Party rules, the Buro of the Georgian Communist Party Central Committee released the first secretary of the South Ossetian Oblast Party Committee, A. Chekhoev, from his post "at his own request" and "entrusted the work of the Buro of the oblast Party committee to M. Gokhelashvili," the oblast second secretary (*AFP* of November 17, quoting *Zarya Vostoka*). Such personnel moves are normally the prerogative of the

Georgian Parliament Sets Up Commission on South Ossetia

oblast organization. This shift came on the heels of strikes and demonstrations in South Ossetia demanding that Ossetian be made the state language of the oblast and that the oblast be united with the North Ossetian Autonomous Republic in the RSFSR. On November 10, some deputies to the oblast soviet and representatives of informal groups called on the Georgian SSR Supreme Soviet to consider upgrading the status of the oblast to that of an Autonomous republic (*TASS*, November 10).

On November 25 fighting was reported near the South Ossetian capital of Tskhinvali. Citing a Georgian dissident, *AFP* reported that ten people had been injured in fighting between Ossetians and Georgians. The latter had traveled to Tskhinvali to hold a demonstration.

On November 26, *UPI* quoted an Ossetian as claiming that the fighting had taken place between Georgians and Georgian MVD troops who had attempted to prevent them from entering Tskhinvali for the demonstration. According to this account, nineteen people, mainly passers-by, had been wounded.

On November 27, Reuters reported that twenty-one people had been hurt and that Tskhinvali was under siege by thousands of angry demonstrators. Hundreds of Georgian MVD troops were reported to have sealed off the city. Appealing for calm, Georgian Communist Party First Secretary Gumbaridze said he would keep troops in Tskhinvali to prevent further clashes (*TASS*, November 27). On December 1, *Izvestia* said workers at most plants in South Ossetia were on strike.

Union of Workers of Kuzbass Created

On November 18 and 19, the fourth conference of workers' committees of Kuzbass took place in Novokuznetsk. At the conference a new unofficial public political organization, the Union of Working People of Kuzbass, was created. A detailed report on the new organization appeared in the Paris-based Russian émigré newspaper *Russkaya mysl'* on November 24. The report revealed that there had been debates at the conference on whether to call the new organization a political party, a free trade union, or a popular front. It was eventually agreed that the Union of Working People of Kuzbass was equivalent to a popular front. The report revealed that local Party officials had attempted to influence the independent workers' movement in Kuzbass and had sponsored their own conference of Representatives of Working People of Kuzbass to coincide almost exactly with the conference of the Union of Working People of Kuzbass (the rival conference was held on November 14). One of the main goals of the Party officials in Kuzbass was to make local miners denounce their striking colleagues in Vorkuta. This plan failed, however, and the Union of Working People of Kuzbass proclaimed their solidarity with the Vorkuta miners.

_____ *Sunday, November 19*

Georgian Supreme Soviet Defies Moscow

At its session over the weekend, the Georgian Supreme Soviet adopted amendments to the republican constitution that give the republic the right to veto all-Union laws, and it declared land, water, and other natural resources, as well as the basic means of production, the property of the republic. These amendments, which conflict with the all-Union constitution, represent a snub to the Presidium of the USSR Supreme Soviet, which on November 10 declared similar amendments to the constitutions of the Baltic republics and Azerbaijan unconstitutional and called on these republics to bring their legislation into line with all-Union legislation. The amendments to the Georgian Constitution also state that Georgia retains the right to secede from the Soviet Union. The Georgian Supreme Soviet also heard a report of the commission set up to make a political and legal analysis of violations of the treaty of May 7, 1920, between Georgia and Russia. The commission concluded that the entry of troops into Georgia had been "an occupation aimed at changing the existing political system." It was not clear from the TASS report whether the Supreme Soviet endorsed this conclusion, but it did rule that the second Congress of People's Deputies, which is to be held in Moscow in December, should be asked to give a political and legal assessment of the treaty. Other controversial topics discussed by the Georgian Supreme Soviet included a report by the working group on the reestablishment of national military formations and on provisions for Georgian conscripts to do their military service in Georgia—both of which have been completely ruled out by Moscow. *Pravda* carried a report on the Georgian Supreme Soviet session on November 20.

Moscow News on Press Restrictions

Moscow News (No.47) carried several articles complaining about recent restrictions on the official press, including purges of editors of the most outspoken periodicals. For instance, the local city Party committee recently ordered

629

the ouster of the chief editor of the Noginsk newspaper, *Znamya kommunizma*, for publishing a commentary by historian Yurii Afanas'ev saying that Marxism-Leninism was outdated. (Afanas'ev is a deputy of the Congress of People's Deputies for the Noginsk territorial district.) In response to the chief editor's ouster, the editorial staff of the newspaper started a strike, which was proclaimed by a local court to be illegal (*AP*, November 20). In this connection, contributors to *Moscow News* urged the adoption of a press law that would regulate relations between the press and the authorities. On November 20, some deputies complained at a session of the USSR Supreme Soviet about the authorities' campaign against outspoken media representatives. They attributed the campaign to the authorities' fear that critical materials in the press would result in local Party officials losing in the upcoming elections to the soviets (Radio "Mayak," November 20).

Remains of Three Ukrainian Political Prisoners Reburied

Several thousand people were reported to have attended the reburial in Kiev of three Ukrainian rights activists who died as political prisoners. The remains were those of Vasyl Stus, Yurii Lytvyn, and Oleksii Tykhi. The three, who were members of the Ukrainian Helsinki group, died between 1984 and 1985 while serving sentences in the Perm labor camp (*RL Ukrainian Service*, November 19). The three were originally buried in a labor camp cemetery. On November 20, Radio Liberty's Ukrainian Service was told that activists were calling for a monument to be erected in Kiev honoring Vasyl Stus. Stus is regarded as one of the best modern Ukrainian poets.

Moscow News on Soviet Media Coverage of Moldavian Events

Moscow News (No. 47) carried an article by its special correspondent Leonid Miloslavsky on unofficial protests in Kishinev during which demonstrators damaged the MVD building in the Moldavian capital. The correspondent said that the Soviet media had based their reports on statements by MVD officials who claimed that "extremist supporters of the Moldavian Popular Front" had attacked the building while the police behaved very cautiously towards the demonstrators. People who disputed this version of events had had no chance to express their views, Miloslavsky complained, and he pointed out that there were both testimony and facts that contradicted some details of the MVD version. In another article in the same issue of *Moscow News*, the Moldavian Popular Front was attacked by Len Karpinsky, an outspoken journalist

630

and critic of Stalinism, who, however, defends Lenin and the Bolsheviks' coming to power in October, 1917. In his article, Karpinsky criticized Moldavian Popular Front activists for blocking a part of the official parade in Kishinev on November 7. Karpinsky also alleged that an alternative demonstration in Moscow on November 7, whose participants shouted "Shame on October," had hurt the feelings of many Soviet people, since, Karpinksy insisted, the October Revolution remains for millions of Soviet citizens "a symbol of inspiring faith."

The USSR protested against a US Senate committee resolution calling for a peaceful settlement of the Nagorno-Karabakh dispute. First Deputy Foreign Minister Aleksandr Bessmertnykh summoned US ambassador Jack Matlock to receive "a vigorous protest" about the resolution. TASS said the protest criticized the resolution as an attempt at "gross interference" in Soviet internal affairs. The Senate Foreign Relations Committee had on November 17 adopted a resolution urging Gorbachev to restore order and reestablish supply routes to Armenia and Nagorno-Karabakh. It also urged the Soviet leader to protect the people of Nagorno-Karabakh from attacks. On November 20, the United States rejected the Soviet protest (*RFE/RL Special*, November 20). On November 21, the International Affairs Committee of the USSR Supreme Soviet criticized the resolution as being "in the spirit of the Cold War" (*TASS*, November 21). On November 22, in contrast with the official Soviet reaction, representatives of Nagorno-Karabkah expressed support for the US resolution (*Radio Erevan*, International Service in Armenian, 1730, November 22, and *Radio Erevan*, Domestic Service in Armenian, 0645, November 22).

USSR Protests against US Senate Resolution on Nagorno-Karabakh

———— Monday, November 20

The Afghan resistance was reported to have handed over to the International Red Cross two Soviet soldiers captured in Afghanistan. *Izvestia* said the soldiers were now in the Pakistani city of Peshawar. The newspaper said a delegation from the Soviet "Nadezhda" (Hope) Committee, which includes the soldiers' mothers, would go to Pakistan in the next few days. On November 27, AP quoted the Afghan resistance as saying there would be no more releases unless there is a suitable Soviet response.

Afghan Resistance Hands Over Two Soviet POWs

Supreme Soviet Again Rejects Economic Autonomy Bill

The USSR Supreme Soviet again rejected as inadequate a bill designed to give the republics more say in controlling their economies. An earlier version of the bill was rejected in October. Reintroducing the measure, Deputy Prime Minister Leonid Abalkin said the country was taking a step forward almost unimaginable a few years ago. But deputies called the bill too timid. Some complained that it fails to treat the republics as sovereign. Some deputies from Lithuania and other republics walked out to protest the lack of time allocated in the present session to discuss a more radical plan (*TASS, Reuters, DPA,* November 20).

Filaret Replaced as Patriarchate's Minister for Foreign Affairs

Metropolitan Filaret of Minsk and Grodno has stepped down from his post as minister for foreign affairs of the Moscow Patriarchate. He has been replaced by the Archbishop of Smolensk and Kaliningrad Kirill, former secretary to the deceased Metropolitan of Leningrad and Novgorod Nikodim (*TASS,* November 20). Nikodim was known for his strong belief in the need to promote dialogue between the Russian Orthodox Church and the Vatican. Kirill is reported to have similar views.

Canadian Prime Minister in Moscow

Canadian Prime Minister Brian Mulroney, who is on an official visit to the USSR, said the Soviet Union could count on Canadian support in carrying out economic reforms. Soviet Foreign Ministry spokesman Gennadii Gerasimov told reporters that Mulroney had delivered this message during talks with Prime Minister Nikolai Ryzhkov. It was reported that Mulroney and Ryzhkov had signed numerous bilateral agreements, including accords on protecting arctic and marine environments (*AP,* November 20). On November 21, Mulroney met with Gorbachev (*AP,* November 21). On November 21, Gorbachev reportedly told Mulroney that leaders in Moscow and Eastern Europe had misjudged the situation a decade ago and that rapid changes were required to make up for lost time. He was not reported to have mentioned Czechoslovakia by name, but reporters said his comments applied to developments there (*Reuters,* November 21, *Pravda,* November 22).

Tuesday, November 21 ————————————————————————————

Lithuanians Told Law Being Prepared on Secession

Mikhail Gorbachev was reported to have told Lithuanian Party leaders that a law was being prepared that will determine the mechanism under which a republic can leave the Soviet Union. Lithuanian Party Second Secretary Vladimir Berezov told a press conference in Vilnius on November 20 that Gorbachev had made the comment during a meeting with the Lithuanian Party leadership in Moscow last week. The Politburo had summoned the entire Lithuanian Party leadership to a meeting to discuss Lithuanian Party plans to hold a special congress next month on the possibility of becoming independent of the CPSU (*RFE Lithuanian Service*, November 21).

Ceausescu and Vorotnikov Assess Soviet-Romanian Ties

Romanian President Nicolae Ceausescu received CPSU Politburo member Vitalii Vorotnikov in Bucharest. TASS said Vorotnikov was heading the Soviet delegation to the Romanian Party Congress. According to TASS, the sides "positively" assessed relations between their countries. The agency said that Vorotnikov had informed Ceausescu about the current stage of *perestroika* in the Soviet Union and that Ceausescu had briefed his guest on Socialist development in Romania.

Yakovlev Supports *Glasnost'* in Media

The Soviet television news program "Vremya" broadcast an address by Politburo member Aleksandr Yakovlev to students of the Komsomol High School in Moscow. In the speech, Yakovlev rebuffed attacks on progressive journalists, which have recently intensified in the USSR. "The impression is," Yakovlev said, "that were we tomorrow to close down the media for a week, everything would be all right: the shelves in the shops would be full, and history would be in order." Yakovlev compared officials who criticize the media with those who killed envoys bringing bad news. Yakovlev also warned against what he termed "a negative and suspicious attitude towards the intelligentsia" and called such an attitude, which he said prevailed among Soviet bureaucrats, "immoral." The abridged text of Yakovlev's address was published in *Pravda*, November 24.

Officials Punished for Cruel Treatment of Prisoners

The Soviet Union said that more than 100 officials had been jailed for mistreating Soviet prisoners and that an additional 5,000 had been punished. A statement made by Yurii Kalinin, a spokesman for the USSR Ministry of Internal Affairs, did not say when the actions were taken. The statement was made last week in Geneva to a UN human-rights panel examining violations of a convention against torture (*RFE/RL Special*, November 21).

Supreme Soviet Approves Culture Minister

The USSR Supreme Soviet approved Nikolai Gubenko as culture minister. Gubenko is the artistic director of the Moscow Taganka Theater. TASS said it was the first time in many years that a professional in the arts had become minister of culture. Gubenko told the Supreme Soviet that it was possible to lead Soviet culture out of its present crisis but that this would take time. Gubenko also said he hoped Yurii Lyubimov would again take over the management of the Taganka Theater (*TASS, Pravda*, November 22). Lyubimov was the artistic director of the theater for twenty years. In the early 1980s, he remained in the West and was stripped of his Soviet citizenship. He now has his citizenship back and is in Moscow.

Zaikov Replaced as Moscow Party Chief

Moscow City Party First Secretary Lev Zaikov was removed from his post and appointed first deputy chairman of the USSR Defense Council. TASS reported that Zaikov had been relieved of his Moscow duties at a plenum of the city Party committee attended by Mikhail Gorbachev. Zaikov, a Politburo member who is considered a hardliner, became Moscow Party chief just over two years ago after Boris El'tsin was ousted from the post for criticizing the slow pace of reforms. Zaikov's replacement as Moscow Party chief is Yurii Prokof'ev, who until now has served as Party second secretary in Moscow (*Pravda*, November 22).

Yazov Again Rejects Idea of Volunteer Army

Soviet Defense Minister Dmitrii Yazov said the Soviet Union could not afford to create an all-volunteer army. In an interview in *Komsomol'skaya pravda*, Yazov said it would cost at least 3.5 billion rubles for servicemen's salaries alone in an all-volunteer army. Yazov also said "a difficult situation" had developed because of the exemption students have received from military service. He said soldiers now want to know whether their ranks will be filled only with people who have failed to get into higher education. He said all students should be required to take military courses in order to maintain a high standard in the Soviet armed forces.

Soviet Newspaper Praises Pope

Komsomol'skaya pravda devoted a special article to Pope John Paul II, praising him. The newspaper said it was not just the pope's service to God but also his "remarkable personality" that made him popular. The newspaper also praised efforts by the Vatican and the USSR to work towards peace and dialogue.

The USSR wants the Union republics to play a more active role in forming Soviet foreign policy. The head of a newly created department at the USSR Foreign Ministry, Yurii Kuplyakov, said the republics' access to the international arena and their contribution to Soviet foreign policy had heretofore been minimal. Kuplyakov said his department wants to change this situation (*TASS*, November 21).

USSR Plans More Active Role for Republican Foreign Ministries

The same day that Lev Zaikov was dismissed as Moscow city Party first secretary, his Leningrad counterpart suffered the same fate. On November 22, *Pravda* reported that Anatolii Gerasimov had been ousted as Leningrad city Party first secretary. (Gerasimov lost in last spring's elections.) Gerasimov was replaced by Boris Gidaspov, who will now combine the posts of first secretary of the Leningrad Oblast and City Party Committees. Western correspondents advanced the theory that both Zaikov and Gerasimov were replaced as part of a move to win votes for the Party in forthcoming elections to the soviets. On November 22, thousands of people attended an officially sponsored rally in Leningrad to support renewal in the CPSU. The rally was called by the Leningrad City Party Committee and was opened by Boris Gidaspov (*Central Television*, "Vremya," November 22). Some speakers at the rally strongly attacked Gorbachev's policy of *perestroika*, saying that it had resulted in a loss of prestige for the CPSU and in an economic crisis. Calls for the removal of the Politburo were also made (*DPA*, November 24; *Central Television*, "Semi dnei," November 26). On November 23, *Pravda* carried a report on the Leningrad demonstration but did not reveal the attacks on Gorbachev. On November 24, *Sovetskaya Rossiya* carried an interview with Gidaspov in which he called for the reassertion of the Party's control over society. For a review of the situation in Leningrad, see also *Ogonek*, No. 51 and *Izvestia*, December 11. On November 28, Gidaspov gave an interview to *Pravda* in which he said there must be no departure from Socialist values. He said "we will stop being ourselves" if we allow people to be fooled with "fairy tales" about "people's capitalism."

Leningrad City Party First Secretary Dismissed

Wednesday, November 22

Deputy Foreign Minister Anatolii Adamishin said members of the banned Ukrainian Catholic Church now enjoyed the same rights "de facto" as other worshipers in

Adamishin on Ukrainian Catholic Church

the USSR. He said the new law on freedom of conscience would "provide equal rights for all religions" (*TASS, Reuters,* November 22). In fact, members of the Ukrainian Catholic Church still have problems in conducting their services, because their church has not yet been legalized and they do not enjoy the same rights as other believers.

Armenians and Azerbaijanis Appeal to Supreme Soviet

Armenians and Azerbaijanis urged the Soviet parliament in separate appeals to help stop violence against their peoples, Radio Moscow said. Both appeals complained about refugee problems created by the conflict over Nagorno-Karabakh. On November 22, workers in Azerbaijan staged a one-day strike in a campaign to end Moscow's rule of Nagorno-Karabakh (*Reuters,* November 22).

Abalkin on *Perestroika*, Ties with EC

Deputy Prime Minister Leonid Abalkin said the failure of *perestroika* would lead to destabilization not only in the USSR but also elsewhere. Abalkin was speaking at a news conference in Brussels after talks with European Community officials. Abalkin attended an EC-sponsored seminar on Soviet economic reforms and on prospects for cooperation between the USSR and the EC. A third round of talks on a ten-year EC-Soviet trade and cooperation agreement opened in Brussels on November 22. Abalkin said an agreement would be "a historic step, not only for the Soviet people, but also for Europe as a whole" (*UPI, DPA,* November 22).

Pollution of Lake Ladoga Continues

Radio Moscow reiterated that continuing deterioration in the quality of the water in Lake Ladoga was threatening the water supply for Leningrad and surrounding areas. It said that, if the dumping of phosphorus in the lake were not stopped soon, the city would find itself in a situation worse than if it were in the middle of a desert (*Radio Moscow-1*, 1000, November 22).

Modrow Says Relations with USSR Must Be Expanded

Sovetskaya Rossiya quoted East German Prime Minister Hans Modrow as saying relations with the Soviet Union were vital for East Germany and must be expanded. In an interview with the newspaper, Modrow was also quoted on the upcoming meeting between West German Chancellor Helmut Kohl and East German head of state Egon Krenz. Modrow said the two German states had a special responsibility for peace in Europe.

TASS said thirty-four people had been killed in a plane crash in the USSR. The news agency said an AN-24 airliner with forty-two people on board had crashed while attempting to land at an airport in the Tyumen Oblast in Western Siberia on November 21 (*TASS*, November 22).

Thirty-four Killed in Soviet Plane Crash

_____ *Thursday, November 23*

TASS said miners at Ukrzapadugol in Western Ukraine had ousted their trade-union officials and voted in their own candidates. It said grass-roots candidates had been voted in at a recent meeting after management had failed to respond to miners' demands that local trade-unions "be purged of official stooges." TASS quoted the miners as saying the officials were "mere *apparatchiks* oblivious to miners' real needs." TASS quoted the newly elected chairman, Sergei Besaga, as saying the new committee had succeeded in increasing night-shift pay and introducing longer holidays. He said it was also working on other benefits.

Trade-Union Officials Ousted at Mine in Ukraine

The Lithuanian Supreme Soviet passed an ethnic minorities law giving equal rights to all nationalities in the republic. TASS said the new law would defuse the tension that was created in the republic after the Lithuanian language was raised to the status of a state language. TASS said the new law guarantees all citizens of Lithuania equal political, economic, and social rights and freedoms regardless of their nationality. The Lithuanian Supreme Soviet also decided to hold elections for the republic's new Supreme Soviet next February 24.

Lithuania Passes Ethnic Minorities Law

Moldavia's Supreme Soviet adopted an election law providing that all Moldavian citizens would be entitled to vote regardless of nationality and length of stay in the republic. The law also stipulates that voting rights will not be restricted by religion, native language, or occupation. Moldavia's parliament further decreed that republican elections would be held in territorial constituencies only, without public organizations being entitled to certain seats. There will be no limits on the number of candidates in each constituency (*Central Television*, "Vremya," November 23). The text of the law appeared in *Sovetskaya Moldaviya*, November 26.

Moldavian Supreme Soviet Adopts Election Law

USSR Supreme Soviet Adopts Law on Leasing

The USSR Supreme Soviet adopted a new law on leasing. Under the law, which is to take effect on January 1, all production resulting from lease arrangements will belong to the work collectives involved. Collectives will also be allowed to "buy out" enterprises they have leased from the state. The head of the parliamentary committee for legislation, Sergei Alekseev, said the law would make it possible to improve the country's economic situation as early as next year (*TASS*, November 23; *Izvestia*, November 24).

Mazowiecki Visits USSR

Polish Prime Minister Tadeusz Mazowiecki arrived in Moscow for his first visit to the USSR since becoming head of Poland's "Solidarity"-led government (*TASS*, November 23; *Pravda*, November 24). The same day, *Pravda* welcomed Mazowiecki's visit. On November 24, Mazowiecki met in the Kremlin with Soviet Prime Minister Nikolai Ryzhkov (*TASS, UPI*, November 24). Ryzhkov was quoted as saying he hoped Mazowiecki's visit would enable Poland and the USSR to solve problems of mutual concern. AP said Ryzhkov and Mazowiecki discussed Poland's massive debt to the Soviet Union. The same day, Mazowiecki met with Mikhail Gorbachev (*Pravda*, December 25). Speaking at a dinner in his honor, Mazowiecki raised the question of the massacre in Katyn of Polish officers during World War II. The Soviet Union still has not officially admitted its responsiblity for the murder. Mazowiecki was quoted as saying the massacre "is not only a matter for our alliance but for a real reconciliation of our peoples." AP and Reuters reported that Mazowiecki also raised the issue of Katyn during his talks with Gorbachev.

On November 25, Mazowiecki briefed reporters on the progress of his talks with Soviet leaders. He said he felt the Soviet leadership appreciated that his "Solidarity"-led government wants closer Polish-Soviet ties (*Radio Warsaw*, November 25).

On November 26, Mazowiecki visited the site of the wartime massacre of Polish officers in Katyn. While Poland at the beginning of this year declared the Soviet NKVD responsible for the massacre, the Soviet Union has still not renounced its traditional version of events, which blames the Nazis for the killing. Soviet television gave details of the arguments of both sides and interviewed several Poles who said they were sure Stalin's secret police were responsible for the massacre. At the time of Mazowiecki's visit to Katyn, human-rights activists in Smolensk staged a demonstration urging the USSR to admit its guilt (*AP*, November 26). On November 25, AP quoted Soviet historian Yurii Afanas'ev as saying at a reception held by Mazowiecki for Moscow intellectuals that the continued Soviet silence about who was responsible for the Katyn massacre was "paradoxical."

On November 27, the final day of his visit, Mazowiecki traveled to Leningrad, where he met with local intellectuals and city officials (*DPA*, November 27). The same day, a joint Soviet-Polish communiqué was issued. The communiqué stressed that relations between the USSR and Poland were based on the right of each country to choose its own social and political path without interference. The statement said clarification of historical issues—above all the Katyn question—would strengthen Polish-Soviet relations (*TASS*, November 27; *Pravda*, November 28).

Friday, November 24

Soviet Media Reaction to Events in Czechoslovakia

The Soviet media gave extensive and relatively frank coverage to events in Czechoslovakia. On November 24, Soviet television showed the mass demonstrations in Prague demanding the resignation of the Party leadership. *Pravda* reported that the Czechoslovak people had lost faith in leaders who did not match words with deeds. On the evening of November 24, the Soviet media reported the resignation of the Czechoslovak Party leadership. Radio Moscow World Service expressed hope that the country's new leadership would work "more energetically to promote democratization in the country." It also reported Alexander Dubcek's address to the crowds in the center of Prague, referring to him as the man "who had led the Party in 1968."

On November 25, TASS quoted Dubcek as blaming the present crisis in Czechoslovakia on "military interference in the affairs and life of the Czechoslovak people." The same day, the Soviet media expressed the hope that the new leadership of Karel Urbanek would be able to "bring the country out of the crisis." TASS called for continued dialogue between the Party and the opposition but suggested that the latter did not yet have "a harmonious and clear-cut program of action."

On November 27, Radio Moscow's Prague correspondent Aleksandr Samylin reported that, "as a public opinion poll has shown, the overwhelming majority in Czechoslovakia does not agree with the incomplete personnel changes in the Central Committee Presidium." Samylin once again emphasized the need for dialogue between the Communist Party and representatives of the Civic Forum and other opposition groups. TASS said today's strike in Czechoslovakia showed that the working people support restructuring and the renewal of society in accordance with humanitarian principles. TASS carried a detailed report on an extraordinary session of the Central Committee of the Czechoslovak Communist Party.

Lithuanian Independence Commission Set Up

Reuters quoted journalists in Vilnius as saying Lithuania had set up a parliamentary commission on the restoration of independence. They said the commission had been formed on November 23. It was reported that the commission would examine various possiblities, including negotiations with Moscow, agreements with the Kremlin on economic and political sovereignty, and a referendum on secession from the USSR.

Saturday, November 25

Starkov Comments on His Position

The embattled editor of *Argumenty i fakty*, Vladislav Starkov, said on Soviet television that the authorities had not yet been able to force his resignation. Appearing on the popular television show "Do i posle polunochi," Starkov produced a suitcase of letters and telegrams supporting his crusading editorial policies. He said these had enabled him to resist the continuing pressure from above. Starkov did not name those putting pressure on him to resign but spoke pointedly about "the highest circles." Gorbachev demanded Starkov's dismissal in a speech to representatives of the Soviet media on October 13.

Earlier this month, Starkov commented on his situation in the US press. On November 3, in an article published by *The Washington Post*, Starkov said he believed a popularity poll published by *Argumenty i fakty* had "touched a nerve" when it came to his attention.

In issue No. 45, the editorial board of *Argumenty i fakty* said it wanted Starkov to remain in his job as chief editor of the journal. The board said it had acknowledged the leadership's criticism of the periodical and would take it into account in the future.

Argumenty i fakty (No. 46) carried an article by Starkov and his three deputies written in response to readers who wanted to know why the authorities wished to dismiss Starkov. The article explained that during the period of *perestroika* many complaints had been voiced by the CPSU Central Committee's Ideological Department about materials published by the periodical. It said criticism had been voiced over the publication of some anti-Stalinist materials, including discussions about the number of Stalin's victims by Roy Medvedev and Vladimir Tikhonov. A piece on the privileges of the Party elite also displeased the authorities. Among the latest materials that the authorities found unsuitable for publication were an article on the work of the Supreme Soviet commission on the Gdlyan and Ivanov affair and a review of Western press opinion on the CPSU Central Committee resolution on the situation in the Baltic republics.

Sunday, November 26

Pravda Publishes Article by Gorbachev on Socialism

In an article published in *Pravda*, Gorbachev said the main aim of *perestroika* was to build socialism with a human face. He wrote that the task at hand was not simply to proclaim this idea but to renew socialism in practice in order to ensure that the entire social system would be geared to the needs of the people. He added, however, that, in the struggle for the renewal of socialism, the Party could not yield the initiative to "populist demagoguery, nationalistic or chauvinistic currents, or unruly group interests." On November 29, *Pravda* carried an editorial devoted to Gorbachev's article. The editorial stressed Gorbachev's rejection of claims by his critics that the leadership had launched *perestroika* without a clear plan of action.

Interregional Group Wants Debate on Role of Party

There was another call for the leading role of the Party to be discussed at next month's Congress of People's Deputies. (Earlier this month, the USSR Supreme Soviet, under pressure from Gorbachev, defeated a similar call to have the role of the Party placed on the agenda of the Congress). This time the call came from the Interregional Group of people's deputies, which held a meeting in Moscow (*TASS*, November 26).

Writer Condemns Soviet Invasion of Czechoslovakia

In what seems to be the strongest condemnation of the Soviet invasion of Czechoslovakia to appear so far in the Soviet press, Leningrad writer Daniil Granin called the crushing of the Prague Spring in Czechoslovakia "a collective murder." In an open letter published in *Moscow News* (No. 48), Granin bitterly criticized the Kremlin's armed suppression of reformists in Prague in 1968 and the Stalinists who took over there afterwards. "Czechoslovakia's desire to move on to a new socialism 'with a human face' was cut short by military force . . . That was the first *perestroika* in the Socialist countries, and we crushed it and slandered it," Granin said.

Yakovlev Says Japan's Claim to Kuriles Spoils Relations

Politburo member Aleksandr Yakovlev, who recently visited Japan, said in *New Times* (No. 48) that Japan was obstructing the development of better cooperation with the Soviet Union. Yakovlev complained that Japan was showing "rare stubborness" in its insistence on the return of the Kurile Islands.

Yakovlev Says No Swing to the Right

Aleksandr Yakovlev said there would be no swing to the right in the USSR, though conservatism was stronger than the present leadership first thought. Speaking on Soviet television, Yakovlev said conservative views, old habits, and parasitic attitudes were deeply ingrained. He also said the leadership under Mikhail Gorbachev had underestimated the country's economic problems when launching its reform program. But Yakovlev said moving to the right would mean going backwards.

Ukrainian Catholics March for Legalization

Approximately 150,000 Ukrainian Catholics marched through Lvov to press for the legalization of their Church. The march appears to have been the largest demonstration of its kind since September 17, when over 100,000 people took part in a similar procession through the city. On November 25, the Moscow Patriarchate's newly named external affairs director, Metropolitan Kirill of Smolensk, told the Milan Catholic daily *Avvenire* that the question of the Ukrainian Catholic Church must be resolved in negotiations between the Patriarchate and the Vatican "without the intervention of the Soviet state."

Estonian Komsomol Plans to Abolish Itself

Komsomol'skaya pravda reported that the Komsomol organization of Estonia had voted to abolish itself in the near future. The newspaper said delegates at a congress of the Komsomol in Tallinn had approved the motion because the group's influence and popularity had declined. The congress resolved to declare a transitional period for the Estonian Komsomol up to March 1, 1990, after which the activities of the organization, based on its existing statutes, would be considered to be concluded," the newspaper said. A motion to abolish the organization immediately had been defeated. On November 29, First Secretary of the All-Union Komsomol Vladimir Mironenko commented on the Estonian Komsomol Congress. He complained that the majority of delegates had only one goal—to abolish the Estonian Komsomol—and did not want to discuss important issues of *perestroika* in Estonia (*Radio Moscow*, 1900, November 29).

Army Union Stages Demonstration

The new armed forces trade union "Shield" staged a rally in Moscow to demand an end to Communist Party influence on military life and better pay for soldiers. At least 200 servicemen, retired officers, and their relatives took part. Mothers of soldiers addressed the crowd, complaining that draftees were physically abused, badly fed, ill-housed, and underpaid. The authorities did not interfere with the rally (*Reuters, AP*, November 26).

Moscow Pushes for Better Relations between North and South Korea

The USSR trade representative in Seoul said Moscow would do what it could to help reduce tensions between the two Koreas (*Reuters* November 27). While acknowledging Soviet "obligations" to North Korea, Valerii Nazarov said that the Soviet goal was to promote a general improvement in relations between the two Koreas. Nazarov has been in Seoul since July, when Moscow opened a Soviet Chamber of Commerce and Industry.

Monday, November 27

Draft Press Law Approved

The USSR Supreme Soviet approved a draft law on the press. The draft bans censorship of the media and allows individuals to set up publications. Following sharp debate, Soviet Vice President Anatolii Luk'yanov, who chaired the session, suggested that the liberal draft be published in the press for public discussion and that alternative proposals—including those put forward by Politburo member Vadim Medvedev—be published shortly thereafter. The Supreme Soviet commissions on *glasnost'*, legislation, and international affairs are to continue working on the draft. Luk'yanov's suggestion was adopted 376 to 8, with 13 abstentions (*Radio Moscow*, "Mayak," 1800-1830, November 27). The text of the draft appeared on December 4 in *Izvestia* and other newspapers.

643

The adoption of the draft followed strong debates in the Supreme Soviet on November 24. The controversy arose when Politburo member and Party chief ideologist Vadim Medvedev introduced changes in Articles 6 and 43 of the draft. From Article 6 Medvedev excluded permission for individuals to set up periodicals and to Article 43 he added permission for the authorities to interfere with the work of the media. During the session on November 24, liberal and conservative deputies clashed, mainly over Medvedev's amendments. (*Radio Moscow,* "Mayak," November 24 and *Izvestia,* November 25).

Law on Economic Autonomy for Baltic Republics Passed

The USSR Supreme Soviet passed a law giving economic autonomy to the Baltic republics. TASS said the law gives the three republics the right to dispose of land and other natural resources, regulate all branches of their economies, and manage the financial system and republican banks. But there are some exceptions: the law says oil and gas centers and other, unidentified items will remain all-Union property. The text of the law was published in *Izvestia,* December 2.

Supreme Soviet Approves Document on Nuclear Testing

The USSR Supreme Soviet passed a resolution on improving the ecological situation in the USSR, which among other things calls on the authorities to consider stopping nuclear tests at the Semipalatinsk testing ground in Kazakhstan. TASS said the resolution also calls for a study of the consequences of nuclear tests at the northern testing ground on the arctic island of Novaya Zemlya. TASS commented that the document reflects growing concern about the extremely grave ecological situation in many areas of the Soviet Union. The resolution also stipulates measures for the improvement of the ecological situation in the area of the Aral Sea, Belorussia, and other regions. The text of the resolution was published in *Izvestia,* December 3. See RL 545/89.

European Community to Aid *Perestroika*

On November 27, the European Community and the Soviet Union concluded a broadly structured trade and economic agreement that should result in a net positive flow of economic and financial aid to the Soviet Union. Perhaps its most important aspect is an easing of restrictions on Soviet exports to the EC in exchange for better conditions for EC business people in the USSR. The ten-year accord touches on a number of key areas, including science and technology, transport, and the environment

(*Reuters*, November 27). In a separate development, the West German government announced that it is willing to help the Soviet Union overcome acute shortages. The announcement came as Soviet Deputy Prime Minister Ivan Silaev began a visit to Bonn (*DPA*, November 27). Silaev met with Chancellor Helmut Kohl on November 29, and on November 30 he discussed economic relations with West German Economics Minister Helmut Haussman (*DPA*, November 30).

Israel's agriculture minister arrived in Moscow for the highest-level Israeli visit to the USSR since the Kremlin broke diplomatic ties with Israel in 1967. Abraham Katz-Oz, who had failed to get a Soviet visa in August, now has meetings scheduled with the agriculture ministers of the USSR and the RSFSR (*Reuters*, November 27).

Israeli Minister in Moscow

————— Tuesday, November 28

The USSR Supreme Soviet voted in closed session to abolish the special administrative commission that has run Nagorno-Karabakh since last January. Armenian deputies interpreted the resolution as a restoration of Azerbaijani authority over the oblast and walked out in protest before the vote was taken. The resolution instructs Azerbaijani officials to take "urgent legislative measures" to increase the autonomy of Nagorno-Karabakh and guarantee the rights of the mostly Armenian population (*TASS*, *AP*, November 28; *Izvestia*, November 29). On November 29, Radio Moscow said a blockade of the Azerbaijani railways and other transport routes leading to Armenia was continuing (*Radio Moscow-1*, 1900, November 29). On November 29, mass demonstrations were held in Erevan and Baku to criticize the Supreme Soviet resolution (*TASS*, November 29). The text of the resolution was published in *Izvestia* on November 29.

On November 30, the Armenian Supreme Soviet met to discuss the latest developments in the dispute over Nagorno-Karabakh (*Radio Erevan*, November 30). Radio Erevan also reported a mass rally in Nagorno-Karabakh at which speakers said the USSR Supreme Soviet had given in to the demands of the Azerbaijani Popular Front. The same day, new killings were reported in Transcaucasia in connection with the dispute. It was reported that at least two Azerbaijanis had been shot dead on November 29 on Azerbaijani territory just outside Nagorno-Karabakh. UPI

Moscow Tries New Approach to Nagorno-Karabakh

quoted a spokesman for the Azerbaijani news agency as saying he knew of two or three other deaths resulting from clashes over Nagorno-Karabakh.

Amnesty for Afghan Crimes

The Supreme Soviet granted an unconditional amnesty to all former soldiers who committed crimes while serving in Afghanistan. The amnesty, which is to take effect on December 15, also applies to deserters and prisoners of war, many of whom may have feared punishment if they returned to the Soviet Union. The new law will directly affect both the 2,540 soldiers already convicted of crimes and the 75 to 100 Soviet prisoners of war (*AP*, November 28; *Izvestia*, November 30).

Zagladin Emphasizes Difference between Baltic Republics and Eastern Europe

Vadim Zagladin, an adviser to Gorbachev on international affairs and chairman of the Soviet Committee for European Security and Cooperation, indicated in Rome that the Soviet Union would not allow the dramatic political reforms that have taken place in Eastern Europe to occur in the Baltic republics. Zagladin stated that the Soviet Union was now laying a legal basis for relations among its republics. He criticized those working for the breakup of the Soviet state and stressed that all problems should be solved within the framework of the Soviet state. He cited the recent local election laws adopted in the republics as proof of their new freedom to shape their own destinies (*Reuters*, November 28).

Invasion of Czechoslovakia in 1968 Criticized

Recent developments in Eastern Europe have prompted Soviet officials to reevaluate Moscow's suppression of the Prague Spring. On November 28, Eduard Shevardnadze indirectly criticized the Soviet invasion. In an interview in *L'Unita*, the Soviet foreign minister said Moscow is now guided by the principles of freedom of choice and noninterference, adding that "these principles were always proclaimed but not always respected." Shevardnadze suggested that the Czechoslovaks themselves must decide whether there is a link between 1968 and now. The same day, Andrei Grachev of the CPSU Central Committee's International Department said on French radio that the suppression of the Prague Spring was "a mistake worse than a crime." He added that the USSR Supreme Soviet should condemn the invasion (*AP*, November 28). On November 27, several Soviet deputies put forward just such a proposal at a session of the Supreme Soviet (*Reuters*, November 27).

Sergei Kuznetsov, a member of the Democratic Union and Sverdlovsk correspondent for the *samizdat* journal *Glasnost'*, was sentenced to three years in a labor camp, according to AP. Kuznetsov was charged with resisting arrest and slandering specific MVD and KGB officials in leaflets calling for public demonstrations. Prior to his arrest last December 11, Kuznetsov was an active organizer of such rallies in Sverdlovsk. Kuznetsov blamed the unpopular Sverdlovsk Party chief, Leonid Bobykin, for his arrest. Kuznetsov's trial was unusually long even by Soviet standards and was marked by the same types of legal violations that characterized such proceedings under Brezhnev. But there was one major difference: this time, certain Soviet publications took the side of the accused. A Sverdlovsk newspaper *Za tyazheloe mashinostroenie* published an interview with Andrei Sakharov supporting Kuznetsov; the Latvian Komsomol newspaper *Sovetskaya molodezh'* on November 15 carried a long interview with Kuznetsov; and *Literaturnaya gazeta* (No. 46) protested against legal violations at his trial. Kuznetsov's defense lawyer Sergei Kotov will appeal the decision.

Independent Journalist Sentenced to Three Years

Speaking at a two-day session of the RSFSR Supreme Soviet, RSFSR Deputy Prime Minister Aleksandr Khomyakov said the Russian republic would cut its subsidies to unprofitable enterprises. The money saved is to be invested in modernization programs. TASS reported that this budget plan had been drawn up under "economic crisis conditions" (*Sovetskaya Rossiya*, November 29). On November 29, the RSFSR Supreme Soviet adopted its economic plan for 1990 (*TASS*, November 29). The text of the plan appeared in *Sovetskaya Rossiya* on December 1.

RSFSR Budget Plans

Soviet and US partners signed a joint venture deal to build and operate a 2 billion-dollar petrochemical complex in Western Siberia. The plant, to be built in Tobolsk, will process petrochemicals that will be used to make consumer products, largely medical and automotive items, for both Soviet and foreign markets (*AP*, November 28).

Major US-Soviet Joint Venture on Petrochemicals Signed

On November 28, the USSR Supreme Soviet directed the USSR Council of Ministers to set up commissions to solve practical questions related to restoring the rights of Soviet Germans and Crimean Tatars. In an interview in *Izvestia* on November 29, Chairman of the Council of Nationalities Commission on Nationalities Policy and Interethnic Rela-

Restoration of Rights for Germans and Crimean Tatars Approved

tions Georgii Tarazevich made clear that the Supreme Soviet had, in effect, approved the restoration of the peoples' autonomy. Tarazevich said deputies had concluded that the re-creation of the autonomy of the Soviet Germans on the Volga was a matter of historical justice. He added that their resettlement would be expensive but that the Germans were prepared to provide their own housing and that the areas they would be leaving would also provide assistance. The Crimean Tatars should likewise be allowed to return to the Crimea, he said, but the tensions caused by their present spontaneous and sometimes illegal resettlement should be avoided. Tarazevich said that the Supreme Soviets of the RSFSR and Ukraine would examine the proposals but that, "since the problem involves constitutional changes," it should also be put before the Congress of People's Deputies.

Moscow Blocks AFL-CIO Delegation

According to AP, Soviet officials refused to issue visas for an AFL-CIO delegation that had hoped to visit striking miners in Vorkuta. The AFL-CIO had assembled a five-man team after receiving a telegram from the Vorkuta miners two weeks ago. The miners reportedly told the AFL-CIO that they were struggling not only for their rights but also to end the Communist Party's leading role in Soviet government.

Wednesday, November 29 _____

Gorbachev in Rome

On November 29, Mikhail Gorbachev arrived in Italy for a three-day state visit. At a state banquet in Rome, Gorbachev said "the Cold War is ending." Arguing that the war had produced neither victors nor vanquished, he said it should be possible to move forward without "a cold peace." Gorbachev also repeated his longstanding call for a reduction in naval forces (*Reuters,* November 29).

On November 30, Gorbachev held talks with Italian Communist Party General Secretary Achille Occhetto. Later he had a meeting with Italian Prime Minister Giulio Andreotti. A joint statement signed by Gorbachev and Andreotti said international order should be based on values of freedom and pluralism, as well as national, ethnic, and religious tolerance (*Reuters, UPI,* November 30). The same day Gorbachev delivered a speech at the Capitol in Rome. In his speech Gorbachev called for a new East-West summit meeting. Gorbachev said the summit, which he called "Helsinki Two," could be held as early as 1990. His proposal would bring forward by two years a meeting originally called for under the 1975 Helsinki accords on human rights and security in Europe. Gorbachev also said the Soviet Union had abandoned its claim to a monopoly on the truth and its idea that those with whom it disagreed were enemies. Gorbachev insisted, however, that it was wrong to think that socialism was collapsing (Western agencies, November 30). See, *Pravda*, November 30 and December 1.

Soviet officials reacted negatively to West German Chancellor Helmut Kohl's plan for a German confederation. Speaking in Rome, Eduard Shevardnadze said the existence of two German states is one of the realities that must be accepted in order to achieve East-West integration. In Moscow, Soviet Foreign Ministry spokesman Yurii Gremitskikh said Kohl had acted without considering the feelings of other European countries, especially East Germany, whose leaders say reunification is not on the agenda (*AFP*, *DPA*, November 29).

Soviet Reaction to Kohl's Plan for Confederation

Because of Soviet delays in admitting Soviet responsibility for the Katyn massacre, Warsaw wants to replace the Polish-Soviet commission of Party historians examining "blank spots" in Soviet-Polish relations with a bilateral government commission. This idea was raised during Tadeusz Mazowiecki's visit to the Soviet Union. For the past two years, the Soviet side of the existing commission has blocked any Soviet acknowledgment of responsibility for the Katyn massacre. Such a situation is clearly unacceptable for Poland; the leader of "Solidarity" in the Sejm, Bronislaw Geremek, complained that things were moving too slowly (*Radio Warsaw*, November 29).

Poland Wants Government Commission on "Blank Spots"

The November issue of *Yunost'* provides a detailed account of the rising number of *samizdat* periodicals in the USSR. The account, together with recent studies in the February and May issues of *Sovetskaya bibliographiya*, reflects growing official recognition of this form of publication. *Yunost'* reported that most of the 323 such serials registered in a *samizdat* reference guide issued by SMOT, the independent trade union, are liberal-democratic in orientation, outnumbering Marxist journals three to one. The journal also reported that Moscow's Historical Archives Institute, headed by Yurii Afanas'ev, now maintains a special library for *samizdat* publications.

***Yunost'* on Unofficial Journals**

Soviet-Turkish Trade Talks

Soviet Deputy Prime Minister Lev Voronin arrived in Turkey for a ten-day visit aimed at boosting still further already booming Turkish-Soviet trade. He is scheduled to meet with Turkish President Turgut Ozal and other officials. Voronin told the Turkish daily *Hurriyet* that bilateral trade would reach a billion dollars next year, triple the amount in 1986.

Broad Support for Right to Strike

According to a recent poll, 63 percent of Soviet citizens support the right of workers to go on strike, TASS reported. A majority also support the idea that trade unions should have the right to veto actions of enterprise administrators that affect the interests of workers.

CIA Director Says Soviet KGB Efforts Intensified

The director of the CIA said that Soviet spying has become more aggressive under Mikhail Gorbachev. William Webster said CIA stations around the world were reporting more aggressive Soviet actions, more robust intelligence collection efforts, and more efforts to recruit US embassy and intelligence personnel. Webster said increased Soviet activity was particularly apparent in KGB efforts to obtain foreign technology (*UPI, AP*, November 30).

Newspaper Discusses Possibility of Solzhenitsyn's Visit

Literaturnaya gazeta (November 29) carried the text of a conversation between journalist Alla Latynina and historian Vadim Borisov, who recently visited Aleksandr Solzhenitsyn in Vermont. (Borisov is in charge of the publication of Solzhenitsyn's works in the USSR.) Latynina raised the question of Solzhenitsyn visiting the USSR, reminding Borisov that the writer's precondition for returning to his homeland—namely, the publication of his works, particularly *Gulag Archipelago*, in the USSR—had now been fulfilled. Borisov said he expected Solzhenitsyn to visit the USSR eventually but indicated that at present he is still hesitant about doing so. According to Borisov, Solzhenitsyn has agreed to return to the USSR only after he has finished his historical epic *The Red Wheel*.

Thursday, November 30 —————————————————————

Girenko on New Central Committee Department on Nationalities

In an article in *Pravda*, CPSU Central Committee Secretary Andrei Girenko described the Central Committee's newly created Department of Nationality Relations. The department, staffed by members of various nationalities, has three subdivisions—one for the non-Russian Union republics, one for the RSFSR, and a third concerned with research and forecasting. Elsewhere in his article, Girenko argued that calls for secession or border changes represent attempts to divert people from solving the main problems. The restoration of the autonomy of the Soviet Germans and Crimean Tatars, however, he says, represents not a recarving of frontiers but rather "the correction of an illegality committed in the past." But he adds that the restoration of their autonomy must take into account present-day realities. As former Party first secretary in the Crimea, Girenko is well aware of the hostility of much of the Slav population there to the restoration of Crimean Tatar autonomy.

Vadim Medvedev Attends Lithuanian CP Plenum

Politburo member Vadim Medvedev flew to Vilnius to attend the twenty-second plenum of the Lithuanian Communist Party Central Committee that is to set the agenda for an extraordinary congress of the Lithuanian Communist Party on December 19. (The congress is to discuss the possibility of the Lithuanian Communist Party breaking away from the CPSU.) TASS quoted Medvedev as saying during his meeting with Lithuanian Party officials on November 30 that "the aspirations of certain forces to drive a wedge between the Lithuanian Communist Party and the CPSU will benefit no one and will only complicate the process of *perestroika.*" Participants in the plenum were read a message from Mikhail Gorbachev in which he cautioned the Lithuanian Communist Party against breaking with the CPSU (*AP*, December 1). On November 28, the Vilnius city newspaper *Vakarines Naujienos* published a statement by some of the delegates elected to the Lithuanian Party Congress asking that the plenum of the republican Party Central Committee be open and democratic. The statement called on other Communist Party members to support an appeal to the Lithuanian Supreme Soviet urging the elimination of Article 6 of the Lithuanian Constitution on the leading role of the Communist Party. On November 30, *The New York Times* published an article saying that the head of the Lithuanian Communist Party's Organizational Party Work and Cadre Department, Viktoras Baublys, had informed local reporters about a resolution signed by all the members of the CPSU Politburo sharply criticizing the Lithuanian Party Buro and First Secretary Algirdas Brazauskas for "allowing hesitations, inconsistencies, and deviations from the resolutions of the CPSU."

El'tsin in Greece

Speaking at the start of a five-day visit to Greece, Boris El'tsin said Gorbachev had failed to take the economic measures necessary to promote *perestroika*. El'tsin also said the major threat to *perestroika* comes from conservative forces who "want to block any path forward." The same day, El'tsin discussed Soviet-Greek relations with Premier Xenohon Zolotas (*RFE/RL Special*, November 30).

Shevardnadze Meets Former Afghan King

Eduard Shevardnadze held talks in Rome with the former Afghan king, Zahir Shah. TASS said the talks were useful. It said a political solution to the Afghan problem had been discussed.

***Rodina* on 1937 Census**

Writing in issue No. 11 of the periodical *Rodina* on the suppressed census of 1937 and the falsified census of 1939, demographer Mark Tol'ts called for the restrictions on all the statistics of the 1930s to be lifted so that estimates of the numbers of people who died in the famine at the beginning of the 1930s and during the war can be based on real and not mythical figures. In his article, Tol'ts described the fate of those in charge of the 1937 census, cited figures from the report of the commission set up to investigate its supposed irregularities, and suggested how the 1939 census data were falsified. Among materials based on inaccurate population figures for the 1930s, Tol'ts named Roy Medvedev's article on the 1932–33 famine in *Znamya*, No. 2, 1989, and A. Antonov-Avseenko's article in *Smena*, No. 11, 1989.

The Month of December

On December 1, the Armenian Supreme Soviet declared Nagorno-Karabakh rightfully part of Armenia. It said the disputed region was now united with Armenia (*Reuters, UPI*, December 1). The same day the Buro of the Azerbaijani Party Central Committee welcomed the decision of the USSR Supreme Soviet to return control over the Nagorno-Karabakh to Azerbaijan (*Radio Baku*, December 1).

Armenian Supreme Soviet Declares Nagorno-Karabakh Part of Armenia

On December 1, Gorbachev held talks with Pope John Paul II in the Vatican in the first meeting between a Soviet leader and a pope. During the meeting, Gorbachev raised the question of the Ukrainian Catholics, saying he hoped all Catholics of the Byzantine rite could "freely practice their religious life." Speaking to reporters after the meeting, Gorbachev said the Vatican and Moscow had agreed in principle to establish diplomatic relations. He said he and the pope had discussed problems that exist in the USSR, including relations between the state and various churches (*Reuters*, December 1; *Pravda*, December 2). Gorbachev said a new Soviet law on freedom of conscience would be adopted soon. Gorbachev also invited the pope to visit the USSR.

Gorbachev Holds Talks with Pope

The USSR Supreme Court has fully rehabilitated more than 150 people convicted of antistate activities during the 1930s, 1940s, and early 1950s. TASS said that, at its session on November 30, the court had proclaimed that those involved had been "convicted without grounds." The news agency did not give the names of those affected but said most had been charged with anti-Soviet agitation and propaganda and with committing terrorist acts against the state and the Party.

More Than 150 People Rehabilitated by USSR Supreme Court

The chairman of the Ukrainian government's Council on Religious Affairs, Nikolai Kolesnik, told Novosti press agency that, from now on, Ukrainian Catholics would,

Ukrainian Catholics Allowed to Register Congregations

653

like other religious groups, be allowed to register their congregations. Novosti said this means de facto recognition of the rights of the banned Ukrainian Catholic Church. The announcement came as Mikhail Gorbachev was meeting with Pope John Paul II. Reuters quoted an activist of the Ukrainian Catholic Church, Ivan Hel, as saying the new rules allowing registration of church congregations fail to meet the Church's demands for full legalization. See RL 559/89.

Saturday, December 2 ————————————————————————————

US-Soviet Summit

On December 2, Mikhail Gorbachev and George Bush began their summit meeting. The two leaders met aboard the Soviet passenger liner "Maxim Gorky," docked in Marsaxlokk bay on the southeast end of Malta. *Pravda* carried an article welcoming the summit. It said dialogue between the two leaders was particularly important now that rapid changes were taking place in the world. The changes in Eastern Europe were on the summit agenda together with arms control. (*AP, AFP,* December 2; *Pravda,* December 3).

On December 3, the Malta summit resumed. The situation in Eastern Europe was again the main topic of discussion. Speaking at a joint press conference at the end of the summit, both Bush and Gorbachev said their countries were entering a new era that could produce a lasting peace. Both leaders declared the summit a success. They agreed to hold their next meeting in the United States in June, 1990. They said they hoped to sign a treaty then halving the US and Soviet strategic arsenals (*AP, Reuters,* December 3). It was disclosed at the press conference that the two leaders had narrowed their differences over Nicaragua. Bush said he accepted Gorbachev's assurances that the Soviet Union had stopped shipping arms to Central America. Gorbachev told the news conference that the Soviet Union understands US sensitivities about Central America, and he said the USSR wants free elections in Nicaragua. The two leaders disagreed, however, over the need for talks on reducing US and Soviet naval forces. Gorbachev said "the time has come" for such talks. Bush said there was "no agreement at all" on the issue at the summit. He said he was "not particularly positive" about the need for negotiations (*Reuters, AP,* December 3; *Pravda,* December 4 and 5). Summing up the results of the summit, US Secretary of State James Baker said it had given a major boost to US-Soviet cooperation

(*CBS*, December 3). Before leaving Malta, Gorbachev gave an interview to Soviet television, which was reported in *Pravda* on December 4.

After the summit, Bush went to Brussels to brief NATO allies on the meeting, while Warsaw Pact leaders gathered in Moscow to hear Gorbachev's report on his talks with Bush (*Reuters*, *AP*, December 4; *Pravda*, December 5). It was the first Warsaw Pact summit to include non-Communist representatives in East European countries' delegations.

Progressive Deputies Call for Two-Hour Strike

Western agencies reported that Andrei Sakharov, Yurii Afanas'ev, Boris El'tsin, and other reformists from the Interregional Group of deputies had called for a two-hour general strike to demand that the article in the Soviet Constitution guaranteeing the leading role of the CPSU be abolished. They called for the strike to be held between 1000 and 1200 on December 11, one day before the Congress of People's Deputies begins its session. On December 6, *Izvestia* carried a letter from a deputy, Yurii Chernichenko, who said he had decided to withdraw his signature from the strike appeal.

On December 10, the Interregional Group of deputies met in Moscow to discuss the strike call. Only 140 members of the group attended the meeting, although the group originally claimed about 400 members. TASS said some of the group's members spoke against the strike. It said the deputies passed a compromise resolution that acknowledged the right of every member of the group to "independent political actions in the interests of radical democratic transformations."

On December 11, reports from the Soviet Union said very few workers took part in a brief general strike urged by the Interregional Group of reformist deputies. AP said that only about 1,500 workers in Moscow observed the strike and that there were apparently also very few strikes in other parts of the country.

Vorgashorskaya Miners Back at Work

TASS said that all miners at the Vorgashorskaya mine in Vorkuta had ended their strike and returned to work but that operations had not yet regained their normal pace. The Vorgashorskaya miners decided to return to work after receiving a document signed by Minister of Coal Industry Mikhail Shchadov promising to meet their main demands. The document stipulates full economic independence for the mine but says the mine must continue to meet state orders for coal.

Protests in Baku over Supreme Soviet Decree

A spokesman for the Azerbaijani Popular Front said tensions in Baku were running high following the adoption by the USSR Supreme Soviet of a decree abolishing Moscow's special administration of Nagorno-Karabakh. (Activists of the Azerbaijani Popular Front think the decree does not go far enough in underlining Azerbaijani control over the oblast. On December 3, Reuters said that on December 2 a mass rally was held in Baku to protest the Supreme Soviet decree.) As quoted by DPA, the spokesman said there was also an increased flow of Azerbaijani refugees from Armenia. Although the Azerbaijani Supreme Soviet welcomed the USSR Supreme Soviet decree on Nagorno-Karabakh, on December 2 Azerbaijani President Elmira Kafarova said on Baku television that Azerbaijanis planned to suspend parts of the decree that they believe infringe on Azerbaijani sovereignty.

On December 4, another rally was held on a square in Baku. A spokesman for the Azerbaijani Popular Front told RFE/RL in a telephone interview that the rally was called to mark the first anniversary of the forcible dispersal of mass demonstrations on the same square. The same day, TASS said goods trains were moving again along the Azerbaijani railway, which had been subjected to a blockade for the past week.

On December 7, Azerbaijani Party First Secretary Abdul Rakhman Vezirov met with members of a new Azerbaijani committee charged with taking over administration of Nagorno-Karabakh. He told them their first task was to quickly stabilize the social and political situation in the oblast (*Radio Baku*, December 7). Meanwhile, TASS said the only guarantee of safety for people in Nagorno-Karabakh was the MVD troops.

DOSAAF Renamed

Radio Moscow (1900) reported that the defense organization known as the All-Union Voluntary Society for Cooperation with the Army, Navy, and Air Force had been renamed the Union of Societies and Organizations Aiding the Defense of the Country. While the change in name does not necessarily portend a change in function, the new title may be intended to forestall any republican-level demands to leave the parent body.

Latvian Social Democratic Workers' Party Convenes

The Latvian Social Democratic Workers' Party began a two-day congress in Jurmala. TASS reported the meeting and said the last such congress of the party was held fifty-five years ago. On December 3, the congress approved party statutes and elected leading bodies (*TASS*, December 3). Valdis Steins, a professor at the State University of Latvia, was elected head of the party. He told RFE/RL in an interview that the party's main task was to work for the election of its candidates to local soviets and to the republic's Supreme Soviet.

Sunday, December 3

Lithuanian Party Defines Sovereignty Aims

In a draft program published in *Sovetskaya Litva*, the Lithuanian Communist Party said it aims to create a sovereign and independent state within the USSR. The program said socialism was not a dogmatic plan but a constantly developing structure based on reality. The program said the Party would pursue the goals of sovereignty and independence by peaceful parliamentary and constitutional means.

On December 7, the Lithuanian Supreme Soviet voted 243 to one to replace the article in the Lithuanian Constitution on the leading role of the Communist Party with an article legitimizing political parties and public organizations and movements, provided they follow republican law (*Sovetskaya Litva*, December 8). Lithuania thus became the first Soviet republic to open the way for a multiparty system.

Lithuanian Social Democratic Congress

The Lithuanian Social Democratic Party held its Fourteenth Congress in Vilnius on December 2 and 3. The party was established in 1896, but held its last congress fifty-eight years ago in 1931. More than a thousand people attended the congress, which had 272 delegates. Social Democrats from Western Europe, Poland, and several Soviet cities greeted the congress. The congress approved a commission to write the statutes and program of the Lithuanian Social Democratic Party (*RFE Lithuanian Service*, December 4).

Newspaper Reports on Formal and Informal Committees of Voters

Moscow News (No. 49) carried an article by a specialist on informal groups, Nina Belyaeva, who commented on the creation of numerous committees of voters in various parts of the USSR. Many of these committees exist as informal groups. Belyaeva complained that the committees selected by the authorities for official registration often tended to be conservative in their political orientation. Thus, among numerous committees of voters in Moscow, official registration was given to a committee that includes

657

representatives of the extremist nationalist societies "Pamyat'" and "Edinstvo." The article also suggested that, whereas in the elections to the Congress of People's Deputies last March democratic forces won a significant victory over conservative Russian nationalists, the results of forthcoming elections were likely to be much closer because conservative nationalist forces in the RSFSR, who condemn Gorbachev's reforms as a betrayal of Socialist ideals, are now much more united than they were last spring.

Timofeev Wins Libel Suit against KGB

Former political prisoner Lev Timofeev has won his libel suit against the newspaper *Sotsialisticheskaya industriya,* according to *Moscow News* (No. 49). On February 12, *Sotsialisticheskaya industriya* published an article entitled "There Is a Limit to Everything" signed with the characteristic KGB pseudonym V. Sashin. The article charged that Timofeev, along with three other former prisoners of conscience, had engaged in "anti-Socialist activities" and should be arrested for them. A court in Moscow proclaimed the article in *Sotsialisticheskaya industriya* slanderous and ruled that the newspaper should publish an apology.

Soviet Press Marks Anniversary of Soviet-Finnish War

The Soviet press carried several articles marking the fiftieth anniversary of the Soviet-Finnish war. The most outspoken article, by historian Boris Sokolov, appeared in *Moscow News* (No. 49). Sokolov described the war as an act of aggression on the part of the Soviet Union and said that the government of the so-called Democratic Finnish Republic under Hertta Kuusinen was installed by Moscow and had no support among the Finnish population. Other articles on the Soviet-Finnish war appeared in *Trud* and *Krasnaya zvezda* on November 30 and in *Argumenty i fakty* (No. 47).

Monday, December 4 ─────────────────────────────────

Warsaw Pact Denounces 1968 Invasion of Czechoslovakia

The USSR has joined Bulgaria, Hungary, East Germany, and Poland in saying the Warsaw Pact invasion of Czechoslovakia in 1968 was wrong. A joint statement issued in Moscow said that the invasion represented interference in Czechoslovakia's internal affairs and was thus incompatible with the norms of relations between sovereign countries. The Soviet Union issued a second statement saying that the Soviet authorities of that time had taken "an unbalanced and inadequate approach" (*TASS*, December 4; *Pravda*, December 5).

Tensions in Moldavia

According to TASS, speakers at a Moldavian Party *aktiv* meeting described the situation in the republic as "still tense," "potentially explosive," and "alarming," owing to "confrontation among social forces" and "the division of people along ethnic lines." New Party leader Petru Lucinschi's remarks, as summarized by TASS, sounded less alarmist, however. He "drew attention to the need to take into account the constructive points in the opposition's stance" and to focus on issues on which consensus can be achieved. Lucinschi's conciliatory tenor appears to reflect his readiness for dialogue with the Popular Front, contrasting with the confrontational attitude displayed thus far towards the front by the republican Party apparatus.

Pravda on Lenin Library

Pravda argued that the USSR Supreme Soviet should assume direct management of the Lenin Library in Moscow. It said that the Ministry of Culture does not have the means or the authority to run the library properly. *Pravda* said this would bring the USSR into line with many other countries.

Ryzhkov Meets Nemeth and Modrow

The Soviet and Hungarian prime ministers, Nikolai Ryzhkov and Miklos Nemeth, met in the Kremlin and discussed bilateral economic ties. Before the talks, Nemeth told a Radio Budapest reporter that he and Ryzhkov would try to find solutions to some of their economic problems. But Nemeth said this would not be easy, and he noted that previous talks on economic problems had not produced solutions (*Pravda*, December 5).

The same day, Ryzhkov also met with East German Prime Minister Hans Modrow. TASS said Modrow and Ryzhkov had stressed their readiness to expand cooperation with all countries, including West Germany, by taking into account existing political and territorial realities.

Gorbachev Meets Ceausescu

Mikhail Gorbachev met in Moscow with Romanian leader Nicolae Ceausescu. Ceausescu was in Moscow to hear a report on Gorbachev's talks with Bush. TASS said Gorbachev and Ceausescu discussed Socialist and Communist development and the international situation as well as bilateral trade and cooperation (*Pravda*, December 5).

Mladenov Interviewed in Pravda

Pravda carried an interview with Bulgarian Party General Secretary Petar Mladenov, who said the country's past leaders did not want real reforms, because they feared they would lose their power monopoly. He said that the people could see through the old leaders' approach and that he believed his task now was to tell the people the truth about Bulgaria's situation, to work out a national stabilization plan, and to democratize institutions.

Urbanek and Adamec Meet Gorbachev

Two senior Czechoslovak leaders told Mikhail Gorbachev that the new Czechoslovak Party leadership wants to get rid of "conservatism." Radio Prague said Czechoslovak Party General Secretary Karel Urbanek and Prime Minister Ladislav Adamec made the comment during a meeting with Gorbachev in Moscow. The radio quoted Urbanek and Adamec as saying that Czechoslovak workers and youth had prevailed in their efforts to speed up restructuring and democratization. During the talks, Gorbachev and the two Czechoslovak leaders also discussed the issue of Soviet troops in Czechoslovakia. Gorbachev's meeting with Urbanek and Adamec was reported in *Pravda*, December 6.

Tuesday, December 5

Armenian Supreme Soviet Besieged

According to Reuters and AP, the Armenian Supreme Soviet building in Erevan was surrounded by thousands of demonstrators demanding that the legislature rename the Armenian SSR "the Armenian republic," release political prisoners, and abolish the Communist Party's "right to rule." The demonstrators also called on Armenian deputies to boycott the forthcoming session of the Congress of People's Deputies. Strikes and further demonstrations took place in Erevan to back these demands.

Shevardnadze Holds Talks with Genscher

Soviet Foreign Minister Eduard Shevardnadze held talks with West German Foreign Minister Hans-Dietrich Genscher (*Pravda*, December 6). The talks centered on West German Chancellor Helmut Kohl's program for a confederation that could lead to reunification of the two Germanys. During the talks, Shevardnadze and Genscher signed two agreements, one for setting up a center to provide artificial limbs to victims of the Armenian earthquake and the second for a bilateral cultural exchange. TASS reported that Shevardnadze rejected Kohl's program on German reunification. He said parts of it bordered on a "diktat" towards East Germany. On December 4, however, DPA quoted TASS as saying that Moscow was ready to participate in talks on German reunification. TASS said that this position was in line with "the spirit of new thinking" in Soviet foreign policy. The TASS item goes beyond what Gorbachev said in public at the summit, but it is consistent with the movement in Moscow's position on this issue over the last month.

TASS Says Grain Imports Must Fall

A TASS commentary saying that the USSR must cut its grain imports, including those from the United States, came at the end of talks between US and Soviet trade officials on current problems in grain trade between the two countries. Negotiations on a new grain agreement began today. TASS said the trade imbalance with the United States forces the USSR to seek trade surpluses with other countries, creating unnecessary tensions in those relationships. Another problem is the scarcity of hard currency needed to buy the grain.

Personnel Changes at Moldavian Plenum

A Moldavian Communist Party Central Committee plenum reshuffled the Party's top leadership. Ideological Secretary Ion Gutsu, in that post barely six months, was demoted to secretary for industry and services. Gutsu took over from Vladimir Semenov, who lost his Buro seat and position as a Central Committee secretary to become minister of transportation. A conservative, who blocked registration of the republican ecology movement, Semenov also encouraged the strikes by Russian-speaking workers to protest against making Moldavian the state language. The new ideological secretary is Eugen Sobor, until now the republic's minister of culture. In an interview with TASS, Sobor repudiated "the ideological immobility and gilded internationalism" that many associate with the previous Moldavian leadership.

The position of Central Committee secretary for agriculture, vacated by Mircea Snegur on his election as chairman of the Presidium of the republican Supreme Soviet, went to the conservative *apparatchik* Nikolai Kutkovetsky. Moldavian KGB chief Gheorghe Lavranciuc was promoted from candidate to full member of the Central Committee Buro. The Buro got two new candidate members belonging to ethnic minorities: the Gagauz Georgii Samsi and the Bulgarian Ilya Arnaut. Their appointment is to be seen against the background of the Gagauz campaign for territorial autonomy in Moldavia and the uncertain attitude of the Bulgarian minority, which could be crucial to the outcome of that campaign (*TASS*, December 5, *Sovetskaya Moldaviya*, December 6).

In addition to these changes, Petru Lucinschi broke precedent by delivering his plenum speech (which was his inaugural) in Moldavian. It was the first time since the Soviet annexation that a Moldavian Party leader and other Moldavian speakers had addressed a Moldavian Central Committee plenum in Moldavian. See RL 558/89.

Trial of Former Karakalpak Party Chief Begins

Kallibek Kamalov, former Party boss of the Karakalpak ASSR, went on trial. TASS reported that Kamalov had pleaded guilty to charges that he took bribes totaling 120,000 rubles. He has also been indicted for abuse of office and nepotism. Kamalov was removed from his Party post in August, 1984, in the early stages of the anticorruption campaign in Uzbekistan, but instead of being held to account for his actions, he was named Soviet consul in Constanta, Romania. On December 6, Kamalov rescinded his admission of guilt.

Bakatin on Situation in South Ossetia and Nagorno-Karabakh

Tension was again reported high in Georgia's South Ossetian Autonomous Oblast. USSR Minister of Internal Affairs Vadim Bakatin said in a television interview that there were blockades in cities in the region and that shots had been fired and one person had been injured. Activists in South Ossetia were demanding that the oblast be given the status of an Autonomous republic. Bakatin also talked about the situation in Nagorno-Karabakh. He said the Armenian Supreme Soviet's decision that the oblast should become part of Armenia was inadmissible.

Vagris on Ties between CPSU and Latvian CP

Latvian Party First Secretary Janis Vagris said an independent Party in Latvia would transform, but not sever, relations with the CPSU. TASS reported the comments and said the Latvian Party was due to hold a congress in January to discuss its status within the CPSU as well as Latvia's status within the USSR.

Wednesday, December 6 _____

Gorbachev Meets Mitterrand

Mikhail Gorbachev held a meeting in Kiev with French President Francois Mitterrand (*Pravda*, December 7). Central Committee official Andrei Grachev called the Kiev meeting "a positive step" of the kind world statesmen must take to keep pace with what he called "the dramatic developments" in Eastern Europe. Briefing foreign and Soviet journalists, Grachev said the French and Soviet presidents had agreed in early July, during Gorbachev's visit to France, to hold more frequent meetings. The initiative for today's meeting, Grachev said, had come from Mitterrand during a telephone conversation with Gorbachev last month (*RFE/RL Special*, December 6).

According to Reuters, Mitterrand said in Kiev that he supports Gorbachev's call for an all-European summit next year. At a joint press conference following their meeting, the two leaders also said that the question of German reunification could only be settled within the framework of improved East-West relations.

Meanwhile, there was a demonstration in Kiev by several hundred people demanding an end to the Party monopoly on power. Reuters said the police did not try to break up the demonstration.

First Anniversary of Earthquake in Armenia

On the first anniversary of the earthquake in Armenia, the Soviet press carried numerous stories on the subject and Erevan proclaimed a day of national mourning. A year after the earthquake, the Soviet media have yet to carry a credible figure on the number of deaths. The figure generally given is 25,000, but 20,000 people are still reported missing, suggesting that the real loss was closer to UN estimates of 50,000–60,000. Commenting on the anniversary of the quake, Foreign Ministry spokesman Gennadii Gerasimov praised foreign relief aid to Armenia. Gerasimov said the aid had through mid-October totaled 586.5 million dollars (*TASS*, in English, December 6). Meanwhile, a Soviet delegation was in the United States to learn more about how to cope with earthquakes (*RFE/RL Special*, December 6).

Pravda's Readers Discuss Party Rules

Pravda continued the discussion of the Party Rules begun on November 12. (A new edition of the Party Rules is to be adopted at the Twenty-eighth Congress of the CPSU.) Among readers' letters is one proposing that primary Party organizations should be created on a territorial rather than a territorial-production basis. Under the present Party Rules, both forms of organization are permitted. The suggestion appears to imply that Party cells in factories, farms, schools and hospitals (of which there are at present 360,000) should be abolished and that all cells should in future be formed on the basis of members' places of residence (there are at present 82,000 cells of this kind). This proposal would drastically reduce the Party's influence over the economy. Another reader made a proposal that procedures be established for those who want to leave the Party voluntarily. At present, members can leave only if they are thrown out or if they fail to pay their dues.

Jewish Emigration Sets Record

The International Organization for Migration said that 55,465 Soviet Jews had arrived at its Vienna reception center from January through November of this year (*Reuters*, December 6). That total easily surpasses the previous record set for all of 1979. The migration group said another 1,600 had gone directly to Israel via Bucharest and Budapest during the past two months.

Soviet-Turkish Trade to Increase 50 Percent

Turkey and the USSR signed a protocol calling for an increase of 50 percent in bilateral trade over the next two years. That will bring the total volume of Soviet-Turkish trade to approximately 3 billion dollars. Turkey also pledged to build factories in the USSR, and Moscow said it would modernize an iron and steel factory in Turkey. The two countries agreed to make a list of items the USSR will buy in Turkey in exchange for Ankara's purchases of Soviet natural gas (*RFE/RL Special*, December 6).

Soviet Official Says New Grain Policy Did Not Come Soon Enough

A Soviet deputy minister for foreign economic relations, Yurii Chumakov, said a Soviet plan to pay farmers hard currency for surplus grain production went into effect too late to meet its goals this year. Chumakov said, however, that the plan could affect next year's grain harvest. Chumakov spoke to reporters in Moscow after the first day of negotiations with US officials on a new bilateral grain agreement (*Reuters*, December 6).

USSR Supreme Soviet Commission on Privileges Reports on Its Work

The secretary of the Supreme Soviet's Commission on Benefits and Privileges told Soviet television that the commission's work would not attempt to track down individual wrongdoers but instead would set overall government policy. Putting forward the idea that senior officials should have a right to decent wages but generally not to special privileges, Ella Pamfilova said the commission is looking into the privileges some have enjoyed in the past. Her own working group, which is examining personal pensions, is focusing on the free transport and medical care such people receive and the fact that spouses have survivor benefits. Pamfilova said her commission had received many letters from the public on this subject, but she made no mention of another privilege much resented by ordinary people—the existence of special food shops. She did say, however, that members of her commission fear that officials deprived of undeserved privileges may turn to corruption to make up the difference.

On December 17, *Komsomol'skaya pravda* reported that, in the voting on the proposed agenda of the USSR Congress of People's Deputies, members of the Politburo split on whether to discuss the report on privileges enjoyed by senior Party and government officials during the current session of the Congress. Five full members— Vitalii Vorotnikov, Lev Zaikov, Vladimir Ivashko, Egor Ligachev, and Aleksandr Yakovlev—voted for inclusion of the report on the agenda, while four—Mikhail Gorbachev, Vadim Medvedev, Nikolai Ryzhkov, and Nikolai Slyun'kov—voted against. Only one of the candidate members—Anatolii Luk'yanov—voted against; the other four supported the proposal. All five Central Committee secretaries—with the exception of Egor Stroev, who was not present—voted in favor of discussion of the report.

Soviet Citizens to Get Western Journals and TV Programs

Soviet citizens will now be able to subscribe to Western publications and satellite television—but only if they can pay for them in hard currency, according to *Izvestia*. *Pravda* said last month that foreign newspapers had been freely available in the USSR for some time. Meanwhile, Moscow is reported to be ready to launch an international edition of the popular weekly *Argumenty i fakty*. According to one account, the newspaper will be published and distributed from Athens (*RFE/RL Special*, December 6).

Secretariat of RSFSR Writers' Union Holds Plenum, Seeks to Dismiss Editor

After a lengthy controversy, the Secretariat of the RSFSR Writers' Union voted to dismiss Anatolii Anan'ev from the post of chief editor of the journal *Oktyabr'* (*AP*, December 5). The secretariat cited alleged "hooliganism" in Anan'ev's editorial decisions. Anan'ev aroused criticism by publishing Vasilii Grossman's *Vse techet* and Andrei Sinyavsky's *Progulki s Pushkinym*, both of which the Secretariat condemned as Russophobic. According to reports from Moscow, however, Anan'ev and his supporters were determined to resist the union's decision.

Anan'ev's case was discussed at length by the Secretariat of the RSFSR Writers' Union at a plenum that took place on November 13–14 in Moscow. In addition to criticizing Anan'ev, speakers at the plenum spoke about the alleged plot of Zionists against the Russian culture and complained about the alleged dominance of Jews in the Leningrad organization of writers. A detailed report on the plenum was published in *Ogonek* (No. 48).

Thursday, December 7

TASS Warns against Attacks on East German Military

TASS warned against civilian attempts to attack East German military bases. TASS cited allegations by the East German government that attacks were being prepared by civilians on the East German armed forces and border guards. TASS said that such attacks and resulting seizures of arms and ammunition could have serious consequences. It said this could undermine political stability and create chaos. The agency said the East German armed forces still play a significant role in the Warsaw Pact.

Estonian Supreme Soviet Discusses Role of Communist Party

The Estonian Supreme Soviet discussed a plan to drop the constitutional guarantee of the leading role of the Party but did not reach a decision. It approved a law calling for Estonian conscripts in the Soviet armed forces to serve only in the Baltic and allowing conscientious objectors to perform community service as an alternative to military service. The Supreme Soviet also adopted a law allowing farmers to keep farm land as long as they wish and to pass the land on to their heirs (*Pravda*, December 7).

***Gulag Archipelago* Now in Soviet Bookstores**

Aleksandr Solzhenitsyn's *Gulag Archipelago* is now available in book form in the Soviet Union. The "Sovetsky pisatel'" publishing house has started issuing the complete text. Excerpts from the work have been published by *Novyi mir*. On December 7, *Izvestia* said Solzhenitsyn and others exiled from the Soviet Union for their dissenting views may have their citizenship restored on request.

Leningrad Demonstration in Support of Gorbachev

On December 7, the Soviet television news program "Vremya" reported that on the previous day supporters of Gorbachev in Leningrad had held a demonstration to protest about another demonstration organized in November by conservative officials of the Leningrad City and Oblast Party Committees, including the head of both committees, Boris Gidaspov. Some of the banners the demonstrators were carrying read "Leningrad Commun-

666

ists for Gorbachev"; others called for Party reform. The meeting was addressed by several progressive members of the Congress of People's Deputies.

_____ *Friday, December 8*

Pravda published an editorial that said the monopoly of the CPSU is now being reconsidered. The newspaper made no comment on the decision by the Lithuanian Supreme Soviet to delete the clause on the Party's leading role from the Lithuanian Constitution, but it did discuss the call by Andrei Sakharov and others for a general strike to press for the deletion of the clause from the all-Union constitution. The newspaper asked those who want the clause deleted not to be "hasty." The issue, *Pravda* promised, will be considered in the near future by the committee set up (under Gorbachev's chairmanship) to draft a new constitution for the USSR.

Pravda **Editorial Says Party's Role is Changing**

The Soviet government urged all countries to stop supplying arms to Central American countries. In a statement published by TASS, the government said the USSR has halted its arms supplies to Nicaragua. The statement urged "a demonstration of similar restraint by other countries." The United States says Nicaragua and Cuba are responsible for distributing weapons in Central America, and it has urged the Soviet Union to help stop this practice. Today's Soviet statement urged an end to military assistance to "nonregular forces and rebel movements." It also said the Soviet Union believed priority should be given to holding free and democratic elections in Nicaragua (*Pravda*, December 9).

USSR Urges End to Arms Supplies to Central America

US and Soviet negotiators said major progress was made during the latest round of strategic arms reduction talks that ended in Geneva. Chief negotiators Richard Burt and Yurii Nazarkin held a joint news conference to review the talks, which began in late September. They said that, while much remains to be done, they think a treaty cutting US and Soviet strategic nuclear arsenals in half could be completed and ready for signing by the end of next year. Burt and Nazarkin signed an agreement allowing reciprocal trial inspections of each side's strategic bombers to determine which are capable of carrying nuclear-armed cruise missiles. They said they expected another agree-

US-Soviet Talks in Geneva End in Positive Mood

ment to be reached "very soon" on allowing trial inspections of nuclear warheads to help develop verification methods (*UPI, Reuters*, December 8).

Intermovement Calls for Estonian Election Boycott

A group of voters and deputies in Estonia associated with the movement "Interdvizhenie" in the republic, whose members are mainly non-Estonians, called for a boycott of the forthcoming local elections in Estonia. Soviet television said the boycotters wanted alternative elections at enterprises and the formation of alternative organs of power. The report said the boycott had been condemned by the majority of Estonian Communists.

Soviet Television Shows Delayed Dubcek Interview

Soviet television showed an interview with former Czechoslovak Party First Secretary Alexander Dubcek some four months after it was filmed. The moderator of the "Vzglyad" show, Dmitrii Zakharov, said the interview was not allowed to be shown earlier, because it would have constituted interference in Czechoslovakia's internal affairs. Dubcek, who led the Communist Party of Czechoslovakia during the Prague Spring, has now become active in the opposition to the present leadership of the Czechoslovak Communist Party. In the interview with Soviet television, Dubcek likened the Prague Spring to Gorbachev's reform drive. He also gave some background information on the Soviet-led Warsaw Pact invasion that ended the Prague Spring.

Nina Andreeva Again Criticizes Gorbachev

Nina Andreeva, the Leningrad teacher who has on several occasions spoken out against Gorbachev, told the Hungarian daily *Magyar hirlap* that Gorbachev had deviated from Leninist norms, adding that "it is well known that nobody is irreplaceable." In other comments, Andreeva said that "Zionists" were pushing for power in the Soviet Union and that reformers were attempting to restore capitalism there as well.

"Pamyat'" Holds Demonstration on Red Square

The Russian nationalist "Pamyat'" group held a demonstration last week on Red Square, "Vzglyad" reported on December 8. The fact that this was the first time an unofficial group had been permitted to hold a meeting there prompted the moderator of "Vzglyad," Dmitrii Zakharov, to remark "obviously they have important sponsors." This was an apparent reference to Moscow's new Party boss, Yurii Prokof'ev, who is widely believed

668

to be a "Pamyat'" supporter. Zakharov went on to interview Konstantin Zatulin, chairman of an unofficial association of enterprise directors, who warned of "an open counterattack" being planned against Gorbachev's economic reforms by organizations such as the United Front of Workers of Russia.

Butenko Criticizes Lenin

Anatolii Butenko, a leading Soviet social theorist, said on "Vzglyad" that Lenin had made serious errors "within a few days" of coming to power. Instead of using economic means to motivate the population, Lenin turned to force, he said. As a result, the Soviet Union was modernized "by barbaric methods." Butenko argued that the country was not in a crisis, as Gorbachev has suggested, but at a dead end and that the only way out is to move backwards. Long an advocate of a revival of private enterprise along the lines of the New Economic Policy of the 1920s, Butenko seemed to be implying that the USSR must return to capitalism to overcome its current difficulties.

Saturday, December 9

CPSU Central Committee Plenum

The CPSU Central Committee held a plenum in Moscow to discuss ways of improving the economy and other issues related to the coming session of the Congress of People's Deputies. The plenum elected Ukrainian Party First Secretary Vladimir Ivashko as a member of the Politburo. Chief editor of *Pravda* Ivan Frolov was elected a Central Committee secretary (*Pravda*, December 10). The plenum made Gorbachev chairman of the newly formed Russian Bureau of the CPSU Central Committee. It also announced plans to hold an extended plenum next month.

At the plenum, Party officials leveled strong criticism at Gorbachev's policies. Details of the criticism were disclosed by Leningrad writer Daniil Granin, who was a guest at the plenum. Writing in *Moscow News* (No. 51), Granin said he heard "direct accusations against Gorbachev that his line was incorrect." Granin added: "It was not surprising that these speeches deeply wounded Gorbachev. And so much so that he declared: if the work done over these past years is assessed in that way, then he was ready to lay down his power." (This is not the first time Gorbachev has threatened to resign in response to criticism.)

669

The plenum also issued an address to the Soviet population (*TASS*, December 11; *Pravda*, December 12). The address was in effect an appeal to voters to support the Party and its candidates in the local and republican elections. The appeal said the Party was open to dialogue and partnership and favored constructive cooperation with all forces acting on a Socialist basis. It also called on Communists to maintain Party unity and rebuff any attempts to tear it apart along national lines. Federalization of the Party, the appeal stated, would have severe consequences for *perestroika*.

On December 18, Politburo member Vadim Medvedev gave an account of the proceedings at the Central Committee plenum. Medvedev reported that some participants in the plenum had said there must be something wrong with *perestroika* because the West and even Pope John Paul II were praising it. Medvedev said Gorbachev then intervened and told the plenum that, if that were really the case and *perestroika* was in trouble, then the Politburo should have resigned. Medvedev added, however, that no one in the Central Committee demanded the resignation of the Politburo. Medvedev said there were heated and critical discussions at the plenum (*Central Television*, "Vremya," December 18). Meanwhile, according to *Izvestia* (December 18), members of the Congress of People's Deputies called for the publication in full of the proceedings of the plenum.

Sunday, December 10 ——————————————————————————

Rallies Held to Mark International Human-Rights Day

Thousands of people were reported to have attended a rally in northern Moscow to mark International Human-Rights Day. Radio Moscow said the rally was organized by various public organizations. Another rally was held on Pushkin Square by several hundred supporters of the unofficial Democratic Union. TASS said about twenty people were detained after it. On December 13, the Frankfurt-based International Society for Human Rights reported that fourteen of those detained had been sentenced to prison terms of up to fifteen days.

Local Elections in Estonia and Latvia

Voters cast ballots in local multicandidate elections in Estonia and Latvia. Fifty-seven percent of the candidates who won in the elections in Riga were supported by the Latvian Popular Front, and 39 percent were candidates of the non-Latvian International Workers' Front (*TASS*, December 11). On December 12, Tanjug quoted the election coordinating center in Latvia as saying that everywhere in the republic except the city of Daugavpils the popular front candidates won a majority. Reporting on the elections to local soviets in Estonia, TASS said the call to boycott the elections made by the United Council of Workers' Collectives and the International Movement, which is dominated by non-Estonians, did not have much influence on voter turnout. Only four election districts in Tallinn had to hold new polls within forty-five days because the turnout was too low. According to preliminary results, environmentalists are likely to receive half the vote in these districts (*AP*, December 11). On December 11, *Pravda* commented on the elections in Estonia and Latvia, pointing out that, for the first time in many decades, there was sharp competition in elections to local soviets. On December 14, TASS said that, of 152 local Party officials running for election in Latvia, ninety had won seats in the first round and twenty-two would contend run-off elections on December 17. The rest were defeated.

Sobesednik (No. 49) carried several articles on preparations in Moscow and Vologda for the forthcoming elections to local soviets. The journal reported that the refusal of the authorities to register the Moscow Popular Front would, according to front members, only increase voters' support for the unofficial organization. The elections were reported to have been one of the main items on the agenda at a recent plenum of the front. Speakers at the plenum were quoted as saying that a preliminary election poll had indicated a conservative swing since last spring's elections. It revealed that at present only 35 percent of Moscow voters support the Interregional Group of People's Deputies. The same issue of *Sobesednik* reported that the Vologda association of voters had received approval from the local oblast committee to publish a journal called *Vybor* whose purpose would be to familiarize voters with the election platforms of the various groups fielding candidates for election.

***Sobesednik* on Preparations for Elections**

Following a preparatory conference, a new Russian Orthodox Church initiative group in support of *perestroika* has been established in Moscow. According to *Sobesednik* (No. 49), the preparatory conference for the new organization took place on November 30. Both priests and laymen spoke at the conference. The new group is

New Church Group Organized

probably intended to support the ideas outlined by Archbishop Kirill, the new head of the Russian Orthodox Church's Department for External Relations.

Expanded Coverage of Eastern Europe

The television program "Mezhdunarodnaya panorama" devoted most of its time to an in-depth analysis of developments in Czechoslovakia and East Germany. Foreign Ministry spokesman Gennadii Gerasimov, who was the moderator, declared that the Warsaw Pact invasion of Czechoslovakia in 1968 had crushed freedom in both countries, adding that the recent denunciation of the invasion was a belated one. Discussing the disintegration of the East German Party, Gerasimov said the career of Erich Honecker had confirmed the old truth that power corrupts and that absolute power corrupts absolutely.

Moscow News (No. 50) carried an article by Academician Oleg Bogomolov on the changes in Eastern Europe. Bogomolov said that, although they had started with reforms much later, East European countries were now far ahead of the USSR. On December 12, TASS said Western leaders, especially those of France and Britain, were worried that a plan to reunify Germany could destabilize Europe.

Tuesday, December 12

Second Congress of People's Deputies Opens

The second Congress of People's Deputies opened with an attempt by radical deputies to schedule debate on the exclusion from the USSR Constitution of the article guaranteeing the leading role of the Communist Party (Article 6) (*Pravda, Izvestia*, December 13). The bid to schedule debate on the issue was, however, rejected by a vote of 1,138 to 839, with 56 abstentions. "It was a noble defeat. We got more votes than I expected," the radical deputy Evgenii Evtushenko told reporters after the tally.

During a discussion of the need to debate Article 6, a deputy from Latvia, Vilen Tolpezhnikov, who is a member of the commission to investigate the Tbilisi violence, attacked Egor Ligachev. Tolpezhnikov said the decision to use force against the demonstrators was taken at a meeting of the Politburo, chaired by Ligachev, on April 7. (Gorbachev, Yakovlev, and Shevardnadze were in England at that time.) Tolpezhnikov said that there was no written record of the Politburo session and that the decision was implemented merely on the basis of Ligachev's verbal communication with Defense Minister Dmitrii Yazov. "Power does not belong to us [the Congress of People's Deputies]," Tolpezhnikov said, "and we cannot be sure that one fine day a member of the Politburo will not again have a chat with Yazov and have us all deprived of our mandates."

In his opening address to the Congress, Gorbachev said there was a need for drastic reforms in the Soviet economy. He said the economic results the leadership had hoped for had not been achieved (*Pravda*, December 13).

On December 13, Nikolai Ryzhkov offered the Congress his prescription for economic reform—namely, traditional Soviet planning and a continued ban on private property (*Pravda*, December 14). He described the nation's economic situation as tense. Reports of Ryzhkov's speech suggest that he has taken a major step backwards with respect to the reform concept that has been evolving in recent months. Pavel Bunich was quoted as saying that, in the struggle between the five-year plan and *perestroika*, the five-year plan had won (*Reuters*, December 13).

Ryzhkov's speech was followed by debates. Economist Gavriil Popov, one of the cochairmen of the Interregional Group of Deputies, said that the group agrees with Leonid Abalkin's ideas for economic reform but finds Ryzhkov's proposals too restrictive. Popov compared Ryzhkov's proposals to an apartment that has no room for a family's children—i.e., market forces—to play. Lithuanian Deputy Kazimiras Antanavicius said Ryzhkov's program consisted solely of ideas that had already been tried and had failed in other Socialist countries. Politburo member Egor Ligachev said a 270-billion-ruble injection of cash was needed to resuscitate Soviet agriculture. He made no reference to the need for fundamental organizational changes in agriculture. (*Radio Moscow*, "Mayak," December 13; *Pravda*, December 15).

On December 14, TASS reported that the Congress of People's Deputies was continuing a detailed analysis of the economic plan proposed by Ryzhkov. In response to criticism by deputies of the slow pace of economic reforms envisaged in Ryzhkov's plan, Deputy Prime Minister Leonid Abalkin said it would take the Soviet Union at least three years to switch over to a market economy. Abalkin was quoted by TASS as saying that trying to move any faster would result in mass unemployment, bankruptcy of thousands of enterprises, and a drop in living standards (*Pravda*, December 16).

On December 15, Boris El'tsin addressed the Congress of People's Deputies and criticized Ryzhkov's economic plan. He called the plan "a rebuff for *perestroika*." El'tsin, who spoke on behalf of the Interregional Group of People's Deputies, also proposed moving towards a multiparty system and suggested reforms in the Soviet armed forces, the MVD, and the KGB. Deputy Prime Minister Leonid Abalkin said in response that El'tsin's economic proposals were "impractical, totally unacceptable, and dangerous from a sociopolitical point of view" (*Radio Moscow, AFP, DPA*, December 15; *Pravda*, December 16).

On December 16, debate of Ryzhkov's economic plan continued. TASS quoted Leningrad Party First Secretary Boris Gidaspov as saying the plan lacked a clear approach to balancing state control and enterprise self-management. Irkutsk deputy Gennadii Filshin said the government was trying to solve the economic crisis with old methods. He called for a new plan that would bring quicker results. He said that, if the old methods were used again, the Congress should pass a vote of no confidence in the government and force it to resign. Ryzhkov agreed that the plan had shortcomings but insisted that it took into account the country's real potential, and he appealed to the Congress to support it. Ryzhkov added that some criticism (he specifically singled out the speeches by Boris El'tsin and Gavriil Popov) had been unconstructive and contradictory (*TASS*, December 16). On December 17, *Sovetskaya Rossiya* carried an interview with Ryzhkov in which he said he sensed that his economic program was gaining support in the Congress of People's Deputies despite the initial negative reaction.

On December 19, the Congress voted overwhelmingly to approve the government's economic plan (*Pravda*, December 20). TASS quoted Leonid Abalkin as saying that, if the program had not been passed, the USSR Council of Ministers would have resigned immediately.

Soviet and US Forces Conduct Communications Tests

The US Defense Department said US and Soviet military forces had conducted joint radio communications tests in the Bering and Mediterranean seas. Spokesman Peter Williams told reporters that US and Soviet ships, aircraft, and ground-based air traffic controllers had taken part in the exercise last week. He said it was the first test of procedures that will be used when a US-Soviet agreement on prevention of dangerous military activities takes effect on January 1. Williams said the test was successful (*RFE/RL Special*, December 12).

Leningrad City and Oblast Party First Secretary Boris Gidaspov denied he was a conservative opponent of *perestroika.* TASS quoted Gidaspov as saying he was among the first group of people to support Gorbachev. He said he still adheres to this position. Gidaspov spoke to reporters during a break in the session of the Congress of People's Deputies. Accusations of conservatism arose after Gidaspov sponsored a rally in Leningrad at which speakers strongly attacked Gorbachev's policies. Earlier, at the Congress session, composer Rodion Shchedrin told the deputies he felt Gidaspov's stance was incompatible with his post as chairman of the Mandate Commission of the Congress of People's Deputies.

Gidaspov Denies Accusations of Conservatism

The latest issue of *Pravitel'stvenny vestnik* is reported by TASS to spell out the details of the first installment of the reverse consumer credit scheme that has been under discussion during the past year. This provides for citizens to put down cash now for the future delivery of specific consumer durables, with the aim of mopping up part of the huge monetary overhang, variously estimated at between 100 and 450 billion rubles. Bonds to the value of 10 billion rubles (the size of the uncovered deficit in the planned budget for 1990) will be offered in 1990. The bondholders will be entitled to collect the desired consumer durables in 1993.

Details of Reverse Consumer Credit Published

Ernst Obminsky has been named a deputy foreign minister, TASS reported. Obminsky, who is fifty-eight, had been head of the Foreign Ministry's Directorate for International Economic Relations. Earlier he had been deputy chief of the Academy of Sciences Institute of the International Working Class Movement. He is the first professional economist to be named a USSR deputy foreign minister, and his elevation thus underscores the commitment Gorbachev and Shevardnadze made last year to subordinate Soviet foreign policy to the requirements of domestic reform. A spokesman for the Foreign Ministry said that the ministry has never been so deeply involved in foreign economic cooperation as it is now, and Obminsky's task will be to establish closer contacts with the International Monetary Fund, the World Bank, and GATT.

Economist Appointed Deputy Foreign Minister

Expanded Legal Protection for Soviet Soldiers

The USSR Ministry of Defense has introduced the position of deputy commander for legal work at major garrisons, Novosti reported. The holders of these new posts, whose job will be to reassure soldiers and their parents that the rights of draftees are not violated, will also be charged with defending the rights of the military itself. This conflict of interest is unlikely to be resolved in the soldiers' favor, and the existence of these posts may further complicate Moscow's efforts to increase military efficiency during the current retrenchment.

Sino-Soviet Border Trade Increases

Border trade between China and the Soviet Union increased substantially last year. Statistics published in today's edition of China's *Economic Daily* show that Sino-Soviet border trade was up more than 50 percent last year compared with the previous five years combined (*Xinhua*, in English, December 13).

Russian Bread Industry in Disastrous State

Pravda reported that the bread industry in the RSFSR was in a disastrous condition. It said that only half the republic's 1,462 bakeries were working properly and that low morale, staff shortages, and poor quality bread were rife throughout the industry.

Official Says USSR Should Rethink Development Aid

Deputy head of the Foreign Ministry's International Relations Department Sergei Lavrov told Reuters that current Soviet aid to developing countries would be rethought. He said the USSR should eventually join the World Bank and International Monetary Fund, which coordinate many Western aid projects. He said that Moscow was considering cuts in military aid to Third-World countries and that specific proposals had already been made to transform military aid into aid for civilian purposes.

Yazov Rebuffs Lithuanians on Military Issues

Defense Minister Dmitrii Yazov had talks with a high-level Lithuanian delegation in Moscow in a meeting that one participant described as "not very friendly." The Lithuanian group included Lithuanian Party First Secretary Algirdas Brazauskas, Prime Minister Vytautas Sakalauskas, and the head of "Sajudis," Vytautas Landsbergis. They met with Yazov to discuss issues relating to military service of Lithuanians. Describing the meeting to RFE/RL, Landsbergis said Yazov had rejected the idea of an alternative to military service and the concept of territorial army units in which Lithuanians would serve in Lithuania. Yazov also refused to discuss the status of Soviet troops in Lithuania, saying that this was a political question for the government. Another member of the Lithuanian delegation reported that the one positive note came when Yazov said the Defense Ministry should be informed of cases in which Lithuanian youths were mistreated during their military service.

Thursday, December 14

Western agencies reported that Academician Andrei Sakharov had died of a heart attack in Moscow during the night of December 14. The White House issued a statement praising Sakharov's efforts on behalf of human rights. On December 14, Sakharov attended a meeting of the Interregional Group of People's Deputies, of which he was a member. At the meeting he delivered an emotional speech, criticizing the leadership for slowing down the pace of reforms. In his last public statement Sakharov also supported a call by Yurii Afanas'ev for the creation of a formal opposition in the USSR.

Political leaders and public figures and organizations in the Soviet Union and abroad paid tribute to Sakharov. Mikhail Gorbachev said Sakharov's death was a major loss for Soviet society (*AP, Reuters*, December 15). On December 16, *Pravda* carried an obituary of Sakharov, which said his seven-year banishment to Gorky had been a gross injustice. The obituary was signed by Gorbachev, several other (but not all) members of the Politburo, Nikolai Ryzhkov, state and Party officials, and members of the Academy of Sciences. Egor Ligachev, who praised Sakharov in commenting on his death to Western reporters, and KGB chairman and Politburo member Vladimir Kryuchkov did not sign the obituary. Several members of the Academy who signed Sakharov's obituary had in the 1970s put their signature to letters critical of Sakharov published in the Soviet press.

A crowd of mourners gathered near the apartment building on Chkalov street in Moscow, where Sakharov lived and died. On the evening of December 15, Sakharov's widow Elena Bonner appeared on "Vzglyad" and announced details of Sakharov's funeral. *Moscow News* printed a special issue devoted to Sakharov.

On December 17, over 100,000 Soviet citizens paid tribute to Sakharov at Moscow's Youth Palace. Soviet television provided extensive coverage; however, *Komsomol'skaya pravda* (December 17) criticized the cover-

Andrei Sakharov Dies

age given to Sakharov's death by the official media as inadequate. It also questioned whether deputies who had previously tried to prevent Sakharov from speaking were now sincere in their grief. The newspaper also carried an interview Sakharov gave a few days before his death. On December 17, Reuters reported that the Soviet Union had refused to grant a visa to former dissident Natan Shcharansky, who wanted to attend Sakharov's funeral.

On December 18, Mikhail Gorbachev and Nikolai Ryzhkov visited the Academy of Sciences, where Sakharov's body was lying in state. The Congress of People's Deputies interrupted its session from 1230 until 1600, Moscow time, to allow deputies to pay their last respects to Sakharov. A ceremony to pay a final tribute to Sakharov was organized on December 18 at the Luzhniki Stadium, where radical people's deputies and members of the Academy of Sciences praised Sakharov as a public figure, human-rights activist, and scientist (*Central Television*, Western agencies, December 18). The same day, Sakharov was buried at the Vostryakovskoe Cemetery in Moscow.

On December 20, KGB Chairman Vladimir Kryuchkov said that the banishment of Sakharov to Gorky in 1980 had been a flagrant error and an injustice (*TASS*, December 20).

For Soviet press reaction to Sakharov's death, see *Pravda*, December 17; *Izvestia*, December 17; *Sovetskaya kul'tura*, December 16; *Sotsialisticheskaya industriya*, December 16.

On December 29, *Izvestia* said the authorities in Erevan had named a city square after Sakharov. The newspaper said the Erevan City Soviet also had plans to name a street, a scientific institute, and a scholarship after Sakharov.

Gorbachev Promises Special Supreme Soviet Session on Nagorno-Karabakh

A boycott by Armenian deputies of the Congress of People's Deputies ended after Mikhail Gorbachev pledged that a special session of the Supreme Soviet would deal with the future of Nagorno-Karabakh. The Armenian deputies started boycotting the current Congress session on December 13 after the Congress refused on December 12 to put Nagorno-Karabakh on its agenda (*TASS*, December 14).

Yurii Afanas'ev Proposes Formation of Opposition

Historian Yurii Afanas'ev proposed the establishment of a formal opposition to the CPSU. Afanas'ev said at a meeting of the Interregional Group of Deputies that a radical democratic opposition was needed to speed up *perestroika*. Afanas'ev told Western reporters after the meeting that the opposition organization he proposed could eventually become a political party challenging the Communists for power (*AP*, *Reuters*, December 14). Western agencies said that some other members of the Interregional Group felt that Afanas'ev's proposals were too radical (*Reuters*, December 15).

US-Soviet Talks on Chemical Weapons End on Upbeat Note

US arms negotiator Max Friedersdorf said the United States and the USSR "are fairly close together" on a proposed global ban on chemical weapons. Friedersdorf led the US side at the latest round of US-Soviet chemical weapons talks that have just ended in Geneva. He said he thinks a worldwide treaty is possible within two years. Separate US-Soviet talks on nuclear testing ended on December 15 in Geneva. They are aimed at meeting US Senate concerns over verification of two existing agreements limiting the size of nuclear tests (*AP*, December 14).

Former Uzbek Party Chief Gets Twelve Years for Corruption

The trial of Uzbekistan's former Party first secretary, Inamzhon Usmankhodzhaev, began in the USSR Supreme Court in Moscow. Usmankhodzhaev was accused of taking bribes of more than 55,000 rubles between 1979 and 1983. TASS said he had denied the charges, which stem from a long corruption probe in Uzbekistan. Usmankhodzhaev was chairman of the Presidium of the Supreme Soviet in Uzbekistan from 1979 to 1983 and republican Party first secretary from 1983 to 1988. He was arrested on bribery charges in 1988. On December 27, the USSR Supreme Court sentenced Usmankhodzhaev to twelve years in prison, according to TASS. Somewhat surprisingly, his sentence was three years shorter than that pronounced on former Karakalpak Party leader Kallibek Kamalov.

Historian Says Moscow Must Take Initiative on German Question

The historian Vladimir Baranovsky suggested that Moscow should take the initiative in finding an answer to the German question by proposing East-West talks on the subject. Writing in *Moscow News* (No. 51), Baranovsky said Moscow should act now to avoid tension in Europe, because the Germans could not be indefinitely deprived of their right to self-determination. Baranovsky proposed that the four World War II allies—the Soviet Union, Britain, France, and the United States—should meet first to discuss the signing of a peace treaty with Germany and should then draw East and West Germany into the process. The results of the six-way talks could be put to NATO and the Warsaw Pact for discussion, he said. In the final stage, an all-European conference could ratify the outcome.

Soldiers Clash at Urals Base

Radio Moscow reported "an armed confrontation" involving soldiers from Uzbekistan and the Caucasus at a military unit in the Urals on December 12. The report, broadcast in Spanish, said that some 700 soldiers had been involved and that there had been several injuries. It said MVD troops had helped to restore order and the military prosecutor's office was investigating the incident.

Orthodox Church Leader Condemns Ukrainian Church Merger

Archbishop Kirill of Smolensk and Kaliningrad, who was recently put in charge of foreign relations for the Russian Orthodox Church, condemned the forced merger of the Ukrainian Catholic Church with the Russian Orthodox Church under Stalin. Speaking on Soviet television, Kirill said dialogue with the banned Ukrainian Catholic Church was the only way to resolve the issue. Kirill said the situation was very tense in Western Ukraine and was becoming tenser and more dramatic every day.

Friday, December 15 ───────────────────────────

No Decision on Leading Role of Communist Party in Estonia, New Party Created

The Estonian Supreme Soviet ended a one-day meeting without acting on a proposal to end guarantees of the leading role of the Communist Party (*Pravda*, December 15). The body discussed the issue eight days ago but delayed action. Meanwhile, a group of leading Estonian political figures—comprising much of the Popular Front leadership—announced the formation of a new political party whose goal would be to establish an independent and democratic Estonia. The new party is called the Estonian Social Democratic Independence Party (*RFE Estonian Service*, December 15 and *Izvestia*, December 24).

Meskhetians Should Be Allowed to Return to Georgia, Commission Says

A USSR Supreme Soviet commission said the Meskhetians should be allowed to gradually return to Georgia, from where they were expelled by Stalin in 1944. TASS said the commission urged the central and Georgian authorities to work out a program to create a favorable moral and psychological climate for their return. The commission reported to the Congress of People's Deputies on its investigation of the clashes, in which about 100 people, most of them Meskhetians, were killed in ethnic violence in the Fergana Valley of Uzbekistan last summer (*TASS*, December 15).

Minister Says East European Changes Will Not Affect USSR Trade

Soviet Finance Minister Valentin Pavlov said political developments in East Germany, Czechoslovakia, and Hungary would not affect their economic relations with the Soviet Union. TASS quoted Pavlov as saying the USSR would continue to honor all its commitments to those countries. The Soviet Union supplies most of the oil and gas for all three countries as well as many other raw materials.

Polish Nuclear Scientists Murdered near Moscow

Poland has sent an investigator to Moscow to look into the murder of Polish nuclear scientist Jerzy Polys. PAP news agency said Jozef Gurgul of the Polish chief prosecutor's office was in Moscow, and TASS said Soviet investigators were also at work on the case. Radio Warsaw said that, by all appearances, Polys had been stabbed to death during a robbery. But, it said, a note was found nearby reading in Russian "for the Lenin monument in Krakow." Youths have tried in recent weeks to demolish a statue of Lenin in the Krakow suburb of Nowa Huta. City authorities have now removed the statue. Polys had worked at the United Institute of Nuclear Research in Dubna, near Moscow, since 1987.

Nikolai Chervov on Military Spending Cuts

Colonel General Nikolai Chervov, chief of the Treaty and Legal Administration of the Soviet Armed Forces, told a news conference in Moscow that the Soviet Union would cut defense spending by 8.2 percent next year. He said the cuts were part of a program to shift the Soviet defense posture from offensive to defensive (*TASS*, December 15).

Petrovsky Says There Are 627,500 Soviet Troops Abroad

Soviet Deputy Foreign Minister Vladimir Petrovsky said a total of 627,500 Soviet troops are at present stationed outside the Soviet Union. Petrovsky gave the figure in a letter to UN Secretary General Javier Perez de Cuellar. The letter said the Soviet government's goal is not to have a single soldier outside the country's borders after the year 2000. Discussing the letter at a press conference in New York, Petrovsky declined to give a breakdown of Soviet forces abroad. He said the countries where Soviet troops are stationed are "well known" and comprise mainly East European nations (*RFE/RL Special*, December 15).

Soviet Press on Solzhenitsyn

Argumenty i fakty (No. 48) carried an installment from Aleksandr Solzhenitsyn's book *Bodalsya telenok s dubom*, and on December 10 *Sovetskaya Rossiya* carried a lengthy article on Solzhenitsyn. The article suggested that the local museum in Kislovodsk, where Solzhenitsyn was born, should collect materials on the period Solzhenitsyn lived in the town.

Draft Law on Archives

The television program "Vzglyad" reported on the unofficial draft law on archives, prepared by a group of jurists and archivists. The text of the draft, guaranteeing free access to archives in the USSR, was published in *Vestnik Akademii Nauk SSSR* (No. 10). The draft also places a limit of thirty years on any ban on access to archival materials containing state secrets and prohibits departmental (*vedomstvennye*) archives, such as those now kept by the KGB and various ministries. It represents a sharp break with current Soviet practice.

Saturday, December 16 ————————————————————————

Gorbachev Sends Sharply Worded Message to East Berlin Congress

Gorbachev sent a message of greetings to the East German Congress of the Socialist Unity Party (SED) in which he denounced "lies and double standards" as poison for socialism. Quoted by TASS, he said the heated debate and drastic decisions in East Germany were a logical consequence of pressures that had been pent up for years bursting out in "a cleansing storm" (*Pravda*, December 17).

Sunday, December 17 ————————————————————————

Primakov Says Deputies Can Create Factions

In his report on the draft regulations governing the conduct of business in the Congress of People's Deputies and the USSR Supreme Soviet, candidate member of the Politburo Evgenii Primakov said that, in future, deputies would have the right to form permanent or temporary groups. According to Primakov's report, published by *Pravda* on December 17, such groups may draw up their own platforms and bills. The right to set up groups (in effect, factions) will not be limited only to those with a national or territorial focus, or to those affiliated with a particular organization.

Yurii Lyubimov Reinstated as Taganka Theater Director

Soviet theater director Yurii Lyubimov has been restored to his old job at the Taganka Theater five years after he was dismissed. TASS said that for the next year and a half Lyubimov would work both at the theater and abroad while fulfilling obligations under Western contracts he had already signed. The post of director of the Taganka Theater fell vacant after Nikolai Gubenko was appointed USSR minister of culture. Gubenko campaigned to have Lyubimov reinstated at the Taganka.

—————— Monday, December 18

Shevardnadze in Brussels

In Brussels, Soviet Foreign Minister Eduard Shevardnadze signed a ten-year trade and cooperation agreement with the European Community. On December 19, Shevardnadze held unprecedented meetings with NATO Secretary General Manfred Woerner and with NATO ambassadors. Western agencies reported that, during his visit to NATO headquarters, Shevardnadze said the Warsaw Pact and the Western alliance had an important stabilizing role to play as Europe changes. Shevardnadze also expressed interest in establishing formal contacts between NATO and the Warsaw Pact. Later the same day, in an address to the European Parliament, Shevardnadze restated his opposition to a unified Germany. He said that, without two German states, Europe would be "fraught with destabilization" (*AP, UPI*, December 19). The same day, Shevardnadze left Brussels for London.

Pravda* Publishes Roy Medvedev's Review of *Gulag

Pravda published historian Roy Medvedev's review of Aleksandr Solzhenitsyn's book *Gulag Archipelago*. *Pravda* quoted Medvedev as saying that, now that Solzhenitsyn's works were being published in the USSR, he believed it was useful and necessary to publish the review. Medvedev praised Solzhenitsyn for writing the best study known of the Soviet labor camp system. Medvedev was critical of Solzhenitsyn, however, for concentrating too much on Lenin as the creator of the Soviet Gulag and for playing down the role of Stalin in the history of Soviet labor camps.

Soviet Press and Officials on Events in Romania

TASS and Radio Moscow (December 18) and *Izvestia* (December 19) provided limited but straightforward coverage of clashes that took place in the Romanian city of Timisoara between police and demonstrators who tried to prevent attempts by the authorities to evict Reformed Church pastor Laszlo Tokes from his house. The reports said the demonstrators had denounced the country's leadership and the existing system, but they avoided speculating on the number of casualties resulting from the clashes.

On December 19, Foreign Ministry spokesman Vadim Perfil'ev told TASS that reports on Romania were contradictory, making it difficult to get a clear picture of events there. Still avoiding any direct criticism of Romania, Moscow began reporting foreign protests over the events in Romania in its Romanian-language broadcasts. The latest issue of *Moscow News* (No. 51) sharply criticized the Soviet press coverage of events in Socialist countries. Describing earlier coverage as completely inadequate, journalist Anatolii Druzenko said that the situation remained unsatisfactory, despite some recent improvements.

On December 20, the Soviet media (TASS, *Izvestia*, and *Pravda*) gave more details of the bloody suppression of protests in Timisoara. *Izvestia* also pointed out that the Romanian media had ignored the clashes, concentrating instead on a current visit by Nicolae Ceausescu to Iran and on "the successful labors of the Romanian working people." In its evening news program, Soviet television reported the severe criticism of Ceausescu's policies by other East European countries. Meanwhile, Moldavian poet and People's Deputy Ion Drutse said a group of Moldavian deputies had formally asked the USSR Congress of People's Deputies to draw up a resolution expressing concern over the situation in Romania (*AP*, *Reuters*, December 20).

On December 21, TASS filed dramatic and detailed reports from Bucharest, making little attempt to hide the mounting protests against Ceausescu. Radio Moscow, in Romanian, quoted Politburo member Lev Zaikov as saying it was necessary for the Romanian authorities to establish a dialogue with the people. He said force should not be used to "strangle" the people's discontent. Speaking in the Congress of People's Deputies, Mikhail Gorbachev said, however, that it was not yet possible to make a detailed and objective assessment of what was going on in Romania (*TASS*, December 21). Meanwhile, the Moldavian Popular Front organized mourning for the Romanians killed in the unrest. A statement by members of the front compared the current violence in Romania with last month's clashes between Moldavian demonstrators and police (*Reuters*, December 21).

On December 22, after Ceausescu's downfall had been announced, the USSR Congress of People's Deputies approved a statement of support for the Romanian people's "just cause" at the request of Gorbachev (*TASS*, December 22). Many radical deputies considered that Gorbachev's reaction had been belated and expressed anger over this fact (*Financial Times*, December 23).

A campaign of solidarity with the Romanian people was launched in Moldavia. On December 22, demonstrations took place in Kishinev condemning Ceausescu. Some of the demonstrators carried posters demanding reunification of Moldavia with Romania (*Financial Times*, December 23). The same day, a service honoring fellow Romanians who had been killed was conducted in the Moldavian capital. It was also announced that the Moldavian government and the Moldavian Popular Front were sending aid to Romania (*TASS*, *RFE Romanian Service*, December 22).

On December 23, TASS carried a joint statement by the Moldavian Party Central Committee, the Presidium of the Moldavian Supreme Soviet, and the Moldavian Council of Ministers expressing deep concern over the events in Romania and protesting against the violence there. TASS also reported concern over the fate of Soviet citizens in Romania. Meanwhile, Bucharest television quoted the Soviet Foreign Ministry as denying that the USSR had offered military aid to Romania.

On December 24, TASS said Soviet Deputy Foreign Minister Ivan Aboimov and US Ambassador Jack Matlock discussed developments in Romania at a meeting in Moscow. On December 25, the Soviet Union recognized the Romanian National Salvation Front (*TASS*, December 25). On the following day, Gorbachev sent congratulations to Ion Iliescu, who was named head of Romania's ruling Executive Buro. Iliescu and Gorbachev first met thirty-five years ago when they were both students at Moscow State University (*The New York Times*, December 25).

Gorbachev's message of congratulation to Iliescu was published in *Izvestia* on December 27. Western agencies noted that it departed from the usual format of such messages in that it was signed simply "M. Gorbachev" and did not bear the title of the Soviet leader. The shorter announcement that followed immediately below congratulating Petre Roman on his appointment as

Romanian prime minister and signed by the USSR Council of Ministers also highlighted this unusual step of recognizing an informal government.

Whereas the United States was critical of the summary execution of Nicolae Ceausescu and his wife without an open trial, the Soviet reaction to the execution was less categorical. Soviet Foreign Ministry spokesman Vadim Perfil'ev said that "the decision to execute the president probably took into account the aspirations and will of the Romanian people" (*TASS,* December 26).

On December 27, TASS reported that Gorbachev had held a telephone conversation with Iliescu, who assured the Soviet leader that the situation in Romania was normalizing. The same day, Iliescu and Roman met Soviet Ambassador to Bucharest Evgenii Tyazhel'nikov. Radio Bucharest said the ambassador had delivered a message from Gorbachev promising Soviet assistance to Romania on its road to renewal. The same day, Soviet television carried an interview with the head of the Romanian Department of the USSR Foreign Ministry's Administration for the Socialist Countries of Europe, Vladimir Lapshin, who said the ministry was surprised by the timing and violence of the uprising in Romania.

Meanwhile, *Izvestia* (December 27) reported that more aid from Moldavia was arriving in Romania. A special bank account was opened in Kishinev for donations for Romania. By noon of December 26, 150,000 rubles had been deposited in the account. Throughout the week, TASS and Soviet television in its news program "Vremya" provided detailed coverage of the events in Romania.

Could Gorbachev Be Recalled?

During debate on the draft election law, a deputy from Voronezh pointed out that under existing regulations even Gorbachev could be recalled from the Congress by his constituency, the CPSU Central Committee. "I would be very distressed," Vladimir Kirillov said, "to learn that a Central Committee plenum had recalled the Soviet president because it does not like his performance." Kirillov asked that the recall provisions—which date to Lenin's day and which were introduced to make the soviets "more democratic" than bourgeois institutions—be abolished. A Latvian deputy, Yurii Boyars, who spoke after Kirillov, proposed a compromise. He suggested that it should be possible to recall any deputy except the president, "since he is elected by the Congress itself" (*Central Television,* "Vremya," December 18).

Radio Moscow (1700) said fourteen of the 100 most polluted cities in the Soviet Union were in Kazakhstan. This report came at the opening in Alma-Ata of a republican seminar on propagating environmental consciousness, which brought together representatives of official environmental protection agencies, informal "Green" movements, and also guests from outside Kazakhstan. While large environmental groups, such as the Nevada-Semipalatinsk antinuclear movement and the society to save Lake Balkhash and the Aral Sea, enjoyed official support, numerous small local ecological groups continued to be opposed by some local officials.

Pollution in Kazakhstan

The Soviet government has decided on measures to try to restrain inflation and to create a system to measure how fast prices are rising. TASS quoted Vyacheslav Senchagov, chairman of the State Committee for Prices, as saying that the government is also considering ways to compensate citizens, especially those with low incomes, for rising prices. According to TASS, Senchagov said these measures are necessary because of rising retail prices and because there is more money available than there are consumer goods. He said the surplus amounts to more than 165,000 million rubles.

USSR to Try to Restrain Inflation

_____ *Tuesday, December 19*

Some 150 Soviet Germans, Crimean Tatars, and Meskhetians demonstrated outside the Moskva and Rossiya hotels in Moscow for the restoration of their rights. According to *DPA*, they were trying to persuade members of the USSR Congress of People's Deputies, who were staying in these hotels, that their problems should be discussed at the Congress, saying that the declaration on deported peoples adopted by the Supreme Soviet in November was not enough.

Volga Germans, Tatars, Meskhetians Demonstrate

Eduard Shevardnadze discussed developments in Eastern Europe with British Prime Minister Margaret Thatcher in London. Before meeting Thatcher, Shevardnadze discussed the Romanian situation with British Foreign Secretary Douglas Hurd. Hurd also gave Shevardnadze a list of unresolved Soviet human-rights cases (*DPA*, December 19).

Shevardnadze Discusses Eastern Europe with British Leaders

Orthodox Church Calls for End to Violent Action in Ukraine

The Holy Synod of the Russian Orthodox Church issued a statement condemning what it called violent action taken by laymen representing the Ukrainian Catholic Church. TASS quoted the Synod as saying the violent activities were directed against Orthodox believers in the western regions of Ukraine. TASS quoted the Synod statement as criticizing the Committee for the Defense of the Ukrainian Catholic Church, some activists of the Ukrainian Popular Movement for *Perestroika*, and some Eastern Rite Catholics. The same day, AP quoted Ukrainian Catholic Church hierarchs in Rome as saying that, since the government had announced that the registration of Ukrainian Catholic communities would be permitted, 100 Russian Orthodox priests and 200 parishes in the Ukraine had registered themselves as Catholic. On December 21, TASS reported that Russian Orthodox Archbishop Makarii had begun a hunger strike to protest against an attempt by Ukrainian Catholics to take over his cathedral in Ivano-Frankovsk in Western Ukraine.

On December 27, Archbishop Kirill of Smolensk and Kaliningrad said Ukrainian Catholics had seized fifteen of Lvov's nineteen Orthodox churches. He also said churches in Ternopol, Ivano-Frankovsk, and other cities had been taken over. Kirill said that one Orthodox priest had died of shock and another had a heart attack as a result of these actions and that an Orthodox archbishop was now conducting a hunger strike to protest against the seizure of his church. (On December 27, UPI quoted Archbishop Makarii of Ivano-Frankovsk and Kolomyya as saying he was in the ninth day of a hunger strike. The beginning of the strike was reported earlier by TASS.)

Kirill Mazurov Dies

Kirill Mazurov, a former CPSU Politburo member and USSR first deputy prime minister, died at the age of seventy-five (*TASS*, December 20; *Pravda*, December 21). His death, which occurred on December 19, was announced at the Congress of People's Deputies on December 21. At the time of his death, he was a member of the Congress and chairman of the All-Union Council of War and Labor Veterans. Mazurov had been first deputy prime minister and a member of the Politburo from 1965 to 1978. During the Soviet invasion of Czechoslovakia in 1968, Mazurov was sent there by the Politburo to supervise the operation. He was stationed in Prague secretly under the name of "General Trofimov."

On December 19, the Lithuanian Party Congress opened with a call for the Party's independence. Party First Secretary Algirdas Brazauskas said in an opening speech that only an independent Lithuanian Party can compete with other political forces. He said power can be attained only through democratic elections. AP quoted a draft declaration as saying the Party belongs to the world Communist movement but is an independent organization with its own program and statutes. On December 20, the Lithuanian Party voted to establish itself as a party independent of the CPSU. The vote to make the Party independent was supported by 855 of 1,038 delegates. A resolution calling for the establishment of "an independent party within a renewed CPSU" was rejected, gathering only 160 votes. Egor Ligachev told reporters in Moscow that the Lithuanian Party's action means "big trouble" and that Lithuanians "just do not realize what grief will descend." A leading member of "Sajudis," Alvydas Medalinskas, said the Lithuanian Party's decision to make itself independent of Moscow will improve the Party's image (*RFE/RL Special*, December 20; *Sovetskaya Litva*, December 21).

On December 21, a group of Lithuanian Communists who voted against the independence of the Party from Moscow established an alternative group that will remain part of the CPSU. They called the group "the Lithuanian Republican Organization of the Communist Party of the Soviet Union" (*Radio Vilnius*, December 21). The same day, Mikhail Gorbachev, obviously angered by the proclamation of independence by the Lithuanian Communists, said the CPSU Central Committee would meet to discuss the situation in Lithuania. He told the Congress of People's Deputies that he shared "the concern and alarm" of many other Communists about events in Lithuania (*TASS*, December 21). The same day, Algirdas Brazauskas was elected first secretary of Lithuania's new Independent Communist Party (*TASS*, December 21).

Lithuanian Party Congress Votes for Independence from CPSU

On December 20, after three days of debate, the USSR Congress of People's Deputies amended Article 95 of the USSR Constitution to exclude the clause that sets aside one-third of the seats for representatives of public organizations. According to the revised text, Union and Autonomous republics will be free to decide for themselves whether to set aside seats for such organizations, but at

Allotment of Seats to Public Organizations Abolished

the all-Union level—i.e., in elections to the USSR Congress of People's Deputies—the allocation of such seats will be abolished. Those deputies already elected to the Congress from public organizations will serve out the remainder of their terms (*Radio Moscow,* "Mayak," December 20; *Pravda,* December 21).

Pravda Carries Criticism of Opponents of Perestroika

Pravda published an article saying some critics of *perestroika* were incompetent officials who were afraid of losing open elections. *Pravda* singled out for mention "many senior Party officials in the provinces." It said they were trying, in "panic-stricken terror," to find out why they were unpopular with voters. The reports said the officials were blaming "evil forces or a secret plot" instead of the true culprits—i.e., themselves. The author of the article was Evgenii Solomenko, *Pravda*'s correspondent in Novosibirsk.

USSR Tells US to Stop Intervention in Panama

The Soviet Union called on the United States to stop its armed intervention in Panama. A Soviet Foreign Ministry spokesman, as quoted by TASS, said the US military action in Panama was a violation of the United Nations Charter and of the generally recognized rules of state relations. The statement urged the world community to condemn the US action.

On December 30, the Soviet Union repeated its call for the immediate withdrawal of US troops from Panama. TASS said Soviet Deputy Foreign Minister Aleksandr Bessmertnykh summoned US Ambassador to Moscow Jack Matlock and outlined the Soviet position on Panama. It said he called for the withdrawal of US troops in "the interests of normalizing and stabilizing the situation."

Challenge to Use of Russian Language Defeated

The USSR Congress of People's Deputies rejected a challenge to the use of Russian as its primary language. TASS said Ukrainian poet Dmytro Pavlychko called the present rules on language discriminatory. The rules require the use of Russian unless a deputy wishing to use another national language notifies the Congress Secretariat of his intention in advance. TASS quoted Pavlychko as saying every deputy should have the right to use his own national language without notifying anybody. The agency said it would not be technically or financially feasible to make provisions for simultaneous translation of the Soviet Union's approximately 130 national languages.

Mikhail Gorbachev held talks in the Kremlin with Czecho-slovak Prime Minister Marian Calfa. Radio Prague said Gorbachev complained to Calfa that he was under attack from "Soviet extremists" on both the right and the left. Accompanying Calfa to Moscow was Foreign Minister Jiri Dienstbier, who met with Eduard Shevardnadze to discuss the issue of Soviet troops in Czechoslovakia. Radio Moscow quoted them as noting the necessity of solving questions stemming from the 1968 invasion and concerning the presence of the remaining Soviet troops (*Pravda*, December 21).

Gorbachev Talks with Calfa

Thursday, December 21

A law on the status of people's deputies was adopted. Published in *Izvestia* on December 27, the law outlines the rights and obligations of people's deputies from the level of the USSR Supreme Soviet to local soviets. The adoption of the law followed a lengthy discussion. Several radical proposals for the broadening of the rights of people's deputies were eventually rejected. The new law is in many ways similar to the previous law on the status of deputies.

Law on Status of People's Deputies Adopted

Friday, December 22

Soviet Deputy Foreign Minister Yulii Vorontsov paid a brief visit to New Delhi to greet the leaders of India's new government and tell them Moscow wants to strengthen the traditionally friendly ties between their two countries. Vorontsov brought a letter to this effect from Mikhail Gorbachev. Vorontsov met Prime Minister Vishwanath Pratap Singh, who has been in office for three weeks, and his external affairs minister, Inder Gujral. A spokesman for the Indian External Affairs Ministry said Vorontsov discussed economic cooperation, Afghanistan, and Eastern Europe (*Reuters*, December 22).

Soviet Minister Visits India to Meet New Leaders

TASS reported that an Azerbaijani archeologist had discovered a mass grave on an island in the Caspian Sea containing the remains of victims of Stalinist repressions. The news service did not say how many victims were found, but it did say that the dead were all male and aged thirty or more.

Mass Grave Found Near Baku

691

Sovetskaya Rossiya Criticizes Baltic Deputy

Sovetskaya Rossiya carried a letter signed by four members of the USSR Congress of People's Deputies from the RSFSR attacking Estonian writer and USSR People's Deputy Tiit Made for his "unfriendly, even offensive" opinion of Russia and the Russian people. The putative occasion for the letter's publication was the recent appearance in Finland of Made's *Empire at the Crossroads*. In fact, the letter seems to have been intended as a more general warning against Baltic moves towards self-determination.

Saturday, December 23 ——————————————————————————

Gorbachev Attacks Separatist Tendencies

Speaking in the USSR Congress of People's Deputies, Mikhail Gorbachev warned that supporters of secession sowed "discord, bloodshed, and death." Gorbachev called for a new kind of federation with various forms of relations and with room for different languages and cultures. Gorbachev said it was essential to make Soviet society more just, humane, and democratic. He said this must be done on the basis of socialism, not capitalism. On December 24, Gorbachev spoke again at the closing session of the Congress. He said people who call for strikes and whip up nationalist tensions in the USSR are trying to wreck *perestroika* (*Central Television*, December 24; *Pravda*, December 25). Gorbachev's attack on the supporters of secession followed the Lithuanian Communist Party's declaration of independence from the CPSU (*TASS*, December 23).

Congress Votes to Combat Organized Crime

The USSR Congress of People's Deputies voted to combat organized crime. TASS said that, at the next session, the Congress would discuss changing the Criminal Codes. The Congress also called for measures to remove the conditions that have given rise to "the shadow economy." These measures include more effective monetary controls. TASS reported that many deputies acknowledged that crime could not be combated solely by law enforcement, but that there must also be an improvement in the country's social, economic, political, and moral climate (*Pravda*, December 28).

Congress Sets Up Constitutional Oversight Committee

The USSR Congress of People's Deputies has approved the formation of a constitutional oversight committee. The approval came after a compromise had been reached with deputies who feared that the committee would

692

infringe on the sovereignty of the republics. One of the committee's responsibilities is to make sure that the laws and constitutions of the republics conform with the USSR Constitution, but the commission is not to have these powers until the planned amendments to the USSR Constitution revising the relationship between the central government and the republics have been made (*TASS*, December 23). The Congress elected lawyer Sergei Alekseev as chairman of the new committee and Professor Boris Lazarev as deputy chairman (*Izvestia*, December 24 and 26).

Responding to increasing public discontent, the USSR Council of Ministers has issued new rules requiring licenses for the export of consumer goods, TASS reported. This step is unlikely to be of any great significance, as the Soviet Union exports relatively few consumer items. It will, however, further complicate Soviet efforts to attract partners for joint ventures.

Export of Consumer Goods Now Subject to Licensing

Sunday, December 24

The USSR Congress of People's Deputies issued a resolution condemning the secret protocols to the Molotov-Ribbentrop Pact of August 23, 1939. The resolution said, however, that the pact itself was a legitimate document for its time. On December 23, the resolution failed to gain the required absolute majority of Congress members. During the discussion of the pact, several deputies, mostly war veterans, still insisted that the existing text of the protocols was a fabrication. The Congressional resolution on the Molotov-Ribbentrop pact was prepared by a commission set up by the Congress under the chairmanship of Politburo member Aleksandr Yakovlev (*TASS*, December 24, *Pravda*, December 24 and 28).

Congress Condemns Secret Protocols

In its closing session, the USSR Congress of People's Deputies adopted a resolution condemning the use of violence by military forces against protesters in the Georgian capital of Tbilisi in April. AP reported that about 200 members of the Congress walked out of the session to protest against a speech by USSR Deputy Prosecutor General Aleksandr Katusev, who attempted to defend the military crackdown. Despite a promise that the proceedings of the Congress would be covered in full by Radio

Resolutions Condemning Tbilisi Massacre and Invasion of Afghanistan Adopted

693

Moscow, the radio dropped the Congress commission's report on the events in Tbilisi from its Sunday broadcast. The Congress also adopted a resolution strongly condemning the Soviet invasion of Afghanistan in 1979 and approved a message to the Soviet people calling on them to "close ranks behind the ideas and aims of *perestroika*" and to take an active role in implementing them (*TASS*, December 24; *Pravda*, December 25).

Report on Commission on Gdlyan-Ivanov Affair

Pravda carried the text of a preliminary report by the commission of the Congress of People's Deputies on the Gdlyan-Ivanov affair. The report stressed that some members of the commission were of the opinion that the disbandment by the USSR Procurator's Office of an investigation commission headed by Tel'man Gdlyan had a negative result on the quality of the corruption probe in Uzbekistan. The report agreed that during their investigation of corruption among Uzbek officials Gdlyan and Ivanov had indeed abused their power. The report stressed, however, that some complaints from defendants and their relatives about misdeeds by the Gdlyan group had no proof. The report also said that the Gdlyan group had a serious conflict with the USSR Procurator's Office and that therefore the current investigation by the Procurator's Office of the wrongdoings of Gdlyan could be unobjective. The report said that the commission of the Congress of People's Deputies found that there was no evidence proving Egor Ligachev's involvement in bribe-taking, as Gdlyan and Ivanov had implied. The report said that in contrast the commission found that the case against V. Smirnov, Central Commission official in charge of Uzbekistan and later Party second secretary of Moldavia, had been closed by the USSR Procurator's Office too early. The Procurator's Office and the KGB, also involved in the case, were said to have ignored many materials showing that Smirnov was in fact guilty of corruption and bribe-taking.

Local Elections in Kazakhstan and Tajikistan

Elections to local soviets were held on December 24 in Kazakhstan and Tajikistan. Although TASS claimed that voters in Kazakhstan now have a better understanding of election procedures than they did at the time of the elections to the Congress, there were contests in only a quarter of the districts. The Party chief of East Kazakhstan Oblast found himself running against five other candidates for a seat on the oblast soviet, but apparently this was an exception. Altogether, fewer than 100,000 candidates competed for some 79,000 seats. Radio Moscow reported on December 25 that 85.6 percent of the registered voters went to the polls. In Tajikistan, where 34,000 candidates sought 16,380 seats, 91.2 percent of those entitled to vote did so.

_____ *Monday, December 25*

On December 25–26, the CPSU Central Committee held an emergency plenum to discuss the Lithuanian Party's declaration of independence. Mikhail Gorbachev delivered an emotional speech at the plenum, saying that there were clear limits to what Moscow would tolerate (*Pravda* and *Izvestia*, December 26). He called for the preservation of a one-party structure and of the union state and said anything else would have fateful consequences for both *perestroika* and international relations. Gorbachev then attacked the Lithuanian Party leadership for "appeasement" of and "endless concessions" to "Sajudis." He said the legislature of the USSR should consider banning the activity of any group pursuing secessionist aims. In his speech, Gorbachev rejected attacks on Russians by people of other nationalities and defended the Russian people as "a huge store of benevolence and humanism." At the same time, Gorbachev urged "maximum restraint" in dealing with the current crisis, and Vadim Medvedev announced that no force would be used in resolving the Lithuanian question. The Central Committee then declared the Lithuanian Party's declaration of independence null and void, but neither Gorbachev nor the Central Committee took any concrete steps to enforce Moscow's will (*TASS*, *AP*, December 25 and 26). It was agreed that the Central Commitee would reconsider the matter after Gorbachev and other senior officials had visited Lithuania.

On December 26, more than 10,000 people took part in a demonstration at Vilnius Cathedral in support of the Lithuanian Party's independence from the CPSU (*AFP*, *DPA*, December 26). DPA said the demonstrators drafted an appeal in support of Lithuanian Communist Party First Secretary Algirdas Brazauskas, who had been sharply criticized by Gorbachev.

On December 27, *Pravda* said that the clash of ideas over the future of the Lithuanian Communist Party was continuing. The *Pravda* article quoted at length two members of the breakaway segment of the Lithuanian Party that retains its ties with the CPSU. The newspaper also quoted Juras Pozela, the president of the Lithuanian Academy of Sciences, as saying that reforms of the CPSU

**CPSU Central Committee
Plenum on Lithuania**

must permit the creation of autonomous Communist Parties. The same day, in an interview given to Radio Moscow, CPSU Central Committee member Vladimir Anishchev said a compromise should be found, since the Lithuanian Party's split from the CPSU would be a blow to the heart of *perestroika*.

On December 28, in its lead article, *Pravda* said that, in reaction to the Lithuanian Party's declaration of independence, meetings of Party members and workers across the country were demanding "energetic measures in defense of the unity of the Party."

On December 30, *Krasnaya zvezda* said the Communists of Lithuania face an unprecedented situation whereby two Communist Parties now exist in the republic. The newspaper said people are asking themselves how and on what basis it is possible to bring the two halves together. It quotes a senior pro-Moscow Lithuanian as saying one solution might be to hold a referendum of all Lithuanian Communists. It also said Lithuanian journalists had been in "no hurry" to report the activities of Communists who want to stay loyal to Moscow.

Meanwhile, *Komsomol'skaya pravda* (December 30) and *Moscow News* (No. 52) refused to join the general chorus of denunciation of the Lithuanian Party's declaration of independence and have tried to provide their readers with more balanced coverage. *Moscow News*, for example, stressed that the decision to form an independent Party was supported by 83 percent of the delegates to the Lithuanian Party Congress.

Karakalpak Party Chief Sentenced for Corruption

The USSR Supreme Court sentenced Kallibek Kamalov, former Party chief of the Karakalpak ASSR, to fifteen years in prison for bribery and abuse of office. Kamalov had been accused of taking advantage of his position and his family connections with former Uzbek Party First Secretary Sharaf Rashidov to extract bribes from subordinates. As TASS noted, the trial was complicated by Kamalov's retraction of his pretrial admission of guilt and by the fact that most of the witnesses also retracted earlier statements incriminating Kamalov. The court ignored the retractions and later initiated proceedings for perjury; it also suggested that the USSR Public Prosecutor's Office reconsider its decision to quash a number of bribery cases that had arisen out of the Kamalov investigation. Kamalov's conviction indicates that recent retractions by other Uzbek officials of earlier admissions of guilt are unlikely to save them.

In a Radio Moscow broadcast, journalist Tat'yana Koru-
paeva reported the findings of one investigator who
claims that the political abuse of psychiatry is continuing
in the USSR. She interviewed Mikhail Tsaregorodtsev,
who in 1987 organized an International Independent
Research Center for Psychiatry. Tsaregorodtsev noted that
some 500 former victims of psychiatric abuse had visited
his center and had complained that those responsible for
the abuses had not been punished.

Psychiatric Abuse Alleged to Be Continuing

An accurate map of Moscow Oblast will go on sale by
New Year's Day, according to TASS of December 25. The
news agency said the new map would be of particular
interest to foreign tourists, who have, until now, had to
make do with inaccurate maps. TASS also announced that
several specialized maps of the city are to appear next
year. Also of interest to foreigners, TASS said, is a new
telephone service that will provide telephone and telex
numbers and the postal addresses of foreign firms in
Moscow. The information will be given in Russian,
English, and German. The new service may also be able
to provide link-ups to the TASS computer network.

Accurate Maps of Moscow to Appear

Major General Viktor Tatarnikov called for concessions by
both NATO and the Warsaw Pact in their negotiations in
Vienna on conventional force reductions in Europe.
Tatarnikov told TASS that mutual concessions were
needed if a treaty were to be ready in 1990. Tatarnikov is
a member of the Soviet negotiating team in Vienna and a
spokesman for the Soviet General Staff. He said that
recent NATO and Warsaw Pact proposals on conventional force reductions were similar in many ways and
provided "new scope for productive work at the talks."
But, he said, the talks have recently become bogged
down as a result of difficulties in reaching agreement on
definitions for various types of weapons.

Soviet Negotiator Calls for Mutual Concessions

Tuesday, December 26

Radio Moscow said that the USSR was in the grip of an epidemic of influenza and that 30,000 cases among children
were being registered daily in Moscow alone. The radio
described the situation as "disturbing." It said winter
school vacation dates were being changed because
children in particular were at risk from the epidemic.

Influenza Epidemic in USSR Reported

697

El'tsin Comments on Session of USSR Congress of People's Deputies

Supreme Soviet deputy Boris El'tsin was quoted by Radio Moscow World Service as saying the session of the USSR Congress of People's Deputies that ended on December 24 had wasted time by not taking action on important laws. According to El'tsin, the Congress should have acted on reforms of land ownership, land use, and the operation of state enterprises. Instead, he said, the Congress had put the country in an extremely difficult position by delaying action for as long as a year pending a nationwide discussion of the changes.

Sakharov's Last Speech Published

At the time of his death, Andrei Sakharov was preparing a speech attacking recent Soviet legislation giving prosecutors the power to prolong pretrial detentions. As published in *Literaturnaya gazeta*, the speech argued that, by attempting to lengthen the amount of time Soviet citizens can be held before trial, the USSR Prosecutor's Office was trying to "free its hands entirely and return the country to the stormy times of illegality, of the cult of personality, stagnation, and other rather gloomy periods." The speech had reportedly been circulated at the USSR Congress of People's Deputies.

Anniversary of Invasion of Afghanistan Marked

TASS reported that Soviet citizens commemorated the tenth anniversary of the Soviet invasion of Afghanistan in a variety of ways. There were memorial services in Russian Orthodox churches in Moscow, the relatives of soldiers who perished in Afghanistan visited cemeteries, and wreaths were laid at the tomb of the Unknown Soldier. The news agency made no mention of memorial services being held in churches other than the Russian Orthodox ones.

Estonian and Latvian Parliaments Hold Sessions

The Estonian and Latvian Supreme Soviets discussed next year's economic policies (*Sovetskaya Estoniya*, December 28). In effect from January 1, the Baltic republics will have independent economic status. TASS said the Estonian Supreme Soviet had rejected a government budget draft for 1990 that included new taxes on tobacco and alcohol. TASS said the Latvian Supreme Soviet had passed a budget draft after rejecting a clause raising prices of alcohol and tobacco. The budget deficit will be covered by issuing Latvian government bonds.

TASS said the Latvian Supreme Soviet had also discussed legislation giving more power to the soviets and economic institutions and an article in the republican constitution dealing with social organizations (*Sovetskaya Latviya*, December 28).

Thursday, December 28

The Latvian Supreme Soviet approved at the first reading changes in the article in the republican constitution on the leading role of the Communist Party. The changes provide for the abolition of the leading role of the Party and for the creation of other political parties. There will be a final vote on the amendments in the Latvian Supreme Soviet in January. (*RFE Latvian Service, AP, AFP*, December 28). The Lithuanian Supreme Soviet has already made similar changes in the Lithuanian Constitution.

Latvian Supreme Soviet Approves Abolition of Party's Leading Role

The Lithuanian Council of Ministers legally registered the Independent Lithuanian Communist Party. Radio Vilnius said the registration took place without any discussion. On December 29, a spokesman for the "Sajudis" information agency in Vilnius told RFE that the Democratic Party had also been registered.

Independent Lithuanian Communist Party Legally Registered

TASS said veteran diplomat Eizens Poch had become the new foreign minister of Latvia. It said the decision had been made by the Latvian Supreme Soviet. In the past, one person served as both foreign minister and deputy prime minister in Latvia. According to TASS, Poch served for six years in the Soviet embassy in Washington and then for five years at the USSR Foreign Ministry in Moscow. From 1985 to 1988, Poch was a Soviet consul general in Indonesia and until now has been the first deputy chief of the USSR Foreign Ministry's consular department (*TASS*, December 28).

New Foreign Minister in Latvia

Soviet authorities will close down 13,000 inefficient kolkhozes and sovkhozes as part of a new plan to boost grain production, a senior Communist Party official was quoted as saying in *Pravda*. Egor Stroev, a CPSU Central Committee secretary, told the newspaper the mass closures were part of the plan for 1991–95 approved by the Politburo. He urged kolkhozes and sovkhozes to transform their

***Pravda* Quotes Official on Closures of 13,000 Farms**

structures with the help of lease-holding schemes introduced this year and called for massive investment to provide basic amenities in backward rural regions.

El'tsin Reported Running for RSFSR President

The Soviet news service Interfax reported that Boris El'tsin had been nominated for election as president of the RSFSR by voters in Ramenki, a town near Moscow. Interfax is a newly created cooperative news agency affiliated with Radio Moscow (*Reuters*, December 28).

Deputies Say Ethnic Conflicts Most Serious Problem

A survey of the USSR Congress of People's Deputies showed that deputies believe that interethnic conflicts are the most serious danger facing the Soviet Union. Novosti said the country's growing economic problems were a close second on the deputies' list of dangers. According to the press agency, other dangers cited by many of the deputies polled include crime, strikes, and increased economic inequality among citizens. Novosti said external factors were at the very bottom of the deputies' list.

Friday, December 29

Violent Clashes between Police and Demonstrators in Azerbaijan

Official reports from Azerbaijan said eighty-five people had been injured in clashes between police and demonstrators. Radio Baku said violence had erupted in the Dzhalilabad Raion when "anti-*perestroika*" elements attacked buildings belonging to the Communist Party and the republican Ministry of Internal Affairs. Unofficial reports quoting local Azerbaijan Popular Front members spoke of an even higher injury toll and one death. The reports said police had opened fire on demonstrators demanding the removal of the raion Party first secretary, Kheirulla Aliev. Radio Baku said thirty-seven people had been detained. Soviet television said a group of deputies from the Azerbaijani Supreme Soviet had gone to the area to look into the situation.

Police in the town of Dzhalilabad in Azerbaijan denied widespread reports that they had fired on a crowd of protesters on December 29, killing one person and injuring 162 others. People claiming to be eyewitnesses to the confrontation told a rally in Baku on December 30 that police had fired on a crowd of 20,000 to 30,000 protesters seeking the ouster of the newly appointed raion Communist Party chief Aliev (*AP*, December 31). On January 1, Azerbaijani officials held talks in Dzhalilabad on setting up new administrative and Communist Party bodies. Nazim Ragimov, an independent journalist in Baku, told Reuters by telephone that all previous state and Party institutions in the town of 20,000 had collapsed and that the town was "in the hands of the people." On January 2, officials of the Azerbaijani Popular Front told Radio Liberty that Aliev had been among those injured in the clash. Reports said calm had returned to the town.

The controversial Soviet television program "Vzglyad" was dropped this evening without advance notice. One of the presenters of the program, Aleksandr Lyubimov, said the show's producers were told by government authorities that it had been dropped "to reduce the number of political programs ahead of the New Year holiday." He gave no other details. Western news agencies quoted Soviet television sources as saying the authorities were worried by some of the show's contents, which were to include a parody of the evening news program "Vremya." Another edition of "Vzglyad" is scheduled to be broadcast on January 5, but the television sources said the show's long-term future was in doubt. The Moscow youth newspaper *Moskovsky komsomolets* said the decision to drop the program from the schedule was reminiscent of pre-*glasnost'* censorship.

"Vzglyad" Unexpectedly Dropped from Schedule

In an article in *Pravda*, Soviet Prime Minister Nikolai Ryzhkov ruled out the possibility of transferring large-scale state enterprises to private or collective ownership. Ryzhkov approved, however, of privately run operations for types of business in which large-scale enterprises are ineffective. Ryzhkov said the key direction of the government's economic program was to increase supplies of consumer goods. He also said the policies of Comecon encouraged isolation from world markets and hindered technological progress. He said schemes to rectify the shortcomings would be offered by the USSR at the forthcoming Comecon meeting.

Ryzhkov Says No Transfer of Large-Scale Enterprises

The South Korean conglomerate, the Hyundai group, said it had signed a thirty-year joint venture agreement with the Soviet Union for logging and wood-processing in Siberia. The partners plan to inaugurate the proposed 50–50 joint venture company, initially capitalized at 64 million rubles, by next April after obtaining approval from their respective governments. Hyundai officials said the

South Korean Firm Signs Logging Joint Venture with USSR

701

accord provides for the joint venture to cut one million square meters of timber in the Svetlaya area annually for thirty years. Hyundai said the entire production would be imported to South Korea (*AP*, December 29).

Memorial to Diplomatic Victims of Stalinism Unveiled

A memorial honoring Soviet diplomats who suffered under Stalin's repressions was unveiled at the Soviet Foreign Ministry. Soviet Foreign Minister Eduard Shevardnadze attended the unveiling ceremony. Foreign Ministry spokesman Gennadii Gerasimov said a special government commission was working to collect the names of diplomats, consular officials, and other ministry employees who fell victim to the repressions between 1934 and 1953 (*TASS*, in English, December 29).

Soviet Miner Prevented from Leaving for United States

The US embassy in Moscow said the Soviet authorities had prevented a miner at the Vorkuta coal field from leaving on a trip to the United States. An embassy spokesman said the miner, Sergei Mosolovich, was one of a group of ten leaders of last summer's coal strike invited by the US government and the AFL-CIO labor organization. A Soviet Foreign Ministry spokesman said the miner's visa had been canceled because the union committee in Vorkuta had ousted him from the strike committee. Mosolovich denied that this was the reason. The embassy spokesman said the US considered the action a violation of the new Soviet free-exit policy (*AP*, *Reuters*, *UPI*, December 29).

Saturday, December 30 ————————————————————————————

Society to Defend Stalin Formed

Admirers of Joseph Stalin, now officially denounced in the USSR, formed a society to defend his memory, according to *Molodezh' Gruzii*. The newspaper said the society held its founding congress in Stalin's home town of Gori on December 21, the 110th anniversary of his birth. Another report said that members of the conservative "Edinstvo" society held a meeting at Moscow University on December 21 to mark the anniversary of Stalin's birth (*Reuters*, January 7).

Gorbachev Tops Popularity Polls in West

Soviet President Mikhail Gorbachev has been topping popularity polls in the West. He was named "man of the year" in a poll conducted for the Paris newspaper *Le Figaro*. In Britain, television viewers last night voted

Gorbachev one of the statesmen of the decade and pronounced him winner of a special "hope for the future" award. The US news magazine *Time* also recently named Gorbachev "man of the decade" (*UPI*, December 30).

Russian Nationalist Groups Issue Joint Election Platform

A group of twelve Russian nationalist organizations issued a joint election platform demanding more rights for ethnic Russians. It also criticized Mihkail Gorbachev's economic reforms. The platform, which was published in *Literaturnaya Rossiya* (No. 52), is critical of attempts to restore private property and expresses concern at concessions made to separatist movements. The group wants an end to large Russian subsidies to other republics and to what it calls anti-Russian discrimination in the non-Russian republics. It criticizes the increase of Western influence and calls for a return to conservative values and for "the rebirth of the real Russia." It also urges the restoration of the traditional role of the woman in the family.

Pravda Says "No" to Separatist Efforts

Pravda sharply condemned any efforts to disband the Soviet federation through separatist moves. It called attempts to dismantle the Soviet federation "historically a step backwards" and a move towards economic disintegration and political destabilization. *Pravda* said Communist Party unity played a special role. Mikhail Gorbachev has sharply criticized Lithuania's recent vote to form an independent Communist Party.

Sunday, December 31

Demonstration over Food Shortages

Komsomol'skaya pravda said police broke up a demonstration in Sverdlovsk on December 29 that began when shops ran out of vodka and other alcohol. It said the demonstrators demanded political reforms, the resignation of local leaders, an end to food shortages, and tougher action against the black market. The newspaper did not mention any arrests. The same day, Western agencies carried interviews with Muscovites, all of whom complained about difficulties they had encountered trying to buy food and drink for the New Year's festivities in the Soviet capital (*AP, Reuters*, December 31). The agencies quoted the interviewees as saying that they did not remember the food supply being so bad since the postwar period.

703

Selyunin on Economic Prospects

Writing in *Sotsialisticheskaya industriya*, Vasilii Selyunin offered his typically outspoken and apocalyptic appraisal of the state of the economy. He reckoned that national income in 1989 had declined by some 3 percent in real terms, and he offered prescriptions for two main bottlenecks—rail transport and electricity generation. He doubted that the present Soviet government would be able to cope with the "the negative political results of these economic troubles."

Gorbachev's New Year's Address

Soviet President Mikhail Gorbachev said that 1989 had been "a year of ending the Cold War" and that the 1990s "could become the most fruitful period in the history of civilization." In a New Year's address, Gorbachev said a common European home had become a realistic prospect as "the postwar division of the continent recedes into the past." On domestic themes, Gorbachev said the Soviet people could now visualize their goal of attaining a humane and democratic socialism and a society of freedom and social justice. Gorbachev described 1989 as the most difficult year for *perestroika*. He cited problems with the consumer market, disruptions caused by mass industrial stoppages, and the exacerbation of interethnic relations. But he said 1989 had also brought events of fundamental importance, including free elections and the first two Congresses of the USSR People's Deputies (*TASS*, in English, December 31; *Pravda*, January 1).

Key

to Articles Published in
Report on the USSR in 1989

RL Numbers	Issue Number	Date of Issue
1–11	1	January 6
12–22	2	January 13
23–34	3	January 20
35–46	4	January 27
47–56	5	February 3
57–68	6	February 10
69–81	7	February 17
82–95	8	Februrary 24
96–108	9	March 3
109–122	10	March 10
123–135	11	March 17
136–145	12	March 24
146–156	13	March 31
157–168	14	April 7
169–181	15	April 14
182–190	16	April 21
191–201	17	April 28
202–210	18	May 5
211–221	19	May 12
222–229	20	May 19
230–239	21	May 26
240–249	22	June 2
250–260	23	June 9
261–273	24	June 16
274–281	25	June 23
282–291	26	June 30
292–302	27	July 7
303–312	28	July 14
313–328	29	July 21
329–343	30	July 28
344–356	31	August 4
357–369	32	August 11

RL Numbers	Issue Number	Date of Issue
370–382	33	August 18
383–394	34	August 25
395–406	35	September 1
407–420	36	September 8
421–431	37	September 15
432–444	38	September 22
445–456	39	September 29
457–468	40	October 7
469–479	41	October 14
480–488	42	October 21
489–497	43	October 28
498–509	44	November 3
510–518	45	November 10
519–527	46	November 17
528–532	47	November 24
533–541	48	December 1
542–551	49	December 8
552–560	50	December 15
561–570	51	December 22
571–587	52	December 29

Name Index

Abalkin, Leonid, 332, 636
  on budget deficit, 46, 78
  and economic reform, 301, 544, 615–616, 673–674
  and economy, 203–204, 312, 336, 517, 548
  and politics, 301, 322, 334
  and republic self-management, 556, 632
Abarinov, Vladimir, 483
Abdel-Maguid, Esmat, 103
Abdulla, Abdulgani, 563
Aboimov, Ivan, 685
Abram, Morris, 324
Abramov, Valerii, 385–386
Adamec, Ladislav, 97, 660
Adamishin, Anatolii, 140, 185, 223, 397, 635–636
Adamovich, Ales, 51, 52, 86, 258, 267, 271, 277
Adleiba, Boris, 187
Adzhievich, Polad, 326
Afanas'ev, Viktor, 99, 161, 561
Afanas'ev, Yurii, 53, 86, 420, 450, 639, 649
  on CPSU, 500, 655
  criticisms of, 399, 551, 565
  and ideology, 51, 401, 630
  and politics, 306, 592, 678–679
Agaev, Ismail, 435
Aganbegyan, Abel, 90, 165, 493–494
  on economy, 72, 189, 299, 336, 475
Airikyan, Paruir, 601, 607
Aitmatov, Chingiz, 179, 284, 459, 587–588
Akhmedov, Khan, 352
Akhromeev, Sergei, 316, 330
  and foreign affairs, 119, 161, 304, 386, 621
  on military reductions, 27, 55, 600–601
  on *perestroika*, 399–400
Akihito, Emperor (Japan), 613
Akselrod, Semen, 308
Aksenov, Aleksandr, 256
Alekseev, Sergei, 285, 540, 619, 638, 693
Alekseev, Yurii, 334
Aleksei, Metropolitan, 160
Aliev, Abulfaz, 124, 382

Aliev, Enver, 124
Aliev, Geidar, 220
Aliev, Kheirulla, 700, 701
Allilueva, Svetlana, 607
Ambartsumov, Evgenii, 343
Ambartsumov, Sergei, 270
Amoli, Abdullah Javadi, 7
Anan'ev, Anatolii, 665–666
Andreev, Sergei, 76–77
Andreev, Vladimir, 71, 358
Andreev, Yurii, 198
Andreeva, Nina, 329, 373, 399, 609, 668
Andreotti, Giulio, 648
Andronov, Iona, 359–360
Andropov, Yurii, 128, 161, 309–310, 457
Anikiev, Anatolii, 294, 476, 548
Anishchev, Vladimir, 696
Antanavicius, Kazimiras, 107, 214, 673
Arafat, Yasser, 103–104, 388, 461
Arbatov, Georgii, 168, 213, 301–302, 464, 621
Arefeeva, E., 361
Arens, Moshe, 16, 103–104, 259, 441–442, 520
Arnaut, Ilya, 661
Arshenevsky, Yurii, 60
Arutyunyan, Ludmilla, 450
Arutyunyan, Suren, 17, 51, 57, 278, 327, 360, 497, 598
Arutyunyan, Usik, 14
Arutyunyan, Vladimir, 128
Arzhannikov, Nikolai, 233, 420–421
Ashkenazy, Vladimir, 608–609
Askarov, Asanbei, 546–547
Aspin, Les, 386
Assad, Hafez, 97–98 , 183
Astaf'ev, Viktor, 166
Astrauskas, Vytautas, 485, 571
Auelbekov, Erkin, 473
Aushev, Ruslan, 330
Avaliani, Teimuraz, 43, 412
Avduevsky, Vsevolod, 578
Averintsev, Sergei, 213

Azimov, Sarvar, 388
Aziz, Tariq, 104, 175, 461

Babakhanov, Shamsutdin, 67
Babitsky, Andrei, 321
Bakatin, Vadim, 272, 361–362, 381, 428,
    556
  on crime, 36, 173, 396, 433
  and domestic unrest, 293, 378, 487, 662
Baker, James, 34–35, 91, 402, 489, 507
  on Eastern Europe, 137, 184
  and Soviet relations, 137–138, 243–244,
    509–510, 654–655
  and Soviet trade, 534, 626
Baklanov, Grigorii, 2, 53, 175
Baklanov, Oleg, 422
Baltaeva, Roza, 35
Baltrunas, Valerijonas, 546
Baluev, Veniamin, 330
Barabashev, Georgii, 141
Baranov, Aleksandr, 600
Baranovsky, Vladimir, 679–680
Barou, Jean-Pierre, 57–58, 72
Baublys, Viktoras, 651
Bauer, William, 318
Bautina, Ninel, 345–346
Begun, Vladimir, 78
Belonogov, Aleksandr, 181
Belousov, Igor, 4, 439–440
Belov, Nikolai, 398
Belyaev, Anatolii, 166
Belyaeva, Nina, 447–448, 657–658
Berdyaev, Nikolai, 13
Berezhkov, Valentin, 249, 466–467
Berezov, Vladimir, 633
Beria, Lavrentii, 131, 462
Berklavs, Eduards, 463
Berkov, Aleksandr, 298–299
Besaga, Sergei, 637
Bessmertnykh, Aleksandr, 63, 631, 690
Bestuzhev-Lada, Igor, 483–484
Bhutto, Benazir, 61, 359
Bielinis, Jonas, 89–90
Billik, Vladimir, 446
Bilyk, Ivan, 597
Biryukova, Aleksandra, 43, 400
Bodiul, Ivan, 94–95
Bogdanov, Petr, 353
Bogomolov, Gennadii, 63

Bogomolov, Oleg, 62, 75, 90, 672
Bogoraz, Larisa, 1, 56
Bolshakov, Vladimir, 19
Bolton, John, 596
Bondarchuk, Sergei, 33–34
Bondarev, Yurii, 317
Bonner, Elena, 69, 56, 98–99, 119, 677
  and Barou interview, 57–58, 72
  and Wallenberg case, 457–458
Borisov, Vadim, 421, 650
Borovik, Artem, 330
Borovik, Genrikh, 51
Bosenko, Nikolai, 391
Botha, Roelof "Pik," 385
Boucher, Richard, 384
Bourdeaux, Michael, 538
Bovin, Aleksandr, 74, 156, 187, 343
Boyarov, Vitalii, 2
Boyars, Yurii, 686
Brakov, Evgenii, 133, 148
Bratun, Rostislav, 527
Brazauskas, Algirdas, 88, 107, 127, 333
  criticisms of, 651, 695
  and Lithuanian independence issues,
    171–172, 504, 546, 583, 622, 689
  and Soviet military, 208, 676
Bresis, Vilnis, 89
Brezhnev, Leonid, 161, 187, 393, 521
Brezhnev, Vladimir, 348
Britvin, V., 330
Brodsky, Joseph, 199
Bromlei, Yulian, 424
Bronfman, Edgar, 85
Bronshtein, Mikhail, 276, 371
Bukharin, Nikolai, 80
Bunich, Pavel, 213, 498, 673
Bunin, Ivan, 168
Buniyatov, Z., 267
Burlakov, Matvei, 59
Burlatsky, Fedor, 120, 310, 392, 397, 540, 616
  and human rights, 28, 519
Burt, Richard, 667–668
Burykin, Vladimir, 362
Bush, George, 37, 52, 104, 309, 488–489
  and arms control, 281, 510, 532–533
  and Eastern Europe, 348–349, 409
  and Soviet relations, 281, 399–400,
    509, 654–655
Busygin, Mikhail, 363

Butenko, Anatolii, 669
Buturlin, Aleksei, 263
Bykov, Vasyl, 34, 166, 342, 450

Calfa, Marian, 691
Cardin, Shoshna, 393
Carter, Rosalyn, 28
Castro, Fidel, 188, 535
Ceausescu, Nicolae, 56, 633, 659, 686
Cekuolis, Algis, 193
Cepaitis, Virgilijus, 107, 485
Chaikovskaya, Ol'ga, 306
Chalidze, Valerii, 476–477, 607
Chanturia, Georgii (Gia), 194, 197
Chazov, Evgenii, 80, 322, 361, 437
    on AIDS, 106, 140, 230, 321–322
Chebotareva, Valentina, 624
Chebrikov, Viktor, 294–295, 470
    and ethnic issues, 429, 444, 468,
    on informal groups, 80, 335
    and politics, 175, 323, 504
    and Tbilisi violence, 537, 490–491
Cheney, Dick, 240, 532
Cherkashin, Vyacheslav, 22
Cherkezia, Otar, 181–182, 197–198
Chernavin, Vladimir, 61, 404
Chernichenko, Yurii, 170, 198, 276, 283,
    404, 655
Chernomyrdin, Viktor, 62, 358–359
Chernyavin, Vladimir, 331
Chernyshev, Albert, 72, 335, 386
Chernyshev, Vladimir, 64
Chertok, Boris, 203
Chervonopisky, Sergei, 284, 373
Chervov, Nikolai, 375, 390–391, 681
Chevenement, Jean-Pierre, 189
Chirac, Jacques, 347
Chkheidze, Zurab, 182, 197–198
Chornovil, Vyacheslav, 372
Chrobog, Jürgen, 525
Chumakov, Yurii, 664
Chung Ju-Yung, 407
Churbanov, Yurii, 3, 24, 212, 250, 393,
    482
Churkin, Aleksandr, 246, 401
Clark, Charles, 53
Coeme, Guy, 351
Conquest, Robert, 176
Craxi, Bettino, 70

Crowe, William, 307
Cuellar, Javier Perez de, 90, 104, 464, 496,
    681
Czapski, Jozef, 483
Czyrek, Jozef, 333

Daniel, Aleksandr, 88
Daniel, Yulii, 1, 17–18
Danilov, V., 176
Dashichev, Vyacheslav, 477
Davletova, Lyudmila, 376
Davydov, Grigorii, 568
Debov, Sergei, 581
Delov, Dmitrii, 45
Dementei, N. I., 400
Demidenko, Nikolai, 611
Deng Xiaoping, 61, 252
Didorenko, Eduard, 296
Dienstbier, Jiri, 691
Dinitz, Simcha, 424
Dinkov, Vasilii, 74, 137
Dobelis, Juris, 172
Dodolev, Evgenii, 319
Doguzhiev, Vitalii, 322, 337
Dolanc, Stane, 125
Dotsenko, Anatolii, 372, 474
Dovyatin, Viktor, 321
Drach, Ivan, 486, 487
Dragunsky, David, 106
Drutse, Ion, 455, 684
Druzenko, Anatolii, 684
Dubcek, Alexander, 121, 500, 585–586, 639,
    668
Dubov, Lev, 186
Dudintsev, Vladimir, 82
Dukhanin, Aleksandr, 264
Dumas, Roland, 621
Dunaev, Aleksandr, 180, 257, 271–272
Durasov, Vladimir, 196, 513
Dzhafarov, V. D., 278
Dzhanibekov, Uzbekali, 4, 315

Eagleburger, Lawrence, 309, 506
Edward, Prince (Great Britain), 207
Efanov, Vyacheslav, 210
Eidel'man, Natan, 352
Elchenko, Yurii, 126, 487
Eligulashvili, Mikhail, 198
Elizabeth II, Queen (Great Britain), 192

El'tsin, Boris, 299, 349, 372, 375–376, 472, 555–556
  criticisms of, 37, 156, 501–502
  on effects of *perestroika*, 19, 25, 261, 415, 453, 515, 652, 674
  and foreign affairs, 146, 161, 297, 488–489
  on the leadership, 15, 105, 428, 555, 596
  and politics, 28, 97, 133, 143, 147, 148, 174, 265, 275–276, 279, 288, 306, 307, 608, 655, 698, 700
  and radical groups, 401–402, 420
  support for, 132, 159–160, 172, 211, 271, 525–526, 540, 551, 602
  and Supreme Soviet, 276, 277, 300–301
Emel'yanov, Aleksei, 286–287
Emel'yanov, Yurii, 440
Endere, Sirge, 507–508
Evtukh, Vladimir, 452
Evtushenko, Evgenii, 34, 51, 53, 78, 99, 139
  and politics, 132, 254, 283, 672

Fabius, Laurent, 624
Fahd, King (Saudi Arabia), 175
Falin, Valentin, 39–40, 126, 525
  and Molotov-Ribbentrop Pact, 390, 449, 450
  and politics, 166, 220,
Fedorov, Yurii, 210
Feoktistov, Konstantin, 430
Filali, Abdellatif, 339
Filaret, Metropolitan, 384, 632
Filimonov, Leonid, 414
Filipov, Petr, 249
Filshin, Gennadii, 569, 674
Friedersdorf, Max, 340, 467, 679
Frolov, Ivan, 561–562, 570, 585, 618, 669
Frolov, Konstantin, 10

Galich, Aleksandr, 199
Galimov, Marat, 415
Galvin, John, 259
Gamkrelidze, Tomaz, 278
Gams, Eduard, 599
Gamsakhurdia, Zviad, 113–114, 186, 197, 280
Gandhi, Rajiv, 92–93
Gaponov-Grekhov, A., 330
Gdlyan, Tel'man
  corruption investigations of, 212, 231, 492–493, 538
  criticisms of, 317, 241, 250

  probe into investigations of, 263–264, 277, 462–463, 511, 522–523, 694
  support for, 362, 540
Gekkiyiev, Mufti Mahmud, 128
Gel'man, Aleksandr, 2
Genoyan, Albrik, 44
Genscher, Hans-Dietrich, 248, 304, 305, 660
Gerashchenko, Viktor, 414
Gerasimov, Anatolii, 218, 635
Gerasimov, Gennadii, 118, 136–137, 268, 300, 663
  on Afghanistan, 60, 90, 138, 214, 245–246, 407
  on arms control, 133–134, 152, 384
  on domestic issues, 21, 42, 179, 197–198, 218, 702
  and Eastern Europe, 494, 502, 576, 672
  and East Germany, 491, 525, 605–606, 621
  and United States, 10, 145, 155, 490, 507
  on Wallenberg case, 31–32, 557
Geremek, Bronislaw, 575, 649
Gidaspov, Boris, 365, 446, 635, 666–667, 674, 675
Gilashvili, Pavel, 181
Ginzburg, Vitalii, 213, 521
Giogannini, Giovanni, 147
Girenko, Andrei, 650–651
Giscard D'Estaing, Valery, 34
Glotov, Vladimir, 412
Golanov, Vladimir, 45
Golovin, Vladimir, 62
Golovko, Dmitrii, 123
Golovkov, Anatolii, 41–42
Golubov, Georgii, 10
Gorbachev, Ivan, 71
Gorbachev, Mikhail, 52, 58, 161, 187, 259, 331, 360, 417, 460, 602, 677, 678, 704
  on agriculture, 26, 127, 153–154, 344
  and arms control, 29, 34, 192, 322
  and Baltic Republics, 495–496, 546, 608, 689, 695
  and Congress of People's Deputies, 276, 277–278, 283, 284–285, 287, 288
  and domestic issues, 38, 52, 291, 404, 407, 431, 503–504, 632–633, 692
  and domestic unrest, 197, 216, 293, 294, 371–373, 380, 455, 463–464, 497, 530, 541, 572, 678

and Eastern Europe, 356–357, 453–454, 493, 537, 543, 545, 632, 638, 659, 660, 682, 684, 685–686, 691
and economy, 16, 162, 378, 38, 516–517, 560, 586, 601, 673
and foreign affairs, 1, 7, 37, 76, 121, 127, 171, 182, 184, 188, 191–192, 226, 234, 244, 251–253, 281, 303–306, 319–320, 324, 339, 346–347, 393–394, 409, 471, 492, 509, 514, 576–577, 610, 648–649, 654–655, 662–663
and ideology, 622, 624–625, 641
and the media, 551–552, 570
and politics, 4, 20, 120, 147, 160, 174–175, 178, 180–181, 220, 270–271, 345, 364–365, 383, 414–415, 506–507, 513, 519, 555–556, 571, 616–617, 669–670
popularity of, 566, 702–703
and public relations, 54, 100–102, 124, 211, 321, 400
on reform, 89, 97, 163, 174, 192, 417, 489
and Vatican relations, 458, 653
Gorelovsky, Ivan, 330
Gorgodze, Shota, 228
Gorodetsky, Lev, 424
Grachev, Andrei, 299, 646, 662–663
Gramov, Marat, 322
Granin, Daniil, 2, 190, 271, 641–642, 669
Grazin, Igor, 522
Greenspan, Alan, 545–546
Gremitskikh, Yurii, 355, 439, 447, 620, 649
Gribov, Vladimir, 326
Grienko, A. I., 216
Grigoryants, Sergei, 3, 132, 136, 147
awards for, 50, 307
criticisms of, 80, 461–462
Grinevsky, Oleg, 49, 141, 520
Groman, Vladimir, 162
Gromov, Boris, 92, 316
and Afghanistan, 18, 60, 90, 119
Gromyko, Andrei, 161, 187, 219, 345
Groshev, Vladimir, 551
Grossman, Vasilii, 329
Grossu, Semen, 109, 115–116, 455, 611, 623
Grosz, Karoly, 171, 182, 393–394
Groth, Heinrich, 431
Gubarev, Vladimir, 51
Gubenko, Nikolai, 634, 683

Gujral, Inder, 691
Gulyaev, Yurii, 62
Gumbaridze, Givi, 197, 215, 236, 287, 379, 381, 626, 628
Gurevich, Leonid, 178
Gurinovich, Anatolii, 544
Gurov, Aleksandr, 294, 307, 362
Gusev, Sergei, 348
Gusev, Vladimir, 336, 518
Gutsu, Ion, 441, 612, 661

Hager, Kurt, 545
Hajek, Jiri, 500
Hallik, Klara, 254
Haq, Abdul, 395
Hassan, Hussein Kamel, 74
Hatemi, Muhammed, 337
Haussman, Helmut, 645
Havel, Vaclav, 109, 190
Havlicek, F., 273
Havriliv, Mikhailo, 248
Hekmatyar, Gulbaddin, 61
Hel, Ivan, 526, 597, 654
Hint, I., 241, 263
Hippel, Frank von, 398
Holst, Johan Joergen, 331
Honchar, Oles, 166
Honecker, Erich, 537, 672
Howe, Geoffrey, 34, 134, 191–192, 268
Hurd, Douglas, 687
Hussein, King (Jordan), 102
Hussein, Saddam, 104, 461

Ibragimov, Mirzaolim, 135, 163
Ignat'ev, Aleksandr, 81
Igrunov, Vyacheslav, 88
Ilchenko, Anatolii, 21–22
Ileshin, Boris, 363
Iliescu, Ion, 685–686
Il'in, Viktor, 68
Ilizarov, Boris, 11
Ioann, Bishop, 618
Ishutin, Valerian, 272
Ivankov, Petr, 267, 317
Ivanov, Anatolii, 254
Ivanov, Ivan, 47, 311, 433, 599
Ivanov, Nikolai, 253, 306, 317
and corruption investigations, 202, 249–250, 289, 538

Ivanov, Nikolai (*continued*)
  probe into investigations of, 263–264, 277,
    462–463, 511, 522–523, 694
  support for, 261, 362, 540
Ivanov, Vladimir, 415
Ivanov, V. P., 453
Ivanov, Vyacheslav, 213
Ivanova, Tat'yana, 331
Ivanovsky, Evgenii, 92
Ivans, Dainis, 13–14, 145, 451
Ivashko, Vladimir, 519, 669
Izrael', Yurii, 368
Izyumov, Aleksei, 413

Jackson, Jesse, 57
Jakes, Milos, 142, 209
Jankowski, Jan Stanislaw, 547
Janowski, Jan, 542
Jaruzelski, Wojciech, 226, 461, 471, 575
Jiang Zemin, 492
John Paul II, Pope, 69, 458, 527, 634, 653

Kacharyan, Robert, 85
Kadar, Janos, 254
Kadyrov, Gairat, 567
Kafarova, Elmira, 324, 656
Kalashnikov, Vladimir, 326
Kalin, Ivan, 611
Kalinin, Nikolai, 92
Kalinin, Yurii, 633
Kalistratova, Sofiya, 419
Kalmykov, Yurii, 264
Kamalidenov, Zakash, 143
Kamalov, Kallibek, 609, 662, 696
Kamentsev, Vladimir, 72–73, 348, 361, 575
Kamshalov, Aleksandr, 374
Kamsky, Gata, 181
Kaputikyan, Silva, 57
Karakhan, Lev, 62–63
Karamanov, Uzakbai, 399
Karimov, Islam, 325, 504
Karlov, Yurii, 458
Karmanov, Konstantin, 209, 437
Karpinsky, Len, 135, 630–631
Karpov, Aleksandr, 209
Karpov, Lev, 225
Karpov, Viktor, 141–142, 281, 368
Karpovich, Ya., 377
Kartashkin, Vladimir, 69

Kartelev, Boris, 56
Karyakin, Yurii, 132, 213, 284
Kashirov, Sergei, 143–144
Kashlev, Yurii, 29, 133
Kasim, Marwan, 461
Katargin, Ivan, 385
Katasonov, Valentin, 351
Katusev, Aleksandr, 170, 216, 693
Katushev, Konstantin, 125, 308–309, 346,
    594, 626
Katz-Oz, Abraham, 645
Kaverin, Venyamin, 236
Kazarezov, Vladimir, 356
Kazdailiene, Teodora, 150
Kelam, Tunne, 493
Kelly, John, 407, 410
Kezbers, Ivars, 190
Khabibullaev, Pulat, 44, 135
Khaddam, Abdel-Halim, 98
Khaeev, Izatullo, 42
Khamenei, Ali, 116–117
Khan, Sahabzada Yaqub, 61
Kharchev, Konstantin, 584
Khariton, Yulii, 552
Khilchevsky, Yurii, 207
Khitrin, Yurii, 318–319
Khmara, Stepan, 597
Khodyrev, Vladimir, 344
Khodzhamuradov, Annamurad, 626
Khomeini, Ayatollah, 7, 85, 116, 118
Khomenko, Nikolai, 481
Khomyakov, Aleksandr, 647
Khrennikov, Tikhon, 164, 523
Khrushchev, Nikita, 81–82, 185, 187, 192–
    193, 208, 343, 411
Khrushchev, Sergei, 81–82, 411
Khudaiberdyev, Narmakhonmadi, 482
King, Francis, 225
Kireev, Genrikh, 309
Kirichenko, Vadim, 374, 564
Kirill, Archbishop, 632, 642, 672, 680, 688
Kirillov, Vladimir, 686
Kirov, Sergei, 97
Kiss, Dezso, 43
Kissinger, Henry, 34
Kiszczak, Czeslaw, 439, 461
Klibi, Chedli, 388
Klimchuk, Fedor, 349–350
Klimenko, Maksim, 356

Klimov, Elem, 2
Klimov, Oleg, 434, 503
Klyamkin, Igor, 442–443
Kochetov, Konstantin, 92, 278
Kochetov, Yurii, 30
Kogan, Evgenii, 391
Kohl, Helmut, 17, 248, 303–304, 305–306, 645, 649
Koivisto, Mauno, 445, 576–577
Kokoshin, Andrei, 145
Kolbin, Gennadii, 178, 285–286, 323, 399
Kolesnik, Nikolai, 653–654
Kolesnikov, Aleksandr, 165–166
Kolesnikov, Viktor, 530
Kolomitsev, A., 40
Kolotusha, Vasilii, 422
Komin, Anatolii, 531
Konarev, Nikolai, 348, 404, 414, 529, 530, 565–566, 570
Kondrashev, Aleksandr, 95
Kondrashev, Stanislav, 68, 355, 372
Kondrat'ev, Vladimir, 491
Kondratovich, Dmitrii, 473
Kondrusev, Aleksandr, 106, 150–151, 210, 424
Kondrusiewicz, Tadeusz, 394
Konev, Sergei, 486
Konnabikh, Anatolii, 144
Konovalov, Aleksandr, 242
Kopasov, Valentin, 572
Kopelev, Lev, 14–15
Koptyug, Valentin, 154
Korchagin, Mikhail, 292
Kornienko, Anatolii, 389, 487
Kornilov, Yurii, 610
Kornylyak, Platon, 318
Korolev, Mikhail, 55–56
Korolev, Sergei, 12
Korotich, Vitalii, 8, 99, 53, 209, 270, 516
    and Congress of People's Deputies, 44, 110, 253
    and Gorbachev, 58, 180–181, 551
Kortunov, Andrei, 413
Koryagin, Anatolii, 559
Koryagina, Tat'yana, 2
Korzhavin, Naum, 540–541
Kosharovsky, Yulii, 149, 256
Kostava, Merab, 197, 550
Kostenko, Yurii, 152

Kostikov, Vyacheslav, 290, 421
Kosygin, Aleksei, 161
Kotov, Yurii, 320
Kozyrev, Nikolai, 407
Kravchenko, Leonid, 166
Kravchuk, Leonid, 486
Kravtsev, Vladimir, 492–493
Kravtsov, Boris, 263
Krekie, Nenad, 125
Kremnev, Roald, 206
Krenz, Egon, 591, 604
Krivenko, Aleksandr, 396
Krolikowski, Werner, 493
Kryuchkov, Vladimir, 334, 375, 461, 494, 505, 597–598, 677, 678
    on border zones, 565, 574
    and crime, 297, 452, 539
    and restructuring the KGB, 284, 325–326, 417, 557
    and the United States, 6, 555
Kubilius, Andrius, 152
Kudryartsev, Gennadii, 9
Kudryavtsev, Vladimir, 201
Kugultinov, David, 110–111
Kulchitsky, Stalinislav, 526
Kulik, Viktor, 172
Kulikov, Viktor, 64
Kuolelis, Juozas, 89–90
Kuplyakov, Yurii, 635
Kuptsov, Vladimir, 541
Kurchatov, Igor, 131
Kuriyama, Takakazu, 164
Kurkov, Anatolii, 501
Kurochkin, Vladislav, 273
Kutkovetsky, Nikolai, 661
Kutsenko, Nikolai, 552
Kutsenko, Viktor, 55
Kutsev, Gennadii, 182
Kuznetsov, Rudolf, 14, 298, 398–399, 452
Kuznetsov, Sergei, 395, 601–602, 647
Kuznetsov, Yurii, 113
Kvilitaya, Otar, 507
Kvitsinsky, Yulii, 220, 242

Lagutina, Irina, 549
Lakhtin, Vladimir, 518
Lakshin, Vladimir, 302
Landsbergis, Vytautas, 463, 464, 485, 676
Lanovoi, Viktor, 146, 209, 377

Lapshin, Vladimir, 686
Lapygin, Vladimir, 330
Larijani, Mohammed Javad, 7
Latsis, Otto, 469
Latynina, Alla, 650
Lauristin, Marju, 276, 603
Laverov, Nikolai, 337, 459
Lavranciuc, Gheorghe, 661
Lavrov, Sergei, 676
Lazarenko, Viktor, 292
Lazarev, Boris, 693
Lebedev, Aleksei, 442
Lemaev, Nikolai, 453
Lenin, Vladimir, 82, 124–125, 178, 669
   removing body of, 224–225, 581
Lerner, Aleksandr, 308
Lesiv, Yaroslav, 302
Levashev, Aleksei, 363
Ligachev, Egor, 285, 493, 504, 677
   and agrarian policy, 127, 142, 153, 185,
      194, 344, 413, 566, 627, 673
   and corruption probe, 249–250, 263,
      289, 315–316, 492–493, 511, 694
   criticisms of, 15, 105, 132, 277, 283,
      402, 555
   and domestic issues, 672–673, 689
   and economy, 162, 542
   and politics, 154, 160–161, 169, 175,
      180, 194, 383, 472
Likhachev, Dmitrii, 158, 160, 235
Likhanov, Dmitrii, 3
Li Peng, 252
Lisauskas, Stasis, 529
Lisichkin, Gennadii, 213
Lisov, Oleg, 279
Litovchenko, Aleksei, 436–437
Litvintsev, Aleksandr, 54
Liu Xiangdong, 395–396
Li Zhaoxing, 36
Lobov, Oleg, 30
Lobov, Vladimir, 92, 228
Lordkipanidze, Tariel, 236
Lordkipanidze, V., 97
Lubachivsky, Cardinal Myroslav, 69–70,
   318
Lucinschi, Petru, 623–624, 659, 662
Lukinov, Ivan, 92
Luk'yanov, Anatolii, 283–284, 427
   and foreign affairs, 319, 492

   and politics, 175, 276, 277, 420, 448, 552
   and the press, 392, 643
Lushev, Petr, 64, 89, 258–259
Lyashko, Oleksandr, 93
Lytvyn, Yurii, 630
Lyubimov, Aleksandr, 701
Lyubimov, Mikhail, 111
Lyubimov, Yurii, 44, 111–112, 272, 608,
   634, 683

Maciszewski, Jarema, 140
Made, Tiit, 429, 692
Makarevsky, Vadim, 610
Makarii, Archbishop, 688
Makarov, Konstantin, 331
Makarova, Natal'ya, 38
Makhno, Nestor, 77
Maksimov, Vladimir, 352
Maksimov, Yurii, 198–199
Malarciuc, Gheorghe, 584
Malashenko, Igor, 480
Malyshev, Vadim, 376
Mamayusupov, Mukhammadsadyk, 155–156,
   194, 254
Mamedov, A., 30
Mamedov, E'tibar, 155, 382, 435, 478
Mamedov, Mehdi, 419, 435, 536
Mamedov, Veli, 420
Manaenkov, Yurii, 521, 606
Manannikov, Aleksei, 356, 384
Marchuk, Gurii, 63
Marin, Vladimir, 214
Markaryants, Vladimir, 497
Markov, Georgii, 8
Markovic, Ante, 125
Markovsky, Frants, 511
Marx, Karl, 22–23
Masaliev, Absamat, 504
Mashchenko, Nikolai, 222
Masik, Konstantin, 198, 389
Maslyuk, Antoi, 597
Maslyukov, Yurii, 322, 413, 416, 505, 514
Masol, Vitalii, 178
Masood, Ahmad Shah, 60
Matlock, Jack, 6, 631, 685, 690
Matrosov, Vadim, 565
Matusevich, Vladimir, 443
Matveev, Vikentii, 441
Matveev, Yurii, 286

Matyukhin, G., 246–247
Mazia, Nina, 47–48
Mazowiecki, Tadeusz, 454, 460, 461, 494–495, 546, 575, 638–639
Mazurov, Kirill, 283, 446–447, 688
Medalinskas, Alvydas, 689
Medunov, Sergei, 170
Medvedev, Roy, 97, 161, 399
  and Gdlyan-Ivanov case, 322–323, 522–523, 533, 552–553
  and historiography, 67–68, 81–82, 94, 208, 526
  and literary criticism, 2–3, 683
  and politics, 198, 226, 271, 277, 420
Medvedev, Vadim, 56, 220
  and domestic issues, 216, 351–352, 651, 695
  and the media, 138, 244–245, 532, 552, 643–644
  on *perestroika*, 215, 594
  on pluralism, 123–124, 156, 271, 274
  and politics, 165, 175, 180, 547–548, 670
Medvedev, Zhores, 131, 607
Mel'nikov, Aleksandr, 416, 572
Mel'nikov, Vladimir, 414
Mercer, Ellen, 146
Michnik, Adam, 486, 575, 581
Migranyan, Andranik, 108, 442–443
Mikhailov, Boris, 86, 296
Mikhailov, Mikhail, 233–234
Mikhoels, Solomon, 84
Miloslavsky, Leonid, 630
Minnullin, Tufan, 480
Mirkasymov, Irakhmat, 567
Mironenko, Viktor, 582
Mironenko, Vladimir, 643
Mironov, Leonid, 84
Mitterrand, François, 346–347, 662–663
Mityunov, Yurii, 38–39, 395
Mladenov, Petar, 660
Modrow, Hans, 636, 659
Mogilnyi, Aleksandr, 236
Moiseev, Mikhail, 75, 84, 92, 551, 578, 581
Moiseev, Nikita, 505
Mojaddedi, Sibghatullah, 18, 314
Mokanu, Alexander, 403
Morgun, Fedor, 227–228, 334
Moroz, Oleg, 622–623
Morozov, Georgii, 22, 564

Morozov, Petr, 559
Mosolovich, Sergei, 702
Motaev, Kh., 390
Mozhaev, Boris, 114, 130
Mubarak, Hosni, 103
Mukusev, Vladislav, 549
Mulroney, Brian, 632
Murav'ev, V., 438
Mustafin, Rafael, 46–47
Mutalibov, Ayaz, 52

Nadiradze, David, 587
Nagy, Imre, 310, 313, 343, 562
Najibullah, President (Afghanistan), 421
Nakasone, Yasuhiro, 34
Nayashkov, Ivan, 18
Nazarbaev, Nursultan, 323, 399
Nazarkin, Yurii, 667–668
Nazarov, Nikolai, 81
Nazarov, Valerii, 643
Nedelin, Mitrofan, 209
Negmatullaev, Sagit, 43
Negovitsina, Elenora, 66
Neizvestny, Ernst, 354
Nekrasov, Viktor, 183
Nemeth, Miklos, 127, 356, 659
Nenashev, Mikhail, 108–109, 256, 322, 374, 504
Nicholas II (Tsar), 207, 265–266, 382
Nikitin, Vladilen, 398, 603
Nikodim, Metropolitan, 632
Nikolaenko, Valerii, 116
Nikolsky, Boris, 278
Nikolsky, Rostislav, 131
Nikonov, Viktor, 114, 162, 175, 484, 504
Nikonov, Vladimir, 437
Nishanov, Rafik, 294, 325, 354
Nosenko, Vladimir, 78
Nou, Urbe, 563
Novikov, Aleksandr, 22
Novikov, Vasilii, 7–8
Novodvorskaya, Valeriya, 132
Nuikin, Andrei, 142
Nyers, Rezso, 356, 543, 393–394

Obminsky, Ernst, 675
Occhetto, Achille, 121, 648
Ogarkov, Nikolai, 161, 219
Ogorodnikov, Aleksandr, 186, 206

Okudzhava, Bulat, 82, 139
Okulicki, Leopold, 547
Olechowski, Tadeusz, 103
Oliinyk, Borys, 130, 414, 623
Oliinyk, Ivan, 521
Olin, Jim, 360
Omelichev, Bronislav, 57
Onikov, Leon, 3–4
Orlik, Mariya, 87
Orlov, Mikhail. *See* Souther, Glenn Michael
Orlov, Yurii, 476
Ortega, Daniel, 594
Osipov, Vladimir, 316
Ost, Friedhelm, 17
Ostrogorsky, Vladimir, 273
Ozawa, Ichiro, 613

Pakdemirli, Ekrem, 346
Pakhtusov, Yurii, 145
Pallaev, Gaibnazar, 115
Palm, Viktor, 401
Pamfilova, Ella, 664–665
Panahov, Ne'mat, 337
Panina, Valentina, 43
Pankin, Boris, 457
Pankin, Vyacheslav, 13, 294–295
Papoyan, Rafael, 3, 14
Pasternak, Boris, 230
Pastukhov, Boris, 494
Patiashvili, Dzhumber, 196–197, 278, 490
Paton, Boris, 428
Patrikeev, Valerii, 484
Pavlov, Aleksandr, 93
Pavlov, Valentin, 416–417, 429, 517, 681
Pavlovsky, Gleb, 212–213
Pavlovsky, Ivan, 447
Pavlychko, Dmytro, 87, 487, 559, 690
Pekshev, Valerii, 577
Peres, Shimon, 39–40
Perfil'ev, Vadim, 6, 184, 227, 423, 586
    and domestic unrest, 216, 478
    and foreign affairs, 184, 430, 471, 479, 510,
        684, 686
Pervyshin, Erlen, 363
Peters, Janis, 184, 276
Petrakov, Nikolai, 90, 213
Petrov, Ivan, 359
Petrov, Stanislav, 92
Petrovsky, Vladimir, 204, 508, 596, 681–682

Pikalov, Vladimir, 92
Pirozhkov, Vladimir, 338
Piskarev, V., 87
Pitirim, Metropolitan, 144, 158, 160, 318
Poch, Eizens, 699
Podrabinek, Aleksandr, 21–22
Pogosyan, Artur, 44
Pogosyan, Genrikh, 40, 278
Pokrovsky, Vadim, 210
Pokrovsky, Valentin, 51, 151, 387
Poldroos, Enn, 463
Polit'kovsky, Aleksandr, 549
Poltoranin, Mikhail, 159, 166
Polyakov, Vladimir, 175
Polyanovsky, Eduard, 219
Polys, Jerzy, 681
Ponomarev, Anatolii, 343
Ponomarev, Boris, 219
Ponomarev, Vitalii, 26
Poplavskaya, Evgeniya, 360
Popov, Boris, 12
Popov, Gavriil, 233, 271, 276, 401, 411, 521,
    551, 673
Popov, Nikolai, 125, 316
Portugalov, Nikolai, 302
Postnikov, Stanislav, 316
Pozdyshev, Erik, 158
Pozela, Juras, 695–696
Pozsgay, Imre, 108
Prelin, Vladimir, 81
Primakov, Evgenii, 220, 284, 480, 505, 521,
    580, 583, 682–683
Pristavkin, Anatolii, 82, 170
Prokhanov, Aleksandr, 313–314
Prokhorov, Boris, 45
Prokof'ev, Yurii, 634, 668–669
Protchenko, Boris, 95
Provotorov, Vladimir, 112
Pshenichnikov, Vyacheslav, 611
Pugo, Boris, 505
Pumpyansky, Aleksandr, 496
Pushkin, Aleksandr, 240
Pyadyshev, Boris, 247

Qian Qichen, 61, 308
Quayle, Dan, 490

Rabinovich, Aleksandr, 53
Racz, Sandor, 310

Rafsanjani, Hashemi, 319–320, 410, 411
Raikhman, Leonid, 483
Rakowski, Mieczyslaw, 453–454, 545, 575
Rao, Narasimha, 93
Rapoport, Aleksandr, 512
Rasputin, Valentin, 33–34, 166, 285
Rau, Johannes, 305
Razgon, Lev, 208
Razmadze, Vakhtang, 380
Razumovsky, Georgii, 197, 216, 364, 490, 616
Reagan, Ronald, 1, 489
Repshe, Einars, 129
Reshetov, Yurii, 111, 374–375, 506
Reshetovskaya, Natal'ya, 200
Revenko, Grigorii, 229–230
Rishanov, Rafik, 493
Rodgers, Dick, 206
Rodins, Askolds, 475–476
Rodionov, Igor, 228, 274, 278, 287, 289, 484
Rogachev, Igor, 83, 164, 220, 308, 562
Roginsky, Arsenii, 88, 272
Rogov, Sergei, 78
Roman, Petre, 685–686
Romanin, Dmitrii, 485–486
Romanov, Grigorii, 249–250, 498
Rostropovich, Mstislav, 44, 75, 607
Roth, Loren, 146
Rozanova, Mariya, 17–18
Rozenbaum, Yurii, 94
Rozhkov, Georgii, 515–516
Rubchenko, Aleksandr, 234
Rucs, Andris, 332
Rudyakov, Aleksandr, 95, 246
Rupsyte, Angonita, 152
Rusak, Nikolai, 414
Rushdie, Salman, 108–109, 118, 139, 155–156, 167, 190, 194
Rutkovsky, Anatolii, 46
Ruutel, Arnold, 112, 276, 279–280, 426–427
Ruutssoo, Sirje, 109
Ryabchenko, Sergei, 616
Ryabev, Lev, 462
Ryabov, Gelii, 207, 266
Rybakov, Anatolii, 51, 245, 357
Rykov, Aleksei, 80
Ryzhkov, Nikolai, 29–30, 261, 289, 539, 595, 620, 677, 678
  and domestic unrest, 294–295, 373, 409–410, 590
  and economy, 28, 139, 162, 281, 287, 327, 335–336, 530, 544, 560, 564, 673–674, 701
  and foreign affairs, 189, 389, 545–546, 555, 632, 638, 659
  and politics, 174–175, 286, 337, 348, 365, 381
  and Supreme Soviet, 301, 322, 333–334
Ryzhov, Yurii, 198

Safonov, Vladislav, 528–529
Sagalaev, Eduard, 243, 614
Sagdeev, Roald, 2, 139, 235, 398
  and deputy nominations, 33, 99, 165, 213
  on space program, 269, 423–424
Sagdiev, Makhtari, 143
Sakalauskas, Vytautas, 676
Sakharov, Andrei, 263, 677–678
  and Congress of People's Deputies, 9, 33, 41, 50, 63, 70, 98–99, 165, 200, 213, 275, 277, 284, 288, 385, 401
  criticisms of, 58, 211–212, 267, 549
  on domestic unrest, 6–7, 205, 235, 312–313
  and foreign affairs, 119, 325, 457–458
  on Gorbachev, 321, 506–507
  on human rights, 37–38, 52–53, 56, 57, 69–70, 698
  and the media, 86, 552
  on political reform, 47, 72, 254, 265, 405–406, 414, 448, 518, 539–540, 561, 655
  support for, 299, 355, 551
Sakhatmuradov, Baba, 48
Salutsky, Anatolii, 90, 548–549
Salykova, Mariya, 134
Samedoglu, Yusuf, 478
Samoilov, David, 448
Samoilovich, Georgii, 191
Samolis, Tat'yana, 502–503
Samsi, Georgii, 661
Samylin, Aleksandr, 639–640
Sarnov, Benedikt, 68
Sarukhanov, Suren, 479–480
Saunin, Anatolii, 519
Savisaar, Edgar, 149
Scowcroft, Brent, 510
Seidov, Gasan, 52
Sein, Vladimir, 468–469
Selyunin, Vasilii, 193–194, 704

Semenov, Boris, 149–150
Semenov, Vladimir, 661
Semenov, Yulian, 368
Semenov, Yurii, 363
Semichastnyi, Vladimir, 309–310
Semiryaga, M. I., 440–441
Senchagov, Vyacheslav, 299, 398, 687
Senderov, Valerii, 80
Sepetys, Lionginas, 107
Serebrov, Aleksandr, 481
Serebrov, Lev, 39, 40
Sergeev, B., 376
Serov, Valerii, 373–374
Shabanov, Vitalii, 27, 330
Shaevich, Rabbi Adolf, 5
Shah, Zahir, 652
Shaimiev, Mintimer, 515
Shakhnazarov, Georgii, 142, 460, 520
Shakhverdiev, Bakhtiyar, 337
Shalaev, Stepan, 411, 445, 481, 544
Shamir, Yitzhak, 104, 149, 441
Shamshev, Igor, 270, 501–502
Sharon, Ariel, 442
Shatalin, Stanislav, 332
Shatalin, Vitalii, 90
Shatalin, Yurii, 295, 379–380, 487, 574
Shatalov, Vladimir, 257, 430
Shatrov, Mikhail, 254
Shchadov, Mikhail, 136, 196, 370, 524, 589, 655
Shcharansky, Natan, 678
Shchedrin, Rodion, 675
Shchelokov, Nikolai, 23
Shcherbak, Yurii, 321, 584
Shcherbakov, Vladimir, 374
Shcherbitsky, Vladimir, 101, 153, 178, 486, 504, 519
Shelenberg, Andrei, 54
Sheltikov, Oktyabr, 315
Shemyatenkov, Vladimir, 96, 511
Shengelaya, Eldar, 205–206
Shevardnadze, Eduard, 337, 587
   and Afghanistan, 26–27, 61, 168, 324–325, 421, 652
   and arms control, 15, 19, 133–134, 281, 305
   and domestic issues, 9, 84–85, 147, 197–198, 205, 484, 559–560, 702
   and Eastern Europe, 299–300, 525, 575, 581, 621, 627, 691

and foreign affairs, 34, 36, 61, 76, 137–138, 191–192, 234, 240, 243–244, 248, 303, 348–349, 402, 405, 410, 492, 509–510, 532, 535, 687
and German reunification, 649, 660–661, 683
and historiography, 125, 646
and Middle East, 16, 97–98, 102, 103–104, 114, 116–117, 139, 175, 319, 410–411, 520
on Soviet foreign policy, 20, 168, 357, 413, 572–573
Shevchenko, Taras, 117
Shevchenko, Valentina, 178
Shikin, Gennadii, 432
Shilov, Ivan, 611
Shilov, Mikhail, 177
Shishlin, Nikolai, 542–543, 583, 594
Shkabardya, Mikhail, 337
Shmelev, Nikolai, 165, 193–194, 213, 270, 286, 346, 534
Shultz, George, 19, 34
Shuralev, Vladimir, 92
Shvyrev, Nikolai, 436
Sibentsov, Andrei, 198
Sidorenko, Viktor, 562, 607
Sidorov, Valerii, 527
Silaev, Ivan, 348, 645
Silanov, Genrikh, 543
Singh, Vishwanath Pratap, 691
Sinopalnikov, Igor, 354
Sinyavsky, Andrei, 1, 17–18
Sirotkin, Vladlen, 363
Sitaryan, Stepan, 523, 575, 591–592
Siyabov, Alesker, 564–565
Sizov, Leonid, 70–71
Skokov, Yurii, 198
Skorobogatov, Vladimir, 528
Skorokhodov, B., 376–377
Skubiszewski, Krzysztof, 558, 575
Skudra, Viktors, 89
Sladkevicius, Cardinal Vincentas, 187, 247–248
Slicite, Zita, 511
Slyun'kov, Nikolai, 125, 175, 321–322, 370, 429, 468, 615
Smirnov, Anatolii, 88, 308
Smirnov, Georgii, 622–623
Smirnov, Mark, 316
Smirnov, Nikolai, 475

Smirnov, Viktor, 24, 109, 263, 538, 552, 694
Smith, Christopher, 433–434
Smolentsev, Evgenii, 286, 617
Snegur, Mircea, 403, 455, 661
Sniukas, Domas, 90, 166
Sobchak, Anatolii, 345, 556–557
Sobolev, Gennadii, 135
Sobor, Eugen, 661
Sokolov, Boris, 148, 658
Sokolov, Efrem, 342
Sokolov, Igor, 12–13
Sokolov, Sasha, 199–200
Sokolov, Vadim, 170
Solomenko, Evgenii, 690
Solomentsev, Mikhail, 249–250
Solov'ev, Yurii, 190, 220, 249, 365, 389,
    504–505
Solzhenitsyn, Aleksandr, 2–3, 406, 607
    popularity of, 199–200, 302, 497–498
    and returning to Soviet Union, 404, 421,
    650
    support for, 132, 170, 443
    works by, 130, 166, 291, 343–344, 434, 488,
    507, 666, 682
Sonnenfeld, Sonja, 457
Sorensen, Theodore, 52
Sorokin, A. M., 406
Sorokin, Igor, 462–463
Sorokin, V., 67
Sorsa, Kalevi, 576
Souther, Glenn Michael, 334
Spadolini, Giovanni, 69
Spath, Lothar, 304
Spiridonova, Mariya, 363
Spizhenko, Yurii, 254
Stalin, Joseph, 8, 94, 97, 125, 483–484, 702
    image of, 36–37, 82
    and World War II, 241, 249, 323, 477
Stankevich, Sergei, 198, 276
Starkov, Vladimir, 580
Starkov, Vladislav, 552, 579, 640–641
Starodumov, Vitalii, 258
Stavrov, Vitalii, 505
Steinberg, Elan, 5
Steins, Valdis, 657
Stolar, Abe, 149
Stoltenberg, Gerhard, 304
Stoltenberg, Thorvald, 195
Stolypin, Arkadii, 374

Stolypin, Petr Arkad'evich, 374
Strelyanyi, Anatolii, 154, 170, 352
Stroev, Egor, 699–700
Stukalin, Boris, 335
Stus, Vasyl, 630
Stuvalin, Boris, 543
Suharto, President (Indonesia), 492
Sukharev, Aleksandr, 73, 264, 286
Sulakshin, Stepan, 356
Suleimanov, Hafiz, 505
Suleimenov, Olzhas, 167, 287
Suslov, Mikhail, 64, 161, 383
Süssmuth, Rita, 624
Sychov, Igor, 132

Tabeev, Fukrat, 296
Talyzin, Nikolai, 505
Tarasov, Gennadii, 223, 387–388, 461
Tarazevich, Georgii, 274, 400, 648
Tarsis, Valerii, 607
Tatarnikov, Viktor, 697
Tatliev, Suleiman, 323–324
Tavchedlidze, Albertas, 273–274
Teimurazov, Rudolf, 193
Teodorovich, Tadeusz, 27
Terebilov, Vladimir, 202, 250
Terekh, Kondrat, 363
Tereshkova, Valentina, 166
Ter-Grigoryants, Norat, 584
Terleckas, Antanas, 282
Ter-Petrossyan, Levon, 598–599
Thatcher, Margaret, 72, 181, 191–192, 325,
    392–393, 514, 687
Thornburgh, Richard, 555
Tian Jiyun, 389, 492
Tikhomirov, Robert, 117–118
Tikhonenko, Vladimir, 122
Tikhonov, Vladimir, 139, 276, 312, 369–370,
    387, 526
Timofeev, Lev, 56, 80, 157, 461–462, 658
Titma, Mikk, 32–33, 392
Tkachuk, Grigorii, 115
Tolpezhnikov, Vilen, 672–673
Tolstaya, Tat'yana, 225
Tolstoukhov, Aleksandr, 265
Tolstykh, Boris, 374
Tol'ts, Mark, 652
Tomachev, Yurii, 553
Tomkus, Vitas, 367

Tomsen, Peter, 470
Tomsky, Mikhail, 80
Toome, Indrek, 427
Tovstonogov, Georgii, 279
Trost, Carlisle, 391, 550–551
Trotsky, Leon, 8, 98, 268–269, 446
Tsaregorodtsev, Mikhail, 697
Tsavro, Yurii, 521–522
Tsibukh, Valerii, 317
Tsipko, Aleksandr, 177–178, 614
Tsybin, Vladimir, 13
Tsykalo, Valerii, 442
Tukhachevsky, Mikhail, 11
Tumanov, Oleg, 104
Tutikov, Vladimir, 527
Tyazhel'nikov, Evgenii, 686
Tykhi, Oleksii, 630

Udovenko, Gennadii, 505
Ulam, Adam, 146
Ulyanov, Mikhail, 2, 53
Umiev, Ruslan, 384–385
Umudov, Djanbakhysh, 435
Uno, Sosuke, 234
Urban, Jerzy, 140
Urbanek, Karel, 639, 660
Usmankhodzhaev, Inamzhon, 609, 679
Usmanov, Gumer, 515
Ustinov, Dmitrii, 161
Ustinov, Vyacheslsav, 223

Vagris, Janis, 13, 172, 432, 464, 491, 662
Vahabadze, Bakhtiyar, 382
Vaksberg, Arkadii, 23, 342
Valjas, Vaino, 136, 426, 495, 576
Valton, Arno, 109
Varennikov, Valentin, 92, 161
Vasetsky, Nikolai, 8
Vashkidze, Mikhail, 229
Vashko, Nikolai, 74
Vasil'ev, Aleksei, 348
Vasil'ev, Boris, 30
Vasil'ev, Nikolai F., 179
Vazgen, Patriarch, 57, 178
Velayati, Ali Akbar, 117, 184, 410, 594
Velikhov, Evgenii, 220, 330
Vertelov, Konstantin, 360
Vezirov, Abdul-Rakhman, 49, 477–478, 573, 656

Vichku, Ivan, 227
Viera, Jose, 535
Viktorenko, Aleksandr, 481
Vinogradov, Igor, 130
Vladimir, Archbishop, 243
Vladimov, Georgii, 41
Vlasov, Aleksandr, 57, 397–398, 524
Vlasov, General Andrei, 165–166
Vlasov, Yurii, 279, 326, 578–579
Voinovich, Vladimir, 68, 190
Volk, Igor, 257
Volkogonov, Dmitrii, 82, 94, 268–269, 468
Volkov, Aleksandr, 349
Volkov, Esteban, 98
Voloshin, Valerii, 228
Vol'sky, Arkadii, 25, 49, 51–52, 120, 475, 595
Vonsovsky, Sergei, 211–212
Voronin, Lev, 115, 517, 650
Voronov, Yurii, 166
Vorontsov, Nikolai, 413, 465
Vorontsov, Yulii, 18, 92–93, 95, 156–157, 265, 494, 582, 691
Voroshilov, Kliment, 63–64
Vorotnikov, Vitalii, 276, 345, 555, 577, 633
    on perestroika, 342, 398
    and politics, 41, 178
    and RSFSR government structure, 431–432, 444, 476
Voss, August, 132
Voznesensky, Andrei, 53
Vranitzky, Franz, 432
Vsevolodova, Maya, 136
Vulfsons, Mavriks, 450
Vyshinsky, Andrei, 23

Wajda, Andrzej, 69, 227
Wakasugi, Genki, 256
Wakil, Abdul, 324–325
Waldegrave, William, 268
Wallenberg, Raoul, 31–32, 289, 457–458, 557
Webster, William, 25–26, 650
Weizsäcker, Richard von, 303
Wellershoff, Dieter, 238
Williams, Peter, 674
Woerner, Manfred, 683
Wojna, Ryszard, 76
Wojzechowska, Urszula, 345–346
Wolf, Frank, 433–434

Yablokov, Aleksei, 214, 261, 338, 594
Yagodin, Gennadii, 374
Yakovenko, Vasilii, 100
Yakovlev, Aleksandr, 89, 126, 633
  and the Criminal Code, 41, 202
  and foreign affairs, 16–17, 163, 303, 492, 612–613, 642
  and 1939 Nazi-Soviet treaties, 441, 450, 522, 693
  and politics, 161, 175, 213, 220
  on reform, 11, 117, 326
  on Soviet ideology, 366, 642
Yakovlev, Egor, 112, 224, 263–264, 552, 605
Yakovlev, Veniamin, 363, 425–426
Yanaev, Gennadii, 578
Yarin, Veniamin, 555, 574
Yaroshenko, Viktor, 198
Yashin, Yurii, 198–199
Yazov, Dmitrii, 345
  and disarmament, 78–79, 110
  and domestic issues, 210, 345, 445, 537, 613
  and foreign relations, 183, 189, 392–393, 532–533, 550
  and military accidents, 331, 350–351, 381–382
  on military issues, 203, 243, 369, 389, 504, 634
  and military service, 208, 367–368, 676–677
  and troop withdrawal from Europe, 118–119, 217
Young, Lord, 72
Younger, George, 393
Yuldashev, Shavkat, 295

Zagladin, Vadim, 58, 603–604, 646
Zagorsky, Vladimir, 369
Zaikov, Lev, 81, 122, 142–143, 173, 555, 684
  and politics, 37, 175, 634, 635
Zakharov, Dmitrii, 668–669
Zakharov, Mark, 224–225
Zakharov, Vasilii, 326–327
Zakharov, Vyacheslav, 82
Zalygin, Sergei, 166, 497–498
Zaslavskaya, Tat'yana, 90, 121–122, 165, 276
Zatulin, Konstantin, 669
Zazubrin, Vladimir, 186
Zemskov, Viktor, 612
Zgursky, Valentin, 198
Zhangelova, Maira, 378
Zhao Ziyang, 252
Zharnikov, Aleksandr, 314
Zhdanov, Andrei, 31, 163
Zhdanov, Vladimir, 186
Zhila, Olga, 83–84
Zhila, Vladimir, 83–84
Zhivkov, Todor, 324, 335
Zhukov, Georgii, 36–37
Zhukov, Yurii, 461–462, 470
Zhu Liang, 492
Zhumashev, D., 335
Zhurkin, Yurii, 333
Zinov'ev, Aleksandr, 199–200, 352
Zivs, Samuil, 106
Zolotas, Xenohon, 652
Zuev, Aleksandr, 262, 300

Subject Index

Abkhazia. *See* Georgia, strikes in Abkhazia

Academy of Sciences, 62, 86, 205, 232–233, 235, 505
  and Congress of People's Deputies, 33, 63, 98–99, 165, 200, 211, 213–214
  Economics Institutes, 78, 92

Aeroflot, 75, 193, 222, 349, 609

Afghanistan
  and Pakistan, 95, 156–157, 181
  political settlement for, 61, 265, 324–325, 407, 421, 510, 652
  and politics, 65, 138
  and POWs, 119, 204, 245–246, 313–314, 332, 359–360, 549–550, 631
  Soviet casualties in, 31, 66, 74
  and Soviet embassy attack, 214, 395
  Soviet invasion of, 84, 146, 161, 168, 235, 694
  Soviet withdrawal from, 18, 27, 40, 60, 90–91
  supplies for, 39, 132–133, 157, 168–169, 275, 470
  and the United States, 195, 402
  war in, 55, 77, 479

Agrarian policy
  and Baltic republics, 206, 239, 245, 349
  and Congress of People's Deputies, 283, 387
  demands to reform, 75, 92, 114, 128, 312
  Gorbachev on, 26, 127, 153–154, 344
  Ligachev on, 127, 142, 153, 194, 542, 566, 627, 673
  and stimulating production, 432, 434, 503, 547, 664, 699–700
  See also Agrarian sector; Property

Agrarian sector, 57, 159
  and transport problems, 593–594
  See also Agrarian policy; Food

AIDS. *See* Health, AIDS

Alexei Mateevici Club, 48

All-Union Voluntary Society for Cooperation with the Army, Navy, and Air Force, 656

Amnesty International, 184–185

Anti-Zionist Committee, 5, 106, 424

"April." *See* Writers' Union, "April"

Aral Sea, 35, 179, 320

Armenia, 139, 327, 363, 468, 518
  declaration on Nagorno-Karabakh by, 653
  earthquake in, 4–5, 13, 17, 29–30, 73, 104, 114–115, 185, 314, 360, 663
  economic blockade of, 496–497, 527–530
  and 1915 massacre in Turkey, 161, 218
  rallies in, 231, 280
  unrest in, 3, 7–8, 12, 13, 98, 113, 119, 147–148, 175, 239, 358, 458–459, 660
  See also Nagorno-Karabakh

Armenian Pan-National Movement, 598

Arms control, 189, 398, 581
  and chemical weapons, 15, 305, 339–340, 384, 467, 679
  and Geneva talks, 322, 667–668
  and NATO, 241, 242, 393
  and naval forces, 78–79, 386, 390–391, 551, 654
  and short-range nuclear weapons, 238, 244, 248, 303
  Soviet position on, 16, 191–192, 347, 368, 576, 600–601
  United States position on, 281, 507
  United States–Soviet talks on, 509–510, 533, 654
  and Vienna talks, 29, 133–134, 141–142, 170, 228, 259, 520, 606, 697
  and Warsaw Pact, 356–357
  See also Weapons

Arrests. *See* Legal system, arrests

Arts, 21, 45, 122
  film, 45, 93, 178, 227
  music, 75, 164, 608–609
  theater, 44, 111, 207, 279, 683
  See also Literature; Ministry of Culture

Auschwitz, 603

Austria, 432

Azerbaijan
  and ethnic relations, 13, 98, 468
  general strikes in, 435, 477–479

Azerbaijan (*continued*)
and language, 67
politics in, 30, 52, 323–324
rail disruption in, 527–530. *See also*
Armenia, economic blockade of
Shaumyanovsk Raion, 430–431
and sovereignty law, 535–536, 571, 608
and trade with Turkey, 346
unrest in, 358, 367, 423, 435, 438, 627,
700–701
See also Azerbaijani Popular Front;
Nagorno-Karabakh
Azerbaijani Popular Front
and administration of Nagorno-Karabakh,
375, 656
founding conference of, 382
registration of, 155, 419, 536
and rail disruption, 528–530
and servicemen's rights, 564–565
and strikes in Azerbaijan, 435, 477–479

Baltic Council, 617–618
Baltic republics, 445, 502, 573, 644
and autonomy/independence issues, 309
369, 397, 493–494, 504, 603, 626, 646
and conflicting Soviet law, 571, 608
and CPSU Central Committee, 463–464,
470
and Gorbachev, 495–496, 503
and 1939 Nazi-Soviet treaties, 440–441,
449–451, 522
See also Estonia; Latvia; Lithuania
Baltic Sea, 475–476, 576
Belgium, 93
Belorussia, 45, 100, 579, 581
leadership in, 342, 400
unrest in, 524
See also Belorussian Popular Front;
Chernobyl'
Belorussian Popular Front, 328, 474, 524
Belorussian Soviet Encyclopedia, 31
Berlin Wall, 16, 34, 305, 610
"Birlik," 403, 435, 483, 516
Black Sea, 594
Bolsheviks, 30, 77, 168, 421. *See also*
Historiography, pre-Stalin era
Border
Tajik-Kirgiz, clashes, 376, 388, 447, 512
Sino-Soviet, 252, 562

trade, 676
zones, 565, 574
Bulgaria
ethnic relations in, 308–309, 334–335, 386
and reform, 620, 660
and Soviet relations, 323, 324

Cambodia, 253, 405, 487
Canada, 98–99, 632
Censorship. *See* Media, and censorship
Central America, 116, 138, 188, 535, 667
Central Committee, CPSU, 219–220, 261, 511,
669–670
and elections, 19–20, 174–175, 178, 547–548
and ethnic relations, 162–163, 172, 503–505,
650–651
journal of, 54
and Lithuania, 695–696
plenum on agriculture, 153–154
and special Party privileges, 665
and statement on Baltic Republics, 463–464,
470, 472, 531
See also Communist Party of the Soviet
Union; Politburo
Central Committee News. *See Izvestiya TsK
KPSS*
Central Intelligence Agency (CIA), 650
Chelyabinsk, 436–437
Chernobyl', 214, 222, 524, 604
aftermath of, 58, 65, 79, 99, 131, 152, 162,
169, 229–230, 258, 403, 428, 452, 520–521,
544, 581, 594
demands to close, 225, 279, 390
and Gorbachev, 100, 102
China, 93
and border talks, 252, 562
Gorbachev on, 305, 347
protests in, 299, 312–313, 343, 568
and Sino-Soviet summit, 251–253
and Soviet relations, 36, 61, 74, 308, 389,
395–396, 492
and Soviet trade, 676
CIA. *See* Central Intelligence Agency
Cinema Workers' Union, 205–206
Collectivization, 13, 27, 173
Comecon, 2, 76, 96, 553
Committee for the Defense of Peace, 225
Committee on Defense and State Security,
330–331

Communist Party of the Soviet Union (CPSU), 81, 226, 417–418, 431, 491, 518
  in Armenia and Azerbaijan, 30–31
  in Belorussia, 342
  changing the, 502–503, 554, 663–664
  and Congress of People's Deputies, 24, 123, 138, 142, 154, 160–161, 178–179, 190, 194
  criticisms of the, 364, 501
  and elections to local soviets, 547–548
  in Estonia, 666, 680
  and federalization, 504, 546, 583, 703
  in Georgia, 197–198
  and Gorbachev, 120, 218, 383, 393, 519
  and informal groups, 222–223, 335
  in Kiev, 389
  in Latvia, 145, 436, 662
  in Leningrad, 364–365, 446
  in Lithuania, 107, 171–172, 512–513, 621–622, 651, 657, 689
  in Moldavia, 109, 441
  and nationalities policy, 443–444, 514, 518
  and perestroika, 3–4, 76–77, 102, 422
  and political pluralism, 363
  and public opinion, 129, 135, 177, 558, 635
  role of the, 286–287, 471, 520, 561, 572, 580, 616–617, 625, 641, 655, 667, 672, 699
  and special privileges, 164, 498, 521–522, 664–665
  See also Central Committee, CPSU; Politburo
Composers' Union, 75, 164
Congress of Consumer Cooperatives, 162
Congress of People's Deputies, 316, 469, 685, 691, 694, 700
  assessments of, 302–303, 306–307, 477, 698
  and constitutional issues, 327, 692–693
  and deputy clubs and groups, 321, 401–402, 420, 526, 682–683
  and election law, 686, 689–690
  election platforms for, 24, 50, 112, 114, 117, 137, 144, 148, 149, 159, 172
  elections for, 71, 110, 123, 126, 141, 142, 152, 153, 154, 158, 159–161, 164, 165, 166, 172, 173–175, 178–179, 180–181, 190, 198–199, 211, 213–214, 253–254, 271, 559
  first session of, 265, 275–279, 283–288
  and Gdlyan-Ivanov commission, 533, 537–538, 694

  and investigation of Tbilisi violence, 672–673, 693
  and language, 690
  mandates of the, 160, 275
  media coverage of the, 270–271, 329–330
  and Molotov-Ribbentrop Pact, 693
  nominations for, 9, 19–20, 28, 33, 35, 40, 41, 44, 47, 63, 66, 70, 97, 98–99, 200
  second session of, 672–674
  See also Interregional Group; Supreme Soviet
Consumer goods
  and economic reform, 251, 498, 544
  exports of, 1–2, 693
  imports of, 38, 193–194, 400
  and reverse consumer credit, 675
  shortages of, 56, 57, 66, 102, 335–336, 397, 429, 503–504, 517, 518, 560, 615
  See also Informal groups, consumer societies; Legal system, draft laws on consumer issues
Cooperatives, 67, 78, 272, 517
  and crime, 46, 169, 539
  first national congress of, 339, 344
  protests against, 232, 364, 534
  restrictions on, 10–11, 67, 134–135, 158, 556–557
  taxes on, 110, 207–208, 369–370
  trade union for, 415
  See also Congress of Consumer Cooperatives
Corruption, 23, 143
  in elections, 141, 153, 198, 232
  and government officials, 109, 170, 231, 249–250, 261, 263–264, 289, 316, 362, 393, 482, 492–493, 543, 609–610, 665
  and Gdlyan/Ivanov affair, 317, 322–323, 462–463, 522–523, 538
  in Kazakhstan, 546–547
  in legal system, 169, 202, 212
  in Uzbekistan, 3, 24, 44, 135, 609, 662, 679, 696
  See also Crime; Legal system
Council of Ministers, 10–11, 28, 301, 438–439
Council of Nationalities, 24, 162, 276
Council of the Union, 284
CPSU. See Communist Party of the Soviet Union

Crime, 4–5, 105, 407, 466, 553
and cooperatives, 46, 169, 539
in correctional institutions, 117–118,
385. See also Legal system, and penal
institutions
involving foreigners, 533–534
journal on, 319
and the KGB, 297, 451–452
and murders, 412, 563, 681
organized, 234, 362, 396, 692
statistics on, 36, 60, 73–74, 88, 169–
170, 173, 307–308, 353, 362, 396,
583, 620
and unrest, 433
See also Corruption; Legal system
Crimea, 17, 23–24, 458, 651. See also Ethnic
groups, Crimean Tatars
Cuba, 61, 188, 535
Cuban missile crisis, 52
Cultural Fund, 158, 160
Culture, 195, 256, 588. See also Arts;
Language; Ministry of Culture
Czechoslovakia, 96
demonstrations in, 37, 56
and 1968 invasion of, 104–105, 446–447,
500, 553, 581, 585–586, 641–642, 646,
658–659
and reform, 97, 142, 209, 639–640, 660,
668
and Soviet relations, 109, 691

Debt, foreign, 125, 212, 287, 512, 524. See
also Foreign aid, reappraising Soviet
program of; Government deficit
Defections, 83–84, 181, 220–221, 236, 262,
300, 505
Democratic Union
criticisms of the, 79, 204, 540
harassment of the, 38–39, 147, 321
newspaper by the, 462
and rallies, 118, 223, 450–451, 670
Detentions. See Legal system, detentions
Dissidents, 2
arrests of, 197, 216, 223
detention of, 321, 337, 435
and psychiatric hospitals, 21–22. See also
Psychiatry, political abuses of
rehabilitation of, 41–42, 357, 419, 476
See also Emigrés

Eastern Europe
Gorbachev on, 409, 576
reform in, 603–604, 613, 620–621, 627,
672
and Soviet military, 20, 59, 118–119, 388
and the Soviet Union, 184, 301–302
See also Individual countries
East Germany, 336, 537, 604, 666
exodus from, 491, 525, 569
and reform, 545, 591, 605–606, 682
and reunification issues, 621, 625, 649
and Soviet relations, 299–300, 493, 636,
659
EC. See European Community
EEC. See European Economic Community
Economy, 315, 346, 480, 704
and Baltic cooperation, 494, 573
and development plans, 413, 428
and foreign investment, 5, 93, 192, 299, 587
and free economic zones, 311, 433, 474–475
and inflation, 475, 687
and international joint ventures, 9, 45, 83,
183, 189, 281, 305, 351, 407, 475, 534–535,
577, 599, 647, 701–702
performance of the, 55–56, 193–194, 217,
220, 286, 336, 398, 564, 582
and plan for 1990, 438–439, 517, 586, 607
in RSFSR, 56–57, 647
in Uzbekistan, 125, 233
See also Agrarian sector; Financial sector;
Foreign aid; Industry; Reform, economic;
Trade
"Edinstvo" society, 702
Education, 59–60, 102, 355, 472, 541
and international programs, 22, 193, 340,
408
and the military, 105–106, 182, 202–203,
634
Egypt, 103
Electoral system, 469
changes in, 365–366, 391, 423, 437, 474,
513, 515, 577–578, 605, 637, 689–690
and Congress of People's Deputies, 123,
160. See also Congress of People's
Deputies, 276
and constitutional changes, 570–571
criticisms of the, 47, 58, 71, 72, 265, 270,
321
and election law, 165, 686

and elections to local soviets, 670–671, 694–695
in Estonia, 425–427, 536, 608, 625
Emigration, 257, 393
regulations, 69, 308, 616
statistics on, 398–399, 452
See also Emigrés
Emigrés, 171, 219, 347, 352–353
intellectuals among, 14–15, 41, 68, 111–112, 183, 190
Jewish, 149, 191, 233, 259, 298, 397, 593, 664. *See also* Jews
Soviet policy towards, 8–9, 19, 62, 69, 111
See also Emigration
Employment, 428, 481. *See also* Unemployment
Energy, 74, 582, 597
and coal miners' strike, 370
and fuel shortages, 456, 465, 561, 572
gas, 35–36, 62
hydroelectric, 56, 418, 472
nuclear, 10, 17, 58, 73, 100–101, 115, 130–131, 158, 214, 225, 235, 238, 255, 333, 367, 405, 428, 524, 545, 562, 564, 579, 580, 607. *See also* Chernobyl'
and pipeline accidents, 98, 358–359, 377, 508, 569
See also Transportation, and unrest
Environment, 91, 195, 499, 508, 644
and Chernobyl', 58, 65, 79, 99, 162, 229–230, 258, 439
and climate conference, 602–603
and pollution, 35–36, 45, 48, 62, 70, 80, 149–150, 233, 235, 320, 351, 377, 394–395, 442, 462, 475–476, 594, 636, 687
protecting the, 35, 58, 120, 179, 227–228, 244, 261, 357, 465
and radiation pollution, 10, 56, 232–233, 366–367, 368–369, 506, 520–521
and water projects, 64, 179, 255, 449, 472
See also Environmental groups
Environmental groups, 58, 87, 232, 584, 687
Estonia
autonomy/independence issues, 112, 172, 258, 279–280, 351, 351–352, 391–392, 448, 615
commemorating Stalin's victims in, 173, 456–457
and economy, 26, 245, 563, 698–699

and election laws, 425–426, 536, 608, 625
and ethnic relations, 351–352, 387, 425–427, 429. *See also* "Interdvizhenie"
labor in, 412
language law in, 32–33
local elections in, 670–671
and politics, 32, 65, 149, 167–168, 234, 236, 666, 680
See also Estonian Popular Front
Estonian Popular Front, 32, 65, 149, 168, 251, 352
and CPSU Central Committee, 463–464
and election of deputies, 179
and Molotov-Ribbentrop Pact, 341, 342
Ethiopia, 582
Ethnic groups, 23, 349–350
Abkhaz, 173, 186–187
Afghans, 7, 18
Bashkirs, 46–47
Crimean Tatars, 23–24, 53, 54, 199, 260, 458, 647–648, 651, 687
Gagauz, 614
Hungarians, 59
Meskhetians, 292–296, 354–355, 373, 680–681, 687
Ossetians, 627–628
Russians, 151–152, 193, 237, 297, 387, 425–426, 495, 625, 703
Soviet Germans, 53–54, 144, 179–180, 235, 256, 311–312, 318, 325, 431, 624, 647–648, 651, 687
See also Bulgaria, ethnic relations in; Ethnic relations; Jews; Religion
Ethnic relations, 87–88, 358, 418, 509, 700
in Armenia/Azerbaijan, 120, 468, 475
attempts to improve, 4, 7–8, 24–25, 49, 51–52, 59, 117, 118, 162–163, 183–184, 231, 285, 311–312, 386, 429, 443–444, 468, 647–648, 650–651
in Bulgaria, 308–309
and CPSU, 314, 503–505, 514
in Estonia, 351–352, 387, 425–427, 429
and government policy, 101, 341, 392, 480, 518, 617, 623
and Lithuania, 637
in military, 578
and tensions in Georgia, 341–342
and unrest in Kazakhstan, 314–315

Ethnic relations (*continued*)
  and Uzbekistan clashes, 292–296, 354–355, 453
  See also Ethnic groups; Nationalism; Unrest
Europe, 55, 58, 73, 167, 471
  pre- and post-1939 status of, 466–467
  and Soviet blocs, 573
European Community (EC), 553, 636, 644–645, 683
European Economic Community (EEC), 76, 96
Exports, 27, 108, 599, 693
  bans on, 1–2, 26, 84, 381
  oil, 47, 128, 137, 189
  See also Trade

Famine, 12–13, 27, 176, 312, 526
Fergana Valley. *See* Uzbekistan
Financial sector, 345–346, 508, 546, 596
  and Baltic currencies, 563, 573
  and banking sector, 82, 535
  and bonds, 150, 593
  and a convertible ruble, 246–247, 414, 534, 599
  and devaluation of ruble, 577
  and monetary supply, 429
  and a two-ruble system, 189
  See also Economy; Trade
Finland, 93, 576–577
Food, 210, 484, 582, 676
  exports of, 1–2
  grain, 92, 133, 139, 237, 413, 547, 603
  imports, 180, 396, 503, 591–592, 661
  production, 4, 26, 39, 56, 142
  shortages, 39, 101, 114, 153, 185, 202, 606, 703
  See also Agrarian policy; Agrarian sector
Foreign affairs
  and Afghanistan, 421, 479. *See also* Afghanistan
  and Austria, 432
  and Bulgaria, 323, 324, 386, 471
  and Canada, 632
  and Central America, 116, 535, 667
  and China, 36, 61, 74, 251–253, 285, 300, 308, 389, 395–396, 492, 562
  and Cuba, 188
  and Czechoslovakia, 581, 639–640, 691
  and Eastern Europe, 301–302, 620–621, 627, 672, 681
  and East Germany, 299–300, 491, 493, 512, 603–604, 610, 659, 666
  and Ethiopia, 582
  and European Community, 636, 644–645
  and Finland, 576–577
  and France, 346–347, 662–663
  and Great Britain, 268, 290, 392–393, 514, 687
  and Hungary, 310, 313, 356, 394, 599, 659
  and India, 691
  and Indonesia, 492
  and Iran, 7, 116–117, 118, 156, 167, 184, 319–320, 410–411
  and Israel, 16, 21, 39–40, 387, 441–442, 645
  and Japan, 164, 220, 234, 256, 430, 612–613, 642
  and Middle East, 97–98, 102, 103–104, 114, 175, 183, 223, 354, 387–388, 461, 520
  and Poland, 226–227, 266, 439, 453–454, 460, 494–495, 502, 542, 545, 558, 575, 638–639, 649. *See also* Katyn massacre, and Soviet-Polish relations
  and Romania, 633, 659, 684–686
  and South Africa, 185, 223, 385
  and Southeast Asia, 9, 45, 405, 407, 643
  and Sweden, 434, 557
  and the United Nations, 508
  and the United States, 1, 10, 32, 37, 68–69, 129, 137–138, 145, 146, 155, 188, 195, 243–244, 257, 399–400, 402, 407, 410–411, 422, 488–489, 490, 506, 507, 509–510, 532–533, 545–546, 550–551, 596, 631, 654–655, 690
  and the Vatican, 458, 604, 653
  and Western Europe, 17, 76, 163, 191–192, 624
  and West Germany, 238, 248, 303–306, 407–408
  See also Foreign policy; Terrorism
Foreign aid, 663
  reappraising Soviet program of, 361, 376, 676
  See also Medical services, and international assistance
Foreign Ministry, 675

Foreign policy, 65, 572–573, 635
and "the Brezhnev Doctrine," 136–137, 182
decision-making process for, 168, 357, 413
and German reunification, 649, 660–661, 679–680, 683
Gorbachev on, 409, 648–649
France, 340, 624, 662–663
Gorbachev visit to, 346-347
GATT. *See* General Agreement on Tariffs and Trade
General Agreement on Tariffs and Trade (GATT), 433, 675
Georgia
and autonomy/independence issues, 148, 280, 507, 600, 626, 629
economic blockade of, 529
energy shortage in, 561
ethnic tensions in, 341–342
and investigation of Tbilisi violence, 273–274, 275, 278, 283–284, 287, 345, 429–430, 490–491, 537, 672–673, 693
leadership in, 181–182, 236
natural disasters in, 15, 156, 215
and South Ossetia, 627–628, 662
strikes in Abkhazia, 484
unrest in, 5, 113, 173, 186–187, 194, 196–198, 205–206, 215–216, 239, 262, 378–381, 411, 418, 586–587
Glasnost', 209, 329, 369
and historiography, 63–64, 477
and the KGB, 126, 237, 377
and politics, 4, 83, 123, 167–168, 392
and Soviet media, ix, 25, 112, 125
Glasnost' (journal), 118, 461–462
Government, 301, 469, 539–540, 561
and constitutional changes, 570–571, 616–617, 625
and constitutional oversight committee, 692–693
and 1990 budget, 416–417, 481–482, 517, 586
restructuring the, 442–443, 444, 448, 451, 580, 703
See also Communist Party of the Soviet Union; Foreign policy; Government deficit; Supreme Soviet
Government deficit, 46, 78, 327, 376, 416, 429, 513

and banking industry, 82
See also Debt, foreign; Military, budget
Great Britain, 204
Gorbachev visit to, 191–192
and human rights, 6, 538
and Soviet relations, 268, 290, 392–393, 514, 687
and Soviet trade, 72–73, 93, 400
Greece, 143, 652
Greenpeace, 232
Health, 43, 195, 264, 554, 600, 697
AIDS, 21, 50–51, 65–66, 106–107, 110–111, 140, 150–151, 210, 218, 230, 254, 262, 321–322, 386–387, 424, 479, 558
and alcoholism, 38, 467, 592
and Chernobyl', 403, 604
"Chernovtsy Disease," 143, 219
and poisonous gas, 229
and pollution, 9, 35–36, 48, 62, 65, 79, 99, 131, 169, 378, 390, 563
See also Medical services; Narcotics
Historiography, 30, 59–60, 368
and access to archives, 11, 19, 239–240, 603, 682
and Brezhnev era, 457
and the Cold War, 125–126
and Hungarian 1956 uprising, 95, 108, 313, 562
and Khrushchev, 81–82, 192–193, 208, 343, 411
and Lenin, 124–125, 669
and 1930s census data, 652
and 1939 Nazi-Soviet treaties, 339, 341, 440–441, 520, 522
and 1968 invasion of Czechoslovakia, 104–105, 446–447, 500, 553, 585–586, 641–642, 646, 658–659
pre-Stalin era, 77, 147, 186, 207, 265–266, 362–363, 374, 421
and Soviet-Finnish war, 658
Stalin era, 8, 23, 36–37, 51, 63–64, 66, 67–68, 76, 80, 82, 94, 97, 102–103, 140, 165–166, 172, 176, 222, 226–227, 249, 266, 344, 383, 419, 438, 462, 468, 477, 483, 501, 526, 538–539, 573, 586, 612, 691
and Trotsky, 446
Housing, 23, 29–30, 46, 51, 102, 172, 174, 217, 360, 373–374, 472

Housing (*continued*)
  auction of, 614–615
  and the homeless, 442
Human rights, 56, 324, 419, 579, 670
  and AIDS victims, 110–111, 479
  and international arena, 45–46, 140, 219,
    425, 509–510, 538
  and international conferences, 6–7, 28, 29,
    34–35, 38, 255
  and joint US-Soviet resolution, 596
  and the military, 676
  and political prisoners, 21–22, 38–39, 41,
    70–71, 124, 146, 433–434, 467–468. *See
    also* Karabakh Committee; Psychiatry,
    political abuses of
  and prison torture, 292, 318–319, 633
  progress in, 37–38, 70, 138, 183–184, 191,
    519
  and Soviet citizenship, 44, 607–608.
    See also Emigrés and Wallenberg
    case, 457–458
  See also Emigration; Jews; Memorials;
    Rehabilitations
Hungary
  and East German refugees, 491
  1956 uprising in, 95, 108, 562
  reform in, 35, 75, 127, 171, 542–543
  and Soviet relations, 59, 96, 254, 310, 313,
    335, 356, 394, 599, 659
  and Warsaw Pact, 583

Ideology
  debate on, 75, 77, 177–178, 366, 622–623,
    624–625, 635, 641, 642, 669, 692
  and education, 541
  and political change, 123–124, 314, 400,
    592, 597–598
  See also Perestroika; Political pluralism
IMF. *See* International Monetary Fund
Imports, 479–480, 597
  of grain, 180, 396, 503, 591–592, 661
  of medicine, 437
  See also Trade
Income, 56
  and cooperatives, 539
  personal, 58, 78, 171
  and reform, 531, 544, 564
  See also Living standards
India, 92–93, 691

Indonesia, 492
Industry, 346, 453, 582
  accidents in, 62, 166, 221–222, 246, 309
  chemical, 189, 261, 336, 357
  coal-mining, 370–373, 438
  converting military, 4, 64, 139, 439–440,
    578
  and pollution, 223, 351. *See also*
    Environment
  state enterprises, 28, 66, 71, 203–204,
    413, 701
  See also Economy; Energy; Labor
Informal groups
  consumer societies, 21, 144
  criticisms of, 79–80, 476, 540
  draft law on, 447–448
  harassment of, 87, 222–223
  and new Kadet Party, 579
  and politics, 82–83, 86, 174, 249, 328–
    329, 352, 383, 472, 499–500, 554, 566,
    586, 628–629, 657–658
  Tatar Public Center, 96
  and unrest, 274, 380, 404–405
  See also Nationalism; Popular fronts; and
    Individual groups by name
Infrastructure, 40, 344
  water projects, 64, 83, 120, 255
Institute of Books, 199–200
Institute of the USA and Canada, 168
Intellectuals, 14–15, 139
  emigration of, 587–588
  and Georgian violence, 197, 205
  and historiography, 48, 51
  and politics, 2, 86, 99, 328, 366
  and Soviet bureaucrats, 633
  See also Emigrés; Writers
"Interdvizhenie," 136, 151–152, 391, 412,
    625, 668
"Interfront," 13–14, 148, 387
International Atomic Energy Agency, 333
International Monetary Fund (IMF), 508, 675,
    676
International Movement. *See* "Interdvizhenie"
Interregional Group, 401–402, 420, 567, 602,
    608, 673, 678–679
  attacks on, 549
  and CPSU role, 641, 655
  support for, 671
  and voters' clubs, 574

Interregional Organization of Democratic Organizations (MADO), 586
Investment, foreign. *See* Economy, and foreign investment
Iran, 85, 421, 594
  and Rushdie affair, 118, 139, 155–156, 167
  and Soviet relations, 7, 116–117, 184, 319–320, 410–411
  and Soviet trade, 143–144, 352, 597
Iraq, 74, 83, 104, 175
Isfara Valley. *See* Border, Tajik-Kirgiz, clashes
Israel
  and peace negotiations, 103–104
  and Soviet relations, 16, 21, 39–40, 387, 441–442, 645
Italy, 69–70, 121, 163
  Gorbachev in, 648–649
Ivan Pavlov Institute of Physiology, 9, 33
Izvestia (newspaper), 5
Izvestiya TsK KPSS (journal), 54

Jamming, 9, 151, 154, 273. *See also* Media
Japan, 164, 220, 234, 256, 430, 612–613, 642
Jewish Anti-Fascist Committee, 48–49
Jews
  and cultural centers, 118, 225
  refuseniks, 127, 140, 191, 245, 256, 393, 397, 512
  status of Soviet, 6, 78, 84–85, 106, 203, 242, 270
  and US immigration rules, 280
  See also Anti-Zionist Committee; Emigrés, Jewish; Jewish Anti-Fascist Committee

Kadet Party, 579
Kaliningrad, 485–486
Karabakh Committee, 80, 394
  and Armenian politics, 327, 598
  and arrests, 3, 7, 14, 35, 38, 113
  demands for release of, 53, 57, 70, 175, 231, 239
  and economic blockade, 529
  release of, members, 271, 282
Katyn massacre
  and memorial service, 586
  NKVD role in, 102–103, 266, 419, 483
  and Soviet-Polish relations, 76, 140, 226–227, 547, 638–639, 649

Kazakhstan, 27, 105, 687
  corruption in, 546–547
  and language law, 513
  leadership in, 143, 399
  and nuclear testing, 538, 567, 620, 644
  politics in, 323, 335, 694–695
  and unrest, 4, 314–315, 385, 394, 498
  See also Ethnic groups, Soviet Germans
KGB, 62, 161, 417, 445, 494
  and crime, 297, 451–452
  criticisms of the, 279, 324
  and Gdlyan-Ivanov affair, 231, 694
  operations, 184, 221, 375–376, 377
  and public relations, 80–81, 126, 325–326, 338–339, 593
  restructuring the, 111, 237, 284, 557
  and US relations, 6, 26, 650
Kirgizia, 169
  language in, 355, 459, 515
  and Tajikistan border clashes, 376, 388, 447, 512
Komsomol, 158, 164, 317, 582
  Estonian, 642–643
Kuropaty Woods massacre, 45, 47–48
Kurile Islands, 164, 220, 234, 279, 430, 565, 613, 642

Labor, 290, 445, 555, 548, 606, 650
  and the AFL-CIO, 648
  coal miners, 136, 196, 338, 370–373, 409–410, 416, 418, 438, 519, 524, 538, 571–572, 589–591, 614, 655
  in Estonia, 412, 425–427
  and law on strikes, 411–412, 541–542
  and transportation, 109, 261, 404
  strikes in Abkhazia, 484
  strikes in Azerbaijan, 435, 438, 477–479
  See also Trade unions
Language, 136, 162, 164, 480, 623, 690
  in Azerbaijan, 67, 124
  in Belorussia, 342
  in Crimea, 458
  in Estonia, 32–33, 352, 448
  in Kazakhstan, 513
  in Kirgizia, 355, 459, 515
  in Latvia, 100, 148, 237, 465
  in Lithuania, 50, 87–88, 107, 193
  in Moldavia, 85, 115–116, 149, 182, 200,

Language (continued)
  328, 405, 441, 454–456, 473–474, 662
  and Soviet Germans, 256
  in Tajikistan, 115, 204, 388, 49
  in Turkmenistan, 543
  in Ukraine, 87, 101, 466, 481, 583
  in Uzbekistan, 163, 270, 317–318, 388, 403,
    516, 567, 585
Latvia, 89, 206, 610
  and agriculture, 206, 239, 349
  and autonomy/independence issues, 100,
    129, 132, 172, 332, 402, 436, 540–541,
    584, 626, 662
  and economic policy, 698–699
  and election law, 608
  and ethnic relations, 183–184
  and historiography, 173, 306
  language in, 237, 465
  politics in, 13–14, 76, 145, 148, 432, 436,
    656–657, 670–671, 699
  See also "Interfront"; Popular Front of
    Latvia
Latvian Journalists' Union, 85–86
Latvian Popular Front. See Popular Front of
  Latvia
Lebanon, 339, 347, 461
  and Western hostages, 410–411, 422
Lebedev Physics Institute, 33, 41
Left Socialist Revolutionaries, 362–363
Legal system, 272, 555, 617
  arrests, 3, 7, 14, 24, 35, 38, 117, 124, 147,
    216, 248, 384, 395
  court trials, 4–5, 32, 44, 45, 121, 147–148,
    157–158, 453, 462, 482, 498, 506, 531, 587,
    647, 658, 662, 679, 696
  and Criminal Codes, 41, 201–202, 243,
    406–407, 413, 619, 623, 682
  detentions, 364, 670, 698
  and draft law on freedom of conscience, 94,
    199, 247–248, 298–299, 563, 653
  and law enforcement, 548, 583. See also
    KGB; Ministry of Internal Affairs; Police
  and laws on consumer issues, 83, 144,
    517
  and laws on political expression, 269,
    288, 406–407, 417, 447–448
  and laws on strikes, 411–412, 416, 541–
    542, 572, 589–591
  and penal institutions, 117–118, 221,

  236, 292, 298, 318–319, 385, 427–428,
    620, 633
  and prison population, 361–362
  See also Corruption; Crime
Leningrad
  leadership in, 635
  politics in, 328–329, 364–366, 420–421, 446,
    472, 605, 666–667
  water supply for, 636
Leningrad Engineering and Physics
  Institute, 63
Library of Congress (US), 462
Libya, 19
Literature, 22–23, 168, 186
  dissident, 1, 78, 173
  and glasnost', 329, 406
  The Satanic Verses, 108–109. See also Iran,
    and Rushdie affair
  and Solzhenitsyn, 2–3, 130, 166, 291, 302,
    343–344, 421, 434, 466, 488, 497–498,
    507, 666, 682, 683
  See also Arts; Writers
Lithuania, 21, 119, 333, 561, 567
  agrarian policy in, 349
  and autonomy/independence issues, 20,
    50, 73, 91, 107, 214, 258, 282, 298, 512–513,
    514, 640
  and citizenship law, 576, 595, 623
  constitution in, 120–121
  and ethnic relations, 87–88, 231, 485,
    637
  and military service, 187, 208, 676–677
  and politics, 657, 695–696, 699
  and special Party congress, 546, 583,
    621–622, 632–633, 651, 689
  See also "Sajudis"
Lithuanian Popular Front. See "Sajudis"
Living standards, 171, 336, 480
  and Congress of People's Deputies
    mandate, 275
  need to improve, 72, 120, 548
  plans to improve, 410, 513
  See also Consumer goods; Income

MADO. See Interregional Organization of
  Democratic Organizations
Market, domestic, 2, 364, 439. See also
  Consumer goods
Marxism, 75, 177–178. See also Ideology

Media, 79, 224, 398
  and censorship, 133, 198, 212–213, 290, 376–377, 411, 549–550, 701
  and circulation, 363, 598
  coverage by the, ix, 4, 37, 53, 56, 63, 70, 73, 79, 85–86, 106–107, 113, 119, 180–181, 205–206, 221, 252, 253, 266, 270–271, 276, 280, 296–297, 302, 329–330, 370–371, 392, 443, 451, 483, 487, 491, 492, 500, 525, 537, 568, 585, 602, 613–614, 630, 677–678, 696
  coverage of changes in Eastern Europe by the, 542–543, 569, 604, 627, 639–640, 668, 672, 684, 686
  criticisms of the, 115, 138, 220, 244–245, 311, 352, 359, 412, 413, 432, 484–485 511, 551–552, 555, 592, 633
  foreign, 133, 215, 243, 268, 273, 377, 462, 470, 665
  freedom, 25, 86–87, 112, 157, 187, 221–222, 364
  and government publications, 54, 417–418, 431, 471
  and harassment of journalists, 147, 256, 356, 507–508, 551–552, 578–579, 629–630, 640–641, 647
  and historiography, 63–64, 102–103
  and ideology debate, 622–623
  and independent publishing, 50, 86, 88, 157, 206, 225, 247, 319, 367, 368, 420, 461–462, 516, 649
  and interethnic relations, 429
  and religion, 316, 360–361
  and Supreme Soviet, 384, 643–644
  See also Glasnost'; Jamming; Technology, Information
Medical services, 81, 108, 288, 424
  and cooperatives, 11, 134
  and Gorbachev, 102, 154, 417
  and international assistance, 145, 291, 292, 601–602
  and medicine shortages, 336, 437
  and Party privileges, 418, 521–522
  See also Health
Memorials
  and Afghanistan invasion, 698
  to "Erna," 456–457
  and Katyn service, 586
  and reburials, 490, 630

  in Riga, 353–354
  to Soviet diplomats, 423
  and Stalin's victims, 45, 62–63, 66, 344, 355, 702
  See also "Memorial" society; Rehabilitations
"Memorial" society, 52–53, 88, 272
  and Leningrad Popular Front, 328
  and mass grave near Leningrad, 344
  and unrest in Moscow, 585
  See also Ukrainian "Memorial" Society
Middle East, 97–98, 102, 103–104, 138, 223, 520
  Soviet military in, 355
Military, 210, 229, 355, 674
  accidents, 195, 209, 232–233, 273, 300, 311, 331, 350–351, 354, 381–382, 396, 404, 422, 494, 582
  and Afghanistan, 18, 26–27, 40, 60, 66, 72, 74, 80, 84, 90–91, 384–385, 395, 444–445, 599, 646
  in Baltic republics, 502
  budget, 16, 20, 34, 49, 68, 75, 286, 480, 517, 681
  debate on a professional army, 330–331, 610, 634
  and domestic unrest, 196–198, 205–206, 228, 278, 290, 484, 490–491, 580, 600
  education, 105–106, 182, 202–203
  and ethnic issues, 504, 578, 680
  and Europe, 20, 55, 59, 78–79, 118–119, 217, 242, 251, 307, 327, 336, 348–349, 511
  exercises, 388, 523, 553–554
  and human rights, 389, 676
  leadership, 92, 198–199, 345
  and politics, 316, 369
  and POWs, 119, 204, 245–246, 313–314, 332, 359–360, 549–550, 631
  service, 65, 84, 182, 187, 208, 367–368, 468–469, 564–565, 584, 600, 613, 634, 676–677
  trade union for, 567, 643
  and troops abroad, 36, 83, 203, 252, 255, 279, 290–291, 492, 535, 681–682
  and unilateral reductions, 27, 34, 55, 57, 110, 145, 152, 307, 347, 581. See also Arms control
  veterans issues, 31, 144, 391

Ministry of Culture, 21, 53, 164, 634
  and Lenin Library, 659
  See also Arts; Culture
Ministry of Health, 95. *See also* Health;
  Medical services
Ministry of Internal Affairs (MVD), 381, 471,
  548
  and crime, 60, 88, 221, 533–534
  and domestic unrest, 205, 216, 228, 278,
    293, 295, 341, 350, 611, 630
  and passes for journalists, 86–87, 113, 221
  and Leningrad politics, 420–421
  size and dispersement of troops, 334, 361,
    574
  and troop training, 333, 574
  See also Legal affairs; Police
Ministry of the Medical and Biological
  Industry, 45
Moldavia, 24, 685–686
  and election law, 637
  and ethnic relations, 527, 614, 659
  language in, 85, 115–116, 200, 405
  leadership in, 94–95, 109, 403, 623–624,
    661–662
  nationalism in, 328, 451
  politics in, 441, 554
  strikes in, 454–456, 473–474
  unrest in, 48, 85, 116, 149, 182, 231, 247,
    359, 568–569, 610–612
  See also Moldavian Popular Front
Moldavian Popular Front, 568–569
  criticisms of the, 630–631
  and Moldavian unrest, 359, 611–612
  and Romania, 684–685
Molodezh' Gruzii (newspaper), 289
Molotov-Ribbentrop Pact, 283, 284, 299, 341,
  351–352, 390, 440–441, 477
  commission report on, 522
  Congress of People's Deputies resolution
    on, 693
  fiftieth anniversary of, 449–451
Mongolia, 83, 252, 255
Moscow, 37, 634, 671
  unrest in, 584–585, 601
  See also Moscow Popular Front
Moscow Aviation Institute, 81–82
Moscow Popular Front, 671
Moslem Religious Board of Central Asia and
  Kazakhstan, 67

Multiparty system. *See* Political pluralism
Muslims, 67, 128, 155–156, 194, 563
  and Iranian relations, 320
  and Uzbekistan clashes, 294, 296
  MVD. *See* Ministry of Internal Affairs

Nagorno-Karabakh, 288, 475, 487, 503
  administration of, 24–25, 375, 595, 598–
    599
  dispute over, 3, 7, 35, 74, 141, 191, 237,
    238–239, 350, 409, 435, 438, 477–479,
    493, 636, 645–646, 653, 656, 678
  economic blockade of, 527–530
  and efforts to stabilize, 40, 49, 51–52, 85,
    120, 414, 448–449, 573
  electoral representation for, 276, 278
  and United States, 388–389, 631
  See also Karabakh Committee
Namibia, 223
Narcotics
  government officials involved in, 543
  and law enforcement, 96, 221, 422, 451–
    452, 466
  statistics on abuse, 176, 592
  See also Health, and alcoholism
National Aeronautics and Space
  Administration (NASA), 145
Nationalism
  in Armenia, 280
  in Azerbaijan, 419
  in Baltic Republics, 451, 463–464, 531
  in Estonia, 32–33, 112, 172, 426
  in Georgia, 113–114, 148, 194, 196–198,
    215, 280, 600
  Gorbachev on, 692
  and informal groups, 79–80, 232
  in Latvia, 100, 129, 172, 584
  in Lithuania, 20, 73, 91, 107, 119, 120–
    121
  in Moldavia, 182, 328, 454–455
  opposition to, 83, 200–201, 208, 215,
    391–392, 476, 495
  Russian, 22, 33, 132, 329, 703
  in Ukraine, 404–405, 500, 531–532
  See also Unrest
NATO. *See* North Atlantic Treaty Organization
Natural disasters
  earthquakes, 42–43, 124, 169, 562. *See also*
    Armenia, earthquake in

landslides, 156, 183, 215
storms, 15, 156
See also Weather
Nicaragua, 257, 535, 594, 654, 667
24 chasa (newspaper), 86
NKVD, 8, 54, 462
and Katyn massacre, 140, 226–227, 266, 419, 483, 547
and Kuropaty Woods massacre, 45, 48
and mass graves, 222, 490, 573
North Atlantic Treaty Organization (NATO), 305
and disarmament, 55, 134, 141–142, 170, 393, 606
and Malta summit, 655
and military balance in Europe, 55, 78–79, 228
and modernizing short-range nuclear weapons, 240, 241–242, 248, 347
and Warsaw Pact, 258–259, 683
North Korea, 643
Norway, 331
Nuclear Research Institute, 43

Oil, 47, 128, 137, 189, 394, 592
pipeline accident, 377
and pollution, 351
OPEC, 47, 137

Pakistan, 95, 138, 156–157, 181
Palestine Liberation Organization (PLO), 103–104
"Pamyat'," 22, 78, 132, 329, 668–669
Panama, 690
PEN, 190, 225, 245, 357
Perestroika, 51, 138, 178, 342, 373, 553
and the CPSU, 3–4, 20, 215, 422, 670
and economy, 56, 72, 78, 111, 139. *See also* Reform, economic
El'tsin on, 15, 19, 25, 279, 415, 488–489
Gorbachev on, 16, 54, 100–102, 163, 174, 178, 305, 347, 365, 415, 417, 489, 576, 641
government officials on, 11, 117, 316, 392, 401, 594
intellectuals on, 2, 47, 82–83, 121–122, 352–353
and international reform, 62, 188, 492

in Leningrad, 366, 446
and the military, 389
opinion poll on, 211, 568
opponents of, 399, 690
Sakharov on, 414, 518
See also Ideology; Reform
PLO. *See* Palestine Liberation Organization
Poland, 260, 333, 547, 558, 681
and Katyn massacre, 76, 226–227, 266
politics in, 69, 439, 453–454
and reform, 460, 461, 546
and Soviet relations, 494–495, 502, 542, 545, 575, 638–639, 649
Soviet troops in, 348–349
Police, 199, 233–234, 272, 353, 531–532
training, 333, 553, 574
and Uzbekistan clashes, 295
See also Legal system; Ministry of Internal Affairs
Politburo, 91, 123, 169
commission on Armenian earthquake, 114–115
and CPSU Central Committee, 670
and economy, 10, 128
and Lithuanian Communist Party, 621–622, 633, 651
personnel changes in the, 504–505
reprimands of officials by, 489–490
role of, 580
and special Party privileges, 665
See also Central Committee, CPSU; Communist Party of the Soviet Union
Political pluralism
and the Bolsheviks, 421
and the CPSU, 123–124, 124–125, 218, 222–223, 335, 363, 520
debate on, 79–80, 132, 133, 142–143, 156, 177, 274, 283, 383, 605, 617
and the Democratic Union, 38–39, 204
in Estonia, 680
Gorbachev on, 16, 89, 127, 171, 174, 181
and the Interregional Group, 678–679
and Latvia, 464, 656–657, 699
and Lithuania, 158, 657, 699
Sakharov on, 561
See also Ideology; *Perestroika*
Political prisoners. *See* Human rights, political prisoners

Politics
  and public opinion, 210–211, 234
  See also Communist Party of the Soviet
    Union; Congress of People's Deputies;
    Political pluralism
Popular Front of Latvia, 145, 251
  and Congress of People's Deputies, 179,
    190, 254
  and CPSU Central Committee, 463–464
  and elections to local soviets, 670–671
  on "Interfront," 13–14, 148
  and program for independence, 100,
    540–541
  registration of, 76, 158
Population, 23, 227
Postal service, 6, 20
Pravda (newspaper), 598
  criticisms of, 53, 99, 322–323, 332,
    500
  editor changes for, 561–562, 570, 618
Presidium of the USSR Supreme Soviet, 12,
  24–25, 91, 95
Prices
  calls to freeze, 481, 534, 544
  and cooperatives, 10, 364, 556–557
  and inflation, 475, 687
  reforming, 35, 46, 71, 139, 417, 531,
    571
  and state enterprises, 66, 71, 101
  for trade goods, 27, 38, 137, 189, 592
  See also Economy; Informal groups,
    consumer societies
Prisons. *See* Legal system, penal institutions
Property
  debate on, 16, 75, 185, 530, 625, 673
  and housing auction, 614–615
  law on, 560, 619
  and leasing, 127, 153, 196, 211, 229, 536,
    638
  See also Cooperatives
Psychiatry
  directives on, 95, 122
  and membership in World Psychiatric
    Association, 437, 558–559
  political abuses of, 21–22, 146, 184–185,
    209, 246, 361, 374–375, 377, 401, 697

Radio Free Europe/Radio Liberty (RFE/RL),
  29, 104, 151, 443

Reform
  calls for, 285, 312, 343, 469
  and the CPSU, 194, 548
  and Eastern Europe, 409, 460, 545, 620–621
  economic, 35, 47, 56–57, 78, 193–194,
    203–204, 251, 254, 326, 378, 414, 417,
    498, 511, 531, 544, 569, 601, 615–616,
    673–674
  Gorbachev on, 9, 89, 253, 277
  intellectuals on, 2, 76–77
  opposition to, 495
  See also Agrarian policy; *Perestroika*;
    Prices, reforming
Refugees
  from Armenia/Azerbaijan, 13, 49, 52, 98,
    120, 139, 332, 636, 656
  from Kazakhstan, 315
  and the United States, 155
  from Uzbekistan, 373
  Vietnamese boat people, 309
Rehabilitations,
  commission on, 338–339
  and declaration on deported peoples,
    619–620
  of former dissidents, 41–42, 43, 44, 170,
    241, 357, 419
  of Polish politicians, 547
  of Soviet diplomats, 423
  of Stalin's victims, 11–12, 48–49, 93, 97, 112,
    129–130, 144, 162, 200, 269, 306, 358, 445,
    653
  of Trotsky, 98
  See also Human rights; Memorials
Religion
  and broadcasting, 360–361
  churches, 71, 110, 127, 141, 167, 182, 186,
    227, 427, 445, 550
  and Council for Religious Affairs, 199
  and Ecumenical Council of Churches, 382
  freedom of, 28, 51, 54, 69–70, 71, 94, 151,
    175–176, 199, 213, 227, 247–248, 298–299,
    384, 406, 561, 563, 584, 635–636, 653
  and politics, 65, 160
  publications on, 316
  and Soviet Germans, 318
  and synagogues, 242
  See also Jews; Muslims; Roman Catholic
    Church; Russian Orthodox Church;
    Ukrainian Catholic Church

Republics
  and autonomy issues, 59, 91, 110, 120–121,
    124, 149, 151, 162, 172, 214, 250–251, 258,
    269, 284, 297, 321, 369, 397–398, 405–406,
    471, 472, 480, 496, 526, 556, 618, 632–633,
    646
  and a confederation system, 424
  development differences in, 96
  and foreign policy, 635
  and military service, 208
  See also Specific republics
Research, 62, 93
  agricultural, 159
  and laser testing, 360
  nuclear, 580
  nuclear testing, 42, 96, 259, 358, 378
  on public opinion, 121, 210–211, 234
  and Radiobiological Congress, 452
  See also Scholarship; Space program
Roman Catholic Church, 187, 394, 634
  and Vatican-Soviet relations, 458, 604, 653
Romania, 56, 633, 659
  clashes in, 684–686
"Rossiya," 574
RSFSR. See Russian Soviet Federative
    Socialist Republic
"Rukh," 93, 126, 486–487, 540, 559
Russian Orthodox Church, 110, 117, 127, 160,
    167, 227, 243, 550, 570, 612
  leadership changes in, 632
  and perestroika, 671–672
  and Shevardnadze, 559–560
  and Ukrainian Catholic Church, 318, 618,
    680, 688
Russian People's Academy of Sciences, 267,
    316–317, 505
Russian Popular Front, 83
Russian Soviet Federative Socialist Republic
    (RSFSR), 47, 566, 700, 476
  and autonomy issues, 397–398
  and economy, 56–57, 647
  election laws in, 437, 577–578
  restructuring the, 431–432, 444, 606

"Sajudis," 158, 367
  criticisms of, 107, 451, 695
  and Congress of People's Deputies, 126–127,
    152, 179, 198
  and CPSU Central Committee, 463–464

  and ethnic issues, 297, 485
  and Lithuanian citizenship law, 576
  on Lithuanian independence issues, 91,
    119, 121, 251, 470
Saudi Arabia, 175, 354
Scholarship, 131, 146, 148, 176, 177–178
  and library fire, 462
  and public opinion polls, 240, 302–303,
    558, 566, 605
  See also Historiography; Research
"Sem' dnei" (Television program), 613–614
"Sister cities" movement, 281
Social services, 152, 327, 399, 416
  law to improve, 410
  and pensions, 595
"Solidarity," 69, 297, 439, 454, 460
  and "Rukh," 486
South Africa, 185, 223, 385
South Korea, 407, 643
  and Soviet joint ventures, 9, 45, 701–702
Soviet Peace Committee. See Vek XX i mir
Space program, 12, 269, 423–424, 521
  and cargo craft, 460–461
  costs of, 167, 203, 271–272
  international ventures, 204
  Mars program, 180, 206–207
  shuttle program, 257, 430
  and space station, 226, 257, 481
Sports, 21
  spectator tragedies, 358, 402–403
Stalinism, 77, 130, 176. See also Ideology;
    Perestroika
Standard of living. See Living standards
State Committee on Inventions and Dis-
    coveries, 18
State enterprises. See Industry, state enter-
    prises
Strikes. See Labor
Suicide rate, 17, 564
Supreme Court
  appointments to the, 286
  criticisms of the, 348
  See also Legal system
Supreme Soviet, 300–301, 303, 516–517, 580
  criticisms of, 306, 617–618
  and economy, 556–557, 560, 607
  and election law, 426–427, 570–571
  elections to, 276, 277
  and the environment, 644

Supreme Soviet (*continued*)
  and ethnic issues, 392, 473, 617, 623
  and Gorbachev, 414–415
  and government appointments, 285–286,
    322, 326–327, 333–334, 337, 348, 363,
    374, 375–376, 381, 398, 413–414, 575
  and the Interregional Group, 420
  and juridical system, 552–553, 617
  and law on strikes, 541–542
  and the media, 384, 392, 502, 511, 630,
    643–644
  on pensions, 595
  and reform, 469, 544
  and republic autonomy, 556, 629, 632, 644
  and Soviet citizenship, 607, 623
  See also Congress of People's Deputies;
    Council of Ministers; Council of
    Nationalities; Council of the Union
Sweden, 227–228, 434
  and Wallenberg case, 457–458
Syria, 183
Tajikistan
  corruption in, 609–610
  earthquake in, 42–43, 124
  and elections to local soviets, 694–695
  and ethnic issues, 499
  and Kirgizia border clashes, 376, 388, 447,
    512
  language in, 115, 204, 388
  and Rogun dam, 120
Taras Shevchenko language society, 87
Tataria, 46–47, 96, 515
Tax
  on cooperatives, 110, 339, 344, 369–370
  incentives for inventors, 18
  and local soviets, 561
  rates, 91, 207–208
Technology, 18, 135, 145, 409, 532, 650
  and control on materials duplication, 536
  information, 123, 224
  nuclear, 130–131, 607
  and nuclear testing, 390, 474, 567. *See also*
    Kazakhstan
  US-Soviet joint venture in high, 534
  See also Space program
Terrorism, 121, 157–158, 184, 499
  and airport security, 222
  Soviet position on, 6, 25–26, 401–402
  United States-Soviet joint actions on, 523

Third World
  and debt crisis, 361, 532
  and Soviet arms sales, 410
Tourism, 697
Trade, 27, 38, 158, 304
  with China, 395–396, 676
  and Comecon, 553
  currency for, 189, 345–346
  and the EC, 96, 644–645
  with Finland, 577
  and Great Britain, 72–73
  and Iran, 143–144, 352, 597
  and Socialist countries, 108, 125
  with South Korea, 407
  with Turkey, 346, 650, 664
  with the United States, 183, 237, 502, 534,
    626, 661
  See also Exports; General Agreement on
    Tariffs and Trade; Imports
Trade unions, 412, 481, 482, 578
  and cooperatives, 415, 534
  military, 567, 643
  and miners, 416, 637
  and RSFSR, 482–483
  See also Labor
Transcaucasia, 49. *See also* Armenia; Azer-
    baijan; Georgia
Transnational Radical Party, 234
Transportation
  accidents, 266, 291–292, 320–321, 342, 415,
    637
  air travel, 75, 109, 193, 349, 609
  bus service, 124, 261
  problems moving goods, 394, 593–594
  and rail mismanagement, 348, 539, 565–566,
    568, 569–570
  and rail strikes, 404, 572
  and unrest, 409, 436, 438, 456, 496–497,
    527–530
Travel, 59, 256, 452, 474
  policy, 14, 53, 69, 220–221, 560, 616, 702
  for Yupik Eskimos, 510
  See also Transportation
Trials. *See* Legal system, court trials
Trilateral Commission, 34
Turkey, 72, 161, 212
  and Soviet trade, 346, 650, 664
Turkmenistan, 221, 543
  and Iran, 352

leadership in, 48, 626
unrest in, 232, 248–249

Ukraine
and Chernobyl', 225. *See also* Chernobyl'
economy in, 152
and ethnic relations, 458
Gorbachev visit to, 100–102
language in, 87, 466, 481, 583
leadership of, 519
"Memorial" Society in, 129–130
and politics, 423, 474, 500
unrest in, 117, 141, 232, 404–405, 531–
532
See also "Rukh"
Ukrainian Catholic (Uniate) Church, 69–70,
117, 174, 248
and legalization demands, 260, 298–299,
302, 318, 386, 500–501, 515–516, 526–527,
552, 584, 642, 653–654
rights of, 635–636
and Russian Orthodox Church, 127,
596–597, 680, 688
United States on, 509
Ukrainian Helsinki Union, 101, 117, 129–130,
153, 540
and coal miners strike, 372
Ukrainian "Memorial" Society, 129–130
Ukrainian Popular Front. *See* "Rukh"
UN. *See* United Nations
Unemployment, 442, 523, 587
Unidentified flying objects, 543
Union for the Independence of Lithuania,
282
Union of Cooperative Associations, 67, 344,
557
Union of Managers, 551
Union of Scientists of the USSR, 337–338
Union of Soviet Composers, 523
Union of Soviet Journalists, 86, 221
Union of Working People of Kuzbass, 628–629
Union of Working People of Moldavia, 554
United Front of Workers, 329, 365–366
United Front of Workers of Russia, 495, 549,
555, 577, 669
United Nations (UN)
and Afghanistan, 181
and assistance to USSR, 42–43, 544, 553
and Baltic Republics, 20, 464

and Cambodia, 405
and the environment, 228, 508
and human rights, 45–46, 219
and politics, 505, 508
United States and Soviet Union at, 510,
596
World Court, 140
United States (US), 145
and Afghanistan, 195, 407
and arms control, 192, 322, 339–340, 360,
375, 386, 390–391, 467
and hostages in Lebanon, 410–411 422
and human rights, 6
and Malta summit, 654–655
and Soviet domestic affairs, 388–389, 529,
555, 590
Soviet immigration to the, 155, 280, 298,
497, 506
and Soviet joint ventures, 22, 183, 193, 534,
647
and Soviet military cooperation, 674
and Soviet relations, 1, 10, 32, 37, 68–69,
104, 129, 137–138, 145, 146, 155, 188, 242,
243–244, 257, 281, 320, 399–400, 402,
488–489, 490, 506, 507, 509–510, 532–533,
534, 545–546, 550–551, 573, 596, 631,
667, 690
and Soviet trade, 237, 502, 547, 626, 661
Unrest, 147, 200–201, 217, 415, 433
in Armenia-Azerbaijan, 3, 7–8, 12, 13, 30–31,
40, 44, 74, 98, 113, 119, 141, 147–148, 175,
237, 238–239, 350, 358, 367, 409, 423, 435,
438, 458–459, 527–530, 606, 627, 645–646,
660, 700–701
in Baltic republics, 20, 87–88, 187, 151–152
in Belorussia, 524
and border clashes, 376, 388
in Eastern Europe, 37, 56, 310
in Georgia, 5, 113–114, 173, 186–187, 194,
196–198, 205–206, 262, 378–381, 418,
586–587, 628, 662
in Kazakhstan, 4, 314–315
in military, 680
in Moldavia, 48, 85, 116, 149, 247, 359, 441,
568–569, 610–612
in Moscow, 223, 353, 584–585, 601
predictions on, 312–313
and revolution anniversary, 602, 614, 630–
631

Unrest (*continued*)
  student, 105–106, 202, 232
  by Tatars, 23–24
  in Turkmenistan, 248–249
  in Ukraine, 101, 117, 130, 141, 232, 404–405, 531–532
  in Uzbekistan, 7, 163, 287, 292–296, 354–355, 506, 585
  See also Labor; Nationalism
US. *See* United States
Uzbekistan
  corruption in, 3, 24, 44, 135, 609, 662, 679, 696
  and economy, 125, 428
  and the environment, 35
  and language, 163, 270, 317–318, 388, 403, 516, 567
  media in, 432
  politics in, 325
  unrest in, 7, 287, 292–296, 354–355, 373, 436, 506, 585
  See also "Birlik"
Vek XX i mir (journal), 166, 212–213
Vietnam, 203
Vilnius Cathedral, 71
Volga German Autonomous Republic, 431
Volga River, 70, 442
"Vzglyad" (television program), 65, 224–225, 245
  and censorship, 549–550, 701

Warsaw Pact, 64, 68, 134, 356–357, 409
  and freedom of political choice, 580, 583
  and Malta summit, 655
  membership in, 75, 460, 606
  and military balance, 55, 78–79, 89, 228
  and NATO, 258–259, 683
  and 1968 invasion of Czechoslovakia, 581
Weapons, 55, 229
  chemical, 15, 19, 357, 459
  held by Soviet civilians, 324, 342, 379, 380–381, 411
  nuclear, 42, 167, 209, 434–435, 552
  and Soviet arms sales, 410

and toxic gas, 205, 215–216, 229, 274, 315
  See also Arms control; Military
Weather
  drought, 413, 456
  landslides, 156, 183, 215
  storms in Georgia, 15, 156
  See also Natural disasters
West Germany
  and East German refugees, 491, 525
  and Gorbachev visit, 303–306
  and Soviet relations, 16–17, 238, 248, 407–408, 624, 645, 660–661
WJC. *See* World Jewish Congress
World Bank, 508, 534, 675, 676
World Court. *See* United Nations, World Court
World Health Organization, 150, 195, 219
World Jewish Congress (WJC), 5, 85
World Psychiatric Association (WPA), 185, 377, 437, 558–559
World War II, 48–49, 164
  and German POWs, 303–304
  and Stalin, 36–37, 468, 241, 249, 323
  See also Historiography
World Zionist Organization, 424
WPA. *See* World Psychiatric Association
Writers
  émigré, 68, 183, 199–200, 377, 406
  and PEN, 190, 245
  and *perestroika*, 82–83, 170, 215
  and politics, 93, 102, 118, 197
  popularity of, 199–200
  and repression in Stalin years, 51, 438
  See also Literature; Writers' Union
Writers' Union, 8, 183, 190
  "April" on, 170, 215
  and Congress of People's Deputies, 44, 166
  PEN on, 190
  and politics, 57, 68, 90, 109, 665–666
  and Solzhenitsyn, 343–344

Yugoslavia, 125, 524
"Yurd" Society, 124

Zagorsk, 369